MERCHANTS
& Marvels

MERCHANTS & *Marvels*

Commerce, Science, and Art in Early Modern Europe

Edited by

Pamela H. Smith & Paula Findlen

Routledge

New York   London

Published in 2002 by

Routledge
29 West 35th Street
New York, NY 10001

Published in Great Britain by

Routledge
11 New Fetter Lane
London EC4P 4EE

Routledge is an imprint of the Taylor & Francis Group.

10 9 8 7 6 5 4 3 2

Library of Congress Cataloging-in-Publication Data

Merchants and marvels : commerce, science, and art in early modern Europe
/ edited by Pamela H. Smith and Paula Findlen.
    p. cm.
    Includes bibliographical references and index.
    ISBN 0-415-92815-X (hb)   —   ISBN 0-415-92816-8 (pbk.)
    1. Art and science. Nature (Aesthetics). 3. Commerce —Europe —
    History. I. Smith, Pamela H., 1957– . II. Findlen, Paula.
    N72.S3 M47   2001
    704.9'43'094—dc21   2001016008

Contents

Acknowledgments

This volume of essays began life in two conferences: a session held at the 1997 History of Science Society meeting in San Diego, and a 1999 workshop at the Clark Library hosted by the Center for Seventeenth- and Eighteenth-Century Studies at the University of California, Los Angeles, and convened by the two editors. We are grateful to all the participants of those two conferences.

Peter Reill, director of the Center for Seventeenth- and Eighteenth-Century Studies at UCLA, encouraged and fostered this conference as he has done so many others over the years. We are deeply grateful for all he has brought to the Center; his presence as Director has made the Clark Library and southern California into a perhaps unlikely, but, most importantly, lively and stimulating intellectual center for early modern studies. Without the help of his staff, primarily Candis Snoddy, Nancy Connolly, Kathryn Sanchez, and Marina Romani, the conference could not have taken place. The volume would have come far more slowly into existence without the enthusiasm and efficiency of our editor, Brendan O'Malley at Routledge, and the capable assistance of Emily Klancher and Stacey Loughrey.

By all reports, edited volumes are the source of many tribulations. Our experience has been otherwise; we feel richly rewarded by the conversations this volume has spurred and by the opportunity the contributors have afforded us to collect their thoughts into this volume. Our thanks to all of them for helping us to bring merchants and marvels together.

Commerce and the Representation of Nature in Art and Science

PAMELA H. SMITH AND PAULA FINDLEN

On May 20, 1515, an Indian rhinoceros *(Rhinoceros unicornis)* arrived in Lisbon aboard the *Nostra Señora de Ajuda,* a Portuguese trading ship from India. It was the first rhinoceros to reach Europe alive since the third century. A diplomatic gift to Alfonso d'Albuquerque, governor of Portuguese India (1509–15) by Sultan Muzafar II (1511–26), ruler of Cambaia, or Gujarat, the animal was passed by Albuquerque to his king, Don Manuel I (1495–1521) in 1515. Later in the same year, Manuel sent the rhino as a diplomatic gift to the Medici Pope Leo X (1513–21) via Marseilles, where it was seen by King Francis I of France. Dressed with a gilt-iron chain and a green velvet collar decorated with gilt roses and carnations, the rhinoceros drowned when its ship sank off the coast of Italy. It followed in the wake of an elephant named Hanno that actually made it all the way to the papal city in 1514.[1]

The rhinoceros, circulating in Europe as part of a gift economy — not yet commodified — was brought to Europe within the framework of global commerce. Large gifts of nature were tangible signs of European overseas expansion, through trade or conquest, into regions where the "marvels of the East" could be found. If the rhinoceros itself was never fully commodified, its portrayal in a drawing of 1515 sent to an unknown acquaintance by Albrecht Dürer did circulate as a commodity of sorts (fig. Intro 1). Dürer had transferred the visual and verbal description of his drawing to a woodcut that served as the model for numerous reproductions in the following centuries and was disseminated very widely. Increasingly the rhinoceros became the artist's image of it. Dürer participated in shaping the verisimilitude of his rhinoceros by describing it enthusiastically although he never saw it himself:[2]

In the year 15[1]3 [this should read 1515] on 1 May was brought to our king of Portugal in Lisbon such a living animal from India called a

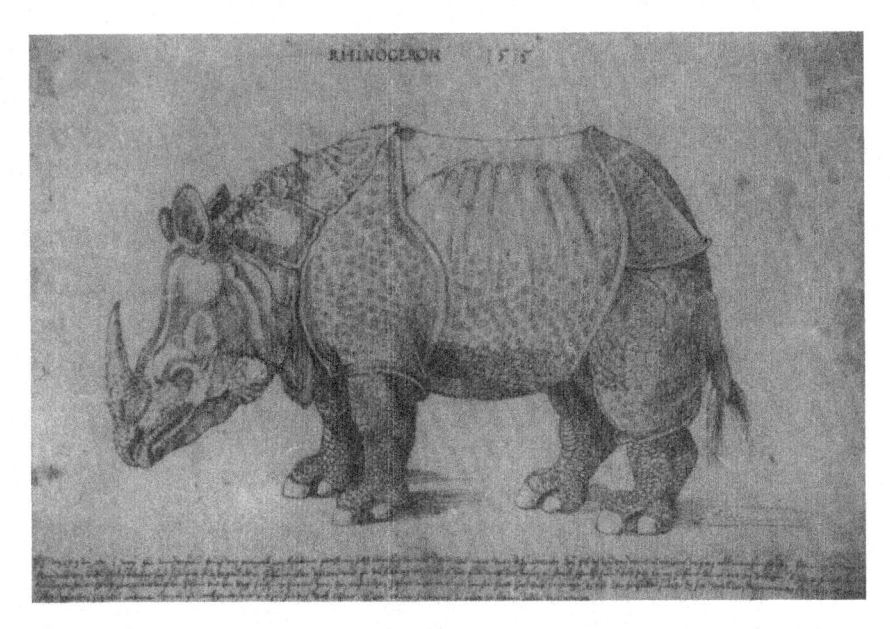

Figure Intro.1 Albrecht Dürer, *Rhinoceros*, 1515. Copyright © The British Museum.

Rhinocerate. Because it is such a marvel I considered that I must send this representation. It has the colour of a toad and is covered all over with thick scales, and in size is as large as an elephant, but lower, and is the deadly enemy of the elephant. It has on the front of the nose a strong sharp horn: and when this animal comes near the elephant to fight it always first whets its horn on the stones and runs at the elephant with its head between its forelegs. Then it rips the elephant where its skin is thinnest and then gores it. The elephant is greatly afraid of the Rhinocerate; for he always gores it whenever he meets an elephant. For he is well armed, very lively and alert. The animal is called rhinocero in Greek and Latin but in Indian, gomda. [3]

Dürer used the term *abkunterfet* to describe his portrayal of the animal, a term that often implied "copied from life,"[4] and thus left open to his correspondent the question of whether he had portrayed this particular rhinoceros from the living model. In reality, he probably copied his description from a report and drawing (now lost) sent to Nuremberg by a member of the German community in Lisbon, yet Dürer's image of this wonder, which went on to have an extraordinary life in copies, was probably taken by most viewers to be an accurate rendering of a strange and exotic beast.[5] It had the descriptive, realist "mark of truth" that became signature in the work of Dürer and his followers, and also appeared in works of scientific illustration

Pamela H. Smith and Paula Findlen

at about the same time.[6] By the mid-sixteenth century naturalists would commonly refer to their illustrations of nature as being done *ad vivum*, which they associated strongly with making a "true portrait" of nature.

The story of Dürer's rhinoceros points to several important aspects of the relationships among art, science, and commerce in Europe that will be considered in this volume. Renaissance and post-Renaissance western Europe played a unique role in the development of various arts and sciences devoted to the imitation of nature. The fact that they did this during the same time that Europeans expanded overseas had profound consequences for Europe and the world. Early modern Europeans sought to master nature through technology on an unprecedented scale, making the conquest of nature a political imperative from the sixteenth through eighteenth centuries.[7] Their activities resulted in the development of various arts and sciences devoted to the imitation of nature, the emergence of new conceptions of nature that responded to political and material changes, and a new discourse about nature that would become a central cultural force in Western society. But these results did not emerge *sui generis*, and we need to understand better the interconnections among diverse aspects of the project of understanding, describing, and conquering nature in order to appreciate fully the significance of these new developments.

During the early modern period a profound transformation in attitudes toward the natural world, the material environment, and their artistic representation occurred within a new environment of global trade and imperial ambitions in which commodities were produced, accumulated, consumed, and exchanged. The essays that make up this book explore many intersections between these developments, such as those suggested by Dürer's rhinoceros. One main conclusion of these essays concerns the importance of the coexistence of patronage and commerce in the early modern period and the way in which these overlapping social and economic systems of establishing value and significance resulted in an expansion of cultural production that greatly encouraged the investigation of and familiarity with nature. In addition, patronage of and commerce in the representations of nature in both art and science raised the status of individuals who claimed to imitate nature, such as many of the artist-artisans, medical practitioners, and other investigators of nature discussed in this book. This volume argues that these individuals helped lay the foundations of the new philosophy, which eventually would come to be called "science." This new natural philosophy, pursued with increasing enthusiasm in the late sixteenth and seventeenth centuries, emphasized practice, the active collection of experience, and observation of nature. One of the central goals of this volume is to invite readers to consider how a greater awareness of the importance of commerce in relation to scientific and artistic representations of nature and the growth of new technologies transforms the conventional story of the Scientific Revolution.

The genesis of Dürer's drawing of the rhinoceros illustrates the interpenetration of gift and commodity exchange in this period. As Europeans sailed down the coast of Africa, around the Cape of Good Hope, and finally across the Atlantic, the world changed. In 1601, as Deborah Harkness notes in her essay here, John Wheeler wrote that "all the world choppeth and changeth, runneth & raveth after Marts, Markets and Merchandising, so that all things come into Commerce . . . [and] all that a man worketh with his hand or discourseth in his spirit is nothing els but merchandise." Like many early modern Europeans, Wheeler was acutely aware of the fact that political, economic, and material changes were also remaking the world of knowledge and culture. How did commodification affect objects and attitudes to nature in early modern Europe? Traditional accounts of the new world of wealth in early modern Europe have drawn a stark contrast between the nobility and the bourgeoisie, seeing them as enmeshed in two different systems of production and as representing two contrasting types of economic actors who inhabited divergent cultural environments. Norbert Elias[8] and Otto Brunner,[9] for example, adduced evidence to show how attitudes to money wealth on the part of the nobility contrasted with that of the bourgeoisie. Marcel Mauss[10] distinguished between the feudal gift economy, permeated with notions of natural values, and the burgeoning new commercial economy, which assigned value to things based on their labor cost, giving them, in Marxian terms, an "unnatural," "fetishistic" value. In this view, nobility and bourgeoisie were enmeshed in two separate systems of exchange—one a world of gifts and favors, and the other a world of cash and commerce.

These categories have been used particularly in examining the activity of collecting. For example, Kryzstof Pomian places the "semiophore-man" (whose objects are "priceless" and bear only mystical significance because they point to the invisible) at one end of the spectrum and the "thing-man" (whose objects are worth only their economic value and thus are not priceless because they reflect only what is visible) at the other end.[11] We might conclude from these arguments that noble objects were taken out of economic circulation and thus did not belong to the same category as the bourgeois commodities. We might even conclude with Max Weber that the material accumulation of Calvinist Holland was a completely different enterprise from the material accumulation of Catholic princes. An initial examination of the activity of collecting appears to confirm this conclusion. The Habsburg *Kunstkammern* of the sixteenth and seventeenth centuries, for example, were intended to establish the *fama* of the ruler, representing his majesty (being shown to the most important "public" at court—visiting

Pamela H. Smith and Paula Findlen

nobles and ambassadors—and being displayed at *Schauessen*, or banquets) and wealth.[12] As an encyclopedia and memory theater of all nature, art, and knowledge, the *Kunstkammer* represented a theater of the world, demonstrating the ruler's mastery of nature. The cosmic themes of these *Kunstkammern* are clear from the decorative scheme in the Prague *Kunstkammer*, for example, which included the seasons, the months, the elements, and the planets, with Jupiter reigning over all in the center. Like many of the paintings commissioned by the Habsburg, their *Kunstkammern* can be read as imperial allegories, representing the ruler's symbolic mastery of the world.[13]

Collections in mercantile Holland in the seventeenth century, on the other hand, like many collections in Italy in the late sixteenth century, were filled with natural things. A survey of ninety Amsterdam citizens reveals that their collections were overwhelmingly made up of *naturalia*, followed closely by prints and paintings,[14] many of which were representations of natural and artificial objects. These collections grew largely out of the "professional" activities of doctors, apothecaries, and faculties of medicine at various universities. By the seventeenth century, however, much of these *naturalia* were natural objects turned commodities, such as shells whose price increased in direct proportion to the rarity of their shape and color. In Amsterdam, exotic plants were traded, collected, and sold in special shops that carried only East and West Indian curiosities. Even paintings could be used to buy "real" property such as land and houses. Neither curiosities nor paintings existed only in the realm of pure representation; they also played an active role in the world of commerce. Everything, it appears, could be bought and sold and given an equivalent value in relation to other goods in the marketplace.

But if we look more carefully at practices of collecting, we find that the situation is far less polarized between noble and bourgeois than appears at first glance. The "commodity collections" of the Dutch burghers did not possess only commercial significance, and in fact they were inferior to the princely collections as investments, for they seldom even fetched their calculated value at auction,[15] while noble collections were far more convertible into commodity value. Nobles collected the old-fashioned commodities of gold and silver, and pieces were not infrequently melted down in times of need, as the famous story of the bronze for Leonardo's equestrian monument of Francesco Sforza reminds us on an even larger scale. Perhaps the important thing to keep in mind is the very instability of these categories since the same object could serve multiple purposes. And both the Dutch commodities and the noble "potential commodities" (to borrow a phrase from the very stimulating work of Arjun Appadurai on commodities) could function as gifts at certain times and as commodities at others. Bourgeois collections functioned perfectly well within a gift economy,[16] and both types of collections had representational value.

Furthermore, although much has been made of the practical bent of Dutch scientific and artistic activity, as of that of their Italian predecessors, even the Habsburg *Kunstkammern* in the sixteenth and seventeenth centuries possessed a utilitarian and practical side (and had a number of leading northern European artists and naturalists employed on the emperor's behalf when they were not in places such as Leiden). Collections contained instruments used to survey noble lands; and painters were often sent to record aspects of forests, villages, and towns in a ruler's domains because they had special skills in representing their patron's dominion. The gardens, ponds, menageries, workshops, observatories, and libraries were used by artisans, artists, humanists, and natural philosophers for models, for the raw materials of knowledge and theories, and as part of an effort to classify and categorize.[17] Moreover, princes frequently showed as much interest in the new natural philosophy as citizens of republics and patronized some of the most important natural philosophers of the sixteenth and seventeenth centuries. Some nobles might have been more interested in display than others, but Landgrave Moritz of Hesse-Kassel, to name one, was more interested in arcane knowledge and processes.[18] At the same time, some of the encyclopedic collections of the northern Netherlands were not so much "professional" collections but results of the activities of rich merchants playing the *honnête homme*, such as Jan Six and Joachim de Wicquefort, and in certain ways, Rembrandt van Rijn, and, before him, Albrecht Dürer himself.[19] Indeed, Mark Meadow's essay places the merchant Hans Jacob Fugger squarely within the genesis of the central European *Kunstkammer*.

Whether noble or bourgeois, however, the objects in each collection pointed to their context: the items in Dutch collections represented objects available to moderately wealthy individuals living in a society enmeshed in a network of global trade. This fact, however, did not obscure other meanings: religious, moral, philosophical, and professional meanings intermingled with the commercial significance of a collection, and the alchemy among them depended to a large extent upon the intent of the collector.[20] While the social structure thus left its traces upon the collection, it did not determine entirely the value or meaning of the object. We must conclude along with more recent literature that commodification of natural objects was neither a sudden nor an absolute process, nor one that caused incommensurable disjunctions in society and culture.[21] In this vein, John Frow has suggested that commodification can be both enabling and productive as well as limiting and destructive. According to his argument,

> The commodity form does three things. First, it channels resources of capital into an area of production in order to expand it to its fullest capacity, at the same time destroying all productive activities which are not them-

Pamela H. Smith and Paula Findlen

selves commodified. Second, it transforms the purpose of production away from the particular qualities of the thing produced and toward the generation of profit; production is the indifferent medium for capital valorisation, and the qualities of the thing produced are incidental to this end. Third, it transforms previously or potentially common resources (both raw materials and final products) into private resources; the allocation of these resources normally takes place according to economic criteria (ability to pay rather than moral or civic entitlement), and it may be either restrictive or expansive in its effects. In the case of most cultural production — for example of books, perhaps the oldest of all commodities . . . which would not have come into being without extensive capital investment — the effects of commodification have been massively expansive.[22]

Historians could argue that at least the first and the third of his effects of commodification applied to patronage in early modern Europe. Recent scholarship on Renaissance consumption, particularly by Richard Goldthwaite and Lisa Jardine, has begun to document the way in which patronage, the gift economy, and commodity exchange all contributed to the expansion of cultural production beginning in the Renaissance.[23] The intersection between patronage and commerce in this period seems to be one key to the amplification of value and cultural significance that certain types of natural and artificial objects and modes of representing nature underwent.

VISUALISING NATURE

Dürer's rhinoceros also points to a new mode of description, which, even when not entirely precise, appeared to be the authentic result of a new emphasis on first-hand observation. Commerce clearly brought to light novelties, and novelty helped occasion new modes of description. The Spanish civil servant Gonzalo Fernández de Oviedo (1478–1557) lamented that he did not have a famous artist with him to record the things that he described in his natural history of the Indies in the early sixteenth century: "It needs to be painted by the hand of a Berruguete or some other excellent painter like him, or by Leonardo da Vinci or Andrea Mantegna, famous painters whom I knew in Italy."[24] In so saying, he articulated the importance of art in rendering knowledge visible for an audience fascinated by nature. Words alone could not adequately represent the marvels of the New World for a European audience. They needed to see these strange and different things in order to comprehend them fully. Fernández de Oviedo was not alone in believing that the skills possessed by Italian Renaissance painters versed in the new science of painting, as articulated by theorists such as Leon Battista

Alberti, would convey aspects of the Indies that verbal representation alone could not capture.

In 1543, the same year that Andreas Vesalius's *De Humani Corporis Fabrica* revolutionized anatomical imagery, Leonard Fuchs published 512 woodcuts of naturalistic plant specimens in *De Historia Stirpium*. He defended his departure from ancient practices:

> Though the pictures have been prepared with great effort and sweat we do not know whether in the future they will be damned as useless and of no importance and whether someone will cite the most insipid authority of Galen to the effect that no one who wants to describe plants would try to make pictures of them. But why take up more time? Who in his right mind would condemn pictures which can communicate information much more clearly than the words of even the most eloquent men? Those things that are presented to the eyes and depicted on panels or paper become fixed more firmly in the mind than those that are described in bare words.[25]

But naturalistic representation, appearing first in northern Italy and then in Flanders, was more than pictorial description. In the course of the fifteenth century, it became a fashion. The particularistic naturalism of Flemish painters, such as Jan van Eyck and Robert Campin, that emerged out of the forced integration of French court culture and the indigenous urban artisanal style of the rich trading cities of the Lowlands, spread rapidly to the noble courts and burgher homes of other parts of Europe.[26] Likewise the peculiar version of naturalism that we associate with Tuscan art between the age of Brunelleschi and Leonardo also found its following in many other parts of Italy in the course of the fifteenth and early sixteenth centuries, and influenced important northern artists such as Dürer.[27] Naturalistic images and natural objects became sought-after objects of patronage and commerce among European nobility and wealthy burghers. In many cases, it is not clear that the object was necessarily preferred over the image. A series of images created an aesthetically pleasing archive of the world that the diversity and fragility of actual artifacts never seemed quite able to capture—which is why "paper museums" such as Ulisse Aldrovandi's collection of thousands of naturalistic drawings and John White's illustrations of North America continue to be fundamental resources for our understanding how early modern Europeans saw and understood their world.[28] For this reason, we should take seriously the role of images in generating a new sense of the natural world, while at the same time preserving traditional images of nature that were less easily rendered as objects because they were acts of imagination.

Dürer's nature studies, which both continued and extended the Flemish innovations of the previous century and benefited from parallel developments in Italy, helped fuel a fashion in the description of nature. In the generation following Dürer, we find "amateur" botanizers and artists who self-consciously became his followers in cities such as Nuremberg, just as we can find communities of artists deeply influenced by Leonardo's style in the vicinity of Milan. They painted insects, small animals, and flowers in imitation of Dürer, but interestingly, they also went out into nature to find subjects for their visual descriptions.[29] The passion for a new kind of naturalistic art had indeed inspired artists, naturalists, and patrons to invest in the objects they sought to represent. It brings to mind the comment of the Veronese apothecary Francesco Calzolari, collector of art and nature and a famous botanist in the late sixteenth century, who told his fellow naturalists that when they climbed to the top of Monte Baldo near Verona the landscape that they would see resembled "a most beautiful Flemish painting."[30]

In the sixteenth and seventeenth centuries, the things of nature and their naturalistic representations were collected, studied, sold, and consumed all over Europe; objects and images claiming to portray and describe nature became a desired fashion, hard to obtain, and sought by princes and scholars for their cabinets of curiosities. The correspondence of the Augsburg merchant Philipp Hainhofer (1578–1647), an agent to several German princes, provides numerous examples of the passion with which naturalistic objects and images were sought. He often praised the "lifelikeness" or "naturalness" of an image or sculpture to his noble patrons.[31] Small animals cast from life in which "nothing is carved, but all is cast after life [nach dem leben]" were especially highly prized.[32] In one case, he even called in medical doctors to attest to the verisimilitude *and* aesthetic effect of a corpse sculpted in wax.[33] In his correspondence, Hainhofer both responded to *and* consciously trained the taste of his patrons (who, as his increasingly frantic attempts to obtain payment indicate, were simultaneously his clients).[34]

The fascination with natural goods and artificial objects made after nature that Hainhofer and others both ministered to and fostered, had the effect of disseminating images of nature, increasing familiarity with nature, and training a taste for naturalism. As Hainhofer was selling naturalism to his northern patrons, Galileo Galilei used naturalistic images in his attempts to convince his "image-friendly" patrons of his claims that the surface of the moon was irregular and imperfect (fig. Intro. 2).[35] We see here another of the effects of the fashion for naturalism that is discussed in the papers in this volume: the formation of a new visual language that would eventually become an auxiliary tool of proof in the natural sciences.

The natural and artificial objects and their images that were brought to the fore by the lively trade in early modern Europe constituted a sustained

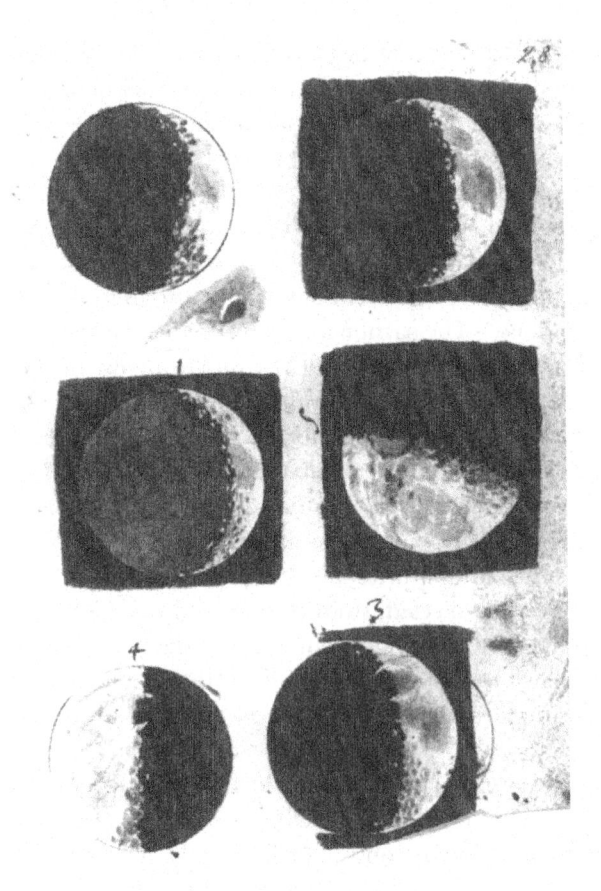

meditation on the boundary between art and nature and on the human capability of transcending this boundary.[36] This meditation went on in artists' workshops, natural philosophical cabinets and academies, and in noble collections and *studioli*. Ultimately, this taste for and interest in nature and naturalism trained the senses. By means of this circulation of naturalistic objects and images, some people learned to observe, record, compare, and, above all, value positively such acts of description, comparison, and recording. The patronage *and* the commodity value of these goods created a climate favorable to the investigation and representation of nature and helped to raise the status of the imitators and knowers of nature. As Claudia Swan has written

> Throughout the sixteenth century and well into the seventeenth, observation, description, and accumulation were the means by which nature came to be ever more systematically encountered, cataloged, published, collected, and studied. The epistemological objectives sponsored a particular kind of image, an image done *ad vivum*.[37]

We might simply say that the peculiar confluence of events made realistic naturalism a model of representation and a measure of the actual objects that were drawn and sculpted in various media. But the important thing to bear in mind is the lesson of Dürer's rhinoceros: such images were deeply enmeshed in political and commercial networks that looked at nature in new ways because it was a tangible sign of one's mastery of the world.

PRODUCING KNOWLEDGE

The turn to naturalism in art reflected a fairly sudden and dramatic transformation of the ways in which European artists represented their world. Its history, particularly in northern Italy and Flanders in the 1400s, has often been recounted in an heroic mode that tends to assume the value of naturalism without exploring what values it reflected at the time. In discussing the remarkable naturalism of the illustrations of the manuscript *Carrara Herbal* of around 1400 (fig. Intro 3), for example, Otto Pächt spoke of the illustrator's "courage to turn his back on all patternbooks and to look nature straight in the face."[38] Similarly, Erwin Panofsky commented on the principle, new in the Renaissance, that a work of art should be a faithful representation of a natural object, writing, "Treatises on sculpture and painting, therefore, could no longer be limited to supplying generally accepted patterns and recipes but had to equip the artist for his individual struggle with reality."[39] This heroic tone might remind us of old narratives of the Scientific Revolution, in which the protagonists finally looked at nature and saw what was "really" there. More recent scholarship has reminded us that naturalistic images did not always imply a theoretical commitment to observing nature for its own sake. The meditation on the boundary between nature and art sometimes produced witty counterfeit images, such as Joris Hoefnagel's imaginary insects that played with viewer's presuppositions about verisimilitude.[40] Just as the history of art has developed a more sophisticated approach to the idea of naturalism, likewise the history of science no longer confines itself to a simple story of seeing what was "really" there. These heroic narratives, however, both speak to the ways in which both modern techniques of representing reality and the advent of a new science traditionally have symbolized the break with the past that observers have discerned between the "premodern" and the "modern." The similarity of these two stories and the coincidence of their arrival make us want to see a connection between a deeper interest in nature that seems to be manifested in naturalistic art and the investigation of nature by the "new philosophy." What connections can we draw between the emergence of the new practices vis-á-vis the natural world and the new naturalistic representation?

• • •

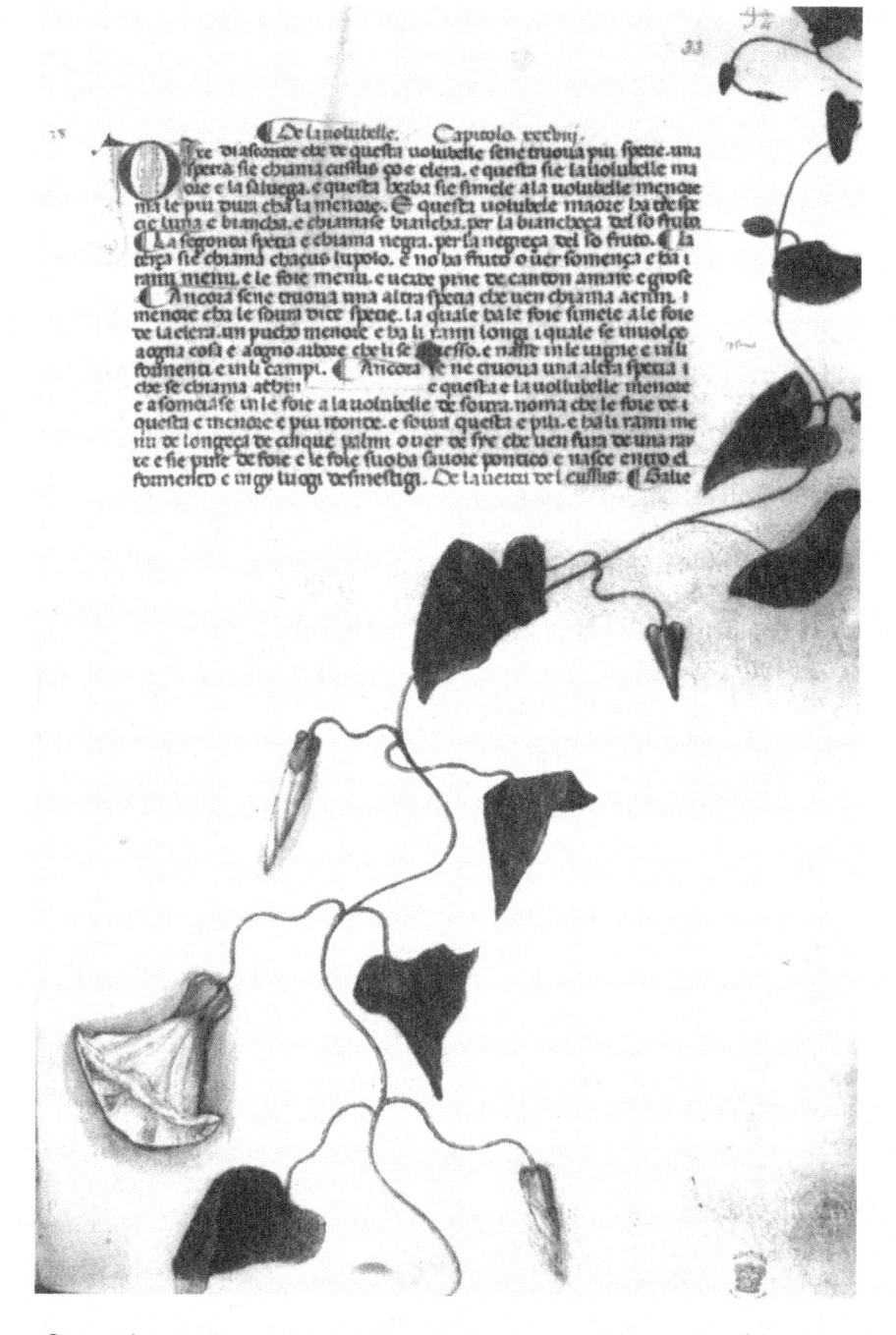

If we look again to Dürer's rhinoceros and recognize the central role he played in disseminating its representation along with other naturalistic images, as well as in establishing a standard and technique of naturalism, we can begin to understand the central role that artisans in the fifteenth and sixteenth centuries played in shaping new modes of description of and new attitudes toward nature. The artisan, after all, was neither wholly an artist nor a technologist in a modern sense but a person with skills that traversed these seemingly different domains. The history of many scientific instruments, such as the telescope, the camera obscura, and the microscope, and their relationship to new techniques of observation indicate similar conclusions. All of these instruments emerged from artisanal and mercantile milieus. Their application and dissemination also reflected the abilities of individuals in early modern society to cross boundaries that we have since installed by creating disciplines in areas which were predominantly defined by skills and techniques rather than specific kinds of knowledge.

Historians of art and of science have treated the convergence between artists-artisans and natural philosophers at length.[41] The subject of perspective, for example, and its mathematical construction has proved to be a *locus classicus* for such interdisciplinary discussions. James Ackerman has made clear the importance of the interaction between craftspeople and scholars in the matter of scientific illustration; Svetlana Alpers has proposed a more diffuse shared sensibility of descriptive analysis that functioned as a "two-way street" between which natural philosophers and artisans traveled in the sixteenth and seventeenth centuries;[42] and Thomas DaCosta Kaufmann has shown in depth the overlapping worlds of humanists and artists in the Holy Roman Empire.[43] In *The Science of Art*, Martin Kemp reconstructs a rich dialogue between artists and naturalists across several centuries, particularly in the matter of perspective construction and the use of lenses, although he concludes that there was no parity and no causal link between realist "art" and realist "science" in the early modern period because science seeks explanation and art seeks to create illusion.[44] Kemp expresses a loosely held consensus among historians of art and science that the investigators of nature and artists shared affinities, but not more. Recent research suggests that we should push this argument further. While the opposition between art and science as two different modes of engaging nature may be true in some sectors today, in the fifteenth and sixteenth centuries, when the methods of the new science were being constructed, artist-artisans were engaged in a kind of philosophizing about nature, and, while so engaged, they articulated a body of claims about nature and about the nature of authority that helped form the basis of the new science.[45]

Panofsky's phrase "the struggle with reality" resonates in this context, because early modern artists, artisans, and natural philosophers were indeed grappling with the problem of what the world really was and how they ought to see it, understand it, and represent it. How could they wrest knowledge, sometimes by bodily force, from nature? How could the information they gained through their senses give them reliable knowledge of nature? And how could they turn that knowledge to the production of works (of art, of technology, or of natural knowledge)? Both artisans and natural philosophers needed such knowledge; they needed to learn by the repeated experience of apprenticeship the characteristics of the material they worked and thus to produce masterpieces, or, in the case of architects and engineers, to build fortresses, canals, and weapons, or, in the case of physicians and natural philosophers, to produce medicaments and knowledge from nature. Moreover, both groups were engaged in a struggle to make sensory knowledge of nature authoritative; that is, they themselves had to gain social authority in order to formulate a picture of the real.[46] Early modern artists and naturalists alike required this social authority and self-consciousness in making the products that resulted from their efforts attractive and persuasive in a marketplace of goods and services that had no obligation to privilege their vision of reality. Practitioners of art and science, then, were both engaged in a quest for new methods of representing nature, as well as representing themselves as representers of nature.[47]

Several essays in the first section of this volume explore the relationship of artists and artisans to nature, and the way in which their values were absorbed into the new philosophy of nature. They make the point, however, that this was not in any way a linear and uncontested process. In the world of fifteenth-century artisans, artists, and natural philosophers we can see how much figures such as Leonardo and Dürer helped to shape subsequent discussions of representing and understanding nature without in any way determining the outcome of the conversation. Moving into the sixteenth century, in a world of learned naturalists such as Leonhart Fuchs, Conrad Gessner, and Ulisse Aldrovandi who created communities of artists around their projects of nature, we see a new set of emerging relations between the artistic, artisanal, and philosophical communities, as each of these groups underwent significant transformation. By the seventeenth century, an artist-naturalist such as Maria Sibylla Merian could travel all the way to Surinam, following the trade routes that had created this Dutch colony in the Indies, in order to pursue the insects that she wished to represent.[48] None of the groups that created the intersections among art, nature, and commerce enjoyed a well-defined or even very stable role. If artists played a dramatic role in ushering forth a new image of the world, naturalists took credit for cataloging the many variations of nature and using the medium of the printed natural history to combine words and images. Likewise the merchants and princes who understood the economic value of nature and of new technologies shaped the material environment in which it became possible, even necessary, to create a new art and science of description.[49]

Art historians have argued that the rise of commerce, as well as the commerce in paintings themselves, brought about changes in style and subject matter. Michael Baxandall famously showed the ways in which the "dancing bankers" of Renaissance Florence changed the face of art.[50] Following some of Baxandall's fundamental insights, Richard Goldthwaite has argued that mercantile and patrician demand for certain kinds of art and architecture played an important role in the development of Italian Renaissance art. John Michael Montias has argued that market demand for paintings in the Dutch Republic led to workshop innovations that brought about greater production, such as the move from fine, detailed, smooth work to quick, rough, painterly techniques in the northern Netherlands in the 1630s,[51] and recent work on the art market in sixteenth-century Antwerp has greatly expanded our understanding of the way in which works of art became regular items of international trade.[52] The issues raised by these works have spawned a literature far too extensive to cover here.[53] Strangely enough, no similar literature on science and commerce exists. It is instructive to explore why this might be so.

Max Weber first linked the rise of science to the rise of capitalism early in this century, regarding such a connection as a by-product of the relationship between Calvinism and commerce.[54] According to Weber, Calvinism was one factor in the emergence of a psychological habit that led to an inner-worldly asceticism that valorized the creation of wealth (as the work of Providence) and eventually resulted in a new rationality, thus tying both science and capitalism to the emergence of a religion of the bourgeoisie. The most famous result of Weber's link in the anglophone world was Robert K. Merton's 1938 monograph, *Science, Technology, and Society in Seventeenth-Century England*, which posited a link between Puritanism and the rise of modern science in the last half of the seventeenth century. Almost two-thirds of Merton's book dealt with the economic factors that made science a "socially countenanced, even esteemed" activity in seventeenth-century England.[55] The link between Puritanism and science came to be known as "the Merton thesis," but for Merton, it was not only Puritanism, but also the rise of capitalist economic activity and social structures that made, as he put it, the "cultural soil of seventeenth-century England peculiarly fertile for the growth and spread of science."[56] The subsequent debates over the "Merton thesis," which occupied so many historians of science, dealt only with the link between Puritanism and science, and did not explore the link between capitalism and science.[57] The reasons for this neglect in anglophone history of science could well be the subject of an entire essay, but important factors include the prevalent influence in the United States and England of Alexandre Koyré's conceptualization of the scientific revolution as a revolution in theory — primarily in astronomy and physics. The professionalization of historians of science that occurred in the United States separated business historians and historians of technology into separate professional societies and discouraged greater consideration of technology and science in their common relation to commerce. No doubt the distaste for examining the social and material relations of scientific knowledge owed something as well to the Cold War.[58] The result was that important scholars of the Scientific Revolution distinguished sharply between the classical, mathematical sciences and the experimental sciences, or the mechanical arts, which they regarded as tied to commercial ends and uninfluential in the Scientific Revolution.[59]

This bifurcation has begun to break down as historians of science, influenced by cultural history and its emphasis on practices, have focused on "practitioners." The old story of the Scientific Revolution was largely the story of theoretical change, in which the story of the invention of "experiment" was also important but was written as the intellectual history of a practice.[60] This story left out the large numbers of individuals who began to show interest in and to practice the "new philosophy," and whose actions brought about the institutionalization of the new philosophy, and, more important, made the new method of pursuing knowledge part of the habits of mind and action of European culture. One of the central components of the Scientific Revolution is now seen to be the emergence of a whole new set of beliefs about, and practices involving, nature. The pursuit of natural knowledge became *active* and began to involve the body; the investigator of the natural world had to observe, record, and engage with nature. This new active element of philosophizing about nature led Francis Bacon to call it a "New Philosophy, or Active Science." "Active science" was for Bacon an oxymoron.[61] Furthermore, one of the aims of this new pursuit of the knowledge of nature consisted in the production of effects — tangible objects or observable phenomena. An important source for this new epistemology was the entry into the knowledge-making process of a new group of people, practitioners, drawn from all social strata, but often occupying a middle ground between university-trained scholars, immersed in texts, and workshop-trained artisans, immersed in a world of technique. These practitioners often saw natural knowledge as an arena in which they could gain new authority and legitimacy. It brought them the attention of humanists, gave them access to the republic of letters, and bestowed upon them the favor of

Pamela H. Smith and Paula Findlen

princes, all predicated not upon their birth nor upon their knowledge of elite learning, but instead upon their ability to undertake particular practices and produce tangible effects or objects. All these practitioners are relative newcomers to the historiography of science, or perhaps a shadowy presence that has always been there but without a clearly delineated role. When we view them as part of the story of the emergence, or, better, the *construction* of science, the connections between early modern natural philosophy and commerce jump out at us with striking clarity. Recent historiography of science has found natural philosophy in new places, and has advanced the argument that entrepreneurial doctors, Spanish juntas, foreign artisans in England, and scholarly merchants all helped shape the habits of mind and action that became the new science.[62] This volume brings together many examples of this recent literature and places it next to a similar set of intersections that have been articulated in the history of art and science.

It is particularly illuminating that for many of these practitioners, attention to nature and to the market sprang from their interest — in both its intellectual and financial senses — in medicine. Recent work on natural history demonstrates the importance of medical practitioners in formulating, articulating, and disseminating the new philosophy.[63] Nor should this surprise us. Medicine always had some manual component to it, and physicians were always involved with the preparation of medicaments, combining theory and practice in a way that would eventually characterize all natural philosophical activity. Moreover, apothecaries and herbalists had long claimed direct access to nature and were among the first to concern themselves with the relationship between word, image, and nature in herbals and other health-related texts.[64]

The essays in the second section of this volume show us just how many individuals in sixteenth- and seventeenth-century Europe were engaged quite straightforwardly both in commerce and the pursuit of natural knowledge, and how many of their scientific ideas and practices had perfectly clear and calculable economic value that could be offered on the market. They make the point that, in some contexts, considerations of use and profit were the main stimulus to the investigation that yielded new "matters of fact" from the sixteenth to the late seventeenth century.[65]

The chapters in this section also show how pursuit of imperial power — and the desire for domination over nature and peoples and their exploitation for income — is integral to the construction of a new mode of rationality; one that stressed eyewitnessing, close observation, group judgment and evaluation of information, and the disciplining of subjects. Anthony Pagden has written very suggestively about the formation of this rationality, making the point that a variety of strategies were used to give authority to these new methods. For example, authors created new genres, often modeled on the natural history of Pliny, they used a new plain prose style, and they often employed the legal category of "fact."[66] The ancient genre of natural history turned out to be a remarkably accommodating rubric under which to ascertain the truth of nature in the service of empire. As Chandra Mukerji shows in this volume, strategies of domination in the seventeenth-century French kingdom also brought to the fore certain practices in relation to nature.

These essays give us the material to conceive of early modern science in new ways and to construct a new social and cultural narrative about the transformation in attitudes to the material world that is sometimes called "the" Scientific Revolution. The story told in the pages that follow includes many more people—ranging from indigenous New World artisans and informants, to Spanish and English bureaucrats, Jesuit missionaries, counterfeiters, and a multitude of others. It brings to light some of the early and explicit connections between political power and knowledge of nature, between the universalist claims of science and those of empire, and between social practices and modes of thought. In contrast to the scholarship that followed Merton, the essays in this volume suggest that it is in fact now difficult to overestimate the importance of the link between science and commerce.

CONSUMPTION, ART, AND SCIENCE

Fernández de Oviedo's desire, quoted above, that an artist would supplement his verbal description of the wonders he encountered, is one obvious link between art, science, and commerce, but a more profound connection between these three areas can be found in their intersection in the body: in sensory observation and sensual consumption, in the use of the senses to know nature, and in the sensory enjoyment of the things of nature and art. Sensuality, desire, and the passions were intimately linked to commerce, and the passions played a part in sensory perception. The first of the passions was curiosity, said by Descartes to be the beginning of knowledge, and it was also the engine that drove the collection and trade of the objects of nature and art.[67] One key to the relationship between commerce, art, and science lies here, in the relation of human bodies and their sensory organs to the material world. The essays in the final section of this volume discuss the connections between consumption and the representation of nature.

Curiosity and the search for profit were insatiable and omnivorous, and the investigation of nature, the creation of art, and commercial exchange were all deeply affected by a new valuation of curiosity in the early modern period. As Lorraine Daston has shown, curiosity moved from an alignment with lust and pride to one with avarice in the early modern period, and this new sensibility oriented scientific investigation toward commodity-like objects, as well as into the hidden secrets and small things of nature. Curiosity drove collection and consumerism, as well as serious scientific inquiry, as was attested to by Isaac Newton, Robert Hooke, and Marin Mersenne.[68] Dürer too, felt his portrayal of the rhinoceros was compelled by curiosity and wonder: "Because it is such a wondrous thing, I had to send you a portrayal made after it (Das hab jch dir van wunders wegen müsen abkunterfet shicken)."[69]

Much work remains to be done in writing a history of the body and the passions in relation to scientific investigation, and the relationship of art, science, and commerce is just one of the areas that will be clarified by such a history. The history that this volume seeks to recapture is not a neatly unified account of the early modern world, but a series of uneven developments — fascinating intersections that emerge when different disciplines discuss the meaning of nature and experience, knowledge and profit, money and materialism in the early modern period. Each contribution highlights a different kind of intersection that defines the world of "merchants and marvels" in the late fifteenth through late seventeenth centuries. They remind us of the importance of careful comparative analysis, lest we be too quick to offer a global definition of any of these categories. Finally, they reflect a new geographic sensibility about the study of science and culture in early modern Europe, one that places as much emphasis on countries such as Spain and the Netherlands as it does on more traditional sites for the Scientific Revolution, such as Italy, Germany, and, above all, England. New questions come from historians' and art historians' interest in new materials. And they also arise from our interaction with old debates — the incomplete vision of science and technology offered by Merton, for example, or the suggestive account of artistic naturalism proposed by Pächt and revised by Baxandall, Alpers, and Kemp. Let us imagine Dürer as he traveled through Europe, carrying the image of a rhinoceros that never arrived. But of course it did — and that is the point of the story.

Notes

1. Silvio A. Bedini, *The Pope's Elephant* (New York: Penguin, 1997).

2. T. H. Clarke points out that prior to the rhino's arrival in Lisbon in 1515, only a few classical scholars and humanists would have been familiar with the animal, from Roman coins, cameos, and Pliny's account. T. H. Clarke, *The Rhinoceros from Dürer to Stubbs, 1515–1799* (London and New York: Sotheby's Publications, 1986), 16. It is most likely that Dürer's drawing and woodcut are based upon a sketch that accompanied a newsletter sent to Nuremberg in 1515 by the Moravian printer Valentin Fernandes, who worked in Lisbon.

Shortly after the original drawing was made and certainly before his death in 1528, the first edition of the woodcut was published. Second and third editions were published in the 1540s–1550s, and it seems that these editions were the ones widely circulated and iconographically influential to later artists. The drawing and woodcut are characterized by decorative and imaginative patterning upon the separate plates of the rhinoceros's body. In 1515, Dürer lived in the street next to the armorers' quarter (the Schneidgasse) in Nuremberg and was actively producing designs for armor. Clarke notes that this patterning bears strong resemblance to Dürer's armor designs of the same period and compares it particularly to his sketch *Visor for a Jousting Helm*, ca. 1515.

3. This inscription written below the image in Dürer's hand is likely a transcription of Fernandes's newsletter account. John Rowlands, *The Age of Dürer and Holbein: German Drawings 1400–1550* (London: British Museum Publications, 1988), 94.

4. Peter Parshall, "Imago Contrafacta: Images and Facts in the Northern Renaissance," *Art History* 16 (1993): 554–579 .

5. Dürer very early on recognized the commercial potential of the new medium of the printing press, writing, "From now on, I shall concentrate on engraving. Had I done so all the time I should today be richer by a thousand guilders." Quoted in Erwin Panofsky, *The Life and Art of Albrecht Dürer* (Princeton, N.J.: Princeton University Press, 1955), 44.

6. Martin Kemp, " 'The Mark of Truth': Looking and Learning in Some Anatomical Illustrations from the Renaissance and Eighteenth Century," in *Medicine and the Five Senses,* ed. W. F. Bynum and Roy Porter (Cambridge: Cambridge University Press, 1993): 85–121.

7. Anthony Pagden, *European Encounters in the New World: From Renaissance to Romanticism* (New Haven, Conn.: Yale University Press, 1993).

8. Norbert Elias, *The Development of Manners*, Vol. 1 of *The Civilizing Process*, trans. Edmund Jephcott (New York: Urizen Books, 1978 [1939]); idem, *Power and Civility*, Vol. 2 of *The Civilizing Process*, trans. Edmund Jephcott (New York: Pantheon Books, 1982 [1939]).

9. Otto Brunner, *Adeliges Landleben und europäischer Geist. Leben und Werk Wolf Helmhards von Hohberg, 1612–1688* (Salzburg: Otto Müller, 1949).

10. Marcel Mauss, *The Gift*, trans. W. D. Halls (New York and London: W. W. Norton, 1990 [1950]).

11. Krzysztof Pomian, *Collectors and Curiosities: Paris and Venice*, trans. Elizabeth Wiles-Portier (Cambridge: Polity Press, 1990 [1987]). See also Antoine Schnapper, *Le Géant, La Licorne et la Tulipe: Collections et Collectionneurs dans le France du XVIIe Siècle* (Paris: Flammarion, 1988).

12. Thomas DaCosta Kaufmann has written eloquently on the political and representational goals of the central European *Kunstkammern* in *The Mastery of Nature: Aspects of Art, Science, and Humanism in the Renaissance* (Princeton, N.J.: Princeton University Press, 1993), especially the chapter, "From Mastery of the World to Mastery of Nature: The Kunstkammer, Politics, and Science," using the examples of the sixteenth- and early seventeenth century *Kunstkammern* of Emperor Rudolf II (1576–1612) and Archduke Ferdinand II of Tyrol (1529–95).

13. The collections of Ferdinand II of Tyrol in Schloss Ambras and those of the emperors in Vienna and Prague, the latter most famously enlarged by Rudolf II, were apparently arranged according to the material of the objects and grouped vaguely under *naturalia* (representing nature), *artificialia* (representing human art and the human place in the scheme of cosmic history as well as the mastery of nature by art), and *instrumenta* (representing human knowledge). See, among others, Christian Gries, "Erzherzog Ferdinand II. Von Tirol und die Sammlungen auf Schloß Ambras," *Frühneuzeit-Info* 5 (1994): 7–37.

14. Jaap van der Veen, "Dit klain Vertrek bevat een Weereld vol gewoel: Negentig Amsterdammers en hun kabinetten," in *De wereld binnen handbereik: Nederlandse kunst-en rariteit-*

Pamela H. Smith and Paula Findlen

enverzamelingen, 1585–1735, ed. Ellinoor Bergvelt, Renée Kistemaker (Zwolle: Waanders Uitgevers, 1992), 232–258. See also T. H. Lunsingh Scheurleer, "Early Dutch Cabinets of Curiosities," in *The Origins of Museums,* ed. Oliver Impey and Arthur Macgregor (Oxford: Clarendon Press, 1985), 116–120.

15. As was the case at the auction of the collection of Jan Swammerdam's father.

16. Arjun Appadurai, ed., *The Social Life of Things: Commodities in Cultural Perspective* (Cambridge: Cambridge University Press, 1986).

17. Kaufmann, *The Mastery of Nature.*

18. Bruce Moran, *The Alchemical World of the German Court: Occult Philosophy and Chemical Medicine in the Circle of Moritz of Hessen (1572–1632), Sudhoffs Archiv,* Supplement 29 (Stuttgart: Franz Steiner Verlag, 1991), and idem, "German Prince-Practitioners: Aspects in the Development of Courtly Science, Technology, and Procedures in the Renaissance," *Technology and Culture* 22 (1981): 253–274; Heiner Borgrefe, Vera Lüpkes, Hans Ottomeyer, eds., *Moritz der Gelehrte. Ein Renaissancefürst in Europa* (Eurasburg: Edition Minerva, 1997).

19. Dagmar Eichberger, "Naturalia and artefacta: Dürer's Nature Drawings and Early Collecting," in *Dürer and His Culture,* ed. Dagmar Eichberger and Charles Zika (Cambridge: Cambridge University Press, 1998), 13–37.

20. See *So wijd de wereld strekt* (The Hague: Mauritshuis, 1979–80).

21. See Appadurai, *Social Life;* Chandra Mukerji, *From Graven Images: Patterns of Modern Materialism* (New York: Columbia University Press, 1983); and Craig Clunas, *Superfluous Things: Material Culture and Social Status in Early Modern China* (Urbana: University of Illinois Press, 1991).

22. John Frow, "The Signature: Three Arguments about the Commodity Form," in *Aesthesia and the Economy of the Senses,* ed. Helen Grace (Kingswood, N.S.W.: UWS Nepean, 1996), 151–200, 192–193.

23. Richard A. Goldthwaite, *Wealth and the Demand for Art in Italy, 1300–1600* (Baltimore: Johns Hopkins University Press, 1995), and Lisa Jardine, *Worldly Goods: A New History of the Renaissance* (New York: W.W. Norton, 1996). See also the AHR Forum on the Renaissance, *The American Historical Review* 103, no. 1 (1998).

24. Fernández de Oviedo, *Historia General,* ii, 7, quoted in J. H. Elliott, *The Old World and the New 1492–1650* (Cambridge: Cambridge University Press, 1970), 21.

25. Leonhart Fuchs, *De historia stirpium comentarii insignes . . . accessit iis succincta admodum difficilium obscurarum passim in hoc opere occurrentium explicatio . . .* (Paris, 1543), Preface, pp. x–xi, quoted in James S. Ackerman, "Early Renaissance 'Naturalism' and Scientific Illustration," in *The Natural Sciences and the Arts: Aspects of Interaction from the Renaissance to the Twentieth Century: An International Symposium,* ed. Allan Ellenius (Uppsala: Almqvist & Wiksell, 1985), 1–17, 17.

26. Wim Blockmans and Walter Prevenier, *The Promised Lands: The Low Countries Under Burgundian Rule, 1369-1530,* trans. Elizabeth Fackelman (Philadelphia: University of Pennsylvania Press, 1999).

27. The classic study of this subject remains Michael Baxandall, *Painting and Experience in Fifteenth-Century Italy* (Oxford: Oxford University Press, 1972).

28. Giuseppe Olmi, *L'inventario del mondo. Catalogazione della natura e luoghi del sapere nella prima età moderna* (Bologna: Il Mulino, 1993); and Roger Schlesinger and Arthur P. Stabler, *Andre Thevet's North America: A Sixteenth-Century View* (Kingston, Ont.: McGill-Queen's University Press, 1986).

29. Heidrun Ludwig, *Nürnberger naturgeschichtliche Malerei im 17. und 18. Jahrhundert* (Marburg an der Lahn: Basilisken-Presse, 1998).

30. Francesco Calzolari, *Il viaggio di Monte Baldo* (Verona, 1565), 11.

31. A brief look at the correspondence of Philipp Hainhofer, the Augsburg merchant and princely factor, confirms this. For excerpts of his correspondence relating to art, see Oscar Doering, "Des Augburger Patriciers Philipp Hainhofer Beziehungen zum Herzog Philipp II von Pommern-Stettin. Correspondenzen aus den Jahren 1610–1619," *Quellenschriften für Kunstgeschichte und Kunsttechnik des Mittelalters und der Neuzeit*, NF Bd. 6 (Vienna: Carl Graeser, 1894).

32. Ibid., 79–82.

33. Ibid., 91.

34. From 1617, Hainhofer's demands for payment became urgent.

35. Mario Biagioli, "Picturing and Convincing: The Discovery and Illustration of Sunspots," unpublished paper read at the Clark Library, Los Angeles, October 2000.

36. Martin Kemp, "Wrought by No Artist's Hand: The Natural, the Artificial, the Exotic, and the Scientific in Some Artifacts from the Renaissance," in *Reframing the Renaissance,* ed. Claire Farago (New Haven, Conn.: Yale University Press, 1995), chapter 9, shows the various and interpenetrating values assigned to objects that teetered on the edge of the nature/art divide. See also Peter Parshall "Art and Curiosity in Northern Europe," *Word and Image* 11, no. 4 (1995): 327–331.

37. Claudia Swan, "Ad vivum, naer het leven, from the life: Defining a Mode of Representation," *Word and Image*, 11, no. 4 (1995), 352–372.

38. Otto Pächt, "Early Italian Nature Studies and the Early Calendar Landscape," *Journal of the Warburg and Courtauld Institutes* 13 (1950): 13–46, 31.

39. Panofsky, *Life and Art of Dürer*, 243.

40. In a study of herbal illustrations, however, Sachiko Kusukawa has pointed out that we should not assume that "naturalistic depiction implies a theoretical commitment to observing nature for its own sake." "Leonhart Fuchs on the Importance of Pictures," *Journal of the History of Ideas* 58 (1997): 403–427, esp. 427. Majorie Lee Hendrix, "Joris Hoefnagel and the 'Four Elements': A Study in Sixteenth-Century Nature Painting" (Ph.D. diss., Princeton University, 1984). Thomas DaCosta Kaufmann and Virginia Roehrig Kaufmann, "The Sanctification of Nature: Observations on the Origins of Trompe L'Oeil in Netherlandish Book Painting of the Fifteenth and Sixteenth Centuries," *J. Paul Getty Museum Journal* 19 (1991): 43–64.

41. Historians of science who have treated art and science include Giorgio Santillana, "The Role of Art in the Scientific Renaissance," in *Critical Problems in the History of Science*, ed. Marshall Clagett (Madison: University of Wisconsin Press, 1959), 33–65; Samuel Edgerton, Jr., *The Heritage of Giotto's Geometry: Art and Science on the Eve of the Scientific Revolution* (Ithaca, N.Y. and London: Cornell University Press, 1991); J. V. Field, *The Invention of Infinity: Mathematics and Art in the Renaissance* (Oxford: Oxford University Press, 1997). Art historians include James S. Ackerman, "The Involvement of Artists in Renaissance Science," in *Science and the Arts in the Renaissance*, ed. John W. Shirley, F. David Hoeniger (Washington, D.C.: Folger Shakespeare Library, 1985), 94–129; idem, "Early Renaissance 'Naturalism'"; Svetlana Alpers, *The Art of Describing: Dutch Art in the Seventeenth Century* (Chicago: University of Chicago Press, 1983); Michael Baxandall, *The Limewood Sculptors of Renaissance Germany* (New Haven, Conn.: Yale University Press, 1980); Thomas DaCosta Kaufmann, *The Mastery of Nature*; Martin Kemp, *The Science of Art* (New Haven, Conn.: Yale University Press, 1990); David Freedberg, *The Power of Images: Studies in the History and Theory of Response* (Chicago: University of Chicago Press, 1989); idem, "Science, Commerce, and Art: Neglected Topics at the Junction of History and Art History," in *Art in History, History in Art: Studies in Seventeenth Century Dutch Culture,* ed. David Freedberg and Jan de Vries (Santa Monica, Calif.: Getty Center for the History of Art and the Humanities,1991); Caroline Jones and Peter Galison, *Picturing Science Producing Art* (New York: Routledge, 1998).

42. "There is a two-way street here between art and natural knowledge. The analogy to the new experimental science suggests certain things about art and artistic practice, and the nature of the established tradition of art suggest a certain cultural receptivity necessary for the acceptance and development of the new science. . . . Didn't northern viewers find it easier to trust to what was presented to their eyes in the lens, because they were accustomed to pictures being a detailed record of the world seen?" Alpers, *The Act*, 25.

43. Kaufmann, *The Mastery of Nature*, and Thomas DaCosta Kaufmann, *Court, City, and Cloister: The Art and Culture of Central Europe 1450-1800* (Chicago: University of Chicago Press, 1995).

44. See the coda to Kemp, *The Science of Art*, esp. 340–341. James Ackerman takes a more developmental view, in which the aims of science and art diverged sometime after Leonardo da Vinci. James Ackerman, "Science and Visual Art," in *Seventeenth Century Science and the Arts*, ed. Hedley Howell Rhys (Princeton, N.J.: Princeton University Press, 1961): 63–90.

45. If we understand art to include other kinds of artisans (as it would have been understood in the early modern period), then there have been numerous studies of the way in which the new science rested on the work of artisans. This view has its origins in early history of science, including the essay by Edgar Zilsel, "The Sociological Roots of Science," *American Journal of Sociology* 47 (1942): 544–562; and the work of Paolo Rossi, particularly *Philosophy, Technology, and the Arts in the Early Modern Era*, trans. Salvator Attanasio (New York: Harper & Row, 1970); as well as Reijer Hooykaas, "The Rise of Modern Science: When and Why?" *British Journal for the History of Science* 20 (1987): 453–473. Arthur Clegg, "Craftsmen and the Origin of Science," *Science and Society* 43 (1979): 186–201, holds a similar view. See also Paolo Rossi, "Hermeticism, Rationality and the Scientific Revolution," in *Reason, Experiment, and Mysticism in the Scientific Revolution*, ed. M. L. Righini Bonelli and William R. Shea (New York: Science History Publications, 1975): 247–273. More recent historians pursuing this approach are James A. Bennett, "The Mechanics' Philosophy and the Mechanical Philosophy," *History of Science* 24 (1986): 1–28; idem, "The Challenge of Practical Mathematics," in *Science, Culture, and Popular Belief in Renaissance Europe*, ed. Stephen Pumfrey, Paolo Rossi, Maurice Slawinski (Manchester: Manchester University Press, 1991), 176–190; William Eamon, in *Science and the Secrets of Nature: Books of Secrets in Medieval and Early Modern Culture* (Princeton, N.J.: Princeton University Press, 1994); Michael Hunter, *Science and Society in Restoration England* (Cambridge: Cambridge University Press, 1983); Pamela O. Long, "The Contribution of Architectural Writers to a 'Scientific' Outlook in the Fifteenth and Sixteenth Centuries," *Journal of Medieval and Renaissance Studies* 15 (1985): 265–298; and idem, "Power, Patronage, and the Authorship of Ars," *Isis* 88 (1997): 1–41; Bruce T. Moran, "German Prince-Practitioners: Aspects in the Development of Courtly Science, Technology, and Procedures in the Renaissance," *Technology and Culture* 22 (1981): 253–274.

46. Lorraine Daston has warned against invoking a struggle to legitimate oneself by claiming access to nature, but in the case of artisans, their claim to legitimacy or authority on the basis of their knowledge of nature was made over and over again and justified by their ability to produce: to effect works and tangible things rather than words. Lorraine Daston, "The Nature of Nature in Early Modern Europe," *Configurations* 6 (1998): 149–172.

47. Among works arguing that artists were seeking to legitimate themselves and their art, see Joseph L. Koerner, *The Moment of Self-Portraiture in German Renaissance Art* (Chicago: University of Chicago Press, 1993); Victor I. Stoichita, *The Self-Aware Image: An Insight into Early Modern Meta-Painting*, trans. Anne-Marie Glasheen (Cambridge: Cambridge University Press, 1997); Hans Belting and Christiane Kruse, *Die Erfindung des Gemäldes: Das erste Jahrhundert der niederländischen Malerei* (Munich: Hirmer Verlag, 1995). In "Augustan Realities: Nature's Representatives and Their Cultural Resources in the Early Eighteenth Century," in *Realism and Representation: Essays in the Problem of Realism in Relation to Science,*

Literature, and Culture, ed. George Levine (Madison: University of Wisconsin Press, 1993): 279–311, Simon Schaffer argues that marginal scientific practitioners in the eighteenth century "worked hard to make a direct access to nature count and then make it clear that they had such access" (296). Such an observation also applies to practitioners and artisans of all kinds in the sixteenth and seventeenth centuries.

48. Natalie Zemon Davis, *Women on the Margins: Three Seventeenth-Century Lives* (Cambridge, Mass.: Harvard University Press, 1997); Charlotte Jacob-Hanson, *Maria Sibylla Merian, Artist-Naturalist* (New York: Brant Publications, 2000).

49. In addition to Alpers's important book *The Art of Describing*, see Brian Ogilvie, *The Science of Describing: Natural History in the Sixteenth Century* (forthcoming).

50. Baxandall, *Painting and Experience*.

51. John Michael Montias, *Artists and Artisans in Delft: A Socio-Economic Study of the Seventeenth Century* (Princeton, N.J.: Princeton University Press, 1982); idem, *Vermeer and His Milieu: A Web of Social History* (Princeton, N.J.: Princeton University Press, 1989); John Michael Montias, Gilles Aillaud, and Albert Blankert, *Vermeer* (Paris: Hazan, 1986). For an overview, see Michael North, *Art and Commerce in the Dutch Golden Age*, trans. Catherine Hill (New Haven, Conn.: Yale University Press, 1997; German ed. 1992).

52. Reindert Falkenburg, Jan de Jong, Dulcia Meijers, Bart Ramakers, Mariët Westermann, eds., *Kunst voor de Markt, 1500–1700* (Zwolle: Waanders Uitgevers, 2000).

53. Many valuable contributions to this discussion will appear in *The Culture of Exchange: Real and Imagined Markets in the Low Countries, 1500–1800*, ed. Liliane Weissberg (in preparation).

54. Max Weber, *The Protestant Ethic and the Spirit of Capitalism*, trans. Talcott Parsons (New York: Harper Collins, 1930).

55. Robert K. Merton, *Science, Technology and Society in Seventeenth Century England* (Bruges: St. Catherine Press, 1938), 231. In the sections he titled "Science, Technology and Economic Development," Merton explicitly tied the rise of science to the rise of capitalism.

56. Ibid., 238.

57. Similarly, other works of the 1930s and early 1940s that treated the relationship between capitalism and science—such as Boris Hessen, *The Social and Economic Roots of Newton's Principia* (London: Kniga, 1931); Edgar Zilsel, *Die Entstehung des Geniebegriffes; ein Beitrag zur Ideengeschichte der Antike und des Frühkapitalismus* (Tübingen: Mohr, 1926); and Edgar Zilsel, "The Sociological Roots of Science"—did not lead to any significant research in this area, at least not in anglophone scholarship. In the late 1950s and early '60s, Paolo Rossi published what came to be titled in the 1970 English edition *Philosophy, Technology, and the Arts in the Early Modern Era*, which took up many of Zilsel's themes.

58. Michael A. Dennis, "Historiography of Science: An American Perspective," in *Science in the Twentieth Century*, ed. John Krige and Dominique Pestre (Amsterdam: Harwood Academic Publishers, 1997), 1–26, gives a very nuanced evaluation of the effects of the particular circumstances of postwar United States on the growth and character of the profession of the history of science.

59. In this light it is perhaps not surprising to find the degree to which science was separated from material relations, which can be seen in A. R. Hall's "The Scholar and the Craftsman in the Scientific Revolution," in *Critical Problems in the History of Science*, ed. Marshall Clagett (Madison: University of Wisconsin Press, 1959) and, somewhat more surprisingly, in Thomas Kuhn's "Mathematical versus Experimental Traditions in the Development of the Physical Sciences," *The Essential Tension* (Chicago: University of Chicago Press, 1977). In this work, Kuhn even naturalized the difference by claiming that it was "rooted in the nature of the human mind" (64).

Pamela H. Smith and Paula Findlen

60. An example of such an orientation is Antonio Pérez-Ramos's excellent *Francis Bacon's Idea of Science and the Maker's Knowledge Tradition* (Oxford: Clarendon Press, 1988).

61. Francis Bacon, *The Great Instauration*, 1620.

62. It should be noted here that in his forgotten chapters, Merton made the relationship between commerce and science quite clear also, but there is a very significant difference between his story and the new historiography of this question: the number and range of people who are relevant to the story of the scientific revolution have been vastly extended in the new history of science. Merton, like his contemporaries, told the well-known story of the Scientific Revolution, which recounted the lives and ideas of a few scholars and dwelled long and lovingly on England in the last half of the seventeenth century.

63. The centrality of medical practitioners in the scientific revolution is suggested by Harold J. Cook, "The Cutting Edge of a Revolution? Medicine and Natural History Near the Shores of the North Sea," in *Renaissance and Revolution: Humanists, Scholars, Craftsmen, and Natural Philosophers in Early Modern Europe*, ed. J. V. Field and Frank A. J. L. James (Cambridge: Cambridge University Press, 1993), 45–61.

64. See Otto Pächt, "Early Italian Nature Studies," on early herbals and *tacuina sanitatis*. From the Middle Ages, the illustrations in these manuals often showed the herbalist digging up the plants, or in some other way making clear his personal eyewitnessing or handling of the plant, even when the herbs themselves were not rendered realistically.

65. Merton made commerce one of the prime legitimators of science in England, but placed this phenomenon in the late seventeenth century: "The development of scientific societies was not unrelated to this interest in enlisting the scientist in the service of industry, commerce and army. For the rising bourgeoisie, science and technology held out a promise which was not to be ignored; for the scientist-inventor, economic developments introduced or emphasized problems which, if attacked and solved, promised some financial reward and more prestige" (159).

66. Pagden, *European Encounters*.

67. Albert O. Hirschman, *The Passions and the Interests: Political Arguments for Capitalism before Its Triumph* (Princeton, N.J.: Princeton University Press, 1977) was one of the first to notice the prevalence of the discourse about the passions in early modern Europe. Recent interest in the passions has yielded Susan James, *Passion and Action: The Emotions in Seventeenth-Century Philosophy* (Oxford: Clarendon Press, 1997); and Stephen Gaukroger, *The Soft Underbelly of Reason: The Passions in the Seventeenth Century* (New York: Routledge, 1998).

68. Lorraine Daston, "Curiosity in Early Modern Science," *Word and Image* 11, no. 4 (1995): 391–404. See also Lorraine Daston and Katharine Park, *Wonders and the Order of Nature* (New York: Zone, 1999). For one preliminary attempt to write a history of the senses, see J. R. R. Christie, "The Paracelsian Body," in *Paracelsus: The Man and His Reputation, His Ideas, and Their Transformation*, ed. Ole Peter Grell (Leiden: Brill, 1998).

69. Translated and quoted in Parshall, "Imago Contrafacta," 561.

Part 1

STRUGGLING WITH REALITY

Visualizing Nature and Producing Knowledge

Splendor in the Grass

The Powers of Nature and Art in the Age of Dürer

LARRY SILVER AND PAMELA H. SMITH

Sheep and oxen, all of them,
Yea, and the beasts of the field;
The fowl of the air, and the fish of the sea;
Whatsoever passeth through the paths of the seas.
O Lord, our Lord,
How glorious is Thy name in all the earth!

—Psalm 8

One of the most striking new images in German art in the era of Albrecht Dürer remains the Virgin Mary situated out of doors. Its combination of natural description and spirituality offers a key to understanding the special yet unarticulated powers associated with nature in early modern Germany. Investigating the new ways in which Dürer and his imitators began depicting nature in the period from 1450 to 1550 can provide an entry point into artisanal attitudes to nature and natural knowledge.

Dürer's Madonna conforms to a late medieval type, associated with the *humus* of the earth, known as the "Madonna of Humility."[1] Late medieval visual tradition also situated Mary in a symbolic enclosed garden, or *hortus conclusus*, of the Song of Songs (4: 12), redolent of her virginity; a notable Rhenish example is the name painting of the Master of the Enclosed Garden (Frankfurt, Staedel).[2] Striking about the images of the Madonna outdoors by Dürer and his contemporaries is the absence of these traditional protective garden walls; these figures sit in wide-open spaces, immersed in expanse rather than confinement.

Dürer's images of the Virgin outdoors on either the ground or a grassy bench begin with his engraving *Madonna with the Mayfly*, ca. 1495 (Meder

Figure 1.1 Albrecht Dürer, *Madonna with a Mayfly*, ca. 1495. Courtesy of the Albertina, Vienna.

42; fig. 1.1), which features a characteristic local landscape, akin to the watercolor settings made in the vicinity of Nuremberg, which Dürer first recorded at around the same time.[3] Yet erupting into this ordinary setting, on the central vertical axis with the Madonna and child in this print, is an extraordinary heavenly epiphany, as God the Father and the dove of the Holy Spirit appear in open clouds directly over Mary, to complete the Trinity with the infant Christ.

In other, slightly later Dürer images of the Madonna outdoors, such as the woodcut *Holy Family with Three Hares* (Meder 212) the same grassy bank recurs, although in front of the extensive, receding landscape setting stands a stone enclosure, reestablishing the tradition of the *hortus conclusus*. Here

Larry Silver and Pamela H. Smith

the Christ child reads precociously from a holy book while a pair of hovering angels above the Virgin bear her heavenly crown, even as she sits humbly on her grassy bank. The presence of the hares has never been explained, but the inevitable association of this most fertile of animals (especially for a group of them together across the bottom of the print) with fecundity suggests generation as an important aspect here of the holy family, although the conception of Christ is expressly not sexual (or worldly or basely animalistic), as the advanced age of St. Joseph assures. The other most important element in the print is botanical: the several large weedlike plants on the favorable right (*dexter*) side of the Virgin. These plants have never been identified, though both position and size suggest their positive, possibly medicinal properties.[4] Indeed, the shorter foreground plant with fleshy leaves resembles the frequent depiction of a mandrake, a plant whose legendary magical and medicinal (chiefly narcotic or poisonous) properties included a perceived homunculus in its forked root system, making it shriek when pulled from the ground.[5] The presence of this plant beside the holy figures lends a particular charge, related to the conception of Christ, which can also be related to the passage in Genesis 30:14–24, where eating mandrake is expressly connected to divine intervention in the pregnancy of Rachel with Joseph, an Old Testament antitype for Christ: "God hearkened to her and opened her womb. She conceived and bore a son." (30:22–23). This combination of mandrake (and grasses, the significance of which remains to be determined) with the fertility of the hares in the enclosed setting of the Madonna suggests her miraculous virgin birth; at the same time, the affinity between the natural world and the holy figures in this work joins with the explicit link between heaven and earth in the *Madonna with the Mayfly* to suggest a cosmic resonance between sacred and profane, celestial and terrestrial, macrocosm and microcosm.

Most commentators on these images of the Madonna outdoors have assumed that the scene has a foundation in narrative, specifically the story of the Flight into Egypt, when the holy family fled for its own safety from the dangers of Herod's Massacre of the Innocents. Yet Dürer never seems to try to represent exotic scenery as the landscape background of these scenes, in striking contrast to his later *Flight into Egypt* woodcut from the *Life of the Virgin* cycle (ca. 1503–04; Meder 201). In that image, the left-to-right movement of the figures across the setting shows their flight, and two distinctly exotic non-European trees, palm tree and "dragon tree," mark the location as "foreign," even close to the lost paradise of Eden.[6] Moreover, the presence of the hovering angels with the crown of Mary in the woodcut offers a hieratic theophany through symbolic royal synecdoche, as if in distillation of the actual vision manifested in the *Mayfly* engraving. Such scenes are not narratives, but instead provide assertions about the nature of the holy figures, especially the incarnate figure of Christ, poised between the world and the divine order of the cosmos.

As if to confirm this mediating role of Christ and the symbolic presentation of theological concepts, Dürer next (ca. 1497–98) produced a more mature engraving, the *Madonna with the Monkey* (Meder 30). Scholars agree in reading this animal as a symbolic image of human sin, the error of old Adam, enchained and redeemed by the presence of Christ.[7] This fettered monkey contrasts with the freedom of the bird in Christ's own hand; wings associate the creature with both angels and the human soul, and the creature is actually nourished by the hand of the child.[8] On the grassy bench to the (favorable) right of the Virgin, a prominent foreground plant, a "star of Bethlehem," surely signals the location and refers unobtrusively to the event of the Nativity.[9] In this print, no structure of enclosure remains to isolate a garden from the wider landscape; in contrast, the background landscape derives closely from a watercolor study from the vicinity of Nuremberg, the *'Weiherhaus'* (London, British Museum, W. 115).[10] This Madonna and child image, which completely eliminates St. Joseph and any suggestion of the holy family, could not be misconstrued as a narrative moment.

Climaxing these suggestions that the natural world responds to the character and virtues of the holy figures, Dürer produced a colored ink drawing in 1503, *Madonna with a Multitude of Animals* (Vienna, Albertina; fig. 1.2).[11] This drawing, a prized cornerstone of the old master collection of Emperor Rudolf II at the end of the sixteenth century, was copied in both an engraving (in the same orientation as the original) by Aegidius Sadeler as well as a painting by Jan Brueghel (1604; Rome, Palazzo Doria).[12] This image does contain background narratives, chiefly the Annunciation to the Shepherds by the angel, as well as the figure of St. Joseph standing at a small distance behind the central Madonna and child. Yet fundamentally it is neither a Nativity nor a narrative scene but rather another image of resonance between these holy figures and the rich diversity of life in nature, exemplified by the multitude of animals that surround Mary and Christ. Again the epiphany of heaven finds expression not only in the form of the hovering angel but also in the form of the star of Bethlehem directly above the holy figures (occupying the spot of God and the dove in the *Mayfly* engraving).[13] If the size of the main figures as well as their seated or enthroned posture on the inevitable grassy bank suggests a hierarchy (with Joseph reduced in size and confined to the middle distance and extreme right), it is noteworthy that plants and animals fill the immediate foreground, which is marked off as the holiest space by another "garden" wall, albeit one only as high as the level of the grassy bench.

Continuity with the *Madonna with the Monkey* can be seen in the two holy figures, their postures and gestures, though here Christ gestures off in the

Larry Silver and Pamela H. Smith

Figure 1.2 Albrecht Dürer, *Madonna with a Multitude of Animals*, 1503, Albertina, Vienna.   Courtesy of Art Resource, New York.

direction of St. Joseph and does not attend directly to an animal like the bird in his hand in the engraving. Mary is now veiled, and her enfolding mantle becomes more noticeable on both sides of her body, evoking the protective *Schutzmantel* of standing Virgin of Mercy figures in German art of the period, which often serves as an image of prophylaxis against plague.[14] Here her sheltering role is focused on the Christ child alone rather than all of humanity, but in effect her benign protection serves to extend grace to the world, including the animals and plants. In this later redaction the fox at the feet of Mary, bound with collar and leash, continues the symbolism of the *Madonna with the Monkey* of restraint for humanity's animal sinfulness.[15] The parrot, the bird of intelligence and speech, was associated with Mary as the Throne of Wisdom and traditionally equated with the Annunciation, even credited with saying "ave."[16] Surrounding the Virgin, as if emanating from her person, are flowers (rose/peony, iris) and fruits (strawberry) that traditionally embody her virtues.[17] Moreover, the hollyhocks beside the owl offer a positive antidote to the evil influences of that bird.[18]

Dürer's imagery of the Madonna outdoors, using animals and other natural items to demonstrate the resonance between holy figures and God's creatures, continued in the works of younger imitators. Shortly after the turn of the sixteenth century, Lucas Cranach painted a 1504 image of the holy family in a forest, which is usually designated as a *Rest on the Flight into Egypt* (Berlin) and was followed in turn by a 1509 woodcut of the same subject (fig. 1.3).[19] This work is not explicitly a narrative either, though there is more suggestion of movement. Here the holy figures, including St. Joseph, pause within a landscape setting of forest or mountain glade in order to rest upon the ground. The forest setting serves principally as a retreat and haven for the holy figures instead of being their visible domain (suitable for showing the Madonna enthroned, even if on her grassy bank). More important, the suggestion of narrative events is underscored by the presence of miracles, such as the drawing of water by a cluster of small angels. In all likelihood, the textual source for this event is an apocryphal gospel, Pseudo–Matthew 20, where the child Jesus bids a palm tree to bend low and offer its fruit at the feet of Mary, while a spring emerges from its roots. In the Cranach woodcut the tree is bent low by angelic agents, and its spring lies below. Symbolic plants in the glade at the foot of Mary suggest the influential presence of her holiness: strawberries, fruits of paradise; cowslip, the plant known in German as "heaven's key" (*Himmelschlüssel*); columbine, traditional Marian flower of sorrow, showing the canonical seven sorrows in its floral shape as well as the mood of melancholy in its purple color.[20] Beside them a thorn serves as contrast and as an anticipation of Christ's Passion. The finch, associated with thorns, is carried (rather roughly) by one of the angels; this bird usually symbolizes Christ's triumph over the Passion in the form of the Resurrection.[21] The presence of this bird in the Cranach scenes could refer to another apocryphal text (Gospel of Thomas), in which the child Jesus (age five, according to the text) fashioned birds out of clay (twelve sparrows) on the Sabbath; these new creatures took flight while he played with many other children.[22] In short, the very landscape in Cranach's *Rest on the Flight into Egypt* becomes energized by their divine powers, visibly denoted by the

Figure 1.3 Lucas Cranach, *Rest on the Flight into Egypt*, 1509.

plethora of angels of various sizes and shapes (possibly of different kinds; there were nine orders of angels, according to medieval theology). Moreover, the site manifests the glory of the holy figures through the presence of meaningful plants and animals, already the case with Dürer's earlier images of the Madonna outdoors.

Related to the model of Cranach's images of the holy family in a forest retreat, a large panel by Altdorfer of *Saints John the Evangelist and John the Baptist* (Regensburg, Stadtmuseum; fig. 1.4) features the two holy men in their roles as hermits, the Baptist on the right in his role as the "voice crying in the wilderness," the Evangelist on the left as the author of the Book of Revelation during his sojourn on the island of Patmos.[23] Here, too, as Behling pointed out,[24] the wilderness is crowded with portraitlike representations of actual plants, highlighted next to the Baptist at right by the large and magnificent mullein plant, known more colloquially for its shape in German as "King's candle" (*Königskerze*; *candela* in Latin). This summer-blooming plant was understood to be a powerful medicament, tied to powerful celestial forces, which would accord with the visionary epiphanies of these two isolated holy men. Moreover, the plant was a prominent decoration associated with the feast day of the birth of John the Baptist, June 24, itself a marker of solstice and a popular folk festival often celebrated with bonfires.[25] Two other prominent plants in the center foreground of the *Two Saints John* (fig. 1.4) are sage and henbane (or "deadly nightshade"), the former a healing herb and digestive, the latter a poison shown just in front of the Lamb of God). One can recall in this context that the normal attribute of John the Evangelist is a chalice with a snake, because of a legend that the saint survived an attempt by a pagan priest to poison him, so the presence of sage and henbane in front of St. John are appropriate opposites, a deadly threat and its natural antidote. Animals, tiny but significant, also populate the Altdorfer image beside the Evangelist: a snail and a butterfly. Traditionally both refer symbolically to Christ's Resurrection (according to medieval beliefs, snails remained buried in the earth for the three coldest months of winter and then emerged as the weather warmed up).[26]

It should be noted that the outlook associating tiny animals with great, even cosmic significance endured through the course of the sixteenth century. This view is particularly vivid in the presentation of insects within the overall luxury miniatures by Georg Hoefnagel illustrating the animal world of the *Four Elements* (Washington, National Gallery of Art), a work produced for Emperor Rudolf II around the beginning of the last quarter of the sixteenth century.[27] As Hendrix's fine study makes clear, insects dominate the volume on the element Fire (*Ignis*), exemplifying the concept of the microcosm, or *multum in parvo*; moreover, the text atop folio 1 of *Ignis* testifies to the significance of connections between earth's creatures and their

Figure 1.4 Albrecht Altdorfer, *The Two Saints John*, 1515. Courtesy of the Stadtmuseum, Regensburg.

heavenly creator: "Of all the miracles made by man, a greater miracle is man. Of all visible miracles, the greatest is the world. Of those invisible, God. If we see that the world exists, we believe God exists."[28]

When Altdorfer painted his 1510 *Rest on the Flight into Egypt* (Berlin; fig. 8), he underscored the visible manifestation of holiness in the landscape through magical transformations.[29] This painting doubtless had strong personal significance for the painter, since he not only signed it but also dedicated it prayerfully with a dedication to the Virgin on the base of the miraculous fountain: *A[l]b[er]tus Altorffer [p]ictor Ratis/ponen[sis] In salutem a[nima]e hoc tibi/munus diva maria sacravit/ corde fideli: 1510* (Albrecht Altdorfer, painter of Regensburg, dedicated this gift to you, St. Mary, with faithful heart in (hopes of) the health of his soul).

At first glance, the Altdorfer *Rest on the Flight* (fig 1.5) offers another instance of the theme of the holy family beside a riverside landscape akin to the Dürer engravings, although one can perhaps make an interpretive equation between the fortified gateway in the background town and the traditional metaphor of the Virgin as both the "portal of Heaven" (*porta coeli*) or the "tower of David" (*turris David*). Again Mary is seated upon a modest,

Figure 1.5
Albrecht Altdorfer,
*Rest on the Flight to
Egypt*, 1510.
Courtesy of Staatliche
Museen Preussischer
Kulturbesitz, Gemälde-
galerie, Dahlem, Berlin.

draped "throne" before or upon a grassy bank. She takes cherries, another fruit of heaven,[30] from the aged Joseph. But the striking anomaly within Altdorfer's vision of this setting is an incongruous, dominant foreground fountain along the left side.[31] This fountain surely evokes recollections — within a worldly landscape — of paradise as well as traditional symbolism of Mary-as-fountain, something that Altdorfer reinforced shortly afterward with a woodcut, *Holy Family by a Fountain* (ca. 1512/15, W. 83).[32] What makes the fountain in the painting so unusual is its figure at the top: a pagan statue on a plinth. But this is not a threatening paganism, for in the lower basin another lively cluster of playful, cherubic angels climb, swim, and make music, while the Christ child, unswaddled and naked, leans from Mary's lap over to the basin to join their play. Moreover, it is at the foot of this astonishing fountain that Altdorfer appended his prayerful Latin inscription, monogram, and date, as if it were his own pictorial "gift" (*munus*) to the Virgin.

The pagan god atop the fountain must be Apollo. Although bearded and muscular, like standard representations of Hercules, he wears a crown of laurel, sacred to Apollo. His quiver of arrows is an ambiguous attribute; on the one hand, Apollo was a renowned archer, who slew Python (perhaps an appropriate serpent analogue to the Virgin and Christ, conquerors of Satan) as well as the children of vainglorious Niobe. Yet Hercules, too, was a noted archer, who slew the Stymphalian Birds with arrows among his celebrated twelve labors.[33] The main figure is accompanied by a blindfolded Cupid, who holds a bow with two arrows, one sharp and the other blunt. This secures the Apollo identification (as well as the divine nature of the muscular bearded figure), because the two contrasting arrows of Cupid refer to the respective shafts that were shot into Apollo (sharp) and Daphne (blunt), after the Python incident, as recounted by Ovid (*Metamorphoses* I, 446–52). Thus the emphatic presence atop the fountain of Apollo, with his pure (and unrequited) love for Daphne, and Cupid suggest pagan analogies, or even typologies, for the divine love principle (including the fruit of cherries) of the Christian holy family alongside that fountain. At the same time, the presence of the fountain itself attests to the extraordinary powers of the holy figures in an otherwise ordinary landscape, akin to the exploits of the Christ child as recounted in the apocryphal pseudo-Gospels.

Still more mysterious on the fountain is the item held by the Apollo figure. It appears to be an egg with wings and ducklike feet and its own laurel crown on top. A similar combination of egglike cup with wings and duck feet (surmounted, however, by a lion rather than a laurel) forms the subject of an emblematic Dürer drawing of 1513 (Berlin; W. 703), along with the inscribed motto *Fortes Fortuna Juvit* (Fortune favors the strong) (fig. 1.6).[34] This combination of lion with egg recalls the presence of lions' heads on the fountain ornament by Altdorfer in both the Berlin painting and the woodcut, which suggests some overlap of meaning with the Dürer drawing. Lions are often associated with Christ not only by virtue of being considered the king of beasts, but also because bestiary lore claimed that lion cubs were born dead but raised to life after three days when breathed upon by their sire.[35]

As Eisler and Hartlaub both observe, Dürer also paired lions with the figure of Apollo (shown with a laurel crown and a bow but beardless) in an early drawing made during his first stay in Venice, ca. 1495 (Vienna, Albertina; W. 87). In that drawing, Dürer also shows a turbaned "oriental" or Turkish alchemist figure holding a skull as a book sits at his feet. On a small tripod between the god and the savant sits a smoking globe, labeled "lutus," that is the *lutum sapientiae*, the "sealing-wax of wisdom" in alchemy.[36] Indeed, the direct association of alchemy with an exotic, Levantine "magus" strongly suggests that this knowledge is both ancient and occult, a frequent belief of early modern natural philosophers.[37] Both its shape and association with Apollo

Figure 1.6 Albrecht Dürer, *Drawing of an Egg Cup with Wings.* Courtesy of Kupferstichkabinett, Berlin.

suggest that this globe should be thought of as the analogue to what Altdorfer produced as an egg on his fountain summit.

Alchemical themes and images were broadly disseminated in manuscript and in print by the sixteenth century, and both Dürer and Altdorfer could well have been familiar with alchemy from Latin or vernacular sources. Historians have debated the esoteric and alchemical meaning of these artists' imagery,[38] but whatever the artists' knowledge of the esoteric aspects of alchemy, artisanal and alchemical practices overlapped.[39] In his 1390 manual for painters, Cennino Cennini described certain pigments as being produced by *"alchemia,"*[40] and Dürer had perhaps learned metallurgical techniques in the workshop of his father, a goldsmith. In any case, alchemy was more than a set of theories or techniques. Throughout the early modern period, alchemy seems to have formed a language for artisans who wanted to articulate their processes of working, as well as for scholars, who were trying to understand how artisans created things from matter. The fact that artisans worked with their hands and learned by apprenticeship separated them socially and intellectually from most scholars, who regarded the mechanical arts as existing across a deep divide. This began to change in the sixteenth century as humanists, such as Petrus Ramus (1515–72) and Juan Luis Vives (1492–1540), exhorted their fellow scholars not to "be ashamed to enter into shops and factories, and to ask questions from craftsmen, and to get to know about the details of their work."[41] The late fifteenth and early sixteenth centuries were crucial for the development of a new relationship between scholars and craftspeople.[42] Because alchemy was one of a few disciplines in which people worked both with texts and with their hands, scholars and craftsmen alike had practiced it since the Middle Ages, and it played a central role in articulating this new relationship.[43] Furthermore, alchemy and artisanry possessed a common essence: the ennobling of matter through manual work. Although today we associate alchemy mainly with the transmutation of base metals into gold, in the early modern period it was indistinguishable from what we would today call metallurgy or chemistry, or even organic chemistry, for alchemists sought the composition of the vital principle through which they could effect transformations of matter of all kinds, as well as heal disease and prolong life. It thus had much in common with medicine as well as with artisanship. Indeed, on a cosmic scale, alchemy was the epitome of all artisanal activity, for it redeemed matter, just as the practice of the arts (and medicine) did. All such activities resulted from the Fall and helped to redeem humankind after the expulsion from Eden.

It is thus not surprising that we would find an interest in alchemy in Dürer's drawings and Altdorfer's paintings, and it is possible to elaborate their alchemical allusions in terms of alchemical theory. For example, their use of Apollo, the classical sun god, points to the privileged position in alchemical thought of solar imagery, which was identified with the metal gold and with a generative male principle, or fiery spirit, that joined with matter.[44] Sulfur, one of the two principles of alchemical transmutation, by which base metals were ennobled, was identified with the sun, gold, and nobility.

Moreover, eggs, placed as central objects by both Dürer and Altdorfer, held special significance in alchemical precepts as the model for the secret, enclosed generation of life out of inanimate matter.[45] The "philosophical egg" of alchemical theory could symbolize a model of the cosmos as well as denote the source of the philosophers' stone, the material by which alchemists transmuted base metals into gold and silver. In addition, a laboratory vessel having a rounded shape and short neck, known as an "egg," or Hermetic vase, was supposed to be particularly effective in generating the philosophers' stone. When artists depicted the alchemical process by which the philosophers' stone was produced, it was often within such egglike vessels. The most fully developed of such depictions, Salomon Trismosin's alchemical *florilegium, Splendor Solis,* produced in Nuremberg in the 1530s, possibly by Albrecht Glockendon or his workshop, shows the progression from the black putrefying material in such a vessel, through the multicolored "tail of the peacock," to the final stage of the transmutation, when the mass in the "egg" turns red, then is suddenly transformed into gold.

One of the illustrations in the *Splendor Solis* displays a hermaphrodite holding an egg in one hand and, in the other, the cosmos, symbolized by the four elements of earth, water, air, and fire. The egg signifies the beginning of all things, out of which the entire cosmos develops.[46] The figure of the hermaphrodite represents the dual principles, sulfur and mercury, involved in alchemical transmutation, which combine to form a unity. Alchemical writers since at least the thirteenth century regarded sulfur and mercury as the primary components of all metals, and they continued to do so well into the seventeenth century.[47] While sulfur and mercury had ordinary forms that could be found in nature and handled by alchemists, in alchemical theory they were understood as principles. Sulfur was viewed as the hot, fiery, male principle, representing the qualities of fire and air and giving metals their combustibility.[48] It combined with the wet, cold, female principle of mercury, combining the properties of earth and water. Alchemical writers identified mercury as the ingredient in metals that gave them their "metallic" qualities, because of its silvery shininess and the fact that it is liquid at room temperature, analogous to the liquidity of metals when heated. In addition, mercury forms amalgams, or alloys, with other metals, particularly gold and silver, in such a way that it is difficult to distinguish the alloy from the pure, noble metal. Mercury also possesses a solid state, a silvery, fluid state, and becomes a volatile spirit when heated. It thus appeared to alchemical writers capable of uniting the qualities of matter and spirit, or fixing the volatile, a common goal of alchemists.[49] Because of its unique qualities, alchemical authors believed mercury played a central part in transmutation, and in the late thirteenth century some alchemists were led to reduce the metallic principles to mercury alone. By the sixteenth century, however, when the *Splendor Solis* was illustrated, the two-principle theory had once again become accepted by most alchemical writers, although the two theories continued to coexist.[50] The "alchemical wedding" of mercury, the female principle, with sulfur, the male principle, resulted in an offspring, the mercury of the philosophers, the main ingredient in the philosophers' stone.

Figure 1.7 "Mercury of the Philosophers" from *Turba philosophorum*, sixteenth century. Ms. lat. 7171, fol. 16. Courtesy of Bibliothèque Nationale, Paris.

A sixteenth-century illustration in a manuscript version of the *Turba philosophorum* shows a naked female figure crowned with a phoenix, standing on the sun and the moon, wings extending to her feet (fig. 1.7). In the hands of this "Mercurius genetrix" are representations of the moon and a chalice out of which shoot flames, perhaps conflating sun, Apollo, and Christ (by reference to the chalice of the eucharist). The verse above this figure reads, "Here is born Sun and Moon's child/ the equal of which no one on

---

earth can find/ but in the world it's nevertheless well known/ it's called Mercurius philosophorum."[51]

A seventeenth-century engraving shows the marriage of Sol (sulfur) and Luna (mercury), from which issues the mercury of the philosophers in a philosophical egg (fig. 1.8). The flowers springing from the neck of the "egg" denote the generative qualities of the philosophers' mercury that led the eleventh-century alchemical author Rhazes, to call it the "water of life." One of the most famous of all alchemical illustrations, the green lion devouring the sun, out of which runs red blood, signified a similar process. It stood for the process of raw antimony ore drawing in the universal generative spirit to produce a vivified mercury, the vital character of which was denoted by the red blood. This living mercury could dissolve and then revivify gold to make it grow and multiply. Such a substance was the common goal of alchemists from Rhazes to Newton.[52]

The fountain in Altdorfer's painting also runs with the "water of life." While the recurring motif in art of the Fountain of Life clearly had a primarily spiritual dimension, ultimately deriving from the source of waters and flowing rivers described in the Garden of Eden (Genesis 2), it could also be understood in an entirely material way: alchemical theory posited a vivifying principle concentrated in the philosophical mercury but also disseminated throughout nature. It fell with the rain and penetrated the earth with the sun's rays, causing all things to grow and flourish. This view was no doubt reinforced by interest in Neoplatonism in the fifteenth and sixteenth centuries, but the concept of a universal spirit already existed in medieval alchemy and popular pantheism.[53] Thus artists like Leonardo da Vinci wrote of a "spirit of growth" that permeated all of nature.[54] Even artistic creativity itself could be understood as a fluid dispensed by the heavens; artist-author Karel van Mander repeatedly characterized artistic talent as a fluid endowed by *natura generans*.[55]

Elements of Altdorfer's *Rest on the Flight* and Dürer's works can thus be read as referring to components of alchemical theory, but they also point to a more general understanding of nature and function as a means for these artists to make claims about their understanding of nature and nature's processes. One such claim that linked artists and alchemists was their common assertion of "mirroring nature" in their work.[56] From the beginnings of Flemish naturalism the painters' efforts to render precise and detailed representations of nature or of reality were viewed by their contemporaries as a striving after exact replication, not just of nature as it appears to the human eye, but also of nature as the source of generation and production, comprising a kind of double imitation of nature. In 1449, Cyriacus of Ancona described a Flemish painting (probably by Rogier van der Weyden) in similar terms:

Figure 1.8 Johann Daniel Mylius, "Coitus" from *Anatomiae auri sive tyrocinium medico-chymicum*, 1628.   Courtesy of the University of Wisconsin, Madison.

multicolored soldier's cloaks, garments prodigiously enhanced by purple and gold, blooming meadows, flowers, trees, leafy and shady hills, ornate halls and porticoes, gold really resembling gold, pearls, precious stones, and everything else you would think to have been produced, not by the artifice of human hands but by all-bearing nature herself.[57]

"All-bearing nature" was regarded as prolific and copious, a creative force that might be imitated by art. Although the idea of art imitating nature or Creation (*ars imitatur naturam*) went back to antiquity,[58] it could mean more than just producing a mirrorlike image of created nature. *Imitating* nature could mean knowing not just how to mirror nature but could also mean imitating (or reproducing or harnessing) the creative power of nature herself.

The Madonnas in Dürer's prints and Altdorfer's paintings can be viewed not only as alluding to the Fountain of Life but also as signifying the mirror of God (as Jan van Eyck adorns the Virgin in heaven in his Ghent Altarpiece with a passage from the Book of Wisdom, reading, "She is more beautiful than the sun and all the order of stars . . . a spotless mirror of God.").[59] The natural surroundings in which these two artists place Mary also alluded to God, for created nature was also seen as the *speculum dei*. But for Dürer, Nature was also a source of certainty and creativity. In his late treatises on perspective (1525) and human proportion (1528), he stated that certainty lay in nature, and that this certainty was expressed through naturalistic representation:

> But life in nature manifests the truth of these things. Therefore observe it diligently, go by it and do not depart from nature arbitrarily, imagining to find the better by thyself, for thou wouldst be misled. For verily art [i.e., *Kunst*, or theoretical knowledge, as opposed to *Brauch*, or simple practice] is imbedded in nature; he who can extract it has it.[60]

Certain knowledge for Dürer lay not in theory, as scholars commonly held, but rather in nature itself, and his naturalism made clear this primacy of nature as a source of knowledge.

Making this same point, Dürer's contemporary, Paracelsus, also articulated an artisanal mode of cognition and a vernacular epistemology. In his written works, he constantly held up artisans and their knowledge of the material with which they work as models for gaining natural knowledge and for creating effects. Alchemy was both the framework for his entire philosophy and the exemplum for all human arts. For Paracelsus, knowledge of nature was gained not through a process of reasoning, but rather by a union of the divine powers of mind and of the entire body with the divine spirit in matter. This he called "experience." In explaining this concept he drew upon the ancient terminology of theory and experience, but he inverted the traditional understanding of these terms in a remarkable way. In the schema that organized the pursuit of knowledge from Aristotle up through the sixteenth century, theory (based on geometric demonstration and syllogistic logic) was regarded as the sole source of certain knowledge, while experience was viewed as knowledge of particulars that could never be certain. Paracelsus inverted this relationship. He defined *scientia*, or certain knowledge, as the divine power in natural things, which the physician must "overhear" and with which he must achieve bodily union in order to gain knowledge of natural materials out of which to make medicaments.[61] Thus for Paracelsus certain knowledge was embedded in nature, while experience was the process by which the physician/natural philosopher united with nature and learned this science. "*Scientia* is inherent in a thing. . . . For instance, the pear tree has *scientia* in itself, and we who see its works have *experientia* of its *scientia*. . . . Thus in this book, I show the way *scientia* enters into you."[62] This is an extraordinary inversion of the concepts of theory and practice, one that Paracelsus derived from artisans. In the late fifteenth and early sixteenth centuries, artisans were experts on the processes and transformations of nature, and individuals who wished to know (and take possession of) nature looked to art as the medium through which to accomplish this. This was true not only for physicians and scholars like Paracelsus but also for princes and city governors, who came to regard artisans as holding the key to unlocking the powers of nature.

Naturalism in artisanal work gained momentum in the North throughout the sixteenth century, as did the image of an artist as privileged interpreter of nature. Dürer's example, extended by the next generation of German artists, produced an extreme form of imitating nature in the technique of actual casting from life. A master goldsmith from Nuremberg, Wenzel Jamnitzer (1508–85), was celebrated for this technique (fig. 1.9).[63] One of Jamnitzer's most famous extant pieces is the Merkel Centerpiece of 1549 (fig. 1.10). It features the artist's specialty: grasses and flowers, cast from life, springing from an egglike vessel at the top, while around the base, reptiles, also cast from life, creep forth from the earth. The central female figure represents Mother Earth, and the whole piece symbolizes the fertility and generative powers of nature. It even bears an inscription, "I am the Earth, mother of all things, beladen with the precious burden of the fruits which are produced from myself."[64] Jamnitzer clearly meant to display his own powers of creation in this work as well as his ability to imitate nature, not only by producing an absolute likeness of nature but by harnessing the processes of metallurgy (alchemy) to create this very representation.

Paracelsus's work also gives insight into the way that nature had, for an artisan, an immediacy and primacy: nature itself, not words about nature,

Figure 1.9 Wenzel Jamnitzer, *Lizard*, life cast.   Courtesy of Staatliche Museen Preussischer Kulturbesitz, Kunstgewerbemuseum, Berlin.

was the certain *scientia*, which the craftsman got to know through individual *bodily* struggle with matter. This awareness emerges from Paracelsus's idea about a bodily union between the natural philosopher and his object of study,[65] as well as in his statement that the creative power of humans resembled God's but lay in the human body rather than in the Word. What God creates through the word, Paracelsus wrote, a human being creates "with his body and his instruments [senses]."[66]

Larry Silver and Pamela H. Smith

Figure 1.10 Wenzel Jamnitzer, *Merkel Centerpiece*, 1549. Courtesy of the Rijksmuseum, Amsterdam.

The bodily aspect of artisanal interaction with nature emerges with particular clarity in the work of the ceramicist Bernard Palissy (ca. 1510–90) and his 1580 account of his discovery of white glaze. His book as a whole discusses processes of generation, growth, and change, and is cast as a dialogue in which Theory attempts to pry out of Practice the secret of his enamel-making.[67] Rather than simply giving a recipe to Theory, however, Practice recounts Palissy's harrowing search for the white glaze, and this account is remarkable for its Paracelsian type of experience–Palissy's body and his home are consumed to form a unity with the materials he works. In the end, his labor redeems him and his household. His ceramic amphibians, fish, and reptiles show the realist products, also molded from life itself, of that experience (fig. 1.11).

A related phenomenon recurs in the account by Benvenuto Cellini (1500–71) of the process of casting his statue *Perseus Beheading Medusa*: his body is wasted by fever and illness, the roof of his house catches fire, he attempts to bring the "corpse" of the metal back to life by throwing all his pewter utensils into the molten mass. While his body and his house are consumed, he finally falls to his knees in prayer.[68] Contemporaries, including the painter Bronzino, saw the realistic blood spouting from the head and torso of Medusa as lifelike, while for Cellini this form mimicked the vivifying force that had sent the life coursing back through both the dead metal as well as his own veins.

By the late sixteenth century, Palissy and Cellini were themselves responding to the evolution of the tradition of the artisan as an interpreter of nature that had begun in the work and writings of figures like Dürer and Leonardo, but their view of the functions and processes of nature shows continuity with the earlier period. Dürer, too, had used similar body language to recount his own process of creation. He wrote that in the process of looking, the painter develops his own *Augenmass* (measure or sense of proportion) in his eyes and that by much *Abmachen* (or reproducing nature from life),[69] he will fill his mind full, and thus accumulate a "secret treasure of the heart," from which he can pour forth in his work, what he "has gathered in from the outside for a long time." For Dürer, the artist was "inwardly full of figures" that he poured out in new inventions, still part of his "direct and faithful representation of a natural object."[70] This bodily experience of the particulars of nature resulted for the artist in knowledge of matter and its transformations, which proved itself through his creation of "effects," or works of art.[71]

As the example of Cellini suggests, the concept of bodily knowledge in the creative process also implicates the bodily labor of the artist's workshop, including the use of body fluids (saliva, urine, blood) along with the natural chemicals of painting pigments, clays, stones, and metals. Artists, like other artisans, were engaged in bodily struggle with and against matter itself, and

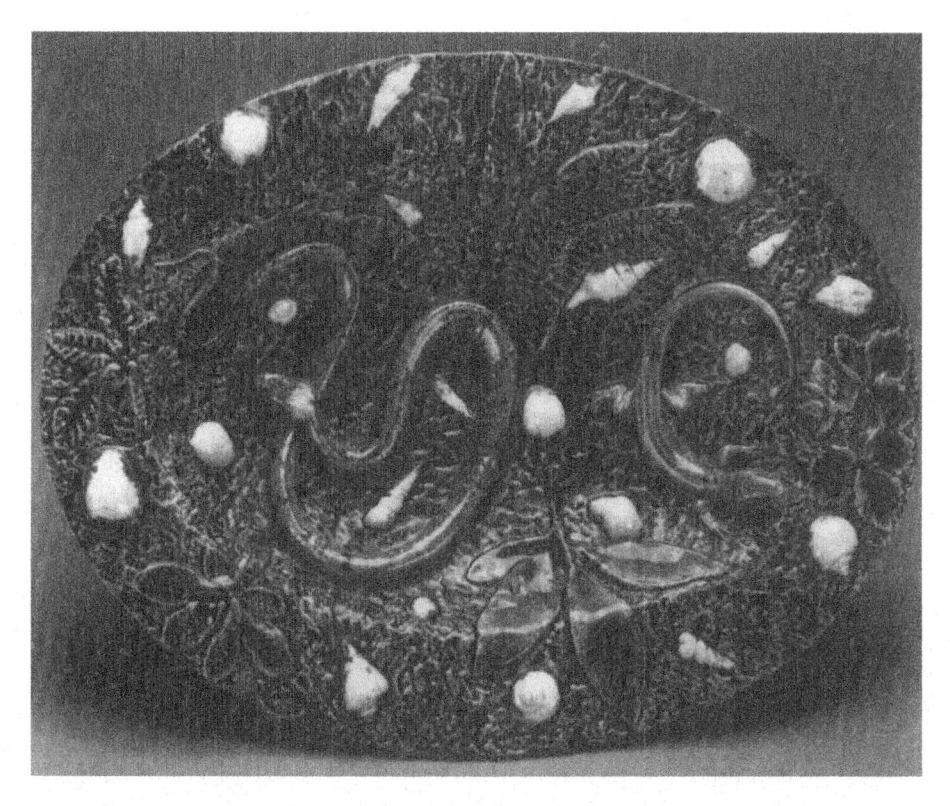

Figure 1.11 Attributed to Bernard Palissy, *Oval Plate*. Courtesy of The J. Paul Getty Museum, Los Angeles.

that matter was not dead, but alive, capable of acting in idiosyncratic fashions, which artisans must come to know–and master–through experience.[72]

One of the central components of alchemical theory was the concept that all generation occurred through a process of putrefaction, that is, decay and regeneration. In putrefaction, particular forms of life appeared first: "serpents, toads, frogs, salamanders, spiders, bees, ants, and many worms," according to the formulation of Paracelsus.[73] The reptiles cast from life in the works of both Jamnitzer and Palissy can thus be seen in a new light, as can Martin Schongauer's engraving *Flight into Egypt*, in which lizards or salamanders creep up the trunk of the Tree of Life.[74] Salamanders were believed to be capable of withstanding fire, and thus were a symbol of generation through putrefaction.[75] In alchemical theory, the salamander could also denote sulfur, the hot, fiery, male principle. A return to the creeping creatures that permeate Dürer's *Madonna with a Multitude of Animals* could suggest that these insects and amphibians, too, could signal the beginning of new life out of the putrefied matter of the old, all under the order and guidance of the divine.

While Altdorfer's *Rest on the Flight into Egypt* does not contain insects, lizards, or salamanders, the winged phoenix egg in Apollo's hand signifies the very same process of regeneration through destruction and putrefaction, for the phoenix, like the salamander, emerges resurrected out of fire.[76] Like Jamnitzer's Merkel Centerpiece, Altdorfer's votive picture appears to have three overlapping themes: the correspondence between spiritual and natural powers, the transformative power of nature, and the place of art in the great work of spiritual and material redemption. Transformation itself is indicated by the arrows in Cupid's hands, those same arrows that eventually caused Daphne to be transformed into a tree. Altdorfer points to the transformational powers of nature in his allusion to the alchemical theory in which Apollo could be seen as sulfur, Mary as mercury, and the fountain as the water of life, the generative principle of nature.

At the same time, Mary, mirror of God and fountain of life,[77] is the vehicle of the macrocosmic transmutation of the world, the process of redemption set in motion by Christ's birth, life, and death. In microcosm, the individual artisan replicates these processes of transformation and redemption. By giving over his painting to the Virgin, Altdorfer alludes to the role that the practice of his art plays in redeeming the "health of his soul." He employs the knowledge of nature, gained by a bodily experience of nature itself, to imitate nature's creative processes and to transform natural materials into a work of art. The powers of nature — inextricably intertwined with divine power — are the wellspring of his own artistic creativity, and the painting as a whole conveys the message that, as an artisan, he is both a knower and a redeemer of matter.

Notes

1. Millard Meiss, *Painting in Florence and Siena after the Black Death* (New York: Harper and Row, 1964), 132–156; H. W. van Os, *Marias Demut und Verherrlichung in der sienesischen Malerei 1300-1450* (The Hague: Ministerie Van Cultuur, Recreatie en Maat Schappelijk, Werk, Staatsuitgeverij, 1969), 77–142. While the prototype images of the "Madonna of Humility" stem from the art of Trecento Siena, this concept spread widely throughout Europe over the course of the century and was widely taken up, for example by Flemish painter Robert Campin. On Campin, see Erwin Panofsky, *Early Netherlandish Painting* (Cambridge, Mass.: Harvard University Press, 1953), 127–128, 143.

2. Panofsky, *Early Netherlandish Painting*, 186; on the larger theological implications of van Eyck's use of the *hortus conclusus*, Carol Purtle, *The Marian Paintings of Jan van Eyck* (Princeton, N.J.: Princeton University Press, 1982), 157–167. More generally, Reindert Falkenburg, *The Fruit of Devotion. Mysticism and the Imagery of Love in Flemish Paintings of*

the Virgin and Child, 1450-1550 (Amsterdam/Philadelphia: John Benjamins, 1994), esp. 8–21 and references at n.11; Mirella Levi d'Ancona, *The Garden of the Renaissance: Botanical Symbolism in Italian Painting* (Florence: L. Olschki, 1977). For the Master of the Frankfurt Paradise Garden, see Ewald Vetter, "Das Frankfurter Paradiesgärtlein," *Heidelberger Jahrbücher* 9 (1965): 102–146; the theme of the enclosed garden in general is discussed by Vetter, *Maria im Rosenhag* (Dusseldorf: L. Schwann, 1956).

3. For Dürer watercolors, still understudied, see Walter Koschatzky, *Albrecht Dürer. The Landscape Water-Colours* (New York: St. Martin's Press, 1973). The banks of open water do not correspond exactly to extant watercolors but do show elements of the south German subalpine lake region in the distant horizon of the print, while the buildings resemble steeply pitched wooden structures around Nuremberg's river, the Pegnitz, as shown in later watercolors, notably the large *Mills on a River Bank* (Koschatzky, no. 30; Paris, Bibliothèque Nationale; W. 113). A slightly earlier Dürer drawing (Berlin, W. 30) anticipates an image of the holy family on a grassy bench before a background landscape, albeit a constructed landscape of receding trees and distant peaks without open water. Among the elements in favor of an early date are the artist's undeveloped monogram, perhaps used here for the first time; in addition, the burin technique and modeling remain comparatively sketchy and irregular. See *Dürer in America: His Graphic Work*, exh. cat. (Washington, D.C.: National Gallery of Art, 1971), 112–113, no. 2, where the date of 1495–96 is suggested, in part because the landscape elements make it likely that the work was done after the artist's first trip to Italy. For the identification of the tiny insect as a mayfly and for a general discussion of this print and other Dürer images of the Madonna with animals, see Colin Eisler, *Dürer's Animals* (Washington, D.C.: Smithsonian Institution Press, 1991), 34–36, who argues that the short life of the mayfly underscores the brevity of Christ's time on earth. Certainly this particular identification of species is more plausible than most of the other insect names (dragonfly, cricket, butterfly, locust) that have been put forward by previous scholars, despite their differing body types.

4. For plants in general in German art of this period, Lottlise Behling, *Die Pflanze in der mittelalterlichen Tafelmalerei*, 2nd ed. (Cologne/Graz: Böhlau, 1967); see also Behling, "Betrachtungen zu einigen Dürer-Pflanzen," *Pantheon* 23 (1965): 279–291. A rigorous analysis of Dürer watercolors of plants (and imitations thereof) is given by Fritz Koreny, *Albrecht Dürer und die Tier- und Pflanzenstudien der Renaissance* (Munich: Prestel-Verlag, 1985), 176–253. There a close comparison to the several plants in the woodcut print is provided by no. 63, p. 182 (German, beginning of 16th century; Potsdam, Sanssouci, inv. 536b), where the combination of plants, identified by Koreny as goose-kress, common Ruchgras, and speedwell (Veronica). Of course, Dürer painted a celebrated watercolor in 1503, usually known as the *Great Clump of Turf* (Vienna, Albertina), discussed by Koreny as no. 61, 176–179, along with some other botanical representations by the artist. Koreny follows both Anzelewsky and Gombrich in suggesting a possible Neoplatonic goal of Dürer's immersion in such minutiae of nature, which might also be implicit in the use of the short-lived mayfly in his earlier engraving, and in his watercolor studies of plants and animals in general (see below). For a later illuminated botanical herbal, painted in Holland in the late sixteenth century (today Cracow, Jagiellonian University Library) for the pharmacist Theodorus Clutius, see Claudia Swan, *The Clutius Botanical Watercolors* (New York: Harry N. Abrams, 1998).

5. Behling, *Pflanze*, 132–136, figs. 19–20, 39; a similar plant occupies the center foreground of Pieter Bruegel's *Beekeepers* drawing (ca. 1568 Berlin), for which see Ethan Matt Kaveler, *Pieter Bruegel. Parables of Order and Enterprise* (Cambridge: Cambridge University Press, 1999), 233–254, but the plant is not discussed; also, *Pieter Bruegel d. Ä. als Zeichner: Herkunft Und Nachfolge*, exh. cat. (Berlin: Staatliche Museen Preussischer Kulturbesitz, 1975), 86–87, no. 100, where the plant is identified as mandrake (German *Alraune*), "a rare

plant, which according to superstition grows under the gallows and consequently is called 'Gallow youth' (*Galgenjunge*) or 'Gallow dwarf' (*Galgenmännlein*)." See also Richard Kieckhefer, *Magic in the Middle Ages* (Cambridge: Cambridge University Press, 1990), 13–14, 66.

6. Götz Pochat, *Der Exotismus während des Mittelalters und der Renaissance* (Stockholm: Almqvist & Wiksell, 1970), 118–136; Robert Koch, "Martin Schongauer's Dragon Tree," *Print Review* 5 (1976) *Tribute to Wolfgang Stechow*, ed. Walter Strauss, 114–119. The 1493 *Nuremberg Chronicle* woodcut of the Garden of Eden shows three trees: a date palm behind Adam, an apple tree with snake between the first parents, and a dragon tree behind Eve and next to the fountain of life, suggesting that it is to be equated with the scriptural Tree of Life. Bosch also puts the same three trees in his Paradise wing from the triptych of the *Garden of Earthly Delights* (Madrid, Prado); as Pochat recognized, the source for this imagery of animals is the pilgrimage guidebook *Peregrinatio in terram sanctam* by Bernhard von Breydenbach, published in Mainz in 1486.

7. For example, *Dürer in America*, 121, no. 14, citing H. W. Janson, *Apes and Ape Lore in the Middle Ages and Renaissance* (London: Warburg Institution, University of London, 1952), 151. Eisler, *Dürer's Animals*, 260–262, discusses monkeys at greater length.

8. Eisler, *Dürer's Animals*, 37, calls the bird a thrush and more explicitly associates its flight with the Resurrection; see also 56–91 for extended discussion on Dürer's birds of various species.

9. This same plant appears in a Leonardo da Vinci drawing (Windsor Castle, no. 12424) and in his two versions (Paris and London) of the *Madonna of the Rocks*. See Kenneth Clark, *Leonardo da Vinci*, rev. ed. (Harmondsworth: Penguin, 1988), 179, fig. 72; Martin Kemp, *Leonardo da Vinci* (Cambridge, Mass.: Harvard University Press, 1981), 273, fig. 74. To my knowledge this plant has not been identified in the Dürer *Madonna with the Monkey*.

10. Koschatzky, no. 25. This pond setting also resembles the background of the *Mayfly* engraving.

11. Eisler, *Dürer's Animals*, 31–55, with discussion of two other drawing versions, an earlier one in Berlin (W. 295), the other in Paris (1503; Louvre, W. 297). Koreny, *Albrecht Dürer*, 114–118, with full references.

12. For background on the print and the Dürer revival at the court of Rudolf II, see Dorothy Limouze, "Aegidius Sadeler," *Bulletin, Philadelphia Museum of Art* 85 (spring 1989), esp. 20 n. 22; for the Jan Brueghel, *Breughel-Brueghel*, exh. cat. (Essen, 1997), 169–171, no. 38.

13. For a later manifestation in the art of Albrecht Altdorfer of starbursts, coronas, and comets in the heavens above religious scenes of the early sixteenth century, see Larry Silver, "Nature and Nature's God: Landscape and Cosmos of Albrecht Altdorfer," *Art Bulletin* 91 (1999): 194–214. This earlier article suggests some of the arguments about macrocosm/microcosm resonances that are pursued further here.

14. Michael Baxandall, *The Limewood Sculptors of Renaissance Germany* (New Haven, Conn.: Yale University Press, 1980), 165–172.

15. Eisler, *Dürer's Animals*, 37–39, discusses the fox in this watercolor drawing as representing "the devil, to be caught by Christ's sacrifice." The two nearby owls also are often associated, as birds of night, with evil. On owls in Dürer, see Eisler, *Dürer's Animals*, 83–85. On the owl in the Netherlands tradition, see Paul Vandenbroeck, "Bubo significans I. Die Eule als Sinnbild der Schlechtigkeit und Torheit, vor allem in der niederländischen und deutschen Bilddarstellung und bei Hjeronimus Bosch," *Jaarboek Koninklijk Museum voor Schone Kunsten Antwerpen*, 1985, 19–136.

16. L. Naftulin comments on the presence of the parrot in van Eyck's *Madonna with Canon van der Paele* (Bruges, Groeninge Museum; 1434–36) in his "A Note on the Iconography of the van der Paele Madonna," *Oud Holland* 36 (1971): 7; see also Purtle, *Marian Paintings*, 92. Discussing the overall significance of the animals in Dürer's *Madonna with the Multitude of Animals*, Eisler, *Dürer's Animals*, 33, cites Francis of Retz's *Defensorum virginitatis Mariae*, a

Larry Silver and Pamela H. Smith

book from the prior generation that used bestiary lore on animals to argue that their behavior heralded both the Immaculate Conception and the miraculous birth of Christ.

17. On flower symbolism in relation to the Virgin, by which her qualities are expressed through "similitudes" of the flowers to her beauty, purity, sorrow and the like, there is considerable literature. See, for example, Falkenburg, *Fruit of Devotion*, 10–11; Robert Koch, "Flower Symbolism in the Portinari Altarpiece," *Art Bulletin* 46 (1964): 70–77. Also Eisler, *Dürer's Animals*, 42–43.

18. Eisler, *Dürer's Animals*, 42–43, notes that "the hollyhock was believed to heal the bite of poisonous snakes, scorpions, and spiders, and thus, like Christ, to save humankind from the serpent–Satan."

19. *Lucas Cranach*, exh. cat. (Berlin, 1973), 13–14, no. 1; Hans Möhle, *Lucas Cranach d. Ä. Ruhe auf der Flucht nach Ägypten* (Stuttgart: Reclam, 1966); for the plants of the Berlin painting, see Behling, *Pflanze*, 120–121.

20. Panofsky, *Early Netherlandish Painting*, 146 n. 6, 333; Koch, "Flower Symbolism." On strawberries as the fruit of paradise, see Behling, *Pflanze*, 19; also James Mundy, "Gerard David's Rest on the Flight into Egypt: Further Additions to Grape Symbolism," *Simiolus* 12 (1981–82): 213–215; more generally, see Falkenburg, *Fruit of Devotion*.

21. The association of the finch with Christ's Passion derives in part from the blood-red mark on the bird's throat; see Herbert Friedmann, *The Symbolic Goldfinch* (New York: Pantheon Books, 1946).

22. M. R. James, *The Apocryphal New Testament* (Oxford: Clarendon Press, 1975), 49; for the text of Pseudo-Matthew and the miraculous fruit and spring, see 75.

23. Larry Silver, "Forest Primeval: Albrecht Altdorfer and the German Wilderness Landscape," *Simiolus* 13 (1983): 4–43, esp. 30–36; Franz Winzinger, *Albrecht Altdorfer. Die Gemälde* (Munich: R. Piper, 1975), 84–86, no. 27, dated there ca. 1513–15 but often situated somewhat earlier. This large work was once, probably originally, located in the monastery of St. Emmeram in Regensburg, where it is documented in the same century as its creation.

24. Behling, *Pflanze*, 125–129.

25. On "St. John's fire," in the context of Pieter Bruegel's 1560 *Children's Games* (Vienna, Kunsthistorisches Museum), see Sandra Hindman, "Pieter Bruegel's Children's Games, Folly, and Chance," *Art Bulletin* 63 (1981): 453–454, esp. n. 37. In commemorating a birthday and falling almost exactly six months away from Christmas itself, this holiday held special calendrical significance. This is the midsummer night alluded to as a lover's holiday by Shakespeare.

26. See Herbert Friedmann, *A Bestiary for St. Jerome* (Washington, D.C.: Smithsonian Institution Press, 1980), 291–293, for the snail; Eisler, *Dürer's Animals*, 119 (snail as a symbol of virginity), 127 (butterfly as image of the soul or Resurrection), 133–134 (snail's virginity tied to belief that air alone impregnated the animal).

27. Marjorie Lee Hendrix, "Joris Hoefnagel and the 'Four Elements': A Study in Sixteenth-Century Nature Painting," Ph.D. dissertation (Princeton University, 1984); Thomas DaCosta Kaufmann, *Drawings from the Holy Roman Empire 1540–1680*, exh. cat. (Art Museum, Princeton University, 1982), 154–157, no. 56.

28. Hendrix, *Joris Hoefnagel*, 215–262, esp. 219 n. 9. She points to the significance of beetles in the illustrations as examples of nature's own artifice and of the succeeding butterflies, both inscribed with biblical quotations such as Psalm 145:5 at folio 6: "They shall speak of the magnificence of the glory of thy holiness; and shall tell thy wondrous works." The last folio of Ignis (fol. 80) quotes Ecclesiasticus 43: "There are many things that are hidden from us that are greater than these: for we have seen but a few of his works." This is nature as both presentation of God's manifold glory as well as nature as enigma, shielding divine secrets. Hendrix points out 257, n. 16, that biblical quotations dominate the epigrams of the *Four Elements* illustrations:

thirty from Psalms, eight from Ecclesiasticus, eight from Isaiah, six from Proverbs, five from Job, and three from Ecclesiastes. See also her appendix of inscriptions, 263–332.

29. Winzinger, *Albrecht Altdorfer*, 75–77, no. 7.

30. Falkenburg, *Fruit of Devotion*, esp. 91–92, citing cherries in particular as "love fruit" in the convergence of erotic imagery of the Song of Songs with the Marian interpretation of divine love for humanity.

31. A fountain, of course, was also an important feature of the Garden of Eden, hence for enclosed gardens evocative of Paradise regained, such as Jan van Eyck's *Madonna of the Fountain* (1439; Antwerp); see Purtle, *Marian Paintings*, 163–166. Falkenburg, *Fruit of Devotion*, 10, refers to the Song of Songs' "sealed fountain and/or garden fountain, a well of living water" (4:12, 15), to be understood as a reference to the Virgin and her chastity. See also Friedrich Muthmann, *Mutter und Quelle: Studien zur ouellenverehrung im Altertum und im Mittelalter* (Basel: Archaölogischer Verlag, 1975), esp. 414.

32. Hans Mielke, *Albrecht Altdorfer*, exh. cat. (Berlin, 1988), 152, no. 73. The rich Renaissance ornament of this fountain further suggests its wonder, in contrast to the ornate Gothic vocabulary of actual contemporary fountains and the surrounding chapel space of the print. For the pictorial sources of the fountain and its relation to other Altdorfer works, see Franz Winzinger, "Der Altdorfer-Brunnen," *Jahrbuch der Berliner Museen* 13 (1963): 27–32. Here as well as in the Berlin painting the presence of accompanying angels and a pagan deity atop the fountain suggest the supernatural forces at work in its manifestation. Mielke points out a logical fact: that during the lifetime of the holy figures, only pagan deities could have been publicly presented; however, as will be discussed below, it is possible to interpret these deities as linked to planetary gods and thus to the natural forces inherent to both alchemy and astrology in this period.

33. Dürer painted the scene of *Hercules Slaying the Stymphalian Birds* (Nuremberg, Germanisches Nationalmuseum; on canvas) for the court of Frederick the Wise in Saxony; see Fedja Anzelewsky, *Albrecht Dürer. Das malerische Werk* (Berlin: Deutscher Verlag für Kunstwisssenschaft, 1971), 168–170. For another German painting of a bearded Apollo with bow and arrow, see the 1530 Lucas Cranach work, *Apollo and Diana* (Berlin; exh. cat., 1973, 21–22, no. 10). The nude Altdorfer figure also lacks the most characteristic marks of Hercules: his club and his lionskin mantle.

34. Rarely analyzed, this drawing does receive attention from Eisler, *Dürer's Animals*, 156–157, plate 22, who follows G. F. Hartlaub ("Albrecht Dürers 'Aberglaube,'" *Zeitschrift des deutschen Vereins für Kunstwissenschaft* 7 [1940], 183–184 n. 23), in asserting that the egg might well be "an alchemical image of the 'philosopher's egg,' that egg-shaped vessel for thought and matter." Hartlaub claims that the Altdorfer fountain in the Berlin painting represents the "bath of Mary" (*balneum Mariae*), which corresponds to alchemical writings that discuss distillation as an act of purification, akin to the rite of baptism. There is also an association in alchemy between virginity and the *prima materia*. A related drawing, also dated 1513, Eisler's plate 36 (Berlin; W. 703) shows a tall bird, a crane (or a heron) with talonlike feet, standing tall. This bird is associated with vigilance (Eisler, 72, citing Ambrose as well as Dürer's own marginal illustrations around the same time for the "translated" *Hieroglyphica* of Horus Apollo), so it also has a virtuous character, appropriately paired with the strengths of the lion.

35. Eisler, *Dürer's Animals*, 139–161, discusses lions in general along with their varied inclusions in Dürer's oeuvre. For the bestiary lore, based on a translation of a twelfth-century "book of beasts," see T. H. White, *The Bestiary: A Book of Beasts* (New York: Putnam's, 1960), 7–11, which makes explicit the identification with Christ by analogizing and allegorizing the qualities of the animal with the mission and nature of the Savior.

36. "Lutum sapientiae" could also refer to the mixture of clay, hair, straw, and horse dung that was used to seal and protect glass vessels from breakage when they were placed in the flames of the distilling furnace.

37. Richard Kieckhefer, on "Arabic Learning and the Occult Sciences," *Magic in the Middle Ages*, 116–150, esp. 144–150 on the Renaissance magus and the intensified interest in Hebrew Kabbalah as an additional source for occult knowledge and potential magical incantation. Wayne Shumaker, *The Occult Sciences in the Renaissance: A Study of Intellectual Patterns* (Berkeley and Los Angeles: University of California Press, 1972), esp. 201–251 on Hermes Trismegistus and associations of occult learning with ancient Egypt. See also D. P. Walker, *Spiritual and Demonic Magic from Ficino to Campanella* (London: Warburg Institute, 1958), esp. 117–156; Frances Yates, *Giordano Bruno and the Hermetic Tradition* (Chicago: University of Chicago Press, 1964), esp. 75–96.

38. G. F. Hartlaub, "Albrecht Dürer's 'Aberglaube,'" and "Arcana artis. Spuren alchemistischer Symbolik in der Kunst des 16. Jahrhunderts," *Zeitschrift für Kunstgeschichte* 6 (1937): 289–324, interpreted Dürer's alchemical imagery as the manifestation of the long enduring workings of the human subconscious. More recently, historians have claimed that Dürer's *Melencolia I* concerns the first stage of the alchemical process: Maurizio Calvesi, *La melencolnia di Albrecht Dürer* (Turin: G. Einaudi, 1993). James Elkins and Didier Kahn have debated the value of such research: James Elkins, "On the Unimportance of Alchemy in Western Painting," *Konsthistorisk tidskrift* 1, no. 1–2 (1992): 21–26, and "Reply to Didier Kahn: What is Alchemical History?" *Konsthistorisk tidskrift* 64, no. 1 (1995): 51–53; Didier Kahn, "A propos de l'article de James Elkins: On the Unimportance of Alchemy in Western Painting," *Konsthistorisk tidskrift* 64, no. 1 (1995): 47–51.

39. Cennino D'Andrea Cennini, *The Craftsman's Handbook (Il libro dell'Arte)*, trans. Daniel V. Thompson Jr. (New York: Dover, 1960), lists the colors made by "alchemy" as vermilion, red lead, orpiment yellow, arzica yellow, verdigris, and white lead (24, 25, 28, 30, 33, 34). Other colors fell into the categories of "natural" or "artificial" (but not manufactured by alchemy). See also A. Wallert, "Alchemy and Medieval Art Technology," in *Alchemy Revisited*, ed. Z. R. W. M. von Martels (Leiden: Brill, 1990).

40. Jacques van Lennep, *Alchemie. Bijdrage tot de geschiedenis van de alchemistische kunst* (Brussels: Gemeentekrediet, 1984) argues that artists' distillation procedures for producing varnishes were regarded as alchemy. Similarly, Laurinda S. Dixon, "Bosch's *Garden of Delights* Triptych: Remnants of a 'Fossil' Science," *Art Bulletin* 63 (1981): 96–113; *Alchemical Imagery in Bosch's Garden of Delights* (Ann Arbor: UMI Research Press, 1981); and "Bosch's 'St. Anthony Triptych'—An Apothecary's Apotheosis," *Art Journal* (summer 1984), maintains that Bosch's familial ties to apothecaries and their procedures of alchemical distillation account for much of the imagery in Bosch's paintings. While both these authors make their arguments in general and expansive terms, they do point out an important convergence between alchemical and artisanal activities, in which material transformation of any sort could be regarded as alchemical. For an interesting recent meditation on the overlap between alchemy and artists' practices, see James Elkins, *What Painting Is: How to Think about Oil Painting Using the Language of Alchemy* (New York: Routledge, 1999).

41. Juan Luis Vives, *De tradendis disciplinis*, 1531, trans. Foster Watson (Totowa, N.J.: Rowman and Littlefield, 1971), 209.

42. For the relationship between scholars and artisans, see Elsbeth Whitney, *Paradise Restored: The Mechanical Arts from Antiquity through the Thirteenth Century*, Transactions of the American Philosophical Society, vol. 80 (Philadelphia, 1990); Paolo Rossi, *Philosophy, Technology, and the Arts in the Early Modern Era*, trans. Salvator Attanasio (New York: Harper & Row, 1970); William Eamon, *Science and the Secrets of Nature: Books of Secrets in Medieval and Early Modern Culture* (Princeton, N.J.: Princeton University Press, 1994); Pamela O. Long, "Power, Patronage, and the Authorship of *Ars*," *Isis* 88 (1997), 1–41; and R. Hooykaas, "The Rise of Modern Science: When and Why?" *British Journal for the History of Science* 20 (1987): 453–473.

43. On the connections between artisanal epistemology and the later New Philosophy of the sixteenth and seventeenth centuries, which helped to shape attitudes toward nature and the pursuit of knowledge about nature in the new science, see Pamela H. Smith, "Artists as Scientists: Nature and Realism in Early Modern Europe," *Endeavour* 24 (2000): 13–21; idem, "Science and Taste: Painting, the Passions, and the New Philosophy in Seventeenth-Century Leiden," *Isis* 90 (1999): 420–461.

44. Christ was likewise frequently associated with Apollo or with the "true sun," *Sol Justitiae*. See also images from the Early Christian period, esp. the Jewish mosaics at Beth Alpha and Hamat synagogues in modern Israel, which feature Apollo in his solar chariot at the center of the zodiac within an alien religious setting (Bezalel Narkiss, "The Jewish Realm," in *Age of Spirituality*, ed. Kurt Weitzmann, exh. cat., New York, 1979, 374–375, no. 342). For Apollo and Christ in Early Christian art, see the mosaic in the Mausoleum of the Julii under St. Peter's basilica in Rome, late third century, where the nimbus around the head of the charioteer Helios/Apollo transfers divine imaging to the figure of Christ, ascending into heaven on the chariot and representing the "victorious sun," *Sol invictus,* for which see Marilyn Stokstad, *Medieval Art* (New York: Harper and Row, 1986), 15–17, fig. 14. Another important connection between Christ and the image of the sun, specifically by Dürer in his engraving *Sol Justitiae* (ca. 1500; B. 79), where the judging God rides upon a lion. This almost neglected print, so redolent of ancient solar iconography transposed into a Christian context, was discussed by Erwin Panofsky, "Albrecht Dürer and Classical Antiquity," *Meaning in the Visual Arts* (New York: Doubleday, 1955), 256–265, also discussing the late antique spirituality tied to "astral mysticism," which even led to Augustine's warning against carrying the identification of Christ with Sol so far as to relapse into paganism (260). Altdorfer's muscular Apollo on the Berlin fountain also resembles the figure type (again without beard) and pose used by Dürer in his drawings of Apollo (W. 261–64), nude and holding an orb in his left hand, for example, the famous Apollo with Diana (London, British Museum, W. 261; Panofsky, fig. 76). While Altdorfer's access to such drawings remains unknown, even doubtful, a more public, visible touchstone of this figure concept by Dürer would have been the engraving *Apollo and Diana* (ca. 1502; Meder 64), where the muscular god (beardless) carries a bow and quiver of arrows and wears a laurel wreath. In this context, it is worth noting the importance of Altdorfer's equation of the *Resurrection* (1518; Vienna) with the rising sun; see Silver, "Nature and Nature's God," 199–201. For Dürer's equation of the resurrected Christ with an Apollonian sun god, see Panofsky, 260–261 n. 77, fig. 81, citing the Latin poem by Benedictus Chelidonius on the reverse of the Small Woodcut Passion *Resurrection* woodcut, translated as follows: "This is the day on which the Creator began to make the world, dedicated, according to the perennial belief, to the Lord of Heaven and Phoebus. On this day the all-seeing Sun, affixed to the cross, hidden and dying when the sun set in darkness, splendidly reappeared when it rose." Moreover, Dürer wrote: "Then, at the same time, as they [the artists of antiquity] attributed the most beautiful human figure to their idol, Apollo, we would praise Christ the Lord, who is the most beautiful in all the world. And as they praised Venus as the most beautiful woman we would ourselves set forth the gracious figure of the most pure maiden Mary the Mother of god. And for Hercules we would substitute Samson, and we would do the same with all the other [gods]." Hans Rupprich, *Dürer's schriftlicher Nachlass,* 3 vols. (Berlin: Deutscher Verein für Kunstwissenschatt, 1956–69), 2: 103ff.

45. Eggs also could be specifically associated with the Incarnation of Christ. In particular, the ostrich egg included by Piero della Francesca above the central holy figures in his *Madonna and Child with Saints* (Milan, Brera) has been interpreted as a symbol of supernatural birth. See Millard Meiss, "Ovum Struthionis: Symbol and Allusion in Piero della Francesca's Montefeltro Altarpiece," *The Painter's Choice. Problems in the Interpretation of Renaissance Art* (New York: Harper and Row, 1976), 105–129. This supernatural role of an

egg's miraculous powers is especially true for an ostrich egg, hatched only by the rays of the sun according to medieval bestiaries. White, *The Bestiary*, 121–122, speaks of the incubation in warm sand. This link between the sun and the eggs corresponds to Altdorfer's association of Apollo and the hatching egg within his hand.

46. H. J. Sheppard, "Egg Symbolism in Alchemy," *Ambix* 6 (1958): 140–148, 144.

47. See the work of Allen G. Debus, B. J. T. Dobbs, and, briefly, E. J. Holmyard, *Alchemy* (New York: Dover, 1990; reprint of 1957 ed.) and John M. Stillman, *The Story of Alchemy and Early Chemistry* (New York: Dover, 1960; reprint of 1924 ed.). In the sixteenth century, Theophrastus von Hohenheim, called Paracelsus (1493–1541), added a third principle–salt–to sulfur and mercury, probably reflecting the importance of the production of salts beginning in the fourteenth century. Gunpowder, saltpeter (from which fertilizer was produced), and the preservative properties of common salt came to have increasing importance in the fourteenth and fifteenth centuries.

48. Sulfur appears in a pure form in nature. On heating, it turns a dark red color, which when rapidly cooled forms a glassy red substance. Similarly mercury is found in a pure form in nature.

49. For an excellent discussion of the significance of mercury in alchemical theory, see Karin Figala, s.v. "Quecksilber," *Alchemie. Lexikon einer hermetischen Wissenschaft*, ed. Claus Priesner and Karin Figala (Munich: Beck, 1998), 295–300; see B. J. T. Dobbs, *The Foundations of Newton's Alchemy* (Cambridge: Cambridge University Press, 1975), 35–37, for the matter/spirit problem in alchemy.

50. Figala, "Quecksilber," 298.

51. Hie ist geboren Solis und Lüne kindt/ Desgleichen nyemant auf Erden findt/ Und in die weldt doch gern erkhennt/ Mercurius philosophorum ist Er gennent.

52. Dobbs, *Foundations of Newton's Alchemy*, 184–185.

53. In alchemical theory and practice, the conception of nature as actively creating, and of *ars* as knowing how to reproduce the natural processes of creation and generation, had long predated the arrival of the Hermetic corpus. See William Newman, "Technology and Alchemical Debate in the Late Middle Ages," *Isis* 80 (1989): 423–445; idem, "Art, Nature, and Experiment in Alchemy," in *Texts and Contexts in Ancient and Medieval Science*, ed. Edith Scylla and Michael McVaugh (Leiden: Brill, 1997), 304–317; idem, *The Summa perfectionis of Pseudo-Geber* (Leiden: Brill, 1991).

54. Quoted by Jan Bialostocki, "The Renaissance Concept of Nature and Antiquity," *The Renaissance and Mannerism* 2 (Princeton, N.J.: Princeton University Press, 1963), 19–30, esp. 25, quoted as an atypical statement of Leonardo, taken from Neoplatonic views that the world was animated. Although this idea was certainly expressed, particularly by Marsilio Ficino, much older sources were available to artists and artisans. One author who regards Leonardo's comments on the vital forces of nature as extremely significant, though he does not precisely know how to categorize them (he calls them "myth"), is James Ackerman, "Science and Art in the Work of Leonardo," in *Leonardo's Legacy*, ed. C. D. O'Malley (Berkeley and Los Angeles: University of California Press, 1969), 222ff. See also Martin Kemp, *Leonardo da Vinci. The Marvellous Works of Nature and Man* (Cambridge: Harvard University Press, 1981), esp. 263, 277 on the earth as an organism with geological flux; 312–319 on the relationship between this geology and the system of the four elements.

55. Karel van Mander, *The Lives of the Illustrious Netherlandish and German Painters from the First Edition of the Schilder-boeck (1603–04)*, trans. and ed. Hessel Miedema (Doornspijk: Davaco, 1994); see esp. the lives of Lucas van Leyden (1: 104–105, with commentary 3: 2), Spranger (1: 330–331; commentary 5: 87), and Aert Mijtens (1: 313; commentary 4: 24).

56. This goal of mirroring nature was the fundamental ambition of Netherlandish painting, for which, see Hans Belting and Christiane Kruse, *Die Erfindung des Gemäldes. Das erste*

Jahrhundert der niederländischen Malerei (Munich: Hirmer, 1995), with references; see also the classic study by Erwin Panofsky, *Early Netherlandish Painting* (Cambridge: Harvard University Press, 1953), esp. the discussion "Reality and Symbol in Early Flemish Painting," 131–148, and the discussion of the epitome of this ambition, Jan van Eyck: "Thus Jan van Eyck's style may be said to symbolize that structure of the universe which had emerged, at his time, from the prolonged discussion of the 'two infinites'; he builds his world out of his pigments as nature builds hers out of primary matter. The paint that renders skin, or fur, or even the stubble on an imperfectly shaved face seems to assume the very character of what it depicts; and when he paints those landscapes which, to quote Fazio once more, 'seemed to extend over fifty miles,' even the most distant objects, however much diminished in size and subdued in color, retain the same degree of solidity and the same fullness of articulation as do the very nearest. Jan van Eyck's eye operates as a microscope and as a telescope at the same time" (181-182). Here it is worth recalling that Jan van Eyck was (falsely) credited as being the inventor of oil paint technique, surely a form of chemistry/alchemy, for which he was praised in the following century in the *Lives of the Artists* by Vasari (1566), who states in the life of Antonello da Messina that one Jan of Bruges, "a painter very much esteemed for the practice which he had acquired in becoming a master . . . began to try [provare] different sorts of colors, especially those which pleased him from alchemy, to make an oil to use as a varnish and other things, according to the notions of the learned men of that age." Cited from the edition of Rosanna Bettarini (Florence: Sansoni, 1971), Vol. 3, 302.

57. Quoted by Panofsky, *Early Netherlandish Painting,* 2, with full citation.

58. Bialostocki, "Renaissance Concept of Nature and Antiquity"; E. H. Gombrich, "The Style All' Antica: Imitation and Assimilation," *The Renaissance and Mannerism* 2: 31–40; Ernst Kris, "Georg Hoefnagel und der wissenschaftliche Naturalismus," *Festschrift für Julius Schlosser zum 60. Geburtstag,* ed. Arpad Weixlgärtner and Leo Planscig (Zurich: Amalthea, 1927); Otto Pächt, "Early Italian Nature Studies and the Early Calendar Landscape," *Journal of the Warburg and Courtauld Institutes* 13 (1950): 13–46.

59. Elisabeth Dhanens, *Van Eyck: The Ghent Altarpiece* (New York: Viking, 1973), 80. Wisdom 7: 29, 26.

60. From book 3 of his work on human proportions, *Vier Bücher von menschlicher Proportion,* 1528, trans. and quoted by Erwin Panofsky, *The Life and Art of Albrecht Dürer* (Princeton: Princeton University Press, 1955), 279–280.

61. Walter Pagel, *Paracelsus. An Introduction to Philosophical Medicine in the Era of the Renaissance,* 2nd ed. (Basel: Karger, 1982), 51.

62. Paracelsus, *Das Buch Labyrinthus medicorum genant* (1538, 1st publ. ed. 1553), in Vol. 11 of *Sämtliche Werke,* ed. Karl Sudhoff (Munich/Berlin: Oldenbourg, 1928), 163–221, chap. 6, 192. Paracelsus also stated that knowledge (*erkantnus*) is not in the physician but in nature, as are the disease and the cure. *Das Buch Paragranum* (1530), in Vol. 8 of *Sämtliche Werke,* ed. Sudhoff (Munich: Barth, 1924), 140. Pagel, *Paracelsus,* 51, 218–223, notes the Neoplatonic overtones of this passage, but in this and other essays, he also points out the multiple sources for Paracelsus's work, including popular pantheism, Salomo ibn Gebirol's (1021–70) notion of "prime matter" (229–230), and medieval alchemical treatises (259ff.). See also Walter Pagel, "Paracelsus and the Neoplatonic and Gnostic Tradition," *Ambix* 8 (1960): 125–166.

63. Ernst Kris, "Der Stil 'Rustique': Die Verwendung des Naturabgusses bei Wenzel Jamnitzer und Bernard Palissy," *Jahrbuch der Kunsthistorischen Sammlungen in Wien* N.F. 1 (1928), 137–207, esp. 147; see also Klaus Pechstein, "Der Goldschmied Wenzel Jamnitzer," *Wenzel Jamnitzer und die Nürnberger Goldschmiedekunst 1500–1700,* exh. cat. (Nuremberg: Germanisches Nationalmuseum, 1985), 60, 219–223, 342–343, nos. 15–16, 299, esp. the Merkel Centerpiece, dated 1549.

Larry Silver and Pamela H. Smith

64. Quoted in Wenzel, *Jamnitzer*, 220, no. 15: "Sum terra Mater Omnium/ Omusta caro pondere/Nascentium ex me fructuum."

65. Although this aspect of the thought of Paracelsus has usually been attributed to Neo-platonic influences, two recent works have suggested the vernacular nature of his ideas. For example, Stefan Rhein, "'Mein bart hat mer erfaren dan alle euer hohe schulen'. Ein Zwischenruf zur Quellenfrage bei Paracelus," 99–104, and Gundolf Keil, "Mittelalterliche Konzepte in der Medizin des Paracelsus," 173–193 in *Paracelsus. Das Werk–die Rezeption,* ed. Volker Zimmermann (Stuttgart: Steiner, 1995).

66. Paracelsus, *Astronomia magna: oder die gantze Philosophia sagax der grossen und kleinen Welt/ des von Gott hocherleuchten/ erfahrnen/ und bewerten teutschen Philosophi und Medici* (finished 1537–38; 1st publ. ed. 1571); in Vol. 12 of *Sämtliche Werke,* ed. Karl Sudhoff (Munich/Berlin: Oldenbourg, 1929), 1–444, esp. 56.

67. Bernard Palissy, *The Admirable Discourses,* 1580, trans. Aurele la Rocque (Urbana: University of Illinois Press, 1957), 188–203; for an illuminating discussion of this point, see Neil Kamil, "War, Natural Philosophy and the Metaphysical Foundations of Artisanal Thought in an American Mid-Atlantic Colony: La Rochelle, New York City, and the South-western Huguenot Paradigm, 1517–1730," Ph.D. dissertation (Johns Hopkins University, 1988). The most important recent works on Palissy are: *Bernard Palissy: Mythe et Réalité* (Niort, Saintes: Museés d'Agen, 1990); Bernard Palissy, *Recepte véritable* (Geneva: Droz, 1988), with introduction by Keith Cameron; Frank Lestringant, ed., *Barnard Palissy 1510-1590. L'Écrivain, Le Réformé, Le Céramiste* (Coédition Association Internationale des Amis d'Agrippa d'Aubigné, 1992); Leonard Amico, *Bernard Palissy: In Search of Earthly Paradise* (Paris/New York: Flammarion, 1996); and the recent exhibition catalog, *Un Orfèvre de Terre: Bernard Palissy et la Céramique de Saint-Porchaire* (Chateau D'Écouen, 1997). Also, with an emphasis on Palissy's Calvinist minority status and architectural and garden designs, Catherine Randall, *Building Codes. The Aesthetics of Calvinism in Early Modern Europe* (Philadelphia: University of Pennsylvania Press, 1999), 44–77. See also Kris, "Stil rustique."

68. Benvenuto Cellini, *Autobiography,* trans. George Bull (Harmondsworth: Penguin, 1956), 343–358, discussed (partly in terms of alchemy) by Michael Cole, "Cellini's Blood," *Art Bulletin* 81 (1999), 215–235. Here the crucial element of the image is precisely its metallic substance and its forging in the crucible of a furnace with the addition of "spirits" to resuscitate the dead metal into flowing, corporeal vitality.

69 While today "Abmachen" means to undo, Panofsky translated Dürer's use here as "reproducing nature from life." (Erwin Panofsky, *Idea. A Concept in Art Theory,* trans. Joseph J. S. Peake [Columbia: University of South Carolina Press, 1968, 121–126.) In Dürer's usage, it was probably closer to the modern "abschreiben," or copying verbatim. Dürer also used the term "abkunterfet" to mean portraying after life or with verisimilitude. Similarly Paracelsus used "ablernen" to denote the process of learning the "scientia" from the plant itself. Paracelsus, *Labyrinthus,* 191.

70. Panofsky, *Art and Life of Albrecht Dürer,* 243–244, discussing the artist's "individual struggle with reality"; Panofsky, *Idea,* 121–126, esp. 123, characterized here as a unique combination in Dürer of contemporary Italian art theory, influenced by Neoplatonism, and the artist's own, "personal," here characterized as artisanal, vision of his creative process. This combination of study from nature and evocation from the memory and spirit corresponds fairly closely to what Dutch art theory at the turn of the seventeenth century, exemplified by Karel van Mander would discuss in the contrasting terms "after life" (*naer het leven*) and "from the spirit/memory " (*uyt den geest*). See Walter Melion, *Shaping the Netherlandish Canon. Karel van Mander's Schilder-Boeck* (Chicago: University of Chicago Press, 1991), esp. 63–66, 243 n. 10.

71 "Effects" were synonymous with the products of (al)chemical experiments and with works of art. For example, Lorenzo Ghiberti's called his naturalistic relief panels on the doors of the Florence baptistery (1425–52) the "effeti" of the biblical stories illustrated in each one. Julius von Schlosser, *Lorenzo Ghiberti's Denkwürdigkeiten (I Commentarii)*, 2 vols. (Berlin: Julius Bard, 1912), Vol. 1: 49.

72. Paracelsus believed that an artisan must perfect the art of reading a thing from its external character through experience, thus understanding the virtue and power of the material, what he calls "chiromancy": "People who work wood, carpenters, joiners and such, have to understand their wood by the chiromancy of it, what it is apt and good for." In the same way a miner will know the chiromancy of the mine. Paracelsus, *Liber de imaginibus*, vol. 11 of *Sämtliche Werke*, ed. Karl Sudhoff (Munich/Berlin: Oldenbourg, 1931), 361–386, esp. 375–376. This translation is taken from Baxandall, *The Limewood Sculptors*, 160, who finds that Paracelsus "throws a more penetrating light on the characteristic forms of sculpture than anything else available."

73. Paracelsus, *Die neun Buecher De Natura rerum* (1537), book 1 in Vol. 11 of *Sämtliche Werke*, ed. Sudhoff, 314.

74. Hartmut Krohm and Jan Nicolaisen, *Martin Schongauer. Druckgraphik* (Berlin: Staatliche Museen, 1991), 83–84, no. 3c (Lehrs 7). For the identification of the Tree of Life as a derivation of the exotic "dragon tree," see Robert Koch, "Martin Schongauer's Dragon Tree"; also Götz Pochat, *Der Exotismus*, 118–136.

75. Robert Koch, "The Salamander in Van der Goes' Garden of Eden," *Journal of the Warburg and Courtauld Institutes* 28 (1965): 323–326; also White, *Bestiary*, 182–184; Edward Topsell, *The Elizabethan Zoo* (Boston: Nonpareil, 1979), 108–115. Benvenuto Cellini's first childhood memory was of seeing a salamander in the fire (*Autobiography*, 20).

76. White, *Bestiary*, 125–128; Topsell, *Elizabethan Zoo*, 22–23; Herbert Kessler, "The Solitary Bird in Van der Goes' Garden of Eden," *Journal of the Warburg and Courtauld Institutes* 28 (1965), 326–329.

77. See the equation of Mary with the fountain in Jan van Eyck's *Madonna of the Fountain* (1439; Antwerp, Koninklijk Museum), as noted above, n. 31. Purtle, *Marian Paintings*, 157–167; Larry Silver, "Fountain and Source: A Rediscovered Eyckian Icon," *Pantheon* 41 (1983): 95–104; Paul Vandenbroeck, *Catalogus Schilderkunst 14e-15e eeuw* (Antwerp: Koninklijk Museum, 1985), 174–178. The fountain as a Marian symbol derives from passages in the Song of Songs, 4:15, where the beloved is described as "a garden fountain, a well of living water, and flowing streams from Lebanon."

Objects of Art/Objects of Nature

Visual Representation and the Investigation of Nature

PAMELA O. LONG

This essay explores some of the ways in which visual representation came to legitimate knowledge claims in the period between about 1490 and the 1540s. The use of images to further knowledge about the natural world represents a significant cultural development. For both philosophical and historical reasons, ancient and medieval thought tended to separate things made by human artifice — paintings and drawings, as well as constructed objects such as machines — from the natural world. In part, this reluctance to use visual images to demonstrate claims about the world came out of the Aristotelian view that art and nature were opposed to one another.[1]

Alan Gabbey frames the issue as it concerns mechanics. He points to the traditional separation between the mechanical arts and Aristotelian physics. For Aristotle, machines and devices rearrange things *against* nature and for human ends; they belong to mechanics as a practical art. The theoretical discipline of physics did not include an interest in mechanical devices or their specific effects in the world. Physics "did not share the concerns of mechanics, since physics did not deal with artificial things *qua* artificial." Traditional Aristotelian definitions of *physica, philosophia naturalis,* or *physiologia* concern "the science [*scientia*] of natural bodies *in so far as they are natural.*" Gabbey investigates the ways in which mechanical arts became mechanics, a discipline in which the ancient distinctions between the mechanical arts and *physica* or natural philosophy came to be seriously eroded or eliminated. Thereby could seventeenth-century experimental philosophers use machines and devices to demonstrate claims about the natural world.[2]

Yet the transformation involving mechanical arts and mechanics is just one episode in a larger cultural development in which the artifactual and the natural moved into closer proximity. The use of visual images (created by human artifice) to represent observed natural objects had to overcome serious impediments, including a focus on the capacity of drawings and paintings to create optical illusions. In ancient times, as the story of Zeuxis attests, the most skillful painter is the one whose painting is radically deceptive. The story as told by Pliny recounts the rivalry of Zeuxis and Parrhasius. Zeuxis, attemping to demonstrate his superiority as a painter, produced a picture of grapes so expertly that birds flew up to it. Then Parrhasius created a picture of a curtain so realistic that Zeuxis, "proud of the verdict of the birds, requested that the curtain should now be drawn and the picture displayed." When he discovered that the curtain was actually a painting by Parrhasius he honorably yielded the prize to him.[3] The story emphasizes the remarkable skill and ingenuity of the painters, but it hardly offers visual representation as a modality for demonstrating truths about the natural world. It underscores instead the capacity of humans both for creating optical illusions and for being deceived by them.

The inherent capacity of visual images to deceive made them suspect as aids to discovering truths about nature. This suspicion was augmented by the sharp medieval social divisions between those who studied natural philosophy at the universities and those who produced images in workshops. Scholastic natural philosophy was not fundamentally experimental, observational, or visual, but was logical and textual involving extensive commentaries, lectures, and formal disputations based on the study of authoritative writings. Artisanal practitioners did not attend universities, but were trained by apprenticeship in workshops. The mechanical arts and natural philosophy were separated physically and socially, as well as conceptually.[4]

Yet gradually during the fifteenth and sixteenth centuries in settings outside of the universities in cities and courts, humanists and others combined an interest in learning with a preoccupation with the constructive arts. The basic context for such a development involves medieval commercial capitalism and urbanism in which the production and exchange of all kinds of goods was aided by the expansion of both local and distant markets. Worldly goods proliferated just as the cultural value of material objects increased. Elite rulers undertook massive building programs to reorganize the urban spaces that they controlled and to legitimate their own power. From the late-fifteen century, they increasingly practiced conspicuous consumption. Finely wrought objects, including paintings, sculpture, and other forms of visual representation gained cultural value.[5]

At the same time, learned culture expanded beyond the universities as humanists took positions as secretaries in cities and courts, or found patronage from oligarchs and princes who also employed workshop-trained painters, architects, and engineers. Across Europe, in many courts and cities, learned humanists, wealthy patrons, and artisan-trained painters, sculptors, and architects lived in closer proximity—both physically and in terms of their mutual interests—than they had in previous centuries. Artisan-trained individuals sometimes wrote treatises about their crafts. Learned humanists such as Leon Battista Alberti also wrote treatises and commentaries on painting, architecture, and other constructive arts.[6] These broad cultural developments took place in the context of a thriving commercial culture involving the production and exchange of everyday and luxury goods within both local and European-wide markets. One result was that objects fabricated by humans, including visual images, came to be used for the study of the natural world.

This essay examines a group of diverse sources in an investigation of the ways in which art and nature came to be closely associated or even interchangeable between the 1490s and the 1540s. Sources include a lengthy architectural romance, the *Hypnerotomachia Poliphili* [*Struggle of Poliphilus in a dream*], a literary work published in 1499; Leonardo da Vinci's *Madrid Codex I*, an extensively illustrated manuscript treatise on machines and mechanics created in the 1490s; some of the paintings and writings of Albrecht Dürer; the treatise on the architectural orders by Sebastiano Serlio, published in 1537; and finally, Andreas Vesalius's famous anatomical treatise, the *De Humani Corporis Fabrica*, published in 1543.[7]

These sources are often placed in separate disciplinary categories. The *Hypnerotomachia Poliphili* is a literary work of interest to architectural and literary historians. *Madrid Codex I* falls into the category of mechanics and is of interest to historians of science. Dürer's paintings and prints are studied primarily by art historians. Serlio is studied by architectural historians, whereas Vesalius draws the attention of historians of anatomy, medicine, and science. Yet these modern disciplinary categories are at least in part anachronistic. They tend to separate these works one from another in ways that are inappropriate for the sixteenth century, obscuring their common culture.

The sources considered here share several characteristics. In diverse ways, for example, they display close relationships, and even interchangeability between artificial and natural objects. This interchangeability is particularly evident in the *Hypnerotomachia Poliphili*, and it is explicit or implicit in the other sources as well. Analogies between natural and artificial objects, and the use of one to demonstrate a truth about the other, are evident in most of them. Leonardo, for example, uses the motions of actual and visually depicted machines to explore principles of motion. Dürer creates the first free-standing images of landscapes and creates other "slices" of the natural world by means of art. Vesalius in his anatomical treatise uses methods strikingly similar to those that Serlio used in his earlier treatise on architecture. He also compares anatomical structures such as bones to artificial structures such as the beams of houses. While the differences among these works are

---

apparent, they share a tendency to closely associate objects of art and objects of nature.

ART AND NATURE IN THE HYPNEROTOMACHIA POLIPHILI

The *Hypnerotomachia Poliphili*, published in 1499, was written possibly by one Francesco Colonna, who probably can be identified as a Dominican monk of Venice of the same name. The authorship of the work is controversial. Whoever Francesco Colonna was, his complex romance encompasses a dream within a dream in which Poliphilo walks through a varied terrain filled with pyramids, ruins, gardens, forests, meadows, and streams, as he searches for his lost love, Polia.[8]

For my purposes here, *Hypnerotomachia Poliphili* is interesting because of the author's persistent interest in itemizing objects of nature and objects of art, including architectural fragments, in profuse detail, and also because of his habit of interchanging constructed artifacts and natural things. For example, at one point in his dream within a dream, Poliphilo comes to an enclosed valley where he encounters an enormous half-ruined pyramid carved out of the surrounding mountains and topped by an obelisk that is dedicated to the sun. The author provides a detailed description of the monument itself including structures, ornamental details, fragments of sculpture and architecture, inscriptions, and the names of many varieties of herbs and grasses growing among the ruins. Poliphilo hears frightening groans and discovers that they are emitted by the colossal statue of a man. The groans are caused by wind blowing through the open mouth of the colossus. Using the hairs of the chest and beard of the statue, Poliphilo pulls himself into the open mouth and then climbs through the viscera. Each part of the body, "intestines, nerves, bones, veins, muscles, and flesh" is present, and each is labeled in Chaldean, Greek, and Latin. The inscribed body parts describe what sickness is generated in each part, the cause, the required care, and the remedy.[9]

Poliphilo emerges from this polyglot body, and looks at other ruins such as the colossal statue of a horse that "seemed almost to tremble in its flesh, and more alive than fabricated." He enters the pyramid through the great portal, encounters a dragon and other amazing things, emerges from the bowels of the great structure into a lovely meadow. He describes the meadow by providing an encyclopedic enumeration of the specific varieties of plants and trees. As he continues on his journey he describes an ancient bridge over a stream with overgrown banks populated with many varieties of birds, and then a plain filled with creatures, flowers, and fruit trees, each of which he specifies by name. He meets the nymphs of the five senses, whose clothing he describes minutely. He finally arrives at the palace of the

Queen Eleuterilyda (free thought), and describes the approach to the palace where the nymphs take him first to the baths. As he draws near to the palace and enters, he describes the courtyard, the exterior, the ornamentation of the entrance, the ornate tapestries of the successive rooms, the decorations, the throne of the queen, her clothing, and jewelry, and each item of the lavish, bejeweled services used at the sumptuous banquet.[10]

After the banquet, the nymphs lead Poliphilo to the lower courtyard where they walk through an orange grove and a series of extraordinary gardens, one made entirely of glass and gold, a second that is an aquatic labyrinth and a third made of silk and decorated with pearls and vines of gold. The glass garden, for example, is filled with pots of artificial plants. In place of real greenery, "every plant was of very pure glass, excellently [made] beyond what one could imagine or believe, intopiated boxes with the roots and stems of gold." Here is just one of many examples in which the natural and the artifactual are interchanged to the delight and stupefaction of the wandering Poliphilo.[11]

The *Hypnerotomachia Poliphili* is a literary work by an author who is enthralled by architecture, fabricated objects, and myriad specific natural species. It contains numerous detailed lists and encyclopedic descriptions of both natural and fabricated objects. Frequently, Poliphilo expresses astonishment at both kinds of objects. The examples mentioned here—the pyramid that is actually a carved-out mountain, the colossal statue of a man that groans, the fabricated horse that trembles as if alive, and the gardens made of beautifully fashioned glass, gold, silk, and pearls—each obscure or transgress the boundaries between the artifactual and the natural. The *Hypnerotomachia Poliphili* exhibits an interchangeability between natural and constructed things as it also displays a kind of descriptive exuberance in which plants, birds, and trees are described in exorbitant detail, as are architectural ruins, structures, inscriptions, and crafted objects of all kinds.

MACHINES AND MOTION IN MADRID CODEX I

Leonardo created the *Madrid Codex I*, a treatise on mechanics and the mechanical arts, between 1492 and 1497 shortly before the publication of the *Hypnerotomachia Poliphili*. It is far different from the architectural romance, but also provides evidence of the view that the natural and the artificial are entities that are closely associated with each other. The folios of *Madrid Codex I* are filled with beautiful drawings of machines and devices surrounded by detailed textual explanations concerning how they work and how they demonstrate the ways in which the natural world works. The treatise as a whole focuses on practical mechanics and the sciences of weights and motion. It treats the motions of toothed wheels, springs, clock escapement mechanisms (what he calls *tempi*), continuous and discontinuous motions of various sorts, counterweights, chain gears, screws, pinions and wheels, endless screws, lifting devices, mills, keys and locks, and crossbows, among others. In this work and in his other writings as well, Leonardo constructs analogies of various kinds between mechanical devices and natural phenomena.[12]

He compares the mechanical and the natural early in the treatise when he equates the earth to a cannonball: "If it were possible," he writes, "to make a bombard having the earth for its ball, and because a bombard throws a ball of one *braccio* to a distance of 3 *miglia*, we can measure the distance 9,000 *braccia* which equals 9000 balls. We could therefore assume that such a bombard would throw our earth to a distance equal to that of 9000 times its diameter. Assuming this to be 7000 *miglia*, it would come to 63 thousand *miglia*."[13] What is interesting about this passage is not that Leonardo makes a multiplication mistake, but that he makes a cannonball and the earth itself interchangeable. He imagines the earth behaving in the same way as a ball shot by a bombard, and attempts to calculate the resulting distance mathematically.

Madrid Codex I contains many illustrations of machines and devices that in part are the result of Leonardo's studies of motion, but are also grounded in his practice as an engineer, painter, and sculptor. In the 1490s Leonardo's relationship with the Sforza court involved him in a system of court patronage, which he acquired primarily on the basis of his abilities as an engineer and productive artist. I suggest a model of patronage here in which the system of court patronage is mixed with a system of production and commerce. The Sforza created a court that included learned humanists and famous artisan practitioners such as Leonardo. They also strenuously involved themselves in the armaments industry and in canal building undertaken to improve transportation and agriculture primarily for commercial purposes. Court patronage, material production, and commerce were not contradictory activities, but functioned together in reciprocal support.[14]

This is the context within which Leonardo wrote *Madrid Codex I*. The folios of the codex are filled with drawings of mechanical devices and machines that illustrate not just themselves, but serve as devices for conceptualizing principles in the natural world and for thinking about how things both natural and artificial work. Leonardo is interested in how devices work in practice. He often describes their specific motions, as well as factors such as friction that cause problems. Yet he is also interested in the principles of motion.

For example, in a section that begins with the heading "Questions," he asks: "Why does the flame rushing to its [natural] place take the shape of a pyramid while water becomes round in its descent, that is, at the end of the drop?" After posing this question involving the differing shapes of two different elements as they seek their natural place, Leonardo launches into a discussion of what I would call the shape of motion of a device consisting of

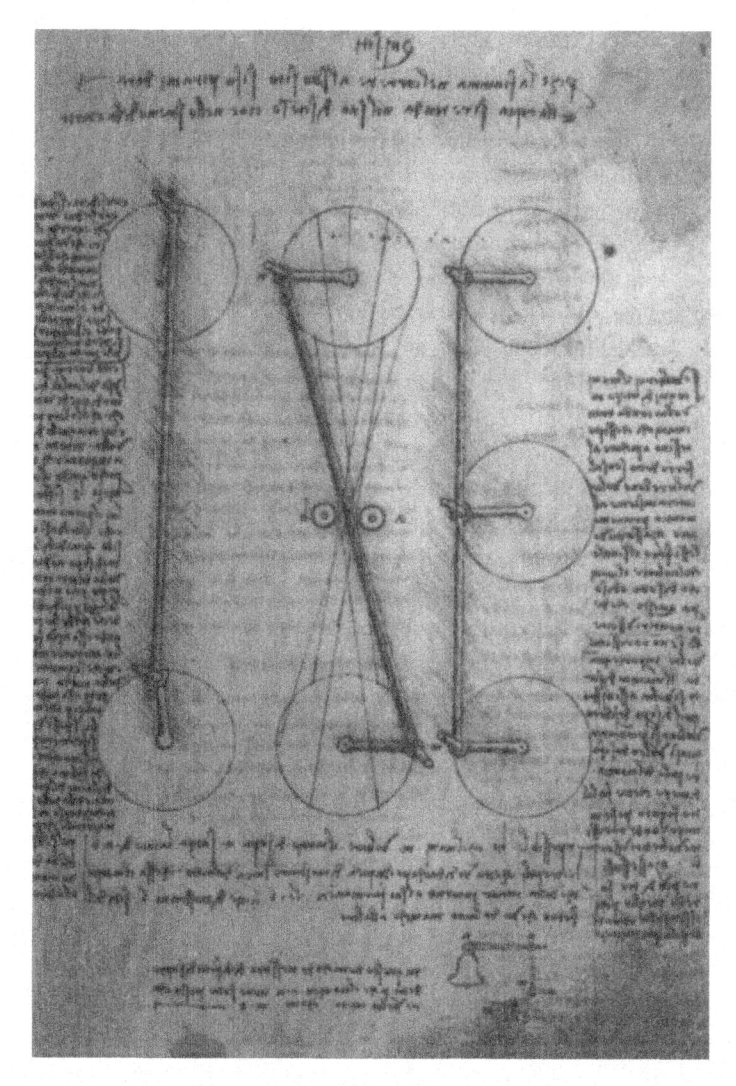

Figure 2.1 Leonardo da Vinci, *Madrid Codex I*, fol. 1r. Cranks with Connecting Rods.   Courtesy of Biblioteca Nacional, Madrid.

two cranks joined by a connecting rod (Fig. 2.1). He illustrates the same device twice within a chronological time sequence, first on the left, and then in the middle after the crank has been moved. (The depiction on the far right shows a variation.) He invites his reader to consider the position of these two cranks. If you move the lower crank to the left, the upper one will go right, he says, but the length of the *sensale* or connecting rod will not permit it to go all the way around because "it could not overcome the perpendicular line that unites the centers of their axles. Therefore, the crank will have more ability to turn back than to make a complete revolution."[15] And indeed, in a model of this device that I constructed, the top crank usually goes halfway around and then reverses itself. Occasionally it makes a full circle.

As this example shows, Leonardo's drawings are not superfluous illustrations of what he explains in the text. Rather the text concerning the motion of these crank devices would not really be comprehensible without the drawings. Text and drawings are necessary to one another. The drawings represent devices that Leonardo may have constructed and used for observation and experiment. The pages show the devices themselves, how they are made and how they work. They illustrate the particular motions of specific devices. Leonardo frequently reiterates the point that slight deviations in construction will cause major problems. Craft skill is necessary in order to construct instruments that will properly demonstrate principles of motion. Leonardo offers hundreds of close-up studies of actual local motions made by various devices in a great variety of different circumstances. The understanding of motion in the natural world, the observed motions of the devices themselves, and the visual images of those devices are closely linked.

As this page demonstrates, Leonardo's devices function on some level as observational tools. He constructs various devices and then observes and describes how they move, in what direction and how fast. It is probable that Leonardo often actually constructed, or had constructed by others, many of the devices that he draws. We know that he frequently hired German artisans to make machines and devices for him. He also mentions from time to time his own experimentation.[16] Some of the effects that he describes probably could be learned only by making the device and actually observing its motions.

For Leonardo, the study of motion entails construction, observation, and explanation using visual images. One can hypothesize that his procedure usually consisted of constructing a particular device, drawing it, moving it, and then describing and explaining its motion. He often adopts Aristotelian assumptions about motion (e.g., his remark about the flame and the water going to their natural places). Yet his mechanics are not fundamentally Aristotelian because they require constructing and then observing the motions of constructed things, thereby ignoring the Aristotelian distinction between art and nature. Neither are his mechanics Galilean, and they should not be read anachronistically in the context of Galileo's mechanics. Unlike Galileo, Leonardo usually does not analyze motion mathematically, nor does he create idealized situations that eliminate such local conditions as air resistance and friction. Leonardo creates machines and devices, and then he watches them move and describes that motion; or perhaps in some cases he does not construct the devices but draws them and imagines how they might move. It is not uncommon for him go back and forth between the motion of a device and motions in the natural world.

For Leonardo, local motion of machines and the motion of wind, air, water, and the earth itself can be reciprocally explanatory. He is in part indebted to Archimedes and to the pseudo-Aristotelian mechanics as well as to some scholastic writings on impetus. Yet his mechanics are uniquely his own. They might be described as an observational and experimental mechanics dependent on visual representation to explain and demonstrate particular motions in a material world in which friction, air resistance, and small glitches of construction are perpetual concerns.

ALBRECHT DÜRER AND THE COMMERCE OF ART AND NATURE

The reciprocity of natural objects and images occurs in a very different sort of way in the work of Albrecht Dürer. Dürer's city of Nuremberg was an important center of trade in the empire, and he was influenced by the commercial environment in which he lived. He made two trips to Italy by accompanying the Nuremberg merchant convoy that regularly traveled to Venice. These trips were important to him both for artistic and social reasons, and he may have met Leonardo or some of his acquaintances (such as Luca Paccioli) on one of these trips. During his lifetime, Dürer used the printing press to gain a degree of economic autonomy and control over his artistic production by managing the marketing of his prints. Rather than following the customary practice of waiting for orders, he created a stock of woodcut prints and copper plate engravings. He kept his worked plates and blocks in his possession and used them whenever he needed a new supply of prints for market. At times he hired salesmen to go from city to city to sell his prints. He also sold them himself in Nuremberg. His wife, Agnes Frey, throughout her husband's productive work life functioned as his business manager and handled many of his print sales, both by selling in Nuremberg and by traveling to markets in nearby cities such as Frankfurt.[17]

Dürer's work in general was far more portable than the work of the average artist of his time. Most of his production consisted of small objects that could be carried, and bought and sold, or offered as gifts. Yet this portability was not limited to prints, as is attested by his watercolor landscapes. In 1494 before he left Nuremberg for Venice, Dürer painted two watercolors of local subjects, the *St. Johannis Kirche* and the *Wire Drawing Mill*. As Peter Strieder describes it, they are "the first known autonomous representations of identifiable localities and served to raise watercolour to the status of an independent medium, the full potential of which Dürer had grasped." Shortly thereafter, on his return from his first trip to Venice in 1495, Dürer painted

Figure 2.2 Albrecht Dürer, *View of the Val d'Arco, in the South Tyrol*, 1495. Watercolor. Louvre, Paris. Giraudon/Art Resource, New York.

watercolor views of places he passed through. An example is his painting of Arco (fig. 2.2) which combines a masterful composition with beautiful and diverse details of rocks, flora, and buildings. One could almost call it a portable view that he carried back to Nuremberg. Yet as Hermann Leber analyses in detail, it is not only a record of a view, but a carefully constructed composition. This is just one of many examples whereby Dürer created portable pieces of "nature" by means of his art; his genius for creating naturalistic representations made such paintings as his renowned hare and *The Great Piece of Turf* (fig. 2.3), the latter a wonderfully detailed painting of a grassy piece of turf, famous in his own lifetime.[18]

For Dürer objects of art and objects of nature became almost interchangeable especially as he traveled and admired and collected a great variety of

Figure 2.3 Albrecht Dürer, *The Great Piece of Turf*, 1503. Watercolor on paper. Vienna, Graphische Sammlung Albertina.
Courtesy of Albertina, Wien.

objects, natural and constructed, including paintings. This interchangeability is especially evident in his diary of a trip to the Netherlands in 1420–21, as has been pointed out by Dagmar Eichberger. For example, in the Nassau house of Margaret, he reports that he saw "the good picture that Master Hugo painted," two fine large halls, treasures everywhere in the house, "also the great bed wherein 50 men can lie." He saw further "the great stone which the storm cast down in the field near the Lord of Nassau." And finally, from the high-standing house, "a most beautiful view, at which one cannot but wonder; and I do not believe that in all the German lands the like of it exists."[19] Various treasures, a painting by Hugo van der Goes, marvels such as a huge bed and a stone, and an extraordinarily beautiful view are all remarked in the same paragraph and seem to occupy the same conceptual realm.

Dürer's delight in both natural and fabricated objects, and his careful itemization of both, resembles in some ways the detailing of specific natural and artificial objects in the *Hypnerotomachia Poliphili*. Dürer's wonderful landscapes, plants, animals, and "slices" of nature such as the *Great Turf* strikingly celebrate the ability of human artifice to create elements of the natural world. In so doing, the artist/creator closely imitates the divine Creator, just as artificial things and natural things come to resemble each other.

SERLIO AND VESALIUS

The proximity of the artificial and the natural increased through the interaction of artisanal and learned cultures in the cities and courts of Europe. Thus the influence of Serlio's treatise on the architectural orders, published in 1537, upon Vesalius's *Fabrica* on human anatomy, published in 1543, resulted in part from the proximity of the two men themselves and their shared culture. Serlio trained in a workshop as a painter, lived in the Veneto in the 1530s and associated with the painter Titian and his circle, which included both painters and learned humanists such as Pietro Aretino. Vesalius lived in Padua and Venice in the late 1530s; he was teaching anatomy at the University of Padua when he wrote his treatise. Vesalius had the illustrations for the *Fabrica* created in Titian's workshop, clearly under his own close supervision (as the level of anatomical detail makes certain). He was probably familiar with Serlio's treatise on architecture. Each man used visual representation in ways that were innovative for their respective disciplines.[20]

Serlio's book, which would eventually become part of a more extensive treatise, focuses upon five architectural styles or orders. Serlio wrote his didactic handbook for designers of buildings and others who were interested in Vitruvius and in classical building styles. Pictures appear on virtually every page and depict various parts of buildings designed in a variety of ways. One example shows pictorially and also describes three different gates. The first, called rustic work, is suitable for a country villa; the second, suitable to the Tuscan style, was seen in Trajan's Forum for a long time before it fell into ruin; the third door with "a segmental arch which is the sixth part of a circle, is a work of great strength." Serlio in this way depicts various kinds of architectural styles pertinent to particular elements of the building, many if not all from observation. He shows them to the architect who can then pick and choose various elements for his own designs. As Serlio says about his drawing of the Trajan Forum: "The two niches on either side are out of place, but I have put them here in order to demonstrate the different

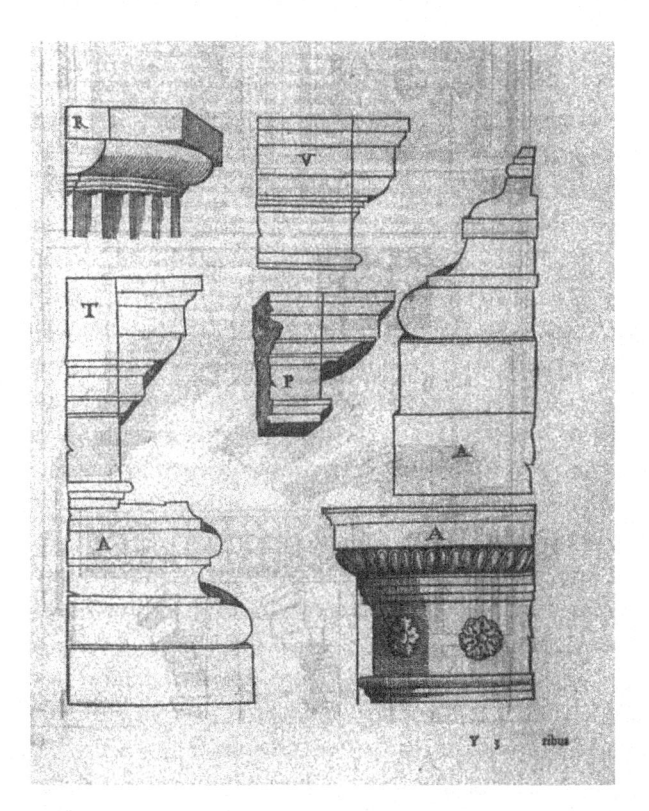

Figure 2.4 Sebastiano Serlio, *De architectura libri quinque* (Venice: Franciscus de Franciscis and Joannes Chriegher, 1569), 235. Elements of architecture. Courtesy of the Burndy Library, Dibner Institute for the History of Science and Technology, MIT.

types of niches which would suit such work, so that the judicious architect can make use of them and put them in the right place."[21]

Serlio often seems to work with Vitruvius's *De architectura* in one hand, and ancient architectural fragments and ruins in the other. For him, the discipline of architecture requires detailed study of the ancient text, careful observation of ancient structures and ruins, and depiction of those observations in the form of copious illustrations. He writes, "Because I find a great discrepancy between the buildings in Rome and other places in Italy and the writings of Vitruvius, I wanted to show some elements which, to the great pleasure of architects, can still be seen on buildings." He provides pictorial representations of various parts of different buildings that he has drawn from observation (fig. 2.4). He labels the parts of buildings with letters and identifies them. R was found outside Rome on a bridge over the Tiber. V is above a triumphal arch in Verona. T is in Rome on a Doric temple in the Tullian Prison. "The capital P was found in Pesaro with many other praiseworthy things: its projection, although it may be large, is nevertheless very pleasing to viewers." The podium, base, and capital A are in the Forum Borarium in Rome.[22] This is a collection of architectural fragments, carefully drawn from actual examples, for the use of practicing architects and students of Vitruvius and of ancient architecture.

It is probable that Vesalius saw Serlio's book while he was working on the *Fabrica* and took some ideas from it. Serlio's architectural representations with their softly shaded renderings look very similar to some of Vesalius's carefully depicted body parts. Vesalius uses illustrations as one way of narrowing the wide gap between university medical learning and the artisanal practice of surgery. He wants to integrate the artisanal practices of the surgeon and the apothecary into the practice of medicine as a whole. He believes that he is restoring anatomy to its ancient splendor. In his view, medicine was destroyed when its various components such as surgery were broken off from it and relegated "to laymen and people with no knowledge of the disciplines that go to serve the healing art." Similarly, the art of drugs and medicines was handed over to apothecaries. Trained physicians only prescribed medicines and regimes for hidden or internal ailments. As a result, "they shamefully cast aside the foremost and most ancient limb of medicine, the limb that above all is founded . . . on the study of nature."[23]

Vesalius emphasizes that the order of books in the *Fabrica* is the same as the order that he has followed during his own dissections in the company of the eminent men of the city. "This means," he notes, "that those who were present at my dissections will have notes of what I demonstrated and will be able with greater ease to demonstrate anatomy to others." Nevertheless, Vesalius believes that his books will be "particularly useful also for those who cannot see the real thing." These individuals will be able, from Vesalius's treatise by itself, to study each part of the body, "its position, shape, size, substance, connection with other parts, use, function and many similar matters." In sum, from his illustrated treatise, they will be able to learn all the things they could study during a dissection. In a remarkable defense of virtual witnessing, Vesalius tells his readers, "pictures of all the parts are incorporated into the text of the discourse, so as virtually to set a dissected body before the eyes of students of the work of Nature."[24] Just as the architect can study the elements of the building by perusing Serlio's treatise, so the student of anatomy can study human anatomical parts by scrutinizing the illustrations and text of the *Fabrica*.

Vesalius is aware of the opinions of some "who strongly deny that even the most exquisite delineations of plants and of parts of the human body should be set before students of the natural world; they take the view that these things should be learned not from pictures, but from careful dissection and examination of actual objects." He concedes that he would never urge students to use the pictures alone without dissecting cadavers: "Rather, I would, as Galen did, urge students of medicine by every means at my command to undertake dissections with their own hands."[25]

Nevertheless, he defends visual representation as a way of learning anatomy. "In fact," he says, "illustrations greatly assist the understanding, for they place more clearly before the eyes what the text no matter how explicitly, describes." In addition, Vesalius insists that his "pictures of the parts of the body" will give particular pleasure to those who do not have the opportunity to dissect real bodies or are too squeamish to do so.[26]

As he gets into the subject of his first book, namely bones and cartilage, Vesalius compares the function of bones to the function of certain elements in constructed things. Bone, he writes is "the hardest, the driest, the earthiest, and the coldest" of all the constituents of the human body. "God the great Creator of all things" formed its substance to be this way for good reason, "intending it to be like a foundation for the whole body; for in the fabric of the human body bones perform the same function as do walls and beams in houses, poles in tents, and keel and ribs in boats." Vesalius later describes the cartilages that form the larynx as resembling "the beams which form the framework of a country cottage before the thatch, the facings and the mud are applied. In fact, when the human bones and cartilages are stripped of their flesh and then assembled together there is no better analogy to describe them than that of the framework of a hut which has been raised but not yet finished off with branches or earth." One gathers from Vesalius's account of how to acquire a corpse and prepare a skeleton, that the usual procedure involved constructing the skeleton from pieces that had fallen apart during boiling. Even if an entire corpse was available at the outset, which was often not the case, it would fall apart during the usually necessary boiling.[27]

Vesalius's many illustrations of particular bones are labeled with numbers and letters that tie them tightly to his explanatory text. Within a discussion of the substance of bone, for example, he shows an illustration (fig. 2.5) of a humerus bone split lengthwise. He uses letters and visual indicators to show the nature of the bony substance: the little holes like pumice in the capula are marked A; the scale over these holes are marked B; C shows the outer surface of the bone, D the large hollow space along the length surrounded by the hardest bone E and F. Underneath the illustration of the humerus, Vesalius shows the navicular bone which is cut through the middle to show pumicelike bony substance. Finally, at the bottom, N is a tiny bone at the end of the toe which is cut through the middle to show it has no pumicelike holes at all. This illustration shows Vesalius's extensive cross-referencing as well. The navicular bone (a small bone of the wrist) can be seen in its entirety, he says, in figure 11 of chapter 33.[28]

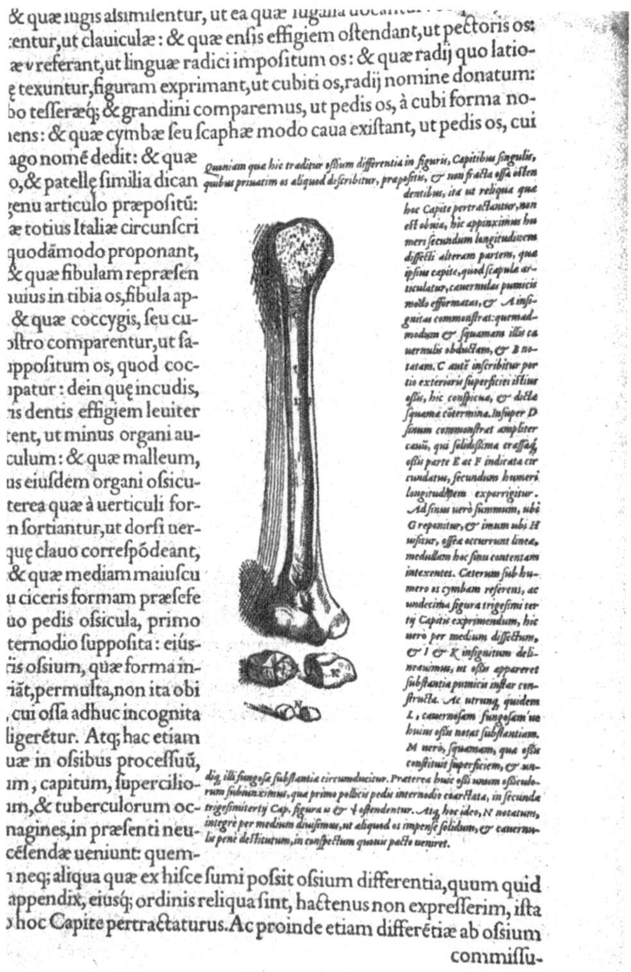

& quæ iugis alsimilentur, ut ea quæ iugula docant...
entur, ut clauiculæ: & quæ enfis effigiem oftendant, ut pectoris os:
æ referant, ut linguæ radici impofitum os: & quæ radij quo latio-
e texuntur, figuram exprimant, ut cubiti os, radij nomine donatum:
bo tefferæq; & grandini comparemus, ut pedis os, à cubi forma no-
iens: & quæ cymbæ feu fcaphæ modo caua exiftant, ut pedis os, cui
ago nomé dedit: & quæ
o, & patellæ fimilia dican
enu articulo præpofitu:
æ totius Italiæ circunfcri
quodamodo proponant,
& quæ fibulam repræfen
iuius in tibia os, fibula ap-
& quæ coccygis, feu cu-
oftro comparentur, ut fa-
ippofitum os, quod coc-
ipatur: dein quæ incudis,
is dentis effigiem leuiter
tent, ut minus organi au-
culum: & quæ malleum,
us eiufdem organi ofsicu-
terea quæ à uerticuli for-
n fortiantur, ut dorfi uer-
quæ clauo correfpódeant,
& quæ mediam maiufcu
u ciceris formam præfefe
uo pedis ofsicula, primo
ternodio fuppofita: eius-
is ofsium, quæ forma in-
iát, permulta, non ita obi
, cui offa adhuc incognita
ligerétur. Atq; hac etiam
uæ in ofsibus proceffuú,
im, capitum, fupercilio-
im, & tuberculorum oc-
nagines, in præfenti neu-
céfendæ ueniunt: quem-

i neq; aliqua quæ ex hifce fumi pofsit ofsium differentia, quum quid
appendix, eiufq; ordinis reliqua fint, hactenus non exprefferim, ifta
i hoc Capite pertractaturus. Ac proinde etiam differétiæ ab ofsium
commiffu-

Figure 2.5 Vesalius, *De humani corporis fabrica libri septem* (Basel: Ioannus Oporinus, 1555), 2. The humerus bone, split longitudinally. Courtesy of the Burndy Library, Dibner Institute for the History of Science and Technology, MIT.

The careful, beautiful drawings of the *Fabrica* and Vesalius's assiduous cataloging of the bones of each illustration by lists of descriptive identifications marked by letters and numbers make this a treatise in which visual representation and textual description are integrated in a remarkably close fashion. This integration is furthered by the fact that each time a bone or bone part is mentioned in the text, an italic indication is given in the margin showing where the illustration of the bone or part mentioned can be viewed—sometimes chapters away.

Serlio and Vitruvius each created new uses for visual representation in their respective disciplines. Both men understood the value of observing the elements of real buildings or real bodies, and both provided detailed illustrations that would allow such observation apart from actual objects by means of detailed drawings. They lived in a world in which artisanal and learned cultures were growing increasingly proximate. Each left the Veneto immediately after the publication of his respective book, attracted by courtly patronage. In 1537 Serlio moved to the court of Francis I in France, and in 1543 Vesalius moved to the court of Charles V in Spain. Each used his authorship for patronage, but each also exploited the commercial book market. Both certainly recognized that their illustrated treatises would find readers and admirers well beyond practitioners of architecture and anatomy, respectively, especially because of the attractive illustrations. As they used their illustrated treatises to acquire courtly patronage, they also had their eye on the commercial book market. In regard to that market, both complained bitterly about the theft of their writings.[29]

The sources treated here provide evidence for the pleasure taken in objects, both natural and artificial, whether it be gardens made of glass and pearls, crank machines, a landscape, a piece of turf, architectural elements, or bones. They also illustrate the increased significance of visual representation of those objects for knowledge about the world. The urban commercial economies of the sixteenth century promoted the cultural value of objects whereas hierarchical social structures increasingly were delineated by means of construction, fabrication of various sorts, and conspicuous consumption. At the same time, interactions among certain workshop-trained individuals and those from more learned and elite backgrounds became increasingly common within certain settings such as cities and courts. One aspect of learned culture, namely natural philosophy, came to be influenced by the rising cultural status of objects and their visual depiction. What is commonly understood as the increased importance of observation within the natural sciences is the result of a complex set of cultural developments having to do with the status of objects, both natural and artificial, and their visual representation.

What was deemed to be knowledge was not separate from the material/ economic/social world that treasured objects. From another point of view, the cultural importance of objects was reflected in the the expansive number of visual representations of natural and mechanical objects in the sixteenth century. Those visual representations in turn functioned to explicate and validate statements about the world whether it be the motion of machine elements, architecture, or anatomy. In most of the examples presented in this essay, textual and visual material belong together and are intricately joined. Both are used to challenge traditions in at least two ways. Works such as

Madrid Codex I showed that machines were not just objects to be constructed to perform certain tasks within the mechanical arts, but objects to be visually depicted and thereby able to produce knowledge about local motion. Treatises such as Vesalius's *Fabrica* challenged the textual emphasis of the previous anatomical tradition by showing anatomical parts visually, associating them with hands-on dissections, and suggesting that visual representations could substitute for such dissections. Objects of art and objects of nature, having lost their ancient distance one from another, became more or less interchangeable instruments in the construction of knowledge.

Notes

1. For a wide-ranging study of some of the relevant issues, see David Summers, *The Judgment of Sense: Renaissance Naturalism and the Rise of Aesthetics* (Cambridge: Cambridge University Press, 1987).

2. Alan Gabbey, "Between *Ars* and *Philosophia Naturalis*: Reflections on the Historiography of Early Modern Mechanics," in *Renaissance and Revolution: Humanists, Scholars, Craftsmen and Natural Philosophers in Early Modern Europe*, ed. J. V. Field and Frank A. J. L. James (Cambridge: Cambridge University Press, 1993), 133–145, citation on 134; and for accounts of the conflict between Aristotelian and experimental approaches, see especially Peter Dear, *Discipline and Experience: The Mathematical Way in the Scientific Revolution* (Chicago: University of Chicago Press, 1995); and Steven Shapin and Simon Schaffer, *Leviathan and the Air-Pump: Hobbes, Boyle, and the Experimental Life* (Princeton, N.J.: Princeton University Press, 1985).

3. Pliny, *Natural History*, trans. H. Rackham, Loeb, (Cambridge, Mass.: Harvard University Press, Loeb, 1952) 9: xxxv. xxxvi. 65–66 (308–311); and see J. J. Pollitt, *The Ancient View of Greek Art: Criticism, History, and Terminology* (New Haven: Yale University Press, 1974), 63–64.

4. For an account of traditional natural philosophy and its transformations, see William A. Wallace, "Traditional Natural Philosophy," in *The Cambridge History of Renaissance Philosophy*, ed. Charles B. Schmitt et al. (Cambridge: Cambridge University Press, 1988), 201–235.

5. For an introduction to this large subject, see especially, Richard A. Goldthwaite, *Wealth and the Demand for Art in Italy, 1300–1600* (Baltimore: Johns Hopkins University Press, 1993); Lisa Jardine, *Worldly Goods: A New History of the Renaissance* (New York: Doubleday, 1996); Pamela O. Long, "Power, Patronage, and the Authorship of *Ars*: From Mechanical Know-How to Mechanical Knowledge in the Last Scribal Age," *Isis* 88 (March 1997): 1–41; and Randolph Starn and Loren Partridge, *Arts of Power: Three Halls of State in Italy, 1300–1600* (Berkeley and Los Angeles: University of California Press, 1992).

6. Long, "Power, Patronage, and the Authorship of Ars"; and Pamela O. Long, *Openness, Secrecy, Authorship: Technical Arts and the Culture of Knowledge from Antiquity to the Renaissance* (Baltimore: Johns Hopkins University Press, 2001).

7. Francesco Colonna, *Hypnerotomachia Poliphili*, ed. Giovanni Pozzi and Lucia A. Ciapponi, 2 vols. (Padua: Editrice Antenore, 1984 [reprint, 1964]); Leonardo da Vinci, *The Madrid Codices*, 5 vols., Vol. 1: *Facsimile Edition of Codex Madrid I*, and Vol. 4: *Transcription and Translation of Codex Madrid I*, trans. Ladislao Reti (New York: McGraw-Hill, 1974); Sebastiano Serlio, *On Architecture*, Vol. 1: *Books I–V of 'Tutte L'opere d'architettura et prospetiva*, trans. with

introduction and commentary by Vaughan Hart and Peter Hicks (New Haven, Conn.: Yale University Press, 1996); and Andreas Vesalius, *On the Fabric of the Human Body: A Translation of 'De Humani Corporis Fabrica Libri Septem*, Book 1: *The Bones and Cartilages*, trans. William Frank Richardson and John Burd Carman (San Francisco, Calif.: Norman Publishing, 1998).

8. A lengthy romance, written in a highly Latinized Italian, it was the first illustrated book and the first vernacular book to be published by the Aldine press. Colonna, *Hypnerotomachia Poliphili*, ed. Pozzi and Ciapponi. See also Maria T. Casella and Giovanni Pozzi, *Francesco Colonna: biografia e opere*, 2 vols. (Padua: Editrice Antenore, 1959), a biography of the Dominican monk of the Venetian monastery of SS. Giovanni e Paolo, Francesco Colonna (1433/34–1527) who is the probable author of the work. The recent claim that the author was Alberti does not seem convincing to me. See Liane Lefaivre, *Leon Battista Alberti's Hypnerotomachia Poliphili: Re-Cognizing the Architectural Body in the Early Italian Renaissance* (Cambridge: MIT Press, 1997).

9. Colonna, *Hypnerotomachia*, 19–28. ("intestini, nervi et ossa, venej musculi et pulpamento.")

10. Ibid., 34, ("vedevasi quasi il tremulare degli sui pulpamenti, et più vivo che fincto") and 53–95.

11. Ibid., 112–123, citation on 116, ("in loco di virentia, omni pianta era di purgatissimo vitro, egregiamente oltra quello che se pole imaginare et credere, intopiati buxi cum gli stirpi d'oro").

12. Leonardo, *Madrid Codices*, Vol. 1, f. 9r., vol. 4, 24–25 (springs, clock escapements, continuous and discontinuous motions); vol. 1, f. 10 r., Vol. 4, 27–28 (chain gears); Vol. 1, f. 15 r., Vol. 4, 39–40 (screws); vol. 1, f. 19 r., Vol. 4, 47–48 (endless screws); and Vol. 1, f. 46 v., and Vol. 4, 89–90 (mills).

13. Ibid., Vol. 1, f. o r., Vol. 4, 2, ("Se possibile fussi fare una bonbarda, che 'l mondo fussi sua ballotta, e che sicome una bonbarda gitta una balotta d'un braccio 3 miglia, che si pò misurare il tal corso 9000 braccia, cioè 9 mila ballotte. Noi possiamo adunque dire, che tal bonbarda gitterebbe il nostro mondo novemila volte le grandeza del diamitro d' esso mondo distante da ssè. [Sare]bono a settemila miglia per monda [sic], sarebono 63 migliara di miglia.")

14. For the Sforza court, see Franco Catalano, *Francesco Sforza* (Milan: dall'Oglio Editore, 1983); Giorgio Chittolini, ed. *Gli Sforza, la chiesa lombardia, la corte di Roma: Strutture e pratiche beneficiarie nel ducato di Milano (1450–1535)* (Naples: Liguori, 1989); Gary Ianziti, *Humanistic Historiography under the Sforzas: Politics and Propaganda in Fifteenth-Century Milan* (Oxford: Clarendon Press, 1988); Evelyn S. Welch, *Art and Authority in Renaissance Milan* (New Haven, Conn.: Yale University Press, 1996); and Gregory Lubkin, *A Renaissance Court: Milan under Galeazzo Maria Sforza* (Berkeley and Los Angeles: University of California Press, 1994). For Milanese canal building, see William Barclay Parsons, *Engineers and Engineering in the Renaissance* (Cambridge: MIT Press, 1968), 367–419.

15. Leonardo, *Madrid Codices*, Vol. 1, f. 1 r, Vol. 4, 3–4.

16. Ibid., Vol. 3, 40–41 for Leonardo's references to the various German artisans that he hired; and for explicit references to experiments, Vol. 1, ff. 77 r., 78 r., 122 v., and Vol. 4, 179–180, 183–184, 325–366.

17. For recent Dürer studies and discussion of the importance of Nuremberg for his work, see especially Jane Campbell Hutchison, *Albrecht Dürer: A Biography* (Princeton, N.J.: Princeton University Press, 1990), 14, 23–26, 57–66, and 78–83 (for his travels and the sale of his prints); Dagmar Eichberger and Charles Zika, ed., *Dürer and his Culture* (Cambridge: Cambridge University Press, 1998); and Peter Streider, "Dürer. (1) Albrecht Dürer," *The Dictionary of Art*, ed. Jane Turner (New York: Grove Dictionaries, 1996), Vol. 9, 427–445.

18. Strieder, "Dürer," 429; and Hermann Leber, *Albrecht Dürers Landschaftsaqarelle: Topographie und Genese* (Hildesheim: Georg Olms Verlag, 1988).

19. Dagmar Eichberger, "*Naturalia* and *Artefacta*: Dürer's Nature Drawings and Early Collecting," in *Dürer and his Culture*, ed. Dagmar Eichberger and Charles Zika, 13–37; and Albrecht Dürer, *Schriftlicher Nachlass*, ed. Hans Rupprich, 3 vols. (Berlin: Deutscher Verein für Kunstwissenschaft, 1956–69), Vol. 1, 146–202. I cite the translation in Albrecht Dürer, *Diary of His Journey to the Netherlands, 1520–1521*, trans. Frank Conway (Greenwich, Conn.: New York Graphic Society, 1971), 64–65.

20. Serlio, *On Architecture*, xix; and Vesalius, *On the Fabric*. My comparison of the two works takes up a suggestion by Vaughan Hart and Peter Hicks that Serlio's treatise bears notable similarities to Vesalius's *Fabrica*.

21. Serlio, *On Architecture*, 266–269.

22. Ibid., 286–287.

23. Vesalius, *On the Fabric*, "To King Charles V," xlvii–xlix.

24. Ibid., liv–lv.

25. Ibid., lvi. The reference is to Galen, *Procedures* 2:1.

26. Vesalius, *On the Fabric*, lvi.

27. Ibid., and 8 and (for finding and preparing bodies) 370–384.

28. Ibid., 4.

29. Serlio, *On Architecture*, xi–xxxi; and Vesalius, *On the Fabric*, xviii–xxi.

Mirroring the World

Sea Charts, Navigation, and Territorial Claims in Sixteenth-Century Spain

ALISON SANDMAN

In sixteenth-century Spain, navigation and cartography were critical industries. Commerce with the New World formed the basis of many fortunes and the hopes for many more. But it was also crucial for the survival of the fledgling Spanish colonies and the interests of the government, which carefully regulated the pilots who guided the ships across the ocean and the charts they used to navigate. Not least among their functions, the charts used by the pilots served as evidence in the ongoing disputes between Spain and Portugal about ownership of territories in the Indies. The tension between the two roles of charts — as navigational tools for the pilots of merchant ships, and as political tools of diplomats in territorial disputes — catalyzed several important changes in early modern Spain. As experts debated the uses of charts in the first half of the sixteenth century, their arguments crystallized ideas about the proper ways of representing the world in a sea chart and the value of systematic theoretical knowledge in navigation.

This chapter uses debates about sea charts as the lens through which to view changing ideas about representations of the world and their links to controversies about the utility of theoretical knowledge. While the practical culture of navigation was shaped by the commercial requirements of the merchants who provided cargo for the ships, and proved adequate to their needs, the territorial implications of sea charts took the debate out of the realm of commerce and brought it into that of imperial politics. This political importance brought new people into the field, cosmographers with closer ties to the royal court than to the pilots or the merchants. Expert in astronomy, geography, and hydrography, these cosmographers tried to reform navigation, focusing on general and systematic knowledge in place of local craft knowledge.[1] They used the newfound official attention to sea charts as a lever to implement their reforms.

Unfortunately, between losses at sea and the routine destruction of out-dated charts, no examples remain of charts used at sea. We are left with a few of the pilots' own notes and sketched charts, and with presentation copies of charts that probably match, more or less, those sold to the pilots.[2] Fortunately, a large variety of sixteenth-century texts survive that chronicle debates about sea charts both in Seville and at the royal court.[3] These texts contain most of the available information about the use of charts in the sixteenth century, and so are an invaluable source for ideas about the proper representation of nature.

Since Seville was the center for travel to the Indies, the debates there focused on the use of charts in navigation, and, more narrowly, on what charts should be sold to pilots. These debates took place within the *Casa de la Contratación* (House of Trade), which had been founded in 1503 to regulate trade with the New World, including the actions of the pilots.[4] In 1523 the growing importance of the new territories led the crown to create a new council, based at court, to take over policy decisions relating to the Indies. As soon as debates about charts were referred to this council, however, it became clear that more was at issue than which charts were most useful at sea. Since 1494, when the Treaty of Tordesillas set the boundary between Spanish and Portuguese overseas territories as a line of longitude, east-west distance had been crucial to territorial claims and disputes. As longitude could not be reliably measured at sea, however, it was not particularly important to the pilots when navigating. Pilots customarily did their best to estimate distance traveled, using their knowledge of currents and winds and the characteristics of the ship. They then set an especially careful watch when they thought they were approaching land. Their craft did not need an accurate representation of longitude on sea charts, which mattered more to diplomats than to navigators. Indeed the Council of the Indies was attuned to precisely such diplomatic concerns.

Abandoning local disputes in Seville, a handful of reforming cosmographers, whom I call theory proponents to distinguish them from an even smaller group of more traditional cosmographers, took their case directly to the council and the king. They used the evidentiary potential of charts to win support for their view that the key to navigation was the ability to accurately locate both the ship itself and the ports to be reached in terms of a coordinate grid of latitude and longitude. Since the only methods to do this involved astronomical observations, they thought navigation necessarily an application of general rules, and as such a science.[5] Though the councillors never ruled on how pilots should navigate, in supporting the charts of the theory proponents they also supported the latter's efforts at reform, undercutting the craft culture of the pilots.

The arguments about the construction and use of the official pattern chart illustrate the key issues in the case: the representation of nature, the disputed uses of that representation, and the ways in which these problems were connected to debates about the nature of navigation and the importance of general knowledge.[6] During the sixteenth century the theory proponents made a concerted effort to gain control of both the institutions of navigation and the practices of the pilots while at sea. The creation of a new pattern chart was central to their endeavors. The royal attention that surrounded the creation of a new pattern chart not only enticed new cosmographers into navigation, increasing the influence of the theory proponents, but also provided them with an audience that was more receptive to their claims than were pilots and merchants, and one that possessed sufficient authority to demand changes.

CONSTRUCTING THE PADRÓN REAL: WHO SHOULD MAKE A CHART

All charts used at sea were supposed to match a central exemplar, known as the *padrón real*, or royal pattern chart.[7] In 1526, after failed boundary talks with Portugal had underscored the inadequacy of the available charts, the Council of the Indies decided there was need for a new pattern chart. In the absence of the pilot major, the person at the Casa de la Contratación in charge of charts and instruments, they entrusted the revision to Hernando Colón, the younger son of Christopher Columbus, ordering him to make both a sea chart and a world map.[8] As a cosmographer and bibliophile with some diplomatic experience, Colón had long been involved in the conflicts surrounding Spain's territorial claims in the Indies.[9] Colón chose as an assistant Alonso de Chaves, arranging for him to be appointed as one of the royal cosmographers at the Casa.[10] Though little is known of Chaves's early life or training, by 1526 he was working as a cosmographer in Seville, and he remained a steadfast supporter of all attempts to increase the pilots' level of education, especially their knowledge of astronomy.[11] With help from Chaves, Colón began to compile a book filled with information from returning pilots, who were ordered to keep daily records while at sea.[12] Though the book eventually contained statements from more than 150 pilots, the attempt to make a new pattern chart seems to have been abandoned unfinished.[13]

Almost ten years later, in 1535, the Council of the Indies sent a letter to Colón in Seville, asking him about the status of the chart and ordering him to finish it as soon as possible.[14] The same letter also empowered the Casa de la Contratación officials to order all of the pilots and cosmographers in Seville to help him finish it. At this point, however, Colón was no longer active in navigation, and without his support Chaves's authority had been much diminished, especially after the return of the pilot major, Sebastian Cabot. Cabot took over most of the cosmographical work in Seville, helped by his friend and ally Diego

Gutiérrez, who made most of the charts used at sea.[15] Both men were allies of the pilots, and resolutely opposed the reforms of the theory proponents.

Cabot had been pilot major since 1518, shortly after Charles I (later Emperor Charles V) came to power, but had spent the years between 1526 and 1530 on a voyage of exploration.[16] He had long identified himself with the pilots and emphasized the importance of practical experience. In fact, he was first hired away from England on the basis of his claims to experience in the northern route to the New World.[17] He himself had little or no cosmographical training and did not place particular importance on the education of the pilots, though as pilot major he was supposed to be in charge of their training. In 1526, Cabot was sent to reinforce the Spanish presence in the Spice Islands, and his absence gave the theory proponents their opportunity to impose reforms. Cabot's voyage was striking for its lack of success, and on his return he was sentenced to fines and several years of exile in North Africa. The sentence seems never to have been carried out, and soon he was again serving as pilot major and struggling to regain his former authority.[18]

Over the next several years Cabot worked to counter the influence of Chaves and Colón, appealing changes in the rules on licensing exams that had weakened the office of pilot major during his absence, and supporting the appointment of Gutiérrez, who shared his emphasis on experience.[19] As with Chaves, little is known about Gutiérrez's early life. He first appeared in the Casa records with an application to be appointed cosmographer, supported by a petition signed by Cabot and a long list of pilots.[20] Though he won the appointment in 1534, his salary was negligible, and the bulk of his income came from selling charts and instruments to the pilots and tutoring them for the licensing exam. He earned enough from such sources to set up his son Sancho as a shipowner as well as a cosmographer.[21]

By 1535, when Colón was ordered to finish the padrón, Cabot and Gutiérrez were firmly in charge. This changed, however, when three new cosmographers responded to the crown's call to help revise the pattern chart, as they were predisposed by training and social status to ally themselves with Chaves. The first of the new cosmographers, Francisco Falero (or Faleiro), had come to Spain from Portugal in 1518 to help organize Magellan's voyage.[22] He did not go on the voyage, but remained in Spain, helping as called upon with various projects. He confirmed his credentials as a learned cosmographer in 1535 with the publication of a commentary on Sacrobosco's *Sphere* and its application to navigation.[23] Though he was certainly not new either to cosmography or to Seville, Falero seems to have stayed out of local politics whenever possible.

The others who helped revise the pattern chart were new to the profession. Alonso de Santa Cruz was just beginning to make a reputation for himself as a cosmographer. He brought to the project an abiding mistrust of

Cabot, gained while sailing under him on his ill-fated voyage as an agent of the investors. Santa Cruz had become interested in cosmography during the voyage, and spent much of the rest of his life writing books on the subject and devising instruments and methods for finding longitude at sea.[24] Pedro Mexía, a local dignitary with some reputation as a humanist and an astrologer, also joined the revision, and in 1537 the council rewarded him with a post as cosmographer.[25] The success of his literary endeavors soon propelled him to more prestigious positions, but even at this point in his career he added weight to the idea of the cosmographer as educated expert.

The addition of the new cosmographers to the *padrón real* project shifted the balance toward people with a more scholarly and theoretical orientation; though Santa Cruz and Falero both had experience at sea, they presented themselves as knowledgeable cosmographers rather than as experienced pilots. The new cosmographers also had closer ties to the royal court than did Chaves or Gutiérrez: Falero had been employed at various tasks since 1519, Santa Cruz held an appointment in the royal entourage to supplement his income in the Casa, and Mexía was later appointed as royal chronicler.[26] Though the three by no means presented a united front, all tended to ally themselves with Chaves rather than with Cabot and Gutiérrez.

With such a large and diverse group, constructing the *padrón* was far from easy, especially as the committee members could not agree on how to reconcile the pilots' reports. The six men spent more than a year in contentious meetings in the house allocated to Juan Suárez de Carbajal, the visiting inspector from the Council of the Indies who was overseeing the project. Finally Suárez de Carbajal ordered them to vote on each point at issue and abide by the majority decision. When they objected, he argued that panels of judges routinely decided legal cases by vote.[27] Why should mapmaking be different? This ruling pleased no one, but it did allow them to finish.[28]

Santa Cruz's objections to the proceedings were so strong that he abandoned the project. Before the chart was even finished he left Seville to complain to the Council of the Indies. He later claimed that because of his report the councillors held the chart in little esteem, though this is hard to reconcile with their subsequent approval of the chart.[29] In any case, his travels were not in vain, for Santa Cruz returned from court with increased authority over cosmographical matters in Seville and with permission to gather the information he thought necessary to revise the *padrón real*.[30] Cabot fought this increase in Santa Cruz's authority, and the issue of their relative precedence was never satisfactorily resolved, though Santa Cruz began to spend more time at court and traveling instead of in Seville.[31] By the end of the 1540s he had returned to Seville but was shut up in his house, writing feverishly but participating little in the cosmographical work of the Casa.[32] Despite all protests, the chart approved by Suárez de Carbajal became the official pattern chart and served as the basis both for making sea charts for pilots and for subsequent revisions.

OBTAINING RELIABLE INFORMATION

Subsequent events, however, revealed more problems in the process, as Cabot, Gutiérrez, and Falero all joined Santa Cruz in disavowing the chart. The ensuing discussions and justifications show the deep disagreements not only about who should make the chart, but also about how to get reliable information and how to decide which information to trust. The pilots' supporters were outvoted, while the theory proponents argued among themselves about whose expertise counted and whether the problems were sufficient to justify junking the chart.

Everyone involved agreed that the pilots were indispensable, for they were often the only available source of information. Access to reports from pilots was considered crucial for anyone interested in correcting charts, so crucial that Santa Cruz, on his return from court, fought the Casa officials for the right to hear reports from returning pilots in a timely fashion.[33] There was also general agreement that oral testimony from experienced pilots could usefully supplement the statements collected over a period of time, so that it made sense to call the pilots to testify at meetings, as indeed happened.[34] Clearly, no one thought the pilots could be ignored.

At the same time, however, most of the cosmographers did not trust the reports of the pilots. As one pointed out in an anonymous pamphlet, when three pilots on the same ship could calculate their position variously as 100 leagues from land, 45 leagues from land, and sailing on dry land, there was clearly some problem in their observations, and thus some role for cosmographers.[35] The author was arguing that since the astronomy behind the methods was unimpeachable, the problems must stem either from the instruments or from the pilots' use of them. Though the example was surely apocryphal, its use illustrates the contempt that many cosmographers felt for the reports of the pilots.

Indeed, Falero gave a masterful summary of the problems of relying on such reports.[36] Most pilots, he said, located positions using compass bearings rather than latitudes. These compass bearings were frequently inaccurate, because many failed to account for magnetic declination, the amount by which the north shown on the compass was offset from geographic north. Those who did correct their compasses for declination often made the wrong adjustment, compounding the error. Furthermore, the few pilots who did determine location by latitude were rarely accurate enough for their observations to be useful. Falero concluded that since the charts made from pilots' reports were based on shaky foundations, it would be best to start anew.

Falero's proposal for reforming the charts involved nothing less than a new survey of the West Indies. He suggested that the survey be done by skilled pilots, all taking frequent latitude observations, using new and accurate instruments, and adjusting their compasses for declination at frequent intervals. He also wanted the pilots to keep a daily written record of their observations, remarking that it would be impossible to give a full report from memory. This plan essentially involved making the pilots behave as cosmographers, and in fact he went on to suggest that if possible a cosmographer should be sent to oversee the survey. Falero's proposal shows how deeply he distrusted the reports and methods of the pilots.

Santa Cruz, on the other hand, felt that the available reports could be made to serve if the pilots could only work without interference from biased cosmographers. He complained bitterly, however, about the qualifications of the other cosmographers involved in the project. He objected that his vote was held equal with that of Pedro Mexía, "who at that time had never in his entire life seen a sea chart nor understood that language," and of Francisco Falero, "who only knew a little about the sphere and judicial astrology," but each "presumed to give his opinion, just like one who understood better," while despite his position Cabot could not be relied on. According to Santa Cruz, he himself was often overruled to the great detriment of the chart, and in sum the whole procedure had made laughingstocks of all the cosmographers involved. As an alternative, he suggested that the pilots be taken one by one into a room with no cosmographers present and asked to point out any flaws in the chart. If each pilot was carefully questioned under oath about where he was licensed to go as pilot, where he had been, and what was good and bad about the chart as it was, they could soon have a chart much better than any that had yet been produced. Santa Cruz never said, however, what should be done if the pilots disagreed. Instead he seemed to assume that the combination of oaths and detailed questioning would yield accurate reports, and hence remove all disagreements.[37]

Chaves and Mexía were working from a similar assumption, but thought that this degree of consensus had already been obtained for most areas of the chart. They argued that the flaws in the pattern chart had been greatly exaggerated, and that most of the problems were in newly discovered areas and so would disappear when there were more reports.[38] They did not, however, solve the problem of disputed testimony. Chaves said that one reliable statement for each area would be enough, provided it was from a man "who knew and had seen what he said," but it is not clear whether he thought any of the pilots reached this standard. Pedro de Medina, who had arrived in Seville only after the chart was completed, took his critique further. The problem with relying on reports from pilots, he said, was that they risked introducing errors rather than fixing them, which was a "very great damage and danger to the seafarers, from the statement of just one person to lose the truth and the statements of many."[39] But he gave no indication of how to tell which statements were reliable.

Cabot and Gutiérrez blamed not the reports of the pilots, but the lack of eyewitness experience among the members of the committee. Gutiérrez did not object to the idea of voting, but thought the wrong people were being polled. "None of those who were there," he said, "had been in the Indies, nor was a sailor, nor had seen the coasts, islands and bays, except only the pilot major who was a sailor and understood the art of navigation." Though this comment discounts Santa Cruz's time at sea, Santa Cruz had shipped as an agent for investors in the voyage rather than as a pilot or sailor. The pilots themselves, Gutiérrez complained, who "knew by the sight of their eyes how the coasts ran and in what latitudes they lay," were completely disenfranchised by the procedures.[40] Cabot used this same argument as a reason to repudiate the finished chart, claiming that he signed only under pressure, a claim the theory proponents indignantly denied.[41]

In fact a group of pilots later rejected the pattern chart on the grounds that experience at sea was crucial to making good charts. A statement signed by more than fifty pilots complained that "it is a harsh thing that we have to navigate by charts made according to the padrón real, which was made by people who have not sailed, nor understand the art of navigation, nor have experience in it, nor have seen the lands or the coasts, bays and islands."[42] But protest as they might, the pilots did not have a vote.

This struggle over whose testimony should be considered reveals a fundamental divide between the theory proponents and their opponents. The pilots thought the most important criterion was having seen the lands in question, and so having a knowledge base to reject inaccurate reports. The theory proponents, however, distrusted the ability of pilots to be adequate witnesses. Though all agreed that the pilots needed to bring back information on the exact locations of places, the theory proponents thought this should be based on astronomical observations, and so distrusted reports based on other methods. The pilots, however, determined locations not from such cosmographical methods, but instead from the compass bearings and distances between places. Since these were deduced from estimates of the course the ship made good and the average speed, the pilots' reports were closely dependent on their knowledge of seamanship and local conditions, knowledge that was impossible without eyewitness experience.

Thus, though the theory proponents did not like having to rely on the pilots' statements about position, the issues in this instance were methods and type of evidence rather than the pilots' credibility per se.[43] Since, however, the pilots' fallibility as witnesses to the positions of lands was central to the theory proponents' claims for authority, they had little incentive to compromise. Furthermore, as is clear from Cabot's having rejected the *padrón real* on the grounds that the pilots were not consulted, the issue of whose testimony was important in making the chart was in practice inextricable from the question of who got to judge if the resulting chart was adequate, and on this issue the theory proponents certainly did not want to yield to the pilots.

TWO EQUATORS AND FOUR POLES: INTERPRETING CHARTS AND CONTROLLING NAVIGATION

The disagreement between the theory proponents and the pilots, Cabot, and Gutiérrez went well beyond a struggle over different methods of determining position and the relative importance of eyewitness testimony. More fundamentally, they disagreed about the relationship between a chart and the world it represented, and what made a chart useful or true. A few years after the construction of the *padrón*, a new cosmographer's bid to enter the market reopened the issue of which charts the pilots should use. Though by royal decree all charts sold to the pilots were supposed to be exact copies of the pattern chart, Cabot and Gutiérrez ignored the *padrón* and instead sold charts that were more popular with the pilots.

This practice was challenged by the new cosmographer, Pedro de Medina, who arrived in Seville in 1538 and tried to establish himself selling charts and tutoring pilots.[44] Though armed with a royal license to make and sell charts and instruments which he had obtained during a stay in court, Medina met with consistent obstruction from Cabot, and had trouble even gaining access to the *padrón real*.[45] Medina's problems may have been increased by the speculation that his presence was intended to act as a check on Cabot's power, since during the same period the sons of Medina's chief rival, Diego Gutiérrez, opened workshops with Cabot's support and without any apparent need to be licensed.[46]

Cabot's support, however, would not have been sufficient to guarantee a good living selling charts, for the charts also had to be acceptable to the pilots. Cabot and Gutiérrez maintained their effective monopoly through the early 1540s, despite Medina's best efforts, in large part by being extremely responsive to the desires of the pilots. Medina and the other theory proponents, on the other hand, thought that they knew which charts were best, and wanted to force that judgment on the pilots. Since the intensive regulation of charts in effect made the court (as regulator) another crucial client to be satisfied, the theory proponents seem to have hoped that court approval would overcome the reluctance of the pilots, and so create a market for charts matching the pattern chart.

Thus when Cabot and Gutiérrez tried to block Medina's entry into the market by denying him access to the *padrón real*, Medina sued for access both in Seville and at court. In the meantime, he began to study the charts sold to the pilots by other makers. When Medina got access to the pattern chart, he discovered that the charts in common use were a novel design by Gutiérrez, rather than being based on the *padrón* as the law required. He then redoubled his efforts, beginning legal proceedings that would drag on for several years.[47] With the support of other theory proponents in Seville, Medina argued that the charts preferred by the pilots were unsafe and unusable because they were false, and, being false, didn't allow the pilots to use proper (i.e., astronomical) methods of navigation. He insisted that the only solution was for all pilots to use charts based on the *padrón real*.

Gutiérrez's charts used two incompatible latitude scales in an attempt to reconcile the observed latitudes of specific places with the compass bearings between them (fig. 3.1). The problem was magnetic declination. A pilot sailing westward using an uncorrected compass would travel farther south than he thought, by an amount that increased as he moved farther west in the Atlantic. By the time he reached the New World he would be about 3 degrees further south than expected. The solution adopted by Gutiérrez was to add a second latitude scale, offset from the first by these same 3 degrees (fig. 3.2). In this way, the chart could still show the customary compass bearings between places, the ones that the pilots were accustomed to using. But by charting latitudes in the Old World on one scale, and latitudes in the New World on the other, he could put places in their correct latitudes without changing the compass bearings at all. On his chart a ship could sail due west by the compass and yet wind up in a different latitude, precisely as the pilots did. Though his charts didn't really reconcile the two sorts of information—latitude and compass bearing—Gutiérrez did find a way to represent both systems at the same time.[48]

The theory proponents objected to this makeshift solution. They claimed that to give a chart two incompatible latitude scales also implied two North Poles, two equators, and other impossibilities, and thus "destroyed and falsified the arts and sciences, principally astronomy, geometry and cosmography."[49] In his unpublished textbook on navigation, written at about this time, Chaves compared a sea chart to "a mirror, in which is represented the image of the world in its absence," showing the "true description and true location and forms of all its particularities."[50] A mirror of the world could not portray poles or equators that didn't exist.

The theory proponents also objected in no uncertain terms to any attempt to modify the representation of the world, even to make the charts more use-

Alison Sandman

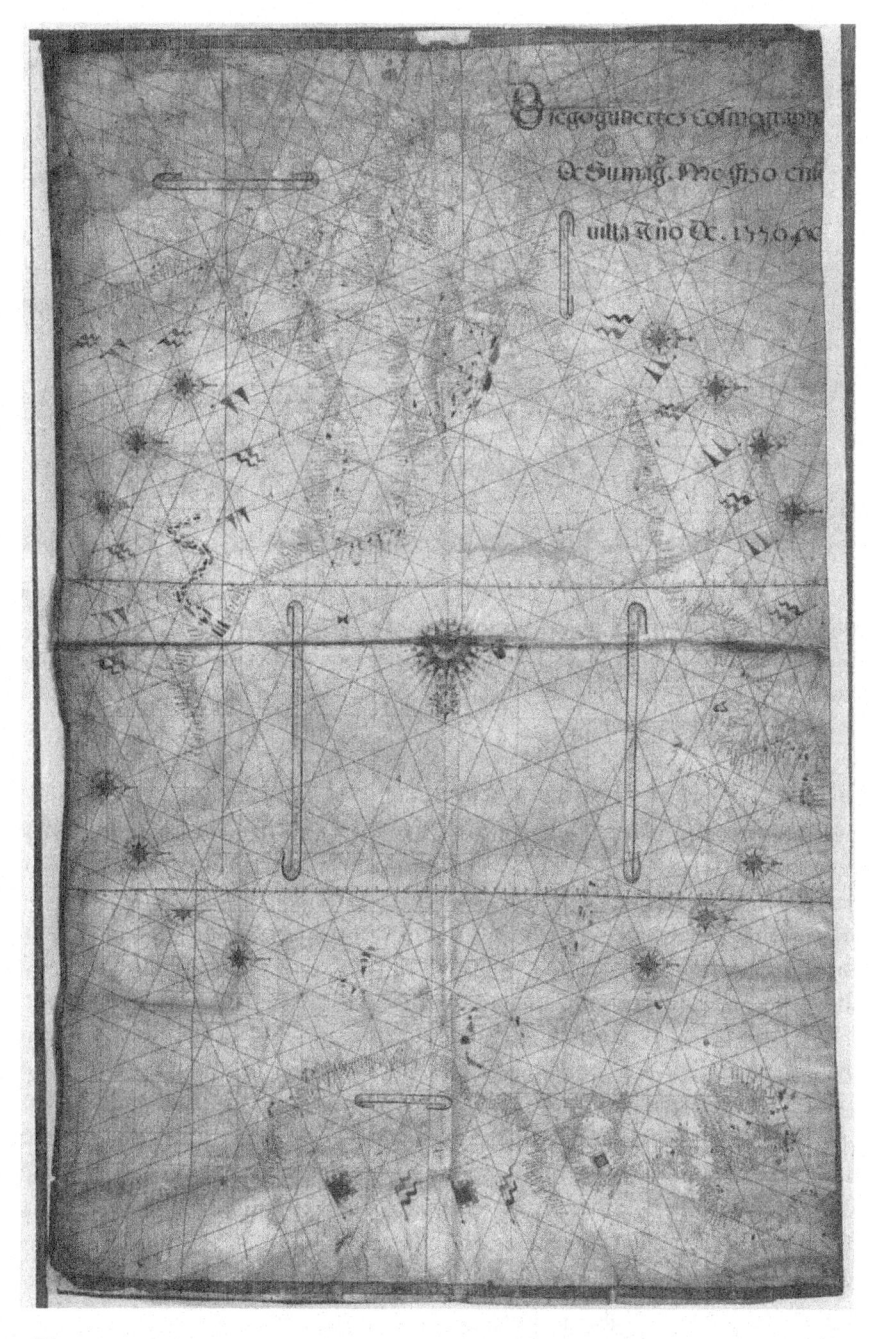

Figure 3.1 Diego Gutiérrez, Atlantic chart, 1550. Note especially the double equators and tropics, more visible in detail.   Courtesy of Bibliothèque National, Paris.

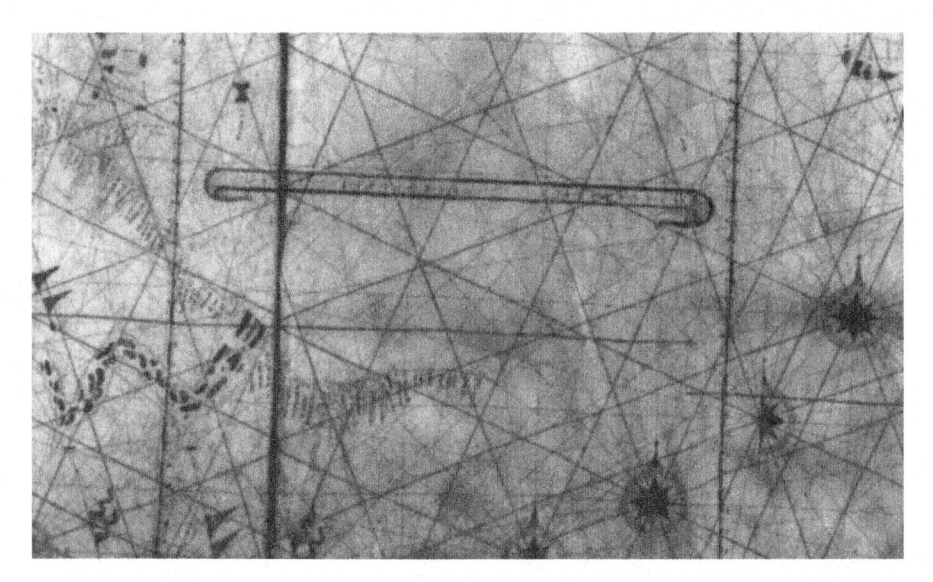

ful. Chaves argued that it was better to teach the pilots to navigate by latitude than to distort the charts, adding that "it is more appropriate that they search for the path on the earth, than to put the earth in the path that they use when it isn't there."[51] Medina compared Gutiérrez's solution to a doctor who treats a man with one arm dislocated by dislocating the other.[52] All the theory proponents agreed that there was no excuse for putting anything on the chart that had no counterpart in nature.

The pilots completely rejected this interpretation of the charts. For them the double scale was a convenience that allowed them to find the latitudes of places, not a claim about the existence of two equators. Several pilots affirmed that they understood the two scales to be one and the same, but drawn as two to put the lands in the right relation to each other.[53] In taking the two equators literally, they claimed, the cosmographers missed the point. The theory proponents, however, did not trust the pilots' opinion of the sea charts, saying that they spoke with the "common voice" and were insufficiently educated to be able to judge.[54]

This was not simply a fight about the propriety of different types of representation, for underlying the debate about which charts should be used was a long-standing disagreement about how pilots should navigate. The theory proponents first became involved in navigation with the appointment of Colón to revise the *padrón* in 1526. From that time on, they had tried to change the way in which the pilots navigated by emphasizing the importance of astronomical methods of navigation. Soon after Colón was asked to revise the *padrón* in 1526, he was appointed as acting pilot major during Cabot's absence.[55] Under Colón's aegis the pilots' licensing exams had become more rigorous; he had even ordered some previously licensed pilots to retake their exams.[56] Chaves, too, was a part of this new regime; one of his first actions after being appointed cosmographer in 1528 was to request permission to give daily lessons to the pilots on the use of charts and instruments.[57]

The composition of Chaves's proposed classes indicates the ways in which the theory-proponents wanted to reform navigation. The authorization letter from the court noted Chaves's desire to give a daily lecture in his house to pilots and seamen on "the use of the astrolabe and quadrant and sea chart, with the treatise of the *Sphere*." Although the ability to use a chart, an astrolabe and a quadrant was already supposed to be part of the licensing exam for pilots, the extent to which pilots found these skills useful at sea was still in dispute twenty years later, as was the extent to which the pilots were learning enough in the classes to use the instruments properly.[58] Since the main use of an astrolabe or quadrant at sea was to find latitude, this emphasis on instruments implied a reliance on latitude measurements, and so on astronomy.

Furthermore, Chaves did not plan to limit his classes to the use of instruments. He also proposed to teach the pilots from the standard introductory astronomy text, Sacrobosco's *Sphere*.[59] This would probably have involved discussions of the sphericity of the earth, the zodiac, the moon and tides, and the equator, tropics, and poles. This curriculum assumed that pilots needed to understand the reference system of elementary astronomy if they were to find latitude at sea. The available methods required them not only to observe the altitude of the sun or north star, but also to know which tables to use, and how to apply the necessary corrections. Most sixteenth-century navigation textbooks included discussions of these issues and offered detailed rules to follow, in addition to tables and explanatory diagrams.[60] In fact, the need for such tables and calculations was one of the reasons cited later for requiring pilots to be able to read and write, another project of the theory proponents.[61] The methods in the textbooks could all be learned by rote, but Chaves, with the strong support of Colón, wanted the pilots to understand the astronomy underlying them, on the conviction that this would help them navigate.

When Gutiérrez gained control of the education of the pilots in the early 1530s, he presided over a distinct decrease in the theoretical content of the classes. In discussing the classes, he made no mention of the *Sphere* or astronomy, but quickly passed on to his expertise in making nautical instruments. Other cosmographers later derided his lack of learning, complaining that a man who didn't know the *Sphere* or understand Latin could hardly be considered an expert.[62] A midcentury investigation into practices at the Casa de la Contratación branded his classes as superficial and corrupt. He was accused not only of accepting bribes to pass unfit candidates (a common complaint in the sixteenth century), but of providing a list of questions and answers for would-be pilots to memorize.[63] Pedro de Medina, Gutiérrez's chief competitor as a teacher during the 1540s, further testified that if the candidate could not read this list (and thus did not qualify as even marginally educated), Gutiérrez would teach it to him orally.[64] The thrust of the complaint was that the candidates could then recite the answers without actually understanding any of the cosmography underlying them. Certainly if Gutiérrez did not understand the astronomical underpinnings of celestial navigation, he could not be expected to teach it to the pilots.

Though the argument over the extent to which pilots needed to master astronomy seems far removed from the concerns involved in making a sea chart, in practice the two were closely linked. Pilots trained in astronomy and the use of instruments could use latitude measurements to navigate, and thus would be more aware of the exact location of lands and ships at sea. Pilots not so trained relied instead on the compass bearings between places, which left them, according to one of the theory proponents, "ignorant and deprived of the general and well-founded science and art [*ciencia y arte*] by which they needed to govern themselves."[65]

The ability to navigate by compass bearings was precisely what Gutiérrez's charts facilitated. According to the pilots, the reason Gutiérrez's charts were more useful than those matching the *padrón real* was because its double scale allowed them to use compass bearings to navigate instead of having to rely on latitude measurements. They considered the compass to be their primary tool; the pilots' guild later compared a ship without a compass to a man without eyes.[66] Though all of the pilots had to know how to take latitude measurements from the sun and North Star, they consistently complained that these were unreliable, since the weather might not permit observations for several weeks at a time, and when it did the results were often inaccurate.[67] Using the two-scale charts they could travel by compass bearing, perhaps using occasional latitude observations as a check, and without having to adjust for magnetic declination. For those sailing by compass, the pilots agreed, the charts were extremely useful.

The charts matching the *padrón real*, which the pilots called latitude charts (*cartas de altura*), could not be used in this way because in making sure that ports were put in the correct latitudes, the chart makers changed the bearings between them. In fact many of the pilots said they didn't know how the latitude charts could be used.[68] The theory proponents explained that the charts were intended to be used with frequent latitude observations, which then corrected courses set by a compass regularly adjusted for magnetic declination.[69] This method, however, was too complicated and cumbersome for most of the pilots. To them, the practical utility of the two-scale charts was both obvious and all-important. Indeed, it was at the request of the pilots that Cabot and Gutiérrez (or so they claimed) had begun to sell two-scale charts in the first place.[70]

In essence, then, everyone agreed that available charts limited the possible methods of navigation. The theory proponents wanted to use this fact to force the pilots to navigate by latitude, by controlling the charts they used. The pilots, with the help of Cabot and Gutiérrez, successfully resisted this move, instead retaining (for a time) the charts that allowed them to navigate by compass bearing. The incentive of a sufficiently large and unified market (the pilots), as well as an ideological commitment that harmonized with the pilots' demands, convinced Cabot and Gutiérrez to defy the rules by making and selling two-scale charts instead of ones matching the pattern chart. They even partially succeeded in convincing the officials in Seville to ignore the regulations they were sworn to uphold.[71] These officials listened to the warnings of the pilots and agreed that forcing them to use charts they did not understand could only cause shipwrecks and loss of life and property; they counseled that any changes be slow and cautious.[72] But the Council of the Indies, more isolated from the pilots by its position at court, found these arguments less compelling, and banned the two-scale charts.[73] By 1545, ten years after they had constructed the chart, and after twenty years of fighting for control of navigation, the theory proponents had won.

SEA CHARTS AS TERRITORIAL CLAIMS

So far this has been a local argument between two factions of cosmographers in Seville. The theory proponents, due to both their ideas of navigation (which privileged latitude over compass bearings) and their ideas of representation (which placed a high value on literal representation) favored the charts matching the *padrón real*, which indeed they had helped construct in the first place. They also placed great importance on the pilots' ability to report back about where they had been so the charts could be improved. This would necessitate their being literate (so they could keep good records) and making frequent latitude observations (so they had data to report). Cabot and Gutiérrez supported instead the arguments of the pilots, that any sea chart that allowed the pilot to guide a ship safely was a good chart. As a group of pilots explained, there were many types of charts for different purposes, but the pilots' own charts served as "nothing more than to go from here to the Indies." They suggested that for other concerns, such as territory and boundaries, the Casa officials instead use charts "of all the universe," which were clearly distinct from the sea charts used by the pilots.[74] The theory proponents, however, rejected this distinction, insisting that one type of chart be fit for all uses.

Once the debate left Seville, it ceased to center on the practical needs of the pilots, and focused instead on other uses of charts. The pilots demanded only that the charts be useful, that is, that they provide an algorithm for crossing the ocean. While the cosmographers did want charts that were useful at sea, they also asked that the charts be accurate reflections of the world. As such, the cosmographers' charts could be used to support Spanish territorial claims as well as to cross the Atlantic, while those the pilots preferred could not. While by no means central to the cosmographers' disagreements with the pilots, these diplomatic implications did give the cosmographers additional leverage with the Council of the Indies. Once sea charts began to take on a larger political significance, the choice of which chart to use became more than a technical issue, and became too important for pilots and cosmographers to settle among themselves.

In sixteenth-century Spain, the exact location of territories was a politically sensitive issue, as all the cosmographers were well aware. To understand this we have to go back to 1494, when the treaty of Tordesillas set the boundary between Spanish and Portuguese territories. Though the treaty specified a line of longitude 370 leagues west of the Cape Verde Islands, it did not specify which island in the group.[75] It also failed to indicate any landmark to locate the line, for the simple reason that no one knew what was there. These details were supposed to be worked out by a bilateral commission, but the commission never met. Despite some diplomatic skirmishes, both countries were too involved in other parts of the world to worry overmuch about the exact boundary line.[76] Though the line of demarcation was officially a line of longitude, and thus something to be determined by cosmographers, at first it was not very important in practice.

All this changed with Magellan. He left Portugal for Spain promising to prove that the Spice Islands fell into Spanish territory (fig. 3.3).[77] In 1522, the successful return of one of his three ships inflamed Spanish hopes of riches in the East, and caused both sides to reopen the question of demarcation. Both agreed that the obvious solution would be to extend the line of demarcation to complete the great circle, thus creating a line in the east. Locating this line, however, was problematic, even in theory. First the parties had to agree on the location of the line in the Atlantic, which involved agreeing on a starting place and on the size of the earth (and so the conversion between leagues and degrees). Then they had to draw a line exactly halfway around the world from the first, and (more important) agree where that line was in reference to known places, since neither side had any reliable longitude measurements.

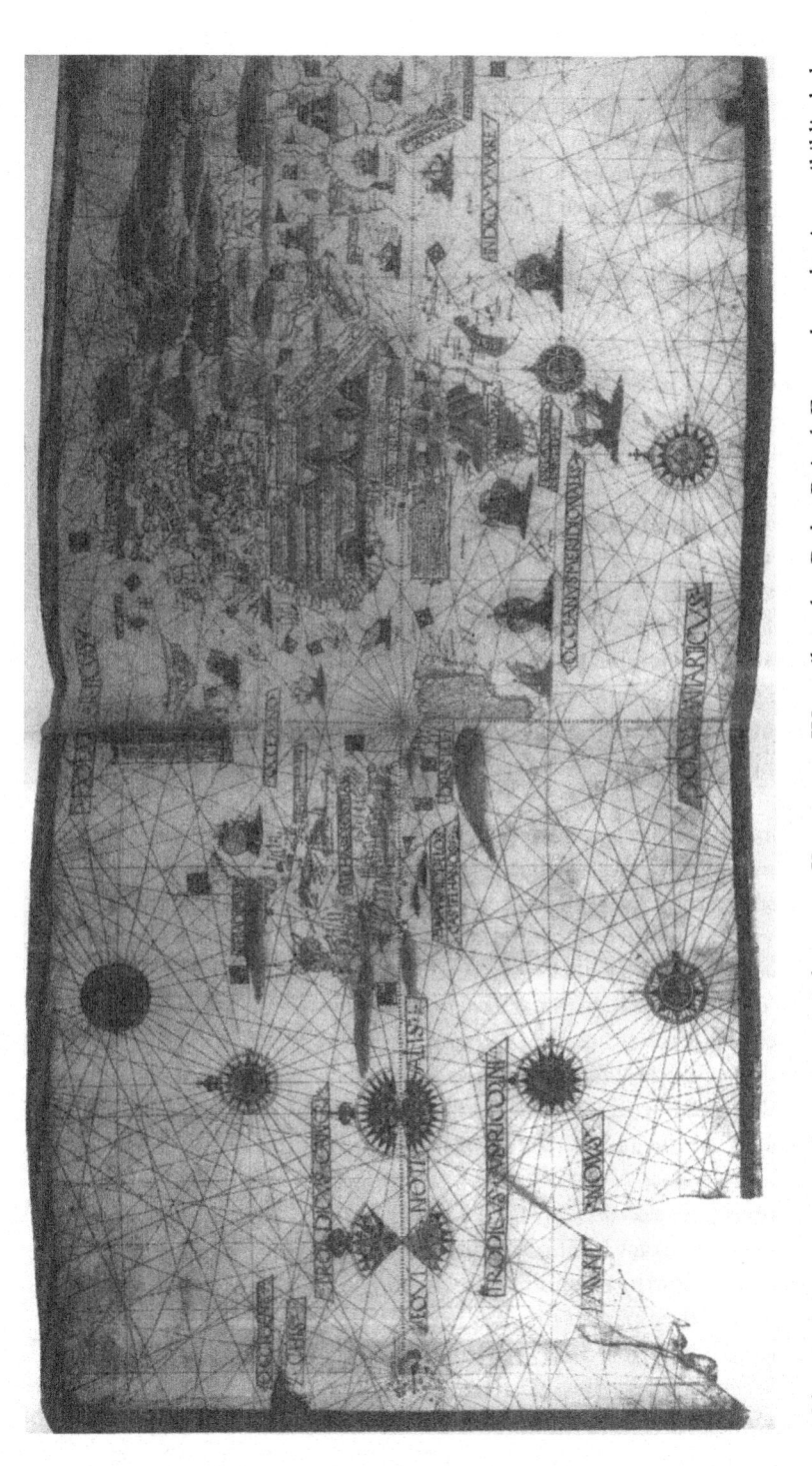

Figure 3.3 Anonymous chart circa 1518, known as Kunstmann IV, attributed to Pedro Reinel. Formerly at the Ameeribibliothek, Munich, present whereabouts unknown. This chart may have been one of those used to convince the Spanish king that the Spice Islands (far left) fell within his demarcation, as their placement on the chart implies.

In 1524 Spanish and Portuguese delegates met to try to decide the locations of the demarcation lines.[78] Hernando Colón served as one of the delegates for Spain. Sebastian Cabot was on hand as an advisor, along with a variety of other pilots and cosmographers. These talks hinged on cosmographical issues—the length of a degree, the locations of certain groups of islands, and the ability to measure longitude at sea. The talks were inconclusive, and the issue remained unsettled until 1529 when the Spanish sold all rights in the Spice Islands to Portugal.

The discussions did, however, serve to underscore both the unreliability of the pilots' reports (since none of them could agree on locations of the islands) and the utility of each side's charts as evidence of the locations of places. In fact, much of the diplomatic maneuvering centered on charts. The Portuguese withdrew from discussion several of the charts and globes they had prepared once it became apparent that they could be used to support Spanish claims. Whether this was a dispute over projections or pure obstructionism, the result of the political maneuvering was to paralyze the discussions.[79] The Spanish, for their part, advocated the use of older charts, since only recently had the Portuguese had any motive for falsifying the distances.[80]

Neither side seems to have expected the talks to be decisive. Perhaps this was due to the considerable technical difficulties in deciding the longitude of the islands, for the uncertainties were huge. The Spanish team pointed out that between their account of travel to the west, and the Portuguese account of travel to the east, they failed to account for almost 50 degrees of longitude, a substantial percentage of the earth. Hernando Colón considered the location of the line of demarcation too uncertain to provide convincing proof of Spanish ownership of the Moluccas. He advised that the Spanish instead assert ownership by right of discovery, and leave to the Portuguese the problem of proving any treaty rights.[81] Perhaps, also, the discussions were hindered by the improbability of either country being willing to give up valuable property to comply with a disputed expert ruling. Only a unanimous decision by all the cosmographers could be expected to exert the necessary moral force, and the technical difficulties were too great to expect such unanimity. It appears that the Portuguese believed the Moluccas were probably on the Spanish side of the line, and so determined to obstruct the talks.[82]

Thus when the committee of Spanish cosmographers gathered in Seville in 1535 to revise the *padrón real*, they were all keenly aware of the political implications of the exact locations of lands. Cabot had been present at the negotiations with Portugal, and one of the aims of his voyage in 1526 had been to reinforce the Spanish presence in the East Indies. Falero, who was born in Portugal, had first come to Spain with Magellan and helped him to convince the Spanish that the Spice Islands would fall within their demarcation. Though the other cosmographers had less direct ties with the territorial dispute, they could not have been unaware of it. Furthermore, when the *padrón* was investigated in the 1540s, one of the issues discussed was whether either of the two competing charts placed territories claimed by Spain on the Portuguese side of the line.

The legal testimony directly reflected concerns about demarcation, especially in the questions asked of each witness. Sancho Gutiérrez made the diplomatic importance of the charts explicit. Discussing the charts made by his father, he argued that "although in the locations of the land the charts do not differ" one type was better to use than the other, because it minimized the risk of foreigners *misunderstanding* the charts, and so coming to the *false* opinion that certain areas were outside of Spanish territory.[83] A representation needed not only to be accurate, but also transparent to even a hostile observer. In rebuttal, Diego Gutiérrez asked the defense witnesses whether the chart misplaced the line of demarcation.[84] Falero, Mexía, and Chaves condemned the two-scale chart on the issue, warning that since the chart misplaced latitudes in the New World, it decreased distances, and so moved the line of demarcation in Portugal's favor.[85] This claim still involved an interpretation of the chart, but an interpretation that they judged valid. This was not an argument the Council of the Indies could ignore.

These cosmographers were not suggesting that anyone falsify charts to support Spanish territorial claims, although perhaps only because they did not think falsification necessary in this case. In their view, however, all charts made claims about the locations of overseas territories, regardless of their intended use. They rejected the pilots' claim, that different types of charts with different uses should be judged only according to that use, on both intellectual and practical grounds: intellectual, because they did not believe that a chart with an inaccurate picture of the world could possibly be useful, and practical, because they did not trust the potential users of charts to respect the intention of the makers. Only a faithful and accurate representation of the world could be useful simultaneously to navigators (provided they used the proper astronomical methods) and to diplomats. All charts should mirror the world.

CONCLUSIONS

The theory proponents and the pilots disagreed about the role that eyewitness experience should play in the construction and evaluation of sea charts, about whether a general knowledge of astronomy was more important to navigation than local knowledge of winds and currents, and about the link between charts as tools of navigation and charts as pictures of the world. Most of these issues, however, were ignored by the Council of the Indies.

The theory proponents were able to gain the support of the council in large part because of the growing political sensitivity of charts. Once the council approved the charts of the theory proponents, however, the rest of their reforms followed. Once the placement of lands on a sea chart was no longer simply a technical matter, but part of a larger constellation of diplomatic claims, the pilots ceased to be the ultimate arbiters of the quality of any given chart, and the ability to describe locations accurately became more central to navigation. Though it did not hurt that the theory proponents were more likely to have friends at court than were their opponents, this contact also made them more sensitive to political concerns. Their ability to speak to concerns about both demarcation and the accuracy of charts brought them the approval of the Council of the Indies, and so support in their attempts to reform navigation. Just a few years later the council chose Chaves to be pilot major and created a new position of professor of cosmography which went to his son. These changes consolidated the control of navigation by cosmographers.

Making sure that ships could safely cross the ocean was important to the Spanish state because they carried the trade that increasingly supported both the Spanish economy and the overseas colonies. The technical side of navigation, including the charts used, was usually relegated to a small team of experts. After Magellan's voyage increased Spanish interest in the East Indies, however, the political importance of the exact locations of territories focused increasing attention on representations of the world, including sea charts. This provided an opportunity for a small group of reformers to argue for the importance of astronomical methods of navigation, on the grounds that they allowed pilots to report accurately on the positions of the ports they visited. The spread of astronomical methods and the subsequent improvements in techniques of navigation thus owed far more to the territorial preoccupations of the Spanish crown than to any practical problems in guiding ships across the ocean. The politicization of cosmography was instrumental in changing the approach to navigation from pragmatic to theoretical, and so in spreading the idea that theoretical knowledge was indeed useful in practice.

Notes

This article forms a part of my dissertation, *Cosmographers vs. Pilots: Navigation, Cosmography, and the State in Early Modern Spain*. I am grateful for research support from the University of Wisconsin, the Fulbright organization, the National Science Foundation, and the Spencer Foundation.

1. Cosmography in Spain has been the subject of much recent research. See, for example, Mariano Esteban Piñeiro, "Los Oficios Matemáticos en la España del Siglo XVI," in *II trobades d'història de la ciència i de la tècnica*, ed. Vicente L. Salavert, Víctor Navarro Brotóns,

Mavi Corell (Barcelona: Institut d'Estudis Catalans, 1994), 239–251; Víctor Navarro Brotóns, "La Cosmografía en la Época de los Descubrimientos," in *Las relaciones entre Portugal y Castilla en la época de los descubrimientos y la expansión colonial*, ed. Ana María Carabias Torres, Acta Salmanticensia Estudios Históricos y Geográficos, 92 (Salamanca: Ediciones Universidad de Salamanca, 1994), 195–205; M. I. Vicente Maroto and M. Esteban Piñeiro, *Aspectos de la Ciencia Aplicada en la España del Siglo de Oro* (Madrid: Junta de Castilla y Leon, 1991). For a review of literature in the field, see Mariano Esteban Piñeiro, "Cosmografía y Matemáticas en la España de 1530 a 1630," *Hispania* 51, no. 177 (1991): 321–337.

2. Ricardo Cerezo Martínez, *La Cartografía Náutica Española en los Siglos XIV, XV, y XVI* (Madrid: Museo Naval, 1994), 141. In his appendix he lists all known sea charts from the period.

3. The majority of these texts are now in the Archivo General de Indias (AGI) in Seville, Spain, primarily in the legal records (section *Justicia*).

4. José Cervera Pery, *La Casa de Contratación y el Consejo de Indias (Las Razones de un Superministerio)* (Madrid: Ministerio de Defensa, Secretaría General Técnica, 1997), 13–18; Ernesto Schäfer, *El Consejo Real y Supremo de las Indias; Su Historia, Organización y Labor Administrativa Hasta la Terminación de la Casa de Austria* (Seville: Universidad de Sevilla, Publicaciones del Centro de Estudios de Historia de América, 1935), especially 82ff.

5. Art (*arte*) and science (*ciencia*) were generally treated as synonyms, contrasted with the office (*oficio*) of a pilot, which involved the traditional methods learned at sea. The cosmographers did not wholly discount these traditional methods, but wanted the pilots to learn astronomical methods in addition. For a discussion of this distinction, see Maria Isabel Vicente Maroto, "El Arte de Navegar," in *Felipe II, la Ciencia y la Técnica*, ed. Enrique Martínez Ruiz (Madrid: Actas Editorial, 1999), 343–344. On navigation as part of cosmography, see AGI, Justicia, 1146, N. 3, R. 2, block 3, image 102, 3 September 1544 statement from Pedro de Medina; on the necessity of astronomical observations and general rules, see images 336 and 339–340, 10 April 1545 statement from Alonso de Chaves.

6. On the chart's construction, see Cerezo Martínez, *Cartografía Náutica Española*, 201–204. Most information on the chart comes from a 1544–1545 dispute (AGI, Justicia, 1146, N. 3, R. 2), which prompted discussion of its construction, and from Alonso de Santa Cruz's 6 September 1549 letter to Hernán Pérez de la Fuente (AGI, Justicia, 945, ff. 168r–171r).

7. On the idea of a *padrón*, see Cerezo Martínez, *Cartografía Náutica Española*, 137–140. On inspections intended to ensure the conformity of the charts, see AGI, Indiferente, 1207, N. 61 (1546 discussion of procedures) and AGI, Indiferente, 2005 (1565 order on the disposition of instruments failing inspection).

8. Cerezo Martínez, *Cartografía Náutica Española*, 190. The relevant orders are dated 6 October 1526 and 16 March 1527, AGI, Indiferente, 421, L. 11 f. 234rv and L. 12, f. 40rv.

9. For a biography of Colón, see Tomás Marín Martínez, "Estudio Introductorio," in *Catálogo Concordado de la Biblioteca de Hernando Colón*, ed. Tomás Marín Martínez, José Manuel Ruiz Asencio and Klaus Wagner (Cabildo de la Catedral de Sevilla, Fundación MAPFRE-América, and Editorial MAPFRE, 1993), 27–351.

10. AGI, Indiferente 421, L. 13, f. 82r, 4 April 1528 letters to Chaves and officials of the Casa de la Contratacíon.

11. His work as a cosmographer is inferred from his possessions listed at the time of his marriage that year. Paulino Castañeda Delgado, Mariano Cuesta Domingo, and Pilar Hernández Aparicio, *Transcripción, Estudio y Notas del Espejo de Navegantes de Alonso de Chaves* (Madrid: Instituto de Historia y Cultura Naval, 1983), 15; José Pulido Rubio, *El Piloto Mayor: Pilotos Mayores, Catedraticos de Cosmografía y Cosmógrafos de la Casa de la Contratación de Sevilla* (Seville: Escuela de Estudios Hispano-Americanos, 1950), 609.

12. AGI, Indiferente, 421, L. 12, f. 40rv, 16 March 1527.

---

13. On the book, see AGI, Justicia, 1146, N. 3, R. 2, image 97, Pedro de Medina, 3 September 1544. Ricardo Cerezo Martínez argued (*Cartografía Náutica Española*, 191–192, 201–203) that a chart was indeed finished at this time, but that later administrators were unaware of it.

14. AGI, Indiferente, 1961, L. 3, f. 276rv, 20 May 1535.

15. AGI, Justicia, 836, N. 6, images 580–625, testimony from various pilots. On Gutiérrez, see Robert W. Karrow, Jr., *Mapmakers of the Sixteenth Century and Their Maps: Bio- Bibliographies of the Cartographers of Abraham Ortelius, 1570* (Chicago: Speculum Orbis Press, 1993), 285–287. See also the discussions in Ursula Lamb, "Science by Litigation: A Cosmographic Feud," *Terrae Incognitae* 1 (1969): 40–57, and Ursula Lamb, "The Sevillian Lodestone: Science and Circumstance," *Terrae Incognitae* 19 (1987): 29–39.

16. On Cabot's appointment as pilot major, see José Toribio Medina, *El Veneciano Sebastián Caboto al Servicio de España, y Especialmente de su Proyectado Viaje á las Molucas por el Estrecho de Magallanes y al Reconocimiento de la Costa del Continente Hasta la Gobernación de Pedrarias Dávilla*, 2 vols. (Santiago de Chile: Imprenta y Encuadernación Universitaria, 1908), vol. 1, 25–33. While this book remains the best source for Cabot's time in Spain, and especially for his voyage, the details of Cabot's early life are contentious. For a brief overview of the historiography, see Karrow, *Mapmakers*, 103–112.

17. Medina, *El Veneciano*, 1: 1–6. The actual extent of Cabot's experience is debated, but there is no doubt that he convinced the Spanish officials interviewing him.

18. Ibid., 303–313, 332. Vol. 2 contains many of the relevant documents.

19. AGI, Indiferente, 2005, undated petition from Cabot, reproduced in Medina, *El Veneciano*, 1: 507.

20. AGI, Indiferente, 1204, N. 21, undated petition from Gutiérrez, supported by pilots' petition with twenty-nine signatures from September 1533.

21. AGI, Contratación, 5784, L. 1, f. 58v, 21 May 1534 cedula giving Gutiérrez a salary of 6,000 maravedís (16 ducados) per year, though most cosmographers were paid 30,000 mrs or more. On prices, see AGI, Justicia, 836, N. 6; in 1551 Gutiérrez charged 4 ducados for a sea chart and 2 to 6 for lessons. On Sancho's inheritance, see Lamb, "The Sevillian Lodestone," 204–206.

22. Ricardo Arroyo Ruiz-Zorrilla, "Estudio," in *Tratado del Esphera y del Arte del Marear con el Regimiento de las Alturas*, by Francisco Falero (Madrid: Ministerio de Defensa; Ministerio de Agricultura Pesca y Alimentación, 1989), 9–10.

23. Francisco Falero, *Tratado del Esphera y del Arte del Marear con el Regimiento de las Alturas, con Algunas Reglas Nuevamente Escritas Muy Necessarias, 1535*, facsimile edition with introductory study and transcription by Ricardo Arroyo Ruiz-Zorrilla (Madrid: Ministerio de Defensa; Ministerio de Agricultura Pesca y Alimentación, 1989).

24. Mariano Cuesta Domingo, *Alonso de Santa Cruz y Su Obra Cosmografica*, 2 vols. (Madrid: CSIC, 1983), 1: 35–61.

25. Antonio Castro Díaz, *Los «Coloquios» de Pedro Mexía: Un Género, una Obra y un Humanista Sevillano del Siglo XVI* (Seville: Excma. Diputación Provincial de Sevilla, 1977), 75–84.

26. Arroyo Ruiz-Zorrilla, "Estudio"; Cuesta Domingo, *Alonso de Santa Cruz*, 1: 81; Castro Díaz, *Los «Coloquios» de Pedro Mexía*, 81–82.

27. AGI, Justicia, 1146, N. 3, R. 2, block 3, image 84, Gutiérrez's account of Suárez de Carbajal's statement.

28. Ursula Lamb ("Science by Litigation," 56) has argued that Suárez de Carbajal was trying to determine scientific truth by majority rule. I would argue instead that he was trying to find a way to reach a decision in the absence of conclusive data.

29. AGI, Justicia, 945, f. 168v, 6 September 1549 letter from Santa Cruz to Hernán Pérez de la Fuente.

30. This involved giving him an appointment as cosmographer. On gathering information, see AGI, Indiferente, 1962, L. 5, ff. 41v–42v, 20 and 21 November 1536. On his authority over Cabot, see AGI, Indiferente, 1962, L. 5, f. 41v, 20 Noember. 1536.

31. For their running battle over authority, see the petitions in AGI, Indiferente, 2005. For Santa Cruz's movements, see Alonso de Santa Cruz, *Crónica de los Reyes Católicos*, edition and study by Juan de Mata Carriazo (Seville: Publicaciones de la Escuela de Estudios Hispano-Americanos de Sevilla, 1951), v.

32. For Santa Cruz's own account of his activities at the time, see AGI, Justicia, 945, f. 168v, 6 September 1549 letter to Hernán Pérez. For Pérez's interpretation, see his letter of 22 September 1549, AGI, Indiferente, 1093, N. 98. On 20 November 1549 Santa Cruz was charged with not attending licensing exams; see AGI, Justicia, 945, ff. 209v–211r.

33. AGI, Indiferente, 2005, various 1538 petitions.

34. AGI, Justicia, 1146, N. 3, R. 2, block 3, image 93, Pedro Mexía, 2 September 1544; block 3, image 97, Pedro de Medina, 3 September 1544; block 2, images 37–38, Alonso de Chaves, 9 September 1544.

35. "Coloquio Sobre las Dos Graduaciones Diferentes Que las Cartas de Indias Tienen," in *Disquisiciones Nauticas*, ed. Cesáreo Fernández Duro, Vol. 6: *Arca de Noé* (Madrid: Ministerio de Defensa, 1996 [1881]), 513. Though Fernández Duro identified the anonymous author as Hernando Colón, Ursula Lamb ("Science by Litigation," 50) has convincingly argued that the *coloquio* was instead written by Pedro de Medina.

36. AGI, Justicia, 1146, N. 3, R. 2, block 1, images 15–17, 5 May 1545 statement by Francisco Falero.

37. AGI, Justicia, 945, ff. 168v and 169rv, 6 September 1549 Santa Cruz to Hernán Pérez.

38. AGI, Justicia, 1146, N. 3, R. 2, block 3, image 94, Pedro Mexía, 2 September 1544, and image 339, Alonso de Chaves, 10 April 1545.

39. AGI, Justicia, 1146, N. 3, R. 2, block 3, image 99, Pedro de Medina, 3 September 1544.

40. AGI, Justicia, 1146, N. 3, R. 2, block 3, images 107–108 (both quotes), Diego Gutiérrez, 9 September 1544.

41. On Cabot and Gutiérrez, see AGI, Justicia, 1146, N. 3, R. 2, block 2, f. 14v and block 3, ff. 12r–13r. For denials, see AGI, Justicia, 1146, N. 3, R. 2, block 2, images 43 (Chaves) and 378 (Mexía). Falero (image 309) testified that there was a lot of controversy but everyone signed.

42. AGI, Justicia, 1146, N. 3, R. 2, block 3, image 371, undated 1545 statement.

43. In this it differs from the English context as described in Steven Shapin, *A Social History of Truth: Civility and Science in Seventeenth-Century England* (Chicago: University of Chicago Press, 1994). For a discussion of the basis for credibility critiquing Shapin, see Barbara J. Shapiro, *A Culture of Fact: England, 1550–1720* (Ithaca, N.Y.: Cornell University Press, 2000), especially 12–26, 70–76, and 120–127. Since the role of juries is central to her analysis of England, her findings are not directly applicable to Spain, but many similar factors apply.

44. For a biographical sketch of Medina see Pedro de Medina, *A Navigator's Universe: The Libro de Cosmographía of 1538 by Pedro de Medina*, ed. Ursula Lamb (Chicago: University of Chicago Press for the Newberry Library, 1972), 9–18.

45. See AGI, Indiferente, 1962, L. 6, f. 156r, granting the right to make and sell instruments; f. 164; ordering that he be given access to the *padrón*; AGI, Indiferente, 1963, L. 7, f. 19; ordering that the other cosmographers inspect Medina's charts and instruments; and f. 84v, ordering that there be no monopoly on making charts.

46. For speculation about Medina's intended role, see AGI, Indiferente, 2673, undated 1551 letter by Alonso Zapata, pilot, decrying rampant corruption among cosmographers in Seville. On the Gutiérrez family, see Chaves's later complaint in AGI, Justicia, 1146, N. 3, R. 2, block 2, f. 10r.

47. The ensuing litigation has been much discussed from a variety of points of view, most recently in Pablo Emilio Pérez-Mallaína Bueno, *Spain's Men of the Sea: Daily Life on the Indies Fleets in the Sixteenth Century*, trans. by Carla Rahn Phillips (Baltimore: Johns Hopkins University Press, 1998), 233–237. The fullest treatment is Lamb, "Science by Litigation." Many of the relevant documents are reproduced in José Pulido Rubio, *El Piloto Mayor de la Casa de la Contratación de Sevilla: Pilotos Mayores del Siglo XVI (Datos Biográficos)* (Seville: Tip. Zarzuela, Teniente Borges 7, 1923), 77–119, and Pulido, *El Piloto Mayor (1950)*, 482–534. The bulk of the original documents are found in AGI, Justicia, 1146, N. 3, R. 2.

48. Many charts of the period tried to deal with this problem by introducing multiple latitude scales; see D. Gernez, "Les Cartes avec Échelle de Latitudes Auxiliaire Pour la Région de Terre-Neuve," *Mededelingen: Academie Van Marine Van Belgie*, book 6 (1952), 93–117. On Gutierrez's charts in particular, see Cerezo Martínez, *Cartografía Náutica Española*, 205–208.

49. 10 April 1545 statement by Alonso de Chaves, AGI, Justicia, 1146, N. 3, R. 2, block 3, image 335; see also similar statements by Pedro Mexía (image 343, undated 1545) and Pedro de Medina (images 100–101, 3 September 1544).

50. Chaves, *Espejo de Navegantes*, 110.

51. AGI, Justicia, 1146, N. 3, R. 2, block 3, image 339, Alonso de Chaves, 10 April 1545.

52. AGI, Justicia, 1146, N. 3, R. 2, block 3, images 100–101, Pedro de Medina, 3 September 1544.

53. AGI, Justicia, 1146, N. 3, R. 2, block 3, image 224 (Francisco del Barrio); 149 (Alonso Martin), 165 (Cristobal Cerezo de Padilla), 170 (Alonso Perez), 181 (Francisco Guzado), and many others.

54. AGI, Justicia, 1146, N. 3, R. 2, block 1, image 8, 24 April 1545 petition from Pedro de Medina; block 3, image 338, Alonso de Chaves, 10 April 1545.

55. AGI, Patronato, 251, R. 22, 2 August 1527 cedula appointing Colón as acting pilot major, to be assisted by Alonso de Chaves and Diego Ribero.

56. See AGI, Indiferente, 2005, 1534 investigation of licensing exams, especially the testimony of Francisco Vanegas and Diego Ramirez, transcribed in Medina, *El Veneciano* 1: 507–512.

57. AGI, Indiferente, 421, L. 13, f. 295v, 21 August 1528 cedula authorizing the classes.

58. For the rules on licensing exams, see AGI, Patronato, 251 R. 22; the entire cedula has been reproduced in Pulido, *El Piloto Mayor (1950)*, 140–143. For pilots' testimony in 1544 about problems measuring latitude at sea, see below, note 67. On licensing pilots who could not use instruments at sea, see AGI, Justicia, 945, ff. 110v–112r (Pedro de Medina, 17 July 1549).

59. On the *Sphere* itself, see *The Sphere of Sacrobosco and Its Commentators*, ed. Lynn Thorndike (Chicago: University of Chicago Press, 1949); on its role in navigation texts of this period, see Pablo Emilio Pérez-Mallaína Bueno, "Los Libros de Náutica Españoles del Siglo XVI y su Influencia en el Descubrimiento y Conquista de los Océanos," in *Ciencia, vida y espacio en Iberoamérica* (Madrid: CSIC, 1989), esp. 477–478.

60. See, Martín Fernández de Enciso, *Suma de Geographía*, 1519, ed. M. Cuesta Domingo (Madrid: Museo Naval, 1987), 113–118 (tables ff. 87–110); Falero, *Tratado del Esphera* part 2, chs. 5–6; Chaves, *Espejo de Navegantes*, 149–160 (book 2, treatise 1, chapters 1–3).

61. AGI, Justicia, 768, N. 2; AGI, Indiferente, 1967, L. 16, ff. 312r–313r.

62. AGI, Justicia, 1146, N. 3, R. 2, block 2, image 38 (Alonso de Chaves, 9 September 1544); block 2, image 380 (Pedro Mexía, undated January 1545); block 3, f. 20r (Pedro de Medina, 3 September 1544).

63. AGI, Justicia, 945, section 4, f. 70rv (Hernando Blas, 27 May 1549); ff. 103r–104r (Sancho Gutiérrez, 11 July 1549); f. 112r (Pedro de Medina, 17 July 1549). This was part of an inspection of the Casa de la Contratación by the Council of the Indies. Gutiérrez died while appealing the sentence.

64. AGI, Justicia, 945, section 4, f. 112r, 17 July 1549 testimony.

65. AGI, Justicia, 1146, N. 3, R. 2, block 3, image 336, Alonso de Chaves, 10 April 1545.

66. AGI, Justicia, 1146, N. 3, R. 2, block 3, image 371, undated statement signed by about fifty-five pilots; AGI, Justicia, 792, N. 4, especially image 74, 1565 petition from the pilots guild to have a certain lodestone made available for remagnetizing their compasses.

67. AGI, Justicia, 1146, N. 3, R. 2, block 3, image 186 (testimony from Martin Lopez), image 203 (Pedro Camino), image 212 (Martin Sanchez), image 218 (Diego Sanchez Colchero), image 223 (Francisco del Barrio), image 234 (Tome de la Isla), image 250 (Hernando Blas), image 371 (statement from fifty-five pilots). All the witnesses cited here were pilots.

68. For being unable to use single-scale charts see the statements in AGI, Justicia, 1146, N. 3, R. 2, block 3, image 244 (Jeronimo Rodriguez), images 355–356 (six experienced pilots), image 371 (about fifty-five pilots). For one pilot who could use both types of chart, see image 347 (Hernan Rodriguez).

69. See for example AGI, Justicia, 1146, N. 3, R. 2, block 3, images 339–340, description by Alonso de Chaves.

70. AGI, Justicia, 1146, N. 3, R. 2, block 2, image 33 (Diego Gutiérrez, 28 August 1544); block 3, image 119 (Sebastian Cabot, 9 September 1544).

71. This charge was brought by Medina, and substantiated by the long-standing use of the two-scale charts even after they were banned; AGI, Justicia, 945, ff. 109v–110v, 17 July 1549 testimony.

72. AGI, Indiferente, 1093, N. 68, 5 April 1545 letter from the officials of the Casa de la Contratacíon to the prince.

73. AGI, Indiferente, 1963, L. 9, ff. 174v–176v, 22 February 1545 letter to the officials of the Casa de la Contratación.

74. AGI, Justicia, 1146, N. 3, R. 2, block 3, images 356–357, undated ca. 1544 petition from six pilots.

75. Antonio Rumeu de Armas, *El Tratado de Tordesillas*, Colecciones MAPFRE 1492 Colección América 92, 12 (Madrid: Editorial MAPFRE, 1992), 141–150, 169–175.

76. The most notable skirmish during this period was probably the arrest of eleven Portuguese sailors accused of being on the wrong side of the line of demarcation, which sparked official inquiries into the location of the line. Rolando A. Laguarda Trías, *El Predescubrimiento del Río de la Plata por la Expedición Portuguesa de 1511-1512* (Lisbon: Junta de Investigações do Ultramar, 1973), 91–113, esp. 96–97.

77. On Magellan, see Tim Joyner, *Magellan* (Camden, Maine: International Marine, 1992). On the cartographic importance of the debate over the Spice Islands, see Jerry Brotton, *Trading Territories: Mapping the Early Modern World* (Ithaca, N.Y.: Cornell Univ. Press, 1998), 119–150.

78. For a brief description of the meetings, see Rumeu de Armas, *El Tratado de Tordesillas*, 222–224. He blamed the lack of results on the obstructionism of the Portuguese representatives. Most of the expert opinions can be found in AGI, Patronato, 48, Ramos 12–17, and have been published in Martín Fernández de Navarrete, *Colección de los Viages y Descubrimientos que Hicieron por Mar los Españoles Desde Fines del Siglo XV, Vol. IV: Expediciones al Maluco = Viage de Magallanes y de Elcano* (Buenos Aires: Editorial Guarania, 1945), 296–335.

79. Ursula Lamb, "The Spanish Cosmographic Juntas of the 16th Century," *Terrae Incognitae* 6 (1974): 51–64, 55; Rumeu de Armas, *El Tratado de Tordesillas*, 223. Rumeu de Armas characterized the Portuguese as obstructive throughout, while Lamb argued that the political maneuvering hindered the experts' attempts to discuss freely all available data and suggested that the differences over the charts involved a disagreement over projection.

80. AGI, Patronato, 48, R. 13, image 5, undated 1524 opinion signed by Hernando Colón, Fray Tomás Durán, Doctor Salaya, Pero Ruiz de Villegas, Maestro Salazar, and Juan Sebastián del Cano.

81. AGI, Patronato, 48, R. 17, image 1, 17 April 1524 opinion of Hernando Colón.

82. Luis de Albuquerque, "O Tratado de Tordesilhas e as Dificultades Tecnicas da Sua Aplicação Rigorosa," in *El Tratado de Tordesillas y Su Proyeccion* (Valladolid: Seminario de Historia de America, Universidad de Valladolid, 1973), 131–132.

83. AGI, Justicia, 1146, N. 3, R. 2, block 3, image 359, undated spring 1545 statement from Sancho Gutiérrez. Emphasis mine.

84. Unsurprisingly, they all said no. AGI, Justicia, 1146, N. 3, R. 2, block 3, images 149ff. (question 13 and answers by pilots).

85. AGI, Justicia, 1146, N. 3, R. 2, block 1, images 13–14 (5 May 1545 statement from Francisco Falero); block 3, image 344 (undated 1545 statement from Pedro Mexía); block 3, images 336–338 (10 April 1545 statement from Alonso de Chaves); Chaves did not mention the demarcation directly, but focused on the errors in distances and positions caused by the double scale.

From Blowfish to Flower Still Life Paintings

Classification and Its Images, circa 1600

CLAUDIA SWAN

A t its broadest span, this essay is about how early modern (pre-Linnaean) natural history organized its experience of the natural world. More narrowly, I am conerned with the *visual* organization of the natural world by means of naturalistic figuration (mimetic pictures) and schematic representation (grids). Much of the chapter will focus on naturalistic representation in the classification of blowfish in the first decade of the seventeenth century in the Netherlands, and on grids and schematic tables in natural history of the period. I conclude by suggesting that the coexistence of these two modes of representation is a crucial feature of early modern natural history and that, taken together, they may help to explain how botanical still-life paintings are structured, compositionally and epistemologically speaking. In other words, this essay treats the organization of the natural world by images and the impact of natural history's modes of visualization on the new genre of flower pictures ca. 1600.

CHAOS IN THE MICROCOSM: THE CASE OF ULISSE ALDROVANDI

Ulisse Aldrovandi, who died in 1605 at the age of 83, ranks among the most renowned sixteenth-century natural historians. Aldrovandi was professor of logic and philosophy and lecturer in simples (medical preparations from plants and minerals) at the University of Bologna. From 1568 until his death he served as director of the university's botanical garden, which he helped found. During his lifetime, Aldrovandi was known to European medics, naturalists, princes, clerics, pharmacists, and scholars as a collector who amassed a truly staggering number of natural specimens, which he housed in a kind of proto-museum, and many of which were illustrated in his massive volumes on insects, birds, wood, metals, monsters, and other classes of *naturalia*.[1] His fame endured: in 1750 the great naturalist Georges-Louis Leclerc, Comte de Buffon (1707–88), dubbed him "the most diligent and knowledgeable of naturalists" and philosopher/encylopedist Denis Diderot (1713–84) referred to him as "the most universal and complete modern naturalist."[2]

Diligent, knowledgeable, universal, and complete: these adjectives were used even in the sixteenth century to describe Aldrovandi's efforts to observe the natural world and to make it available for observation. Buffon and Diderot, taken together, offer an apt, if antithetic, introduction to Aldrovandi's natural history. Unlike his exact contemporary Carl von Linné/Carolus Linnaeus (1707–78), Buffon did not believe in the necessity of systematic taxonomy. Diderot in his turn drove the production of that immense and powerful machine of calibrated knowledge, the *Encyclopédie*. While Aldrovandi amassed, arranged, studied, taught, and published as many specimens of the natural world as he could get his hands on, he did not find it necessary to offer a systematic mode of organization for them. In the sixteenth century, naturalists resorted regularly and without apology to what subsequent natural historians would take to be arbitrary and convenient modes of organization.[3] The alphabet, for example, was sufficient for Leonhart Fuchs, one of the three so-called fathers of German botany and the author of a suite of volumes on the plant world first published in the 1540s. Generally speaking, very broad morphological or Aristotelian classes served as the brackets between which sixteenth- and seventeenth-century naturalists arranged the stuff of nature, which they so eagerly tracked down, studied, observed, dissected, dried, bought, sold, taught, published, displayed, advertised.[4]

In 1595, Aldrovandi described his collection as follows:

> Today in my microcosm, you can see more than 18,000 different things, among which 7000 in fifteen volumes, dried and pasted, 3000 of which I had painted as if alive ("*al vivo*"). The rest — animals terrestrial, aerial and aquatic, and other subterranean things such as earths, petrified sap, stones, marbles, rocks, and metals — amount to as many pieces again. I have had paintings made of a further 5000 natural objects — such as plants, various sorts of animals, and stones — some of which have been made into woodcuts. These can be seen in fourteen cupboards, which I call the Pinacotheca. I also have sixty-six armoires, divided into 4500 pigeonholes, where there are 7000 things from beneath the earth, together with various fruits, gums, and other very beautiful things from the Indies, *marked with their names, so that they can be found* (emphasis added).[5]

Contemporary observers were regularly stupefied by the contents of Aldrovandi's collection — his microcosm, as he calls it here. One visitor wrote of his heart being aflutter and his breath bated in anticipation of seeing all that Aldrovandi had amassed.[6] In the final years of his life, Aldrovandi arranged to have ownership of what he even called the "eighth wonder of the world" transferred to the city of Bologna, a gift accepted gladly by the city's senators.[7] Aldrovandi's efforts are exemplary of what Paula Findlen has called Renaissance curiosity (as opposed to Baroque wonder), of the efforts to contain the infinite manifestations of nature in a single space — also called a museum.[8] Curiosity, however, did not always sponsor recognizable modes of classification.

One organizing principle for Aldrovandi's efforts, as for his possessions, is to be found in the praxis of medicine. Some of the most noteworthy contents of his museum and others of the time had or were thought to have medicinal application — from bezoar stones to dragon skeletons to myriad plants and spices. But if his own notes are any indication, to enter the space of Aldrovandi's microcosm was to give way to what seems from the present perspective of the life sciences relative chaos — chaos in pigeonholes and armoires. Likewise, the headings under which he collated his working notes were distinctly rudimentary from the point of view, say, of systematic taxonomy. They were arranged alphabetically, topically, and geographically. The staggering number of images of the contents of the collection he had made and that he stored in the collection itself is important too. Not because these images contributed to the classification of the contents, but because the net effect of their presence would have been to mirror, and to multiply, the vast number of items at hand. It comes as something of a relief when Aldrovandi tells us that the forty-five hundred pigeonholes in the sixty-six armoires in which he had placed seven thousand dried specimens were "marked with their names, so that they can be found."

THE ENDS OF NATURALISM: BLOWFISH

In the brief description of his collection cited above, Aldrovandi enumerates the specimens he owns in the same breath as images of such objects, which in their turn constitute a substantial portion of the whole. The images Aldrovandi cites are continuous with the rest of the collection in a significant regard: they are, as we know from the woodcuts made for publication in the volumes he authored, naturalistic representations of natural specimens. They were, as he specifies here and elsewhere, drawn or painted *al vivo*.[9] What role do such images — purposefully morphological characterizations — play in contemporary classificatory schemes and efforts?

The blowfish and, specifically, the blowfish as it came to be represented in the context of Dutch natural history ca. 1600 may offer an answer to this question. The blowfish was a widely popular specimen in natural history ca.

Figure 4.1 Jacques de Gheyn II, *Blowfish*, pen and ink drawing, ca. 1605 (Rijksmuseum, Amsterdam). Photo courtesy of the Rijksmuseum–Stichting, Amsterdam.

1600, prized for its exoticism.[10] On the evidence of contemporary prints we know blowfish to have been displayed prominently in a number of illustrious collections, where they frequently were hung from ceilings.[11] A single specimen was also depicted by the Dutch artist Jacques de Gheyn II (1565–1629). De Gheyn cultivated close contacts with members of the medical faculty at Leiden University during the years that he lived in the city of Leiden and his drawing of a blowfish is coeval with published accounts by the great botanist and fellow Leidenaar Carolus Clusius (1526–1609) of what Clusius declared to be four different kinds of blowfish. Close analysis of de Gheyn's and Clusius's verbal and pictorial descriptions of the blowfish is especially revealing—of the difference between an artistic representation of a natural historical specimen and a natural historical representation of the same, as well as of the ways in which naturalistic representation served the ends of contemporary classification strategies.

De Gheyn's drawing of a blowfish (*Diodon hystrix;* fig. 4.1), preserved in its inflated form, is dated on stylistic grounds to the first decade of the seventeenth century. It consists of two views of the dead fish, frontal and lateral, and a lengthy inscription. In translation, the inscription reads:

Claudia Swan

Sea-Hedgehog—this fish is umber white and iron black grayish/ becoming lighter from the back down to the belly/ this is white toward the tail it is even browner and spotted/ with Cologne earth the spines are yellow ochreish light gray/ the fins are umber and Cologne earthish against the body yellow ochre/ and white somewhat red and also somewhat blueish in color/ and also spotted with Cologne earth and the jaw/ rather umber-like in color.[12]

De Gheyn may have observed this fish in a private collection, or among the natural historical specimens belonging to Leiden University. In 1601, he was commissioned by Dr. Pieter Pauw, professor of anatomy and botany, to engrave a plan of the botanical garden (fig. 4.2).[13] De Gheyn's is a schematic plan, intended to describe the layout of the garden. It contains individual plots in which botanical specimens were planted and from which their identification and uses were taught to students of *materia medica*—the makings of medicines. This practice is illustrated by the figure of the robed professor,

Figure 4.2 Jacques de Gheyn II, *Leiden University Hortus Publicus*, engraving, 1601. Photo courtesy of National Herbarium of the Netherlands, Leiden.

surrounded by an attentive audience, in the distant center of the image; he points to one of the plots in the garden, in much the same way as we know the medical faculty to have taught from the contents of the garden in the years around 1600.[14] In effect, de Gheyn's plan of the garden records its physical characteristics as well as its function within the university curriculum; like the anatomical theater, constructed in the mid-1590s, the university's collection of *naturalia* served as a focal point in medical instruction.

In the gallery at the far, western edge of the garden, which was constructed in 1599, specimens of a variety of *naturalia* were housed. A carcass of a blowfish is listed in the two existing inventories of the gallery, alongside a number of rarities including coral, an imbricated shell, the beak of a foreign bird, an Indian ink pot, a crab, pygmy clothing, two Indian hammocks, walrus teeth, and the like.[15] That the blowfish was a prized item in the collections of the Leiden University is also shown by its inclusion in another plan of the garden, by William Swanenburgh and dated 1610 (fig. 4.3), by which time the garden and the anatomical theater had become tourist attractions.[16] The blowfish was also recorded in a major natural history text written by a close associate of de Gheyn's and the director of the university garden—Clusius's *Exoticorum Libri Decem* (Ten books of exotica), a vast

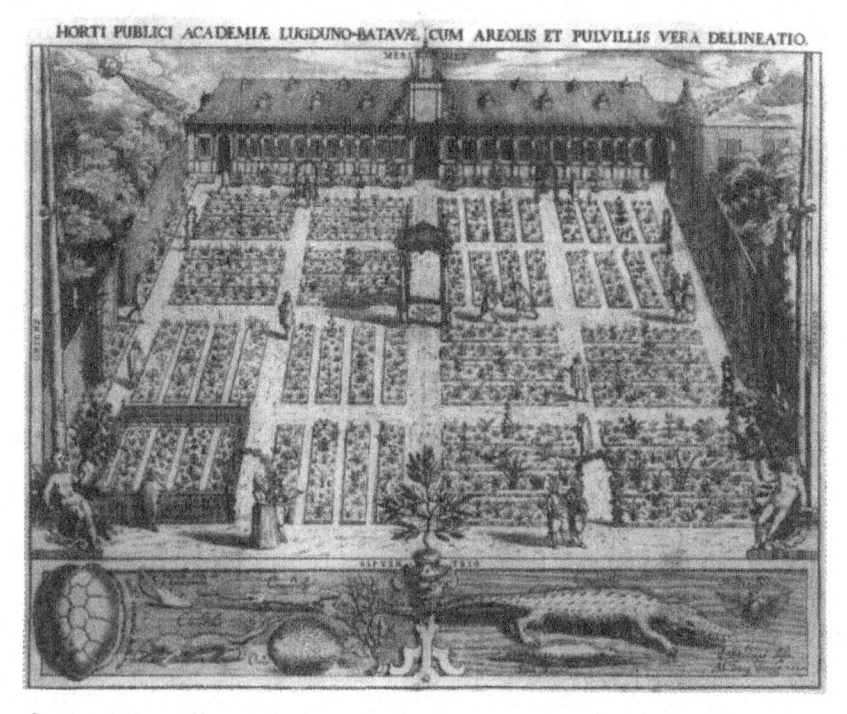

Figure 4.3 Willem Swanenburgh after I.C. Woudanus, *Leiden University Hortus Publicus*, engraving, 1610. Photo courtesy of Rijksmuseum-Stichting, Amsterdam.

Claudia Swan

compendium of wonders of the natural world Clusius compiled in Leiden and published there in 1605.[17] That de Gheyn would have had access to a specimen of the *Diodon hystrix* in Leiden seems clear; moreover, the status of this fish as an object of curiosity at the time is amply documented.[18] How de Gheyn views the blowfish and the modes of verbal and visual description he engages to describe it are what is crucial here.

De Gheyn scanned the surface of the prickly orb of fish before him, first from in front of it and in line with its line of sight and then, in the rendering at the right of the sheet, from its right side. Finally, he scanned it again in order to record, in the inscription below, the shifting colors of its body. The continuity between the abbreviated and spiky forms of the drawing and the forms of the text below is suggestive, and the pace with which he describes the alterations of color from the back to the belly and from the fins to the body (the text is entirely without punctuation) is consistent with the sustained pattern of lines defining the fish above. Significantly, the descriptive responsibilities of the verbal and the visual accounts de Gheyn provides are distinct: the drawing of the fish conveys the form, and the inscription the color. De Gheyn's written description does not reiterate what is made visible in the accompanying image; it supplements it. And by describing the colors of the fish in the colors of pigments (Cologne earth, umber white, iron black grayish, yellow ochreish light gray) de Gheyn describes the fish *as a picture*.

De Gheyn's drawing offers a verbal description that is functionally distinct from the visual description it provides. His verbal description is of a different order — the order of color, of a painter's colors. The inscription does not allude to an external frame of reference beyond the palette, and in this sense the description de Gheyn proposes is entirely self-referential: "This fish" to which de Gheyn refers in the opening line of the inscription is no longer the fish hanging in the Leiden gallery, or the fish returned to the Netherlands after long voyages, the component of a collection of *naturalia*, or this fish as compared to any similar or other fish. "This fish" is the fish of de Gheyn's drawing, the fish of a picture in the making.

Reconstituted according to de Gheyn's indications — colored in — such a picture would effectively convey the forms and colors of this exotic natural specimen. To a very significant extent these were the characteristics according to which distinctions of class and sort were made within contemporary natural history.[19] That this is so is borne out in Clusius's accounts of the natural world in general, and in his description of the *Diodon hystrix* in particular, which is directly relevant to assessing the status of de Gheyn's description. In his voluminous *Exoticorum*, Clusius documents the four fish he identifies as blowfish in the course of four separate chapters of book 6. Of the first three of the fish he describes, Clusius writes that he had observed them hanging in "museums" belonging to individuals in Amsterdam and in Montpellier.[20]

Each of Clusius's entries on these four fish—what he calls the *Histrix piscis* and three related fish, which, following Guillaume Rondelet, the French icthyologist, he names the *Orbis spinosus*, the *Orbis muricatus*, and the *Orbis muricatus alter*—is accompanied by a woodcut that represents the fish described (figs. 4.4, 4.5, 4.6, and 4.7).[21]

In his text, Clusius makes reference to drawings that served him variously in the process of classifying the specimens he describes. One acquaintance, Jacob Plateau, donated drawings of two of the fish;[22] the Leiden pharmacist Christian Porret is credited with having provided Clusius with another.[23] At one point Clusius states that a drawing was made for him to enable him to compare specimens.[24] Clusius's dependence on images in the course of assembling his account of the *Diodon hystrix* is noteworthy; that each of his entries is illustrated with a woodcut reflects a conviction, amplified in his text, that images convey information crucial to description and some form of rudimentary classification. Within the context of late sixteenth-century natural history, the combination of text and image here is entirely conventional. But if Clusius's descriptive method exemplifies the industry standard insofar as it corresponds to the manner in which verbal and visual description are coupled throughout natural history writing of the time, his account of these four fish also provides an excellent example of the limits of contemporary classificatory strategies.

The degree to which Clusius relies on external, observable characteristics in order to describe and classify the specimens he records is typical of contemporary natural history. Clusius's verbal description of the *Histrix piscis*, for example (fig. 4.4), amounts to a meditation on the impenetrable surface of the spiny fish. Its dimensions are given, measured from its shriveled lips to the root of its tail and around its center, and then the specimen is, as it were, fleshed out by a description that dwells on its superficial characteristics. He seems to write as he scans the object: it is "without scales and covered merely with a whitish skin or hide, strewn with firm and sharp spines on all sides." A description of its somewhat protuberant mouth and wrinkled lips and teeth follows, with conjectures about the predatory techniques of the fish; from the eyes, with their raised eyebrows and four prickly spines, Clusius moves along the body. The dimensions of the fins and the coloration of the body are noted ("the skin of the belly is white, and the back is dark, with many distinct dark spots") and, finally, the orifice through which the fish is thought to breathe and the differing inclinations of its spines are recorded.[25] Ultimately, he informs the reader that he is unable to discuss the internal structure of the fish, which was not native to local waters, because it was available to him only in dried form.[26]

If on the one hand the lack of live blowfish in the Netherlands compounded their exoticism, it also made for highly unstable classification.[27] Depending on

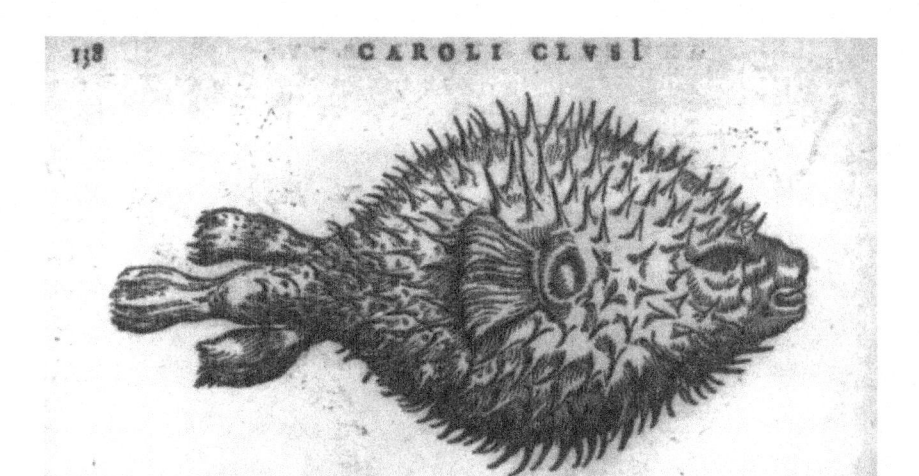

§4. ERAT porrò ab extremo ore ad caudæ initium, five radicem, viginti uncias longus, medio corporis ambitu viginti novem craffus, fquamis carens, & cute five corio albefcente dumtaxat tectus, undiquaque firmis & acutis fpinis obfitus, quarum bafis in binas alias breves & fub cute latentes definebat: oris aperti diameter trium unciarum erat, & aliquantulum prominebat, labra rugofa, binaque offa pro dentibus habebat, fuperné unum, inferné alterum, utrumque fornicatum, & anteriore parte nonnihil, ut oris rictus; pro

Figure 4.4   Anonymous, *"Histrix Pisicis,"* woodcut in Carolus Clusius, *Exoticorum Libri decem*, Leiden, 1605.   Photo courtesy of the National Herbarium of the Netherlands, Leiden.

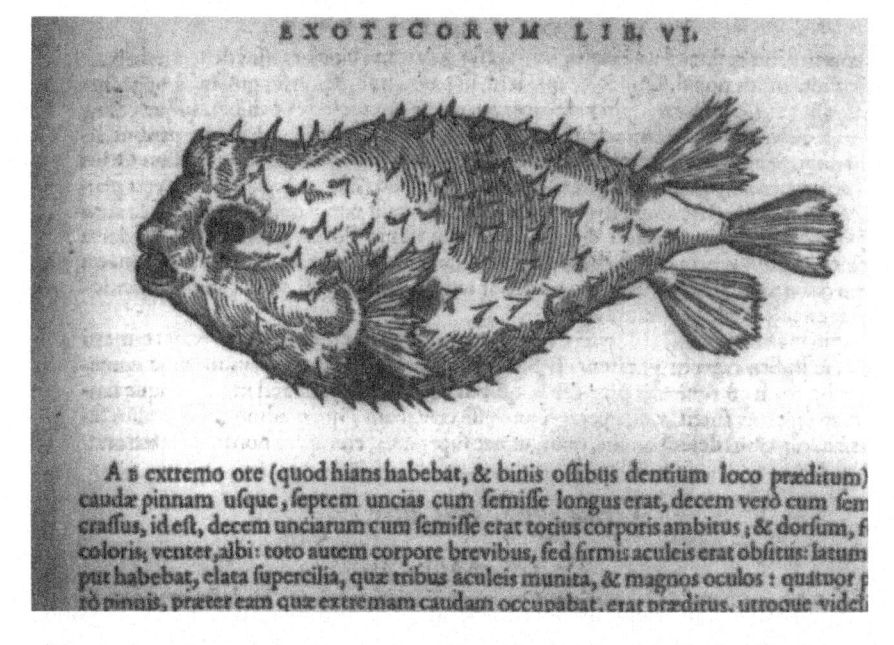

A B extremo ore (quod hians habebat, & binis offibus dentium loco præditum) caudæ pinnam ufque, feptem uncias cum femiffe longus erat, decem verò cum fem craffus, id eft, decem unciarum cum femiffe erat totius corporis ambitus; & dorfum, f coloris; venter, albi: toto autem corpore brevibus, fed firmis aculeis erat obfitus: latum put habebat, elata fupercilia, quæ tribus aculeis munita, & magnos oculos: quatuor p rô pinnis, præter eam quæ extremam caudam occupabat, erat præditus, utroque videt

Figure 4.5   Anonymous, *"Orbis spinosus,"* woodcut in Carolus Clusius, *Exoticorum Libri decem*, Leiden, 1605.   Photo courtesy of the National Herbarium of the Netherlands, Leiden.

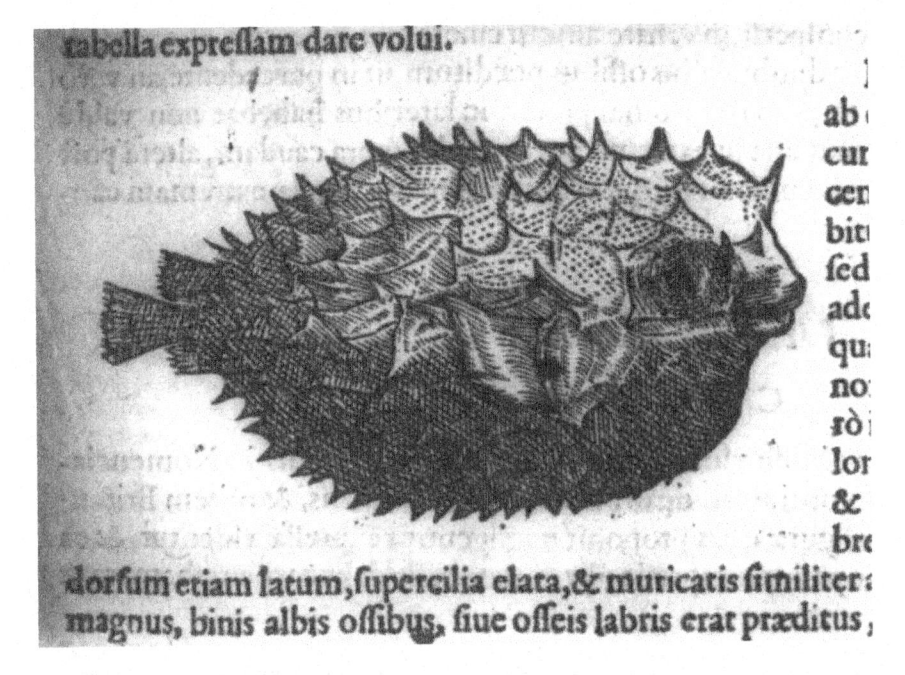

tabella expreſſam dare volui.

dorſum etiam latum, ſupercilia elata, & muricatis ſimiliter; magnus, binis albis oſſibus, ſiue oſſeis labris erat præditus,

Figure 4.6 Anonymous, *"Orbis muricatus,"* woodcut in Carolus Clusius, *Exoticorum Libri decem*, Leiden, 1605. Photo courtesy of the National Herbarium of the Netherlands, Leiden.

the conditions under which they were imported, specimens were not always intact, or they had been carelessly dried and so were deformed. To Clusius and his contemporaries, variegation of form, however, pointed to differences of biological sort or kind, rather than to the uncontrolled means of procuring specimens. In fact, the four fish Clusius describes and names individually are probably all of a single species — the *Diodon hystrix*. It is on the basis of external, visible, quantifiable characteristics that Clusius isolated what he perceived to be four separate kinds of fish, and his dependence on images in the classification of varieties of the *Orbis* demonstrates this to a fault.

Throughout Clusius's *Exoticorum*, as also in most contemporary natural history publications, images served to complement verbal description; they also, where they were the only available evidence, served as a basis for it, as well as for classification. Insofar as the criteria for classification Clusius uses are reducible to form and color, they amount to information an image can impart. It is especially significant that, within Clusius's account of these types of fish, the *Orbis muricatus alter* (fig. 4.7) is recorded as a variant solely on the basis of an image provided by an acquaintance. It was not possible, Clusius writes, for him to observe this particular fish, "but I received from Jacob Plateau a colored picture of it." This image was later supplemented,

Claudia Swan

nen menſes à me admonitus, hujus & ſequentis menſuram, longitudinem & ambit
ſignantem, mittebat.

ꝑISCIS igitur, cujus hoc capite iconem damus, ab extremo ore ad extimam cauda
ꝛè undecim uncias erat longus, ejus verò ambitus multo major, ut qui ſedecim unc
a menſuram expleret, per univerſům corpus muricatis ſpinis munitus, coloris in do
ꞔi, & multis nigris maculis conſperſi, in ventre autem cineracei: ſupercilia elata era
liquantulum prominulum, & duobus albis oſſibus præditum, ut in præcedente, an ve
ꝛtes etiam introrſum habuerit, me latet: binas pinnas in lateribus habebat non va

Figure 4.7 Anonymous, *"Orbis muricatus alter,"* woodcut in Carolus Clusius, *Exoticorum Libri decem*, Leiden, 1605. Photo courtesy of the National Herbarium of the Netherlands, Leiden.

Clusius notes, by information Plateau provided regarding the dimensions of the fish.[28] Because the criteria for classification Clusius engages are more or less exclusively descriptive and quantitative, images may even play a subversive role: classificatory strategies were woven around images taken on faith.

That Clusius depended on images to supply him with the information necessary for purposes of classification is evident in his works on the plant world as well. Given Michel Foucault's arguments for the "epistemological precedence enjoyed by botany" among the natural sciences of the classical age, it is perhaps surprising that Clusius should have relied on images of fish to the extent that he did. Foucault writes:

> The area common to words and things constituted a much more accommodating, a much less 'black' grid for plants than for animals; in so far as there are a great many constituent organs visible in a plant that are not so in animals, taxonomic knowledge based upon immediately perceptible variables was richer and more coherent in the botanical order than in the zoological. . . . Because it was possible to know and to say only within a taxonomic area of visibility, the knowledge of plants was bound to prove more extensive than that of animals.[29]

In his works on plants, which culminated in the publication in 1601 of his *Rariorum Plantarum Historia*, Clusius supplemented his descriptions of flowers, for example, with considerations on relative scale, the time of the year they blossom, and their provenance; but the characteristics most crucial to their classification are those that can be observed in the immediate presence of the specimen.[30] Or, as we have seen in the case of the *Orbis muricatus alter*, those that can be recorded pictorially. In his groundbreaking chapter on tulips in the *Rariorum*, Clusius describes a variety of dwarf tulip within the category of the "intermediates"; it blossoms between the "early" and the "late" varieties. This class is described generally as follows:

> The dwarf [intermediate] tulip is not more than a foot high, usually even less, and in its leaves and flower it strongly resembles the early tulip. All its segments are pointed, but the outer ones are much longer, externally dull red but at the outermost margins greenish; the inner segments are of a brilliant, fiery red throughout. The claws are yellow and radiating, but marked with a jet-black patch in such a way that the latter appears encircled by a mere golden aureole and bears some likeness to an eye; the filaments and their anthers are blackish. It should be noted that its bulbous root is woolly; the outer membrane enveloping and covering the substance of the bulb is so tightly filled with an abundance of dense, white, soft stuffing that it must form a very soft resting place for the bulb.[31]

From the opening sentence of his description, Clusius moves the reader to imagine the plant described. The dwarf tulip resembles the early tulip in its overall appearance; and in the more specific rendering of the appearance of this flower, we are led from part to part by gradations and shifts of color. At the center of the plant, and of the description, we encounter in an almost specular manner (we are looking into the tulip from above, observing the appearance of the golden aureole) "some likeness to an eye." The sensual engagement with the object, which culminates in an empathic description of the outer membrane of the bulb ("a very soft resting place" for it) is driven by a single organ—the eye.

One further example of the dwarf tulip is discussed by Clusius in the text immediately following that cited above. Here again, as in the case of the *Orbis muricatus alter*, Clusius incorporates this specimen into his account on the basis of an image alone, and in the absence of actual experience of the specimen. "Also another kind of dwarf tulips is found," he writes, "which, however, I have not seen."

> But I received a drawing in natural colors [*"iconem suis coloribus expressam"*] of it in the year 1596 from the learned Johan de Jonge, Minister at Middelburg, to which had been added the following description:

"I send you a picture ['*contrefeytsel*'] of a certain tulip, drawn after the plant itself, that is to say of natural size in regard to the plant as well as to the stalk, the flower, the leaves (which should have been drawn slightly longer and narrower) and the bulb, which I dug up in order to enable the artist to properly draw it. . . . "

The whole plant, then (as far as I have been able to gather from the drawing), is not bigger than the palm of a hand, producing four narrow, keeled leaves resembling those of the Montpellier tulip, from among which arises a little stalk of the height of an inch or a little higher, leafless (in contradistinction to the habit of other tulips), purplish green, and carrying on its top a flower consisting of six segments, externally somewhat purplish, internally whitish, its center occupied by an oblong pistil fenced in by six yellow little stamens. . . . That it has flowered in April I deduce from the fact that my correspondent sent me the drawing by the beginning of May.[32]

Sustained observation and morphological comparison are the means to classification, and to the extent that these processes depend on the visual aspects of the specimen to be classed, an image "drawn after the plant itself" and "in natural colors" was deemed sufficient to supply the necessary information.

Such images as Clusius cites and publishes mark the limits of his analysis, which depended crucially on visually apprehensible information. The case of Clusius is exceptional to a degree: unlike many of his contemporaries, he had relatively little interest in the pharmaceutical properties of the plants and other natural objects he described. In fact, it is Clusius who is most renowned for having studied and cultivated rare and exotic species of flowers — tulips, lilies, and other foreign bulbous varieties — as curiosities rather than as remedies. This is not to say that the images he relied on were any different from the images his fellow "fathers of Netherlandish botany" Rembertus Dodonaeus (1517–85) or Matthias Lobelius (1538–16), for example, included in their voluminous accounts of the plant world. Indeed, many of the woodcuts in Clusius's publication were printed from woodblocks in the possession of his publisher Cristoffel Plantin that were also used in Dodonaeus's and Lobelius's great herbals.[33] Clusius's taxonomic efforts, though, were driven by morphological rather than utilitarian (pharmaceutical) concerns. And in this sense images could be said to play a distinct role in his efforts, in principle if not always in fact.

There are two crucial differences between Clusius's verbal description of the "porcupine fish" and de Gheyn's inscription on his drawing of the *Zee-Eeghel*. De Gheyn shows no concern with the dimensions of the fish or its origins or the relation of this dried specimen to the living fish; and the terms in which he describes its coloration are in effect painterly. It is in the verbal, not the visual, information imparted by de Gheyn's image that we can locate its functional prerogatives; it is only its inscription that distinguishes de Gheyn's image from those published by Clusius. It should be clear from the foregoing that sixteenth-century natural history depended on morphological description to such an extent that it would have allowed for the assimilation of precisely this kind of image for scientific ends. Nothing is intrinsically scientific about either de Gheyn's or any of Clusius's or his acquaintances' images; they are capable of being impressed into service of a scientific kind. They become the labels, in a sense, behind which names may be stored.

This circular tale is intended to call attention to the ways in which naturalistic representation served and furthered the ends of a natural history concerned, as Foucault put it, with "the nomination of the visible."[34] Elsewhere, I have written at some length about the role of verifiably naturalistic images — images that could stand in for what they represent — in natural history of this period.[35] I want now to call attention to a different form of visual representation common, not to say integral, to this natural history. This is the grid, the schematic, rectangular representation that so very frequently occurs in the context of the practice and publication of natural history in the sixteenth and early seventeenth centuries.

TABULATION

It is difficult, when examining the relations between visual representation and the praxis of natural history in the early modern period, to overlook the grid and its affiliate, the tabular diagram.[36] Examples abound. Matthias Lobelius's 1581 volume on plants, one of the most renowned botanical publications of its time, concludes with a striking section, "Vande Succedanea," which consists principally of a series of nearly twenty schematic grids (fig. 4.8).[37] Lobelius's herbal shares the distinction, with the publications of his contemporaries Dodonaeus and Clusius, of being copiously illustrated — each of the roughly thirteen hundred pages of text contains at least two woodcuts. The grids in the concluding section of the book come as something of a surprise, given the predominance of naturalistic images overall. The title of this last section of Lobelius's voluminous publication specifies that the individual tables illustrate which dried substances — herbs, roots, flowers, seeds, resins, gums, stones, woods — may be substituted for others for medicinal ends. Lobelius's grids or "tables," as he calls them, offer suggestions for the organization of dried specimens in what Aldrovandi called

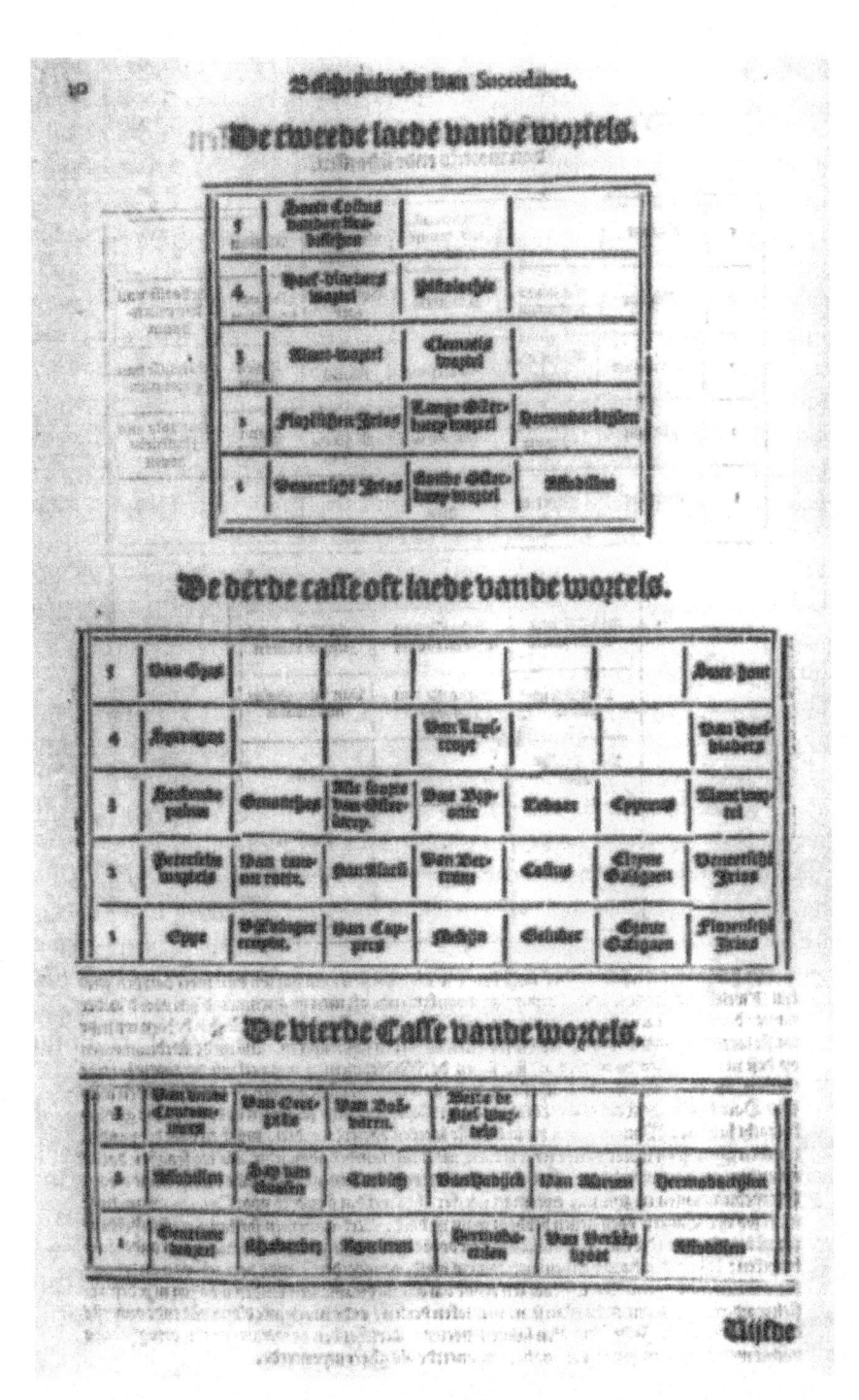

Figure 4.8 Anonymous, woodcut in Mathias Lobelius, *Kruydtboeck*, Antwerp, 1581. Photo courtesy of the National Herbarium of the Netherlands, Leiden.

"pigeonholes"—that is, compartments or drawers in larger pieces of furniture. The pigeonholes schematically represented in the Lobelius woodcuts were intended to correspond to the drawers of a pharmacist's cabinet; the scheme according to which their contents are ordered is a functional—and distinctly pharmaceutical—one.

The kinds of specimens itemized in these woodcuts were, as we have seen in both Aldrovandi's case and the case of the Leiden botanical garden, collected and studied in the immediate proximity of living specimens—plants in particular. The basic units of the Leiden University garden (figs. 4.2, 4.3) are similar to those of numerous early modern academic gardens: multiple individual plots, which in Leiden were arranged in larger rectangular beds. They are itemized and numbered in the plot at the lower left of de Gheyn's plan and in the plot at the far lower left of the upper left quadrant (fig. 4.2). Each small plot of the Leiden garden—in 1594, there were fourteen hundred—contained five specimens at most, and generally speaking one or two.[38] None of those specimens, incidentally, is represented in de Gheyn's plan of the garden. This is particularly interesting in light of the fact that this engraving was produced in conjunction with Professor Pieter Pauw's publication, in 1601, of a catalog of the "Hortus publicus" or public garden.[39] Pauw's is a strange catalog, for it consists of a text preface followed by pages and pages of sets of rectangular boxes (fig. 4.9).[40] Pauw explains in the preface that students of plants were to adapt the catalog to their own experience—to take it with them to the garden and to fill in the rectangles with the names of the plants growing in the rectangular plots of the garden. The space of phytographic experience was, indeed, the rectangular grid. Active phytographs translated their experience of the plots de Gheyn represents in bird's-eye view into the spatially coordinated charts, or tables, of the plants the plots contained. This translation corresponds more or less directly to the way in which the contents of Lobelius's herbal—a series of individual, naturalistic descriptions of plants—are staged against the pigeonholes of the schematic cabinet.

The assemblages of medicinal, protobotanical, zoological, icthyological, ethnographic, mineralogical data such as we know Aldrovandi to have cultivated, and medical professionals throughout Europe in the sixteenth and seventeenth centuries to have studied, were consistently structured and represented by way of the grid. The great and widely traveled Dutch doctor Bernardus Paludanus (1550–1633), for example, amassed a collection of *naturalia* (plant, animal, and mineral specimens) and *artificialia* (primarily ethnographic specimens) at the end of sixteenth century that, although holed away in the northern port town of Enkhuizen, was renowned throughout Europe.[41] In a series of brilliant protocapitalist moves he sold, reconstructed,

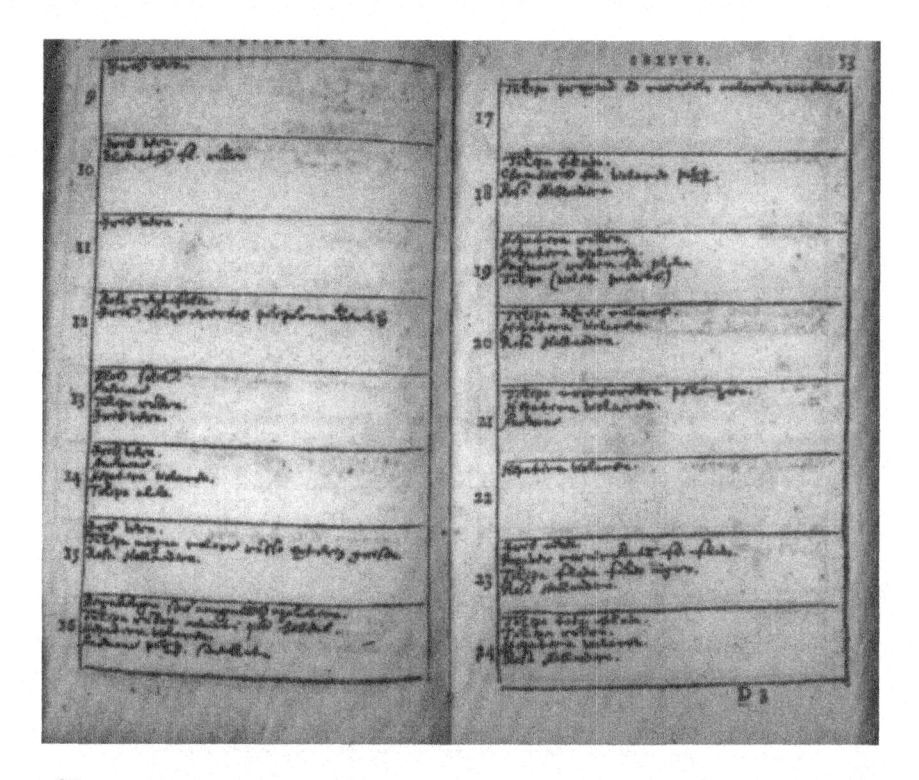

Figure 4.9 Pieter Pauw, *Hortus Publicus*, Leiden, 1601, pp. 52–53. Photo courtesy of the National Herbarium of the Netherlands, Leiden.

and sold again his curiosities, dried animals, minerals, fossils, plants, tusks, and so forth. His collection was the focus of intense admiration on the part of foreigners and native Hollanders alike; hardly a naturalist of the time failed to mention, let alone pay homage to or visit, Paludanus's collection, and the total number of visitors is in the thousands. An elaborate description of Paludanus's collection was compiled by Friedrich of Wurtemberg (1557–1608), one of the doctor's many distinguished guests. The future duke, who was at the time of his visit expanding his own *Wunderkammer* in France, published a catalog of the contents of the Enkhuizen collection in 1603.[42] Notably, it consists of several pages of grids, in which the contents of the collection are itemized (fig. 4.10). These grids seem to correspond to the actual storage of the specimens in the collection, in cabinets or drawers; in all likelihood, Friedrich transcribed the collection in this manner in order to transpose it to his own.

The reason for the widespread use of grids may well be directly related to the problem evident in Aldrovandi's description of his own collection:

Myrrhinum siue Murrhinum vasculum India extrema Orientali: vulgo porcellana vocant.	Vasculum sictile artificiosum flamma Italicum eleganter pictum.	Vasculum aliud ex Chynarum regione minus priore.	
Vasculum antiquissimum ex Lemnia sphragide pretiosum.	Vasculum aliud sictile candidum pictum.	Murrhinum vasculum Chinitum eleganter pictum valdè paruum.	Pars quædam vasculi antiqui rubra eleganter picta.
Vasculum aliud sictile natiuum dono Illustris: Principis Friderici Comitis Wurttembergici.	Vasculum Waldeshurgica.	Vasculum liquationis & separationis metallorum candidum Numantinum.	Vasculum aliud nigrum liquationis.
Vitrum antiquissimum triangulare cum effigie antiquissima.		Cylindri purissimi ex Cryssallo natiuo fossili vitro.	
Flos alius vitreus elegantissimus.	Dæmonis effigies vitrea vitro aqua plena inclusa.	Alius flos ex vitro coloribus tinctis.	Conspicilium ex Cryssallo montano vitro.
Terna alia nauicula minora ex vitro.	Lucretia Romana effigies vitrea.	Ornamenta vitrea.	Vitrum fractum Gallicum æreum.
Antimonium præparatum.	Fibula elegantior ex vitro tincto.	Clepsydra vitrea parua elegantior.	Vitrum aliud nigrum fractum.
Globus ex vitro variegatus elegantissimus.	Cineres kali Alexandrini unde sit vitrum.	Cineres herba kali alij unde sit vitrum.	Vitrum fractum candidum.
Spherula siue coralli differentes ex vitro.	Ornamenta seu sibula quæ auribus appenduntur ex vitro.	Gelosata vitreum est quo olim parietes incrustabant.	Speculum vitreum.

N   S E.

Figure 4.10 *Warhaffte Beschreibung zweyer Raisung*, Tübingen, 1603. Photo courtesy of Amsterdam University Library (ZKW).

Where to put it all? How to pigeonhole the vast ranges of data and specimens that were accumulated? The grid asserts no necessary genetic or relational order between the things it organizes and, crucially, it is infinitely expansive. Nonhierarchical and nonchronological, the grid allowed for precisely the kind of serial differentiation that drove natural history at this moment in its development.

Generally speaking, the death of the naturalist Conrad Gessner (1516–65) is lamented as untimely and said to have deprived contemporary natural history of one of its greatest agents.[43] In a sense, his death by plague was productive, for it encouraged a posthumous production — edited by friends and hangers-on — that invokes and represents Gessner's efforts in telling ways. In 1587, Caspar Wolf (1532–1601), a student of Gessner's and his successor as municipal physician in Zurich, published a handbook under Gessner's name, called *De Stirpium Collectione Tabulae tum Generales, tum per duodecim menses . . .*, or "The general and annual tables for the collection of plants."[44] This small volume consists entirely of a series of lists, called tables. Page after page contains a typographically sparse accumulation of names and various qualities of plants. Wolf's volume is divided into four parts, each of which amounts to a different organizational grid, mapped onto the plant world. The first part, called "The General Table of Plants," contains enumerations of the sorts and parts of plants, which serve as means for differentiating them.[45] The qualities surveyed range from "Substance," which covers both the type of plant (tree, herb, fruit, legume, and so on) and its "constitution" (hard, soft, dense, fragile) to "Quantity," and "Qualities of the Object," to "Location" (where it grows), and, finally, "Virtues" and "Uses." The remaining sections of the book are: "On the Collection of Plants in General," which provides general instructions on when to pick and how to dry plants and seeds;[46] "The First Table of Plants, Flowers and Fruits, enumerated in alphabetical order," a list of plants, by Latin name, with indications of when the plants flower, bear fruit, and seed;[47] and "The Second Table, containing plant names in German and in Latin," which is organized according to the months of the year, and in which the plants are listed according to when they flower, bear fruit, and seed.[48] What do these "tables" add up to? Generally speaking, they provide evidence of the extent to which the tabular model — the serial categorization of entities — structured the experience of the natural world, for Gessner as for Wolf. In the final section of Wolf's handbook, one rudimentary scheme of classification (*Tempus*, or when plants mature) is crossed with another — the alphabet. That overlay of schemes is indicative, of the consistency with which use (and specifically medicinal or pharmaceutical application) structures natural historical experience. Wolf's preface to this volume contains the following specification for "The Use of these Tables":

These tables will be useful not only for those concerned with pharmacy, or for apprentices to this science, but for all those who have an interest in the study of plants. All those who enjoy, be it winter, summer, or fall, going out in the countryside, following partly their own impulse toward knowledge, and partly driven by the necessity of taking a break and exercising their own bodies—let them take the opportunity, thanks to these tables, to go looking for plants, those they know, and to hope to find new ones.[49]

Here, as in the case of Pauw's interactive catalog of the Leiden garden, a tabular model or grid structures experience of the natural world.

Very much remains to be said about early modern classification. Generally speaking, the period under discussion, the later sixteenth century, is just about the time in which a medicinal, pharmaceutical, use-oriented botany gives way to a more purely morphological botany. As mentioned earlier, Carolus Clusius is often cited as a primary agent of this shift. What is implicit in such claims for a transition from a more or less alchemical relation to the natural world—What are its intrinsic properties? What can it do for me?—to a pre-Linnaean move to systematically account for the natural world, is that the transition brings order with it. One of the aims of this article has been to demonstrate that a certain order—visually represented by the grid—was already operative; recuperating it and reconstructing its applications are crucial in understanding early modern experience, and representations, of the natural world. The coordinates of this order might be reduced to serial differentiation; above all the grid allows for comparison of specimens, which have been extrapolated from their "native" contexts and offered up to the language of Gessner and Wolf, for example. Are such specimens soft? Hard? Oily? Dry? Two-part? Three-part? Trees? Legumes?

The grid or tabular model of organization is artificial and schematic, but not necessarily hierarchical. It is, rather, serial. What is perhaps most remarkable about this mode of natural historical observation and schematization is that it is fundamentally nonconclusive. Just because the vanilla bean is long, brown, and contains a certain number of seeds does not legitimate placing it in any privileged relation to other beans, seeds, or foreign plants. The market will do that. This brings us to a class of images I want to adduce by way of conclusion. More or less contemporaneously with the blowfish and the grids discussed here, a "new" genre of painting emerged full force in northern Europe. The first decade of the seventeenth century saw the production of a significant number of these paintings, which conform in technique and subject matter, and had not previously been widely produced or generally marketable. By the mid-seventeenth century, they were countless. Jacques de Gheyn II himself is credited with having painted one of the first three. This "new" genre is the flower still-life painting which

Claudia Swan

Figure 4.11 Jacques de Gheyn II, *Flowers in a vase and small animals*, watercolor and gouache on vellum, 1600. Photo courtesy of the Fondation Custodia (Coll. F. Lugt), Institut Néerlandais, Paris.

typically, in the early years, consists of numerous flowers gathered together in isolation, and offered statically to the viewer's gaze.[50]

The flower still-life attests to sustained interest in naturalistic representation of the blowfish kind; each painstakingly rendered specimen stands in for its real counterpart and, taken together, they come to be referred to as microcosmic representations of gardens (see fig. 4.11). Simultaneously, it makes sense to think about the structure of these pictures, and of their viewing, as pertaining to the tabular model. Consider, for example, that many of the flower still-life paintings, or botanical portraits, produced in the early seventeenth century consist of vases filled with more stems than could readily be fit into the vases and that the flowers represented are more often than not shown blossoming simultaneously, whereas in fact, or in nature, they do not. The counternaturalistic impact of these pictures is crucial. If these paintings were — initially at least, in the first decades of the seventeenth century — painted and collected as "botanical portraits,"[51] and served to record and preserve the appearance of the individual specimens so carefully arranged, to what degree does the sequential, nonnarrative structure of such pictures bear comparison with the grids and tables of natural historical experience? Conventional art historical interpretations have read these images — the flower still-life paintings of the early seventeenth century — as allegories of vanity and the brevity of life.[52] By way of a counterproposal, I want to cite a passage from a philosophical dialogue written in the 1580s by the great neo-Stoic Justus Lipsius (1547–1606), which goes some way in suggesting that attempting to recuperate modes of experience might be more productive than insisting on emblematic or allegorical readings of paintings of the natural world. And that the apparently disjunctive range of scientific representation I have cited — from naturalistic renderings of blowfish and tulips to schematic diagrams of gardens — are not only compatible, but inseparable.

This passage is from Lipsius's *De Constantia*, a dialogue that takes place in a garden, as befits a good Erasmian encounter.[53] The garden of *De Constantia* may well be fictional, but the story of Lipsius's actual gardens is entirely relevant to the foregoing. Lipsius, from the city of Louvain in the southern Netherlands, was professor at the Leiden University from 1578 until 1591.[54] When Lipsius left Leiden, he left two gardens behind, one of which was impressed into immediate service as the university teaching garden before the plots of that garden were dug in 1594, and the official garden opened.[55] Lipsius writes:

> Observe for me these numerous flowers/ how they grow: how these are brought out of their sheaths/ those out of their buds/ see how this one dies suddenly and falls down/ and another one grows on its stem. Finally/ see how one sort of flower is distinguished from and can be compared to/ thousands of others/ solely on the basis of its form/ color, and appearance/. . . . Now/ bring your scrupulous eyes here/ and regard for a moment this sheen and the beautiful colors. See/ how this flower [is] a beautiful purple in color/ this one blood red/ this snow white/ this one like a flame/ this shines like gold . . . even the very best painter cannot possibly replicate them . . . Would that God would allow me to live peaceably among these treasures. . . . among these flowers of the known and the new unknown world.[56]

For Lipsius, the garden is a spectacle, a source of wonder. He encourages "scrupulous eyes" to follow the forms of the individual plants as they change over time and as they vary from one to the next. The "treasures . . . of the known and new unknown world" offer their incomparable colors and sheen for careful, sustained observation. The terms of Lipsius's description are fairly pat; where he lapses into simile it is to compare the coloring of the flowers to gold or to fire — the visible properties of these treasures exceed the products of humans, and of the painter in particular. At the same time, he invokes specific patterns of observation when he states that each sort of flower can be distinguished from and compared to others on the basis of its visually apprehensible, external characteristics. It is this comparative morphology that motivates the use of naturalistic representations (which will strive to equal the "sheen and beautiful colors" Lipsius records) and, at the same time, drives the tabulation of the natural world.

Notes

Many thanks to Pamela Smith, Paula Findlen, and Peter Reill for the invitation to present this material at the colloquium *Commerce and the Representation of Nature in Early Modern Europe* (UCLA, October 1999), and for the helpful commentary they and many other participants offered. I am also grateful to Mary Fissell and other members of the History of Medicine, Science, and Technology Colloquium at Johns Hopkins University, for offering both the opportunity to present these materials and a variety of productive responses; to the Department of Geography at the Pennsylvania State University; to the History and Philosophy of Science program at Northwestern University; to Cees Lut, Librarian, National Herbarium of the Netherlands, Leiden; to Carla Teune, Hortulana, Hortus Botanicus, Leiden; and to Londa Schiebinger, Amy Greenberg, Rich Doyle, Peter Parshall, Roelof van Gelder, Florike Egmond, Paolo Bernardini, and David Freedberg.

1. See, principally, Sandra Tugnoli Pattaro, *Metodo e sistema delle scienze nel pensiero di Ulisse Aldrovandi* (Bologna: Cooperativa Libraria Universitaria Editrice Bologna, 1981); Giuseppe Olmi, *L'inventario del mondo. Catalogazione della natura e luoghi del sapere nella prima età moderna* (Bologna: Il Mulino, 1992); Paula Findlen, *Possessing Nature. Museums, Collecting, and Scientific Culture in Early Modern Italy* (Berkeley and Los Angeles: University of California Press, 1994).

2. As quoted by Giuseppe Olmi, "Arte e Natura nel Cinquecento Bolognese: Ulisse Aldrovandi e la Raffigurazione Scientifica," in *Le Arti a Bologna e in Emilia dal XVI al XVIII secolo. Atti del XXIV Congresso Internazionale di Storia dell'Arte*, ed. Andrea Emiliani, 4 vols. (Bologna: CLUEB, 1982), 4: 151–173, esp. 151.

3. See, e.g., Pattaro, *Metodo e sistema*, 19: "Infine, come esempio del procedimento (*modus*) col quale l'Aldrovandi tentò di realizzare il proprio ideale erudito ed enciclopedico, si può portare la sua *Selva universale della scienze* o *Pandechion epistemonicon* [unpublished]. Quest'-opera, che fu completata nel 1589, è una sorta di dizionario, in ottantatre volumi, ove le materie più disparate sone prese in esame per ordine alfabetico con amplissimo corredo di riferimenti e d'informazioni, e fu concepita esplicitamente dal naturalista bolognese affinché fosse di guida a chiunque desiderasse 'sapere o comporre sopra qual si voglia cosa naturale o artificiale,' onde trovare 'a quel proposito quel che n'hanno scritti i poeti, i teologi, i legisti, i filosofi, gli istorici.'" More generally, on early modern classification, see F. S. Bodenheimer, "Towards the History of Zoology and Botany in the XVIth Century," in *La science au seizième siècle. Colloque de Royaumont 1957* (Paris: Hermann, 1960), 285–296; Michel Foucault, *The Order of Things. An Archaeology of the Human Sciences* (New York: Vintage Books, 1970); David Knight, *Ordering the World. A History of Classifying Man* (London: Burnett Books, 1981), esp. chaps. 2 and 3; Scott Atran, *Cognitive Foundations of Natural History. Towards an*

Anthropology of Science (Cambridge and Paris: Cambridge University Press, 1990); Brian W. Ogilvie, *Observation and Experience in Early Modern Natural History* (Ph.D. diss., University of Chicago, 1997), esp. 337–343. My thanks to David Freedberg for allowing me to read his unpublished lecture, "Naming the Visible: Art and Natural History in the Circle of Galileo" (Munich, 1991).

4. See references cited in previous note and Agnes Arber, *Herbals, Their Origin and Evolution. A Chapter in the History of Botany (1470–1670)* (Cambridge: Cambridge University Press, 1986; 1st ed. 1912); Allen J. Grieco, "The Social Politics of Pre-Linnaean Botanical Classification," *I Tatti Studies* 4 (1991): 131–149, esp. 139ff.

5. As quoted by Lorraine Daston and Katharine Park, *Wonders and the Order of Nature, 1150-1750* (Cambridge: MIT Press, 1998), 154; see also Findlen, *Possessing Nature*, 17–31.

6. Findlen, *Possessing Nature*, 24; the visitor was Pietro Andrea Mattioli (1501–78), one of the most famous Renaissance doctors and botanical authors.

7. Ibid.

8. Ibid., passim.

9. See Giuseppe Olmi, "Osservazione della natura e raffigurazione in Ulisse Aldrovandi (1522–1605)," *Annali dell'Istituto storico germanico italiano in Trento* 3 (1977), 105–181; Olmi, *Inventario del mondo, passim*; Claudia Swan, "*Ad vivum, naer het leven*, from the Life: Considerations on a Mode of Representation," *Word and Image* 11 (October–December 1995): 353–372.

10. Blowfish is the common name for the porcupine fish, which is of the order *Tetraodontiformes*, and is most visibly characterized by spiny or plate-form scales. The stomach of two families of this order—*Diodontidae* (porcupine fish) among them—is highly modified such that it can inflate to enormous sizes; hence "blowfish." Inflation is caused by ingestion of water into a ventral diverticulum of the stomach when the fish is frightened or annoyed; deflation occurs when the fish expels the water. Inflation by air can also occur, when the fish is removed from the water or on death. The bodies of all porcupine fish are covered with sharp spines, which may become erect when the fish inflates. They generally have two fused teeth. Joseph S. Nelson, *Fishes of the World* (New York: J. Wiley, 1984), 379–386. Blowfish are native to the Pacific and Indian Oceans.

11. Examples of engravings showing the blowfish hanging from the ceiling of a collection include "The Museum of Francesco Calzolari" by Hieronymus Viscardus after Io. Bapt. Bertonus, in Benedictus Cerutus and Andrea Chiocco, *Musaeum Franc. Calceolari* (Verona: Apud Angelum Tamum, 1622); anonymous engraver, "The Museum of Ferdinando Cospi," in L. Legati, *Museo Cospiano . . .* (Bologna: Giacomo Monti, 1677). These prints are frequently reproduced in studies of cabinets of curiosities; see, for example, Ellinoor Bergvelt et al., *Verzamelen. Van Rariteitenkabinet tot Kunstmuseum* (Heerlen: Open Universiteit, 1993), figs. 64, 76, and 82.

12. "Zee eeghel/ dese vis is van omber wit en swart ijser graeu achtich/ van den rugghen neerewert al lichter tot den buijck/ die is wit nae de staert is hij noch bruijnder hij al gestippelt/ met keulse aerden de penne sijn geelenoocker achtich licht graeu/ de vinne sij omber en keulse aerdeachtich teghen tlijf geleoocker/ en wit wat root oock wat [illegible mark] blaeu achtich gekolleureert/ ende oock met keulse aerden gestippelt omden muijl/ wat omber achtiger gecollereert." Rijksmuseum, Amsterdam, inv. no. A3971 (149 x 197 mm, pen and brown ink on gray-brown paper). I. Q. van Regteren Altena, *Jacques de Gheyn. Three Generations*, 3 vols. (The Hague: M. Nijhoff, 1983), vol. 2, cat. no. 896, pl. 370; see also vol. 2: 119. Cf. K. G. Boon, *Netherlandish Drawings of the Fifteenth and Sixteenth Centuries. Catalogue of the Dutch and Flemish Drawings in the Rijksmuseum*, 2 vols. (The Hague: Govt. Pub. Office, 1978), cat. no. 242; and *Jacques de Gheyn II. Drawings*, exh. cat. (Rotterdam and Washington: Museum Boymans-van Beuningen, 1986), cat. no. 83: *Two Studies of a Porcupine Fish* (*Diodon hystrix*).

13. Jan Piet Filedt Kok and Marjolein Leesberg, The New Hollstein. *Dutch and Flemish Etchings, Engravings and Woodcuts, ca. 1450–1700 (Jacques de Gheyn)*, 2 vols. (Rotterdam: Sound and Vision, 2000), no. 213. On de Gheyn in Leiden, see Florence Hopper, "Clusius' World: The Meeting of Science and Art," in *The Authentic Garden. A Symposium on Gardens*, ed. Leslie Tjon Sie Fat and Erik de Jong (Leiden: Clusius Stichting, 1991), 13–36; Claudia Swan, *Jacques de Gheyn II and the Representation of the Natural World in the Netherlands ca. 1600* (Ph.D. diss., Columbia University, 1997).

14. See, *inter alia, Leidse Universiteit 400. Stichting en eerste bloei 1575–ca. 1650*, exh. cat. (Amsterdam: Rijksmuseum, 1975); Swan, *Jacques de Gheyn II*, chapter 5, "'t Onderwijs der cruyden*: The Leiden University *Hortus* 1587–1600." The practice of teaching *materia medica* from the garden became widespread throughout Europe at this time; see Karen Meier Reeds, *Botany in Medieval and Renaissance Universities* (New York and London: Garland, 1981), passim.

15. For the inventories of the collection of *naturalia*, see *Leidse universiteit 400*, cat. nos. D24–26; Erik de Jong, *Natuur en Kunst. Nederlandse tuin- en landschapsarchitectuur 1650-1740* (Amsterdam: Thoth, 1993), "*Hortus Sanitatis*. De hortus botanicus en de hortus medicus als wetenschappelijke tuin," 190–234, esp. 202ff. In an appendix de Jong provides transcriptions of the two most important inventories of the collection housed in the *ambulacrum* (1617 and 1659) and cross-references them to Carolus Clusius, *Exoticorvm libri decem: Quibus Animalium, Plantarum, Aromatum, aliorumque peregrinorum Fructuum historiae describuntur* . . . (Leiden: Ex Officinâ Plantinianâ Raphelengii, 1605) and to a copy hereof that Clusius revised by hand, presently in the Leiden Universiteitsbibliotheek (UB nr. 755 A3). A version of this essay by de Jong was previously published as "Nature and Art. The Leiden Hortus as 'Musaeum'," in Tjon Sie Fat and de Jong, *The Authentic Garden*, 37–60. A very early source, to the best of my knowledge never cited, is the catalog by P. Pauw of the Leiden garden; see below, note 38.

16. Hollstein, vol. 29 (1984), Swanenburg(h), H. 32.

17. See above, note 15; the relevant chapters are Clusius, *Exoticorum* 21–24: 137–140.

18. Cf. the passage from *The Tempest* in which Trinculo exclaims, on finding Caliban: "What have we here? a man or a fish? dead or alive? A fish: he smells like a fish; a very ancient and fish-like smell; a kind of, not of the newest, Poor-John. A strange fish! Were I in England now, as once I was, and had but this fish painted, not a holiday fool there but would give a piece of silver: there would this monster make a man: when they will not give a doit to relieve a lame beggar, they will lay out ten to see a dead Indian (II.ii)." That fish and other sea creatures were put on public display in Leiden and Amsterdam is amply recorded in Clusius's *Exoticorum*.

19. See esp. Atran, *Cognitive Foundations of Natural History*; Ogilvie, *Observation and Experience*, 337–343.

20. Clusius writes that the *Histrix piscis* and the *Orbis spinosus* were available to him in a "museum" of a merchant in Amsterdam; see Clusius, *Exoticorum*, 137–138. The third kind he describes, the *Orbis muricatus*, he saw in Guillaume Rondelet's "museum" in Montpellier (139). Cf. (written of the *Orbis spinosus*) "Exenteratus autem erat hic piscis, quemadmodum & alij ejusdem generis, quos istîc variæ magnitudinis apud diversos mercatores videbam: satis enim diligentes sunt in ea urbe rerum exoticarum conquisitores, quas à nautis ex sua navigatione reducibis redimere solent" (139).

21. Clusius cites book 25 of Guillaume Rondelet, *L'histoire entière des poissons* . . . (Lyon: Bonhomme, 1558); Clusius, *Exoticorum*, 139.

22. These are the *Histrix piscis* (Clusius compares the specimen he describes and illustrates to the fish in Plateau's drawing) and the *Orbis muricatus alter*; see Clusius, *Exoticorum*, 138, 140. Plateau is also mentioned in Carolus Clusius, *Rariorum Plantarum Historia* (Antwerp: Ex. Off. Plantiniana, apud Ioannem Moretum, 1601), passim.

23. Namely, a drawing of the *Orbis muricatus*; Clusius, *Exoticorum*, 139. Porret is cited throughout the *Exoticorum*; see F. W. T. Hunger, *Charles de l'Escluse (Carolus Clusius) Nederlandsch Kruidkundige 1526-1609*, 2 vols. (The Hague: Nijhoff, 1927; 1943), Vol. 1: 268.

24. The woodcut of the *Orbis spinosus* is, Clusius explains, based on a drawing that was made in order for him to compare this specimen with the *Histrix piscis*; images of the *Orbis spinosus* and the *Histrix piscis* face each other head-on across the binding of the volume. "Ut autem faciliùs utriusque differentia observari possit, illum, permittente Mercatore, idem Volcardus in meam gratiam delineabat, ego verò in adposita tabella deinde exprimi curabam" (*Exoticorum*, 138).

25. Clusius, *Exoticorum*, 138.

26. Ibid. "De internis partibus nihil pronunciare queo, quandoquidem à recens capto fuerant exemptœ & abjectœ, & corium dumtaxat à nautis funiculorum fragmentis suffarcinatum, ut commodiùs resiccarent & conservarent, mihi fuit conspectum."

27. "In quo mari captus esset hic piscis, nemo certi quidpiam pronunciare poterat," he writes of the *Orbis muricatus*; Clusius, *Exoticorum*, 140. On p. 137, however, he identifies the *Histrix piscis* as having been captured in the "American Ocean."

28. "Horvm trium subsequentium Orbium historiam adeò exactè describere non licebit, ut superiorum [*Orbis muricatus*], quia ipsos pisces videre mihi non contigit, sed eorum icones coloribus expressas dumtaxat accipiebam à Iacobo Plateau, nullis adscriptis notis, è quibus magnitudinis corporis & ejus partium conjecturam facere possem: post aliquot tamen menses à me admonitus, hujus & sequentis mensuram, longitudinem & ambitum designantem, mittebat" (Clusius, *Exoticorum*, 140).

29. Foucault, *The Order of Things*, 137.

30. More generally, on the representation of variable qualities of plants, see also David Freedberg, "The Failure of Colour," *Sight & Insight. Essays on Art and Culture in Honour of E.H. Gombrich at 85* (London: Phaidon Press, 1994), 245-262.

31. Clusius, *Rariorum*, lib. 2: 147; as trans. by W. Van Dijk, *A Treatise on Tulips by Carolus Clusius of Arras* (Haarlem: Enschedé en Zonen, 1951), 50.

32. Clusius, *Rariorum*, lib. 2: 148; Van Dijk, *A Treatise on Tulips*, 52. The letter from Johannes de Jonghe, dated 14 May 1596 and received by Clusius in Leiden on 2 June, is in the Leiden University Library (Cod. Vulc. 101); it and seven others written to Clusius by residents of Middelburg were transcribed and published by F. W. T. Hunger, "Acht Brieven van Middelburgers aan Carolus Clusius," *Zeeuwsch Genootschap der Wetenschappen* (1925), 110-133; for the letter from de Jonghe, see 111-113. See also Laurens J. Bol, *The Bosschaert Dynasty. Painters of flowers and fruit* (Leigh-on-Sea: F. Lewis, 1980), 17-18, who suggests that the Middelburg flower painter Ambrosius Bosschaert may have painted this (lost) drawing and another drawing sent to Clusius by another Middelburg resident in 1597.

33. See F. de Nave et al., *Botany in the Low Countries (End of the 15th Century–ca. 1650)*, exh. cat. (Antwerp: Plantin Moretus Museum, 1993); Swan, "*Ad vivum, naer het leven.*"

34. Foucault, *The Order of Things*, 132.

35. C. Swan, "*Ad vivum, naer het leven.*"

36. By grid I mean a rectangular diagram, divided into small rectangles. On dichotomized and bracketed outlines, and on class logic, see W. J. Ong, *Ramus, Method, and the Decay of Dialogue. From the Art of Discourse to the Art of Reason* (Cambridge, Mass.: Harvard University Press, 1958), esp. chaps. 8 and 9; cf. *idem*, "From Allegory to Diagram in the Renaissance Mind: A Study in the Significance of the Allegorical Tableau," *Journal of Aesthetics and Art Criticism* 17 (June 1959): 423–440.

37. *Kruydtboeck oft Beschrijuinghe Van allerleye Ghewassen, Kruyderen, Hesteren, ende Gheboomten* (Antwerp: Christoffel Plantijn, 1581): "Vande Succedanea, dat is te seggen/ van drooghen oft cruyden die by ghebreke d'een voor d'ander ghebruyckt worden . . . " (15 pp).

On p. 1, Lobelius complains that prior publications on medicinal simples were "sonder eenige ordeninghe/ onderscheydt oft verstant" ("lacking all order, distinctions, and judgment"). "Vande Succedanea" and its tables were reprinted in *Den Leytsman ende Onderwijser der Medicijnen, oft ordenlijcke uytdeylinghe ende Bereydingh-boeck vande Medicamenten*, eds. Pieter van Coudenberg and Matthias Lobelius (Amsterdam: Hendrick Laurentsz., 1614).

38. See Peter Pauw, *Hortvs Pvblicvs Academiæ Lvgdvno-Batavæ. Eivs Ichnographia, Descriptio, Vsus. Addito quas habet stirpium numero, & nominibus* (Leiden: Ex Officina Plantiniana apud Christopher Raphelengius, 1601) fol. 4r. Actual evidence of what was planted—and grew—in the garden in 1601, 1602, 1604, and later years is provided by the copies of Pauw's catalog, which were filled in by Pauw himself and others for presentation to the trustees of the university; several of these are in the National Herbarium of the Netherlands, Leiden.

39. Pauw, *Hortvs Pvblicvs*.

40. There are a total of 176 pages in the catalog. In 1603, the catalog was printed in Leiden by Ioannes Patus (Ex. Officinâ Ioannis Patii, Academ. Lugduno-Bat. Typographi), in revised edition; the page size is smaller, and there are minor changes to the text. That de Gheyn's engraving of the garden was intended for inclusion in the book when it was first published is clear from the marginal note in the 1601 edition that reads, "ad ea quæ sequuntur, inspicienda erit Horti ichnographia, inserta pagina" (fol. 7v.); this marginal note does not occur in the 1603 edition.

41. See F. W. T. Hunger, "Bernardus Paludanus (Berent ten Broecke) 1550–1633. Zijn verzamelingen en zijn werk," in *Itinerario voyage ofte schipvaert van Jan Huygen van Linschoten 1579–1592 IIIe deel*, ed. C.P. Burger and F. W. T. Hunger (The Hague: M. Nijhoff, 1934), 249–268; H.D. Schepelern, "Naturalienkabinett oder Kunstkammer. Der Sammler Bernhard Paludanus und sein Katalogmanusckript in der Königlichen Bibliothek in Kopenhagen," *Nordelbingen. Beiträge zur Kunst- und Kulturgeschichte* 50 (1981): 157–182; E. Bergvelt and R. Kistemaker, eds., *De wereld binnen handbereik. Nederlandse kunst- en rariteit-enverzamelingen, 1585-1735* (Zwolle/Amsterdam: Waanders Uitgevers/Amsterdams Historisch Museum, 1992); Roelof van Gelder, "Paradijsvogels in Enkhuizen. De relatie tussen Van Linschoten en Bernardus Paludanus," in Roelof van Gelder, Jan Parmentier, and Vibeke Roeper, *Souffrir pour Parvenir. De wereld van Jan Huygen van Linschoten* (Haarlem: Uitgeverij Arcadia, 1998), 30–50, esp. 35–41.

42. *Index Rervm Omnivm Natvralivm, a Bernhardo Palvdano, Medicinæ Doctore, et Civitatis Enckhvsensis Physico experientissimo, collectarum*, in *Warhaffte Beschreibung Zweyer Raisen* (Tübingen: In der Cellischen Truckerey, 1603), 46ff. (24 unnumbered pages); see Van Gelder, "Paradijsvogels in Enkhuizen," 36–38.

43. The classic study is Hans Fischer, *Conrad Gessner. Leben und Werk* (Zurich: Kommissionsverlag Leemann, 1966); cf. Hans Fischer, G. Petit, J. Staedtke et al., *Conrad Gessner 1516–1565. Universalgelehrter, Naturforscher, Arzt* (Zurich: Orell Fussli, 1967). See also the facsimile edition of the watercolors by Gessner of plants, which he died before publishing; H. Zoller and M. Steinmann, *Conradi Gesneri Historia plantarum. Gesamtausgabe*, 2 vols. (Zurich: Urs Graf Verlag, 1987–1991).

44. Caspar Wolf, *De Stirpivm Collectione Tabulæ Tvm Generales, Tvm per Dvodecim Menses, cum Germanicis nominibus, & alijs hactenus à nemine traditis, olim per Conradum Gesnerum conscriptæ ac æditæ* . . . (Zurich: Ch. Froschauer, 1587); Universiteitsbibliotheek Amsterdam, 613 H 27.

45. "Conradi Gesneri de Partibvs et Differentiis Plantarvm Physica Syn-nopsis . . . in tabulas methodicè digesta," fols. 1r.–40v.; a header runs throughout these folios, identifying them as "Tabulae stirpivm in genere."

46. "De Collectione stirpivm in genere," fols. 41r.–55v; the page header for this section is "De Collectione in genere."

47. "Tabvla Stirpium prima, alphabetice envmerans . . . ," fols. 56r.–116r.

48. "Tabvla secunda stirpivm nomina Latina et Germanica continens, quæ singulis mensibus aut florent aut fructum maturant . . . ," fols. 116v.–147v.

49. "Tabvlae istæ non pharmacopolis tantùm, tyronibus præsertim & minus exercitatis, vtiles sunt futuræ, sed omnibus stirpium notitiæ studiosis. Qui cum singulis ferè mensibus vernis, æstiuis & autumnalibus, partim cognitionis, partim animum remittendi & corpus exercendi gratia, rusticatum exire soleant, occasionem ex hisce tabulis capient, quænam eis plantæ potissimum quærendæ aut sperandæ sint."

50. The literature is vast. See especially Beatrijs Brenninkmeyer-de Rooij, *Roots of Seventeenth-Century Flower Painting. Miniatures, Plant Books, Paintings,* ed. R. E. O. Ekkart; trans. Ruth Koenig (Leiden: Primavera Press, 1996); Paul Taylor, *Dutch Flower Painting 1600–1720* (New Haven, Conn.: Yale University Press, 1995); Sam Segal, *Flowers and Nature. Netherlandish Flower Painting of Four Centuries* (The Hague: Government Publishing Office, 1990); Norbert Schneider, "Vom Klostergarten zur Tulpenmanie. Hinweise zur materiellen Vorgeschichte des Blumenstillebens," in G. Langemeyer and H. A. Peters, *Stilleben in Europa* (Münster: Landschaftsverband Westfallen-Lippe, 1979), 294–312.

51. Bol, *The Bosschaert Dynasty,* 46; see also, on this phenomenon in France, Antoine Schnapper, *Le géant, la licorne, et la tulipe. Collections et collectionneurs dans la France du XVIIe siècle. I - Histoire et histoire naturelle* (Paris: Flammarion, 1985), 354 and 358–360, where Schnapper speaks of "les 'portraits' de fleurs ou de fruits commandés par un amateur désireux de péerenniser le souvenir des pièces les plus précieuses, mais essentiellement périssables, de sa collection."

52. For a recent example of such an approach, see A. Chong, W. Kloek et al., *Still-Life Paintings from the Netherlands 1550–1720,* exh. cat., trans. R. Koenig et al. (Zwolle: Waanders Publishers, 1999), passim. For another counterproposal, the focus of which is on the social and economic formations that inform still life paintings, see E. A. Honig, "Making Sense of Things: On the Motives of Dutch Still Life," *Res* 34 (autumn 1998), 166–183.

53. *De Constantia* was first published in Leiden in 1584, and was reprinted in a variety of European languages (Dutch, French, German, English, Italian, Spanish, and Polish) in as many as eighty editions throughout the seventeenth century. The first Dutch translation, by Jan Moretus, was published as *Twee Boecken vande Standvasticheyt,* Leiden, 1584 (*Over standvastigheid bij algemene rampspoed,* trans. and annotated P. H. Schrijvers [Baarn: Amboboeken, 1983]). The Erasmian model of the humanist's garden is set out most famously in the colloquy *The Godly Feast* (*Convivium religiosum,* 1522); trans. and ed. C. R. Thompson, *The Colloquies of Erasmus* (Chicago: University of Chicago Press, 1965), 46–78, esp. 46–47 and 51–52.

54. In 1578, at the age of thirty, Lipsius was made a professor of history and law at Leiden University; he and his wife lived at Leiden for thirteen years, until 1591, at which time he returned to Flanders (Louvain) and to Catholicism, from which he had converted to Lutheranism when he took a post at Jena in 1572.

55. Mark Morford, "The Stoic Garden," *Journal of Garden History* 7 (1987): 151–175, esp. 165–167.

56. Trans. mine, from German (1st German ed., 1601); bk. 2, cap. 2.

"Strange" Ideas and "English" Knowledge

Natural Science Exchange in Elizabethan London

DEBORAH E. HARKNESS

During the reign of Elizabeth I, a public well—the traditional neighborhood locus for gossip, news, and information—stood at the crossroads of Bishop's Gate and Threadneedle Streets in London, near the Royal Exchange. Given the colorful occupations of many area residents, and its proximity to Bedlem hospital, one can but imagine that the quality of gossip there was high. Within a few square blocks lived an extraordinary assortment of characters, many of whom made hands-on investigations into the marvelous workings of nature. When John Dee was in London he lived right in the thick of this neighborhood, along with his mathematics pupil Sir William Pickering, and Sir Thomas Gresham, builder of the Royal Exchange. Several members of the Royal College of Physicians also made Bishop's Gate their home, such as the botanically inclined Peter Turner, and the Venetian-born Dr. Caesar Aldemare, who had been trained at the famous medical school in Padua. Aldemare was one of the many foreigners in Bishop's Gate, and the voices of Bedlem would have had to be very loud to drown out the cacophony of tongues generated by the Flemish, French, Dutch, German, Italian, and Spanish residents. These "strangers" included many natural science practitioners: instrument makers, surgeons, midwives, alchemists, and distillers. Neither a humanistically informed natural philosophy, nor a university-taught Galenic medicine, nor a hands-on skill in technology is sufficient to describe the range of interests and activities within the metropolis of London. And so I fall back on "science," which was used commonly in the period to describe those things that required knowledge, but not exclusively theoretical or exclusively practical knowledge. As John Securis explained in his *Detection and querimonie of the daily enormities and abuses co[m]mited in physick*, "science is an habite, . . . [a] ready, prompt and bent disposition to do any thynge, confirmed and gotten by long study, exercise, and use." Securis's emphasis on study, exercise, and use defines how most Elizabethan science practitioners interested in the natural world occupied their time and made their living.[1]

To locate these English and alien practitioners—many of whom did not publish—we must turn to the minutiae that historians of science wade through when they conduct their research: the tortured book prefaces that introduce nearly every scientific work of the period, the roll books of the Barber-Surgeons and College of Physicians, the annals of Oxford and Cambridge Universities, and the diaries of those few men like Dee who left written remains of their practices. But we must also look beyond these sources to the minutiae that historians of science seldom consult: parish registers, the addresses on the back of state papers, petitions for patents and monopolies addressed to the queen, probate cases, and the censuses that were intended to account for the names and occupations of every Stranger living and working in London.[2] Together, these documents can provide historians of science with a richer and more textured sense of natural science practitioners in Elizabethan London—a mapping of who they were, whence they came, how they were educated, and where and with whom they lived and practiced.

While this mapping process would, in and of itself, constitute valuable factual information for historians of early modern science, it also sheds light on the daily practice, the economic imperatives, and even the contemporary conception of science in the period. The evidence also provides an intriguing glimpse into the exchange of ideas and the importance of intellectual community in Elizabethan London. We learn from the mapping process that distinct neighborhoods of science sprang up throughout the city, some housing mainly medical practitioners, one constituting the instrument-making center of London, and still others providing communities for chemical distillers, alchemists, compass makers, and gardeners. While we might think of science practitioners in Elizabethan London as a few scattered individuals, it is clear that one had only to walk down the street to St. Martin Ludgate to have a discussion about anatomy,[3] visit St. Antholin's parish to debate the significance of comets with John Dade and Richard Forster,[4] mingle with the gardeners of St. Giles Cripplegate to learn how to propagate olive trees,[5] or procure a novel remedy for sciatica from the Paracelsian apothecaries and innovative physicians and surgeons of St. Benet Paul's Wharf.[6]

Natural science neighborhoods and practitioners in London were not exclusively English, however, but were international in composition and outlook. It is thus important to recognize that there was no purely English natural science in the period, but only a natural science practiced in England by a variety of individuals both native and foreign, some university trained and others barely literate. As early as 1571, the official census of strangers indicated that the city of London was home to 4,850 non-native workers, who made up approximately 4.9 percent of the total population.[7] More than

Deborah E. Harkness

75 percent of that number were from the Low Countries; the remainder included French, Italian, Spanish, Scottish, Portugese, Danish, Greek, and even Turkish men and women.[8] The numbers of Strangers in the city only increased during the remainder of the century, mostly because religious and political conflicts on the continent forced many people to seek protection in Protestant England.

A healthy proportion of these immigrants possessed skills that brought them to the attention of London citizens interested in the properties of nature. The 1571 census lists twelve Strange physicians, for example, only a few of whom were licensed to practice by the authorities. Sixteen men and women from Burgundy, Antwerp, and Amsterdam professed to being surgeons, while three apothecaries — one Italian, one from Flanders, and a woman from Holland — also worked in the English medical marketplace. Eight professional gardeners from other countries lived in the city in 1571, working both inside and outside the city gates in the garden plots of the wealthier citizens. In addition, many skilled Strangers engaged in trades that supported natural science — glassmakers who made alchemical vessels, potters who shaped apothecary jars, and clock-makers who could craft any number of mechanical marvels such as intricate clocks and astrolabes.

The presence of so many Strangers among London's natural science practitioners suggests that a wide-ranging intellectual atmosphere pervaded the streets and neighborhoods of the city. London provided a lucrative and vital environment for natural science practitioners, and the sheer number of practitioners who lived and worked in the City during the period was much higher than the number who were maintained at, or even circulated through, the royal court.[9] Yet the influx of "strange ideas" was bitterly resented by some because alien natural science practitioners drew clients away from citizens in the tight London market, and because their very unfamiliarity made them stylish to urban consumers.

English natural science practitioners complained frequently about the inroads their alien competitors were making into London commerce. One medical practitioner wrote of the "runners about called cutters for the stone," Strangers who

> have suche a great name at their first coming. But after . . . their work be tried and then the proof of them seen: the people for the moste parte are wery of them. . . . Such is the foolish fantasyes of our English nation that if he bee a Straunger: he shall have more favourers then an English man, though the English mans knowledge doo far passe the others. . . . "[10]

A physician charged that a few of London's popular medical practitioners were actually feigning alien behaviors in order to gain a clientele: "Sometimes, [popular physicians] fain themselves to be of some straunge countrey, and wyll counterfayte their language."[11]

English and alien practitioners competed with each other for economic survival by relying upon a variety of time-tested strategies to carve out a niche for themselves. Some resorted to advertising to draw potential clients to their doors, such as surgeon Edward Parke (fl. 1564–88), who in 1568 erected a sign outside his shop that described him inaccurately as "the skoller [scholar] of St. Thomas of Willyngforde." Parke was competing with three surgeons in the parish of St. Dunstan in the West, and though he undoubtedly knew that the Barber-Surgeons would demand he take down the sign, the opportunity to set himself apart from his commercial competition by claiming some education was too great to resist.[12] Other practitioners favored more theatrical demonstrations of their knowledge in the homes of clients or in the open, as did the surgeon John Smythe (fl. 1556–73) who was admonished by the Repertory Court of Aldermen in 1573 to "make open show" of his surgical skills "against his own house and dore and not elsewhere."[13]

Others settled in a neighborhood already reputed to offer the latest designs in compasses and other scientific instruments, chemical preparations, or surgical techniques, as did a host of foreign clock, instrument, and watch makers who flooded into the former ecclesiastical Liberty of the Blackfriars following in the footsteps of the well-known engraver, instrument maker, and medical empiric Thomas Gemini (fl. 1540–1562). Most of London's natural science neighborhoods were based, like the Blackfriars, on one or more parishes, and were anchored by a parish church where the English and some immigrant households worshipped. Though many of the Strangers attended their own Protestant churches — either the French, Dutch, or Italian congregations — all those residing in the parish at the time of death were recorded in the parish's register of births, marriages, and deaths. The size of London's parishes varied widely from the minute St. John the Evangelist not far from St. Paul's Cathedral to the suburban sprawl of St. Botolph Aldgate. Even the smallest — and some were less than one square acre — could house a surprisingly large number of residents by today's standards.[14]

Because of trade restrictions that were enforced by the City's guild and livery companies, many immigrants gravitated toward those areas in the city where corporate control was at its weakest, namely the former ecclesiastical Liberties, the suburbs, and the areas within the city walls just adjacent to the old gates. What these areas had in common was greater freedom, greater space, and a more equitable mix of English and Strangers than could often be found in the center of the City in neighborhoods that were largely controlled by the guilds and livery companies. There the organizations fostered their own sense of community that was based not on neighborhoods, but on allegiance to the company, and thus acted as a counterweight to neighbor-hood associations.[15]

The masters of London's guilds and livery companies, who were charged with the task of regulating commercial behavior and restricting nonmembers from engaging in their trades, were keen to apprehend both Strangers and English citizens who impinged on their privileges. The Royal College of Physicians, for example, vigorously sought out the French medical practitioner Charles Cornet (fl. 1555–98), whom they described as "an Ignorant Fleming and a most shameless buffoon," after he put up bills of advertisement "on all the Corners of the City." The college punished Cornet by seizing "his feigned and unwholesome remedies" and throwing them into a bonfire in Westminster's public market.[16] Such efforts were a particular hardship to the alien practitioners, who were technically restricted from guild membership except in special circumstances: at the request of the queen or high-placed noble, for example, or if the alien practitioner met guild standards through an examination or demonstration. Those few Strangers who managed to become foreign members of the City's guilds and livery companies paid steeply for the privilege.

As a result, many Stranger practitioners resorted to higher governmental authorities, such as the City's Repertory Court of Aldermen and the queen, for permission to advertise their services and practice their natural sciences. Peter van Duran (fl. 1559–84), a brewer in St. Olave Southwark who was also known by his colorful nickname "Pickleherring," for example, satisfied the Aldermen that he "professethe ye knoledge & science of surgery," and he was given permission in 1563 to "sette up bylles upon posts in such p[ar]ts of the Cytye as to him shall seeme good to give the people knowledg of his said science."[17] The Dutch empiric Margaret Kemmex (fl. 1576–83), following persistent efforts of the Royal College of Physicians to close down her medical practice, successfully appealed to the queen and Sir Francis Walsingham for protection. In 1581, Walsingham found it necessary to remind the College that "it was her highness pleasure that the poore wooman should be permitted by you quietly to practise and mynister for the curing of diseases, and woundes, by the meanes of certaine simples."[18] Walsingham cited two reasons why Kemmex should be allowed to practice unmolested, one knowledge-based and one shaped by economic imperatives: "god hath given her an espetiall knowledge [of simples] to the benefit of the poorer sort," and also for "the better maintenaunce of her impotent husband and charge of family, who wholy depend un the exercise of her skill."[19] Unwilling to let Walsingham have the last word on such an important matter, the College responded on 22 December 1581 that Kemmex's "weaknes and insufficiency is suche as is rather to be pitied of all, then either envied of us or maintayned of others."[20]

Royal patents often became the vehicle for immigrants to secure the right to practice their skills despite guild and livery company restrictions, and for the queen to ensure that some English citizens were trained in the process. Patent petitions often contain evidence of heated intellectual debates between Strangers and English citizens during which expertise and knowledge were called into question. It was in the best interests of the crown, however, to arrange a collaborative détente. The responsibility for this kind of brokerage and peacemaking fell to Elizabeth's secretary of state, William Cecil. For decades Cecil vetted and supervised natural science projects like an early prototype of today's National Science Foundation, judging the merits of each proposal and, whenever possible, turning would-be competitors into scientific collaborators, as will be seen below. One factor always governed his decisions: the profit that the patent holders would be able to bring to the crown.

The spirit of commerce is vividly captured in many of the exchanges that took place between natural scientists, their clients, and the crown in Elizabethan London. Given London's competitive markets, we should not be surprised that natural science ideas and expertise, be they English or alien, had definite economic worth. Few doubted that some profit could be gained by more highly trained mathematicians who might keep your accounts in order, for example, or from a more fuel-efficient furnace, and most were prepared to invest money in far riskier schemes to transmute metals, mine for precious minerals, and construct water mills on London Bridge. Natural science practitioners thus competed in a commercial world in which ideas and materials were quickly transmuted into merchandise. This transformation was part of a general trend toward merchandising of which John Wheeler, in his *Treatise of Commerce* (1601), complained: "There is nothing . . . so ordinarie, and naturall unto men, as to contract, truck, merchandise, and traffike one with an other, so that it is almost impossible for three persons to converse together two houres, but they wil fal into talk of one bargaine or another." Commerce and exchange, Wheeler noted, were no longer the sole province of merchants, but preoccupied everyone, high and low: "The Prince with his subjects, the Maister with his servants, one friend and acquaintance with another . . . the Husband with his wife, [and] women with and among themselves." Wheeler regretted the emphasis on commodities that resulted when his world went mad for merchandising. "[A]ll the world choppeth and changeth, runneth & raveth after Marts, Markets and Merchandising, so that all thinges come into Commerce," Wheeler lamented, "[T]his man maketh merchandise of the workes of his owne handes, this man of another mans labour, one selleth words . . . [and] all that a man worketh with his hand or discourseth in his spirit is nothing els but merchandise."[21]

Deborah E. Harkness

The ways in which natural science practitioners struggled for economic survival in this mercantile atmosphere provide us with important insights into the conditions of intellectual exchange and the dynamics of commercial competition in Elizabethan London. For some, as we will see in the examples below, economic survival could best be fostered through collaboration with Strangers that would blend their alien ideas and practices with English traditions. This was particularly true for practicing alchemists and engineers who preferred syncretism, in which the resulting ideas or products represented an innovative blend of English and non-English knowledge and practice. Other English and alien practitioners, especially clock makers and other instrument makers, preferred to work apart from each other in distinct neighborhoods. For medical practitioners who faced enormous competition, however, there was a blend of conflict and collaboration that could bitterly divide some practitioners while bringing others more closely together in the face of their detractors. When taken as a whole, these examples are evidence of the complicated ways in which natural science practitioners faced challenges in an urban, mercantile environment.

PARACELSIAN THERAPEUTICS AND THE MEDICAL MARKET: COMPETITION, COLLABORATION, AND CONFLICT

Because medical practitioners were by far the largest group of natural science practitioners within the Elizabethan City, encompassing physicians, empirics, surgeons, and barber surgeons, midwives, "cutters for the stone," occulists, dentists, midwives, and nurses, understanding the challenges that faced these practitioners and the negotiations that took place between alien and English ideas represents an important contribution to our understanding of urban-based natural science practice. In addition, medicine often provided the means by which English and immigrant practitioners could engage in other, less lucrative branches of natural science such as natural history, astrology, and alchemy. It is all the more important, therefore, that we understand the tensions between English and Strange practitioners, how they were resolved, and the conditions under which intellectual exchange could take place.

Medical practitioners represented a wide array of educational backgrounds, from illiterate empirics who learned most of their skills from demonstration and hands-on experience, to university-trained members of the Royal College of Physicians. Despite these differences, there were often strong links among what might seem on the surface to be entirely different types of practitioners. The evidence suggests that physicians, surgeons, and apothecaries did indeed form strong friendships through shared patients, remedies, and neighborhood ties. The close working relationships that could occur between physicians and apothecaries can be seen in the medical and alchemical papers of the apothecary Edward Barlow (fl. 1581–94), which mention which physicians he provided with drugs and medicines on a regular basis, including Strangers Johann Vulpe (fl. 1581–89), Hector Nonez (fl. 1553–92), and John Shoring (fl. 1592/3) and Englishmen Thomas Penny (fl. 1569–89), Richard Forster (c. 1545–16), and Walter Baylie (fl. 1580–91/92). Barlow's notes also indicate that English and alien physicians shared cases, as did Christopher Atkinson and Hector Nonez.[22] The relationships that Barlow forged with members of the Royal College of Physicians are all the more interesting because he was reprimanded in 1581 for practicing medicine without the organization's consent.[23]

It was not uncommon for husband-and-wife partnerships to exist among the surgical practitioners in Elizabethan London, or for surgeons to marry midwives and establish a joint practice. Such is the case with surgeons Hugh and Ann Vellam, immigrants who operated a joint practice in the late 1560s which continued to be active after Hugh's death in 1568.[24] William Baxter, a member of the Barber-Surgeons Company, was married to Emma Philipps (fl. 1571–1603), whose brother, Edward Philipps, was an apothecary. Emma Philipps was a medical empiric, and drew the ire of the Royal College of Physicians, which described her as "an ignorant and bold woman" and committed her to prison.[25] Guillaume Alaertes, a Stranger surgeon, was married to a midwife, Lieven Alaertes, who was described, much like Emma Baxter, as "an ignorant old woman" by the Royal College of Physicians.[26]

Given such a variety of backgrounds and expertise it is not surprising that there was both fruitful collaboration and tense competition amongst medical practitioners. Though many English practitioners resented the success of the Strangers, for others the presence of alien ideas presented an opportunity to share new ideas, books, and techniques. Surgeon George Baker (fl. 1577–1607), for example, praised the diverse backgrounds and expertise of London apothecaries, and complimented the work of "Maister Kemech an English man," "mayster Geffray, a French man," and John Hester, whom he called "a paynfull traveyler in those matters, as I by proofe have seene."[27] But Baker did not approve of all alien ideas: in his book on the preparation of *oleum magistrale* he scathingly criticized the London followers of Paracelsus for putting their patients' health at risk.[28]

John Hall's (fl. 1565) translation of Lanfrank's *Chirurgia parva* (1565) recounts a fascinating tale of exchange which took place during his walk along Bucklersbury, the London street famous for its grocery, spice, and drug stores.[29] There he met a "woman [who] came to sell hearbes, to the Apothecaryes." She offered the apothecaries maidenhair, but Hall was aghast when the herb gatherer produced "Nothinge agreeinge with that whiche she named: But only it had rounde leaves, standinge in good order on eche syde [of] the stalke, as maiden heare hathe." Hall took a sample of the plant, in case he "might meete with anye, that knew it, and so to attaine the name therof." Within an hour Hall was encouraged to consult with an alien physician by his friend "master Gale Chirurgien of London" who lived nearby on Lime Street in the parish of St. Dionysius Backchurch.

Lime Street was full of foregin-born practitioners with excellent intellectual credentials, including the physician and botanist Matthew L'Obel.[30] While we cannot be sure that Gale and Hall consulted L'Obel, it is certainly possible. Whoever the physician was, he exchanged "divers communications" before meeting with Gale and Hall to view the troublesome specimen. Hall and the alien physician soon parted company after the Stranger "sayde it made no matter to be so precise in the knowledge of herbes." This single anecdote is laced through with all sorts of exchanges: between the herb woman and the apothecaries, between the apothecaries and Hall, between Hall and his friend Thomas Gale, and between Gale, Hall, and the immigrant population of physicians and surgeons. In this case, the potential collaboration between the English surgeon and alien physician did not come to fruition because the physician's "strange ideas" were incompatible with the English surgeon's beliefs and practices.

It was Paracelsus and his remedies, however, that most polarized the English and alien medical practitioners. One of the most notorious and well-documented showdowns between Paracelsian advocates and opponents involved Valentine Russwurin of Schmalkald.[31] Self-described as a "Medicus spagirirus opt[halamistus],[32] Russwurin was made denizen by Elizabeth in 1574 at the same time that he was practicing his Paracelsian remedies on the London population.[33] Russwurin's London career became problematic when he took up the cure of Helen Currance, a musician's wife, on 3 April 1574. In the presence of witnesses, Russwurin "did attempt with his instruments to have taken out of her bladder a stone." The witnesses later alleged that "finding none there, privily he tooke a stone out of the pocket of his hose . . . conveyed it into a spunge . . . [and] forst it in Pudendo."[34] When this procedure failed to relieve her discomfort, Russwurin sent her a powder that made it impossible for her to urinate. Uncomfortable side effects from the powder included blisters in her mouth, nose, face, and "inward parts of her bodie," which rendered her unable to eat.

Russwurin continued to treat patients for bladder stones, and branched out to treat various illnesses of the eye, including cataracts. Most egregiously affected was Mr. Castleton, a scholar of Cambridge, who still retained some vision when he contracted for a cure with Russwurin. Shortly after their agreement, Valentine "by his rustical dealings, put out his eyes cleane, and so deprived him of all his sight." Castleton had Russwurin arrested at the Royal Exchange, "wher he did display his banners and wares . . . being in the middest of his pontificalibus."[35]

Finally the matter was brought to the Court of Aldermen on 22 April 1574 who heard "certen complants and objections" from Russwurin's patients as well as surgeons George Baker and William Clowes.[36] According to Clowes, Russwurin left behind him a very long list of dead patients — twenty-three in all — from all walks of life including Master Mace, a grocer, the servant of goldsmith Master Dummers, and two Strangers.[37] The court put together a committee of two aldermen and two physicians, with instructions that they should call upon the expertise "of the Discretist and best skylled surgeons of this cytie" to judge Russwurin's "knowledge & skill in s[ur]gerye."[38] Safely incarcerated in the Newgate Prison, Russwurin was examined by a new, largely English committee on 10 May 1574.[39]

No account survives of Russwurin's trial, and so we must rely on one of his fiercest critics, William Clowes, for our insights into what transpired. According to Clowes, Russwurin had only one defender: a "proud bragger . . . of the foresaide Adders broode . . . a man of little skill, and lesse honestie . . . [who] practiseth Chirurgerie, without all order or aucthoritie." An unascribed note in a sixteenth-century hand in the British Library's copy of Clowes's work states that this was "John Hester Alchymist at Paul's Wharf," who was a known supporter of Paracelsian ideas.[40] Hester claimed that "Velentine Rasworme was a wise Alchymist, " and that Clowes and Russwurin's other opponents were "ignoraunt fooles and asses."[41] Clowes felt unable to judge Russwurin's alchemical skill, but did report that "I doe know wise Alchimistes, of mine opinion, that accounts him in deede, an arch coosener, and loper, and Quacksalver."[42]

According to a treatise on the chemical analysis of urines and other opthamalgic matters addressed to William Cecil, Russwurin may well have impressed John Hester as a "wise Alchymist" because of his knowledge and incorporation of Paracelsian ideas into his medical practices. Russwurin chemically analyzed Cecil's urine, weighing it carefully to find that it was "eyght ounces and a lytle more, wherein it hath no difference from a sound man his water at all."[43] He also discussed the problems Cecil's mother was having with her cataracts, focusing on their hard "Tartar."[44] These preoccupations put Russwurin's practices well within the concerns of Paracelsian therapeutics and would have resonated with anyone who had read works by the author.[45]

While much more needs to be done to tease out the full implications of the Russwurin case for a better understanding of the influence of Paracelsian medicine in London, it is clear that such an analysis must take into account the connections that were made between commercial success and alien ideas within the city.[46] For there was more at stake than just theoretical concerns when an English practitioner decried a Paracelsian cure — economic and nationalistic matters were of at least equal importance. Eleven medical treatises making reference to Paracelsus were printed in the six years following the Russwurin case, marking a definite spike compared to print trends prior to 1574. This evidence suggests that Russwurin, no matter his fate at the hands of the English authorities, had an effect on the commercial exchange of ideas in Elizabethan London.[47] While conflict might overshadow collaboration and influence when viewed from the distance of nearly five hundred years, the Russwurin case reminds us how complicated intellectual exchange could be in the early modern period.

While medicine was a feature of life for nearly all residents in Elizabethan London, the city was also a feast for the eyes of anyone interested in machines, engineering, and visual displays of technological prowess. Those interested in mechanical marvels could visit the windmills and glasshouses in St. Giles Cripplegate just northwest of the city walls, or feel the heat of the brick kilns and gun foundry in St. Botolph Aldgate to the northeast of the city center. Smaller-scale industries also thrived within London's walls, including clock- and watchmakers, mathematical instrument makers, and a variety of smiths working on copper and iron. Public interest in viewing such marvels is evident in the Court of Aldermen's decision on 17 October 1588 to exhibit in the Guildhall an "artificial motion" devised by Henrick Johnson from Utrecht in the Netherlands. The Guildhall was the symbolic center of the City's civic power and judicial prerogatives, and it is striking that the Aldermen permitted a Stranger to display his invention there. The Aldermen did so at the request of Sir Thomas Heneage, Queen Elizabeth I's chamberlain of the household, with the stipulation that the display be for "such inhabitants of this city [and] others who shall be willing to see the same."[48]

Instruments, artifical motions, clocks, and watches were much in vogue in the period, their importance raised to new prominence through England's naval expeditions and the influx of European-style watches and clocks that accompanied the immigrants when they entered England. While the desire to possess such items did not always indicate the purchaser's interest in the finer points of natural science, the expense and stylishness of mechanical marvels indicate their cultural currency. William Bourne, a well-known author of navigational and mathematical texts, explained that prices for some instruments put them out of reach for those natural science practitioners who could make most use of them, such as the "Mariners heere in Englande for that the charges is so muche in the making of them." Bourne was especially thinking of equinoctial dials, which indicated "the houre of the day, & to shew the true shadowe of the Moone," which were not "used by any English Master or Pylot, but only by one man, which person had not it for the proper use therof, but rather had it, to say that he had suche an instrument as no English man had the like, & to bragge that he had such an instrument that he could do great feates therewith in the going of long viages."[49]

The relative rarity of instruments and their high asking price provided skilled English and non-English technicians with the economic incentive to produce more and more of the highly desired watches, clocks, and mathematical instruments. Yet unlike the medical practitioners — for whom there is so much evidence of collaboration and conflict — alien and English instrument makers in Elizabethan London appear to have had little contact except in two neighborhoods: the areas just outside the western walls of the city between the parishes of St. Clement and St. Dunstan in the West, and the neighborhood around St. Bartholomew's Hospital, which included parish churches of St. Bartholomew the Less, St. Bartholomew the Great, and St. Sepulchre.[50] Otherwise, the two groups tended to settle in different neighborhoods in the city, and few English practitioners worked for Strangers and *vice versa*.

This division of instrument makers into separate districts mirrors a striking division in workshop production: Strangers dominated the clock- and watchmaking industries, while English makers took preeminence in the field of mathematical instrumentation such as quadrants, astrolabes, staffs, balances, and other navigational instruments. Such a firm division of labor may well have had long-term implications for the development of a highly instrumental natural philosophy in seventeenth-century England.[51] Despite these differences, instrument makers shared some characteristics with medical practitioners, namely that family ties and interconnections featured strongly in their communities.

Two neighborhoods dominated by English instrument makers were the printing district centered on St. Paul's Cathedral Churchyard and the extramural parish of St. Botolph Aldgate. Five English instrument makers settled in St. Botolph Aldgate, which is striking because so many foreign-born surgeons, apothecaries, physicians, and aquavita distillers lived there. Three of these men—Richard Stevens (fl. 1569), Thomas Hearne (fl. 1592), and John White (fl. 1602/1603)—made compasses.[52] Yet the parish, in addition to housing many Strangers, also was home to a number of sailors, mariners, and shipwrights, which may indicate that there was a ready market of potential consumers. In addition, the distribution of active dates may be evidence of a single workshop.

Two notable instrument makers, James Kynvin (fl. 1570–1610) and Humphrey Cole (fl. 1568-91), lived around the precincts of St. Paul's Cathe-

Deborah E. Harkness

dral. Kynvin was highly recommended by William Bourne. Gabriel Harvey, a staunch supporter of experiential knowledge who considered Kynvin "A fine workman, & mie kinde frend," noted in his copy of John Blagrave's *The Mathematical Jewel* (1585) that the paper dials which Blagrave set forth in his treatise could now be purchased in brass from his shop.[53] Some members of Elizabeth's court purchased instruments from him, including the Earl of Essex, who bought from him a combined compass and sundial enclosed in a box in 1593.[54] Humphrey Cole was a steady producer of mathematical instruments including pocket compendiums, navigational instruments, astrolabes, armillary spheres, ring-dials, sectors, gunners' scales, and theodolites.[55] Even Elizabeth purchased instruments from Cole, who like Kynvin received special mention by Gabriel Harvey who described him as a "Mathematicall Mechanicia[n]" in *Pierces Superogation*.[56]

Alien instrument makers, alternatively, preferred to settle in two former ecclesiastical Liberties: the Blackfriars and St. Martin le Grand. Of the two the Blackfriars was the more dynamic, with thirteen instrument makers known to have lived there during the Elizabethan period. The first alien instrument maker to settle in the Blackfriars was Thomas Gemini, whom Leonard Digges recommended to his readers in *A Boke Named Tectonicon* (1556), stating that Gemini was "dwelling within the blacke Friers ... [and] is there ready exactly to make all the Instrumentes apperteynyng to this booke."[57] Another instrument maker, Eloy Mistrell, was one of the Blackfriars' more notorious residents. Mistrell was a French goldsmith who was arrested for counterfeiting and went on to be employed at the Royal Mint after receiving a patent for his novel machine for stamping coins.[58] Other instrument makers residing in the Blackfriars included three members of the Vallin family of clock- and watchmakers from Brussels; three members of the Noway family; Francis Rozean; Peter de Hind; Laurence Dauntenay; Thomas Tiball, a balance maker; and Mark Sara, a scale maker. It is difficult to assess their full importance in the history of Elizabethan instrumentation because so few of their works survive, but it is in clockmaking that the neighborhood appears to have made its reputation.[59]

Because of their expertise with clocks, many Stranger instrument makers found additional employment in London's parish churches, whose clocks were in perpetual need of repair and opened up a bottomless pit for parish revenues. The clock of All Hallow's Staining was fixed repeatedly by a number of experts between 1558 and 1579, including the royal clockmaker Nicholas Orshawe.[60] The clock at St. Helen's Bishopsgate was similarly troublesome, and French clockmaker John De Mellayne kept busy continually from 1565 to 1569 mending, keeping, and, most important, oiling it.[61] Similar positions in parishes all over the city provided the clockmakers with an additional source of revenue, and heightened English residents' awareness of their skills and abilities.

Large-scale engineering and mechanical feats gave foreign-born technicians an opportunity to exercise their technical skills by bringing continental inventions into England. Elizabeth, who could be difficult in patronage matters, was unusually appreciative of the hard work that went into many inventions, as demonstrated by the case of William de Berger (fl. 1535–67), a coppersmith born in Utrecht. In 1559 he was given a seven-year license to make and sell a unique corn mill whose invention had "cost him much money and study during the past seven or eight years."[62] James Acontius, an Italian engineer from Trent, even received one of Elizabeth's rare annuities in exchange for his service to the crown.[63] Acontius's exemptions from guild control which were implicit in the patent became an issue for contention in 1566 when representatives from the Masons, Tilers, and Blacksmiths were called to the Repertory Court of Aldermen to be reminded of "the hole contents and effects of the Quenes Ma[jes]tyes hir patentes . . . in consideracon of a certon & goodly and wyttye devise by hym fyrst found and taught to her hygh[n]es subiectes for the makyge of furnesses."[64]

The importance of engineering and inventions to the state is demonstrated by the role that Elizabeth I's chief minister, William Cecil, played in supervising the patent process. Cecil's efforts ensured that there was an emphasis on output, adherence to a timely schedule, and ultimate English proprietorship over the skills of the inventors. To ensure that the crown's investment in the project was fruitful, patents were typically granted only if the work commenced within a proscribed time frame. When George Gilpin, an English merchant, and Peter Stowghberghen, a Stranger, were given the monopoly on "making ovens and furnaces after a new pattern, more economical of wood and other fuel, which they have invented," they were required to begin work within two months.[65] Failure to produce the anticipated results within another stipulated time frame was grounds for Elizabeth to pull her support entirely, as is vividly illustrated in the patent granted to Philip Cockerman, mercer, and John Barnes, haberdasher, who took over a monopoly on the manufacture of saltpeter once held by a German mineral expert, Garrard Honricke. They were granted a twenty-year monopoly, but were warned that they had only one year to demonstrate the usefulness and profitability of the process or their exclusive rights would be revoked.[66]

The influx of new skills and techniques that accompanied the Strangers into London was highly regarded by the City and the crown. Unlike other forms of natural science practice, instrumentation and engineering caught the attention of both common citizens and high-placed officials in Elizabeth's government. I would argue that such a wealth of technical expertise specifically caught the eye of Francis Bacon, who lived a stone's throw from the St. Clement-St. Dunstan instrument-making neighborhood from 1576 when he enrolled in Gray's Inn. Though Solomon's House in the *New Atlantis* (1627) has always been seen as a prescriptive for scientific practice, it is clear from the examples above that Bacon did not need to actually dream up the displays of ingenuity and inventiveness that he described there. Elizabethan London—Bacon's London—had its own "engine-houses, where are prepared engines and instruments for all sorts of motions," its neighborhoods that produced "divers curious clocks," and its mathematical houses "where are represented all instruments, as well of geometry as astronomy, exquisitely made."[67]

ALIEN ALCHEMISTS AND THE ENGLISH ALCHEMICAL TRADITION IN LONDON

While Elizabethan instrument makers and engineers made visual spectacles of their inventions for the delight of the populace, London's alchemists labored in more private quarters conducting experiments and expounding upon theories that also promised great profit and rewards. Seventy-four alchemists are known to have practiced in the city during the reign of Elizabeth, and because this number is based on written remains it may well underrepresent the number of actual practitioners. Alchemical practitioners came from many occupations, including medical, metallurgical, apothecarial, and distilling trades. The alchemical papers that survive reveal a wide range of approaches, from the traditional to the Paracelsian.

No one neighborhood marked the center of alchemical practice; instead, alchemists were distributed throughout the city, from its crowded center to its more spacious suburbs. The highest concentrations of alchemists occurred in St. Botolph Aldgate, a relatively industrial area outside the city walls to the northeast, boasting four alchemists. St. Helen's Bishopsgate, which was just inside the city walls near St. Botolph Aldgate, had three alchemists. Most other parishes in London had one or two alchemical practitioners. Alchemists may have spread out in this fashion because their practices were so likely to annoy their neighbors with smoking stills, fires that were kept hot all day and night, noxious smells, and regular explosions.

There were instances, however, when the normally secretive practice of alchemy was performed on the public stage. One such incident involved a Polish alchemist, Cornelius Alnetanus, who defaulted on an agreement to transmute lead into gold after Elizabeth gave him a stipend and access to raw materials at the Tower of London's Mint. Hounded by William Cecil, who was determined to make him produce something useful given the substantial investments made by the Queen, Alnetanus became so concerned for his safety that he tried to escape the crown's clutches by fleeing the country with the bankrupt Princess Cecilia of Sweden.[68] Even more public, however, were the alchemical controversies surrounding Frobisher's gold.

While much scholarly attention has been paid to this episode in the history of English navigation, the events surrounding the Frobisher's gold assays have not been investigated for what they can tell us about alchemical practice and the interactions between English and alien alchemists in Elizabethan London. The episode does indeed reveal rich information about these topics and highlights the place that alchemy could have in the English commonwealth. In addition, though alchemists lived all over London, the key players in the Frobisher assays all lived in close proximity in three adjacent areas of northeast London. Within the streets of the Bishopsgate, Aldgate, and Tower Hill were John Dee, Sir Thomas Gresham, the Muscovy Company, the Mint, the Royal Exchange, and virtually all of the alchemists involved in the controversy.

When Martin Frobisher returned from the New World with a dead Eskimo, a black rock, and some other curiosities, he had no idea of the excitement he was about to unleash. In October 1576 Frobisher gave Michael Lok, a London merchant and member of the Cathay Company, a small black stone that was discovered in present-day Baffin Bay.[69] Lok handed it to his wife, who, in a gesture of disdain for Frobisher's adventure, threw it into the fire, where it began to burn. Her curiousity stirred, Mrs. Lok retrieved the stone from the fire, washed the ashes away with vinegar, and discovered that it glittered like gold. [70]

Michael Lok was prompted by this discovery to give samples of the ore to three investors in the Frobisher voyages: Queen Elizabeth I's assay master at the mint and two members of London's powerful Goldsmith's company. When all three failed to achieve anything as encouraging as had his wife, Lok turned for assistance to a Venetian alchemist living in London, Giovanni Baptista Agnello, who may have been introduced to him through their mutual friend, John Dee.[71] Agnello was able to produce "a very little powder of gold" from the stone in early 1577. [72] Lok expressed astonishment, but Agnello assured him that his methods could be trusted because he knew "how to flatter Nature."[73] While Agnello continued to coax golden powder from the black rocks in subsequent trials, gossip began to circulate in London and the court about the mysterious substance. As the gossip swelled, so too did the reported value of the ore and the quantity thought to be available in the New World.

By the second week of January 1577, controversy erupted over the nature of Frobisher's gold. The controversy coalesced around three related issues: First, was the ore of any value? Second, who should be trusted with the heavy responsibility of assessing and then certifying the ore's value? And

Deborah E. Harkness

finally, what method or methods should be used to extract anything of value that might be embedded in the ore? Once three English goldsmiths, a housewife, and a Venetian alchemist arrived at three conflicting assessments of the ore's value, it became a matter for open speculation within the metallurgical and alchemical communities of London, and separate trials of the ore began. The queen's master of ordnance, Admiral William Winter, set his own metallurgist, a Saxon named Jonas Shutz, to work on the ore assisted by his alchemically minded friends Sir John Barklay and Sir William Morgan.[74] The queen's notoriously suspicious advisor, Francis Walsingham, alarmed at the growing involvement of powerful people in London, sent his own samples to "certayne very excellent men" who reported that there was "nothing therein, but . . . a little sylver."[75] Walsingham's experts included the courtier-poet Sir Edward Dyer, who conducted his trials under Walsingham's skeptical eye; and a French alchemist living near the Tower, Geoffrey Le Brum.

While the ore was sent to various experts, Elizabeth became convinced of its value through the promising results achieved by a collaboration of Agnello and Shutz. Working together in furnaces at William Winter's house on Tower Hill, the two men "by . . . meanes of the learning of the sayd Baptista in alchimia and the knowledge of the said Jonas in myneralls and metalls handling," repeatedly gleaned gold from the ore.[76] While Jonas contributed the practical metallurgical knowledge for which Saxony was famous, Agnello's alchemical "learning" is more difficult to characterize, but it seems to have been a deft combination of medieval notions with a sprinkling of Paracelsianism for good measure.[77]

Working with metallurgical and alchemical techniques, Agnello and Jonas convinced Elizabeth and her Privy Council of the richness of the ore and were put into partnership. Disputes soon surfaced about the rightful place of alchemical practices in the trials of the ore, but a compromise method was reached: Agnello would handle the ore before it was put in the furnaces and supervize the chemical additives that would make the melting process easier; Jonas would then complete the process of melting and refining the gold in furnaces he had invented himself.[78] With Agnello tagged as the "chemical" man, and Jonas as the "furnace" man, the two men should have been able to work together in Winter's house toward their common objective.

The compromise failed when a second alchemist, an Englishman named George Woolfe, was brought in to assist Agnello. Lok was forced to admit that Agnello, Shutz, and Woolfe had irreconcilable differences in method and approach which threatened the progress of the trials. In late November 1577, Lok wrote: "the iij workmasters cannot yet agree together, eche is jelous of [the] other" and fears "to be put out of the work." What had been productive collaboration had turned into competition, and Lok reported that the men were now "lothe to shew their conynge or to use effectuall conferens" with each other.[79]

While the disagreements raged on, other voices were raised. Urged by an unknown party to lend his experiences to the project, the queen's German physician, Dr. Burcot, "assayed and proved" that Frobisher's gold wasn't as rich as all had been led to expect. Instead of Agnello's gentle, alchemical flattery Burcot advocated a more aggressive and controlling approach to the materials in which the "roughe wyeld and forrayne" ore would "be well husbanded by a skyllfull and expert man."[80] Frobisher, smelling the first whiffs of disaster at the gap between Agnello's alchemical courtship and Burcot's metallurgical marriage, quickly threw in his lot with the queen's physician, and tried to sabotage the proceedings by spying on Jonas and Agnello.

At court, the Privy Council became concerned and sought the advice of "the goldesmithes and goldefyners of London and manye other namyd counynge menn," all of whom "had made many prooffes of the ewer and could fynde no whitt of goolde therein."[81] In response, Frobisher urged yet another collaboration — this time between Burcot and Jonas Shutz — and the controversy surrounding the ore and its parting turned into a tale of espionage and skulduggery. Throughout December 1577 and into the first months of 1578 the two Germans exchanged insults: Jonas accused Burcot of "evell manners" and of ignorance in "divers points of the works" while Burcot responded by announcing that "yf Jonas had any couninge" it surely should have yielded gold by now. The collaboration ended a few weeks later when Shutz and Burcot refused to have anything to do with each other, leaving only one line of communication between the two camps: the English goldsmith Robert Denham (d. 1605).[82] After all the controversy and contention, only Denham was able to turn the dross of the situation into a more profitable career. Denham was probably spying on both Jonas and Burcot and reporting directly to Elizabeth's Privy Council, resulting in his appointment as chief assayer on Frobisher's third voyage in the summer of 1578. Later, Denham became the director of operations in the royal mines.

As the evidence from the medical, instrumental, and alchemical practices makes clear, in the Elizabethan period natural science practitioners interested in the production of knowledge and the exchange of ideas were increasingly caught up in the international commercial environment that could be found at the Royal Exchange, where national independence was tempered by foreign contributions. The building itself reflected the blend of alien ideas and English knowledge that characterized natural science during the period much more than the local well at Bishop's Gate ever could. For the Exchange — supposedly the symbol of English economic independence — was built with English workers and European know-how and materials. The architect was Flemish; the stones came from Flanders; the windows and wainscoting came from Amsterdam; and the design was modeled after the Bourses of Antwerp and Venice. While the Exchange may have been intended to announce that England had fully arrived on the international economic stage, it also served as a reminder of the country's ongoing relationship with the Continent and the Strangers in its midst. Approaching the history of science from below helps us to focus on the complex ways in which alien ideas and English knowledge were negotiated in the neighborhoods of London and then transformed into commodities to be exchanged. In doing so, it adds a new dimension to our understanding of scientific practices and practitioners in the early modern period.

Notes

1. John Securis, *A Detection and Querimonie of the daily enormities and abuses co[m]mitted in physick, Concernyng the thre partes thereof: that is, The Physitions part, The part of the Surgeons, and the arte of Poticaries* (London, 1566), sig. Biiiiv.

2. Elizabethans called residents who came from abroad "Strangers" or "Aliens," and those who came from parts of England outside of London "Foreigners." One of the greatest resources for studying these individuals is the four-volume *Returns of Aliens Dwelling the City and Suburbs of London from the Reign of Henry VIII to that of James I*, ed. R. E. G. Kird and Ernest F. Kirk (Aberdeen: Huguenot Society of London, 1900–08).

3. St. Martin Ludgate was home to nineteen surgeons between 1558 and 1603, including two masters of the company, Thomas Bird (fl. 1577–1607) and Edward Griffin (fl. 1563–96). One physician who lived in the parish during the Elizabethan period, William Harvey, was deeply interested in anatomical studies and went on to set forth theories on the circulation of the blood.

4. Richard Forster (or Foster, ca. 1546–1616) and John Dade (fl. 1589–1614) were both physicians. Forster taught Sir Christopher Heydon astrology, and published an ephemerides dedicated to Robert Dudley, earl of Leicester, titled *Ephemerides Meteorographica* (London, 1575) which is an extremely well-designed blend of technical and narrative information. His astrological manuscripts can be found in British Library MS Sloane 1713, ff. 1–9.

5. Forty-eight people who identified themselves as gardeners lived in the parish during the period from 1558 to 1603.

6. St. Benet Paul's Wharf was a small parish on the Thames where novelty and innovation were prized. Residents included foreign-trained physician John Osborne (fl. 1577–93), physician Richard Caldwell (ca. 1505–84) who possessed a number of instruments for use in surgical practice, and John Hester (fl. 1570–93), whom Gabriel Harvey described as "the alchemist of London" in his annotations on Hester's broadsheet *These Oiles, Waters, Extractions, or Essence Salts, and other Compositions* (London, 1585?), now in the British Library.

7. Population figures for the period are extremely difficult to state with great precision, but most historians estimate that London's population grew from about seventy thousand in 1550 to two hundred thousand in 1600. In 1571, the total population of London was approximately seventy-three thousand. Most historians use the figures generated by Robert Finlay, *Population and Metropolis: The Demography of London 1580–1650* (Cambridge: Cambridge University Press, 1981). See Finlay, p. 68, for estimates of the Stranger population, and p. 53 for figures regarding the London population more broadly.

8. There is a large and growing literature on the Stranger population and its significance in Elizabethan London. See Joan Thirsk, *Economic Policy and Projects: the Development of a Consumer Society in Early Modern England* (Oxford: Clarendon Press, 1978); Steven Rappaport, *Worlds within Worlds: Structures of Life in Sixteenth-Century London* (Cambridge: Cambridge University Press, 1989); Ian Archer, *The Pursuit of Stability: Social Relations in Elizabethan London* (Cambridge: Cambridge University Press, 1991); Andrew Pettegree, *Foreign Protestant Communities in Sixteenth-Century London* (Oxford: Oxford University Press, 1986); *Huguenots in Britain and Their French Background, 1550–1800*, ed. Irene Scouloudi (Totowa, N.J. : Barnes & Noble Books, 1987); Raingard Esser, "Germans in Early Modern Britain," in *Germans in Britain since 1500*, ed. Panikos Panayi (London: Hambledon Press, 1996), 17–27; Edward Chaney and Peter Mack, eds., *England and the Continental Renaissance: Essays in Honour of J. B. Trapp* (Woodbridge, Suffolk: Boydell Press, 1990); J. Arnold Fleming, *Flemish Influence in Britain* (Glasgow: Jackson, Wylie, 1930), Vol. 1; Henri Gorain, *Les Français a Londres* (Paris: La Vague, 1933); J. Van Dorsten, *The Anglo-Dutch Renaissance: Seven Essays*, ed. J. van den Berg and Alastair Hamilton (Leiden: E. J. Brill, 1988); J. Van Dorsten, *The Radical Arts; First Decade of an Elizabethan Renaissance* (Leiden: Leiden University Press, 1970).

9. My research to date has uncovered information regarding 1450 natural science practitioners who lived in London and its immediate suburbs who were active during the period from 1556 to 1603. Because of the patchy survival of Elizabethan records (whole volumes of state papers, parish records, and court cases have not survived), no accounting of practitioners can ever hope to be complete. Still, this number is much higher in every category (such as female practitioners, medical empirics, and alchemists) than one might expect.

10. George Baker, *The composition or making of the moste excellent and pretious Oil, called Oleum Magistrale* (London, 1574), 44v.

11. Securis, *A Detection and Querimonie*, sig. Ciiiv.

12. The three surgeons consisted of two English surgeons, Robert Clarke and Richard Wistowe, and foreign-born surgeon James Markady. On 16 March 1567/68 Parke was ordered by the company to remove this flattering self-description and "to sette his signe as other Surgeons do without any Superscription." Records of the Barber Surgeons, now London Guildhall MS 5257/1, f. 52r. Hereafter, London Guildhall manuscripts will appear as GH.

13. Repertory Court of Aldermen, Corporation of London Records Office Rep. 18, f. 107v. (hereafter CLRO Rep.)

14. Parishes that were one acre or less included St. John the Evangelist, All Hallows Honey Lane, and St. Mary Mounthaw. Finlay, *Population and Metropolis*, 170.

15. There is a vast literature on London's livery companies and guilds, but Joseph Ward's *Metropolitan Communities: Trade Guilds, Identity, and Change in Early Modern London* (Stanford, Calif.: Stanford University Press, 1997) is the finest account of the efforts of these organizations to foster community within the City. See also A. L. Beier, "Engines of Manufacture: the Trades of London," in *London 1500–1700: the Making of the Metropolis* ed. A. L. Beier and Roger Finlay (London: Longman, 1986), 141–167. Studies of specific organizations relevant here include Joyce Brown, *Mathematical Instrument-Makers in the Grocers' Company, 1688–1800, with Notes on Some Earlier Makers* (London : Science Museum, 1979); Michael A. Crawforth, "Instrument Makers in the London Guilds," *Annals of Science* 44 (1987): 319–377. Harold J. Cook, "Good Advice and Little Medicine: The Professional Authority of Early Modern English Physicians," *Journal of British Studies* 33 (1994): 1–31; Raymond S. Roberts, "The London Apothecaries and Medical Practice in Tudor and Stuart England" (Ph.D. thesis, University of London, 1964).

16. The Royal College of Physicians, London has a series of unpublished manuscript volumes of its proceedings in the period, known as the *Annals*. For references to Cornet see *Annals* 1: 8a.

17. CLRO, Rep. 15, f. 156r. The Royal College of Physicians attempted in that same year to shut down his practice. *Annals* 1: 22b.

18. *Annals* 2: 7a.

19. Ibid.

20. Ibid., 2: 7b–8a

21. John Wheeler, *A Treatise of Commerce* (London, 1601), 6.

22. For Barlow's medical prescription books of 1588–90 see Bodleian Library MS Ashmole 1487. The manuscript also contains a description of his library, which contained 172 books and his original manuscripts.

23. See *Annals* 2: 6b.

24. See Ann Vellam's will proven and registered in the Archdeaconry Court of London on 14 February 1570/1, now Guildhall MS 9171/3/269. In her will Ann bequeaths a case of knives to the Barber-Surgeons Company.

25. *Annals* 1: 33a.

26. Passing mention is made of Lieven Alaertes in Margaret Pelling and Charles Webster, "Medical Practitioners," in *Health, Medicine and Mortality in the Sixteenth Century* (Cambridge: Cambridge University Press, 1979) 179 (where she appears as Lieven Allette) and in Thomas Forbes, *Chronicle from Aldgate: Life and Death in Shakespeare's London* (New Haven, Conn.: Yale University Press, 1971), 194. Margaret Pelling has done more than any other historian to uncover the importance of empirical practitioners in early modern England. In addition to numerous pathbreaking articles she is the author of *The Common Lot : Sickness, Medical Occupations, and the Urban Poor in Early Modern England* (New York: Longman, 1998) and coeditor, with Hilary Marland, of *The Task of Healing: Medicine, Religion, and Gender in England and the Netherlands, 1450–1800* (Rotterdam: Erasmus Publications, 1996), both of which are germane to the subject of this paper.

27. George Baker, *The newe Iewell of Health, wherein is contayned the most excellent Secretes of Phisicke and Philosophie, devided into fower Bookes* (London, 1576), sig. *iiiv, sig. [*ivr] and p. 187v.

28. George Baker, *Oleum Magistrale* (London, 1574), sig. Ciir.

29. John Hall's translation of Lanfrank's *A Most excellent and learned woorke of chirurgeri, called chirurgia parva Lanfranci, Lanfranke of Mylayne his briefe* . . . (London, 1565), sig. [Miiir–Miiiir].

30. For a more detailed discussion of the Lime Street community, see Deborah E. Harkness, "Living on Lime Street: The Anatomy of a Natural History Community in Elizabethan London," forthcoming. For more on L'Obel and his significance in the history of botany, see Edward Lee Greene, *Landmarks of Botanical History*, 2 vols. (Stanford, Calif.: Stanford University Press, 1983), Vol. 2: 876–937; and A. Louis, *Mathieu De L'Obel 1538–1616. Episode de l'Histoire de la Botanique* (Ghent-Louvain: Story-Scientia, 1980).

31. The spelling of Russwurin's name appears to have given Elizabethan writers an unusually hard time. He is also known Valentyne Rawnsworm and Valentine Rushworm. Evidence surrounding the Russwurin case must be pieced together from the Patent Rolls, records of the Repertory Court of Aldermen, a treatise on the chemical analysis of urine and ocular medicine by Russwurin (British Library MS Landsdowne 101/4) which is undated but which must have been written by 1587, given its references to William Cecil's mother, who died in that year, and William Clowes's *A briefe and necessarie Treatise touching the cure of the disease called Morbus Gallicus, or Lues Veneres* (London, 1585). In modern scholarship I have found only passing references to Russwurin in R. Theodore Beck, *The Cutting Edge: The Early History of the Surgeons of London* (London: Lund Humphries, 1974), and Charles Webster, "Alchemical and Paracelsian Medicine," in *Health, Medicine and Mortality in the Sixteenth Century,* ed. Charles Webster (Cambridge: Cambridge University Press, 1979), 301–334, 317. For a more detailed analysis of

this incident, see Deborah E. Harkness, "Paracelsian Therapeutics in Elizabethan London: The Case of Valentine Russwurin of Schmalkald," forthcoming.

32. British Library MS Landsdowne 101/4, f. 15v

33. Webster, p. 305, where he cites *Calendar of Patent Rolls Elizabeth* 6: 261, 25 February 1574. Russwurin was made denizen only a few weeks before he ran afoul of Mrs. Currance.

34. Clowes, *Briefe and necessarie Treatise*, 10r.

35. Ibid., 11r.

36. CLRO Rep. 18, ff. 196r–v.

37. Clowes, *Briefe and necessarie Treatise*, 11r–v.

38. CLRO Rep. 18, f. 196r–v. The doctors consulted were Peter Symons and the Italian physician Julio Borgarucci.

39. CLRO MS Rep. 18, f. 211r. The second committee was far more English in its composition: Dr. Smith of Oxford, Dr. Smith of Cambridge, Dr. Waller, Dr. Gyfford, Dr. Borgarucci, and the Portuguese physician Hector Nonez.

40. Clowes, *Briefe and necessarie Treatise*, 12r. John Hester is a fascinating Elizabethan science practitioner who is well deserving of further study. William Eamon, in *Science and the Secrets of Nature* (Princeton, N.J.: Princeton University Press, 1994) refers to Hester in relationship to his association with the Italian practitioner Fioravanti on 254–255. Allen G. Debus also refers to Hester in *English Paracelsians* (Cambridge: Cambridge University Press, 1965), 101.

41. Clowes, *Briefe and necessarie Treatise*, 12r.

42. Ibid., 12v.

43. British Library MS Landsdowne 101/4, f. 12r. Though the treatise is undated, Russwurin's claim that "from my first co[m]minge into this lande . . . there hath not escaped, as I am credibly enformed, a meale or meetinge where any of the universitye Doctores have bene present, wherin I have not been backbytten, sclaundered, and also impudently . . . belyed," is in keeping with the general tenor of the events of 1574, f. 8r.

44. British Library MS Landsdowne 101/4, f. 14r.

45. For the Paracelsian emphasis on the chemical analysis of urine, see Allen G. Debus, *The Chemical Philosophy: Paracelsian Science and Medicine in the Sixteenth and Seventeenth Centuries*, 2 vols. (New York: Science History Publications, 1977), Vol. 1: 59, 109–110. For the medical implications of tartar in Paracelsian medicine, see Vol. 1: 107.

46. The historiography surrounding the adoption of Paracelsian ideas in Elizabethan England has split between the Kocher/Debus approach (which emphasizes the "compromise" between Galenic and Paracelsian ideas that was made by medical practitioners who disagreed with Paracelsian theories while being attracted to Paracelsian therapeutics) and the approach of Charles Webster, who emphasizes the enormous range and importance of Paracelsian ideas that circulated within England during the period. I believe that the evidence presented here and included in my larger study of natural science practice in progress points more in the direction of Webster's approach. See P. H. Kocher, "Paracelsian Medicine in England: (ca. 1570–1600)," *Journal of the History of Medicine* 11 (1947): 451–480; Allen G. Debus, *The English Paracelsians* (Cambridge: Cambridge University Press, 1965); Charles Webster, "Alchemical and Paracelsian Medicine," in *Health, Medicine, and Mortality in the Sixteenth Century*, ed. Charles Webster (Cambridge: Cambridge University Press, 1979), 301–334.

47. I have been unable to find any references to the outcome of the trial. No mention of Russwurin appears in the records of the Barber-Surgeons Company, and the *Annals* of the Royal College of Physicians for that year does not survive. For a list of works published in London that discuss Paracelsian theories and therapeutics between 1574 and 1580 see Webster, "Alchemical and Paracelsian Medicine," 333, Appendix 2.

48. CLRO, Rep. 15, f. 598v.

49. William Bourne, *A Regiment for the Sea: Conteyning most profitable Rules, Mathematical experiences, and perfect knowledge of Navigation, for all Coastes and Countreys: most needefull and necessarie for all Seafaring men and Travellers, as Pilotes, Mariners, Marchants &c. Exactly devised and made by William Bourne* (London, 1574), 58. For the importance of such recommendations to the London instrument-making trade, see D. J. Bryden, "Evidence from Advertising for Mathematical Instrument Making in London, 1556–1714," *Annals of Science* 49 (1992): 301–336

50. The area from St. Dunstan in the West to St. Clement contained the highest number of instrument makers, including four Strangers (Awdrian Gaunte, Robert Grynkin, Peter Dellamare, and Lawrence Fortuna) and English practitioners Thomas Brome, James Ilsberye, Richard Blunte, Charles Whitwell, John Modye, and Bartholomew Newsam. The St. Bartholomew's neighborhood had fewer practitioners, but they were relatively well-known and influential, such as Maryan de Lander and Michael Nowen (both immigrants) and Christopher Paine and John Reade. For a brief notice of Nowen, see Brian Loomes, *The Early Clockmakers of Great Britain* (London: NAG Press, 1981), 415. For brief notices of Christopher Paine and John Reade see E. G. R. Taylor, *The Mathematical Practitioners of Tudor and Stuart England* (Cambridge: Cambridge University Press, 1954), 189–190 and 185, respectively. Taylor's monumental contribution to the history of English mathematics was one of the first works to attempt to map mathematical practitioners (including instrument makers) within London.

51. The most recent and influential studies of the importance of instrumentation in England during the Scientific Revolution are Steven Shapin and Simon Schaffer, *Leviathan and the Airpump* (Princeton, N.J.: Princeton University Press, 1989) and Steven Shapin, *A Social History of Truth: Civility and Science in Seventeenth-Century England* (Chicago: University of Chicago Press, 1995).

52. Information taken from the will of Richard Stevens in the Archdeaconry Court of London, now GH MS 9171/3/225, and the parish registers of St. Botolph Aldgate, GH MS 9221.

53. Virginia F. Stern, *Gabriel Harvey: A Study of His Life, Marginalia, and Library* (Oxford: Oxford University Press, 1979), 85, 202. Harvey's copy of Blagrave is now at the British Library, and has copious notes. The notes on Kynvin were probably made between 1585 and 1590.

54. Loomes, *Early Clockmakers*, 346.

55. Taylor, *Mathematical Practitioners*, 171–172.

56. For further information on Kynvin see Loomes, *Early Clockmakers*, 158; Taylor, *Mathematical Practitioners*, 187.

57. Leonard Digges, *A Boke Named Tectonicon, briefelye shewynge the exacte measurynge, and speady recenynge all maner Lande, squarted Tymber, Stone, Steaples, Pyllers, Globes, &c.* (London, 1556), title page.

58. See PRO State Papers Domestic, Elizabeth: 12/19/35, 12/19/46, 12/22/22, 12/22/52. *Calendar of Patent Rolls Elizabeth* 2: 153 (a 1561 pardon for Mistrell's 1558 offense of counterfeiting) and British Library Landsdowne MS 14/8 (his 1572 petition for patents on new and improved machines for stamping coin).

59. Most of the information on these practitioners must be pieced together from extremely fragmentary evidence. Nicholas Vallin and Michael Noway are the exceptions, as a few items from their workshops do survive. There are references to the Vallin and Noway families in Loomes, as well as in George White, *The Clockmakers of London* (Hants: Midas, 1998), 1–8.

60. See GH MS 4956/2, f. 84v–132r for repeated references. In addition to Nicholas Orshawe or Urseau, John Portar, John Skrewens, Bruce Awsten, John Goldar, and John Newsam all worked on the clock between 1558 and 1579.

61. See references to John De Mellayne in GH MS 6836, f. 2r–9v.

62. *Calendar of Patent Rolls Elizabeth* 1: 39.

63. Ibid. 1: 254.

64. CLRO Rep. 15, f. 502r.

65. *Calendar of Patent Rolls Elizabeth* 2: 470.

66. Ibid. 2: 98.

67. Francis Bacon, *The New Atlantis* (1627), ed. Jerry Weinberger (Arlington Heights, Ill.: Harlan Davidson, 1989), 79–90.

68. James Bell provides an account of the scandalous visit of Princess Cecilia to England, and her connections to Alnetanus in *Queen Elizabeth and a Swedish Princess: Being an Account of the Visit of Princess Cecilia of Sweden to England in 1565*, ed. Ethel Seaton (London: Hawlewood Books, 1926). The state papers surrounding the case are scattered between the PRO, the British Library, and Hatfield House. For further information on Alnetanus see Deborah E. Harkness, "Queen Elizabeth's Alchemists," forthcoming.

69. Many of the state papers pertaining to the Frobisher voyages and the assays associated with them have been reproduced in Richard Collinson, *The Three Voyages of Martin Frobisher* (London: Hakluyt Society, 1867). For ease of reference, I will give references from Collinson unless the manuscript consulted was not included in his collection. For references to the exchange of the stone, see Collinson, 91. As for the stones themselves, they appear to have been some form of hornblende pyroxenite. See Stuart K. Roy, "The History and Petrography of Frobisher's 'Gold Ore'," *Geological Series of the Field Museum of Natural History* 7 (1937): 21–38.

70. George Best, *A True Discourse* (London, 1578), 98.

71. For Agnello, see Deborah E. Harkness, *John Dee's Conversations with Angels: Cabala, Alchemy, and the End of Nature* (Cambridge: Cambridge University Press, 1999), 204; Webster, "Alchemical and Paracelsian Medicine," 307, and Harkness, "Queen Elizabeth's Alchemists." From 1547 to 1549 "J. B. Agnelli & Co." were authorized by Wriothesley and Peckham to import gold bullion for use in the royal mint (see PROE/101/303/9). For more information on this incident see C. E. Charles, *The Tudor Coinage* (Manchester: Manchester University Press, 1978), 181. Agnello's alchemical treatise *Apocalypsis spiritus secreti* (London, 1566) was later translated by R[obert] N[apier]as *A revelation of the secret spiriti of alchymie* (London, 1623).

72. Collinson, *Three Voyages*, 92.

73. Ibid., "Bisogna sapere adulare la natura."

74. Ibid., 97–98.

75. Ibid., 97.

76. Ibid., 174–175.

77. There are scattered clues to Agnello's alchemical views. Agnello gave John Dee a Venetian book on alchemy—Giovanni Pantheus's *Voarchadumia contra alchimiam*—in 1557. See Julian Roberts and Andrew Watson, *John Dee's Library Catalogue* (London: Bibliographical Society, 1990), #D16 and p. 157. Though relatively unknown today, Pantheus, who proposed that practitioners return to a true, cabalistic alchemy, was one of those "most famous" alchemists mentioned by Agricola. Dee's marginalia in the *Voarchadumia* indicates that it was instrumental in the genesis of his *Monas Hieroglyphica* (1564). See Deborah E. Harkness, *John Dee's Conversations with Angels*, 88–89. Agnello's own alchemical text, *Revelation of the Secret Spirit*, is consistent with the ideas expressed in medieval alchemical texts, but in the second part, Agnello emphasizes the importance of salts to alchemical processes. Robert Napier, who translated the text from Italian and Latin into English in the first quarter of the seventeenth century, enthused about Agnello's "practical search . . . [for] that Chrystalline . . . Salt" which was so prominent in the writings of Paracelsus.

78. Collinson, *Three Voyages*, 175

79. Ibid., 192.

80. Ibid., 194

81. Ibid., 176.

82. Ibid., 176–178, 181.

Deborah E. Harkness

Part 2

NETWORKS OF KNOWLEDGE

Commerce and the Representation of Nature

Local Herbs, Global `Medicines`

Commerce, Knowledge, and Commodities in Spanish America

ANTONIO BARRERA

On 14 September 1501, Diego de Lepe, a resident of Palos, Spain, received a royal license for trading in the New World with gold, silver, copper, mercury, and other metals, jewelry, and gems. In addition, the royal license acknowledged the possibility of valuable unknown entities by granting Lepe the right to trade in "plants and animals of any quality, fish, birds, species and drugs, and any other thing of any name and quality even if they are of a higher value than those already mentioned."[1]

This royal license assumed that there would be new entities of unknown qualities and names, with potential commercial value in the European market. If there were new entities of unknown qualities and names, how to discover their qualities and economic value? In general, how did the Spaniards study the New World entities and how did they find the qualities of these new entities? What practices did they establish for organizing and using information about the nature of the New World, and with what purpose?

Spaniards needed to learn about these things not only for commercial purposes, but for their own health and living conditions (food, construction, ornaments). Health issues were particularly important because many Spaniards who arrived in the New World soon became sick, melting in their European clothes. Many would die in the Caribbean islands, weak and sick after a long and difficult voyage.[2] They passed on their diseases to the Native Americans, who would die in massive numbers, weakening the survivors' ability to halt the new invaders.[3] In the early phases of contact, health issues might have constituted a common concern for both indigenous people as well as for Spaniards. Moreover, sometimes the medicines the Spaniards brought with them were already dated, or did not last long in the new environment.[4] It is not difficult to imagine an apothecary or a physician asking the native inhabitants of the Santo Domingo port (the main port of entrance to the New World in the early sixteenth century) for their medicines and herbs—not only to replace their own medicines but for commercial purposes. This article explores the interactions between commerce and knowledge in the production of empirical practices as well as the roles played by the Spanish state and entrepreneurs in shaping those practices through the case study of a drug found in the Hispaniola, the Santo Domingo balsam.[5]

The story of the Santo Domingo balsam belongs to the intersection between the history of European state formation, the history of science, and the history of the Atlantic encounter. As the Spanish Empire established institutions and laws in the American kingdoms and as commercial interests brought New World commodities and curiosities to Europe, empirical practices developed for taking possession of nature in the New World.[6] In the case of Spain, these empirical practices were institutionalized first at the Casa de la Contratación (f. 1503) and later at the Council of the Indies (f. 1524), as well as at the royal court, the viceregal courts in the American kingdoms, and the Royal Academy of Mathematics in Madrid (f. 1584).[7]

The history of science and the history of the New World are intimately related. The European understanding of the New World's nature passed through a rapid process of transformation after Columbus's landing.[8] It shifted from an image of paradise as described by Columbus to an overtly pragmatic image deriving from personal accounts such as that of Dr. Chanca to the city officials of Seville in 1494, or the letter of Michele de Cuneo to his friend Hieronymo Annari, both of which discussed natural resources in concrete and practical terms.[9] This shift occurred largely as a result of the material culture that shaped the European encounter with the New World. The encounter of new lands provided merchants and royal officials with untapped commercial possibilities. Europeans explored the new lands to find new routes to the East and commodities for the European market. In the process Europeans occupied and colonized the New World. The main purpose of these explorations was to find new sources of revenues for the state. During the explorations, some European notions of nature and experience were displaced from their traditional literary contexts. Classical notions did not account, for example, for the size of earth, a new continent, life in the Torrid Zone, manatees, and guayacan (a New World medicine, later used to treat syphilis).

Experience gained in exploration and in contact with other cultures increasingly displaced classical sources as the authority for knowledge. The natural products of the New World lacked referents in the classical sources. An avocado was nowhere to be found in Pliny or Aristotle, thus the empirical information about avocados—or pineapples, iguanas, mountains, rivers, or herbs—became an alternative and more reliable source of knowledge than the imperfect knowledge contained in classical sources. Thus, the traditional notion of experience, bound to Aristotelian texts, gained a new autonomy within the commercial and imperial needs of the encounter, where experience assumed a new role in validating knowledge.

The need to control faraway lands brought together royal bureaucrats, merchants, pilots, and cosmographers in an effort to produce practical knowledge that could be used to govern the new lands and profit from its resources.[10] This effort led to the development at the Casa de la Contratación of intensely scrutinized and increasingly standardized mechanisms for gathering, producing, and distributing useful knowledge about the New World.

The institutionalization of these offices and practices created a veritable Chamber of Knowledge at the Casa de la Contratación: a set of offices and professionals in charge of collecting navigational and geographical knowledge about the Indies, systematizing this knowledge, disseminating it (teaching), and making new tools with this knowledge (instruments and charts). The practices developed there reshaped the status and application of personal experience in the creation of authoritative knowledge about nature, particularly in the guise of cosmography and navigation. The use and development of navigational techniques and instruments, and the establishment of juntas of theoretical experts and practical people at the Casa de la Contratación played as important a role in those domains as it did in the realms of natural history and medicine.[11] Years later, the Council of the Indies would implement similar empirical practices also with the aim of establishing valid knowledge in natural history and medicine.

At the center of these empirical practices was the need to control human and natural resources in the New World and, in particular, to control the search for things that could bring profits in the Old World. The case of the Santo Domingo balsam shows how empirical practices emerged from entrepreneurial, imperial, and commercial contexts in sixteenth- and seventeenth-century Europe. It also illustrates how empirical practices that emerged from commercial interests influenced the development of knowledge production practices regarding resources from the New World.

TESTING NATURE

Balsam was an old and celebrated classical medicine. According to *Dioscórides*, Judea and Egypt produced balsam, but only in very small quantities; a circumstance that encouraged the selling of fake balsam. The liquor of balsam was better than its fruit or wood. The liquor "was very effective, for its very hot quality."[12] It was used to cure vision problems, to purge, to provoke menstruation and childbirth. It also helped to heal wounds, to provoke urine, and to mitigate fatigue; it was a good antidote against poison.

Balsam was almost an all-purpose medicine in this period and in high demand. However, the production of Egyptian balsam had already stopped by the early fifteenth century as the traveler Pero Tafur, to his consternation, discovered when he visited Matarea, Egypt, in the late 1430s.[13]

The garden of Matarea had been, according to legend, the place where the Virgin Mary had found water when she and her son escaped to Egypt. This water irrigated the balsam of Matarea. A well-informed humanist such as Peter Martyr (1457–1526) did not know that the production of the Matarea balsam had come to a halt until he visited this garden in 1502 and found that the fountain of water was already dry and the production of balsam had stopped.[14] When Antonio de Villasante, a resident of Santo Domingo, claimed to have found a similar product in Hispaniola and that he was willing to exploit it with royal help, the crown supported him. There was already a high demand for balsam in the international drug market, and the discovery of balsam in Hispaniola came just in time to supply this market.

The discovery of the Hispaniola balsam, however, came not only as the result of commercial demand but also as the result of an informal search for curiosities in the New World. In 1525, the humanist Peter Martyr obtained a royal decree that ordered ships' masters to bring animals and plants such as parrots, "turkeys from Tierra Firme," "other strange birds," fruits, iguanas, chilies, cinnamon, roots, blue stones, amber, or "any thing" that the officials from Hispaniola would want to send him.[15] At the same time, Charles V asked Gonzalo Fernández de Oviedo to write a natural history of the New World; Oviedo published a *Sumario de la Historia Natural* in 1526. It was in this context of interest in curiosities from the New World that Antonio de Villasante would a few years later present his report on balsam.

We know little about Antonio de Villasante. The scholar Ernst Schäfer maintains that Villasante was already a resident of Santo Domingo by 1514.[16] He received thirty-five indigenous people, Tainos, in encomienda.[17] He married Catalina de Ayahibex, a chief, or *cacica*, who had converted to Christianity. He became friend of the viceroy Don Diego Colón and later obtained a license from him to exploit balsam and other drugs on the island. Villasante then traveled to Madrid to secure a monopoly for the exploitation of this and other drugs (escormonea, rhubarb root, aturbin, polipondyo, acubebas, atiribinro, and myrrh) in the Caribbean.

Early in 1528, Villasante had obtained from the crown the right to exploit balsam on the condition that he present before the Council of the Indies "a long and very complete report about the tree to obtain the already mentioned liquor, and what its shape is and where this tree is found and what method is used to obtain the liquor; and similar [information] about other drugs."[19] The crown requested an empirical and practical report about balsam and other drugs, and a few months later Villasante complied, presenting a report on Santo Domingo balsam before the Council of the Indies.[19]

Villasante told the council that his wife, whom he described as "an Indian, *cacica*, and Christian," and her family had taught him about the properties and uses of diverse medicinal plants from the island, one of which was balsam.[20] Villasante thus established the authority of his native, female informant. Because Catalina de Ayahibex was a *cacica* and a native, she knew about the resources of her island. She may have been one of the last survivors of the island by this time.[21] Moreover, she was Christian and thus trustworthy. Villasante declared that he would state everything he knew about the plants, so the king or his officials could, eventually, find and exploit them. The issue of secrecy became irrelevant, for Villasante's purpose was to obtain a commercial monopoly over balsam. It was to his benefit to provide all the necessary information for its commercialization and sale.

After establishing the authority of his sources and information, Villasante continued with a description of balsam. He explained that he knew from experience that in Hispaniola, near Santo Domingo, there was a tree called balsam in Spanish and *boni*, *guacunax*, or *canaguey* in the native language, depending on the province. He described the tree, its height, girth, color, and leaf shape, the color and smell of the bark, type of fruit, and habitat.

The tree was three yardsticks tall, and grew around rivers and wet areas; it was about as thick as a human arm. The mature ones were bushy-topped trees; the leaf was very green and in the shape of a rhombus. He then provided the royal officials with a very schematic drawing of a leaf. The bark smelled and looked like cinnamon and tasted good, although it was a little hot and sour. The tree produced a fruit like the pepper tree, he concluded, but thicker.[22]

Villasante knew that the credibility of his report depended on the authority and knowledge of the indigenous people and on his direct access to that knowledge. And the council was by then well aware that Spaniards needed the knowledge of the indigenous people to survive and move around the New World; in this area, as in many others, indigenous people had the advantage. Villasante told the council that "the indigenous people affirm that there are many other beneficial trees and drugs in the Indies," and he promised to send reports on these as he learned about them.[23]

Villasante, however, relied not only on indigenous knowledge to support his information but also on the language of commerce. His intended audience, the Spanish bureaucracy and his commercial partners, shaped his description of balsam. The very name *balsam* that he used to translate the indigenous names *boni*, *guacunax*, or *canaguey*, was connected with an existing commercial drug. But to make his point even more explicit, Villasante compared the Santo Domingo balsam with pepper and cinnamon, two valuable spices in the international trading system at this time. The search for spices and medicines, which had begun with Columbus, continued with Villasante and with the efforts of merchants and the crown to find new drugs and spices as well as plants and animals "of any quality and name" in the New World for commercial purposes.[24]

Villasante confirmed his wife and her family's knowledge and the commercial possibilities of the balsam by performing tests with it—what he called *"esperiencias."* After describing the tree, Villasante provided the method he used for preparing balsam brew. Villasante cut the branches with a knife and took off the leaves and seeds with his hand; using his hands, he shredded the pruned branches together with bark from the trunk; he pounded this mixture with rocks; and finally he chopped it into pieces with a knife. He then warmed the mixture in a clay pot with water. Once the mixture had soaked awhile, he took it out of the clay pot and squeezed it to obtain a liquor. Villasante finally heated the liquor in a small pot, which was inside a bigger one full of ashes, until it was reduced to a thick liquor.[25] Sometimes he would put the liquor to dry under the sun with the same results. He also mentioned that he once had cut the trunk of the tree with a knife and that a "liquor" came out. This sap, "as it was coming out, hardened like gum," he said, "and of this hardened [substance] I did not make any other test or experience."[26]

According to Villasante's "experiences" in the New World, in Seville, and at the court, balsam was effective for healing wounds in a short time. It was also useful for healing all types of abrasions, and for relieving stomach pain. Balsam was therapeutic for the liver and gallbladder, for treating gout, and, finally, for relieving toothache. Villasante expected that the knowledge about his balsam would increase, accumulate, and become more perfect with time and new tests since, as he himself reported:

> This [balsam], by experience, shows already that it is beneficial for the diseases that I have mentioned. With time it may be shown by experience or reports from physicians whether it might be beneficial for other things, and they could also reveal the method for the perfection of this liquor and balsam.[27]

Villasante assumed that knowledge about balsam was cumulative and would be based on the experience of physicians. This was a common tendency in the production of knowledge related to the New World, and echoed the model used at the Casa de la Contratación. Only through the accumulation of information and the correction of previous information through new empirical information could physicians, cosmographers, and natural historians complete their study and understanding of the New World.

Villasante called on his own experience in the preparation and uses of balsam to, first, mediate the transfer of knowledge from the indigenous people to the Spaniards, and, second, validate his commercial interests. Villasante based his knowledge about balsam upon the expertise of Catalina de Ayahibex and, more important, upon his own tests with balsam in the New World as well as in the Old World. Note Villasante's method of presentation here. He did not place balsam within the Galenic framework, for instance, as the physician Garciperez Morales would do a few years later:

> Of this precious liquor, commonly called balsam, which is brought from Santo Domingo of the Indies: its first virtue is hot in the second grade, or a little less; dry in the first metha of the third [grade], or a little more.[28]

Garciperez Morales would write his treatise at the request of the crown in 1530. His audience consisted of royal physicians at the court and regular physicians in Spain, such as his student Nicolás Monardes, who would become well-known for his research on American plants.[29] Morales framed his treatise in classical and traditional terms familiar to him and to his audience. Villasante, by contrast, framed his account in empirical terms for his audience of Council of the Indies members and his commercial partners. The difference in audiences, with their diverse interests and backgrounds, explains the difference between Villasante's and Morales's approach to the Santo Domingo balsam, a difference not unlike that between the practical pilots and learned cosmographers at the Casa de la Contratación. In addition, Villasante had firsthand experience of the New World and knowledge provided by indigenous people while Morales had neither this experience nor this knowledge.

Villasante's empirical approach to nature was not new to the Spaniards in the New World. Since the mid-fifteenth century, both nominalists and humanists had emphasized the collection of empirical evidence to solve internal problems in their textual sources. What was new to Villasante and the Spaniards in the Indies was the intense use of empirical evidence in describing the things they encountered, the elaboration of their reports outside the traditional frameworks of knowledge, and the institutional role played by the Spanish monarchy in this not yet formalized project of research. The relevant framework here was the exploitation of commodities for the European market.

The interest of the crown in the commercialization of balsam, for instance, shaped its decision regarding not only the production of balsam, but also the validation of empirical knowledge about balsam. For the production of balsam, the crown granted Villasante, his heirs, and whomever else he deemed appropriate a complete monopoly on the Santo Domingo balsam as well as on the other drugs he would find in the New World.[30] Villasante also obtained, in perpetuity for himself and his heirs, the alcaldía of the fortress of Santo Domingo, Indian labor, tax exemptions, and other prerogatives.[31] The exploitation of balsam seemed to be ready. Other experts in the field, however, soon challenged Villasante's report.

TESTING EXPERIENCE

In 1529 a competing report about balsam came to Spain from the Hispaniola physician Licenciado Barreda, challenging Villasante's report. Barreda, who has been the Inquisition's physician, left Spain for Hispaniola with Pedrarias Dávila's expedition to Panama (1513–14).[32] In December 1513, the crown had ordered the Casa de la Contratación to pay 12,000 maravedis to Barreda for his travel expenses.[33] In Hispaniola, he held the title of royal physician for some time until 1519, when the crown suspended his title.[34] In 1526, Barreda was appointed official physician of Santo Domingo.[35] By the time Barreda wrote his report on the so-called balsam of Santo Domingo in 1528, he had been in the New World almost fifteen years.

In his report, Barreda argued that the crown had been deceived by the physicians who "approved as balsam the liquor that the aforementioned Villasante" took with him to Spain.[36] Barreda claimed that the royal support for this drug, "approved" as balsam by physicians in Spain, would harm the person and property of the crown's subjects. He criticized the fact that the physicians in Spain did not discuss the matter of the balsam with their colleagues in Santo Domingo:

> [Spain's physicians] know or should know that they [Santo Domingo's physicians] do not lack letters, nor extensive experience, nor knowledge of the tree, its fruit and leaves and the methods to apply the aforementioned liquor that comes from this tree.[37]

For Barreda the lack of interest on the part of the Spanish physicians in sharing their opinions and in consulting their learned and experienced counterparts in the New World were an offense and a great mistake, which led the crown into a dangerous deception. He emphasized the possible financial and health consequences of using a fake balsam for the kingdom. Barreda's report helps to uncover the link between knowledge and political and economic power in sixteenth-century Spanish America. Knowledge pertaining to the New World, claimed Barreda, had to be articulated by those with direct experience of the New World. Physicians in the Old World, despite their "letters," did not have this experience. For this reason, they needed to consult with their counterparts in the New World. Otherwise political and economic decisions regarding the New World could harm the subjects of the king. In the interest of the common good, personal experience was a better source of knowledge than "letters" alone. The crown and its institutions, the Council of the Indies and the Casa de la Contratación, adhered to and supported this view. The issues at stake concerned who would control the production of knowledge — the crown in collaboration with entrepreneurs such as Villasante, or physicians such as Barreda?

Once Barreda had established his authority based on his expertise and personal experience, he moved into the description and uses of Villasante's liquor and compared it to balsam. Villasante had applied the same empirical model to his own account of the balsam, but he did not compare his liquor with the original, Old World balsam; he assumed that they were similar. Personal experience is always fragmented and based on the personal background of the informer or informers. How could these two accounts, both based on experience, be reconciled? Which one was more reliable?

Both Villasante and Barreda argued that their respective accounts were true because each one was based on personal experience and experimentation. What mechanism could be established to determine the truth of the matter? In the case of the pilots and cosmographers, the crown established the mechanism of juntas to determine the truth of different accounts by consensus. In these juntas the experience of pilots together with the formal knowledge of cosmographers came together to produce new knowledge about the New World.[38]

The crown established a similar solution in the case of the New World balsam — perhaps taking a hint from Villasante's suggestion that "with time it may be shown by experience or reports from physicians whether it might be beneficial for other things." The crown, after learning of Licenciado Barreda's account and other similar accounts, requested that different Spanish physicians and hospitals carry on experiments with the balsam. Barreda had provided a convincing case for his own account. He noted the differences between classical balsam and the "liquor that Villasante" took to Spain:

> [The] main virtue of this liquor is to restrain the blood in fresh wounds by pressing it over them, and [to restrain] the flow of blood from below [rectum], this virtue, either called opilativa . . . or constritiva . . . , in what books does it appear that balsam has this virtue?[39]

Certainly classical texts on medicine such as Dioscórides's *Materia medica* did not list this virtue among those attributed to balsam.[40] Barreda also compared the trees and the different methods to obtain the liquor from each type of tree before concluding that Villasante's liquor was not the authentic balsam. By the mid-sixteenth century, such scholars as Gonzalo Fernández de Oviedo, Andrés Laguna, Nicolás Monardes, Pedrarias de Benavides, and Conrad Gessner would agree with him.[41] Nevertheless, Barreda found that this "liquor has other virtues experimented by me [*por mi spimentadas*]."[42] He found that the Santo Domingo balsam was efficient for healing rheum, and kidney and stomach "passion."[43]

Dr. Barreda was not alone in his criticisms. In 1530, the crown claimed that there were already "some physicians, surgeons and other people who, without complete information on the balsam recently discovered in our Hispaniola and without yet having made any experience with it, have published and continue to publish some publications (*ynpreciones*)"[44] against it. Moreover, people had decided not to buy the new balsam because of these publications, which "harms the health of the sick and wounded, and our royal treasury."[45] Such publications indicated that criticism had merit, but the battle for true knowledge about the balsam had just begun.

The crown sought to control and discipline this group of dissident physicians by ordering that

> physicians, and surgeons of any city, town and place of our kingdoms and possessions should have unequivocal information [*cierta noticia*] about this balsam before they talk or publish works, and when, by experience or by other method, they find out that it is harmful for wounds or any other illness, they should declare and reveal it to our local magistrates.[46]

Meanwhile, local magistrates should try to foster the sale of balsam "in the best way they see fit."[47] The crown sought to control dissident physicians by ordering them to speak or publish only after they had made experiments with the balsam, for which they had to buy it. Furthermore, they had to bring their experimental findings before local magistrates, who would send them to the crown. By asking physicians to experiment with balsam and then to show their reports to royal officials, the crown controlled the production of knowledge about the balsam. This situation shows the interplay between the production of new medical knowledge and the political and economic interests of the crown in controlling this knowledge and its products. In this particular case, controlling knowledge about balsam amounted to controlling the possibility of its commercialization.

With the 1530 decree to royal officials, the crown established a protocol for the articulation of empirical information about Santo Domingo balsam, namely, experimentation with samples and the recording of findings. Again, this model resembles that of the Casa de la Contratación case in which cosmographers and pilots appointed by the crown organized empirical information about navigation and geography provided by pilots. In the interplay between the interests of the crown and the interest of individual subjects there arose a scientific practice based on empirical experimentation (*"experiencias"*) and the collective articulation of the resulting information.

The crown, however, not only attempted to discipline dissident physicians into experimenting with the balsam; it also ordered particular physicians, surgeons, and hospitals to carry out experiments with the New World balsam. The crown had listened to the dissidents and sought to produce accurate knowledge about the balsam. Following its own protocol, the crown sent samples of balsam to physicians and hospitals for experimentation. In one case, the crown sent a sample of balsam, useful to "cure injuries and many illnesses," to the hospital of the cardinal in Toledo for use on patients chosen by the physicians and surgeons of the hospital. The crown requested the hospital administrators "to be attentive to inform us of the cures and experiences realized in the hospital with this balsam."[48] Hospitals in Seville, Burgos, Galicia, and Granada received similar orders.[49]

Furthermore, the crown brought particular physicians into the project for testing the Santo Domingo balsam. The physician Andrés de Jodar, for instance, a resident of Baeza, received the order to use balsam for those "cures and experiences" that he would deem appropriate.[50] Moreover, whatever he found, by means of "art" and experience, "certain and true," he should "put in writing," "sign" his report, and send it to Villasante's partners in Spain. Twenty-two physicians and surgeons in different cities of Spain received similar orders.[51] Villasante's partners, Franco Leardo and Pedro Benito de Basniana, would use these reports for the commercialization of balsam in Spain. They hired some physicians and surgeons to help them in the commercialization of balsam.[52]

By 1532, information was already arriving to the court. A certain Juan de Vargas had been using the "balsam from the Indies" to heal the sick.[53] He seemed to have been quite successful, for the crown ordered the officials of Cuellar to collect information from patients who had been healed with Santo Domingo balsam. The scribe of Cuellar, Melchor de Angulo, received the information and sent it to the crown. He received 108 reals for the eighteen days he worked on this assignment.[54] The crown also requested Juan de Vargas to come to the court, which he did in late 1532 or early 1533.[55] During his stay there, he tested the balsam and was paid for his work.[56] Still some medical practitioners opposed the use of this balsam and maintained it was fake. In 1539, the physician and apothecary of the village of Amusco denounced Vargas for using the New World balsam. The authorities of Amusco arrested him and took his balsam. He was later released; the crown asked the authorities of Amusco to explain the matter.[57]

In the end, the crown could not dismiss Barreda's contention that the Hispaniola balsam was not authentic. However, the only thing that mattered to the crown was the fact that this balsam was especially good, as both Villasante and Barreda had argued, at treating wounds. The crown sought, first, to develop the right method to use it; second, to end the confusion between New World balsam and classical balsam; and, finally, to convince other physicians that it was a worthy medicine. The dissident group of physicians in Santo Domingo and Spain were controlled and disciplined by requesting them to experiment with the balsam and to send their results to royal officials — they could not publish or discuss their findings without royal approval. Simultaneously the crown and Villasante's partners hired a group of physicians to legitimize the use of balsam in their practice. The name balsam, given by Villasante, was a propagandistic device to sell this new drug. The physician Monardes, years later, commented that the liquor "received that name because it produces great effects and cures many illnesses,"[58] as had the classical, Old World balsam.

The economic possibilities of balsam shaped the research on it. This research was characterized by, first, empirical observation, that is, knowledge about products of the New World came from "experiences"; second, professionals and experts collectively articulated this knowledge; and, finally, the crown arbitrated the outcome of disputes about knowledge in light of its economic and political goals. In its role as knowledge broker, the crown established a protocol for research, which fostered economic and commercial interests. From these interests emerged the empirical practices that characterized the long-distance control of the New World. The balsam episode helps to understand the significant emphasis placed on empirical approaches to natural products of the New World, approaches that resulted from the commercial and imperial activities of Europeans outside Europe.

The encounter with the New World slowly displaced European notions of nature and experience, which had been closely tied to textual practices.[59] Physicians such as Barreda and entrepreneurs such as Villasante as well as cosmographers and pilots at the Casa de la Contratación, natural historians, and explorers reexamined those notions to accommodate the increasing flow of new knowledge circulating between Spain and America. Certainly, initial information about new drugs came from books, but it was the testing of new drugs, for instance, that provided final knowledge about them. European notions about nature were adapted thus to incorporate discrete local settings, soon to become gardens of knowledge, into an emerging global framework of communication and trade.[60]

Simultaneously, local natural settings were adapted to fit European objectives and strategies with regard to trade and the exploitation of natural resources. Contact with the New World accelerated this process of transforming and exploiting nature. In this emerging global context, nature was largely secularized and approached in empirical terms. Nature became a con-

Antonio Barrera

tingent reality adaptable to human plans and needs and a collection of commodities, such as balsam, or curiosities ready for exploitation or collection.

From about 1500s through the 1560s, this secular or practical approach to the natural world fostered informal, nonsystematic empirical research into the natural products indigenous to the New World. During the sixteenth century nature was described and studied increasingly through empirical terms as more groups joined this collaborative enterprise. The balsam episode illustrates this development. By the late sixtenth century there was already an international network of scholars, including such well-known figures as Carolus Clusius and Antonio Recchi, studying American nature through Spanish gardens, books, and collections.[61] Nature's commodities were tested at the courts, hospitals, and gardens; nature's curiosities were collected, studied, and described. These empirical practices would first become practical knowledge at the Casa de la Contratación and at the Council of the Indies before becoming institutionalized as science in the form of natural history, cosmography, geography, and choreography.

The balsam case constitutes just one episode in the establishment and institutionalization of empirical practices for controlling natural resources in the New World. As the Spanish crown faced particular problems about understanding and exploiting new products, it sought to create systematic methods for the production of knowledge about the New World. As the American enterprise developed, and as more groups became involved in it, empirical information became increasingly more relevant and significant in the production of knowledge. But one report, even if it is based on direct personal experience, does not constitute knowledge. Consequently, the crown sought to establish conditions for the production of several reports based on testing and experimentation. The balsam case illustrates this method. The first notice comes from Antonio de Villasante, who learned about this medicine from the Tainos, in particular, from his native wife. Soon, competing reports challenged Villasante's characterization of this medicine as balsam, and the crown sent samples of the balsam to several hospitals and almost two dozen physicians in Spain for testing the medicine on patients. Whether or not this medicine was placed in a Galenic theoretical framework, the issue at stake remained an empirical one: the practical uses of the medicine, which could be found only through experience, as was the case with the navigation to and mapping of the New World, the exploitation of other resources, and the control of its human resources. The development of empirical practices are at the center of the American enterprise; they made possible the conquest and commercialization of the new resources. Such practices are also at the center of the modern world.

I would like to thank the staff at the Archivo General de Indias (Seville, Spain) for their help locating some of the material for this article, in particular, Pilar Lázaro de la Escosura and Socorro Prous Zaragoza; my advisor, Paula Findlen, for her intellectual and personal support during my research; and Pamela Smith for her advice and comments.

1. Cédula Real a Diego de Lepe on 14 September 1501, Archivo General de Indias, Indiferente, 418, L. 1, ff. 29v–32v. From now on I refer to the Archivo General de Indias as AGI.

2. Columbus was particularly concerned with this problem. In his second voyage many of his people arrived sick or became sick afterward, and there were not enough medicines for them. See the so-called Torres Memorandum of 30 January 1494 in *Cristobal Colón: Los cuatro viajes, testamento,* ed. Consuelo Varela (Madrid: Alianza Editorial, 1986), 209, 211. The expedition of fray Nicolás de Ovando, who was appointed governor of the Indies in 1501, was well provided with medicines and some medical instruments. See the list of medicines in Angel Ortega, *La Rábida. Historia documental crítica* (Seville: Impresora y editorial de San Antonio, 1925), 315. From Santo Domingo, however, Ovando asked the crown to send more medicines and apothecaries, a request that was granted. See Cédula Real a Fray Nicolás de Ovando, 11 November 1505, Salamanca. AGI, Indiferente, 418, L. 1, ff. 185v–186r. On occasion the crown sent orders to treat those arriving in the Indies. Thus, in 1544, the crown ordered the officials of Hispaniola to cure the friars arriving on the island because they would probably arrive sick. See Cédula Real a los oficiales de la Española, 23 February 1544. Valladolid. AGI, Santo Domingo, 868, L. 2, f. 208v. There was a name for a particular sickness that the Europeans suffered as they arrived in the Indies: *chapetonada.* According to the surgeon Pedro Arias de Benavides, those who survived it would live for many years. See Arias de Benavides, *Secretos de Chirurgia, especial de las enfermedades de Morbo galico y Lamparones y Mirrarchia, y assi mismo la manera como se curan los Indios de llagas y heridas y otras passiones en las Indias, muy util y provechoso para en España y otros muchos secretos de chirurgia hasta agora no escriptos* (Valladolid: Impresor Francisco Fernández de Carbona, 1567).

3. On the role played by disease in the conquest of the New World see Alfred Crosby, *The Columbian Exchange: Biological and Cultural Consequences of 1492* (Westport, Conn.: Greenwood Press, 1972); and Noble David Cook, *Born to Die: Disease and New World Conquest, 1492–1650* (Cambridge: Cambridge University Press, 1998). Cook also discusses the consequences of diseases for Europeans as they arrived in the New World, or soon afterwards. See *Born to Die,* 29ff.

4. In 1538, the crown was informed that many of the medicines taken to the New World arrived, or became, "corrupted" there. The crown ordered its officials in Tierra Firme to check the medicines and destroy those that were decayed. See Cédula Real a los oidores de Tierra Firme. 16 April 1538. Valladolid. AGI, Panamá, 235, L. 6, ff. 195v–196r.

5. When I began my research on the Hispaniola balsam in 1996 there were very few references to it in the secondary literature, and only an article on Antonio de Villasante by Ernesto Schäfer, "Antonio de Villasante, descubridor droguista en la isla Española," *Investigación y Progreso* 9, no. 1 (1935): 13–15. In 1996, I presented a paper at the Escuela Libre de Investigadores (Seville, Spain), and, with few changes, at the Consejo Superior de Investigaciones Científicas (Seville, Spain) which discussed the balsam case and its commercialization. Later Esteban Mira-Caballos published an article that discusses the Hispaniola balsam. See his article "La medicina indígena en la Española y su comercialización (1492–1550)," *Asclepio* 44 (1997): 185–198.

6. On this subject see Antonello Gerbi, *Nature in the New World* (Pittsburgh: University of Pittsburgh Press, 1985), and Raquel Alvarez-Peláez, *La Conquista de la Naturaleza Americana* (Madrid: Consejo Superior de Investigaciones Científias, 1993).

7. For the establishment of the Casa de la Contratación see the royal decree of 14 February 1503, AGI, Contratación, 5784, l.1, ff. IV–2. See also Antonio de Herrera, *Historia General de los Hechos de los Castellanos en las Islas i Tierra Firme del Mar Oceano. Escrita por Antonio de Herrera Coronista (sic) Major de Su Magestad de las Indias y su Coronisata de Castilla*, ([Madrid: Imprenta Real, 1601–15]; Madrid, 1730), década I, p. 144; Joseph de Veitía Linage, *Norte de la Contratación de las Indias Occidentales* ([Seville, 1672], Buenos Aires: Publicaciones de la Comisión Argentina de Fomento Interamericano, 1945), 4–5; José Pulido-Rubio, *El Piloto Mayor de la Casa de la Contratación de Sevilla: Pilotos Mayores, Catedráticos de Cosmografía y Cosmógrafo* (Seville, 1950); David C. Goodman, *Power and Penury* (Cambridge: Cambridge University Press, 1988), pp. 74ff.; J. H. Parry, *The Spanish Seaborne Empire* (Berkeley and Los Angeles: University of California Press, 1990), 54f.; and Clarence Henry Haring, *Trade and Navigation between Spain and the Indies* (Cambridge, Mass.: Harvard University Press, 1918), chap. 2. The Casa de la Contratación awaits its modern historian. On the establishment of the Council of the Indies see Ernesto Schäfer, *El Consejo Real y Supremo de las Indias*, 2 vols. (Seville: M. Carmona, 1935) as well as his article, "El Origen del Consejo de Indias," *Investigación y Progreso* 7 (5 May 1933): 141–145. For an overview of the scientific activities of the Casa de la Contratación, the Council of the Indies, and the Royal Academy of Mathematics, see Ursula Lamb, "Cosmographers of Seville: Nautical Science and Social Experience," in *First Images of America: The Impact of the New World on the Old*, ed. Fredi Chiappelli (Berkeley and Los Angeles: University of California Press, 1976), vol. 2: 675–686.

8. See Columbus's development through his diaries in J. Cecil, *The Four Voyages of Cloumbus*, 2 vols. (New York: Dover, 1988). See also Valerie I. J. Flint, *The Imaginative Landscape of Christopher Columbus* (Princeton, N.J.: Princeton University Press, 1992); Stephen Greenblatt, *Marvelous Possessions* (Chicago: University of Chicago Press, 1991); and Gerbi, *Nature*.

9. See the letter of Dr. Chanca (1494) in Martín Fernández de Navarrete, *Colección de los viages y descubrimientos que hicieron por mar los Españoles desde fines del siglo XV con varios documentos inéditos concernientes a la historia de la Marina Castellana y de los Establecimientos Españoles en Indias* (Buenos Aires: Editorial Guarania, 1945); and the letter of Michele Cuneo (1495) in Samuel Eliot Morison, *Journals and Other Documents on the Life and Voyages of Christopher Columbus* (New York: Printed for the members of the Limited Editions Club, 1963), 209ff.

10. On this topic see John Law, "On the Methods of Long-distance Control: Vessels, Navigation, and the Portuguese Route to India," *Sociological Review Monograph* 32 (1986): 234–263; Steven J. Harris, "Confession-Building, Long-Distance Networks, and the Organization of Jesuit Science," *Early Science and Medicine* 1 (1996): 287–318 as well as his article "Long-distance Corporations, Big Science, and the Geography of Knowledge," *Configurations* 6 (1998): 269–304.

11. The name "Chamber of Knowledge" is my own characterization of the scientific aspects of the Casa de la Contratación. By Chamber of Knowledge I mean the offices and practices developed and institutionalized within the *Casa* for collecting and disseminating information about the New World, for training lay people (pilots) in the new navigational techniques, and for hiring professionals (cosmographers and pilots) for research and teaching activities. Haring calls it a "Hydrographic Bureau and School of Navigation, the earliest and most important in the history of modern Europe" (*Trade and Navigation*, 35).

12. Andrés Laguna, *Pedacio Dioscórides Anazarbeo, acerca de la materia medicinal, y de los venenos mortíferos. Traduzido de la lengua Griega en la vulgar Castellana, e illustrado con claras y substanciales Annotaciones, y con las figuras de unnúmeras plantas exquisitas y raras por el doctor . . . , Médico de Julio III, Pontífece Máximo* (Anvers, 1555), ff. 26ff. On the importance of balsam for sixteenth-century naturalists, see Paula Findlen, *Possessing Nature: Museums, Collecting, and Scientific Culture in Early Modern Italy* (Berkeley and Los Angeles: University of California Press, 1994), 270ff.

13. Pero Tafur, *Andanças e viajes de Pero Tafur por diversas partes del mundo avidos (1435-1439)* (Madrid, 1874), 85–86.

14. Ibid., 575 n.: *bálsamo*

15. Cédula Real del Rey don Carlos. January 29, 1525. Madrid. AGI, Contratación, 5787, N. 1, L. 1. ff. 33–34v.

16. Ernesto Schäfer, "Antonio de Villasante," 13. Villasante's name appears in a document signed in Santo Domingo in February 1515. In this document, Villasante was proposed as a witness (together with other residents) to answer questions about Rodrigo de Albuquerque's activities on the island in 1514. AGI. Justicia 1003, transcribed in Luis Arranz-Márquez, *Repartimiento y Encomiendas en la Isla Española (El Repartimiento de Albuquerque de 1514)*, (Santo Domingo: Ediciones Fundación García Arévalo, 1991).

17. Arranz-Márquez, *Repartimiento*, 560. On the Tainos, see Irving Rouse, *The Tainos: Rise and Decline of the People Who Greeted Columbus* (New Haven, Conn., Yale University Press, 1992). Cook suggests that the Taino population around 1492 might have been half a million, by 1518–19 the numbers had fallen to around eighteen thousand and by 1542 the native population was less than two thousand. Villasante's information came from a group that was disappearing from the earth. See Cook, *Born to Die*, 23–24.

18. Provisión Real proponiendo un asiento con Antonio de Villasante sujeta a la presentación de un reporte de Villasante sobre el bálsamo y otras drogas. 4 April 1528. Madrid. AGI, Indiferente, 421, L. 13, ff. 85r–86v.

19. Fernández de Oviedo comments that this balsam is not the real balsam but something different that Villasante called balsam. Oviedo also says that Villasante either learned the secret of balsam from his *cacica* wife or from an Italian physician who went to the Indies in 1515 and died there. See Gonzalo Fernández de Oviedo y Valdés, *Historia General y Natural de las Indias*, 5 vols. (Madrid: Biblioteca de Autores Españoles, 1959), vol. 2: 11.

20. Relación de Antonio de Villasante, n/d, but it was probably presented in mid-1528. AGI, Indiferente, 857. On 4 April 1528 the king ordered Villasante to present a report before the council. By 14 June 1528 he had already submitted his report, see Indiferente, 421, L. 13, ff. 213v–214r. Ernst Schäfer thinks that this document dates from around 1526, for, according to him, Villasante was in Spain in 1525, see Ernst Schäfer, "Antonio de Villasante," 14. Perhaps Villasante was in Spain in 1525 or 1526 and at that time sought support for his project. The call number given by Schäfer for this Villasante's report, Indiferente, 856, is a mistake; it is Indiferente, 857; see also a document in *Colección de documentos inéditos relativos al descubrimiento, conquista y colonización de las posesiones españolas en América y Oceanía,* (Liechtenstein: Kraus Reprint, 1966), series 2, 14: 31.

21. See note 17.

22. Villasante, Indiferente, 857.

23. Ibid.

24. The Spaniards also took spices and medicines for agricultural and commercial purposes to the New World. Thus, Don Francisco de Mendoza, son of the first Mexican viceroy, signed in 1558 two capitulations with the princess Doña Juana (approved by Philip II in 1559) to cultivate ginger, sandalwood and pepper, cinnamon, and clover. See María Justina Sarabia-Viejo, *Don Luis de Velasco, virrey de Nueva España (1550–1564)* (Seville: Escuela de Estudios Hispano-Americanos, 1978), 403–405. The Council of the Indies considered this project unfeasible. See Consulta del Consejo. 21 March 1559. Valladolid. AGI, Indiferente, 738, N. 47.

25. Villasante, Indiferente, 857: "La maña que hasta agora yo he tenydo en el sacar del licor con otros cosas de estos arvoles asy lo? que con un cuchillo cortados los rramos destos arboles con su hoja y grano y con la mano arrancaba los granos y tambien la hojarada cosa por sy y tomaba los rramos asy mondos y tambien tomaba de la corteza de lo grueso del arvol hacia el tronco y lo desmenuzava y ... taba? y lo majava encima de unas piedras o losas con otras piedras

o madero despues de picado con cuchillo y asy majado lo ponya en unas vasijas de barro de? m . . . ? de barreno?nes? o labrillos? y . . . ? calentaba en un caldero con una cantidad de agua competente y la echava en el dicho barreno? y desde a un poce despues de enpapado y enbevido en el agua lo apretavba en un tornyllo de madera y sacaba dello todo el çumo y . . . d? que tenyz y lo colava y colado lo ponya en un caldero pequeno y despues tomaba otro caldero grande lleno de ceniza hasta la mytad del . . . ?/ y dentro de aquel caldero de ceniza ponya y asentaba el otro caldero pequeño con el dicho licor del balsamo colado y ponya fuego debajo del caldero de la ceniza de maña que el calor dela ceniza consumyese el agua que estaba en dicho licor hasta tanto que se espesava y tornaba del color y maña que yo ho he tenydo y entregado a su mag/ . . . ".

26. Villasante, Indiferente, 857.

27. Ibid.: explained that balsam was "en la verdad provechoso asi en las Indias donde lo experimente muchas veces como algunas en estos reinos en sevilla y en la corte y pues para estas enfermedades que he dicho ha parecido por experiencia ser provechoso adelante podra parecer por experiencias o por relacion de los medicos si aprovechara a otras cosas y tambien ellos diran la forma que se podra tener para mas perfeccion del dicho licor y balsamo y otras cosas del dicho arbol."

28. Garciperez Morales, *Tratado del Bálsamo y de sus utilidades para las enfermedades del cuerpo humano. Compuesto por el Doctor . . . catedrático de prima en el colegio de Sancta Maria de Jesus de la ciudad de Sevilla. Dirigido al yllustrissimo señor don Pedro Giron Duque y Conde de Ureña* (Seville, 1530), ff. 2r.

29. Nicolás Monardes was a physician and entrepreneur very interested in the natural resources of the New World. His father, Niculoso de Monardis was a Genovese bookseller established in Seville. It is unclear when Nicolás Monardes was born; he died in 1589. Monardes obtained his B.A. in art and philosophy in 1530 and a B.A. in medicine at the Universidad Complutense in 1533. In 1547 he obtained the *licenciatura* and doctor's degree from the Colegio-Universidad de Santa María de Jesús de Sevilla. Monardes's medical practice in Seville was very successful. He worked with the doctor Garciperez Morales and, in 1537, Monardes became Morales's son-in-law when he married Morales's daughter Catalina. Monardes was also very successful in his commercial activity in the Indies. He obtained many plants and herbs for his medical practice and his garden through his commercial contacts in the Indies. See Juan Jiménez-Castellanos y Calvo-Rubio, prologue to *Historia medicinal de las cosas que se traen de nuestras Indias Occidentales que sirven en medicina . . . por Nicolás Monardes* (Seville: Padilla Libros, 1988), v to xi. See also Nicolás Monardes, *[Primera y Segunda y Tercera partes de la] Historia Medicinal de las cosas que se traen de nuestras Indias Occidentales que sirven en Medicina* ([Facsimile edition, 1574] Seville: Padilla Libros, 1988); for a discussion of Monardes's work see José M. López Piñero, "Las 'Nuevas Medicinas' Americanas en la Obra (1565–1574) de Nicolás Monardes," *Asclepio* 42, no. 1 (1990): 3–67. The work of Monardes was translated into English (Nicolás Monardes, *Ioyfull Newes Out of the Newe Founde Worlde* [London, 1577]) as well into French, Latin, and Italian.

30. Provisión Real a Antonio de Villasante. 20 April 1528. AGI, Indiferente, 421, L. 13, ff. 110r–111r.

31. Ibid. 22 April 1528. AGI, Indiferente, 421, L. 13, ff. 111r–112r; Real Provisión a Antonio de Villasante. 14 June 1528. AGI, Indiferente, 421, L. 13, ff. 213v–214r.

32. Cédula Real a los oficiales de la Casa de la Contratación. 16 December 1513. Madrid. AGI, Panamá, 233, L. 1, f. 126r.

33. Ibid.

34. Cédula Real al licenciado Rodrigo Figueroa, juez de residencia de la isla Española. 26 July 1519. Barcelona. AGI, Indiferente, 420, L. 8, f. 97v.

35. Cédula Real a los oficiales de la Española. 14 September 1526. Granada. AGI, Indiferente, 421, L. 11, ff. 202v–203r.

36. Carta del licenciado Barreda al rey Carlos V. 26 October 1528. Santo Domingo de la Española. AGI, Patronato, 174, R. 43.

37. Carta de Barreda, AGI, Patronato, 174

38. See Alison Sandman's contribution to this volume, "Mirroring the World: Sea Charts, Navigation, and Territorial Claims in Sixteenth-Century Spain"; and Ursula Lamb's fascinating articles, "Science by Litigation: A Cosmographic Feud," *Terrae Incognitae* 1 (1969): 40–57, and "The Spanish Cosmographic Juntas of the Sixteenth Century," *Terrae Incognitae* 6 (1974): 51–64.

39. Carta de Barreda, AGI, Patronato, 174: "la virtud mas principal que se halla en el dicho licor/ es restreñir la sangre en las llagas frescas sobre ellas aplicado/ y dado por la boca el fluxo de sangre por abaxo/ dest avirtud agora se opilativa que sua viscositate aut g?oficie inplendo venari orificia rectineat sanguyneus/ agora sea constrictiva que sua frigiditate /r? stiticitate? constringat venas. digo que entanta manera aprieta que puesto sin ligadura parece el miembro estar atado// pues donde se vido ni en que libros se hallo tener el balssamo esta virtud antes de todo en todo contraria en lo qual por ser muy manifiesto dexo de ser prolixo//."

40. Laguna, *Dioscórides*, 26–27.

41. See Andrés Laguna, *Pedacio Dioscórides Anazarbeo, acerca de la materia medicinal, y de los venenos mortíferos. Traduzido de la lengua Griega en la vulgar Castellana, e illustrado con claras y substanciales Annotaciones, y con las figuras de unnúmeras plantas exquisitas y raras por el doctor . . . , Médico de Julio III, Pontífece Máximo* (Anvers, 1555), 26 and 27; Nicolás Bautista Monardes, *Historia Medicinal,* ff. 9ff; Conrad Gesner, *Evonymus C. Gesneri Medici de Remedis secretis, Liber Physicus, Medicus & partim etiam Chymicus, & Oeconomicus in vinorum diversi saporis apparatu, Medicis & Pharmacopolis omnibus praecipue necessarius, nunc primum in lucem editus,* n/p, n/d [This seems to be the edition from Zurich, c. 1565; for the date and place see Klaus Wagner, *Catálogo abreviado de las obras impresas del siglo XVI de la Biblioteca Universitaria de Sevilla* (Seville: Universidad de Sevilla, 1988)], ff. 131r–v; Pedrarias de Benavides, *Secretos de Chirurgia, especial de las enfermedades de Morbo galico y Lamparones y Mirrarchia, y asimismo la manera como se curan los Indios de llagas y heridas y otras passiones en las Indias, muy util y provechoso para en España y otros muchos secretos de chirurgia hasta agora no escritos* (Valladolid, 1567), ff. 30v–31r.

42. Carta de Barreda, AGI, Patronato, 174.

43. Ibid.

44. Cédula Real de la Reina a las justicias de Sus reinos. 5 April 1530. Madrid. AGI, Indiferente, 422, L. 14, f. 67v.

45. Ibid.

46. Ibid., 67v–68r.

47. Ibid., f. 68r.

48. Cédula Real a los visitadores del Hospital del Cardinal de la ciudad de Toledo. 5 April 1530. Madrid. AGI, Indiferente, 422, L. 14, f. 72v.

49. Cédula Real a los visitadores de varios hospitales. 5 April 1530. Madrid. AGI, Indiferente, 422, L. 14, f. 72v.

50. Cédula Real al bachiller Andrés de Jodar médico, vecino de Baeza. 5 April 1530. Madrid. AGI, Indiferente, 422, L. 14, ff. 73r–74v.

51. Cédula Real a varios médicos y cirujanos. 5 April 1530. Madrid. AGI, Indiferente, 422, L. 14, ff. 73r–74v.

52. Cédula Real a Pedro Benito de Basniana y Franco Leardo para que puedan subir los salarios asignados a los médicos que contribuyen a la propaganda del bálsamo. 12 July 1530. Madrid. AGI, Indiferente, 422, L. 14, ff. 102r–103r.

53. Cédula Real a los oficiales de Cuéllar. 16 October 1532. Madrid. AGI, Indiferente, 422, L. 15, ff. 197v–198r.

54. Ibid.; Cédula Real a Diego de la Haya para que pague a Melchor de Angulo. 27 November 1532. Madrid. AGI, Indiferente, 422, L. 15, f. 199v.

55. Cédula Real a Juan de Vargas para que venga a la corte. 21 November 1532. Madrid. AGI, Indiferente, 422, L. 15, f. 199r.; and Mandamiento a Diego de la Haya para que pague a Juan de Vargas por haber estado en la corte. 27 February 1533. Madrid. AGI, Indiferente, 422, L. 15, f. 199r.

56. Mandamiento a Diego de la Haya para que pague a Juan de Vargas por haber estado en la corte. 27 February 1533. Madrid. AGI, Indiferente, 422, L. 15, f. 199r.; Cédula Real a Diego de la Haya para que pague cierta suma a Juan de Vargas. 3 October 1533. Monzón. AGI, Indiferente, 422, L. 16, f. 43v., Real Cédula a Juan de Vargas. 18 April 1534. Toledo. AGI, Indiferente, 422, L. 16, f. 75v.

57. Cédula Real a los alcaldes ordinarios de la villa de Amusco. 23 May 1539. Toledo. AGI, Indiferente, 423, L. 19, ff.247–248.

58. Monardes, *Historia*, ff. 9r.

59. See Flint, *Christopher Columbus*; Richard H. Grove, *Green Imperialism* (Cambridge: Cambridge University Press, 1995); Steven Greenblatt, *Marvelous Possessions*; Gerbi, *Nature*; and John H. Elliott, *The Old World and the New* (Cambridge: Cambridge University Press, 1970).

60. On this topic see Grove, *Green Imperialism,* 32ff.

61. In 1564 and 1565, the botanist Carolus Clusius (1526–1609) visited Spanish botanical gardens, such as Simon de Tovar's well-known garden. Later he would receive samples of plants and curiosities from Spain for his books. For Clusius's visit to Tovar's garden, see Carolus Clusius, *Rariorum Plantarum Historia* (Antwerp, 1601), 50: 2. 173. For his contacts in Spain, see Asso, *Hispaniiensium atque Exterorum Epistolae cum praefatione et notis Ignatii de Asso* (1793), 53–70. The physician Nardo Antonio Recchi brought the work of Dr. Francisco Hernández on American plants and animals to Italy in the late sixteenth century. Recchi's summary of Hernández's work was published by the Academia dei Linceii between 1630 and 1651. See Raquel Alvarez-Peláez, "La obra de Hernández y su recuperación ilustrada," in *La Real Expedición Botánica a Nueva España, 1787–1803* (Madrid: Consejo Superias de Investiganes Científicas, 1987), 156 n. 1, as well as her article, "La historia natural en la segunda mitad del siglo XVI: Hernández, Recchi y las relaciones de Indias," in *Nouveau Monde et Renouveau de L'Histoire Naturelle,* Vol. 3, ed. Marie-Cécile Bénassy et al. (Paris: Presses de la Sorbonne Nouvelle, 1994).

Merchants and Marvels

Hans Jacob Fugger and the Origins of the Wunderkammer

MARK A. MEADOW

TRADE, TRAVEL, AND THE PROCUREMENT OF CURIOUS OBJECTS

In the cultural world of sixteenth-century Europe, few institutions offer a more compelling venue to study the intersection of art, nature, science, and economics than the *Kunst-* and *Wunderkammern* (commonly in English: curiosity cabinets) of such figures as the Wittelsbach Duke Albrecht V of Bavaria or the Habsburg Holy Roman Emperor Rudolf II of Prague.[1] These *Wunderkammern* served many functions within the great courts of transalpine Europe, being not only instruments of diplomacy and display, but also pragmatic tools of economic statecraft, repositories of ready funds for unexpected wars and disasters, sites of cultural and technological production, and active, functional, and practical laboratories for a variety of crafts and disciplines.

In order to think about the role of trade objects in these collections, let me begin by posing a scenario and a question. In these great collections of Albrecht V, Rudolf II and others, visitors encountered a vast and marvelous range of *naturalia* (natural objects) from across the globe: narwhal tusks from near the Arctic, camel bezoars from the East, ivory and ostrich eggs from Africa, birds and featherwork from the New World. *Artificialia* (works of human craftsmanship) were also present in various forms, including Limousin enamel, majolica pottery, and Venetian glass. Other human artifacts came from well beyond the European world: Indian and Turkish carpets, Tunisian textiles, carved African ivory, South American and Mexican gold and featherwork, Syrian metalwork, shoes from Lapland, and kayaks from Greenland, to name but a few. The question I want to raise is a simple one: How did these varied and heterogeneous things make their way to the Munichs or Pragues of the sixteenth century?

The answer is, of course, much more complicated than the question. In this essay I will address one part of that answer, speaking to the crucial role played by the extraordinarily wealthy and powerful merchant-banking families — such as the Fuggers, Welsers, or Medicis, but especially the first — in bringing these sorts of objects and materials from their points of origin to the courts and collections of Europe. In particular, I will discuss one member of the Fugger family, Hans Jacob Fugger, 1516–75, and the part he played in the material and conceptual formation of the *Wunderkammer*.

We know, for example, of several instances in which the Fuggers were involved in the procurement of particular objects, as for example two ivory caskets they secured from Ceylon via Lisbon, and provided for Albrecht V in 1566.[2] Ivory importation as a raw material was a substantial business in itself, with the Fugger offices in Antwerp making a contract in 1548 to exchange 6,750 hundredweight of brass rings (the family controlled enormous copper mining resources) for large shipments of ivory from Benin, to be crafted into fine objects for resale.[3] Max Fugger, in the 1560s, was very active in procuring gemstones, finished necklaces, and other pieces of jewelry for Albrecht V, both for his own collections and as gifts to figures such as King Philip II of Spain.[4] In the latter part of the century, via Antwerp and through its connections in India, the House of Fugger imported monkeys, parrots, peacocks, wildcats, and other live animals; orange trees, almond trees, rosemary bushes, and other live botanicals; camphor, pearls, leopard skins, indigo, gemstones, and similar natural by-products.[5] These examples of *naturalia*, living or not, ended up in the Fuggers' own collections as well as those of their patrons. Craftsman were employed to work on the raw materials, transforming them into finished products to be sold or given to wealthy and noble clients. In a similar vein, the Fuggers may have been the means by which the merchant-scholar Philipp Hainhofer gained access to South American objects for his own *Kunstkammer*, again through the Fugger offices in Portugal.[6]

The question of how the Fuggers, or other firms like theirs, contributed to the procurement of exotica for these collections, and the implications thereof, is not a trivial one. The objects collected in *Wunderkammern*, especially the exotica, flooded in from throughout the known world, and even at times from beyond it. In an era before the establishment of disciplines such as zoology or botany, ethnography or anthropology, the stories these objects told derived in no small part from the biographies they acquired moving from hand to hand. Their original contexts, uses, and narratives were filtered through the numerous people involved at each stage of their journey. The Fuggers and their representatives, and those of other families, were critical participants in the life histories of these objects. Furthermore, the diverse interests of the Fuggers themselves inevitably affected the procurement process. Certainly business concerns were paramount, and an eye was always kept on the bottom line. But the Fuggers, by the time of Hans Jacob, were intimates of dukes, kings, and emperors, serving at times as courtiers, advisors, financial consultants, and bankers. They were humanists and scholars, trained at the finest universities in Europe. They were also avid collectors of books, ancient coins, exotica, musical and mathematical instruments, fully conversant with the thematic collecting interests of their clients. And perhaps most important, they combined their intellectual and acquisitory pursuits with the practical matters of running a business and communications empire. The sheer vastness of their wealth, of their land holdings, and of their power made them coequals in many ways with the nobility they served.

The Fugger's own collecting practices are central to understanding their role in relation to princely collections. In this period, collecting by its very nature was a communal activity. Princes, scholars, merchants, or apothecaries assembled their collections through complex systems of exchange, gift giving, commerce, patronage, and other forms of social and financial intercourse. To some extent, the activity of collecting provided a social nexus, in which noble, scholar, tradesman, and even craftsman could participate in the same realm. By participating in this system as collectors as well as purveyors, the Fuggers and other such families placed themselves within an intellectual and social milieu that furthered much more than their business goals. As a result, at least in part, the Fuggers gained the rank of minor nobility, status as legitimate scholars and humanists, and a role as patrons of the arts, scholarship, and technology.

Lorraine Daston and Ken Arnold have both stressed the importance of travel in relation to curiosity cabinets. As Daston has written, "Travel was the alpha and omega of collecting, being both the source of the bulk of the objects — voyages of exploration and subsequent trade with the newly discovered lands created a steady flow of exotica — and the occasion for inspecting them in Amsterdam, Oxford, Venice, Paris, Augsburg, Uppsala, or wherever the curious and peripatetic tourist might land."[7] Arnold discusses the close affinities between travel and collecting, noting that "the relationship between the two was precisely reciprocal: one traveled in order to collect, but also one collected in order to travel."[8] Indeed, as Arnold notes, viewing a curiosity cabinet was itself a microcosmic form of travel, "through a world brought back and reassembled in a cabinet."[9] I would like to deviate slightly from the general question of travel and instead consider the importance of trade in the formation of the cabinets. The two issues are closely intertwined, but it is especially instructive here to consider the commercial aspects of travel. Intellectual history often places trade, and the commercial world in general, in the silent shadows when considering perceptions and models of the cosmos.[10] We can use the Fuggers and *Wunderkammern* to bring to light some of the implications of their close relationship.

In particular, I will discuss the relationship of sixteenth-century commercial networks to both the material and the conceptual formation of microcosmic collections north of the Alps. In the course of the larger research project here outlined, I want to situate this commercial world within the broader framework of similar networks, such as the travel and epistolary networks of the humanists; the closely related networks joining together universities and their faculty and students; and the tightly woven fabric of Europe's courts, stitched together through intermarriage and political alliances.

These various skeins of interrelationship are themselves interdependent and interwoven. Hans Jacob Fugger stands as an excellent example of this, bringing together in a single individual the worlds of the university, humanism, the courts, and commerce. As we will see in greater detail below, Fugger plays not one, but several significant roles in the founding moments of the *Wunderkammer*: he was himself a patron, scholar, and collector, but also, following a financial reversal, he worked as a librarian and procurer of books and objects for one of the very earliest of the collections under consideration, that of Albrecht V, elector of Bavaria.

I have been pushing very hard at the metaphors of threads and cloth in order to allow myself to bring in an enlightening fable from Italo Calvino. In his *Invisible Cities*, he includes, under the rubric of "trading cities," a place called Ersilia. In this city,

> to establish the relationships that sustain the city's life, the inhabitants stretch strings from the corners of the houses, white or black or gray or black-and-white according to whether they mark a relationship of blood, of trade, authority, agency. When the strings become so numerous that you can no longer pass among them, the inhabitants leave: the houses are dismantled; only the strings and their supports remain.[11]

The web of many-colored strings that Calvino describes serves as a map of relationships, and those relationships are themselves markers for what we would now call data flow. Reconstructing such threads may therefore serve as a critical analytical tool. We might well say that the houses of the sixteenth century have been dismantled, and certainly the inhabitants of the period have long since departed. But we can still make out the tapestry of social and cultural life that remains in the various strands of relationship. While calling attention to one color of string, the gold and silver strings of commerce, I will also be touching on many of the others. Indeed, in the world of the curiosity cabinet, as in any other place or period, the strands of blood, trade, authority, and agency were all present, and were all interdependent. To touch any of these strands is to set all the others in sympathetic vibration.

The essay that follows, I should note, is more a blueprint for an ongoing research project than the finished results of one. Tracing any one of the social, intellectual, economic, or political networks of the period is itself a daunting task. Examining all of these, and their points of intersection, is Herculean. Nonetheless, if we are truly to understand the conceptual matrix in which the *Wunderkammer* functioned, this line of research must be pursued. The larger study that will develop from this report is a component of a major research initiative undertaken within the University of California. Called "Microcosms: Objects of Knowledge," this broader project is examining the history, functions, and future of material collections in the contemporary university.[12] As is appropriate for a place that calls itself a university, these vast holdings are universal in scope, and when examined holistically bear a surprisingly close resemblance to the range of objects found in a *Wunderkammer*. The Microcosms Project considers these collections, and the university itself, from an historical perspective, turning especially to the sixteenth century, and the *Wunderkammer*, as one point of origin for the modern university and its collections. As we are all aware at the beginning of the twenty-first century, the university is itself intimately bound into a vast range of networks, including those of commerce. Nor is it any coincidence that I have chosen to emphasize metaphors of threads, networks, and skeins, considering how intimately bound the worlds of information and trade have become in the digital community that we have come habitually to call the "net" or the "web."

THE HOUSE OF FUGGER

Before turning to our particular Fugger, Hans Jacob, I will briefly sketch some of the family history. The Fuggers arrived in Augsburg in 1367 in the person of one Hans Fugger, a clothmaker who appears to have founded the family business by importing his own raw materials, rather than relying upon local merchants for them. The firm developed slowly in the next generation, first through Hans's sons Andreas and Jacob I, and then through Jacob's capable widow, Barbara Bäsinger, who ran the business until her children were of age to assume control themselves. From the widow Fugger, the business passed on first to her eldest and youngest sons, Ulrich and Georg. Ulrich and Georg first established a Fugger presence in the German merchants' trade building in Venice, the *Fondaco dei Tedeschi* (German business house).

Finally in 1485, the middle child, Jacob II, who was later to become known as Jacob the Rich, entered the management of the business by taking charge of the Innsbruck office and aggressively pursuing mining opportunities in the Tyrol. Jacob II had trained in bookkeeping and other aspects of business management at the Venetian *Fondaco* since 1478. Ulrich, Georg, and Jacob II formed a trade partnership in 1494, in which the business theoretically was equally shared among them. Although he did not formally become the director of the company until Ulrich's death in 1510, it was Jacob II who contributed most to creating the enormous fortune that catapulted the Fuggers into the center of sixteenth-century European commerce and political power. Jacob II, surviving his two brothers and desiring to extend his control over the firm, later changed the partnership model of governance to that of a single, autocratic director.

Jacob's basic strategy was a very simple but highly effective one. He lent money to the ruling houses of Europe at very high rates of interest, with the loans secured against the income-generating resources that such dukes, princes, kings, popes, and emperors could provide: silver and copper mines, agricultural communities and land, and so forth. A frequent formula employed by Jacob II was to lend large sums of money on a long term basis, with the stipulation that until the loan and its interest were repaid, the production of a particular site, usually a mine, went directly to the Fuggers. In certain instances, should the loan not be repaid in the allotted time, the secured property reverted permanently to the Fuggers. In this way, massive amounts of capital were quickly acquired, together with more stable sources of future earnings in the form of real property. Jacob built especially upon the relations his brother Ulrich had already established with the Habsburgs; the Fuggers, for instance, were one of the main, perhaps even the single most crucial, resource in assuring the election of Charles V as holy Roman emperor in 1519. This same connection to the Habsburgs eventually led to the fading of the Fugger family star, as improperly secured loans and even private family capital went to sustain Charles and his son Philip II, king of Spain, only to result in Habsburg defaults in 1557, 1574, 1575, and 1596. The first of these financial crises was among the main reasons why Hans Jacob Fugger was eventually forced out of the family business and into the service of Albrecht of Bavaria and his collections, thus indirectly setting into motion the story with which we are concerned.

From the time of Jacob I on, as the business grew increasingly large and complex, the Fuggers followed a strategic program of education for their offspring to ensure that the successors to the firm were properly prepared in languages, mathematics, law, and the humanist cultural background that would allow them to converse with the ruling elite. At first this involved sending them to the Fugger outposts in Europe, initially, as in the case of the young Jacob II, to the *Fondaco dei Tedeschi* in Venice, but eventually young Fuggers set out on a grand tour throughout the continent. A bit later, in the time of Hans Jacob's youth, this period of educational preparation also specifically included university education. Here is one of the key points where, for the Fuggers and other such families, the worlds of commerce and humanism intersected.

A business of the scale of the Fuggers', spread across all of Europe and into the vast lands beyond, necessitated efficient lines of communication. The Fuggers operated what are called "factories," that is, places of business run by individuals authorized to conduct business for the family, the "factors," throughout Europe and beyond. Among the places in which the Fuggers had offices were Lisbon, Seville, Madrid, Saragossa, the Tyrol, Vienna, Innsbruck, Munich, Leipzig, Nuremberg, Frankfurt, Cologne, Antwerp, Amsterdam, Paris, Lyon, Strasbourg, London, Helsingör, Malmö, Danzig, Riga, Narva, Poznan, Warsaw, Krácow, Ofen, Breslau, Pest, Venice, Rome, Florence, and the Levant. Through these sites, and many, many others too numerous to list, the Fuggers acted as brokers for trade flowing throughout the known world. In fact, Fugger factors were located in virtually every community of any economic significance in Europe, which means down to locales of only a few thousand residents, with (largely for political reasons) a somewhat more modest presence in France and Spain. But the Fugger mercantile operations were by no means limited to Europe. The Fuggers were involved in all areas of international trade, including between the New World and Europe, where they had offices in Santo Domingo, the Yucatan peninsula, Brazil, and elsewhere.[13] In 1531, the same year that Pissaro reached Peru, the Fuggers were granted a contract to colonize and economically exploit the western coast of Latin America from the southernmost point of Pizzaro's dominion to the tip of Tierra del Fuego.[14] They financed commercial ventures in India and Ceylon through Lisbon, traded in goods and slaves from Africa, and brokered merchandise from as far away as East Asia.

All of the Fugger outposts were expected to stay in constant touch with the home office, and, where necessary, with each other. This led to the creation of a very efficient system of communication, with letters flowing constantly in and out of the home office; paralleling a similarly efficient mechanism for transporting goods in bulk.[15] Primarily from library purchases, the facet of Fugger collecting that has been most thoroughly researched, we know that acquisitions were made along these lines of communication.[16] As business letters were sent out from Augsburg, they would include requests to secure one or another book or object, which in turn would accompany the reply, bringing the desired purchase safely home in very short order.

If we think only of two of the major Fugger factories, those in Venice and Antwerp, we can begin to understand something about the position the Fuggers were in to tap into the fullest range of natural objects and human artifacts as they traveled along the veins and arteries of the early modern commercial world. Venice remained the single most important port in southern Europe, with particular connections to Africa, the Middle East, and on into Asia. Antwerp played a similar role in the North, being the center of commerce with Scandinavia, the Baltic, England, the Iberian peninsula, and various Spanish and Portuguese territories in Africa and the New World. The Fuggers quickly came to dominant positions in both of these markets, and between the two had access to virtually any materials or goods that could be commercially transacted. This is the beginning of the answer to the question I posed at the start of this chapter; important research remains to be done on the specific relationship between the formation of any given princely collection and the financial / mercantile web with which that court was linked. If we take a *Kunst-* or *Wunderkammer* to be a representation of the world, a microcosm, then the accessibility of particular markets, trade routes, and therefore particular objects will have a direct bearing on the model of the world thus created.

HANS JACOB FUGGER

As I turn to Hans Jacob Fugger, I also shift to a different aspect of the question. That is, however important the biographies of objects are to their significance within a collection, and however central the Fuggers are to the formation of those biographies, in the person of Hans Jacob we come to a figure who had a direct bearing upon the activity of collecting as a necessary part of sixteenth-century statecraft and also upon the ordering systems employed in these collections.

Hans Jacob was born in December 1516, the son of Raimund Fugger and nephew of Anton, who was then in charge of the company.[17] Anton and Raimund were the children of Georg Fugger, the brother of Jacob II, who had died childless. Raimund was a renowned collector of antiquities and encouraged his son in similar directions. Hans Jacob had an unusually thorough education, with studies in Germany, Italy, France, Spain, and the Netherlands. His education was primarily classical and linguistic—he was apparently fluent in Latin, Italian, French, Spanish, Polish, Hungarian, and, in all likelihood, Dutch as well.[18] Among those with whom he studied were Wolfgang Bosch, later tutor to Albrecht V of Bavaria, and Johannes Secundus, later court humanist to Margaret of Austria and Philip of Burgundy.[19]

His advanced studies, first with Viglius Zwichem van Aytta, were oriented toward law.[20] He followed Viglius from Dôle to Bourges. While in Bourges he also studied with Andreas Alciati, and appears already to have become a bibliophile, lending Alciati his own copy of Titus Livius.[21] From Bourges he moved to the university in Padua, and then to Bologna by 1534, where he was named syndic of the German Trading Nation while still a student.

It is worth briefly looking at some of Hans Jacob's fellow students, who make a very impressive list. These include such humanist scholars as

Hieronymus Wolf, translator of Demosthenes; Sigmund Gelenius, translator of Josephus; and Roger Ascham, tutor to Elizabeth I of England.[22] In Bologna, Hans Jacob counted among his fellow students Alessandro Farnese, duke of Parma, governor general of the Netherlands, cardinal, and patron of the arts, and someone who was later to name Fugger his own "patrone"; Christopher Madruzzo, later bishop of Trient and Brixen, cardinal, and governor of Milan; Stanislaus Hosius, later cardinal and bishop of Augsburg; Otto Truchsess von Waldberg, also a future bishop of Augsburg; and Wiguleius Hund, later chancellor to the court of Bavaria.[23]

Hans Jacob Fugger was an author in his own right, drafting a history of his own family in 1541–45 and a history of the Habsburgs in 1555, which itself was a sort of collection, containing scores of portraits, images of places, genealogies, images of monuments, insignia, and thousands of coats of arms.[24] This assemblage of images and charts, in fact, corresponds very closely to the first of five classes in Samuel Quiccheberg's *Inscriptiones vel tituli Theatri amplissimi* (Inscriptions or headings of the most complete theater), a treatise on collecting and an organizational plan for Albrecht V's collections, and the earliest known treatise on museums.[25] Hans Jacob was furthermore a prolific patron of scholarship: Maasen lists more than sixty works dedicated to him, including Sigismund Gelenius's work on Flavius Josephus, Conrad Gessner's work on libraries and ordering systems, Jacopo Strada's scholarship on antiquities, Panvinius's history of the church and four works of Hieronymus Wolf.[26]

In 1535, Hans Jacob's father died, and he was summoned back to Augsburg by his uncle Anton to assume his position in the firm. While Hans Jacob was contractually given the equivalent of second-in-command of the family firm, Anton decided he was still not quite ready to take up the reins. So Hans Jacob was sent on a second tour, now specifically oriented toward familiarizing him with the business. Beginning with an extended stay in Antwerp, he traveled very widely among the Fugger factories in Europe.

Before his return to Augsburg, Hans Jacob entered service in the court of the Habsburg Ferdinand I, then king of Bohemia, brother to Holy Roman Emperor Charles V, and from 1556 emperor in his own right. While at Ferdinand's court, Hans Jacob served as tutor to Ferdinand's children, including Maximilian, holy Roman emperor following his father's death in 1564, and Archduke Charles. These figures loom large in the history of the *Wunderkammer*. Ferdinand is traditionally credited with founding the Habsburg *Kunstkammer*, with a particular interest in mechanical devices such as clocks and in antiquities and coins. Maximilian II continued his father's interests in collecting, especially antiquities and coins, but also artifacts of natural history. He later hired Jacopo Strada as architect of his collections, both conceptually and literally, as Strada designed the first Habsburg buildings devoted to the family collections. The more famous collections of Maximilian's son Rudolf II built upon these foundations. The young Hans Jacob was introduced to more than just princes and princely collections while in Ferdinand's service; he also met his first wife, Ursula von Harrach. On 21 June 1540 the couple was wed, with the chief steward of Charles V's court in attendance.[27]

Fugger's return to Augsburg in 1540 heralded a lengthy period of involvement in politics and government, which included membership in different parts of the Augsburg city councils, and a stint as a mayor. His connections with the Habsburgs were exploited by the city during the religious troubles, with Hans Jacob being sent out on more than one occasion to mollify Cardinal Granvelle or the emperor himself.[28] Cardinal Granvelle and Emperor Charles V both were later houseguests of Hans Jacob while visiting Augsburg. After having attended at least two Reichstäge, Hans Jacob reached the pinnacle of his political career in 1549, when he was named imperial councilor by Charles V. At some point during this period, Hans Jacob also developed very close ties to Albrecht of Bavaria, indicated by records of Albrecht serving as godfather to some of Hans Jacob's twenty-one children.

In 1560, Anton died, leaving the business in the hands of Hans Jacob and his brothers. Anton, largely through circumstances beyond his control — the Habsburg financial crises mentioned earlier — left the business in comparatively bad shape. Things were not to improve under Hans Jacob, who by 1565 found himself personally bankrupt and the family fortune in not much better shape. Hans Jacob did not even have enough funds to cover his own tax debts, despite selling off most of own possessions. His friendship with Albrecht here paid off, when the latter personally extended him the money required to stave off complete disaster. Albrecht mediated negotiations between Hans Jacob and the rest of the family, which resulted in a return of the business to Anton's own children and Hans Jacob's permanent removal from the firm. One of the terms of the agreement appears to have been that Hans Jacob enter the service of Albrecht as court librarian, here returning to his earlier and perhaps more temperamentally suitable profession as humanist and scholar.[29]

Serving as a librarian must have suited Hans Jacob well. Even before his time, the Fugger family library was quite famous, but he had turned it into a collection nearly without equal. The Fugger library ranged from the latest vernacular books off the presses of all Europe, and a very comprehensive set of classical texts, to medieval, Byzantine, and even Syrian manuscripts.[30] In his heyday, Hans Jacob had hired as librarians and curators such individuals as Hieronymus Wolf;[31] Jacopo Strada, who may have had his first significant employment from Fugger;[32] and Samuel Quiccheberg, who would move into Albrecht's service at the same time that his former employer did and would write the *Inscriptiones vel tituli* there in 1565.[33]

Given the later activities and careers of Strada and Quiccheberg, we must seriously consider their common link to Fugger. The Fugger collections were not by any means limited to books. We have already noted Raimund's interest in antiquities, which Hans Jacob continued.[34] Raimund also had a considerable interest in musical instruments, with a passion above all for the lute, and amassed a collection of instruments so vast it is difficult to imagine how it could be stored.[35] The Fuggers were active patrons of the arts who commissioned sculpture, architecture, and large numbers of paintings from artists such as Hans Maler and Titian.[36] Hans Jacob, working with Strada, acquired a very significant collection of antique coins, which put them in an excellent position to produce jointly a thirty-volume catalog of drawings of ancient coins, an enormous undertaking.[37] Another Fugger, Marx, had an avid interest in mathematics and collected mathematical instruments. We know much less about the family's interest in *naturalia*, this being virtually unexplored territory in Fugger studies. The Fuggers collected gemstones and jewelry, including four pieces originally from the Burgundian treasury, and not infrequently resold them to such clients as the Habsburg emperors, the Medicis, and the sultan of Turkey.[38] We know of individual purchases of coral objects and so forth, but much work remains to be done on the full extent of Fugger collecting.[39] Antiquities, coins, gems, and scientific instruments are among the objects that formed the core of any humanistically oriented collection, that is, the type of collection we find among the nobility of Europe north of the Alps.

While in Hans Jacob's service, Quiccheberg apparently devised a thematic ordering system for the Fugger library, perhaps in direct collaboration with Fugger himself, based upon the work of Conrad Gesner.[40] Once Quiccheberg and Fugger moved to the court in Munich, they put into place a similar cataloguing system for Albrecht's library. This system certainly formed the conceptual basis for the organizational scheme Quiccheberg developed for the Wittelsbach collections and presented in his *Inscriptiones vel tituli*.

The exact circumstances of Strada's and Quiccheberg's employment and activities under Hans Jacob Fugger remain to be researched, as does a detailed study of the collecting activities of Fugger under Albrecht V. But it should already be clear that Hans Jacob played a key role in the formation of the *Kunst-* or *Wunderkammer* in the Germanic territories. Albrecht V's collections, while predating the arrival of Fugger, underwent a massive increase in scale and a change in nature just as his association with them begins. And the Bavarian collections, while not the very earliest in the region, Ambras in particular predating them, are the first to lay claim through their variety and their mode of display to being a site for the study and accumulation of universal knowledge, and to the practical application of that knowledge in the governance of the state. The more famous collections of Maximilian in Vienna and Rudolf II in Prague are conceptually related to those of Munich, which should hardly be surprising given the role of intermediary played by Jacopo Strada. It is tempting to think, and may well be the case, that two qualities of the Munich collection relate directly to the connection with Fugger: here I speak of the collection as systematically arranged, and of the clear imperative to put the collection to direct practical use. The Fugger's own collections shaded imperceptibly into the conduct of their business, with the library being the clearest indication: the Fuggers effectively compiled two different sorts of library. One was a magnificent example of a humanist and antiquarian collection, primarily of intellectual and aesthetic interest, with precious manuscripts, a remarkably complete set of standard and obscure works of the Greeks, the Romans, Patristic texts, and works of humanist scholarship. The other library was a more immediately pragmatic reference source for business, that would have contained atlases and travel literature, treatises on accounting, mining, law, and so forth. On a more conceptual level, we would do well to recognize that the vast amount of data necessary to the running of the Fugger firm, in the form of business records, newsletters, and other accounts of current events, inventories, and even the commercial goods themselves, presented a powerful challenge in terms of efficient storage and retrieval. Hans Jacob Fugger's interest in ordering systems had a practical origin as well as a humanist one.

COMMERCE IN THE CABINET OF CURIOSITIES

In closing, I would like to think a bit about commerce *in* the *Wunderkammer*. Certainly the financial basis of the collections of the nobility is clear. The earliest of these assemblages were neither collections of art nor of curiosities, although they may well have contained such objects, but rather were treasuries. Gold and silver work, gems and jewelry, even reliquaries were assets that could be and were sold off to raise ready cash. In the case of Munich, in 1565 (not coincidentally the year Quiccheberg's treatise was published, and the year Hans Jacob Fugger entered Albrecht's service) Albrecht V was the first Wittelsbach ruler to declare certain objects, including two narwhal tusks, the inalienable property of the dynasty, to be passed on to later generations with the stipulation that they never be sold.[41] By and large, collections of the *Wunderkammer* type continued to emphasize monetarily valuable objects, most of them acquired through mercantile houses like those of the Fuggers. These objects moved in and out of the collections in an economy of their own, both to generate cash and to cement relationships with other princes and scholars.

The *Wunderkammern* served also as repositories for intellectual capital, functioning in a not dissimilar way to universities and their collections today. Antiquities and numismatic collections were fundamental resources for study of the histories, languages, and cultures of the ancient world.[42] Products of metalsmiths, turners, jewelers, and armorers served to stimulate technical developments both by injecting capital into the higher ends of production and by acquiring examples of nonlocal techniques. *Wunderkammern* and other such collections similarly encouraged the development of scientific instruments, and therefore of scientific endeavor. We can even think of the *Wunderkammern* as assemblages of examples of local and exotic raw materials and processes; there is for instance a consistent interest in mining to be found in these collections — think back to the origins of Fugger wealth, and noble wealth, in mines for precious ores.

Objects were not the only items collected in *Wunderkammern*. Scholars, craftsmen, and other specialists were just as eagerly acquired. Jacopo Strada, for instance, begins working with Fugger, is brought into Albrecht's service, and ends up with Maximilian. Quiccheberg, a physician by training, moves from a university setting at Ingoldstadt to work for Fugger and then Albrecht. Hans Jacob Fugger himself was acquired by Albrecht V in what was essentially a financial transaction between Albrecht and the house of Fugger. These were the elite of the collections personnel, but there were also printers and bookbinders, turners and jewelers, armorers, equerries, and others attached to the service side of the collections.

This brings us to another very interesting point that emerges from looking closely at the infrastructure of Albrecht's collections, using Quiccheberg's text as a lens to help us focus. Almost all attention to these collections has gone into reconstructing first their contents and then their arrangement. Scholars have looked at Quiccheberg, deservedly so, primarily for the intriguing evidence he presents about what was collected and about how it was ordered. But the system of classes and inscriptions for objects is only a part of his treatise. He argues also for conceiving of the collections as one part of a larger complex of workshops and ateliers, including a printing room, a mint, and a pharmacy.[43] In turn, this brings us to a question of access: we expect the collections to be open to the duke and his family, to distinguished guests of the house and to resident and visiting scholars of high repute. But it is also clear that craftsmen and artisans could make use of it as well, for the good of regional technology and the economy.

Let me end with a quote from Quiccheberg:

> For I sense that it cannot be expressed by any person's eloquence how much wisdom and how much use for administering the state — in the civil and military spheres and the ecclesiastical and literary — can be gained from examination and study of the images and objects that I have described.[44]

This passage is found in the section of Quiccheberg's treatise in which he amplifies on the purposes and structure of the collection. In this passage and the one immediately preceding, he compares and contrasts the accumulation of objects with the training suggested by Cicero (the epitome of eloquence for the Renaissance) for the ideal orator. That person should be able to enumerate and learn about all things because all in the world that pertains to mankind is the natural domain of the orator. The collecting of objects, as enumerated by Quiccheberg, is an equivalent to the Ciceronian collecting of knowledge and ideas. But the equivalence is not exact, because however eloquent an orator may be, be it Cicero himself, the pragmatic value of the collection could not be conveyed as well by him as it could by the objects themselves.

And it is with the question of the practical use of the princely *Wunderkammern* that we reach the heart of the matter: these collections aided in the "administering of the state," the business of governance, and did it in very pragmatic ways. Certainly they were means of projecting images of princely wealth, power, erudition, and identity, but they were also very practical repositories of practical knowledge. As I have argued here, we must see this insistence on practicality as having origins in the dual concerns of merchants such as the Fuggers. It was they who dealt with and dealt in all the material things of the world, they who acquired these objects for themselves and for their clients, they who had the necessity and experience of ordering the world for both business and scholarly ends, they who best understood how these were the warp and woof of collecting, and how the two combined to create a representation, a self-portrait, of the collector. Certainly commerce and the merchants who practiced it largely determined which objects ended up in the *Wunderkammer*, and helped create and convey their life histories as well, points that deserve more scholarly attention. But we must also recognize that they played a strong hand in founding and shaping the *Wunderkammer* itself, bringing the threads of their long-established habits of organizing repositories into the tapestry. In this regard I think it is telling that Quiccheberg and Strada both got their start working with Hans Jacob in the Fugger collections, where business came first, and that Albrecht V's collections only started to take their full form as a *Wunderkammer* with the arrival of Fugger. Hans Jacob Fugger, rather like the Zelig of sixteenth-century collecting, turns up surprisingly often in the picture of the founding moments of the *Wunderkammer*.

Many of the conceptual underpinnings of this paper derive from discussion and debate with the members of the Microcosms Residential Research Group, which convened at the University of California Humanities Research Institute from January to June 1999: Ken Arnold, Rosemary Joyce, Rebecca Lemov, Sonnet Retman, and Bruce Robertson. I owe all of these colleagues and friends a great debt. As a visitor to the UCHRI Residency, Dirk Jansen was instrumental in bringing the significance of Hans Jacob Fugger for the *Wunderkammer* to my attention, and has since been an invaluable resource. The writing of this chapter was aided enormously by my indefatigable research assistants, Emily Peters and Amy Buono. This research was made possible by a Getty Grant Program Senior Collaborative Research Grant and funding from the University of California Office of the President, the Interdisciplinary Humanities Center of the University of California Santa Barbara, and the UCSB Committee on Research.

1. I introduce these terms from the beginning as a gesture toward the pioneering research on these early collections written by Julius von Schlosser. It is important to note that collections of the period were quite diverse in form and function, and we should be cautious about speaking about them as a unified phenomenon. For the sake of convenience, I shall use the term *Wunderkammer* for the remainder of this essay, recognizing that its use was infrequent in the period under consideration. For the purposes of this paper, I use the term to refer to heterogeneous collections that aspired to produce, store, and represent universal knowledge. Julius von Schlosser, *Die Kunst- und Wunderkammern der Spätrenaissance*, Vol. 11 of Monographien des Kunstgewerbes (Leipzig: Klinkhardt & Biermann, 1908).

The literature on curiosity cabinets, *Kunstkammern*, *Wunderkammern*, and the many other equivalent forms of early modern collecting is too vast to be given here. An excellent introduction to the topic and overview of many of the most important collections can be found in Oliver Impey and Arthur MacGregor, eds., *The Origins of Museums: The Cabinet of Curiosities in Sixteenth- and Seventeenth-Century Europe* (Oxford: Clarendon Press, 1985). For Albrecht V's collections, see especially Lorenz Seelig, "The Munich *Kunstkammer,*"1565–1807, in the volume just mentioned; Jacob Stockbauer, *Die Kunstbestrebungen am Bayerischen Hofe unter Herzog Albrecht V. und seinem Nachfolger Wilhelm V.*, vol. 8 of *Quellenschriften für Kunstgeschichte und Kunsttechnik des Mittelalters und der Renaissance* (Vienna: Wilhem Braumüler Universitäts-Verlagbuchhandlung, 1874); and Herbert Brunner, *Die Kunstschätze der Münchner Residenz* (Munich: Süddeutscher Verlag, 1977). For Rudolf II's collections, see Robert John Weston Evans, *Rudolf II and His World: A Study in Intellectual History: 1576-1612* (Oxford: Oxford University Press, 1973); E. Fucikova, *Die Kunst am Hofe Rudolfs II* (Prague: Artia Verlag, 1988); and Thomas DaCosta Kaufmann, *The School of Prague: Painting at the Court of Rudolf II* (Chicago: University of Chicago Press, 1988).

2. See Seelig, "The Munich *Kunstkammer,*" 83.

3. Michael Gorgas, "Animal Trade between India and Western Eurasia in the Sixteenth Century—The Role of the Fuggers in Animal Trading," in *Indo-Portuguese Trade and the Fuggers of the Sixteenth Century*, ed. Kuzhippalli Skaria Mathew (New Delhi: Manohar, 1977), 195–225, esp. 218–222.

4. Stockbauer, *Die Kunstbestrebungen am Bayerischen Hofe*, 91–107 passim.

5. Gorgas, "Animal Trade," 218–222.

6. See Hans-Olaf Boström, "Philipp Hainhofer and Gustavus Adolphus's *Kunstschrank* in Uppsala," in *Origins of Museums,* 90–101, here 91. Hainhofer's cabinet, here more literally a piece of furniture, was later purchased and presented to King Gustavus Adolphus, thus illustrating the migration of objects from source to merchant-trader to merchant-collector to royal collection.

7. Lorraine Daston, "The Factual Sensibilitys" *Isis* 79 (1988), 455.

8. Ken Arnold, *Cabinets for the Curious: Practicing Science in Early Modern English Museums*, Ph.D. diss., Princeton University, 1991 (UMI Dissertation Services, 1992), 139.

9. Ibid.

10. An admirable exception is Lisa Jardine's recent *Worldly Goods: A New History of the Renaissance* (London and New York: W. W. Norton, 1996). Her insights into the relation of commerce and intellectual life have helped shape the more specialized argument here presented.

11. Italo Calvino, *Invisible Cities*, trans. William Weaver (New York: Harcourt Brace Javonovich, 1974), 76.

12. The Microcosms Project is described in Mark Meadow and Bruce Robertson, "Microcosms: Objects of Knowledge," *AI & Society* 14 (2000), 223–229.

13. For Fugger trade with the New World, see Karl Heinz Panhorst, *Deutschland und Amerika; ein Rückblick auf das Zeitalter der Entdeckungen und die ersten deutsch-amerikanischen Verbindungen unter; besonderer Beachtung der Unternehmungen der Fugger und Welser* (Munich: E. Reinhard, 1928), Konrad Häbler, *Die Geschichte der Fugger'schen Handlung in Spanien*, Vol. 1 of Socialgeschichtliche Forschungen, Ergänzungshefte zur Zeitschrift für Social- und Wirthschaftsgeschichte (Weimer: E. Felber, 1897); Hermann Kellenbenz, *Die Fugger in Spanien und Portugal bis 1560: Ein Großunternehmen des 16. Jahrhunderts* (Schriften der Philosophischen Fakultäten der Universitäten Augsburg, 33:1), 3 vols. (Munich: Verlag Ernst Vögel, 1990).

14. Panhorst, *Deutschland und Amerika*, passim, esp. 278–283. A shift in Iberian politics effectively ended this venture before it began.

15. The Fugger newsletters have never been published in their entirety. Nonetheless, several extensive sets of selected examples give a good sense of their contents and breadth of coverage. See, for example, Victor Klarwill, *Fugger-Zeitungen: Ungedruckte Briefe an das Haus Fugger aus den Jahren 1568–1605* (Vienna: Rikola Verlag, 1923); Victor von Klarwill, ed., *The Fugger News-Letters: Being a Selection of unpublished letters from the Correspondents of the House of Fugger during the years 1568–1605* (London: John Lane The Bodley Head, 1924); V. von Klarwill, ed., *The Fugger News-Letters, Second Series: Being a further Selection from the Fugger papers specially referring to Queen Elizabeth and matters relating to England during the years 1568–1605* (London: John Lane The Bodley Head, 1924); and George T. Matthews, ed., *News and Rumor in Renaissance Europe (The Fugger Newsletters)* (New York: G. Putnam's Sons, 1959).

16. For the Fugger libraries, the standard references remain Otto Hartig, *Die Gründung der Münchner Hofbibliothek durch Albrecht V. und Johann Jacob Fugger*; (Munich: Verlag der Königlich Bayerischen Akademie der Wissenschaften, 1917); and Paul Lehmann, *Eine Geschichte der alten Fuggerbibliotheken*, 2 vols., Studien zur Fuggergeschichte, 12 (Tübingen: J. C. B. Mohr, 1956–1960).

17. For Hans Jacob Fugger, see Wilhelm Maasen, *Hans Jakob Fugger (1516-1575): Ein Beitrag zur Geschichte des XVI. Jahrhunderts*, Vol. 5 of Historische Forschungen und Quellen (Munich: Datterer, 1922); Lehmann, *Eine Geschichte der alten Fuggerbibliotheken*, Vol. 1, esp. 41–73; and Hartig, *Die Gründung der Münchner Hofbibliothek*, 193–223. For Anton Fugger, see Herman Kellenbenz, *Anton Fugger (1493-1560)*, Weissenhorn (1993) and Johannes Burkhardt, ed., *Anton Fugger (1493-1560): Vorträge und Dokumentation zum fünfhundertjährigen Jubiläum*, Vol. 36 of (Studien zur Fuggergeschichte) (Weissenhorn, A. H. Konrad, 1994).

18. For Hans Jacob Fugger's education, see Lehmann, *Eine Geschichte der alten Fuggerbibliotheken*, Vol. 1, 42–44; Hartig, *Die Gründung der Münchner Hofbibliothek*, 194–196; and Maasen, *Hans Jakob Fugger*, 3–12.

19. See Maasen, *Hans Jakob Fugger*, 6. For Johannes Secundus, see Dougall Crane, *Johannes Secundus, His Life, Work, and Influence on English Literature* (Beiträge zur englischen

Philologie, 16) (Leipzig: B. Tauchnitz, 1931), and Clifford Endres, *Johannes Secundus: The Latin Love Elegy in the Renaissance*, (Hamden, Conn.: Archon Books, 1981).

20. For Viglius, see E. H. Waterbolk and Th. S. H. Bos, eds., *Vigliana : bronnen, brieven en rekeningen betreffende Viglius van Aytta* (Estrikken, 50) (Groningen: Frysk Ynstitut en Historisch Instituut R. U. Grins, 1975); and Folkert Postma, *Viglius van Aytta als humanist en diplomaat (1507-1549)*, (Zutphen: Walburg Pers., ca. 1983).

21. This anecdote is recounted by Hans Jacob in Cod. Vat. Lat. 6412, fol. 105. For Alciati, see Ernst von Moeller, *Andreas Alciati (1492-1550): Ein Beitrag zur Entstehungsgeschichte der modernen Jurisprudenz* (Studien zur Erläuterung des Bürgerlichen Rechts, 25) (Breslau: M. & H. Marcus, 1907); Frederik Willem Gerard Leeman, *Alciatus' Emblemata: denkbeelden en voorbeelden* (Groningen: Bouma's Boekhuis, 1984); and Johannes Köhler. *Der "Emblematum liber" von Andreas Alciatus (1492-1550): Eine Untersuchung zur Entstehung, Formung antiker Quellen und pädagogischen Wirkung im 16. Jahrhundert*, (Beiträge zur historischen Bildungsforschung, 3) (Hildesheim: A. Lax, 1986).

22. For Hieronymus Wolf, see Hieronymus Wolf, *Der Vater der deutschen Byzantinistik: das Leben des Hieronymus Wolf von ihm selbst erzählt*, trans. Hans-Georg Beck (Miscellanea Byzantina Monacensia, 29) (Munich: Institut für Byzantinistik und neugriechische Philologie der Universität, 1984). For Ascham, see Alfred Katterfeld, *Roger Ascham: Sein Leben und seine Werke* (Strasbourg: K. J. Trübner, 1879), esp. 140–41, and Lawrence Ryan, *Roger Ascham*. (Stanford, Calif.: Stanford University Press, 1963). In 1551, Ascham was a houseguest of Hans Jacob Fugger.

23. For Farnese, see Léon van der Essen, *Alexandre Farnèse, prince de Parme, gouverneur général des Pays-Bas (1545-1592)*, (Bibliothèque du seizième siècle) (Brussels: Librairie nationale d'art et d'historie, 1933); Antonio Bezzi, *Alessandro Farnese: una vita per un ideale* (Collana di storia, arti figurative e architettura, 12) (Parma: L. Battei, 1977); and Alessandro Pietromarchi, *Alessandro Farnese: l'eroe italiano delle Fiandre* (Le Storie della Storia, 13) (Rome: Gangemi, 1998). For Madruzzo, see Antonio Monti, *Filippo II e il card. Cristoforo Madruzzo, gobernatore di Milano (1556-1557)* (Milan: Società editrice Dante Alighieri di Albrighi, Segati & Co., 1924). For Hosius, see Joseph Lortz, *Kardinal Stanislaus Hosius: Beiträge zur Erkenntnis der Persönlichkeit und des Werkes* (Braunsberg: Herder, 1931). For Truchsess, see Bernhard Schwarz, *Kardinal Otto Truchsess von Waldburg, Fürstbischof von Augsburg; sein Leben und Wirken bis zur Wahl als Fürstbischof von Augsburg (1514-1543)* (Geschichtliche Darstellungen und Quellen, 5) (Hildscheim: F. Borgmeyer, 1923).

24. Hans Jacob Fugger, *Geheimen Ehrenbuch Mannsstammens und Namens der Eerlichen und altloblichen Fuggerischen Geschlechts*, 1541–1545. Copies of this manuscript may be found in the Nuremberg Germanisches Museum and in the Fugger Museum in Augsburg. Hans Jacob Fugger, *Warhafftige Beschreibung Zwaier Inn ainem Der aller Edlesten vralten vnd hochloblichisten Geschlechten der Christenhait des Habspurgischen vnnd Osterreichischen geblüets, sampt derselbigen lobwurdigen herkommen, Geburten, leben, Regiment vnnd Ritterlichen gethaten, Von dem anfanng biss auff die Vnuberwindtlichisten Grossmechtigisten Fursten vnd herren, herrn Carolum, den funfften vnd Ferdinandum, der ersten, Römischen Kaiser vnd Könige, auch recht ordenliche Erwölte vnd gekrönte, Obriste haupter der Christenhait*, 1555. Maasen doubts that Fugger was in fact the author of this compendious work, suggesting instead that he may have served merely as editor and that the writing itself was by the Augsburg cobbler and historian Clemens Jäger. See Maasen, *Hans Jakob Fugger*, 59–73, esp. 67–68. Copies of this work reside in the Staatsbibliotheken in Munich and Vienna. Bibliographic refs. to Fugger and Habsburg histories.

25. Quiccheberg, *Inscriptiones vel tituli Theatri amplissimi complectentis rerum vniuersitatis singulas materias et imagines eximias, ut idem recte quoque dici possit: Promptuarium artificiosarum miraculosarumque rerum, ac omnis rari thesauri et pretiosæ supellectilis, structuræ atque*

*pictura, qua hic simul in theatro conuqiri consuluntur, ut eorum frequenti inspectione tracta-
tionecque, singularis aliqua rerum cognitio et prudentia admiranda, citò, faciliè ac tutò comparari
possit.* (Munich: Adam Berg, 1565).

26. See Maasen, *Hans Jakob Fugger,* 74–90, on Hans Jacob Fugger's role as a patron of scholarship and the books dedicated to him as a result.

27. For Hans Jacob Fugger at the court of Ferdinand, see Maasen, *Hans Jakob Fugger,* 8–10.

28. For Hans Jacob Fugger's role in Augsburg politics, see Maasen, *Hans Jakob Fugger,* 12–30.

29. For Hans Jacob Fugger at the court in Munich, see Maasen, *Hans Jakob Fugger,* 45–58.

30. For the Byzantine holdings, see B. Mondrain, "Copistes et collectionneurs de manuscrts grecs au milieu du XVIe Siècle," *Byzantinische Zeitschrift* 84 (1991/92): 354–390.

31. Wolf began his employment as librarian to the Fuggers in 1551. The great librarian Conrad Gessner had been offered the position in 1545, but the arrangements never came to fruition. Wolf remained in this post until 1557. See Lehmann, *Eine Geschichte der alten Fuggerbibiliotheken,* Vol. 1: 50–57.

32. Jacopo Strada began working for Hans Jacob Fugger while living in Nuremberg in 1544. At Hans Jacob's request, and with his financial support, Strada prepared a thirty-folio volume set of numismatic drawings to serve as a standard reference for Fugger's collections. He continued to serve Fugger as an intermediary in the purchase of antiquities and coins in Rome. Strada produced architectural drawings for Albrecht V's Antiquarium in Munich, as well as designing his own house in Vienna. He entered the service of the Habsburgs in 1558, and continued in their employ until 1579. For Strada's work in the German-speaking world, see Renate von Busch, *Studien zu deutschen Antikensammlungen des 16. Jahrhunderts* (Diss. Tübingen: 1973). For other aspects of Strada's career, see Dirk Jansen, "Jacopo Strada (1515–1588): Antiquario della Sacra Cesarea Maestà," *Leids Kunsthistorisch Jaarboek,* I (Leiden: 1982), 57–69; E. Fucíková, "Einige Erwägungen zum Werk des Jacopo und Ottavio Strada," *Leids Kunsthistorisch Jaarboek,* I (Leiden: 1982), 339–353; Dirk Jansen, "Jacopo Strada et le commerce d'art," *Revue de l'art* 77 (1987), 11–21; idem, "Gli strumenti del mecenatismo: Jacopo Strada alla corte de Massimiliano II," in *"Familia" del Principe e famiglia aristocratica* (Biblioteca del Cinquecento, 41) ed. Cesare Mozzarelli (Rome: Bulzoni, ca. 1988), 681–715; idem, "Example and examples: The potential influence of Jacopo Strada on the development of Rudolphine art," in *Prag um 1600: Beiträge zur Kunst und Kultur am Hofe Rudolfs II,* (Freren/Emsland: Luca, 1988), pp. 132–146; idem, "Der Mantuaner Antiquarius Jacopo Strada," in *Fürstenhöfe der Renaissance: Giulio Romano und die klassische Tradition* (Vienna: Kunsthistorisches Museum, 1989), 308–323; idem, "Jacopo Strada's Antiquarian Interests: A Survey of his Musaeum and its Purpose," *Xenia: Semestrale di Antichità,* 21 (1991), 59–76; and idem, "The Instruments of Patronage: Jacopo Strada at the Court of Maximilian II: A Case Study," in *Kaiser Maximilian II: Kultur und Politik im 16. Jahrhundert* (Wiener Beträge zur Geschichte Neuzeit, 19), ed. Friedrich Edelmayer and Alfred Kohler (Vienna: Verlag für Geschichte und Politik; Munich: Oldenbourg, 1992), 182–202.

33. Quiccheberg came into the employ of the Fuggers in 1555, first as physician to Anton Fugger "dero leib zu warten und zu artzneyen," but was working as librarian at least as early as 1559. For Quiccheberg, see esp. Harriet Roth, *Der Anfang der Museumslehre in Deutschland: das Traktat "Inscriptiones vel tituli theatri amplissimi" von Samuel Quiccheberg; lateinisch-deutsch,* Berlin, 2000; and Patrice Falguières, "Fondation du Théâtre ou Méthode de l'exposition universelle: les *Inscriptions* de Samuel Quicchelberg (1565)," *Les Cahiers du Musée National d'Art Moderne* 40 (1992), 91–109. For Quiccheberg at Munich, see Otto Hartig, "Der Arzt Samuel Quicchelberg, der erste Museologe Deutschlands, am Hofe Albrechts V. in München," *Bayerland* 44 (1933), 630–633.

34. For Raimund Fugger's collections of antiquities, see Norbert Lieb, *Die Fugger und die Kunst,* Vol. 2 of Studien der Fuggergeschichte (Munich: Verlag Schnell und Steiner, 1952–58), 46–51, 349–351.

---

35. Raimund Fugger's astonishing collection of lutes and harpsichords was cataloged in 1566, at the time they were acquired en masse by Albrecht V. See Stockbauer, *Die Kunstbestrebungen am Bayerischen Hofe*, 81–84.

36. The best work on the art patronage of the Fuggers remains Norbert Lieb, *Die Fugger und die Kunst*, see esp. Vol. 2, 303–305 for Titian.

37. Jacopo Strada, *Antiquorum numismatum*. Later an excerpted version was published as *Epitome Thesavri antiqvitatvm, hoc est, impp. Rom. Orientalivm et Occidentalivm Iconvm ex antiquis Numimatibus quam fidelissimie deliniatarum* (Lyon: 1553). For Albrecht V's numismatical collections, see Stockbauer, *Die Kunstbestrebungen am Bayerischen Hofe*, 70–72.

38. For the Fugger collections and trade in jewels, see Lieb, *Die Fugger und die Kunst*, Vol. 2, 133–138, and esp. 137–138 concerning the Burgundian gems and their eventual resale.

39. For the purchase of coral, see Lieb, *Die Fugger und die Kunst*, Vol. 2, 140.

40. See Lehmann, *Eine Geschichte der alten Fuggerbibiliotheken*, Vol. 1, 57.

41. See Seelig, "The Munich *Kunstkammer*," 76. Albrecht V was preceded in this by the Habsburgs Maximilian II and Ferdinand II, who declared certain artifacts inalienable property only a year earlier in 1564. These included an agate bowl and a "unicorn" horn, another narwhal tusk. See Elisabeth Scheicher, "The Collection of Archduke Ferdinand II at Schloss Ambras," in *The Origins of Museums*, 29–38, here 30; and Rudolf Distelberger, "The Habsburg Collections in Vienna during the Seventeenth Century," in *The Origins of Museums*, 39–46, here 43.

42. For the intellectual importance of antique collections, see esp. Horst Bredekamp, "Antikensehnsucht und Maschinenglauben," in *Forschungen zur Villa Albani: Antike Kunst und die Epoche der Aufklärung* (Frankfurter Forschungen zur Kunst, 10), ed. Herbert Beck and Peter Bol (Berlin: Gebr. Mann, 1982). For the conceptual importance of ancient coins to the intellectual premises of the curiosity cabinet, see Arnold, *Cabinets for the Curious*, 42–87.

43. Quiccheberg, *Inscriptiones vel tituli*, Civ r–Di r.

44. Ibid., Di v–Dii r.

Practical Alchemy and Commercial Exchange in the Holy Roman Empire

By the mid-sixteenth century, alchemy was of widespread interest in the Holy Roman Empire. No longer the preserve of learned natural philosophers and initiates alone, the alchemical arts engaged princes, pastors, and craftspeople, both male and female. This diverse group of enthusiasts devoured alchemical literature as publishers ushered ancient and modern authors into print; they also traded techniques with fellow students of nature and bought recipes from peddlers of alchemical secrets. Not surprisingly, given alchemy's wide purview of the theoretical and the practical as well as the mystical and the material, alchemical practitioners differed about how precisely to define their art, how to master it, and what to do with it. By the end of the century, practitioners increasingly disagreed: what exactly was alchemy, and, as it gained publicity and the support of political leaders, what were its goals to be?

In this paper, I argue that in the late sixteenth century, alchemists offered at least two different answers to these questions. The first view, rather traditional, saw alchemy as a natural philosophy which sought to understand God through his greatest revelation: nature. From this perspective, even the practice of alchemy was pious. In using his art to heal natural bodies (whether human or metallic), the philosophical alchemist sought nothing less than the regeneration of the world by cleansing it of impurities resulting from the Fall of Adam and Eve. A second strain in early modern alchemy took a much more pragmatic perspective, emphasizing instead alchemy's utility and productivity in the world of things. This practical alchemy was markedly commercial in the sense that it was both accessible through and supported by a growing market in alchemical goods and services. Though these two threads in early modern alchemy were not identified exclusively with particular individuals or groups (indeed, a single individual could exhibit both tendencies), nonetheless, they were increasingly in conflict in this period. Both had potential to triumph and determine whether alchemy was ultimately to be about understanding God and learning or profit and the production of things.

Over the past few decades, historians have done much excellent work on the philosophical and spiritual aspects of alchemy. They have shown that early modern European scholars and political elites viewed alchemy not only as *possible*, but often as *central* to their intellectual, religious, and political activities.[1] In focusing on alchemy as an idea, philosophy, or metaphor, and explaining why it made sense to early modern Europeans, these historians have been pivotal in reevaluating alchemy's marginality and demonstrating its importance and legitimacy both before and during the formulation of the new science. It has been much more difficult, however, to appreciate alchemical practitioners who claimed to be able to *do* alchemy successfully, to actually transmute metals or create the philosophers' stone, largely because it seems so obvious to us in the twenty-first century that it is *not* possible to create gold out of iron.[2] And yet alchemy as a practice and the alchemical production of things was just as important to early modern patrons and practitioners as it was as an idea. As alchemists' contracts, proposals, and laboratory reports reveal, a vital community of practitioners was at work in the Holy Roman Empire on a range of alchemical projects. If we wish to understand the relationship between alchemy and commerce, we must first understand the *practice* of alchemy and its relationship to emerging markets and the world of goods.

ALCHEMY AS COMMODITY

Interested patrons and practitioners could find a great deal of alchemical knowledge for sale in the sixteenth century. Novices who wished to pursue their interest in alchemy would have found a variety of literature in the book stalls, where ancient and medieval Islamic and Christian authors joined more modern authorities such as Paracelsus (ca. 1493–1541).[3] Practical books in the vernacular sold particularly well and did much to expand the audience for alchemy. William Eamon has noted how printers often amended these "how-to books" to make them more accessible for audiences from the middling classes, inserting indexes, prefaces, and translations of difficult or technical terms.[4] The 1570 version of the *Kunstbüchlein* (or skills booklet) titled *Alchimia*, for example, began with an "Explanation of Some Latin Words" that translated *sol* to gold, *corpus* to "any metal or material," and so on.[5] With these sorts of additions, Eamon notes, "philosophical traditions such as alchemy were given a new relevance by being placed within the reach of general readers."[6] Furthermore, students of alchemy who did not wish to (or could not) buy an entire book might come across a fellow enthusiast willing to share a recipe for a small fee or a skilled practitioner willing to instruct them in a particular process in exchange for pay. Alchemy had become much more accessible and widely dispersed than it had been to its medieval devotees.

The career of the Wolfenbüttel alchemist Philipp Sömmering (ca. 1535–75) provides a rare glimpse of a practical alchemist negotiating this market of alchemical expertise. The son of a pastor in Thombach, Sömmering attended school before taking up a series of positions in the Lutheran Church. When war and a dispute disrupted his position as a pastor in 1555, Sömmering set off to wander, by his own account, two hundred miles throughout the Holy Roman Empire. On his journeys, Sömmering met two men from whom he obtained his first alchemical book. Sömmering procured from a fellow pastor a second book, in which he reportedly read about certain distilling techniques. With only these two books, Sömmering later reported, he began to try his hand at alchemy. He furthered his studies by paying a woodcarver in Erfurt 5 thaler to teach him distillation and sublimation, then copied down the varieties of plants and bought 11 thaler worth of herbs from an apothecary.[7]

Still in Erfurt, Sömmering discussed the art of alchemy with someone he identified as a "Philosopher" and bought two more books: the *Book of Isaac* ("in which there are many good things") and the *Hexameron of Bernardus*.[8] Together these two books cost Sömmering the considerable sum of 400 thaler, an expense he shared with Abel Scherdinger, confessor to the Count of Hennenberg. Scherdinger and Sömmering clearly viewed these books as an investment, for they made an agreement to pursue alchemy together and to split their profits equally. Sömmering had the further good fortune of learning "a highly secret art, namely the regulation of the fire" from an alchemist named Martin Gurlach. This cost Sömmering nothing more than perhaps the price of a few beers, inasmuch as he reportedly got the information from Gurlach "while drinking." Having purchased books, recipes, and skills from a variety of people, Sömmering was thus ready to work as an alchemist. In 1566 he and Scherdinger signed a contract to produce the philosophers' stone for Duke Johann Friedrich of Sachsen-Gotha.[9]

Several aspects of this story are remarkable. The impressive array of people from whom Sömmering bought his knowledge — including pastors, another alchemist, an apothecary, and a philosopher — is an indication of how widely dispersed alchemical knowledge had become. Similarly, that knowledge came in a wide variety of forms. Sömmering not only bought books, but gleaned alchemical secrets during official lessons (from the woodcarver) and casual conversation (from the alchemist). Most strikingly, however, Sömmering's tale illustrates the extent to which alchemy was for sale by the mid-sixteenth century. Alchemical knowledge itself had become a commodity.

Alchemy's entrance into the marketplace created new forms of alchemical knowledge and new standards for measuring it. Finding it difficult to place lifetimes of learning and vast philosophical systems in compact (and marketable) books, sellers often repackaged this knowledge in the form of recipes and processes, eliminating (or at least deemphasizing) larger theoretical frameworks.[10] At the same time, the market forced buyers and sellers to place a monetary value on alchemical knowledge. As a result, the kind of alchemy which enthusiasts bought and sold at the end of the sixteenth century increasingly came to emphasize qualities that promised immediate returns and highlighted profit and utility.

Nowhere was this new emphasis on alchemy's productive potential clearer than in the manner its practitioners promoted themselves to likely patrons. One strategy alchemists used to peddle their wares was to highlight the potential profits their processes could offer. When the metallurgist, mint official, and technical author Lazar Ercker (ca. 1530–94) wrote to Duke Julius of Braunschweig-Wolfenbüttel (1528-89), he underscored the money, quite literally, that he could help generate.[11] In this 1585 letter, Ercker described a process by which "using a powder, I can bring Rheinisch, or other low quality gold, in a few days to proper Ducat-quality gold," which was worth twice as much. Ercker claimed that he could transmute 100 marks (about 233.85g) of Rheinisch Goldgulden a week, with an extra cost of 10 thaler "for the coals and all the Instruments." Promoting the efficiency of his process, Ercker noted that he could make use of the by-products as well. "The silver which the Rheinisch Goldgulden have in them will be melted out of the powder again," he boasted, "and the gold which the powder has also absorbed, of which there is little, will be separated out and used as is useful."[12]

Ercker emphasized the profits his process would generate. "I am of the humble opinion," he wrote, "that for every hundred Marks of Rheinisch Goldgulden, given the initial costs, there should be a surplus and financial profit of at least seventy or eighty Thaler."[13] As support for his claims, Ercker cited his own results using the technique to mint coins for a merchant from Nuremberg. The merchant profited handsomely (according to Ercker) producing as much as 2,000 thaler in a year. In Duke Julius's case, Ercker pledged, the profits promised to be even greater. "In my opinion," he wrote to Julius, "it would be much more lucrative and useful to Your Princely Grace because Your Princely Grace can invest [*verlegen*] much more than a merchant—which, however, can not happen at all without this invented art of mine."[14]

As Ercker's pledge suggests, practical alchemists often marketed their skills not only by underscoring productivity, but also efficiency. Their claims were usually very specific, outlining the exact ingredients, in precise quantities, and the resulting amount of precious metal. Petr Hlavsa of Liboslav, the manager of Bohemian magnate Vilém-Rožmberk's (1535–92) Prague alchemical laboratories, described one alchemist's technique in just such detail in 1574.[15] For this process, which according to Hlavsa was "truly in accordance with the alchemical art," the alchemist Cristoff von Hirschenberg started with 8 Loth gold and 8 Loth silver.[16] Using "the accompanying powders and materials," Hirschenberg increased the proportion of gold, producing 5 Loth silver and 11 Loth gold "which should pass any tests and should remain fixed."[17] The alchemist Michael Polhaimer (1566/67–98) signed a contract in 1595 with Count Wolfgang II von Hohenlohe (1546–1610) to perform a slightly different process: an "augmentation" that would transmute 2 pounds (or 64 Loth) of mercury into 10 Loth of "fine silver."[18] Such processes were typical among practical alchemists in their specificity and accuracy; they also reflect an awareness of the patrons' desire to know exactly how much money they would have to invest in this type of work and what kind of rewards it could yield.

When practical alchemists did win the support of patrons, they typically set down the terms of employ in a very businesslike contract. These contracts transferred the specific details of the proposals into a legally binding document, stipulating in detail the type of processes the alchemist was to carry out and the deadline for completion, as well as the patron's duties in terms of payment, facilities, and materials. The contract that Philipp Sömmering and Abel Scherdinger entered into in 1566 shortly after they acquired their two prized books was typical. After demonstrating their art at the court of Duke Johann Friedrich of Sachsen-Gotha, the alchemists agreed to give the duke 10 percent of the proceeds from their philosophers' stone in exchange for an advance of 760 thaler, raw materials, and equipment.[19] This kind of arrangement differed from a more general patronage relationship in its specificity. Whereas many philosophical alchemists counted princes as their patrons, they never signed contracts of this type. Instead, they were typically hired as court physicians, expected to perform a variety of duties associated with their position. The contracts that practical alchemists signed, on the other hand, were ordinarily limited to the performance of a single, specific process.[20]

USEFUL ALCHEMY AND THE WORLD OF THINGS

The range of skills that practical alchemists claimed to possess, however, could encompass anything from medicine to metallurgy. The entire laundry list appeared in a 1597 text written by Alexander Lauterwald in praise of the alchemical arts.[21] Lauterwald's interlocutor in the treatise and the embodiment of alchemy, Chimia, proclaims proudly that "no one can do without me" before outlining the full range of activities — from cooking to the fabrication of precious stones — in which she can be of use. Chimia reserves her strongest claims of utility, however, for mining and medicine.

> To that I must add even more / The minerals must choose me as well / when they want to separate themselves from others, / from the ore, in which they languish, / despairing that they are not bright. All of this I do without danger. / Indeed, I make all the metals right. / [Without me] they can not come clean, / nor can they please people; / Since they aren't properly worked, / They crumble under use. / Nor can the ore be used / If it isn't first cleansed through my breath, / [made] pure and clean / Such things know my children alone. / They are the goldsmiths and assayers, / The mint masters and jewelers / I can bring forth gemstones as well / Make glass that can bend light / Many lovely distillations / Are used for medicine / In which the great secret is buried / He who achieves this, need not worry.[22]

Although today we tend to think of medicine, metallurgy, and the production of jewels as separate activities, Lauterwald's poem reminds us that in the minds of early modern Europeans, they were closely related activities, all of which could fall within the provenance of the alchemist.

Practical alchemy was, therefore, by no means limited to the production of noble metals. Alchemists frequently carried out their metallurgical projects alongside medicinal ones, such as the "theophrastian universal medicine" that alchemist Michael Heinrich Wagenmann vom Hoff contracted with Duke Friedrich of Württemberg (1557–1608) to make in December 1598.[23] Some of these medicines were more obviously connected to precious metals, such as the *olium solis et lunae* (oil of sun [gold] and moon [silver]) which Melchior Hornug prepared with "a little of our gold" from his patron's mine in Reichenstein, Silesia, or the seemingly omnipresent medicinal golden liquid, potable gold.[24] The close connection that Paracelsus and others drew between the new chemical medicine and alchemy, in addition to the overlap in distilling skills involved in both, ensured that most practical alchemists might turn their attentions to medicine as easily as to metals. The proper powder or liquor might just as easily "heal" or purify a human body as a metallic body.

Practical alchemy could be useful in other ways as well. A female alchemist named Anna Zieglerin (ca. 1556–75) extended the alchemical concern with generation beyond metals to animal and vegetable material. In an unpublished booklet written in 1573 for her patron, she described a method "for when one wants to have cherries, grapes or other good, ripe fruit early in winter."[25] Most remarkably, Zieglerin shared with Duke Julius of Braunschweig-Wolfenbüttel her unique understanding of the homunculus, imparting a method by which the tincture used for transmuting metals might also be used to engender children. Zieglerin recommended that women having difficulty getting pregnant drink the alchemical tincture daily. When the pregnancy succeeded and the baby was born, the mother should "let the baby taste no mother's milk and give it nothing to eat or drink . . . [but] three times a day let it have three drops [of the tincture] in its mouth."[26] Here Zieglerin demonstrated yet again just how interconnected minerals, plants, and animals could be in view of the alchemist. Just as metals like gold could be used to cure humans, so too could babies thrive on the same tincture that brought noble metals out of base.

Despite all of these other activities, the transmutation or multiplication of metals remained the heart of the practical alchemical enterprise and the skill for which patrons seemed most to value its practitioners. Proposals and claims varied widely, but practical alchemists ordinarily had either a tincture or a "process" for this purpose. Although tinctures also had medicinal uses, in the context of metallic transmutation or multiplication the term designated a liquid or powder that could "tinge" or transmute metals.[27] Typically alchemists already possessed the tincture and asked only for the chance to demonstrate its potential. The Cypriot alchemist Marco Bragadino (ca. 1545–91), for example, arrived in the Veneto in 1589 with his "medicine" and successfully demonstrated it by transmuting 1 pound of quicksilver under the critical eyes of two officials from the Venetian Mint and an assemblage of local nobility.[28] Occasionally practitioners claimed only to have a sure-fire recipe for the tincture rather than the substance itself, but they swore that they could produce it given the necessary materials and equipment.[29] A "process" or *Kunstwerk* (work of artistry or skill) most often described a recipe or method for multiplying metals, and characteristically required an initial investment from a patron to perform.

When practical alchemists successfully secured positions at the princely courts of the Holy Roman Empire, they frequently found themselves working alongside others in large alchemical laboratories. Such laboratories sprouted up in Saxony, Bavaria, Bohemia, Braunschweig-Wolfenbüttel, and Württemberg in the late sixteenth century, mini-alchemical workshops dotting the map of the Holy Roman Empire. The activities in these laboratories illuminate the extent to which practical alchemy was productive work. Although the types and extent of alchemical activity in each of these laboratories certainly varied, we can get a sense of the kind of work it was from a 1608 inventory of the laboratories that Duke Friedrich I set up in his southern German territory of Württemberg. This inventory, taken upon the Duke's death, provides a snapshot of the kind of alchemical activity that went on at noble courts in the Holy Roman Empire. Friedrich's court physicians Abraham Schopf and Ulrich Porta, together with the manager of the alchemical laboratories Chrystoff Wagner, drew up a list of "all the transmutational and medicinal processes (*Stück*), in addition to raw and prepared materials, instruments, ovens, glasses, crucibles, cappels, and other tools required for work" found in the ducal laboratories. According to the list, Wagner himself was in the middle of eight different projects when the inventory was made.[30] In addition, the inventory listed five others at work in the laboratories. Andreas "the chamberboy," for example, had already finished two vials of a tincture, soon to be demonstrated in a projection, and was in the midst of a process which was to produce gold from mercury combined with a certain elemental substance. Daniel Keller, another assistant, was working on both a tingeing process and the multiplication of a tincture, while Johan Geißler was also finishing a tincture which he was shortly to demonstrate. Georgius Butina was earning four gulden weekly working on an unnamed process for the duke and simultaneously working on a process of his own involving gold. The last assistant, Adam Wiera, had just finished a process that produced an entire pound of gold and would double in another six weeks (thus producing 2 pounds). There were apparently others at work in the laboratory as well, as the inventory noted that "what the other workers are carrying out . . . can also be inquired about."[31]

Taken together, these laboratories worked as a sort of alchemical manufactory-cum-workshop. Under the direction of Duke Friedrich's manager Chrystoff Wagner, each of these assistants annually earned from 52 to 208 gulden (plus, in several cases, two new outfits yearly) to work on various processes.[32] Interestingly, few of the assistants were working on processes that they had proposed to the duke; rather, Friedrich handed out processes he collected elsewhere, assigning them to individual assistants. We learn from the inventory, for example, that Daniel Keller's task was "a work of great importance at the command of His Princely Grace." Similarly, Andreas labored at "a work, which was mentioned to His Princely Grace by Gerbelium of Strasbourg." The exception was Georgius Butina, who was lucky enough to have "arranged with His Princely Grace license [to work on] his own invention of a process." Butina, however, was unusual. For the most part these assistants were hired hands, paid a yearly salary for producing alchemical goods on their sovereign's behalf.[33]

The activities in Duke Friedrich's laboratory demonstrate the extent to which early modern alchemy was involved in the production of *things*. This was productive knowledge, and its practitioners put it to work in creating a variety of useful items. Indeed, this kind of alchemy seems strikingly mundane. Because we imagine alchemical laboratories to be dark, smoky solitary rooms and the work there to be highly secretive, it is tempting to say that the kind of alchemical practice in Friedrich's laboratories was actually something else, metallurgy perhaps, or medicine. The practitioners, however, believed that they were alchemists and that what they were doing was alchemy. The market had given them access to the art, and their skills were appreciated by patrons quite willing to pay for them. Their activities were just as much a part of alchemy as were the mystical meditations of their more spiritual colleagues.

PATRONS AND THE USES OF ALCHEMY

Why did princes like Friedrich devote such substantial resources to practical alchemical projects? Historians such as R. J. W. Evans and Bruce Moran have argued convincingly that alchemy could offer a solution to the political and religious problems plaguing central Europe. As Evans noted decades ago in his exploration of Emperor Rudolf II's well-known occult pursuits, the alchemical view of nature posited a single divine order that underlay and connected the natural and the human worlds. As such, the alchemist's work in the laboratory was also work on the world, and "alchemists sought not only the regeneration of metals through the [philosophers'] stone, but also the moral and spiritual rebirth of mankind."[34] This idea held particular promise in a fractured Holy Roman Empire still reeling from the religious wars following the Reformation.[35] Bruce Moran emphasized the political side of this same coin. "The occult vision of unity and universality," he noted, "offered an intellectual balsam for religious and political confusion. As such, it became a surrogate reality, and it is in this sense that its patronage, as much at Hessen-Kassel as at other German courts, became finally a patronage of despair."[36]

Certainly alchemy appealed to some princes on these abstract (yet very real) levels. The increased appeal of alchemy just as the political and religious structure of the empire seemed to be falling apart is an important connection, and does much to explain the power of alchemical ideas. Princes also had more practical concerns, however, and alchemy addressed these as well. We can well understand why it would have appealed to princes concerned about their health, for example. Whether practitioners sought to create a panacea in the philosophers' stone or simply the newly fashionable chemical drugs vaunted by Paracelsus and his followers, alchemy certainly promised medical marvels. And few Renaissance princes would have turned down the pearls and gemstones some alchemists offered, let alone Anna Zieglerin's wintertime fruit. Renaissance princes' delight in such wonders is well-known and would have disposed them to appreciate alchemy's more opulent productions.

A number of central European princes saw even more potential in practical alchemy and understood it as a solution to the financial and mining crises afflicting their territories in the second half of the sixteenth century. Nearly constant warfare combined with Renaissance building projects and courtly splendor drained princely coffers over the course of the sixteenth century. At the same time, the rich central European mines, a fruitful source of income through the mid-sixteenth century, began to stagnate.[37] Whereas new technologies and financial investments had increased silver production in central Europe fivefold between 1460 and 1550, this growth leveled off in the second half of the sixteenth century as the balance shifted definitively toward imported American silver. Silver imports to Europe increased more than thirty-fold in sixty years, in fact, surging from 86 metric tons in the 1530s, to 1,118 in the 1570s and 2,707 in the 1590s.[38] By 1600 the golden age of central European mining had clearly come to a close.

Despite this slump, and perhaps in reaction to it, German and Bohemian princes continued to take an active interest in mining, and several territorial rulers quite actively pursued projects designed to exploit their territories' natural resources. Duke Julius of Braunschweig-Wolfenbüttel, for example, commissioned a report in 1572 on "all kinds of mountains, metals and other uses which are found in [the mining regions of] the Harz and Rammelsberg" and hired mining expert (*Bergmeister*) Hans Fischer to search the ducal territory for natural resources.[39] In addition to these kinds of exploratory projects, Julius invested heavily in his various mines, spending roughly a third of his budget on them in 1579–80, a sum justified by the fact that his mining enterprises were his largest source of income.[40] Other princes took similar measures to develop their mining industries.[41]

For these princes, practical alchemy was intimately related to the pursuit of profits through mining. Alchemical expertise, particularly that of *Scheidekunst*, or smelting, could be extremely useful in mines where difficulties in extracting precious metals from ore had caused a decline in productivity. Recall Chimia's claim in Lauterwald's text: "The minerals must choose me as well / When they want to separate themselves from others." This seems to have been the case with the mine that Bohemian magnate Vilém Rožmberk bought in Reichenstein (Lower Silesia), where the gold ore was particularly thinly dispersed and difficult to smelt. The alchemical laboratory Vilem established there immediately after he purchased the mine may well have been intended to solve this problem.[42] Two alchemists proposed similar processes to Duke Julius of Braunschweig-Wolfenbüttel in the 1570s. Caspar Uden offered a process "by which copper and silver may be separated," and Theophil Töpfer proposed a somewhat vague process for separating metals "resulting from an alchemical technique."[43] Although Uden and Töpfer were not successful in their proposals, Duke Julius clearly valued alchemy's contribution to his mining enterprises and credited it with their renewal. Responding favorably to another proposal in 1576, Julius commented, "Like our beloved Lord and Father, we have been so involved with alchemy that we have paid dearly with thousands of thaler. Nevertheless, it has also taken us so far that for one thing, we have improved our mines during our reign, such that we now enjoy from our various mountains 480,000 gulden coins more yearly."[44]

Not only could alchemists assist princes whose ore was difficult to smelt, but they also promised either to multiply existing precious metals or to turn metals of lesser quality into gold or silver. The alchemist Georg Honauer (d. 1597) held out this possibility to Duke Friedrich I of Württemberg when he claimed to possess a process with which two men could produce one zentner (100 pounds) of gold weekly from the iron in Friedrich's iron-rich territory of Mömpelgard. ("One could also organize it like a large mine," Honauer added, "with a thousand men.")[45] Honauer arrived just as Duke Friedrich had demonstrated his commitment to developing his mining industries by announcing a reward for the location of new ore deposits. Friedrich did not hesitate to hire Honauer; he brought him to Stuttgart in 1596 under ducal protection, converted the old garden house into an alchemical laboratory, and provided Honauer with thirteen assistants. After the alchemist proved his skill in several small trials, Friedrich got down to business: he imported 25 zentner (2,500 pounds) of iron from Mömpelgard and charged Honauer to get to work.[46]

Duke Friedrich I and Georg Honauer may have hoped for unusually spectacular results, but their basic understanding of alchemy as an extremely productive and versatile art was common among central European patrons and practitioners in the decades before the Thirty Years' War. Above all, these practitioners and patrons viewed practical alchemy as a means to generate profits, whether through sales of books, recipes, processes, or the application of those processes to large-scale mining enterprises. This was primarily a utilitarian use of alchemy, aimed ultimately less at the production of broad hypotheses about the natural order than at understanding how to manipulate nature in order to make it more prolific.

At the end of the seventeenth century, Johann Joachim Becher (1635–82) would develop a much more sophisticated formulation of the relationship between alchemy and commerce that linked them metaphorically through the production and consumption common to them both. By equating the two, Becher hoped to translate his patrons' interest in alchemy into support for commercial projects in the German lands.[47] At the end of the sixteenth century, however, neither the projects nor their promoters articulated such a comprehensive view. Practical alchemists around 1600 focused their proposals on specific processes and their immediate yields rather than on large-scale economic projects. For their part, princely alchemical schemes did not situate alchemy within a broader reconceptualization of their economies, nor did they engage yet in the global economies we associate with seventeenth- and eighteenth-century commerce.

Instead, these alchemical projects sought to employ new means in order to maintain traditional ways of generating money (such as mining). The goal — to increase the production of precious metals in a territory — was still fairly traditional, even if the means were somewhat more innovative. In this context, Ercker's comment that Duke Julius could produce "much more than a merchant" with his alchemical process may be even more revealing. Unlike Becher's equation of commerce and alchemy, which sought to engage the emperor in the commercial activities of the merchant, the practical alchemy that flourished a century earlier may have been a way to do just the opposite: find a way to improve on traditional methods of making money precisely *without* involving the empire's princes in the suspect world of the merchant. As such, the princely amalgam of alchemy and mining was a curious blend of tradition and innovation, indicative of the halting emergence of early modern commerce.

CRITIQUES OF THE NEW ALCHEMICAL COMMERCIALISM

Alchemists' participation in the world of commerce did not go unnoticed. Critics of alchemy as a whole expressed doubt about whether alchemy actually could achieve the creation of wealth it promised. At the same time, those who believed in alchemy but pursued it with more philosophical or spiritual priorities in mind attacked profit-seeking practitioners in print. Drawing on older conflicts about whether alchemists should use the art solely to make gold and silver, these critics raised a new objection about the buying and selling of alchemical secrets. In fact, they denied that alchemists with commercial tendencies were "true" alchemists at all and dismissed them as impostors and frauds. As the sixteenth century came to a close, the alchemical community seemed divided between those who believed that alchemy's objective should be the production of profit, and those who pursued alchemy as a spiritual act with the potential for the regeneration of the world.

The Protestant clergyman and rector Johannes Clajus (1532–92) was among those who were highly skeptical of alchemy altogether. In his satirical treatise, *Altkumistica, Das ist die ware Goldkunst . . . aus Mist gut Gold zu machen* (Old-cow-manure, or, the true golden art . . . of making good gold out of manure, 1586), Clajus expressed traditional doubts about the use of alchemy to create wealth. He used a clever play on words to contrast the practice of alchemy (*Alchemisterey*) with the traditional agricultural method of making a living by fertilizing fields with cow manure (*Altkuhmisterey*, or "old-cow-manure-istry").[49] Clajus listed an abundance of products that could ultimately result from such a well-fertilized field: eggs, meat, milk, wool, pelts, leather, hemp oil, and flax, all of which had commercial value. In this way, he argued, the practitioners of traditional farming, or *Altkuhmisterey*, could turn manure into gold.[49]

Clajus's treatise juxtaposed this peasant *Altkuhmist* with the alchemist, setting up an opposition between the traditional agricultural livelihood and what he clearly saw as a new method: manufacturing it alchemically. Clajus rejected the possibility of alchemically manufacturing gold and feared that with so many fixated on an impossible alchemical dream, society would ruin itself. "Because just now all over this land," he wrote,

> Alchemy is growing rampant / And is wreaking havoc more and more / Many apply themselves diligently to making gold / But end up only falsifying metal / Scattering false coins all over the place. / The fact that many are seduced / as one can easily establish with examples / makes a mockery of alchemy / which is nothing but fraud.[50]

Clajus felt that alchemists were most dangerous to themselves. They wasted their money pursuing a hopeless fantasy, perhaps, like Sömmering, spending a fortune on books and materials. (Practitioners of *Altkuhmisterey*, on the other hand, would find that their fields always provided plenty.) Clajus also noted that the unlucky could face pitfalls even worse than poverty. "Many lose eyes and hands, many are beheaded, many burned," Clajus warned, hinting at several prominent alchemists who went to the gallows for failing to produce gold for their patrons.[51] Given alchemy's capacity to both impoverish and incriminate its practitioners, Clajus concluded, alchemists ought to stick to more traditional (and certain) ways of making a living, such as farming. He ended with an admonition: "This is why I recommend Altkuhmisterey . . . / With God it is certain and secure / It bears gold out of manure / it is to be tried."[52]

Proponents of the alchemical arts disagreed with Clajus's denunciation, of course, and wrote treatises praising alchemy's virtues. Many of alchemy's advocates found themselves walking a fine line, however, with regard to criticisms like Clajus's. As much as they rejected arguments about alchemy's futility, a number of alchemists found themselves sympathetic to concerns about alchemists' participation in the marketplace. Rejecting both the use of alchemy solely to create gold and silver and the practice of selling alchemical knowledge for money, critical alchemists increasingly argued that by definition, practitioners engaged in alchemy's commercial dimension were not "true" alchemists at all.

The notion that alchemy was about much more than gold and silver had a long history; for centuries some practitioners of the art had struggled to distance themselves from what they saw as the corruption of alchemy. In the early modern period, Paracelsus insistently reminded his readers that he used the term "alchemy" to mean a technique, usually medicinal, not the preparation of gold or silver.[53] The Paracelsian Alexander Lauterwald expressed these sentiments as well in two treatises which responded directly to Clajus: *Widerlegung der Altkuhmisterey* (*Refutation of Altkuhmisterey*, 1597) and *Colloquium Philosophicum* (*Philosophical Colloquium*, 1597). In the *Colloquium Philosophicum*, a dialogue between the three sisters Chimia, Sapientia, and Natura and a young novice in the alchemical arts, Lauterwald's interlocutor Chimia warned the boy to beware:

> If you hear someone openly say / . . . he wants to make silver and gold / you mustn't give him any money, / for what does such a man need? / He should earn his own living. / You mustn't seek gold; / people will easily judge you. / Those lads [who do] are the bad seeds / whom I named before. / Many honorable men have been cheated by them / parted from their things / finally separated from their goods and possessions; / Only then have they realized / that such lads deal in tricks. / And so seek the truth / wherein you will find me / you find me also in my dear children / they are the true philosophers.[54]

Lauterwald's Chimia challenged the novice with a higher calling instead. She explained that the alchemist's true purpose was to use the philosophers' stone to heal all bodies, "human, animal and metallic," of the worldly corruption that followed the Fall of Adam and Eve. In this sense, alchemy was spiritual work, aimed at the regeneration and ennobling of a corrupt and fallen world.[55]

Although the vociferousness with which spiritual and philosophical alchemists tried to distance themselves from gold-making reached a crescendo around 1600, their objections were hardly unique to the sixteenth century.[56] Beginning in the 1590s, however, critics began to react to the burgeoning market in alchemical goods and princes' increasing interest in alchemy's commercial application. In response, critical tracts began to focus on a new issue: the sale of alchemical recipes and processes for profit. Lauterwald's treatise reflects this trend as well. He denounced market-oriented alchemists (or "process-sellers," as another observer called them[57]) as frauds who seduced others with alchemy's promise of riches and eternal life only to trick them out of their money. Again speaking through Chimia, Lauterwald issued a stern warning to stay away from such impostors.

If such a visitor comes to you / Of whom you have heard before and / Who claims that he can make gold / Ask him what kind of pay he wants. / He will come finely dressed, / Finished off with a golden visage. / He will require three hundred ducats / For this he will counsel / A tincture that spews a thousand. / Stay away from such a wicked type . . . / This is what I want to say to you / You mustn't support processes.[58]

Lauterwald simply assumed that anyone who sold alchemy's secrets was a fraud because the "true" alchemist would never do such a thing. Chimia's words reflect a deep suspicion that most practitioners simply wanted to cash in on alchemy's appeal to wealthy princes.

The Leipzig-born physician and mystical alchemist Heinrich Khunrath (1560–1605), best known for the engraving of the alchemist in his Laboratory-Oratory that appeared in his *Amphitheatrum Sapientiae*, took a slightly milder approach.[59] In a nineteen-page "Heartfelt warning and admonition by a faithful devotee of the truth to all true devotees of the natural transmutory alchemy, which one need keep an eye on because of the villainous grip of the fraudulent malicious chymists," Khunrath merely issued a caveat emptor.[60] "If a goldbeetle flies up to you and says that he can make silver and gold and wants to teach you how," Khunrath warned, "do not believe him quickly and easily; because it is not as mean an art as many let themselves dream it to be."[61] Khunrath certainly did not spare harsh words for "the goldbeetle guild of villans and ill-intentioned and fraudulent alchemists," but he did put the burden not to be tricked on the buyers of alchemical secrets.[62] Khunrath's remedy was to expose the sleights of hand and tricks he believed the impostors used to dupe potential backers. A well-informed buyer, he evidently felt, would make sounder decisions in the alchemical marketplace and stay away from common alchemists.

The physician and occult philosopher Michael Maier (1569–1622) offered a much deeper and more nuanced critique of commercial alchemy. Like Lauterwald and Khunrath, Maier believed that alchemy was fundamentally a spiritual art because it dealt with God's greatest secrets, and he disapproved of those with lesser interests.[63] In his 1616 *Examen fucorum pseudo-chymicorum* (Swarm of drones, or a critical examination of the pseudo-chymists),[64] Maier publicized his vitriolic attack on those he considered "pseudo-chymists." His "four marks of the false alchemists" wove together moral, intellectual, and commercial arguments into a damning denunciation of practical alchemists, concluding that "such men are very harmful both for the state and for Chymica."[65]

The second of Maier's four marks of the impostor explicitly took up the issue of commercial exchange, imparting his disapproval of practical alchemists who traded in the marketplace. Like Lauterwald, Maier registered this censure by defining those who sold alchemical knowledge as false alchemists. "It is an unmistakable sign of the pseudo-chymicus that he wants to sell gold for gold, something uncertain as a fact and something priceless for very little," Maier reasoned. In particular, he questioned the very idea of alchemy as a commodity by focusing on the issue of prices:

> It goes against all reason that someone who really had really mastered this great art, tested over and over again in experiments, would want to sell this knowledge to another for a piece of bread or a bit of gold. If he really doesn't possess it, then it is as if he had sold wind and empty words for money. If the latter is the case, then the scoundrel receives too much money for the wind, and the buyer is cheated. If the former is the case, then the seller is cheated."[66]

If a practitioner truly possessed the secrets of alchemy, in other words, why would he or she sell it for a bit of gold, for surely it would be worth much more? If, on the other hand, the supposed alchemist sold only empty promises, then a bit of gold was far too high a price.[67] In Maier's view, alchemy was either priceless or worthless.

Beneath Maier's discussion of the logic of selling alchemical secrets, one can detect a broader agenda. The rest of his treatise fired moral, epistemo-logical, and philosophical salvoes at the folly of those who thought they could become alchemists with a little training, almost as easily as one could become a goldsmith or pharmacist. Maier viewed alchemy as a sacred art, a lifelong project to understand God's mysteries, which required learning, piety, and years of hard work. He was troubled by the popularization of alchemy and what he saw as its dilution to the point of not being alchemy at all. In the context of commerce, however, what is striking about the *Examen fucorum pseudo-chymicorum* is that Maier chose to articulate this point in the language of profit and commercial exchange. As much as he felt that the market for alchemical goods was responsible for the proliferation of a type of alchemy of whose goals and practices he despised because it created shoddy practitioners and the patrons to support them, he also knew that that market was both vibrant and undeniable. Unable to argue it out of existence, he chose instead to attack it on its own terms, exposing what he saw as the flaws of a system that viewed alchemy in terms of profits and prices.

THE VALUE(S) OF ALCHEMY

The critiques of alchemists like Maier, Lauterwald, and Khunrath reveal a fundamental divide in the community of alchemical practitioners about the value of their art. Those who purchased and peddled alchemical knowledge in the decades around 1600 operated in a world in which alchemical value was defined in terms of utility and profit. Practitioners like Sömmering purchased books and recipes, hoping in turn to sign contracts with patrons and sell acquired knowledge for thousands of thaler. Patrons like Duke Julius of Braunschweig-Wolfenbüttel, in turn, purchased this kind of alchemical knowledge, investing their fortunes in alchemy in order to multiply the natural resources in their territories. Such practitioners and patrons may have appreciated more intellectual or spiritual aspects of alchemy as well, of course, but these considerations rarely entered into their contracts, laboratories, or alchemical work. These were evaluated in terms of how useful and productive buyers perceived the alchemy to be. Critics like Michael Maier, on the other hand, operated in a different value system. They too circulated in courtly circles and depended on princely patronage, but as alchemists they located their own worth elsewhere, in their status as pious, learned men with a deep understanding of God's mysteries. For them, recipes or processes isolated from that larger learning were both impossible and, ultimately, worthless.

The irony was that, as much as philosophical and spiritual alchemists wished to remove alchemy from the marketplace, they ultimately could not. Even if they did not directly compete with their more practically minded colleagues for contracts, alchemists like Michael Maier did perceive them as competition for the right to define what the "true" alchemy was. For even if philosophical alchemists scorned practical alchemists as frauds and impostors, princes did not — and noble support gave legitimacy to practical alchemy. As the sixteenth century came to a close, in fact, practical alchemy seemed to be gaining more and more princely support as princes placed their fortunes in the hands of its practitioners. The sudden appearance of treatises like Maier's *Examen fucorum pseudo-chymicorum* testifies to the vitality he and others ascribed to this new breed of alchemy, and the extent to which they feared its triumph. In the end, of course, they were right: enthusiasm for purely transmutational alchemy would eventually dissipate and come to be mocked as it is today. This would take centuries, however; even in 1796 a contributor to a German newspaper would declare that "thousands of hands and minds" were still at work on alchemy in the Holy Roman Empire.[68] In the sixteenth and even early seventeenth centuries, both strains of alchemy — one commercial, one philosophical — might have claimed the right to define whether alchemy was to be a pious natural philosophy or a useful practice immersed in the expanding world of early modern commerce.

I wish to thank Janice Neri, Daniel Stolzenberg, Seth Rockman, and the participants of the 1999 Clark Library workshop on "Commerce and the Representation of Nature in Early Modern Europe" for their insightful comments on early versions of this paper.

1. See, for example, B. J. T. Dobbs, *The Foundations of Newton's Alchemy or, "the Hunting of the Green Lyon"* (Cambridge: Cambridge University Press, 1975); R. J. W. Evans, *Rudolf II and His World: A Study in Intellectual History* (Oxford: Oxford University Press, 1973); Bruce Moran, *The Alchemical World of the German Court: Occult Philosophy and Chemical Medicine in the Circle of Moritz of Hessen (1572–1632)* (Stuttgart: Franz Steiner Verlag, 1991).

2. One important exception to this trend is Pamela Smith, *The Business of Alchemy : Science and Culture in the Holy Roman Empire* (Princeton, N.J.: Princeton University Press, 1994).

3. Of course, students of alchemy had always spent money on books. Roger Bacon (c. 1215–after 1292) noted as much in his 1267 *Opus Tertium* (Third work) when he wrote, "Through the twenty years in which I laboured specially in the study of wisdom, careless of the crowd's opinion, I spent more than two thousand livres in these pursuits on occult books [*libros secretos*]." As cited (and translated) in E. J. Holmyard, *Alchemy*, 2nd ed. (Baltimore, Md.: Penguin Books, 1968), 119.

4. William Eamon, *Science and the Secrets of Nature: Books of Secrets in Medieval and Early Modern Culture* (Princeton, N.J.: Princeton University Press, 1994), 125–126.

5. Peter Kertzenmacher, *Alchimia Das ist alle Farben, Wasser, Olea, Salia, und Alvmina, damit mann alle Corpora Spiritvs unnd Calces Prepariert, Sublimiert unnd Fixiert Zubereyten : und wie man diese ding nutze, auff dass Sol und Lvna werden möge : Auch von Soluieren unnd Scheydung aller Metall, Polierung allerhandt Edelgestein, fürtrefflichen Wassern zum Etzen, Scheyden unnd Soluieren: Und zuletzt wie die gifftige Dämpff zuuerhüten, ein kurtzer bericht* (Frankfurt am Main: C. Engenolff's heirs, 1570), iv. On the various editions of Kertzen-macher's text and their differences, see Eamon, *Science and the Secrets of Nature*, 114–133.

6. Eamon, *Science and the Secrets of Nature*, 126.

7. Philipp Sömmering's testimony, 1 Alt 9, Nr. 311, fol. 14ff. Niedersächsisches Staats-sarchiv Wolfenbüttel (hereafter NStA Wolfenbüttel). For printed accounts of Sömmering's life, see Albert Rhamm, *Die betrüglichen Goldmacher: am Hofe des Herzogs Julius von Braun-schweig: Nach den Processakten* (Wolfenbüttel: Julius Zwißler, 1883), 3–5, and Jost Weyer, *Graf Wolfgang II. von Hohenlohe und die Alchemie: Alchemistische Studien in Schloß Weiker-sheim, 1587–1610*, ed. Stadtarchiv Schwäbisch Hall, the Hohenlohe-Zentralarchiv Neuen-stein and the Historischen Verein für Württembergisch Franken, (Forschungen aus Württembergisch Franken, 39) (Sigmaringen: Jan Thorbecke Verlag, 1992), 283–285.

8. *Librum Isaacij* and *Hexameron Bernardij*. I have been unable to identify these books and their authors, although I assume that the latter were hexameral writings attributed to Bernar-dus of Treves (fourteenth century). On Bernardus of Treves, see William Newman, "Bernardus Trevirensis," in *Alchemie: Lexicon einer hermetischen Wissenschaft*, ed. Claus Priesner and Karin Figala (Munich: C. H. Beck, 1998), 78. The *Book of Isaac* may refer to the writings of "Isaac Hollandus," a possibly mythical alchemist whose writings first appeared in the 1560s. See Julian Paulus, "Hollandus, Isaac and Johann Isaac," in *Alchemie*, ed. Priesner and Figala 181.

9. Philipp Sömmering's testimony, 1 Alt 9, Nr. 311, fol. 14ff. NStA Wolfenbüttel. For printed accounts of Sömmering's life, see Rhamm, *Die betrüglichen Goldmacher*, 3–5, and Weyer, *Graf Wolfgang II*, 283–285.

10. William Eamon makes this point in *Science and the Secrets of Nature*, chap. 1.

11. Clearly Lazar Ercker did not identify himself as an alchemist; in fact, as Pamela Long correctly has pointed out, he is quite critical of alchemy in his published treatises. In practice,

however, Ercker's projects seem little different from those of self-identified alchemists. Compare his process here, for example, to Hirschenberg's below. The lines between metallurgy, mining, and practical alchemy are extremely difficult to draw in this period. One person may call a particular process alchemy, and another may choose not to use the term. I take the broadest possible understanding of alchemy, one which is defined by practices rather than the rhetoric that often appeared in printed treatises. On Ercker and alchemy, see in particular Pamela O. Long, "The Openness of Knowledge: An Ideal and Its Context in 16th-Century Writings on Mining and Metallurgy," *Technology and Culture* 32, no. 2 (1991): 318–355.

12. Lazar Ercker to Herzog Julius in Wolfenbüttel, 3 May 1585, 1 Alt 9, Nr. 394, fol. 1–2, NStA Wolfenbüttel.

13. Ibid., fol. 1.

14. Ibid., fol. 2.

15. Petr Hlavsa's exact dates are unknown, though he did serve as mintmaster to the kingdom of Bohemia from 1553 to 1561. See Václav Březan, *Zivoty Posledních Rožmberků*, 2 vols., ed. Jaroslav Panek (Prague: Svoboda Praha, 1985), 283, 701, 801.

16. One Loth = approximately 14.62 g, thus the amount of metal involved in this transaction was actually quite small: 16 Loth = 233.85 g. On Hirschenberg, whose exact dates are unknown, see Joachim Telle, "Der Alchemist im Rosengarten. Ein Gedicht von Christoph von Hirschenberg für Landgraf Wilhelm IV. von Hessen-Kassel und Graf Wilhelm von Zimmern," *Euphorion* 71 (1977): 283–305.

17. Petr Hlavsa to Vilém z Rožmberku (alias Wilhelm von Rosenberg), 18 January 1574, Rožmbersky roddiny archiv 25, Státni oblástní archiv Třeboň (hereafter SOA Třeboň), Czech Republic.

18. On Polhaimer, see Weyer, *Graf Wolfgang II.*, 228–271 and his "Der 'Goldmacher' Michael Polhaimer—Alchemistischer Betrüger am Hof des Grafen Wolfengang II. von Hohenlohe," *Beitrage zur Landeskunde. Regelmäßige Beilage zum Staatsanzeiger für Baden-Württemberg* 4 (1993): 7–11.

19. For a description of this contract, see Rhamm, *Die betrüglichen Goldmacher*, 5. Sömmering left Gotha in the chaos of war and Reformation politics, abandoning his obligations, while Scherdinger subsequently took a new post as a pastor elsewhere. In 1571, however, Sömmering signed another contract with Duke Julius of Braunschweig-Wolfenbüttel.

20. Cost- and risk-sharing arrangements like these worked to the benefit of both parties involved. By giving up a share of their future profits, alchemists gained the initial investment they needed to put their knowledge to work (not to mention, of course, the social and political benefits that accompanied such a position at court). For their part, princes could hope to earn back their initial capital outlay once the alchemical work was under way.

21. Alexander Lauterwald, *Colloquium Philosophicum. Von der warenn Chimia, Sapientia, vnd Natura rerum, Wie die von menniglichen vnd allen Liebhabern der Kunst von aller Sophisterey vnd betriegery/mag vnterschieden vnd verstanden werden. Alles zu Gruendlicher vnd warhafftiger widerlegung des groben Phantasierens M. Johan Claij/Bengellebischem Pfarherrs/der durch die Altkumisterey/andere lerer Gold machen/Vnd also das herrliche/vnd verborgenste Geheimnis/so vnter allen Natuerlichen dingen/vnd fuertrefflichsten Gaben Gottes/sehr wenigen bekant vnd offenbaret ist/aus lauterm vnuerstand vnd grobheit/dem stinckenden Kuhemist vorziehen thut etc.* (Cologne: Heinrich Netessem, 1597). Lauterwald's dates are unknown.

22. Ibid., fol. A4v.

23. In exchange, Wagenmann received 4,000 gulden, which he pledged to pay back should he fail. Agreement between Michael Heinrich Wagenmann vom Hoff and Duke Friedrich, Stuttgart, 23 December 1598, Bestand 47 (Alchemie Sachen), Büschel 3, Number 6, Hauptstaatsarchiv Stuttgart (hereafter HStA Stuttgart).

24. Melchior Hornug to Vilém z Rožmberků, 4 April 1585. SOA Třeboň. On potable gold (*aurum potabile*), see Lawrence Principe, "Aurum potabile," in *Alchemie*, Priesner and Figala, ed. 66, and the bibliography there.

25. "Präparation des Stein der Weisen, von A. M. Ziegler, in eigenhändiger Anschrift des Hzg. Julius," 1 April 1573, 1 Alt 9, Nr. 308, fol. 52–70, NStA Wolfenbüttel.

26. Ibid., fol. 64–65.

27. This double meaning makes sense since, in Paracelsian terms, the healing of the body was analogous to the healing of base metals; in both cases, a chemical medicine was necessary.

28. For an account of Bragadino's life, see Ivo Striedinger, *Der Goldmacher Marco Bragadino* (Munich: Theodor Ackerman, 1928). Also Hatto Kallfelz, "Der zyprische Alchimist Marco Bragadino und eine florentiner Gesandtschaft in Bayern," *Zeitschrift für bayerische Landsgeschichte* 31, no. 2 (1968): 476–500, and Kallfelz's article "Bragadino, Marco," *Dizonario Biografico degli Italiani, 13:* 691–694.

29. Marco Bragadino, Michael Sendivoj, Edward Kelley, and Heinrich Müller von Mühlenfels are examples of the former, while Anna Zieglerin and Philipp Sömmering are instances of the latter. See Hermann Kopp, *Die Alchemie in älterer und neuerer Zeit* (Heidelberg: Carl Winter's Universitätsbuchhandlung, 1886).

30. These included an "oil from gold" (the recipe for which was to be found in the ducal apartments (in "a special table in which all the alchemical things are together"), a "salt from gold," an *aurum potabile*, the coagulation of a "red water which is supposed to have come from Prag," a process for "finishing" gold learned from another alchemist named Thurnheuser (Leonhard Thurneisser?), a *praecipitat* from Müllenfels, one of the duke's former alchemists who had been hanged two years earlier for fraud and *lèse-majesté*, a vial to be set in the fire for two years, eventually to yield a projection of gold, and one last, somewhat mysterious, "special process." Inventory from 28 January–3 February 1608, Bestand 47, Büschel 9, HStA Stuttgart.

31. Ibid.

32. Ibid. (These salary figures are also listed in the 1608 inventory.)

33. Ibid.

34. Evans, *Rudolf II and His World*, 201.

35. Ibid., 276.

36. Moran, *The Alchemical World of the German Court*, 25.

37. See Long, "The Openness of Knowledge"; Phillippe Braunstein, "Innovations in Mining and Metal Production in Europe in the Late Middle Ages," *Journal of European Economic History* 12 (1983): 563–591; Hans-Joachim Kraschewski, *Wirtschaftspolitik im deutschen Territorialstaat des 16. Jahrhunderts: Herzog Julius von Braunschweig-Wolfenbüttel*, ed. Prof. Dr. Ingomar Bog (Neue Wirtschaftsgeschichte, 15) (Cologne and Vienna: Böhlau Verlag, 1978); Danuta Molenda, "Technological Innovation in Central Europe between the XIVth and the XVIIth Centuries," *Journal of European Economic History* 17 (1988): 63–84.

38. Richard Bonny, *The European Dynastic States, 1494-1660* (Oxford: Oxford University Press, 1991), 420.

39. Kraschewski, *Wirtschaftspolitik im deutschen Territorialstaat*, 127–128.

40. Ibid., 157. The same year, Julius received 42 percent of his income from his mining enterprises in Rammelsberg and the Harz (152).

41. Duke Friedrich of Württemberg, for instance, displayed his desire to exploit the natural resources in his territories in 1596 when he announced a reward for the discovery of ore deposits in his lands. The following year, Friedrich established the city of Freudenstadt and founded a silver mine nearby. In Bohemia, the Czech magnate Vilém Rožmberk bought a silver mine in Reichenstein (in Czech Rychleby — today Liberec — in Polish Złoty Stok, located

in Lower Silesia) and immediately established an alchemical laboratory there. See Václav Březan, *Životy Posledních Rožmberků*, 703.

42. Five different methods had been tried earlier in the sixteenth century to deal with this, which may explain why the mine was bankrupt by the end of the century. See Danuta Molenda, "Technological Innovation in Central Europe," 75. Also Březan, *Životy Posledních Rožmberku*, 703.

43. On Uden: "Schreiben vom August 1576, Unterschrift und Datum fehlen," 2 Alt 24, NStA Wolfenbüttel. On Töpfer: "Schreiben des Theophil Töpfer an Sander vom 5.2.1575," Fach 2a, 10, Oberbergamt Clausthal.-Zellerfeld Archiv des Oberbergamtes. As quoted in Kraschewski, *Wirtschaftspolitik im deutschen Territorialstaat*, 159–160.

44. "Neigung des Herzogs Julius zur Alchemie; Befehl an die Beamten," 5 June 1576, 2 Alt 24, NStAW. As quoted in Kraschewski, *Wirtschaftspolitik im deutschen Territorialstaat*, 159. When Duke Julius hired Sömmering (after he had left Gotha and his employment with Duke Johann-Friedrich there), the alchemist signed a contract that reflects this close link between mining and alchemy: Sömmering promised not only to teach Julius how to make the philosophers' stone, but also to increase the yield of Julius's mines to 200,000 thaler a year. Rhamm, *Die betrüglichen Goldmacher*, 8–9.

45. Georg Honauer to Emperor Rudolf II, 5 January 1597, Bestand 47, Büschel 1, Number 10 (part 1, unpaginated), HStA Stuttgart.

46. "Documents regarding the trial of Georg Honauer," Bestand 47, Büschel 1–2, HStA Stuttgart. Similarly, Alchemists Moritz Lam and Georg von Minden offered Duke Julius of Braunschweig-Wolfenbüttel a process in 1576 "by which copper can be made from the Rammelsberg lead." "Die angegeben Neue Alchimisten, Moritz Lam und Georg v. Minden betr., Vernehmungsprotokoll vom 6.6.1576," 2 Alt 24, NStA Wolfenbüttel. As quoted in Kraschewski, *Wirtschaftspolitik im deutschen Territorialstaat*, 159.

47. Pamela H. Smith, "Curing the Body Politic: Chemistry and Commerce at Court, 1664–70," in *Patronage and Institutions: Science, Technology, and Medicine at the European Court, 1500-1750*, ed. Bruce T. Moran (Rochester, N.Y.: Boydell Press, 1991), 195–209, and Smith, *The Business of Alchemy*.

48. I have looked at the later 1616 edition: Johann Clajus, *Altkumistica: Das ist / Die ware Goldkunst / aus Mist durch seine Operation vnd Process gut Goldt zu machen / Wider die betrieglichen Alchymisten vnd vngeschickten vermeinten Theophrastisten von Herrn Johanne Clajo beschrieben: Neben angehencktem Special Bericht / von allerhand geheimen vnd subtilen raenken vnd Handgriffen / dadurch die Arg Chymisten vnnd des uebrigen Geldes fein artig zu endledigen / und an statt der verhofften gueldenen Berge Aschen / Kohlenstaub vnd den lehren Beutel zulassen wissen. Auch wie mit dergleichen Kuenstlern vnd Gabalierern zu verfahren seige. Mennigklichen zur Nachrichtung und Warnung zusammen gebracht / Durch Aletophilum Parrhesiensem*, 3rd ed. (Mülhausen: Johann Stangen, 1616).

49. "A commendable art is here described / Which became widely accepted / Long ago among the ancients / From the beginning and the Creation / [This art] is called "old-cow-manure" (*Altkumisterey*) / In which there is no sophistry / No false dealings nor fraud / Just that which one turns up with a plow / On a field which is / well-fertilized and enclosed." Clajus, *Altkuhmistica*, "Vorrede" [unpaginated].

50. Ibid.

51. Ibid.

52. Ibid.

53. See Massimo Luigi Bianchi, "The Visible and the Invisible: From Alchemy to Paracelsus," in *Alchemy and Chemistry in the 16th and 17th Centuries*, ed. Piyo Rattansi and Antonio Clericuzio (Dordrecht: Kluwer Academic, 1994), 17–50.

---

54. Lauterwald, *Colloquium Philosophicum* [unfoliated, 16r–v].

55. Ibid. [unfoliated, 23v.]

56. See Berend Strahlmann, "Chymisten in der Renaissance (16. Jahrhundert)," in *Der Chemiker im Wandel der Zeiten; Skizzen zur geschichtlichen Entwicklung des Berufbildes*, ed. Eberhard Schmauderer (Weinheim: Verlag Chemie, 1973), 47–55.

57. Michael Maier, *Examen fucorum pseudo-chymicorum detectorum et in gratiam veritatis amantium succincte refutatorum* (Frankfurt: printed by Nicolai Hoffmann, published by Theodor de Brij, 1617), 23. Reprinted (and translated into German) in Wolfgang Beck, "Michael Maiers Examen Fucorum Pseudo-Chymicorum—Eine Schrift wider die falschen Alchemisten" (Ph.D., Fakultät für Chemie, Biologie und Geowissenschaft der Technischen Universität München, 1992).

58. Lauterwald, *Colloquium Philosophicum* [unfoliated, 26–26v].

59. On Khunrath, see Elmar Gruber's introduction to *Vom Hylealischen, das ist, Pri-materialischen catholischen oder allgemeinen natürlichen Chaos, der naturgemässen Alchymiae und Alchymisten.* (Magdeburg, 1597; reprint, Graz: Akademische Druck- und Verlagsanstalt, 1990), v–xix.

60. This text, "Wahrnungs-Vermahnung an alle wahre Alchymisten, sich vor den betrügerischen Arg-Chymisten zu hüten," is appended to his *Vom Hylealischen, das ist, Pri-materialischen catholischen oder allgemeinen natürlichen Chaos, der naturgemässen Alchymiae und Alchymisten* (Magdeburg, 1597).

61. Khunrath, *Vom Hylealischen*, 268.

62. Ibid., 286.

63. See Karin Figala and Ulrich Neumann, "'Author Cui Nomen Hermes Malavici': New Light on the Bio-Bibliography of Michael Maier (1569–1622)," in *Alchemy and Chemistry in the 16th and 17th Centuries*, ed. Piyo Rattansi, and Antonio Clericuzio (Dordrecht: Kluwer Academic, 1994), 138–139.

64. Michael Maier, *Examen fucorum pseudo-chymicorum.*

65. Ibid., 10.

66. Ibid., 22.

67. "Maier even cited the law to support his point: "The Civil Code permits people doing business to haggle with one another while buying and selling, but not that more than one and a half times the true worth [of the wares] be paid or asked . . . Regarding this, see the commentary to the section [of the Civil Code] regarding buying and selling. With regard to the wares of pseudo-chymici, nothing is in proportion, because they offer only words and promises for gold. How much empty wind must one accept for the equivalent of a gold drachma, is impossible to determine. In sum: he who touches tar gets dirty hands, and he who gets involved with these people only ends up with an empty purse." Maier, *Examen fucorum pseudo-chymicorum*, 22

68. *Kaiserlich Privilegirter Reichs-Anzeiger* (Gotha), 8 October 1796 (Num. 234), col. 6095.

Time's Bodies

Crafting the Preparation and Preservation of Naturalia

HAROLD J. COOK

S cientific investigation deals with the secular world: the world of time. Scientists study manifestations of the universe as they unfold. Time may be the fourth dimension, but it is so important as to commonly become one of two axes on graphs and charts. Consequently, many of the methods employed by investigators of nature attempt to slow or quicken events. In recent decades, some of the most famous visual examples of this method include serial photographs of movement, slow-motion films of various behaviors too quick to be observed with the eye, or fast-forward films of slow transformations. In the seventeenth century, studies such as William Harvey's on generation involved the serial examination of fertile chickens' eggs and does' uteruses; his even more famous discovery of the circulation of the blood equally involved vivisectional techniques that slowed the heartbeat and pulse to events that could be seen with the naked eye. Some of the important investigations into the material structures of animal bodies carried out in the seventeenth-century Netherlands also had their roots in attempts to alter the processes of ordinary time, especially those associated with decay. The consequences of such trials proved to yield unexpected results, in making visible structures that could not otherwise be ascertained.

TIME'S VALUE: ACCUMULATION, PRESERVATION, AND THE FUTURE

Most historical discussion of changing concepts of time has focused on the development of a sense of its uniformity. Time may be an indivisible wave or a composition of streaming quanta, but in either case the principle that it is uniform, allowing one moment to be compared to another, is fundamental, even in an Einsteinian universe where the speed of matter can "slow" or "accelerate" the time of one object in relation to another. It was famously the invention of mechanical timekeepers that conveyed the view that time is uniform. The sense that time changes with the seasons, with one's age, with peace or war, during moments of stress or bliss, accords with human felt experience. Classically, night and day were divided into twelve parts which varied with the season: the hours of night were longer in the winter, whereas the hours of light were longer in the summer. An advantage of hourglasses and water clocks is that they could be easily altered to accord with such variations. But mechanical clocks moved steadily, invariably (aside from mechanical inconsistency), dividing the day into equal hours. Now it was the night or day that changed according to the hour, not the hour that altered according to the light. Clocks quickly made their appearance in the towers of guildhalls and other municipal buildings, striking the hours to regulate commerce and other activities of large numbers of people: workers in the Low Countries had been complaining of "working to the clock" from at least the fourteenth century.[1] By the lifetime of Galileo and Descartes, both natural philosophers and musicians could take the uniform nature of time for granted, "timing" events according to regularized beats.[2] As Norbert Elias put it, "The significance of the emergence of the concept of 'physical time' from the matrix of 'social time' can hardly be overrated."[3]

In the same period, however, another sense of the relationship between time and human life that had importance for the development of investigations into medicine and natural history: a growing sense that new methods of using time could bring material good. The ways of life developing among early modern capitalists helped to make questions of manipulating the ordinary processes of time seem natural. Capitalist forms of economy depended not only on drawing attention to the rapid passage of time, but also on making work more regularized. The Dutch financial world also depended on new methods of commerce that extended time: long-term arrangements. As a world of markets was being transformed into a world market, "the beating heart of the Dutch economy" was its "entrepôt function." That is, the Dutch Republic functioned as a kind of clearinghouse, to which surplus goods were shipped from all over the world for exchange and redistribution. The goods (and their abstractions in the form of bills of exchange) were traded daily at the Amsterdam Exchange (*Beurs*) rather than at periodic fairs, making it "a mustering field not only for the coincidental surplus production . . . but also for information" about commodities and exchanges worldwide, helping to stimulate collective decisions by merchants on the allocation of capital.[4] Moreover, not only the commodities themselves, but their future worth, could be bought or sold in the form of "stocks," which were paper representations of accumulations of material things. Accumulation of inventory for later (sometimes much later) sale allowed the universal principle of "buy low and sell high" to operate over the middle and long term: items could be kept back from the market when they were otherwise too plentiful, and sold when demand increased. Inventory investment therefore reduced and spread out financial risk, making trade more predictable, and allowing for stabler calculation of future income and expense.

Inventory investment also required that goods set aside for future use or sale made it into the future in good condition. The building boom in dock- and canal-side warehouses is the clearest sign of the new form of merchant capitalism: here nutmeg or tea, there Persian rugs or Chinese silks, were collected, itemized, and assigned an estimated value for the market. In the warehouse, goods could be safeguarded and stored in a manner that prevented decay. Nutmeg, for instance, was shipped back from the Indies dusted with lime. Some other very valuable fruits came preserved in sugar. Salting and pickling kept other fish, meat, and vegetables from putrefaction. Most other goods could simply be dried and kept dry. It was this combination of methods of accumulation, preservation, and calculation of future value that allowed the merchant capitalists of the period to flourish. For instance, the Dutch East India Company (VOC) was able to manage the price of cloves by accumulating and preserving the spice in its warehouses. When the price of cloves fell in 1623, they held back cloves from the auctions to drive the price back up; when the price was so high that the English broke into the Dutch monopoly, they resorted in turn to dumping to drive the English out. With the accumulation and storage of commercial goods, therefore, a "certain measure of control over the prices" could be achieved, which together with "the concentration of the East India trade in the intimately connected London and Amsterdam markets must have meant a greater transparency of the market."[5]

As the simple example of cloves illustrates, "investing in inventory [was] crucial to a smooth functioning of the market." The permanent staple market that developed in places like Amsterdam and Rotterdam served to concentrate supply and demand, which "reduced the commercial risk, so that the cost price decreased. As supply was less regular than sales, prices fluctuated. These price fluctuations offered the prospect of future profits and thus stimulated stockpiling which, in turn, had a stabilizing effect on the price." Holland consequently became "a central storehouse and exchange" for the world market. "And inventory investment was — as already indicated — at the very heart of the Dutch entrepôt trade, which in turn was the focal point of the commercial expansion of the Dutch economy."[6] In short, inventory investment helped to create stability in "the market," hence increasing confidence in it, while growing confidence in turn helped to lower interest rates and raise the amount of available credit for more investment in exchange and accumulation. The calculation and sale of future value gave rise to new forms of material life, with ramifications for intellectual culture as well.

Like the developing world market, the investigation of nature depended on the transportation of information and specimens back to the home metropolis. There collections were accumulated, housed, and preserved, inventories were taken and sometimes published, and redistribution of the value-added information and objects occurred. The ways of life that so valued the accumulation of bulk commodities also valued the accumulation of unique objects, whether works of art or nature. Among the items brought back to the Dutch entrepôt from all over the world were natural rarities and curiosities of all sorts. These things at first tended to be one-of-a-kind, or at least scarce, objects, brought back in the bags of seamen or the chests of officers and merchants. Other specimens were cultivated in botanical gardens. Over time, a steady trade in *naturalia* developed, with a few brokers even buying up objects at dockside and later selling them to collectors. In short, many people began to collect various kinds of objects from nature, although they placed them not in shelters by the docks but in rooms in their homes: the "curiosity cabinets" of burgers, physicians, magistrates, and nobles (fig. 9.1). As in business, too, the collectors of *naturalia* kept detailed inventories of what they had. To make their collections more valuable, they tried to fill them out with new specimens, and they bought books describing the collections of others as a way of substituting for what they could not acquire directly. The accumulation and warehousing of material objects — investment in and preservation of inventory — was part of the creation of value for both naturalists and merchants.

In the sixteenth and early seventeenth century, most objects kept in curiosity cabinets had to be dried. Inventories of later sixteenth- and early seventeenth-century cabinets make this clear. For instance, one of the earliest cabinets of natural history and art assembled in the Netherlands, by Bernardus Paludanus (Berent ten Broecke), contained fruit, grains, and woods from the tropics, skins with feathers prepared from many birds (such as the bird of paradise of New Guinea), many species of fish and reptiles, the horns of a variety of animals, insects, shells, corals, types of earths, stones, minerals, marbles, precious stones, coins, medals, weapons, clothes and other objects used by "savages" and foreigners, objects of art done in ivory, rare woods, precious metals, mummies and funerary furnishings from Egypt, and so on.[7] Perhaps the fruits were pickled or preserved in sugar as well as dried; some of the skins were tanned; everything else could have been kept dried. In another example, the first inventory of the natural history collection assembled at Leiden University shows that it contained skeletons and diverse bones of humans, animals, birds, fish, and other items such as horns; rarities such as mummies and their parts, seven stones surgically removed from the bladder of Joannes Heurnius (the first medical professor of Leiden), a stone from the kidney of a young girl, and so forth; various lists and

Figure 9.1 Title page from Ole Worm's catalog of his collection of curiousities, mainly *naturalia*, published in 1655. All the specimens are dried. They include human artifacts; stuffed fish, birds, and animals; and skulls, horns, minerals, stones, salts, earths, shells, corals, seeds, leaves, and roots. Courtesy of Wellcome Library, London.

placards; portraits and paintings, large and small; surgical and anatomical instruments; a large Egyptian mummy, windings of Egyptian linen, Chinese paper, and paintings of exotic fruits, nuts, woods, stones, and so on; and other odds and ends. There was also the liver of a young woman of seventeen anatomized by Otto Heurnius in 1620, and the vital organs of pigs. While it is possible that these items were pickled or kept in brine (neither of which preserves the structures for close later inspection), they, too, were more likely dried.[8] So it goes with other collections of *naturalia*: they were based on dried specimens. The result was that collectors could see the shape of things, their forms, but with few exceptions, not their inner structures.

Physicians and pharmacists had long investigated methods for the preservation of small quantities of valuable biologicals. Apothecaries had helped to foster the majolica pottery industry and perhaps helped to stimulate the early modern glass industry as well, since both kinds of containers helped enormously in preserving medicaments by keeping out light, moisture, and air. Apothecaries and physicians were also among the first to pioneer the use of chemical processes for the preparation of medicines; in addition to other advantages, chemical preparations were not as subject to decay as their biological counterparts. In the sixteenth century, a new technique for preserving botanical material became indispensable for the study of herbal medicines and botany: the first professor of simples at Bologna and first director of the botanical garden at Pisa in the 1530s and 1540s, Luca Ghini, developed a method of taking plants or parts of them and pressing them firmly between sheets of paper while they dried, which preserved their form (and temporarily their color) for later study.[9] These herbaria gave tremendous aid to botanical study, although there remained no substitute for studying living plants in gardens, which consumed huge investments of time and money in the period. Not all plants could be studied in European gardens, however, since many exotics, from tropical climates in particular, died within a season or two. Not until techniques came along like the building of glass houses coupled with special furnaces in the mid to later seventeenth century — a subject handled so well recently by Chandra Mukerji — could the inner structures of many plants be studied.

The study of animals and their parts was even more difficult. Anatomies had to be carried out with some rapidity, especially when working with soft tissue, because of the rapid onset of putrefaction; this is one reason that public anatomies tended to take place in the cold winter months, despite the darkness of the season. Animal parts could be studied at leisure only if dried (as with skeletons) or tanned, neither of which allowed for the investigation of the structures of the body.

Methods to counteract the natural senescence that came with time had been long sought, however. Roger Bacon, for instance, argued that "men used to know what to do about premature physical deterioration: 'per experientias secretas' it had been discovered and written that this rapid aging is accidental (having avoidable side-effects) and therefore can be treated. The medical art cannot achieve this but the experimental art can."[10] His works on the subject were translated into English in 1683.[11] Many other philosophers and alchemists — to say nothing of Ponce de Leon and the search for the fountain of youth — hoped to discover means to prolong human life to at least the age of the biblical patriarchs. Sir Francis Bacon believed that the classical third part of medicine (after preserving health and curing disease), the prolongation of life, would be much improved by his reform of natural philosophy.[12] René Descartes, too, believed that one of the most important results of his own intellectual reforms would be the prolongation of life.[13] Similarly, finding better means to prevent decay and putrefaction also became subject to study. By the middle of the seventeenth century, the rapid growth of new methods of forestalling time's natural processes can be discerned. Although it was a goal which today seems more modest than the prolongation of life, this seems so only in retrospect, probably because solutions to problems of decay began to be found whereas medicines to prolong life remained the stuff of legend. We may think the development of methods for preserving biological specimens worthy of little remark only because we take them for granted. But in ordinary experience, decay and aging appear to be closely related. In the seventeenth century, then, methods to preserve the bodies of living things seemed almost miraculous. They also made the transition from "dry" to "wet" collections possible. The resultant spin-offs for the investigation of nature had important implications.

PRESERVING A LIFELIKE BODY

At first blush, the motivations for trying to preserve animal bodies in a natural-like state seem obvious. As Herman Boerhaave explained in his account of Jan Swammerdam:

> Having gone through his courses [in medicine] with the most sudden and unexpected success, he immediately began to consider how the parts of the body prepared by dissection, could be preserved and kept in constant order and readiness for anatomical demonstrations; as such a discovery would free him not only from the trouble of repeated dissections, but likewise from the difficulty of obtaining fresh subjects, and the disagreeable necessity of inspecting such as were already putrefied.[14]

The details of how Swammerdam and others came to develop methods for preserving whole bodies and body parts is somewhat more complicated, however.

University-educated physicians and surgeons like Swammerdam were preceded and stimulated by the work of Louis de Bils, lord of Coppensdamme and Bonem (both modest fiefs in Flanders).[15] According to the report of Samuel Sorbière, De Bils (b. about 1624) had begun dissecting at the age of thirteen when living in Rouen, and afterward in Flanders and Rotterdam. Why he developed his interest and how he obtained bodies to dissect are both unknown. His father and brothers were merchants, and he himself seems not to have had the kind of good classical education expected of *savants*. Yet by 1646–47, De Bils had a family and was in Amsterdam, where he met the anatomist and surgeon Paul Barbette and the physician-chemist and anatomist François dele Boë Sylvius; a few years thereafter he had taken up residence in Sluis, in Dutch Zeeland not far from Middelburg, a flourishing port city. He continued his anatomical studies and in 1651 gave the University of Leiden a number of preparations made at great expense, acknowledged in a written testimonial by the new professor of anatomy,

Joannes Van Horne. It contained a particularly remarkable specimen: "Above all else is a dried human cadaver that appears to be freshly dead, the most worthy work for such a theater" of anatomy, Van Horne attested.[16] Shortly thereafter Van Horne saw in The Hague another body "balsamed" by De Bils, in which the sinews and plump muscles were displayed as if alive. Apparently working alone, De Bils had found means to prepare human bodies so that they appeared to be full of life rather than dessicated. His secret process of "balsaming" was a fantastic new art in both senses of the word.

De Bils's method was apparently stimulated by the example of Egyptian mummies. Mummies were common objects in the curiosity cabinets of the late sixteenth and early seventeenth centuries, and the period also saw the flourishing of speculation about the wisdom of the Egyptians.[17] Because the brain and viscera were extracted and the remaining skin and muscle were hardened by the preservative process,[18] Egyptian mummies had little to offer the anatomist. But they had long held people fascinated by the length of time they lasted without decay. In an age before modern methods of embalming, they were true wonders. Most European churches and grave-yards were places where bodies were buried and decayed, the grounds being continually redug for the burial of additional bodies; sometimes the bones that were recovered in the process were collected in heaps under eves around the outer walls — the charnel houses. Shakespeare's famous "alas poor Yorick" soliloquy is located in such a graveyard, contemplating the skull of a past acquaintance. While the wealthy and powerful might have a stone tablet or other enduring memorial erected in their memory, it was the sign of a miracle to possess a body that did not rot after death.[19] De Bils himself was involved in an investigation of the bodily remains of Maria Margaretha van Valckenisse, mother of a cloister in Oirschot who died in 1658 yet did not decay but rather gave off a sweet oil, declaring the causes to be natural and fraudulent rather than miraculous.[20] Mummies were therefore quite unusual for lasting so long after death.

The power of overcoming putrefaction also made mummies and pieces of them, or more often the powder from pieces of them (both called *mumia*), a sovereign remedy in all kinds of complaints. Karl Dannenfeldt has given us an excellent account of the early modern debate over mumia. He explains the historical process as one by which the use of bituminous products in medicine was transferred to embalmed or desiccated bodies. The precious seepage of black rock-asphalt or pissasphalt from a mountain in Persia, locally called "mumiya," became particularly well regarded. By the thir-teenth century, the resinous, aromatic substance exuded from bodies found in Egyptian tombs was considered to be a very similar product. Since asphalt was said to be used by the Egyptians for embalming their dead, the true mumia could be found in the cavities of the head and body in the "mummies." It was a short step to considering the embalmed flesh—and even the wrappings—to contain the precious resin.[21] Antonius [Musa] Brasavola's *Examen omnium simplicium medicamentorum* (1537), defined *"mumia* as the remains of an enbalmed body and the same as bitumen judiacum."[22] The textbook on chemistry by Joachim Tanckius, professor at Leipzig, simply stated that *"Mumia* is the arcanum and secret of the microcosm."[23] Consequently, European demand for mummies became so high that the Egyptian government was forced to outlaw the export of mummies, although a large contraband trade in both true and counterfeited mummies continued through the early modern period.[24]

Medical practitioners also attempted to make mumia themselves. Paracelsus and his followers, for instance, described mumia as a force in living tissue that attacked invading disease semina. Andreas Tentzel's *Medicina diastatica* (1629) "was primarily devoted to mumia, of which he enlarged the scope and definition. Now there was extraction of the mumia of the aerial body by interception of the dying breath."[25] More practically, however, flesh from those who died healthy and without disease—especially those who died a violent death—was thought by Paracelsus and his followers to still radiate the power of mumia, so that the flesh of the recently deceased could be used after exposing it to the air for a day and a night. Oswald Croll was even more precise: the best tincture of mumia was prepared from the flesh of a "red-haired man twenty-four years old, who had been hanged, broken on the wheel, or thrust-through, exposed to the air for a day and a night, then cut into small pieces or slices, sprinkled with a little powder of myrrh and aloes, soaked in spirits of wine, dried, soaked again, and dried." From this could be extracted a red tincture, "a quintessence, which could be used for cures of pestilence, venin, and pleurisy."[26] (Perhaps the trade in mumia affected the debate about cannibalism in early modern Europe).[27] It is no surprise, then, to find Dutch physicians setting recipes for making mumia alongside receipts for embalming bodies.[28]

As for the process by which the Egyptians mummified their dead, the main ingredients were thought to be myrrh and aloes, as well as other resins. It is probably needless to remind anyone that in the Christmas story Magi bear gifts of myrrh and frankincense, two resins from "Arabia" (as Europeans knew the Near and Middle East) very valuable in medicine; closely related to the resins, according to Dioscorides, were the substances in the category pitch, including asphalt and other substances related to the original "mumiya." As one commentator explained: in order to thwart the usual course of putrefaction, the Egyptians disemboweled the dead and repeatedly steeped them in bitumen and stuffed them with precious aromatics.[29] Aromatic and oily resins were also those things that often went under the rubric of "balsam," or in English, "balm." It is clear that De Bils was experimenting with various expensive oils and resins such as myrrh when he engaged in "balsaming" (*balsemen* remains the Dutch verb for the English "embalming"). Given the high prices of the imported balms, his experimental costs must indeed have been enormous.

What De Bils was trying to do went further than what the Egyptians had done, however. For mummification preserved only the external form of the body. While the body endured permanently and could be examined without any effusion of blood or fluids that might offend those with delicate sensibilities, mummies were useless for the anatomist. The bodies were hardened and the viscera absent.[30] De Bils, however, was developing methods of preserving the whole body in a lifelike manner.

De Bils's personal affairs suffered badly in the early 1650s, but he kept up his investigations. After the death of his father, he and his brothers, merchants in Rouen, became embroiled in various lawsuits against one another about the inheritance. Although he obtained the office of bailiff of Aardenburg, the pay was slight, and he seems not to have invested much energy in the position.[31] But two medical friends in Sluis, Drs. Abraham Parent and Laurens Jordaen, both of whom had studied at Padua, helped De Bils with his anatomical work and jointly published a pamphlet on De Bils's investigations on the anatomy of the inner ear. They both moved away in the mid-1650s, however, lessening De Bils's opportunities for anatomical study.[32] By 1657, De Bils was searching for new means of support. A physician in Brugges (not far from Sluis), Burchardus Wittenberg, wrote a tract highly praising De Bils's achievements and calling on a prince to support him, so that his work was not paid for out of his own pocket. Through an intermediary De Bils tried to interest professor Van Horne in working with him, but Van Horne seems to have balked at the probable expense. De Bils did finally get the financial support of a physician from Middelburg for his research and publication on the lymphatics. But this publication hit a nerve with Van Horne, who expressed complete surprise at De Bils's work. Van Horne quickly turned out a Latin translation of the book, although criticizing it at the same time.[33] According to the historian G. A. Lindeboom, Van Horne himself "now applied himself to the making of fine anatomical preparations"[34]—a matter to which we will return in a moment.

Given De Bils's successes, the States General of the Dutch Republic issued an order on 9 August 1658 for the public provision of bodies to De Bils, while new translations into Dutch of anatomical works by Thomas Bartholinus and Paul Barbette allowed De Bils to study further. His friend Parent also published a notice again urging support for De Bils's work, which was so costly — especially the balsams. The city of Rotterdam, to which De Bils had followed Parent, set up an anatomical theater over the former English merchants' courthouse. De Bils used it for further studies on his secret method of dissecting and balsaming, and for the display of at least four dissected and balsamed cadavers. Apparently a "sovereign power" sought to get him to sell his secret several times, but he refused in favor of setting up his show in Rotterdam, for which he charged an admission of 1 rijksdaalder. Despite the high entry fee, his display was heavily attended by physicians and students as well as the public, from ordinary people to ambassadors and princes. He also held public anatomical demonstrations. His special technique was to dissect without losing any blood or other moisture from the body. For such theatrical presentations he charged even more.[35]

But after initial support, encouraging students and others to attend De Bils's displays and demonstrations, Van Horne turned against De Bils in writing. He had become proud, telling the world that students learned more from him in half an hour than from Van Horne in two years. Van Horne in turn decided that De Bils was a pretender, with neither learning nor gentlemanly behavior. The Amsterdam surgeon Barbette also turned against De Bils. He, too, underlined the absence of academic education in De Bils: "Philosophy, chemistry, astronomy, medicine, and daily practice" were absolutely necessary for understanding the workings of the body, but for two years the unlettered De Bils had pretended to be the great master overturning all established learning. De Bils replied to these two sallies with his own pamphlet of March 1660, in which he ascribed Van Horne's and Barbette's criticisms to jealousy. But in attacking them he also further attacked, and further alienated, learned physicians generally. The debate continued throughout De Bils's life (he died in 1669)—he had some supporters in the Dutch Republic as well as antagonists. But the one matter that continued to be praised even by his strongest opponents was his balsaming of cadavers.[36]

De Bils promised to reveal the secret of his process for 120,000 guilders. But he was willing to part with two balsamed cadavers to one Duke Christiaan for 16,000 guilders. At the end of 1661, it was rumored that he had sold his secret to a nobleman. This may well have been prompted by the attempts of Luis de Benavides Carillo y Tolede, marquess de Caracena, a follower of Don Jan van Oostenrijk, stadtholder of the southern Netherlands, to purchase De Bils's collections for the University of Louvain. After inspection of some of De Bils's cadavers in November 1662, Gerard van Gutschoven, a professor of medicine there, became quite enthusiastic about the possibility of obtaining De Bils's specimens. Oostenrijk proposed to the states of Brabant that they purchase De Bils's cadavers and his secret method. By June 1663, eighteen articles had been drawn up by which De Bils agreed to provide Louvain with five cadavers and all his knowledge, including his secret embalming process. The process, and his method of bloodless dissection, would be written in duplicate in Latin, with a Dutch version for De Bils; the two Latin copies would be deposited in separate places, in strongboxes sealed by two keys, one key to be held by the states of Brabant and the other by the professors of Louvain. Various other provisions ensured that De Bils swore that he had not and would not reveal the secret to anyone else. In return, the states promised a payment of 22,000 Rhenish guilders, and a professorship salaried at 2,000 guilders per year, which would revert to his son after his death. De Bils would also establish an anatomy theater in Louvain without charging for admission. By October some changes were made to this draft contract, and Van Gutschoven began to learn De Bils's secret under his tutelage. At the same time, as word of the arrangement got out, people began to insist in their wills that their bodies be embalmed by De Bils's method.[37]

Finally, on 16 April 1664 De Bils's secret was handed over in writing and shown to Van Gutschoven, who was allowed eleven minutes in private to read it, after which he stated that he understood the methods of bloodless dissection and balsaming of bodies. By May, the five bodies De Bils owed the Louvain faculty were in hand, and the states paid out the 22,000 guilders. There was as yet no place prepared for the cadavers, and so they were placed in the basement of the library; after four hot months, they were laid out on tables under a roof with holes in it, subject to rain and snow, which not only damaged books in the library but caused some signs of rot to appear in three of the five cadavers by 1666. This later became known to De Bils's opponents, who claimed it proved him a fraud. But despite these and financial difficulties, De Bils remained well regarded in Louvain and the southern Netherlands: in early 1669 Flanders awarded him the benefice of a canon of 's Hertogenbosch and St. Oedenrode, and made him an honorary professor of anatomy at the Illustrious School. During that same year, several public demonstrations of his method were to be undertaken in the northern Netherlands with the assistance of Tobias Andreae—but De Bils sickened and died. Andreae lent his help to trying to sell De Bils's secret in Amsterdam, coming into difficulties with the Leiden-educated physician and surgeon Frederick Ruysch in doing so.[38]

The process De Bils had developed and written down in 1664 was as follows: A tin box [tinne kiste] 8 feet long by 2 1/2 feet wide by 3 feet high was placed in a wooden box trimmed and caulked so as to let in no light and fixed with iron bands; into the lid of the wooden box was cut a trap door [schuyve] that could be opened and completely sealed. The tin box would also be covered at the appropriate time with double wool blankets so that no light could enter. Into the tin box was introduced 60 pints of the very best rum, freshly made; 50 pints of Roman alum very finely ground; 50 pints of pepper very finely ground; 1 sack of salt finely ground, which must be poured in at this point; 200 large glasses [stoop] of the very best brandy of Nantes; 100 large glasses of the very best wine vinegar, all of which were well mixed in the tin box as quickly as possible so as not to let the power of the mixture get lost [*opdat de kracht niet te veel en verlighe van ditto substantie*]. Twenty pounds of finely ground myrrh of the best kind and 20 pounds of the best finely ground aloes [*allouwe*] could also be added to the mixture. The dead body, wound about with a white linen sheet, was immediately dunked in this mixture, lying on and tied to a wooden platform [*stellinghe*] so that at least two feet of fluid covered it. The boxes were closed for thirty days, except that three days after the body was put in the fluid, the mixture was well stirred, as it was twice more during the thirty-day period. Each time the fluid was stirred, the body was also taken out, unwrapped, washed in fresh brandy, flipped over so as to drain out any moisture via the mouth (being careful not to damage the hair or finger- and toenails), rewrapped in sheets, and replaced. After the thirty days, the body was transferred to another box made like the first with a mixture of rum, pepper, alum, salt, brandy, and vinegar in the previous proportions, in which it was left for sixty days (with three stirrings and turnings). The above mixtures were for kings or others whose bodies were to be displayed in public. If this was not to be the case, the rum and alum could be left out of the first mixture and the spices had to be added, and in the second mixture no salt was added, nor rum and alum. Between the second and third soaking, the body was allowed to dry. The first box was in the meantime cleaned and filled with a third mixture, which excluded the rum, alum, and salt but included the myrrh and aloes; this mixture was stirred several times and the clear liquid that came to the surface was skimmed off. Then 44 pounds of aloes, 44 pounds of myrrh, 20 pounds of *foullie*, 20 pounds of cloves, 20 pounds of cinnamon, 20 pounds of nutmeg (all of the best kind, finely ground), 1/4 pound of ambergris, 1/4 pound of black balsam, with a 1/2 pound of oil of cinnamon were all mixed together and applied several times to the exterior of the body and allowed to dry. The body must lie in the third mixture for two months, being turned over periodically as before, being washed and rinsed with the clear liquid skimmed off previously. If after all this the body fat had not completely dried up, the body would be placed in a small, tight stone room with two ovens burning low, one of which burned 2 pounds of mastix. After the body was thoroughly dried, the ambergris mixture was applied to the body again. The specimen could be best kept in a tin box that let in no air.[39]

UNFORESEEN CONSEQUENCES: THE STRUCTURES OF THE BODY

Because De Bils had kept his method secret, however, others had to guess at the means and experiment with possibilities themselves. In March 1661 it was rumored that a Dr. Hubertus of Leiden had discovered some of De

Bils's secrets, and later in the year a story was circulating that De Bils had sold his secret to a nobleman who passed it on to one Burrhus in Leiden—although nothing more is known.[40] A student at Leiden at the time, Theodorus Kerckring, "is said to have invented," a means of "preserving dead bodies by covering them with varnish."[41] In another version, he "performed experiments with liquefied amber to preserve corpses."[42] Another contemporary, Gabriel Clauder, thought that De Bils was using salts. A medical student at Leipzig (and later physician to the electors of Saxony), Clauder was making a grand tour of Europe and England in 1660 and 1661[43] when he visited De Bils's cabinet. According to his 1679 *Methodus balsamandi corpora humana*, he "applied his moistened finger to one of the bodies, and carrying it to his lips recognized the taste of salts. He started from this fact to attempt numerous researches, and succeeded in forming different compounds." His salt was composed as follows: "Dissolve one pound of common salt with a pound of oil of vitriol [sulfuric acid] in a crucible, apply a cover closely luted, and distill it gradually in a sand bath; you may pour off a spirit very excellent for a lotion; in the bottom of the crucible will remain a *caput mortuum*, which should be dissolved according to art, and after evaporation, you will have the salt so much esteemed by the author."[44]

Better known are the investigations of Jan Swammerdam, who matriculated in medicine at Leiden in 1661 after already having had experience with anatomical work at home in Amsterdam; he quickly became one of the favorite pupils of Van Horne and of François dela Boë Sylvius. In 1652 Van Horne had announced the discovery of the thoracic duct; in the early 1660s, Swammerdam made a durable preparation of it by soaking it in alcohol and then drying it.[45] But the centerpieces of Swammerdam's cabinet were a preserved child of one month, and a whole lamb, both of which he balsamed using a process simpler but similar to De Bils's. According to Justus Schrader—a slightly younger student of Van Horne's—Swammerdam's technique of balsaming was as follows: First, a tin vessel large enough to receive the corpse was prepared. Into this was set a grate or screen resting two fingers' width above the bottom, on which the body was placed. Then oil of turpentine was poured in to a height of three fingers' breadth from the bottom. The vessel was covered tightly except for a tiny opening, and set aside for time to do its work. This most penetrating oil entered the pores and replaced the fluids that caused fermentation and decay, which due to their weight descended through the screen to the bottom of the vessel while at the same time the volatile oils evaporated through the small opening in the top, leaving the specimen coated throughout with the hardened oil, which prevented it from decay.[46] Different organs required longer or lesser times: an embryo took six months, a skeleton about two, the parenchymia of the heart three, a liver and a placenta one, a spleen ten days, and intestines a month.[47]

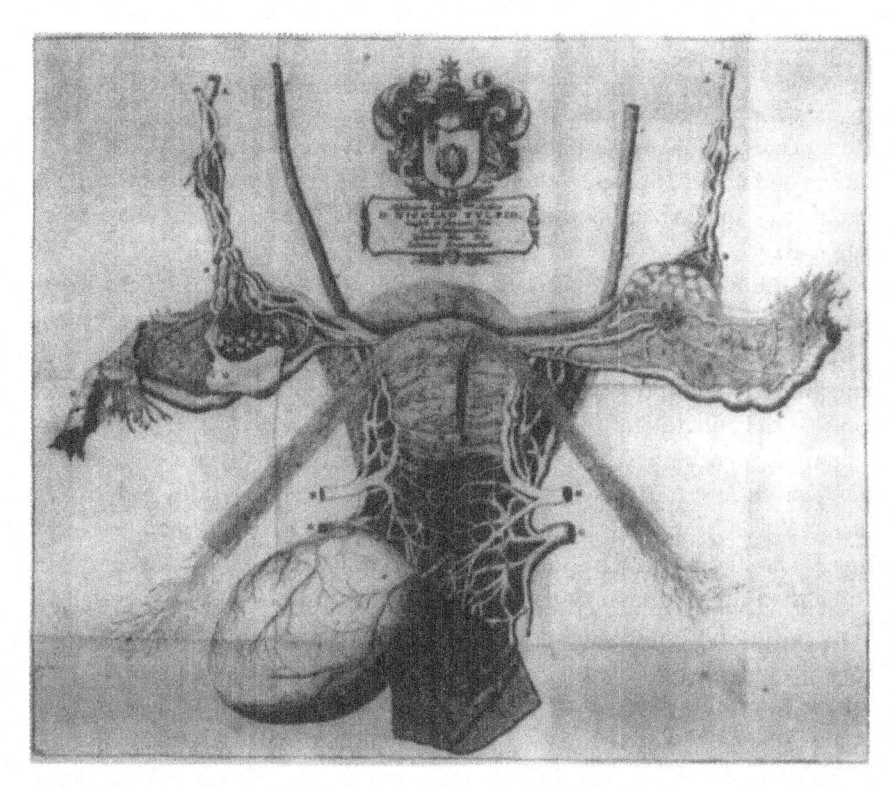

Figure 9.2 Engraving of a preserved female human uterus as depicted by Jan Swammerdam, from his *Miraculum Naturae Sive Uteri Muliebris Fabrica* (1672). The structures of these soft tissues were discovered using preservatives and injections of various kinds. Courtesy of the Universiteit Bibliotheek Leiden.

A few other techniques helped prepare more complicated specimens. With bodies and organs properly prepared, one could also inflate the vessels with air, wax, mercury, and other substances. Using such techniques, Swammerdam was able to examine the structure of the lung, the follicles of the human uterus, the ramifications of the vessels of the placenta, and so on[48] (fig. 9.2).

With a few elaborations, the method developed by Swammerdam continued to be taught at the University of Leiden. For instance, Carel Maets (or De Maets, Dematius), who had been teaching experimental chemistry at Leiden since 1669, explained his private method of preserving bodies from at least 1674.[49] He elaborated the method in his *Chemia rationalis* of 1687: "After first removing the intestines, viscera, brain, and all other soft parts, it is then placed in a lead coffin [*cysta*] commodious enough for it, where it is soaked in clear oil of turpentine. After fourteen days, or when the oil has well penetrated all the parts of the muscles, remove it and wash it with spirits of wine, and put it in a place where it will dry." To preserve the soft tissues, they were first inflated and injected with lukewarm water so as to evacuate all the blood; then they were washed out with spirit of wine until no trace of blood remained, after which they were dried in appropriate shape and soaked in oil of turpentine.[50] Another former Leiden student, Stephen Blankaart, also wrote about the use of oil of turpentine for balsaming bodies.[51]

Thus, the key ingredient for the Leiden experimenters was oil of turpentine. The turpentine commonly in use at the present day, a product of fir and pine trees, has little relation to the substance called turpentine or terebinth, much less its oil, in the seventeenth century. At that time the word applied only to an exudation of the terebinth tree (now called *Pistacia terebinthus*, or Chian turpentine). As John Goodyer explained in his 1655 edition of Dioscorides, the tree grew in "Arabia Petraea" as well as "Judea and in Syria & in Cyprus, & in Africa, & in the Islands called Cyclades." He also noted that "The Resina Terebinthina doth surpass all other rosins."[52] Twenty years later, the English military surgeon James Yonge warned that "there is a base Turpentine-like substance called commonly Terebinth, brought from France, drawn from the Fir and other Trees, . . . which is no more the gum of the Turpentine tree, than Tar is."[53] This is confirmed by the reports of major sixteenth-century investigators: "Champier said larch-tree resin was sold for terebinth but Brasavola reported in the mid-sixteenth century true terebinth was now imported in round lumps from Cyprus to Venice."[54] The oil of true turpentine, as Yonge explained, itself "contain[s] in it the Balsam."[55] Moreover, one definition of balsam itself was "an aromatic oily or resinous medicinal preparation . . . specifically, of various substances dissolved in oil of turpentine."[56] The oil or "spirit" of turpentine ("they being names promiscuously given to one and the same kinds of thing") was obtained after a slow distillation of the resin of the terebinth tree in a retort, which produced first a white, then a yellow, and finally a red oil, the last of which was the best.[57] When the red oil was mixed with blood, Yonge explained, curious things happened, among which was a coagulation that made it a very useful styptic for stanching wounds. For chemists of the day, experiments with oil of turpentine were common. One of the experiments most often repeated by Robert Boyle was the action of oil of vitriol distilled in a retort with turpentine, which yielded sulfur.[58]

Perhaps it is even significant that "oil of turpentine was regarded as very similar to spirit of wine,"[59] for in England, sometime in the 1650s, apparently at the suggestion of William Croon, Robert Boyle discovered that the spirit — or oil — of wine (something resembling today's brandy) could be used to preserve anatomical specimens. He had been so excited by news of De Bils's invention that he published a translation of one of De Bils's pam-

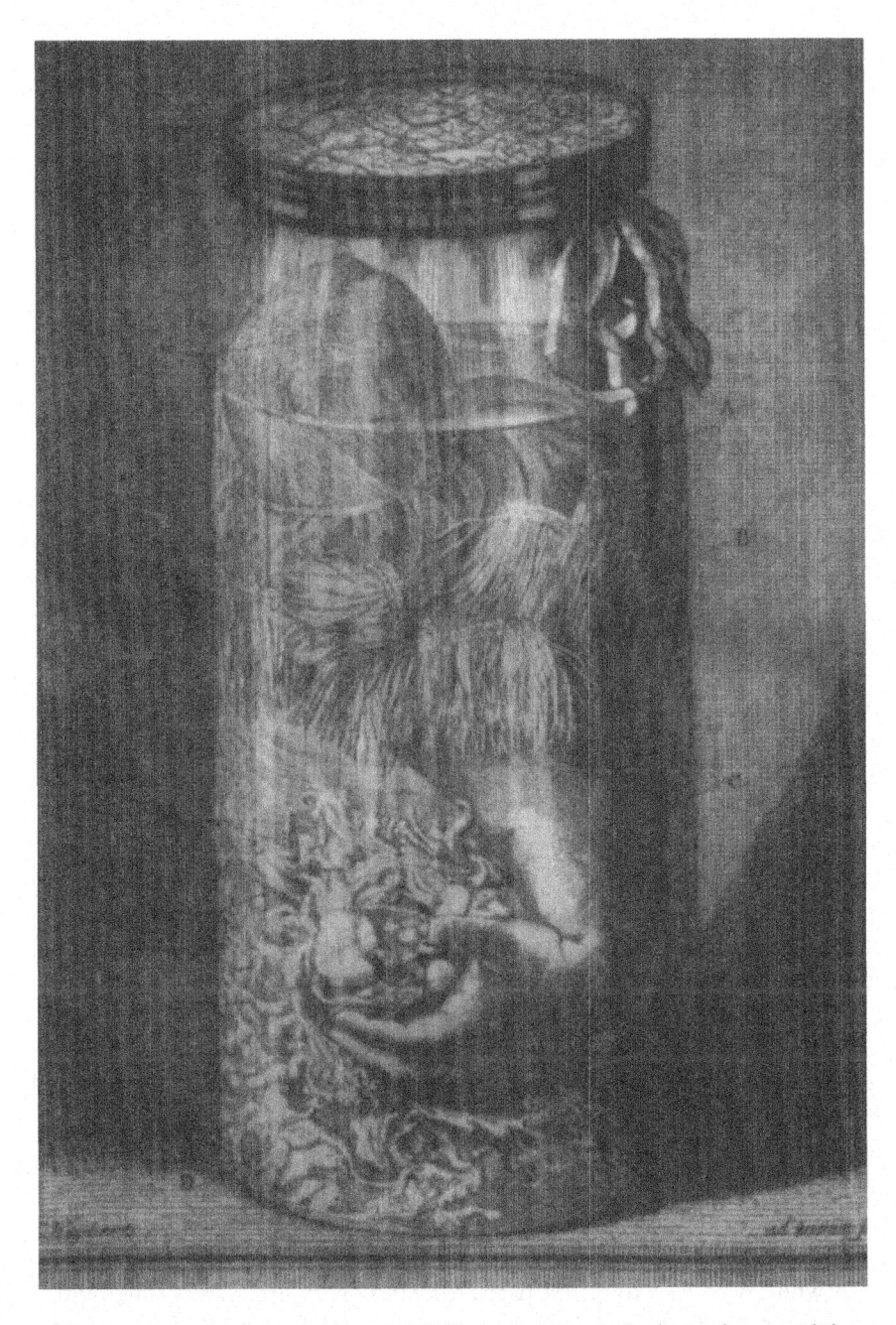

Figure 9.3 A prepared child's arm holding *naturalia*, clothed in a sleeve with lace (specimen prepared by Rachel Ruysch, Frederik's daughter). From Ruysch, *Opera omnia.* Courtesy of Metamedica, Rijksuniversiteit Leiden.

phlets. In 1663 his specimens of "a linnet and a little snake, preserved already four months, entrails and all, without any change in colour, in some spirit of wine," were to be found in the Royal Society's repository.[60] Whether such trials were stimulated by news of the efforts of De Bils and others is unknown. Although the results were slightly imperfect, and the liquid had to be periodically refreshed, the simplicity of suspending specimens in spirit of wine in a glass container made it a very important discovery. As one can tell from some of the methods used by the Dutch, spirit of wine was also used together with oil of turpentine to produce preserved specimens that could be handled.

The use of oil of turpentine and other materials for the preservation of anatomical specimens was rich in unintended consequences, however. For instance, Swammerdam was the first to see the anatomy of insects as something other than an almost undifferentiated jelly. He could do so because of his technique using very fine scissors and tweezers, excellent microscopic technique, mounting platforms of his own design, and oil of turpentine. The latter preserved the bodies of insects that could not be dried, but more: oil of turpentine turned the body fats of insects into a kind of lime, which could be carefully washed away, leaving their fibrous tissue exposed to the eye.[61] When the young Cosimo de' Medici visited his cabinet in 1668, therefore, Swammerdam famously dissected a caterpillar to show how the wings of the future butterfly were already contained in the body of the caterpillar. The demonstration held great importance in showing that metamorphosis was not an alchemical transformation of one kind of matter into another, but rather an unfolding of parts already present. The grand duke was so impressed with the skill and novelty of Swammerdam's work that he offered him 12,000 guilders for his collection of insects—an enormous sum—if he would bring it to Florence and enter his service, an offer Swammerdam declined.[62]

Methods for preserving bodies also allowed for the development of other techniques of anatomical investigation. For instance, working with Van Horne on 21 January 1667 on a human uterus (preserved with oil of turpentine, as Schrader noted above) Swammerdam found means to inject the uterus with wax—a technique he further developed, together with injections of air—filling out vessels that could not otherwise be discerned.[63] His cabinet contained a preparation of the lungs in which the trachea was filled with white wax even to tiniest parts, the pulmonary artery was filled with red wax, the pulmonary vein with rose wax, and the small orifices of the arteria bronchialis with a fire-red substance; he showed a liver similarly differentiated in balsam and wax.[64] He was able to show that the human spinal marrow was composed of fibrous nerves by suddenly placing the yet warm spinal vertebrae in cold water, leaving them there for twenty-four hours, and then carefully breaking off the bone to expose the marrow—which again had turned from an undifferentiated mass into tissues.[65] What had begun as an attempt to defy time by preserving bodies from the process of decay had also become an experimental technique crucial to the development of new anatomical knowledge.

Frederik Ruysch developed the Leiden methods to a high pitch. A fellow student of Swammerdam's, Ruysch became perhaps the most innovative anatomist of the late seventeenth century. His cabinet was an extraordinary sight, full of embalmed and preserved specimens in lifelike poses and dress, and strange fish and organs in bottles. The centerpieces of his displays were his thesaurii: dioramas of tiny human skeletons in poses memorializing the fleeting world of time by (for instance) playing violins made from hardened body parts, all standing among woods made from hardened arteries and veins, and rocks made from bladder stones (fig. 9.4). At the same time that they drew the viewer's attention to the instabilities of time, the specimens themselves represented permanence in the face of the forces of decay. When Tsar Peter visited Ruysch's cabinet, there in a cradle lay an embalmed baby with glass eyes that looked so lifelike and peaceful that he bent down to kiss the child. In 1717, the tsar purchased this emblem of the new science, along with the rest of the specimens in the cabinet, for 30,000 guilders; parts of the collection remain in St. Petersburg. (Ruysch had sold his collections before, laboriously building up new ones.)[66]

CONCLUSIONS

By the mid-seventeenth century, the process of secularization—of investigating the world of time by altering time's previously unalterable movement—was well under way, in the world of science as well as commerce. Perhaps it is not surprising that the most notable investigators had powerful ties to the world of business: De Bils came from a merchant family, Swammerdam from a family of apothecaries located next to the VOC warehouses in Amsterdam, Ruysch from civil servants so down on their luck that he became apprenticed to a pharmacist. Probably all lost more money than they made from their investigations. They turned their material inheritances into wonders of nature. Yet in distorting the "natural" actions of time as they did, De Bils, Swammerdam, and Ruysch also "capitalized" on their work by turning it into money, or could have.

For naturalists, like merchants, the accumulation and preservation of things was in anticipation of later demand. For the sake of future generations as well as immediate curiosity, they undertook the investment in intellectual capital: in specimens and an inventory of details about them (fig 9.5).

Figure 9.4 One of Ruysch's thesaurii (the third) depicting the shortness of life, constructed from kidney, gall, and bladder stones, trees made from dried veins and arteries, topped with fetal skeletons in various poses: a central figure looks heavenward, singing a lament ("Ah fate, bitter fate!") while accompanying itself on the violin; a small figure to its immediate right conducts the music with a baton set with minute kidney stones; on the far right is a skeleton girded with sheep intestines injected with wax, a spear made from a hardened male vas deferens conveying a message about man's first hour also being his last; to the left is a figure with a feather, a symbol of vanitas; and in front is a tiny skeleton holding in its hand a mayfly—an insect on which Swammerdam had written a famous book, centering his moral argument on the supposed fact that the creature lived in its adult form for only one day. From Ruysch's *Opera omni anatomico-medico-chirurgi* (1721–1727). Courtesy of Middleton Health Sciences Library, University of Wisconsin, Madison.

Figure 9.5 The cabinet of Bernard Sigfried Albinus, who carried on the tradition of anatomical preparation and study at Leiden, illustrating how a professor's cabinet had become replete with wet specimens by the 1740s. Courtesy of Metamedica, Rijksuniversiteit Leiden.

Material progress and utility became the watchwords of contemporary naturalists even when reveling in curiosities. They wished to create enduring knowledge from fragile and perishable objects by thorough-going investigation and reporting, which could be handed down to others. But they, too, as much as merchants, depended on preserving their accumulated objects. Just as a warehouse of nutmeg would lose much or even most of its value should mold take over (hence the dusting of it with lime), so a cabinet of curiosity lost value as its specimens were lost or destroyed. Investing for the long term might add value to one's transactions, but it also required a struggle against the processes of decay and putrefaction. New methods of both capitalism and science therefore depended on working against the forces of transitory nature in favor of longer term durability. Given an outlook that valued not only material bodies themselves but the accumulation and preservation of them, coupled with methods of investigation linked to thinking about how to get value from time, ingenious people like De Bils and Swammerdam added to the store of knowledge, now part of our intellectual capital.

1. David S. Landes, *Revolution in Time: Clocks and the Making of the Modern World* (Cambridge, Mass.: Harvard University Press, Belknap, 1983), 72–76.

2. On musical horology, see Penelope Gouk, *Music, Science, and Natural Magic on Seventeenth-Century England* (New Haven, Conn.: Yale University Press, 1999), 202–204.

3. Norbert Elias, *Time: An Essay*, trans. by Edmund Jephcott, reprint, 1987 (Oxford: Blackwell, 1992), 115. Elias emphasizes the phenomenological approach to understanding time. For one who argues for the absolute existence of space and time, in which space-time points "stand in causal relations to one another," see Michael Tooley, *Time, Tense, and Causation* (Oxford: Clarendon Press, 1997), quotation on 379. For a collection of essays informed by modern physical science, see Steven F. Savitt, ed., *Time's Arrows Today: Recent Physical and Philosophical Work on the Direction of Time* (Cambridge: Cambridge University Press, 1995).

4. Jan de Vries and Ad van der Woude, *The First Modern Economy: Success, Failure, and Perseverance of the Dutch Economy, 1500–1815* (Cambridge: Cambridge University Press, 1997), 691, 692.

5. Niels Steensgaard, *The Asian Trade Revolution of the Seventeenth Century: The East India Companies and the Decline of the Caravan Trade* (Chicago: University of Chicago Press, 1974), 142–143, 149.

6. P. W. Klein and J. W. Veluwenkamp, "The Role of the Entrepreneur in the Economic Expansion of the Dutch Republic," in *Economic and Social History of the Netherlands*, Het Nederlandsch Economisch-Historisch Archief, Vol. 4 (Amsterdam: NEHA, 1993), 28, 31–32, 33, 49.

7. F. W. T. Hunger, "Bernardus Paludanus (Berent ten Broecke) (1550–1633)," *Janus* 32 (1928): 361.

8. J. A. J. Barge, *De oudste inventaris der oudste academische anatomie in Nederland* (Leiden: H. E. Stenfert Kroese's, 1934), 34–55.

9. Karen Meier Reeds, *Botany in Medieval and Renaissance Universities*, Harvard Dissertations in the History of Science (New York: Garland, 1991), esp. 35–36.

10. Faye Getz, "Roger Bacon and Medicine: The Paradox of the Forbidden Fruit and the Secrets of Long Life," in *Roger Bacon and the Sciences: Commemorative Essays*, ed. Jeremiah Hackett (Leiden: Brill, 1997), 337–364.

11. *The Cure of Old Age, and Preservation of Youth. By Roger Bacon . . . Translated out of Latin; with annotations and an account of his life and writings. By Richard Browne* (London: Tho. Flesher and Edward Evets, 1683).

12. Sir Francis Bacon, "De augmentis scientiarum," translated as "Of the Dignity and Advancement of Learning," in his *Works*, ed. and trans. James Spedding (London, 1860), Vol. 4, book 4, chap. 2, 390–394.

13. See, for example, his letter to Chanu of 15 June 1646; AT IV:441–442.

14. Swammerdam, *The Book of Nature; or, the History of Insects*, trans. Thomas Flloyd, revised with notes by John Hill (London: C. G. Seyffert, 1758), ii; for the original, see Swammerdam, *Bybel der Natuure/Biblia Naturae*, ed. Herman Boerhaave, with facing-page translation into Latin by Hieronimus David Gaubius (Leiden: Isaak Severinus, Boudewyn vander Aa, Pieter vander Aa, 1737), sig. B.

15. For what follows, I am heavily indebted to Jan Reinier Jansma, *Louis de Bils en de anatomie van zijn tijd* (Hoogeveen: C. Pet, 1919).

16. " . . . sed fidem superat omnem, exsiccatum hominis Cadaver Recenter Mortuum Diceres tanto Theatro Dignissimum opus." The wooden plaque containing Van Horne's testimony is reproduced on 47 of Jansma, *De Bils*. De Bils later claimed that he had spent *f* 40,000 on the preparations, not including his time (66).

17. On Egyptian mummies in cabinets, see both examples above. The famous work of Hermes Trismegistus was thought to have been written at the beginning of Egyptian civilization; on the fascination with Egypt, see for example Frances A. Yates, *Giordano Bruno and the Hermetic Tradition*, reprint, 1964 (New York: Vintage Books, 1969); Thomas C. Singer, "Hieroglyphs, Real Characters, and the Idea of Natural Language in English Seventeenth-Century Thought," *Journal of the History of Ideas* 50 (1989): 49–70; Anthony Grafton, *Defenders of the Text: The Traditions of Scholarship in an Age of Science, 1450–1800* (Cambridge, Mass.: Harvard University Press, 1991), 145–177.

18. Alfred Lucas, *Ancient Egyptian Materials and Industries*, 4th ed., revised by J. R. Harris (London: Edward Arnold, 1962), 270–326.

19. See esp. Katharine Park, "The Criminal and the Saintly Body: Autopsy and Dissection in Renaissance Italy," *Renaissance Quarterly* 47 (1994): 1–33; Katharine Park, "The Life of the Corpse: Division and Dissection in Late Medieval Europe," *Journal of the History of Medicine* 50 (1995): 111–132.

20. Jansma, *De Bils*, 70–74.

21. Karl H. Dannenfeldt, "Egyptian Mumia: The Sixteenth-Century Experience and Debate," *Sixteenth-Century Journal* 16 (1985): 163–180.

22. J.R. Partington, *A History of Chemistry,* (London: Macmillan, 1961) 2:98.

23. Lynn Thorndike, *A History of Magic and Experimental Science* (New York: Columbia University Press, 1923–58), 8: 106.

24. Dannenfeldt, "Egyptian Mumia," 169–171.

25. Thorndike, *A History of Magic and Experimental Science*, 8: 414.

26. Dannenfeldt, "Egyptian Mumia," 173–174; Partington, *A History of Chemistry,* 2:444.

27. William Eamon, "Cannibalism and Contagion: Framing Syphilis in Counter-Reformation Italy," *Early Science and Medicine* 3 (1998): 1–31.

28. For example, see Carolus de Maets, *Chemia Rationalis* (Lugd. Batav.: Jacobum Mocquee, 1687), 162–164, and a manuscript of his chemistry course from 1675 and 1676, British Library, Sloane MSS 1235, fols. 5–5b.

29. Justus Schrader, *Observationes et Historiae* (Amsterdam: Abraham Wolfgang, 1674), 236: "Notum est, cadaverum artus ac viscera sibi relicta necessariò ruere in putredinem, eorumque compagem nunc citiùs nunc tardiùs foedâ corruptione dissolvi, nec ullum pristinæ integritatis aut formæ vistigium tandem retinere. Hunc consuetum naturæ cursum arte non solùm refrænari sed & cohiberi posse, dudum evicerunt medicata Ægyptiorum funera bitumine ac pretiosis subinde refinis & aromatibus abundè infarcta."

30. Ibid., 236: "quae tamen quum externam solummodò speciem servent, idque obscurè, non item interiorum habitudinem, meritò isti Ægyptiaco operi præfertur illa ars, quae cadavera & eorum fragmina ita obdurat, ut salva permaneat ipsorum textura, idem supersit color, eadem conformatio, nullo non tempore ac pro lubitu ab Anatomico contemplanda, & quidem absque cruoris effusione, aut fastidioso madore, quibus delicatiores offendi, & ab inspiciendis demortuorum visceribus communiter arceri solent."

31. Jansma, *De Bils*, 48–53.

32. G. A. Lindeboom, *Dutch Medical Biography: A Biographical Dictionary of Dutch Physicians and Surgeons 1475–1975* (Amsterdam: Rodopi, 1984).

33. Jansma, *De Bils*, 53–54.

34. Lindeboom, *Dutch Medical Biography*, col. 909.

35. Jansma, *De Bils*, 54–58.

36. Ibid., 58–67.

37. Ibid., 65, 67, 68–69.

38. Ibid., 77, 78–79, 83–88, 90.

39. Ibid., 96–99.

40. Ibid., 67.

41. Partington, *A History of Chemistry*, 2:208.

42. Lindeboom, *Dutch Medical Biography*, 1031.

43. N. F. J. Eloy, *Dictionnaire historique de la médecine ancienne et moderne: Ou mémoires disposés en ordre alphabétique pour servir a l'histoire de cette science* (Mons: H. Hoyois, 1778), 655–656.

44. Jean Nicolas Gannal and R. Harlan, trans. and eds., *History of Embalming, and of Preparations in Anatomy, Pathology, and Natural History; Including an Account of a New Process for Embalming* (Philadelphia: Judah Dobson, 1840), 91–92, 96; see Gabriel Clauder, *Methodus Balsamandi Corpora Humana* (Iena: Oan Bielckium, 1679), chap. 5, sec. 3, 128–140, on his view of the method of De Bils, and chap. 6, 140–181, for his own method.

45. Reported by G. A. Lindeboom, ed. and comp., *Het Cabinet van Jan Swammerdam (1637–1680)* (Amsterdam: Rodopi, 1980), xii, from a letter of Olaus Borch to Bartholin (which I have not yet seen), which places the event around 1661–62, when Borch was in the Netherlands.

46. Schrader, *Observationes et Historiae*, 237: "Paretur itaque vas stanneum corpori præparando quoad capacitatem aptè respondens, huic immittatur & duorum digitorum à fundo distantiâ probè firmetur craticula lignea minutis foraminibus constans, super quam corpus collocetur, mox oleum terebinthinæ infundatur ad trium digitorum eminentiam, & vas leviter ac minus arctè opertum per justum temporis intervallum in quiete servetur: Sic penetrantissimum istud oleum, cadaveris, cui circumfusum est, poris paulatim sese insinuabit, & aquosum laticem, præcipuam fermantationis ad corruptelam tendentis causam, extrudet, qui vi ponderis descendens, & per craticulam stillans, spatium inter ipsam & fundum progressu temporis occupabit; interea verò simul subtilior balsami portio, ob minus perfectè clausum vas, exhalabit, quâ magis magisque evanescente, tandem corpus concretâ olei amurcâ tanquam gummosa medullâ penitus imbutum duritiem acquiret, ac idcircò posthac extra liquorem in aperto aëre incorruptum absque situ aut tineis perennare facilè poterit."

47. Ibid., 238.

48. Ibid., 238–240.

49. Sloane MSS 1235: "Collegium Chymicum Secretum / A / D. Carolo de Maes apud Lugdunenses," 1675 and 1676: f.5, "Modus Condiendi Cadavera."

50. De Maets, *Chemia Rationalis*, 162–163.

51. Stephan Blankaart, *Neue und besondere Manier alle verstorbene Cörper mit wenig Ukosten der Gestalt zu Balsamiren* (Hannover und Wolffenbüttel: Gottlieb Heinrich Grentz, 1690). I owe this reference to Tomomi Kinukawa.

52. Dioscorides, *The Greek Herbal of Dioscorides*, ed. Robert R. Gunther, reprint, 1934 (New York: 1959), 49.

53. James Yonge, *Currus Triumphalis* (London: Printed for J. Martin, Printer to the Royal Society, at the Bell in St. Paul's Churchyard, 1679), 50.

54. Partington, *A History of Chemistry*, Vol. 2, 97.

55. Yonge, preface to *Currus Triumphalis*.

56. *Oxford English Dictionary*.

57. Yonge, *Currus Triumphalis*, 48–50. Also see William Davisson, *Philosophia Pyrotechnica* (Paris: Joan Bessin, 1640), 325–326 and William Davisson, *Le Cours de Chymie* (Amiens: Michel du Neuf-Germain, 1675), 308.

58. Partington, *A History of Chemistry*, Vol. 2, 494.

59. Ibid., 267, citing Libavius, Alchemia, 1597, bk. 2I, tract. ii, c. 36.

60. L. de Bils, "Large Act of Anatomy" (1659), in *The Works of Robert Boyle*, ed. Michael Hunter and Edward B. Davis (London: Pickering and Chatto, 1999), Vol. 1; D. H. Tompsett and Cecil Wakeley, J. Dobson, historical intro, *Anatomical Techniques* (Edinburgh and London: E. & S. Livingstone, 1956), x.

61. Jan Swammerdam, *Bybel der Natuure/Biblia Naturae*, ed. Herman Boerhaave, Latin translation by Hieronimus David Gaubius (Leiden: Isaak Severinus, Boudewyn vander Aa, Pieter vander Aa, 1737), sig. l.

62. G. A. Lindeboom, ed. and comp., *Ontmoeting met Jan Swammerdam*, Ontmoetingen Met Mystici, no. 3 (Kampen: Uitgeversmaatschappij J.H. Kok, 1980), 12.

63. Swammerdam, *Bybel der natuur*: "Hier was it, in Van Hornes huys, op de 21 Januarius, 1667, dat hy de eerste reys, medwasch opvulde de vaten des Lyvmoeders van eene Vrouw, door een seer nutte onderneminge, dien hy daar naa heeft verbeterd meer, en meer." [sig C] "Hy verder oeffende vlytig een bysondere konstgreep, door welke hy de deelen der lighaamen suyver rynigde van al, wat daar in was; hier naa blies hy die op, dat sy vol lucht waren, droogde die dan; waar door die styv geworden, haare gedaante behielden, en door die konst naauwkeurig kosten beschouwd werden, jaa ook net beschreven. Eene uytvinding waarlyk van de uyterste nuttigheid."[C2]

64. Lindeboom, *Het Cabinet van Jan Swammerdam*, xvii.

65. Swammerdam, *Bybel*, sig. C: "het ruggemerg, nog warm, med de wervelbeenen, waar in her bevat is, ten spoedigsten moet gelegd in koud water, en 24 uuren daar in gelaten; waar na de wervels omsigtig gebroken moeten werden; dan werd dit alles so gesien."

66. Antonie M. Luyendijk-Elshout, "Death Enlightened: A Study of Frederik Ruysch," *Journal of the American Medical Association* 212, no. 1 (1970): 121–126; Julie V. Hansen, "Resurrecting Death: Anatomical Art in the Cabinet of Dr. Frederik Ruysch," *Art Bulletin* 78 (1996): 663–679.

Cartography, Entrepreneurialism, and Power in the Reign of Louis XIV

The Case of the Canal du Midi

CHANDRA MUKERJI

In seventeenth-century France, it was quite normal for infrastructural projects like roads, drainage systems, canals, and bridges to be carried out not through direct state action, but rather through political funding of contracts with entrepreneurs. Such structures were often deemed essential by the central government, and imposed as a duty on regional governments, but they were constructed by local engineers and laborers under the supervision of a financier, functioning as entrepreneur. Commerce and political power were allied with technical skills for material effect.

Since such engineering brought together political, technical, and commercial powers to rework the *landscape* for politicoeconomic effect, representing nature — in this case the countryside — was instrumental to the process. Infrastructural work was, almost by definition, a product of political geography. Places where improvements might be plausibly tried were identified with surveys, and the results of these projects were recorded in representations that connected the work to larger schemes of territorial integration and communication. The local political bodies that were given some responsibility for these projects also commissioned surveys to assess the feasibility of the work, address any traditional claims to the land in question, and evaluate the potential usefulness of the results. And the entrepreneurs who risked their capital in these endeavors used models and maps to design and promote their constructions, paying particular attention to the specificities of place that would affect the costs of the work (such as natural resources available as construction materials). Their engineers, in turn, used measures of elevation, distance, soil quality, and topography to choose building strategies. Some combination of commercial calculation and representation was at the heart, then, of these infrastructural efforts, and commerce itself was furthered through the cultivation and deployment of representational techniques.

How this kind of engineering depended upon entrepreneurialism and imagery in late seventeenth-century France is apparent in the case of the Canal du Midi, which was built in the 1660s to the 1680s in southwest France, running from Toulouse to the Mediterranean. It was an interesting project because it was so much more ambitious in scope than most infrastructural efforts, but it also shared so many features with them. It was as though a common system for knowing and acting on nature was blown up in scale so its social and technical contours were made more visible.

In principle, the canal was meant to link the Mediterranean Sea to the Atlantic Ocean. At Toulouse, the canal approached the Garonne River, which discharges into the Atlantic Ocean, and near Béziers the canal was to reach the sea. The structure would not only link two regions, but also two vast sea-based trading systems, making the canal huge not only in length but in possibility. More pressingly, however, such an ambitious project was technically difficult to realize. It had to cross a major watershed to link valleys with water draining in opposite directions toward two seas. Flooding the highest point of a canal in this region (particularly in the dry summers) was a difficult task — one that many saw as impossible — because opening locks to move boats would also discharge vast amounts of water. Even the port for the canal on the Mediterranean was a problem. There was no natural harbor to use, since the coast along the Mediterranean in the region tended to be flat, full of salt marshes, and easily silted up. Worse, that region of the sea was plagued by devastating storms that easily destroyed ports or filled them with run-off sand. Making a harbor substantial and deep enough to accommodate trade was not easy. In fact, it was not satisfactorily done in the period. But despite of the difficulties, a canal was built, and commerce along it followed. State-based entrepreneurialism, and representations of nature yielded a new nature — a second nature — a work of "genius" that was a tribute to and improvement upon the land of France.

We can get a better sense of how geographical representation and commercial culture met at the Canal du Midi first by studying the canal as an economic enterprise, and then turning to its development as part of a layered system of representations. With this background, we can consider more systematically links between the two.

THE CANAL DU MIDI AS A COMMERCIAL ENTERPRISE

The Canal du Midi (in roughly the form it was built) was proposed to Jean-Baptiste Colbert, controller general of finance, by Pierre-Paul Riquet, a salt tax (*gabelle*) collector from Languedoc. He was an odd man to take on this task. He was neither an engineer nor a scientist. He was not even an experienced entrepreneur who had built large numbers of roads and bridges already for the state. He had, of course, a fortune and his own businesses, but nothing on a scale to match this canal. In the humanist language that has mainly typified him, he was a simple man of vision whose genius was recognized by Colbert and manifested in the canal's successful completion. More to the point, he was a money man who knew how to use finances to deploy labor power and natural resources for economic effect.

There are a number of political questions that need including in any account of the canal's success. Why did Riquet think that a powerful minister like Colbert would authorize and help him finance such a vast enterprise? Why would a tax collector (a despised social type) from a region known for its dissidents and tax revolts become capable of retaining a loyal labor force to realize his dreams? How could a salt tax collector acquire the capacity to locate a water supply adequate for the canal's watershed area, when so many others had failed? And how did a man with no engineering background imagine he could build a port to serve sailors and fishermen? Most of all, how could a man like Riquet find solutions to technical problems that had evaded the more demonstrable genius Leonardo da Vinci, who had been asked to plan a canal for this region a century before? The mythology of the heroic Riquet that haunts this bit of history raises as many questions as it resolves. But the fact of the canal's engineering remains, and so does the role of Riquet in making the venture succeed. As unlikely as the story might be, a not-so-simple regional tax man whose French was not so good did indeed propose and bring into being a canal that ran from Toulouse to the Mediterranean — not quite before his death but shortly afterward.

There were, as one might expect, indeed some good reasons for Riquet's eventual success. He could propose this project — although he lacked connections at the French court and engineering experience —*precisely because* he was a tax collector and financier. Colbert had been encouraging those with capital, such as tax men, to use their wealth to invest in infrastructural work.[1] They could enrich themselves while serving the state, and he would give them special privileges or revenue to help them. Riquet had a reliable source of income already because he was an *homme de gabelle*. Colbert simply had to give him permission to increase taxes and use that income to finance the project. At the moment he proposed the canal project, Riquet had even recently obtained a new territory to tax. The Treaty of the Pyrenees made Rousillon part of France, and Riquet was one of the few men sent to raise revenue there. Unfortunately for him, however, since Catalonia had no traditional salt tax, violence erupted in Rousillon when it was imposed, leaving Riquet angry and with very little additional revenue. His attention to the dissidents in the region became a sore point with Colbert when the minister thought Riquet was spending too much time in the Catalan city of

Perpignan and away from the canal. Still, when the project was first proposed at Versailles, Riquet's position as a tax farmer (and proven skills at raising money) made him a more attractive candidate for this commission.[2]

Colbert, of course, did not simply share costs with Riquet, using treasury funds. He exercised his political muscle to extract financial contributions from local political authorities, mainly the États de Languedoc. He used also the power of the state to acquire the land for the canal, set down principles for assessing the value of the properties, and force local authorities to help with the financing of their acquisition. The minister additionally signed edicts setting price limits on construction materials and their transport to the canal; he ordered the roads in bordering towns to be improved; and he gave Riquet mining rights in nearby mountains — presumably to make him his own supplier of iron for the locks. Later in the process, he also (and more reluctantly, against local opposition) supported the sale of (lucrative) offices related to the canal's administration, which gave Riquet a new revenue stream for the project.[3] Colbert even authorized the imposition of a new tax on public houses, inns, and bars in the region (perhaps because they were profiting so much from the workers), and required nearby towns to house the workers at local expense.[4]

These schemes for financing the canal's construction were both Colbert's ways of orchestrating the state's participation in the work, and the tax man's ideas about how to make his investment work. Just as much as Colbert tried to control Riquet with his favors, the entrepreneur extracted from his patron means for financing and managing the project. Riquet knew the limits of state influence in his region, and let the minister know when Colbert needed to enforce his edicts or extend his list of required contributions from local authorities. The tax man also was the one to notice when suppliers were price gouging, and he asked for legal relief from these practices. The assiduousness with which Riquet attended to his financial interests may have raised Colbert's suspicions about the tax man's true interest in engineering. But the record suggests that both men used their own forms of financial experience to make the project work. Riquet (an extractor of local revenues and creator of economic opportunities) was skilled in recognizing where money could be found, natural resources exploited, and labor power put to work for politicoeconomic advantage. Colbert was good at recognizing political and economic opportunities for the state, and using political incentives to promote them and reduce their risks to the treasury and the reputation of the king. Both men needed all their wits to keep up with the rising costs and risks of the project, and despite their mutual distrust they managed to make their alliance work.[5]

For dealing with local elites and resources, Riquet had family connections and associations forged through his work to keep his authority intact against the powerful opponents who tried to block his efforts. Local hostility to the project was predictable. Confiscating tracts of estate properties from landholders and demanding large sums of regional tax revenues on top of this—particularly to finance a canal that would (in principle) yield personal economic gain—was unlikely to appeal to stakeholders in the region's economic arrangements. But Riquet had connections in this group and was schooled (if not always skilled) in local politics. His father had been a member of the États de Languedoc—even when an earlier proposal for a comparable canal had been evaluated and rejected by the local authorities. He was aware of the foot-dragging that was endemic to fund raising for state-sanctioned projects from the États. But he was also trained in making people give up the money they owed him—against their will. The elites of Toulouse, Carcassone, Montpellier, and Béziers may have been more visible and powerful than the persons who usually owed him tax money, but once Riquet had Colbert behind him, he had the political connections that could (at least at times) intimidate them. The tax man also cultivated a loyal cohort of supporters for his scheme among these powerful men. He recruited as investors many leading politicians, financiers, landowners, and entrepreneurs, making loyal advocates for his engineering scheme from this group of local elites.[6] These were allies he desperately needed and too frequently alienated as the work progressed and as the list of his local enemies grew.

No skill in political maneuvering was of any value to Riquet, however, until he first persuaded Colbert to endorse the project, and this was no simple task. But he had a trump card. He lived in a land known for its tradition of religious heresy, tax revolts, and antagonism toward the central French state. French troops had been so frequently called into Languedoc (since the Wars of Religion in the sixteenth century) that the region was better mapped (from military surveys) than most other parts of France. The region was mainly peaceful in midcentury, but the nobility in southwestern France of the seventeenth century remained Huguenot, and Protestant ranks seemed to be increasing in size and power. In this context, Riquet chose as local patron for the canal project (the man he hoped would bring his proposal to the attention of Colbert) d'Aglure de Bourlemont, who was about to become the archbishop of Toulouse. This respected cleric agreed to inspect the plans and engineering mock-ups for a canal already set up by Riquet at his estate at Bonrepos. He was impressed enough with what he saw to take the proposal to the very Catholic court at Versailles, and to the minister himself.[7]

Colbert had other than religious reasons to be predisposed toward this tax man and the proposal introduced to him by d'Aglure de Bourlemont—politicoeconomic ones. The minister was already strategically placing new commercial ventures in dissident regions to create a permanent state presence, and Languedoc was on his list of sites with economic assets but needing better control by the crown. Riquet was a good agent for Languedoc. He had financial skills, knew the land from firsthand experience, was not a dissident, and was more than willing to function as an informant about the activities of locals that he deemed threatening to his interests and state power. Important, too, was the fact that he was willing to risk his fortune in a commercial project of imposing scale that might indeed make his fortune but could also serve the regime. If the canal were built, the propaganda value of the structure alone would be enormous. Early in the project, the canal even seemed to have strategic military appeal. The great military engineer Vauban argued that the waterway could be made wide and deep enough to carry military vessels from the Mediterranean to the Atlantic, thereby avoiding pirates by Gibraltar—a great problem for the French navy. Although this military dream was soon scrapped, the political value of the canal remained high.[8]

Infrastructural improvement also had a particular political resonance in seventeenth century France. The *mesnagement* tradition of politics in France—which defined the state as a great estate that needed proper management[9]—had put great emphasis on strategic use of the countryside as a route to collective wealth and power. By using rational land management practices, one could (according to this political theory) yield a landscape that was more Edenic, and that would allow the people in rural areas (rich and poor alike) to enjoy greater prosperity, increased trade, and more stable social relations. The canal was easy to identify as just the kind of improvement needed in the countryside to make it more perfect—a water system that was less prone to flooding and the strong currents of local rivers and streams. Linking the Mediterranean to the Atlantic through such a peaceful waterway was not only a way to increase trade, but—in theory at least—create a better political environment. Trade, of course, was meant to be a clear benefit of the canal. The economies of the Atlantic and Mediterranean areas were so different that there was every reason to think that demand for goods that could be moved through the waterway would be strong. The canal's construction in any case made the countryside around the structure more of an economic asset, and placed the pursuit of trade into the visual field of all those who lived by it, suggesting new possibilities for commercial activity.

Riquet's strategies for managing the work process also impinged upon and added a new commercial element to local social arrangements. The canal was constructed using an innovative and unusually generous wage labor system. In some sense, the contractual labor force he raised to build the canal helped to constitute a working class in this area at a very early moment. There were roughly forty thousand people who participated in the construction, giving this region a surprisingly extensive set of capitalist social relations.

Riquet paid and treated his workers extremely well because he was a money man and knew the power of the purse to deliver what he wanted. But he also needed some way to attract a stable labor force for this vast project. If locals were inclined to hate the tax man who (at least nominally) directed the project, they did not object to sharing his wealth. The pay scale at the work-site was something of a scandal, since common laborers were paid half again what they would be given for farm work. They also could take sick days off and were paid for periods of bad weather, when it was physically impossible to work, and even holidays. This regularity in compensation was practically unheard of in the period, even in Paris, much less among laborers of Langue-doc.[10] It is true, as Le Roy Ladurie has pointed out,[11] that the peasants of this region were already independent farmers rather than serfs in the thirteenth century, suggesting that there were long-standing modernizing forces affect-ing labor relations in the region. Still, Riquet's labor contracts were revolu-tionary, and shocking enough to his contemporaries that they raised questions about his character and honesty. Local nobles who opposed the canal apparently suggested that Riquet was only claiming to pay such high wages so he could actually pocket more money for himself. That is one of the main reasons Colbert sent a trusted confidant and engineer, La Feuille, down to check on Riquet, but there was no evidence of impropriety. La Feuille's reports back to Colbert were, on the contrary, quite clear that many expenses of the project were legitimately large. Wages were eventually cut, but not to the level of local agricultural labor.

It should be no surprise that nobles objected to Riquet's labor policies. Field hands and shepherds from local estates constituted the bulk of the workforce, and nobles lost power over the laboring poor because of Riquet's contracts. Moreover, the tax man did achieve surprising loyalty in the work-force. Even when Riquet raised taxes to supply more revenue for the canal and there were movements against paying the *gabelle*, the workers did not rebel against him.[12] The stability of the workforce meant that the experience gained from early efforts to build the canal was not lost by exhausted and dis-affected workers who left to seek employment elsewhere. It was carried over to the next stage of the project by those who liked the pay scale and work rules. For a canal that was so complicated to achieve, this kind of continuity was very valuable; creating a stable workforce was a good investment.

Given the entrepreneurial logic behind the proposal for the canal and the process of its construction, it is surprising, in the end, that Riquet sought as his reward for this work *not* commercial rights to the canal's use, but domainal rights to the land on which it lay. Riquet demanded (no matter how inappropriate it seemed to Colbert) to create a landed family of title through his entrepreneurial skill. In this region of France, where the well-being of the household (as Le Roy Ladurie has suggested in *Montaillou*) was the central cultural value, this probably made sense. Colbert expected social mores akin to those of the Parisian bourgeois elites, who bought domains with their profits rather than demanded domains as part of a contract. But Riquet was not from Paris. Because of his stubbornness on the subject, Riquet infuriated Colbert, and lost the support from the treasury for the second stage of the project, but his household was indeed given as domain a long, thin stretch of land that meandered Toulouse to the Mediterranean.[13]

In the end, Riquet brought to the engineering of the Canal du Midi not technical expertise and probably not personal genius, but financial experience in extracting resources and creating a loyal workforce that could learn on the job. He was not a thoroughly modern man of finance, but he was an entrepreneur who was clever with contracts, and he respected the expertise of others (even laborers). He used the canal as a means for making a commercially more tractable "second nature" whose profitability would better serve both the interests of his family and the glory of his king.

THE CANAL DU MIDI AND LAND SURVEY METHODS

Cartographic skills, survey measurements, and other means of representing the landscape were invaluable for this project, but less as a source of accurate *information* to shuttle between bureaucrats at Versailles and entrepreneur/engineers in Languedoc than as tools in an ongoing system for learning about and solving problems of land control.[14] The distinction is important. We often assume that states need information, and that they acquire it by deploying experts who feed bureaucrats with the kinds of information they need or want to make administrative decisions. But a project like the Canal du Midi could not have been developed around the formal knowledge of geography in the region, and the engineering depended on a continued pattern of problem solving. Subtle characteristics of the topography, soil, watersheds, and the like became more apparent as the work progressed, and had to be taken into consideration. New information about the project was gathered at every step in the project and pointed to problems that had not been anticipated in the plans. Of course, *good* data were vital. The more accurate the information at any stage of the process, the more useful it was to the outcome. But the most important thing to the project was the capacity to learn — to engage in ongoing decision making and problem solving. Accurate information about how to build a channel through one part of the landscape was useless if the canal was finally routed elsewhere. The project needed good maps of the area to help route the canal correctly, but it needed even more the capacity to survey and assess in complex and changing ways whatever portion of the landscape required engineering attention.[15]

The primary problem for Colbert (as the political patron for the project) and Riquet (as the entrepreneur investing his family's wealth and future in the scheme) was risk. This was an attractive venture that would clearly have enormous benefits if it could be realized, but the "if" was very large. Projects of this sort had been proposed for centuries, but they had not been realized because of technical problems. Certainly Colbert had no interest in undermining the reputation of Louis XIV by sponsoring a project of this visibility that would fail. (The military's later efforts at the Eure River aqueduct would do just that in the 1680s, but Colbert was much more averse to risk than was Louvois or Vauban.)[16] Riquet, too, had no desire to waste all of his personal strength and financial assets. But this was not a project that was guaranteed of success. By all accounts, it was too difficult to achieve. There was no one person in France who really knew enough about the huge area that the canal traversed or enough about canal engineering even to say whether this scheme was practical and whether Riquet's plan was feasible. Instead, the major actors accepted the risk and took a leap of faith in supporting the canal project. What made them do it? One plausible explanation is that they had multiple mappings of this region that made them feel they knew the local countryside and what to do with it. They had canal plans, road maps, military surveys, maps of water sources, and legends about the local landscape. This array of formal and informal representational systems for rendering the countryside not only yielded large amounts of information, but a set of perspectives on land which addressed a surprisingly broad range of human needs and interests.

The growth of humanist geography in the sixteenth and seventeenth centuries had already provided in western Europe a particularly rich set of cartographies, emphasizing human material achievements on the land (cities, wall systems, ports, canals, roads, bridges, monasteries, managed forests, territorial boundaries, and property lines). These images provided a wealth of evidence that human beings could indeed rework the landscape for commercial and political effect.[17] The problem with these maps as guides to building the Canal du Midi is that they were developed by *different* groups with *distinct* ways of measuring, recording, and acting on the land. To reduce the risk of the project and actually create the canal, these distinct *visions* and *traditions of practice* had to be combined. Colbert and Riquet — for a range of reasons — succeeded in doing this, creating a social learning system that allowed experts to bring different ideas into the project. The *ironic result* was that in this period of so-called state absolutism the solution to the material problem of territorial control lay not in centralized and absolute control of the engineering process, but precisely its opposite: the development of a system of distributed learning that allowed diverse strands of surveying and engineering to be combined for a common purpose.[18]

There was a range of skills in geographical measurement available in France used for representing and acting on the natural world. Measurement techniques for making elevation studies with precision were taken from men of the Academie des Sciences; mapmaking repertoires developed by military engineers for planning battles and building fortresses were used to manage the canal's incline, build reservoirs, control water intakes, and design the canal basin and some aspects of its locks; civil surveying techniques from road engineering and property disputes were employed to manage the land acquisitions for the canal, help build the bridges, and design the route; and geographical folklore and traditions of practice from the region identified places to avoid or use in planning the canal and acquiring resources for its construction.

Military surveys were the most frequently employed forms of scientific cartography in France during the early modern period. Maps of coastlines, cities, strategic canals, and drainage projects, mountainous areas and roadways were important strategic tools that took advantage of the measurement techniques being refined in the period. There are thousands of unsigned maps made for building fortresses, planning sieges, setting cannon, deploying troops, re-creating battles, and describing terrain in border regions that remain obscure testimony to a widespread practice. The maps were a clear form of political cartography, obsessed with details of the local landscape that could affect the army's ability to control it.[19]

Military cartographers, whether engaged in fortress engineering projects or planning how to move troops or set up cannon, learned to think primarily topographically. Topographical features of the landscape were natural barriers and conduits, so they had vital strategic importance. Fortresses reconfigured the topography artificially, using walls, ditches, and canals to constitute a new terrain. A set of high bastion walls with a canal between them was (ideally) an artificial version of a deep gully surrounded by mountains and filled with a daunting river. Army engineers and surveyors who helped in mounting sieges, tunneling into the battlement walls and rolling temporary bridges across streams or canals, were in the process also erecting a countertopography of their own. No wonder military surveyors became particularly adept at measuring the subtle changes in elevations that gave character to local regions.[20] A comparable refiguring of the landscape was precisely what Riquet proposed to deliver with the Canal du Midi, and what Colbert hoped to bring to fruition when he sent Chevalier de Clerville, France's leading military engineer, to evaluate and oversee the project in the name of the state.

Also during the reign of Louis XIV, Colbert stimulated and set apart scientific cartographic work when he established the *Académie Royale des Sciences* and the *Observatoire*. The point of these institutions was to promote the sciences in France. To be a center of European civilization — to rival or even eclipse Italy — France needed to be a leader in the sciences as well as the arts. A French system of academies, based on Italian precedents but better funded and organized, seemed the best way to surpass the Italians.[21] Unlike the military surveyors who worked in a range of locations but still paid greatest attention to the peculiarities of a particular place (for obvious strategic reasons), the mathematicians of the academy reduced all lands to planar measurements. The point was to increase the accuracy of simple measures, not try to account for geographical complexity. This was still valuable to an engineering project like the Canal du Midi because the canal would work only if the elevations were accurate enough to create a stable water supply and build a viable system of locks. That is why the commission that first inspected the area under the direction of Clerville used academic techniques for taking elevations to check on Riquet's claims.[22]

The least studied of the pertinent survey traditions of the period was the kind of simple measuring done for plot plans, resource assessments, or civil engineering projects. This genre of mapmaking became a routine political tool for policy making under Henri IV, when infrastructural improvements became important to state policy. Rational land management techniques of the sort used on individual estates were applied to state policy to promote the economic well-being of the kingdom. This political approach put great emphasis on knowing the countryside as a repository of natural resources and site of potential improvement. Surveying and engineering were closely aligned as political tools. Although this strategy seemed to be buried along with the Protestant King Henri IV, the politics of *mesnagement* was revived by Colbert in the period of Louis XIV and became part of the territorial politics used to serve state-based absolutism. This gave civil, forestry, tax, and estate surveyors new work and social importance.[23]

These surveyors did not place their findings in grids of latitude and longitude like Cassini and Huygens. Like the academicians, the *arpenteurs* paid less attention to topography than the military surveyors, but similarly cared about the specific characteristics of local areas. Like *géographes du roi*, they were called upon to address the political status of land holdings, but unlike all the rest, they acquired skills in resource assessment and worked on civil engineering projects with local entrepreneurs. They were the ones attentive to road construction, forest management, estate planning, and hydraulic engineering — techniques of land improvement. This kind of localism, so different from that of the military, was obviously essential to the building of a great canal like the one from Toulouse to the Mediterranean.

The least scientific of local means for representing the land was not a form of survey at all, but regional narratives describing places. Folklore might have seemed to have no place in a process of "rationalizing" the landscape through engineering, but that was not the case for the Canal du Midi. Stories about the countryside as a site of spiritual as well as natural powers were crucial to understanding where to build a tunnel or how to recognize the exact position of a watershed. Stories marked sites of natural anomalies and indicated where human (or superhuman) forces had changed patterns in nature. This region of France, as part of a pilgrimage route to Campostella in Spain, was particularly rich in sites of miraculous streams, devilish rock formations, and stories of saints and heretics. This region of France had also been an important part of the Roman Empire, and stories of past glory made visible the webs of roads, canals, bridges, and burial sites from this early period that could be used a models for construction of a great canal. Narratives of place, then, were means of representation that carried local knowledge about the character of the local countryside, and passed on understandings of the natural world and past engineering ventures that were important to the Canal du Midi.

RISK ASSESSMENT AND REPRESENTATION AT THE CANAL DU MIDI

There were two major problems that plagued the project for the Canal du Midi, which made the risks of trying to build the canal sometimes seem too great to be worth trying. The first was the alimentation system for flooding the high point of the canal. If the canal could not be supplied with water, it could not be built. The other was the port on the Mediterranean. If the canal could not link trade on the Garonne River to trade on the Mediterranean, it had less purpose in propaganda value and economic usefulness. The definition of the canal as the Canal des Deux Mers — the canal of two seas — depended on finding solutions to these two fundamental problems. But the project was begun without either of these problems being fundamentally resolved. The canal was started when the problems seemed soluble, and Riquet seemed able to solve them — with the kind of help and supervision that Colbert insisted upon for the work. What made these problems seem no longer real impediments, but rather practical issues to work through on the ground, was a demonstration that diverse groups of experts could be deployed to fashion solutions.

For the first stage of the project, when the water system was in question, Riquet developed his scheme by assembling his small cadre of experts to guide him, and Colbert tested his capacity to do the work by setting up a commission of diverse (and much more powerful) experts to challenge and refine Riquet's proposal. At the second stage of the project, when the port and routing of the canal were more pressing, Riquet (already used to but annoyed with Colbert's continual stream of spies/experts coming from the north) enrolled all those who came to assess the project in thinking through the problems. He allowed or even encouraged in this period a much more fluid social arrangement of participants, and gave more autonomy to those working at different sites. He also took more risks in the project itself as he became confident that the engineering process would finally yield a canal. In these ways, the project clearly changed in its second stage. But the result was still a pattern of distributed problem solving and group learning, using diverse means of representing land to act on it.

The water system. The first great obstacle to building this canal was designing a water supply system that would flood the high point of the structure, and the basic system for the Canal du Midi was designed for Riquet with help from Pierre Campmas, a *fontainier* from Revel, a small mountain town where Riquet had some land and financial interests. A *fontainier's* job was to find water supplies for the town and get them where they were needed. This work entailed subtle knowledge of local topography, some hydraulic engineering, and experience with seasonal weather patterns. The *fontainier* had already worked for Riquet, diverting water to a mill on his property, so Riquet was aware of his expertise.[24]

Campmas was able to reduce the risk of a water shortage for the canal because he understood so much about the water supplies of the Montagne Noire. He also knew how to follow the topographical contours of the landscape, designing conduits for carrying water safely downhill to where it could be used. He already knew the rivers on the mountain and the gorges that could be dammed to collect water during the rainy season.[25] Still, Campmas was in no position to think about how to design a water supply system for a large canal. He could deliver water and build supply channels, but he had no way to know if the supplies would be enough to keep vessels afloat in the summertime. He could not compute the amount of water necessary for a canal because he had no experience in assessing how many locks were appropriate for a particular incline. Without an educated guess about the number of these structures the canal would need, he could never estimate the amount of water the canal would require to stay filled when it was in use and the locks were dumping water downstream. So his expertise alone left too much unknown to make the project seem reliable enough to fund and try.

The adequacy of the water supply could be better estimated, however, with the expertise of a hydraulic engineer like Riquet's other collaborator, François Andréossy. Andréossy had no local knowledge of the watershed, but he was trained in principles of surveying and engineering. Moreover, he had recently visited Italy, where he inspected some of the well-known Italian canals. He could consider the number of locks needed for the Canal du Midi

Chandra Mukerji

and thus the necessary water supply (although he vastly underestimated the eventual requirements), so he could assess the results of Campmas's efforts. He was also a fine cartographer, so he could represent the proposed canal and its relationship to the region in which it would be laid, not only showing its route but suggesting its fit with the local topography. Thus, he made the canal project seem conceptually viable and strategically visible in ways important to gaining the confidence of Colbert and the king.[26]

While these three men were individually in no position to think through the construction of this large canal, together they had the expertise to make the project seem feasible. Riquet could calculate finances, Campmas could find and direct water from the Montagne Noire, and Andréossy could design the structure and define its technical requirements. Still, the three had little social standing and no obvious authority for making such a grand proposal. Their solution was to build a mock-up of the canal on Riquet's estate at Bonrepos to test their engineering designs. They had two little ponds for a water supply, a set of locks, supply channels, and even a tunnel to take the water downhill and through the mock canal. If anyone doubted that these men could actually construct a canal, this was their answer. The team had already made such a construction — at least on a small scale. It was a matter of demonstration, not dispute. Riquet showed the model to the future archbishop d'Aglure de Bourlemont, who then brought Riquet's plans to the attention of Colbert.[27]

Colbert was interested in, if not convinced by, Riquet's proposal and sent Clerville to assemble a commission of experts to study Riquet's plans. Under Clerville's supervision, this group was to travel through the Montagne Noire and along the proposed route of the canal, making surveys and assessments of the engineering proposed by Riquet, and then report back to the minister.[28]

The commission had the social authority that Riquet, Campmas, and Andréossy did not. It included many local notables who had no expertise in canal construction, but who, like Bourlemont, were necessary to secure political support for the enterprise. The "experts" on engineering and surveying on the commission were, first, Clerville himself, with his experience in building fortresses, including canal construction (at least over short distances). Next there was Henri de Boutheroue de Bourgneuf, whose father had completed the Canal de Briare, linking the Loire to the Seine,[29] and who himself now managed that canal. As the man with the greatest practical knowledge about comparable waterways, Bourgneuf was expressly charged with estimating the amount of work it would require to build Riquet's project, and what it would cost. In addition, there was the sieur de La Feuille, an *ingénieur* who seemed to have the trust of Colbert, and who was put in charge of supervising the canal work from 1667 to 1683. The group also included four *niveleurs*, two of whom are known: Riquet's colleague

François Andréossy, and Jean Cavalier, a *géographe du roi*. Cavalier had started in the military, but he had become a skilled regional cartographer, drawing the region's best map, one that was repeatedly copied and reproduced for almost a century.[30] The other two surveyors, whose names do not appear elsewhere in cartography, presumably had some local knowledge and civil survey skills. This meant that the commission contained not only members of the region's political elite but established experts in the intellectual traditions pertinent to the job. The survey team included a civil engineer/surveyor (Andréossy), a *géographe du roi* (Cavalier), a hydraulic engineer (Bourgneuf) and two military engineers/surveyors (Clerville and La Feuille). There was no academician, but the elevations made by Cavalier were done using the techniques developed by La Hire, one of the most able surveyors from the academy, so even academic surveying had its effects on the development of the plan.[31]

The members of the commission trained in different traditions of French surveying and engineering not only tried to anticipate and reduce the risks of the venture, but also checked the assessments made by the original team. Riquet's financial expertise was set against Bourgneuf's experience at the Canal de Briare; Andréossy's designs for the canal and reservoirs were checked by Clerville and his assistants for their soundness; and Campmas's water supply plans (as well as the overall canal trace) were scrutinized by Cavalier, Bourgneuf, and La Feuille to see if the inclines were well computed and the routes topographically well placed. The commission members did not so much challenge the plan as revise it to make it more effective, apparently reducing the risk of this daunting but intriguing project. [32]

Since the crucial risk facing the commission had to do with whether the water supply system would be effective in supporting a navigational canal, delivering adequate supplies when and where they were needed, the commission spent most of its time considering this issue. One important element in the plan had to be the location of a watershed where the supplies could be delivered to the canal to flow both toward the Atlantic and toward the Mediterranean. Although historians have sometimes admired Riquet's skill in swiftly locating the watershed between the two river systems linked by the canal, in fact there was little argument about where to do this. There were known watersheds in the area, the best recognized of which was La Grave de Naurouze. These were represented less on topographical maps than in folklore. Riquet and his colleagues simply confirmed with their elevation studies what was already common conjecture among locals.[33] The problem was not finding the watershed but making a convincing case for its usefulness for the project. Physical geographers, following Hondius, generally believed that mountain chains existed between all major river systems. In fact, many period maps of southwestern France actually depicted a set of mountains running through the proposed route of the canal. They were fictional constructs, theoretical assertions, unbased on measurements or observations of any kind. But they had the authority of respected science.[34] So, much of the effort of the survey work was *nivellement* or studies of elevation to prove that the canal could in fact be built across the proposed set of valleys and be supplied with runoff from the Montagne Noire carried to Naurouze. Given the serious problems of scientific credibility of the project, it should be no surprise that the surveyors, apparently under the tutelage of Cavalier, the *géographe du roi*, used La Hire's measurement techniques for the commission's elevation studies. This gave their findings the authority of science, so that they could be trusted as a basis for countering Hondius.[35]

Even with good elevations, however, the plan for the water system was so complicated that it was not entirely convincing on paper. This is why the commissioners also asked Riquet to make a channel along the proposed route from the Sor River (on the Montagne Noire) to the Fontaine de La Grave à Naurouze. This *rigole d'essai* was meant to be a small ditch just to prove the inclines, but it was nonetheless built with some difficulty. Torrents of rain kept disrupting construction of the *rigole*, but in October 1665, the waters arrived as expected at Naurouze, and the demonstration of the alimentation system was complete.[36]

The result of the commission's studies on the Montagne Noire and the test of the water system with the *rigole d'essai* was not only an engineering plan for the alimentation system, but also confidence in the canal scheme itself. The risks entailed in designing a canal that crossed a watershed, which had impeded the development of such a waterway in this region before, now seemed small enough to face. Once the commissioners endorsed Riquet's proposal (with their revisions), Colbert was willing to give out a contract for at least the first stage of the process. He authorized beginning the canal at Toulouse, connecting it to the Montagne Noire supplies, and carrying it (with an impressive set of locks) across the watershed. Completing the work to the Mediterranean would have to wait until another set of vexing technical issues were made less daunting.[37]

The Port. The port of Cette or Sète, built as the terminus of the Canal des Deux Mers, was in some ways the exact opposite of the water supply system on the Montagne Noire. While designing an effective complex of reservoirs and ditches in the mountains to deliver water to a faraway canal seemed an obviously difficult engineering task, an outlet for the canal on the Mediterranean appeared relatively straightforward. Building breakwaters and dredging harbors might not have been simple ventures, but they were at least more familiar ones.[38] The risk of diminishing the effectiveness of the canal by giving it no good port at one end seemed small at first, but it loomed larger as the work progressed. To offset the anxiety that resulted from repeated failures of the seawalls and dredging, more and more information about the site was accumulated and discussed by different kinds of experts. The representations of Sète multiplied, providing new hopes for solving engineering difficulties that seemed intractable. By the time the difficulties at Cette had become chronic there was no way to reroute or stop work on the canal. It was already too far advanced. The point was to reduce the risk to the canal's success that a poor port would create, and to increase the chance of making the whole enterprise into the flourishing and politically dramatic system that had been imagined. Each new layer of representation was accumulated to achieve this end, and gave new reason to revive this hope.

Importantly, thought had already gone into the construction of a new harbor in Languedoc even before Riquet first sent his original proposal to Colbert. Clerville had been asked to survey the coast near Béziers to propose a way of constructing a new harbor. He suggested building one at Cette or Sète. The engineer was given this task because for both military and economic reasons; having no safe harbor in this area was a strategic problem for France. Colbert was concerned on both grounds because not only was he finance minister and worried about the French economy, but he was also in charge of the French navy (such as it was). His success in empowering the state, pleasing the monarch, and satisfying his own sense of order depended on making some improvements in this area.[39]

The southwestern region of the country was also among the richest in foodstuffs and manufactures, but poor in transportation. The population (in this period before the Revocation of the Edict of Nantes sent the industrious Protestants in large numbers to the Netherlands and England) was relatively large and productive. There were textiles and leathers being produced in the Montagne Noire. There were marbles and wood to be extracted from the Pyrenees. And wine and other foodstuffs were produced in excess in the rich inland valleys. All these goods could find new and more profitable markets if they could be transported along the Mediterranean.[40] But the sea was full of pirates, the storms in this area frequent and intense, and France was a country too weak in naval power to support a merchant marine without a better infrastructure. The lack of safe harbors was simply dangerous. For these reasons, Colbert had asked Clerville to survey and design a new harbor somewhere to the west of Marseilles. Near Agde, a large rocky hill rose from the otherwise flat and sandy coast. This appeared to be the only natural barrier in the region that could be used to protect ships from storms. The hill was also strategically useful. The promontory provided a site to look out for enemy vessels coming to attack ships in harbor. On the inland side of the hill, there was also a large and relatively deep étang or marsh where water already collected naturally. It seemed possible that dredging this area for a harbor and providing a more substantial barrier between the sea and interior with a well-designed seawall could yield an effective new port. Clerville was already planning this project when Colbert asked him to head the commission to study the Canal des Deux Mers.[41]

This helps explain why, when the commissioners were reviewing the plans for the canal route, they recommended constructing a new port on the Mediterranean just where Clerville had wanted it. It was immediately obvious to him (and perhaps to Colbert before him) that Riquet's canal could be connected to Clerville's port and help serve doubly Colbert's plan for stimulating trade in the region. It also seemed possible to Riquet that if he could construct and have a fundamental economic interest in a vital new French port, he could become an even richer man and safeguard his family's future better than he could with the canal alone. In turn, if Colbert could give this project to Riquet to complete, he would not have to use so much treasury money or become too reliant on the military engineers for realizing his economic policies. (Keep in mind that Colbert and the minister of war, Louvois, were rivals and even perhaps enemies vying for the king's ear and limited resources.) The project seemed a way to reduce risk for both the minister and the tax man. The canal would give more commerce to the port; the port would make the canal a more effective trading route; Riquet would risk his fortune and reputation; and Colbert would create a whole new trading system that would be a wonder of the world and an asset to the French navy.

Unfortunately, dreaming of a new harbor was quite a bit easier than actually building one along this coast. Silt in local rivers and the storms plaguing the Mediterranean in this area made the easy discharge of the canal and its cargo into the Mediterranean more problematic than anyone had thought.[42] Creating a large seawall to enclose the entrance to the harbor was itself a difficult task, but knowing how to design it was more taxing. It had to be constructed so that high seas would not damage ships during storms, vessels could move easily in and out of the harbor, and sand could be normally discharged along with outflows of water from rivers and streams. Because the mouths of existing rivers that ran into the sea produced no natural harbors in this region, there were some fears about the silting up of the new port. But no one at first realized what a persistent problem this would be for Sète.

The reason that the silting problems were not well anticipated for the port was that there was no equivalent to Campmas for the harbor. There were no local harbor masters to consult on design because there were no natural harbors. In the other parts of France where harbors (mostly on the Atlantic) had been improved through engineering, the expertise that had been accumulated in the process was not useful to transfer to Sète. First, the problems of engineering on the Atlantic were substantially different, and second, these harbors tended to be part natural as well as engineered, which the port of Sète simply was not.

Riquet grew up in Béziers and was good at imagining the *town* he would build at Sète to make it a great depot; he knew how to design a major center of wealth and power. But he had no obvious solution to the problems of designing and building the port, and he was spending a great deal of time in Perpignan rather than Agde. Nonetheless, he became impatient with Clerville, La Feuille, and others sent by Colbert, who had their own ideas about the harbor and felt authorized to speak their minds. Colbert was writing to him as the man responsible for the success of the venture, but he was also not letting him make the decisions. The result was another nightmare of diminished control for Riquet. But it also set up a new system of distributed cognition for addressing the problems of the port — using different traditions of land representation and design. In the end, this situation also gave Riquet allies when Colbert abandoned him. La Feuille and Morgues could speak authoritatively about Riquet's honesty and real need for money to complete the work.

The experts consulted on the port brought a range of skills to the task: knowledge of mathematical technique (the Jesuit Père Morgues), Dutch and Italian traditions of hydraulic engineering (La Feuille), military engineering (Clerville), and land management/building techniques used by local surveyors and entrepreneurs in the region.

The authority for the work was as layered as the representational techniques used on site. Riquet, of course, was now sure that he was a world-class engineer, and lost no time in telling Colbert that he should be given more control of the work. Colbert, who was increasingly concerned about costs and the losses that resulted from earlier mistakes of measurement and design on the canal, was not so impressed, but still needed the entrepreneur to deliver on this project. Clerville, in turn, felt he still had the commission of building a harbor in Languedoc, and knew more about this kind of operation. But he was often called elsewhere to work, and this left La Feuille and Riquet to share primary authority. When the problems with the port were mounting, La Feuille was sent first to Holland and then Italy by Colbert to see how more experienced engineers worked with comparable situations.[43] Colbert then insisted that Riquet not proceed on the port until La Feuille brought the results of these study trips back to Languedoc. This rankled Riquet, and locked the two men in a struggle for power that deprived both of them of control.

It is important to notice that unlike the group who worked on the water system for the Montagne Noire, the men charged with creating Sète included a military engineer, a school-trained engineer, and a mathematician, but lacked a man like Campmas. There was no one from the area who had routinely worked on local harbors, knew the coast intimately, shared local narratives of place and used these strands of knowledge for engineering. The closest equivalent this group had was an odd outsider, Louis de Froidour.

Froidour was one of the most unlikely contributors to the port design because he was France's leading forestry surveyor, not an engineer or local fishing or shipping expert. But what Froidour could provide were a set of ethnographic techniques that he used to learn insider, local knowledge about the place where the harbor was being built, and characteristics of the sea that impinged on design. The first problem in designing Sète was defining what local fishermen, merchants, and sailors thought would make a good harbor, and what they understood about the problems in building it. Froidour then recommended design changes based on what he heard.[44]

Interestingly, Froidour seemed to have been called to the canal site originally not to study the port but to look at the water system in the Montagne Noire, where he wrote enthusiastically about the great dam being built at St. Ferréol, and the ingenious system of ditches constructed to carry water to the Seuil de Naurouze. Froidour was not particularly informed about the region or even its forests. He had until this point in his career been busy mainly in the north inventorying the timber reserves there. He had just been called to the south by Colbert to map the much more dramatically depleted forests of this drier region. He was the forestry surveyor whom Colbert trusted the most, but not because he was such a mathematically adept surveyor or knew the forests personally. It was because he was deemed an honest man who sought accurate knowledge more than bribes. His trip to the Montagne Noire made sense as one more instance of surveillance orchestrated by Colber, both resulting from and underscoring the minister's insecurity about the water system. Froidour was a good spy for Colbert to assess the technical work because the forestry bureau was actually the office of water and forests. When he measured France's forests, this often meant Froidour was studying mountainous areas in which large timber trees grew and rivers ran downhill that could carry logs to towns. Additionally, as an "honête homme," Froidour was also a good person to check for signs of impropriety. A large part of his forestry "surveying" was really interviewing people about where old forests had gone. If there was nothing to survey where a forest had been, or an old forest was much smaller in the surveys than it appeared to be in old maps, Froidour was charged to determine who had done the cutting, what taxes they owed on the profits, and what fines they should pay if they cut trees for which they had no authority. He was, then, someone whose job was in part to locate and document improprieties and punish transgressors. These were fine credentials for a spy sent to the Montagne Noire.[45]

While it made sense for him to inspect the water supply system, Froidour was not someone who had any apparent experience in building ports. But his skills as a kind of ethnographer — someone who could acquire local knowledge about places and their uses — made him the next best thing to Campmas. If he had no firsthand acquaintance with local understandings of the coast, the problems with storms there, fishing practices, uses of and seasonal changes in the marshes, and the effects of the rivers discharging into the sea, he was at least experienced in taking oral testimony from local populations (*procès verbaux*). Froidour had learned how to ask pertinent questions that would reveal patterns (good and bad) of resource use.[46]

Froidour interviewed sailors and fishermen about the sea, its character, and uses in the region. He talked to them about why the rivers there had dug no natural harbors into the sea. He learned in what direction the winds blew during the fiercest storms to make sure the port would be designed to provide appropriate protection for vessels in the harbor. An early storm proved the potential protection of the seawall, but later ones were more destructive, raising questions of design that Froidour could address. Through his efforts, he brought more of the local, folk (and oral) representations of the area to this part of the canal's design and construction.[47] Unfortunately, no permanent solution was found to the problem of silting in the port. No matter where the seawalls were placed and replaced, the harbor soon collected sand. But each new representation raised hope for a solution as the area near Agde became known in increasingly complex ways.

The insistent nature of the silting led to more careful consideration of silt accumulation in the canal itself, which was contributing to the load of particulate matter that was settling into the harbor. A number of small rivers and streams in the area between Carcassone and the Mediterranean had been tapped to provide water for the canal in this region, but these water courses carried from the steep nearby mountains runoff that was filled with mud and sand. At first, the water was sent directly into the canal, but this was almost immediately revealed to be a poor plan. The powerful floods that periodically plagued the region damaged the canal walls as surges of mud and debris crashed into the fragile ditch. The flood-driven materials either floated on the surface of the water (sticks and small logs) where it damaged vessels, or sank to the bottom of the canal (silt) where it clogged the waterway and required dredging. To solve the problems, these feeder streams were now either (if they were small enough) routed over slightly elevated stone containers at the side of the canal that held back debris and mud, or (if they were larger rivers) redirected into aqueducts, running either over or under the canal. Conduits (with doors) from the diverted rivers were designed to allow some of the water from these sources to enter the canal when it was needed. Drains were also built into the side of the main channel, particularly near these inputs, not only for expelling excess water that threatened to make the canal overflow in wet periods, but also to wash out some of the silt. Along most of the sides of the canal, ditches were dug parallel to the main channel to capture general runoff and keep excess water from the canal.[48] All these efforts were meant to reduce the myriad silting and flooding problems that plagued the canal, but particularly the Port de Sète. Nonetheless, storms ravaged it, and silt collected without cease. New soundings, land surveys, and harbor plans continued to be drawn, and the experts from the different traditions of representational practice and engineering experience were called in to help — without stable success.

The lack of a reliable port made trade down the whole length of the canal less appealing than it might have been. The high cost of paying tolls through the locks also contributed to keeping long-distance trade low. But the canal as a whole functioned well by the end of the 1680s, and short-distance trade through it was lively from the start. Commercial dreams and cartographic skills not only proliferated representations of the landscape in the area, but made a new landscape in the southwest that was identified with its canal. This in turn became part of the imagery of the region and of France.

THE CANAL DU MIDI

This story tells us a great deal about how cartographic learning and systems for representing the landscape were mobilized in the end of the seventeenth century for commercial and political purposes. They constituted cognitive tools that allowed French entrepreneurs, engineers, and laborers to achieve a project that was technically beyond the means of the period. Representational techniques from land surveying to ethnographic work were mobilized for the project, and provided means for reworking the landscape for advantage.

The engineering of the Canal du Midi or Deux Mers constitutes a good science studies story about social learning, scientific expertise, and state power. But it is also a story about entrepreneurialism in late seventeenth-century France. The entrepreneurs who built the infrastructure for the state in this period absorbed a great deal of the risk involved in the massive social changes that we call in retrospect the growth of the modern state or the development of state absolutism. They helped to rework the landscape in ways that transformed places into states, and made them something politically and economically new. They sought and were given economic benefits from their efforts. They took economic risks for economic gain. But they were interested less in taking risks than reducing them; they wanted to do things they knew they could do. Since they did not have the personal expertise for such assessments, what kind of "knowing" did they rely upon to make good choices in their schemes? An answer perhaps lies in the understudied connections between representations of nature and commercial activity. If someone could see what to do to promote trade and make a map or plan for it, there was reason to invest in it. When Riquet had a map of the Montagne Noire and models to demonstrate his alimentary system, it was time to start building a canal. And so they did, and reworked this region of the southwestern France to make it a tribute to human ingenuity and territorial power.

Notes

1. See, for example, Marie-Joelle Paris, *Versailles: Le Grand Aqueduc de Buc ou de la manière de conduire les eaux au parc*. (Buc: Office municipal des associations de Buc, 1986), 47–58.

2. A. Marcet-Juncosa, " L'opposition catalane à P.P. Riquet" in Ed. Jean-Denis Bergasse, *Le Canal du Midi, Vol. 3: Des siècles d'aventure humaine* (Millau: Maury, 1984), 143–150. On 15 December 1662, Riquet wrote Colbert from Rousillon describing his ambitions for this project.

3. Archives du Canal (AC) Liasse 46, pièce 1—"Edit créant un droit annuel sur les cabaretiers (hotelleries, cabartets, tavernes et marchands de vin) dan toute l'entendue du Languedoc; pièce 2—arrêt du Conseil d'Etat ordonnant une imposition de 40,000 livres sur les contribuables aux tailles de la Généralité de Montauban en remmplacement du droit annuel sur les cabaretiers." 19 October 1671.

The local resistance to the sale of offices is illustrated in exchanges of letters between Colbert and Riquet mentioning the opposition he was facing from the elites in Toulouse, and reluctance to pay from Montpellier.

AC Riquet to Colbert 20 August 1670 mentions that the "scindics de Languedoc" are opposed to the sale of :

> offices des greffiers consulaires et de preudhommes. Mais comme . . . je vous envoyeray un arrest du conseil pour en ynterdire un, j'ay lieu de croise qu'aprés cet example vous trouverez toutes les facilités que vous pouvex désirer à en tirer les sommes qui vous doivent revenir de la ventes desdits offices.
>
> Je parleray au sieur de Bersan des advances que vous souhaitex qu'il vous fasse sur les gages des greffiers consulaires et preudhommes, encore que M. de Senes me mande que vous avez touché les trois quarts de revenu des deux année 1669-1670, et si je puis l'obliger à vous fournir quelque somme considerables je le feray voloniers.

AC Riquet to Colbert 1-10-7: The problems at Montpellier seem to have been less opposition to the sale of offices than routine non-payment of the fees for the sales.

4. For the opposition, see, AC Liasse 46. In AC Liasse 548 pièce 2, there is an order from the intendant enjoining the communities near the canal's construction site to repair the roads to facilitate transport to these areas. 23 Mai 1669. AC, Liasse 191 describes the acquisition of lands. This is a listing of the sales of lands for the canal, which names the seller, the quality of land, the size of the parcel, and the price of sale. The land is valued by what is grown on it.

So, wheat fields are valued less than orchards and gardens. There is no mention of water rights in these early records, although there are some buildings included on the lands where the canal is to go. This is particularly the case in the area of Toulouse where the canal enters a populated area.

5. AC Liasses 35, 37, 39, 45, 46, 48, 191. It is important to keep in mind that although the *gabelle* in Rousillon was new, it was not given to Riquet just to finance the project. In fact, he was given this area to "farm" before he first proposed the canal to Colbert, and it was because of his success as a tax farmer that he was in a position to write to Colbert about his scheme on 15 December 1662.

6. The kinds of connections he had through the *gabelle* are visible in the list of those who invested both small and large amounts in the project. These were people with multiple ties to Riquet and politicians of many statuses. See Pierre Burlats-Brun and Jean-Denis Bergasse,"L'Oligarchie Gabelière, Soutien Financier de Riquet" in *Le Canal du Midi*, Vol. 4: Grands Moments et Grands Sites. 125–141.

7. L. T. C. Rolt, *Le Canal Entre Deux Mers* (Paris: Euromapping, 1994), 23–24.

8. For indication of the value placed on this project in this period and before, see AC Liasse 1.

9. For a discussion of the *mesnagement* tradition, see Chandra Mukerji, *Territorial Ambitions and the Gardens of Versailles* (Cambridge: Cambridge University Press, 1997), 41–42, 45; Thierry Mariage, *L'Univers de Le Nostre* (Bruxelles: Pierre Mardaga, 1990), 43. For more details of this political tradition and garden design see also Chandra Mukerji, "Bourgeois Culture and French Gardening in the 16th and 17th Centuries," paper presented at Dumbarton Oaks 1998, and to be published in Michel Conan (ed.), *Bourgeois and Cultural Encounters in Garden Art*, 1550–1850 Dumbarton Oaks 2001. For the relationship between this political philosophy and the Canal du Midi, see Chandra Mukerji, "The Modern State as Material Accomplishment: Territorial Culture and the Canal du Midi," paper presented at Bad Homburg 2000.

10. For a discussion of the work on the canal including the contract, wages, and working conditions, see Bertrand Gabolde, "Les Ouvriers du Chantier" in *Le Canal du Midi*, vol. 4, 235–239, and André Maistre, *Le Canal des Deux-Mers: Canal Royal du Languedoc 1666–1810* (Toulouse: Éditions Privat, 1998), 72–77.

11. Emmanuel Le Roy Ladurie, *Montaillou: The Promised Land of Error*. New York: G. Braziller, 1978.

12. Rolt, *Le Canal Entre Deux Mers*, 72.

13. Maistre, *Le Canal des Deux-Mers*, 95–111.

14. Bruno Latour, "Visualization and Cognition: Thinking with Eyes and Hands," in *Knowledge and Society: Studies in the Sociology of Culture Past and Present*, ed. H. Kuklick and E. Landfed (Greenwich, Conn.: JAI Press, 1986) 6, 1–40.

15. This distinction between information and learning is crucial for understanding state power and the deployment of experts. Experts often work with partial knowledge and are asked for advice on which they can give only preliminary judgments. Nonetheless, states make their policies on these assessments, and they have, over many centuries, managed to maintain a certain level of legitimacy. Having good information helps, but it is not always possible to get. What is more important to states is the development and cultivation of learning systems—like the research branch of DOD. See Chandra Mukerji, *A Fragile Power: Scientists and the State* (Princeton, N.J.: Princeton University Press, 1989).

16. Paul Bondois, *Deux Ingénieurs au Siècle du Louis XIV: Vauban et Riquet* (Paris: Librairie Picard, n.d.); André Corvisier, *Louvois* (Paris: Fayard, 1983). For the risks of trying to build a canal in this region along with the desire to do it, see AC Liasse 1.

17. François de Dainville, *La Géographie des Humanistes* (Génève: Slatkin Reprints, 1969).

18. I have argued elsewhere that a system of distributed learning developed at this site and that it worked as a means of problem solving for the engineering of the canal. See Chandra Mukerji, "Distributed Cognition and the Canal du Midi," paper presented at the 1997 annual meeting of the American Sociological Association. I don't want to spend time here belaboring the point. I will not elaborate either the concept of distributed cognition, or how it should or should not be applied to this history. That is complex issue that requires a long argument in itself. For work in this tradition of analysis, see Edwin Hutchins, *Cognition in the Wild* (Cambridge: MIT Press, 1995). See also Philip Agre, *Computation and Human Experience* (New York: Cambridge University Press), 1997; Yjro Engestrom and David Middleton, *Cognition and Communication at Work* New York: (Cambridge University Press, 1996).

19. Anne Blanchard, *Les Ingénieurs du Roy de Louis XIV à Louis XVI* (Montpellier: Université Paul-Valéry, 1979), 42–54. See also Chandra Mukerji, "Engineering and French Formal Gardens in the Age of Louis XIV," paper presented at the University of Pennsylvania symposium "New Approaches to French Garden History," 1998. Unfortunately for the army, topographical mapping was a technically difficult discipline. The survey work itself was physically and cognitively taxing. It required attention to two dimensions of measurement (elevation as well as distance), and drew surveyors to work in rugged landscapes, trying to join lines of sight in environments in which it was often hard to see. There were drawing problems as well; contour lines had not yet been developed so there were no good standardized conventions for rendering elevations accurately. Still, military cartographers became skilled at noting localized changes in topography and came to know the landscape in these terms along France's borders. P. D. A. Harvey, *The History of Topographical Maps* (London: Thames and Hudson, 1980).

20. For material techniques and military engineering, see Alain Manesson Mallet, *Les Travaux de Mars . . .* (Amsterdam: Henri Desbordes, 1696); John Muller, *The Attack and Defense of Fortified Places. In Three Parts* (London: T & J. Egerton, 1791), particularly plates 9 and 11; M. Belidor, *Les science des ingenieurs dans la conduite des travaux de fortification.et d'architecture civile.* (Paris : Claude Jombert, 1729); Nicolas de Fer, *Introduccion à la Fortification dedié à Monseigneur le duc de Bourgogne* (Paris: Chez l'auteur dans l'Isle du Palais sur le Quay de l'Orloge à la Sphere Royale. avec. priv du Roy, n.d.); Pierre Rocolle, *2000 ans de fortification française*, tome I. (Limoges and Paris: Charles-Lavauzelle, 1973), 175–212; Sébastien Le Prestre Vauban, *De l'attaque de de la défense des places* (La Haye: Chez Pierre de Hondt, 1736). The importance of surveyors and the military engineers to the politics of the period was symbolic as well as practical. Military engineering had been a hallmark of ancient Rome. "Monuments to the greatness of Rome" were celebrated by Louis XIV and his contemporaries, and stirred them to use French soldiers for comparable work. The army engineers were first employed for the obvious jobs of building of ports, garrisons, and arsenals, but they were also used to improve the water supplies for Versailles and Paris, and in setting out drainage and flood control ditches around rivers and swamps, and laying out canals that flowed where rivers did not. All these projects required some survey work, and all of them showed up again on maps. Tantalizingly, these efforts reshaped precisely what was recorded on maps—the shape of the shoreline, the course of rivers, the topography, and the roads crossing the landscape. See Mukerji, "Engineering and French Formal Gardens in the Age of Louis XIV" 1998; John A. Lynn, *Giant of the Grand Siecle: The French Army 1610–1715* (Cambridge: Cambridge University Press, 1997); and Josef Konvitz, *Cartography in France, 1660–1848* (Chicago: University of Chicago Press, 1987).

21. Frances Yates, *The French Academies of the 16th Century* (Warburg Institute: University of London, 1947); Institute de France, *Académie des Sciences: Troisième Centenaire 1666–1966* (Paris: Gauthier-Villars, 1967), ch. 1.

22. The canal would work only if the segments met and the elevations worked. Alice Stroup, *A Company of Scientists: Botany, Patronage, and Community in the Seventeenth-Century Parisian Royal Academy of Sciences* (Berkeley: University of California Press, 1990), ch.1.

23. Mukerji, *Territorial Ambitions* 1997. For a discussion of this political approach and its effects on the region of Languedoc, see Maistre, *Le Canal des Deux-Mers*.

24. Bertrand Gabolde, "Revel: Des Eaux du Sor à la Rigole de la Plaine," *Le Canal bu Midi*, vol. 4, 241–244; François Gazelle, "Riquet et les Eaux de la Montange Noire," in *Le Canal du Midi*, 145–147; Malavialle, "Une Excursion dans la Montagne Noire," *Société Languedocienne de Géographie* Bulletin, part 2, 135.

25. Maistre, *Le Canal des Deux-Mers*, 72; Gazelle, "Riquet et les Eaux."

26. For the hydraulic expertise in Italy in the period, see Gazelle, "Riquet et les Eaux," vol. 4, 147–150; Malavialle, 120–121. For Andréossy's interest in Riquet and Languedoc, see Jean Robert and Jean-Denis Bergasse, "L'Étrange Destin des Andréossy," *Le Canal du* Midi, vol. 3, 199–201.

27. Rolt, *Le Canal Entre Deux Mers*, 24–27; Inès Murat, "Les Rapports de Colbert et de Riquet: Méfiance pour un homme ou pour un système?" in *Le Canal du Midi*, vol. 3 (Cessenon: J.-D. Bergasse, 1984), 108. For a discussion of demonstration and representation, see Mukerji, *Territorial Ambitions* 1997, ch. 7; Chandra Mukerji and Patrick Carroll, "Material Culture Methods and Historical Sociology," paper presented at the1996 annual meeting of the American Sociological Association.

28. Rolt, *Le Canal Entre Deux Mers*, 30–31; Maistre, *Les Canal des Deux-Mers*, 38–41; Murat, "Les Rapports de Colbert et de Riquet," 111–112.

29. Hubert Pinsseau, "Du Canal de Briare au Canal des Deux Mers: Origines et Conséquences d'un Sysème inédit de Navigation Artificielle" in *Le Canal du Midi*, vol. 4, 27–54.

30. For a discussion of Cavalier's work, see François Dainville, *Cartes anciennes du Langue-doc, XVIe–XVIIIe siècles* (Montpellier: Sociète languedocienne de gèographie, 1961, 38–40); Robert and Bergasse, "L'Étrange Destin," 203.

31. Rolt, *Le Canal Entre Deux Mers*, 31. Dainville, *Cartes anciennes du Languedoc, XVIe–XVIIIe siècles*, 55, 60–61; M.L. Malavialle, "Une Excursion dans la Montagne Noire," *Sociète Languedocienne de Gèographie Bulletin*, part 3, tome 15, 283–314. The first map published of the canal plan and its water supply was actually made by the géographe du roi, P. du Val. See Malavialle, part 4, tome 15, 436–439, 475–476.

32. Rolt, *Le Canal Entre Deux Mers*, 32.Some of the changes they initiated had to do with the route of the canal itself. Under their influence, Riquet abandoned the idea of making the Fesquel and Aude Rivers navigable, and instead agreed to dig a separate canal in these river beds to connect his new canal with the ancient Canal de la Robine, which could then carry boats to the Mediterranean. The reason for this shift was probably Bourgneuf's acquaintance with the Canal de Briare. He knew about the tie-ups in shipping that resulted from problems in navigating these wild rivers. Trade would be easier in a more contained set of canals.

33. Gazelle, "Riquet et les Eaux," 145–146; M. L. Malavialle, "Une Excursion dans la Montagne Noire," Part I. *Société Languedocienne de Géographie Bulletin*, tome XIV, 1891, 280–284.

34. Henri Enjalbert, "Les Hardinesses de Riquet: Données Géomorphologiques de la Région que Traverse le Canal du Midi," *Le Canal du Midi*, vol. 4, 129–142.

35. Dainville, *Cartes anciennes du Languedoc, XVIe–XVIIIe siècles*, 47. The idea of using the Sor River as a source of the water supply for a canal between the Garonne and Mediterranean had been discussed by a géographe du roi, Pierre Petit in 1663. See Malavialle, "Une Excursion dans la Montagne Noire," *Sociète Languedocienne de Gèographie Bulletin,* part I, 273 ff.

36. Rolt, *Le Canal Entre Deux Mers*, 35–37; Froidour, *Lettre à Monsieur Barrillon Damoncourt, Conseiller du Roy en ses Conseils, Maître des Requestes Ordinaire de son Hostel, Intendant*

de Iustice, Police et Finances en Picardie, contenant la Relation & la description des Travaux qui se sont en Languedoc, pour la communication des deux mers, 9–10; Gazelle, "Riquet et les Eaux," 162–164; Dainville, *Cartes anciennes du Languedoc, XVIe–XVIIIe siècles,* 1961, 47; Malavialle, "Une Excursion dans la Montagne Noire," *Sociètè Languedocienne de Gèographie Bulletin,* part 2, 146. Is this the route that Clerville opposed, according to Malavialle (Part I, p. 259)? Although Riquet's project was vindicated by the study, his plan was not adopted without revision. While the commission was checking surveys and Riquet was preparing the rigole *d'essai,* the main proposed *rigole* was rerouted. We have no direct evidence about the socio-cognitive context for the switch. Clerville was the first to make note of it in a plan for Colbert, but the new channel seemed more the work of a local surveyor than a fortress designer; it followed the contours of the land more exactly, requiring a longer course but fewer of the costly tunnels and less complex terracing that military engineers tended to build. Still, Campmas was not part of the survey team; Andréossy was Riquet's expert there; and we have no knowledge of the backgrounds or contributions of the two unknown surveyors in the party. On the other hand, the canal engineer, Bourgneurf, was on the mountain at the time, and he tended to favor simple systems that were less prone to break down. Whatever the dynamics that led to it, all we know is that the shift occurred when the commission's survey team was working on the mountain, checking elevations and routes for the waterworks; any or all of the experts may have contributed to this change of plans. The resulting *rigole* followed a path between the original one developed by Campmas, Andréossy and Riquet, and the suggestions being made for revision by the commissioners. In this way, it was apparently (even from the scanty evidence we have of its design) a socially negotiated solution to a technical problem in the water supply. The alimentary system was changed more dramatically and explicitly by a redesign of the reservoirs on the Montagne Noire. Riquet originally proposed a set of small reservoirs to capture and hold the water, but Clerville thought it would be simpler to construct one great holding facility at Saint-Ferréol. There was a rock base at the end of this high valley where the Laudot River ran; a huge dam could be built on such a solid base and provide, Clerville surmised, all the needs of the canal. The great dam erected at Saint Ferréol was a majestic piece of military engineering, designed for strength using three distinct stone walls filled between with compacted dirt. This was a common pattern of construction at the fortresses built by French military engineers. The tailoring of the design to local material conditions was also typical of military engineering in the period, and so it should be no surprise that Clerville would have made such a proposal. The dam, however, was not just a creature of the military. It contained elements of hydraulic engineering that were also advanced for the period. There was a complex set of sluices for different purposes. Some were near the top for letting out water for use in the canal; at the bottom was a door to drain the reservoir for periodic cleaning, and to let out the inevitable buildup of silt on the floor of the valley. There was a diversion channel, too, for carrying off excess water or for diverting the river when the reservoir was being cleaned or repaired. The great dam, then, was constructed using principles from both civil and military engineering. The holding system originally proposed by Riquet, with its complex set of small reservoirs, would have resulted in less reliable dams built on more unstable surfaces; the Saint-Ferréol plan was in this way an improvement. But in fact the one reservoir was not adequate to its task. Ironically, the great fortress designer Vauban, after he had replaced Clerville as France's top military engineer, was brought in to correct faults in the system, and recommended the construction of additional small reservoirs precisely where Riquet first wanted them. Once again a combination of civil and military engineering-surveying was used to improve the alimentary system. See also Gazelle, "Riquet et les Eaux," *Le Canal du Midi,* vol. 4, 155–158, 169; Froidour, *Lettre à*

Monsieur Barrillon Damoncourt, Conseiller du Roy en ses Conseils, Maître des Requestes Ordinaire de son Hostel, Intendant de Iustice, Police et Finances en Picardie, contenant la Relation & la description des Travaux qui se sont en Languedoc, pour la communication des deux mers, 16–31; Malavialle, "Une Excursion dans la Montagne Noire," Sociètè Languedocienne de Gèographie Bulletin, part I, 266–272.

37. Details of the *rigole d'essai* are contained in AC Liasse 2.

38. For some of the literature that started to appear in the late seventeenth and eighteenth centuries on hydraulic engineering, see, for example, Bouillet, *Traite des Moyens de rendre les Rivieres Navigables avec plusieurs desseins de jettées. . . . Ouvrage tres-utile à tous les Ingenieurs, & à tous ceux qui semêlent de Bâtimens & de Machines.* (Paris: Chez Estienne Michallet, 1693); Belidor, *Architecture Hydraulique seconde partie qui comprend l'Art de diriger les eaux des la Mer & des Rivieres à l'avantage de la défense des places, du Commerce & de l'Agriculture,* (Paris: Jombart, 1756). For the work done on ports in the period, see Josef Konvitz, *Cities and the Sea.* Baltimore: Johns Hopkins Press, 1978.

39. Alain Degage, "Le Port de Sète: Proue Méditerranéenne du Canal de Riquet," in *Le Canal du Midi*, vol. 4, 265–285.

40. For the riches of the region, and their importance in the discussions of the canal in Toulouse, see AC Liasse , piece 14- Avis à Messieurs les Capitouls de la Ville de Toulouse et reponse par Iean de Nivelle, ancien Capitaine Chassvants du Canal. 1667, 7:

> Pour rendre ce Canal Royal encore plus glorieux & donner une tres grande commodité au commerce qui se fit au Royaume d'Espagne pour porter les laines de France, & de faire tranporter les marchandies & dentrées de France & les Royaumes là, faire porter sur la riviere de Garonne depuis sa source, les marbres precieux de toutes sortes de couleurs, & jaspres de plus beaux qui soient en l'Europe, les pierres à taille pout bastir, le bois à construire les maisons & à faire des Vaisseaux qui faire porter sur la riviere de Lariege, le fer & le jayer tiré des Montagnes de Foix desdites Pirenées *** seroit necessaires de faire un Canal depuis la riviere de Garonne au dessus de moulin Chasteau, d'environ deux ou 300 toises de pong pour joindre le Canal Royal, pour lequel il ne faudroit consruire qu'une seule écluse contre la Riviere pour recevoir l'eau necessaire pour porter les Batteaux au Canal Royal.

41. For a discussion of the political economy of the region during this period, see Maistre, *Les Canals des Deux-Mers*, 15–33.

42. Rolt, *Le Canal Entre Deux Mers*, 35, 49, 76–77; Alain Degage, "Le Port de Sète: Proue Méditerranéenne du Canal de Riquet," *Le Canal du Midi*, 265–285. See also Froidour, 35–37; Froidour, *Lettre à Monsieur Barrillon Damoncourt, Conseiller du Roy en ses Conseils, Maître des Requestes Ordinaire de son Hostel, Intendant de Iustice, Police et Finances en Picardie, contenant la Relation & la description des Travaux qui se sont en Languedoc, pour la communication des deux mers,* 48–72 who also participated in the discussions about designing Sète. He brought from his forestry experience skills in civil surveying and the politics of engineering the landscape. Dainville, "Cartes anciennes du Languedoc, XVIe–XVIIIe siècles (Montpellier: Sociètè languedocienne de gèographie, 1961) 56–62.

43. AC 10-10-70- Letter from Colbert to Riquet about sending La Feuille to Holland.

44. Louis de Froidour, *Lettre à Monsieur Barrillon Damoncourt, Conseiller du Roy en ses Conseils, Maître des Requestes Ordinaire de son Hostel, Intendant de Iustice, Police et Finances en Picardie, contenant la Relation & la description des Travaux qui se sont en Languedoc, pour la communication des deux mers.* (Toulouse: Chez Dominique Camusat, 1672).

45. M. Devèze, "Une Admirable Réforme Administrative: La Grande Réformation des Forêts Royales sous Colbert (1662–1680)," in *Annales de L'École Nationale des Eaux et Forêts*

et de la Station de Recherches et Expériences. (Nancy: Ecole Nationale des Eaux et Forets, 1962); André Corvol, *L'Homme et l'Arbre sous l'Ancien Régime* (Paris: Economica, 1984).

46. Froidour, *Lettre à Monsieur Barrillon Damoncourt, Conseiller du Roy en ses Conseils, Maître des Requestes Ordinaire de son Hostel, Intendant de Iustice, Police et Finances en Picardie, contenant la Relation & la description des Travaux qui se sont en Languedoc, pour la communication des deux mers,* 1672.

47. Ibid.

48. The rebuilding of the canal is described in AC Liasse 16- Travaux d'amélioration. These documents are mostly describing work by Niquet, but some was by Vauban.

'Cornelius Meijer inventor et fecit'

On the Representation of Science in Late Seventeenth-Century Rome

KLAAS VAN BERKEL

Among the many explanations of the so-called Scientific Revolution, one of the more attractive relates to the temporary lowering of the social divide between the technical expertise of the craftsmen and the theoretical knowledge of the scholars. In several countries in Europe, architects, navigators, craftsmen, and surgeons contributed both to the construction of scientific knowledge and to the introduction of new methods and instruments. Italian engineers and architects led the way in the fifteenth century, but even as late as the last quarter of the seventeenth century an ordinary Dutch merchant like Antoni van Leeuwenhoek was able to stupefy the Royal Society of London with his most detailed microscopic observations of "small animals."

The contribution of these engineers, merchants, and craftsmen to the new science was not restricted to unconventional ideas, unorthodox methods, or newly invented instruments. A vital aspect of modern science is also the introduction of new ways of representing nature and science. Whereas mathematical sciences in principle needed no more than some crudely drawn diagrams and figures, the experimental sciences depended heavily on the skills of artists who could represent the newly discovered worlds in a way that was convincing for those who were not present. The credibility of the new experimental science not only required statements of trustworthy eyewitnesses and elaborate verbal descriptions, but precise, lifelike, and attractive visual representations. Precise technical drawings were not enough (not yet, at least); seemingly irrelevant ornamental details and a lifelike setting of the configurations were just as important. In a sense, precisely these irrelevant aspects of the representation were the most essential because more than anything else they generated the illusion of lifelikeness that mattered so much to the representatives of the new science. Therefore, the craftsman who was also an artist could be of utmost importance for scholars and scientists who wanted to promote experimental natural philosophy.[1]

A little-known, but intriguing example of the craftsman who also operated as an artist and cooperated with practitioners of experimental science is offered by a near contemporary of Leeuwenhoek, a Dutchman called Cornelis Meijer. He was born the son of a humble wheelmaker in Amsterdam, but in Rome he rose to the the position of a distinguished member of the Accademia Fisicomatematica, the most important local scientific society. He was regarded as a successful engineer and an expert in astronomy, but he was also valued for his contacts with painters and artists and, more to the point, for his own artistic talents. In the 1680s and 1690 he published lavishly illustrated books in which he documented his own inventions, and elaborated on some of the experimental designs of the Accademia Fisicomatematica. As a would-be astronomer he may not have left his mark on seventeenth-century science and the scientific circles he associated himself with may not have become as famous as the Royal Society or the Académie des Sciences, but still his career is instructive for the value even rather conservative scholars in a place like Rome attached to a lifelike representation of their experimental investigations.

THE RISE OF CORNELIS MEIJER

Cornelis Meijer is an unknown figure in the history of science, but in the history of art the experts are not unfamiliar with his name. Actually, the first historian ever to devote some serious attention to Meijer was an historian of art, the assistant director and future director of the Dutch Historical Institute at Rome, G. J. Hoogewerff. His 1920 article on Meijer in the art historical journal *Oud-Holland* still is the essential point of departure for all research on Meijer.[2] For art historians, Meijer's claim to fame was his relation to the famous painter Casper van Wittel, well-known for his *vedute*, his views of Rome and its surroundings. Van Wittel went to Rome just after Meijer had arrived there and was hired by Meijer to execute the drawings for the report Meijer had to write concerning his investigations into the navigability of the Tiber. There is some discussion about the relative share of Meijer and Van Wittel in drawing the illustrations in this report, of which several copies and versions exist.[3] Some claim that Meijer can be held responsible only for the cruder drawings, the more sophisticated ones being ascribed to Van Wittel. But the technical details in even the most refined drawings are unmistakenly inspired by Meijer (who also hired other artists to work out his drafts), and, considering his involvement in the representation of science in the context of the Accademia Fisicomatematica somewhat later, it is quite likely that his share in the cooperation with Van Wittel was more important than most art historians are prepared to admit.

Cornelis Meijer, born in Amsterdam in 1629, belonged to the Lutheran community in Amsterdam, a fact that might explain why later in his life he so smoothly changed religion and turned into a pious Roman Catholic. (The history of the Lutheran community in Amsterdam is full of reconversions to Roman Catholicism.) Not much is known of his early life, but he seems to have been an ambitious craftsman who applied for patents for new technical equipment by the early 1670s. He apparently moved in semiscientific circles, discussing hydraulics with university scholars and participating in the research of Jan Swammerdam. If we are to believe what he told his Roman audience much later, he even acquired enough riches in Holland to collect a large cabinet of curiosities, containing for instance quite a number of precious stones; indeed there is some archival evidence that Meijer's claim is correct. On his departure for Italy, he had his cabinet taken care of by some of his relatives.[4]

In 1674 Meijer left Amsterdam and went to Venice, where he tried to sell his technical expertise to the Republican government. Why he did so is not quite clear. In Rome, Meijer told his friends that he had come to Rome in the Holy Year 1675 to obtain the indulgences the Church had promised to those who repented their sins, converted to Catholicism, and visited a specified number of churches in Rome. But Meijer, while still in Amsterdam, had printed a leaflet that showed all kinds of hydraulic constructions and is explicitly addressed (in Dutch, that is!) to the Venetian government.[5] Therefore it seems more likely that Meijer's main intention was to go to Venice to make a profit out of his technical expertise and that the excursion to Rome (where he would stay for the rest of his life) was just a side trip.

Venice had been a longtime ally of the Dutch Republic in its resistance against Spanish tyranny and popish imperialism. Since the city was confronted with the same problems as the Dutch Republic — rivers and harbors that were silting up, low-lying farmland that had to be drained, and so forth — Dutch engineers found ample employment in Venice.[6] Meijer succeeded quite rapidly in his plans. Some of his proposals were tried and adopted, and Meijer was put in charge of all the operations. He also obtained the official title of engineer, a title he valued even more than the monetary gains to be made in Venice.

However, in April 1675, before Meijer even had started to execute his plans, he left Venice for Rome. He promised the Venetian government to return as soon as possible in order to supervise the clearing of the harbor, but in Rome he found new opportunities for his engineering skills and in the end never returned to Venice. In Rome, Meijer became involved in a complicated project regarding the defense of the well-known Strada (or Via)

Flaminia against the Tiber.[7] North of Rome, the meandering river threatened to undermine the road that led straight to the Porta del Popolo, which most pilgrims took as they entered the Eternal City. Clement IX (1667–69) had ordered the best engineers and architects in Italy to devise a plan to rescue the threatened Via Flaminia. A number of them presented their plans to the cardinals in charge of the project, and the competition was won by the young Roman architect Carlo Fontana, a pupil of Bernini. But the pope died, and the new pope, Clement X (1670–1676), hesitated; according to his advisors, Fontana's plan was too expensive. Then, as Fontana and the cardinals were still discussing the details of the project, Meijer came along and suggested, through the Venetian ambassador to the Holy See, a completely different construction to check the river. Since Meijer's plan was indeed less expensive than Fontana's, the pope decided to put Meijer in charge of the rescue operation, passing over Fontana. In March 1676 Meijer began the work by first removing some obstacles from the river bed and then driving a large row of piles in the river, in this way deflecting its current, which from then on no longer threatened to undermine the Via Flaminia (see fig. 11.1). With this row of piles, in Italian a *passonata*, Meijer managed to do what a number of renowned Italian architects had not been able to do. All of a sudden, he was a well-known figure in the world of Roman architects and engineers.[8]

Not long after the beginning of the construction of his *passonata*, the pope also asked Meijer to concern himself with another complicated problem for which Italian engineers had been unable to find a workable solution. Clement X was very eager to make the Tiber suited for navigation, since this would greatly stimulate trade and commerce in the papal dominions. Now that Meijer had proved his abilities, he of course seemed to be the perfect candidate for writing a report and making proposals to improve the navigability of the Tiber. Although Meijer was eager to return to Venice and perhaps to Holland after finishing his commission in Venice, he was more or less forced to stay in Rome and to accept the pope's orders. During the construction of the *passonata*, Meijer had spent — as was common in those days — some of his own fortune to pay workmen and buy materials necessary for the construction. Of course the pope had promised to pay for all the expenditures and to reward him with an additional and considerable amount of money, but Meijer soon discovered that unlike the Venetian government, which had paid him on the spot, Roman officials were very slow in paying their bills. Only by accepting a second commission could Meijer hope to regain what he had paid out of his own pocket for the *passonata*. Perhaps that was the way papal officials strengthened their ties with their clients without paying them what they were entitled to.

Within a few months, Meijer had traveled all the way to Perugia, had seen what obstacles there were and had devised plans to overcome all these

Figure 11.1 A view of Rome including Meijer's *passonata* in the Tiber. From Cornelis Meijer, *Delinationi con discorsi delle Reparationi* (Rome, 1670). Copyright © Amsterdam University Library.

difficulties. With the help of Caspar van Wittel and some other artists, he composed an extensive report on the project and offered it to the two cardinals who were in charge. The first version was written in Dutch and Italian, a second one in Italian only. Meijer did not speak or write Italian fluently enough to be able to write the report himself, so an assistant had to translate the Dutch text into Italian.[9] But before the report was finished, Clement X died, and a new pope was elected: Innocent XI (1676–89). With the new pope new clients, including architects, engineers, and artists, came to Rome, so Meijer had to do all his best not to fall into disfavor with the new pope and his courtiers. In this respect he succeeded, but his plans were not executed, and it is almost certain that despite his pleas and requests, he never was reimbursed for all the expenditures made during his travels to and from Perugia. This continual effort to regain some of his money kept extending his stay in Rome beyond what he had anticipated; his intention to stay in Rome for a longer period of time is also illustrated by the fact that about this time he sent for his wife, and that she left Amsterdam for Rome.

The construction of the *passonata* had turned the foreigner from Holland into a public figure in Rome. Perhaps his fame was also enhanced by the bitter dispute that erupted once the *passonata* was under construction. Technically the *passonata* was a success, but it also made him a number of influential enemies, who tried to block his further career in Roman society. In a sense, Meijer's career in Rome after 1678 was a constant fight to defend the *passonata* and his own reputation against detractors and envious critics.

The most important of these enemies was the architect Meijer had displaced in the project that made him famous: Carlo Fontana, distantly related to the famous sixteenth-century Roman architect Domenico Fontana and one of the most promising pupils of the great Bernini. It must have been a severe blow to the ambitious Fontana that a total stranger, a Dutchman who could not even speak Italian, was commissioned to do—and did, apparently successfully—what Fontana had very much wanted to do. From the start of the operations, he and others (including other pupils of Bernini) tried to prevent the execution of Meijer's plans. They complained about his materials, the constructions, the amount of money it would cost. Several times during the construction of the *passonata*, the work had to be stopped so the papal administrators could do some investigations. Every time, Meijer was proved right and his critics proved wrong.

The result of what proved to be only the first round in this conflict between Meijer and Fontana was the publication, in 1679, of a small book on the construction of the *passonata*. Actually, it is not a book, but rather looks like a portfolio collection of some engravings representing Meijer's work on the *passonata*. It is dedicated to the pope and has an introduction in which Meijer tells his readers why he published his inventions, but there is no title or title page. The most complete copy I was able to consult includes two broadsheets concerning two completely unrelated plans, first to drain the Pontine marshes and second to dig a new canal between Rome and the sea in order to avoid the silted-up mouth of the Tiber. In his introduction, Meijer makes it clear that his "book" is meant as a simple and true record of what had been accomplished in building the *passonata*, by no means glorifying the man who had devised it. "By presenting this to the public eye, I do not pretend," Meijer said, "to acquire the reputation of a learned and scientifically trained person" ("d'acquistare nome d'addottrinata, ò scientificata persona").[10] Nevertheless, this booklet was an effective means to defend his reputation and his *passonata*.

The booklet was only the first move in a long struggle with Fontana. Evidently, Meijer did also worry about his work on the navigability of the Tiber, fearing that others might publish his inventions without duly acknowledging his part in the project. He therefore decided to write a more extensive report on his engineering skills, including both his construction of the *passonata* and the solutions for the problems encountered by ships traveling on the Tiber between Rome and Perugia. The first edition of this book, titled *L'arte di restituire a Roma la tralasciata navigatione del suo Tevere*, was published in 1683 by the printing office of the Camera Apostolica. A second edition, or so it seems, was published in 1685.[11]

Actually, there is some reason to believe that the second edition was not a second edition at all, but just the completed version of a book that was published partially in 1683. On the title page of the "first" edition, the Camera Apostolica is mentioned as the printing office, but at the end of the book a private publisher is mentioned, Lazzaro Varese. Varese is also mentioned as the printer and publisher of the "second" edition, but it is more likely that during the publishing of the book Meijer changed publishers and that when the book was complete in 1685, he had the publisher print a new title page with the name of the new printer. This seems to indicate that Meijer had some urgent reason not to wait until the book was complete, but to publish the first part upon its completion. And indeed he had every reason to speed up the publication, because in 1683 Fontana once again went public with an attack on Meijer's *passonata*. After 1678–79, Fontana had become silent on the *passonata*. Apparently Meijer had done a fine job, and the destruction of the banks of the Tiber no longer threatened the Via Flaminia.[12] Behind the *passonata* some of the ground once lost to the river was reclaimed, making further losses improbable. In early 1683, however, Fontana and his followers charged Meijer once again with having used the wrong material and with having driven the piles too shallowly into the bottom of the river and so on. According to Fontana, it was just a matter of weeks or months before the *passonata* would collapse, giving free reign to the river again and eventually destroying the Via Flaminia. The pope was alarmed and ordered a careful investigation into the firmness of the *passonata*. Curiously enough, Fontana himself was put in charge of these investigations, and he immediately started to drill holes into the *passonata* in order to establish whether they were rotten or otherwise weakened. Meijer, who had denied all the charges, protested and argued that exactly by investigating the *passonata* in this way the investigators were destroying his constructions, and he urgently called for a halt in the investigations. The papal administrators accepted his protests and ordered Fontana to stop the investigation. In the end, it was shown that the *passonata* was as healthy as could be and that there was no need to be afraid of its being ruined by the river. But apparently, Meijer did not feel satisfied and once again resorted to the means of publication to establish his reputation, now not only as an experienced craftsman. He hastily collected his inventions and published his *L'arte di restituire*.

In a sense, this book is of course a direct continuation of his efforts in the 1670s to persuade future employers to hire him and assign him certain technical projects. Although it is lavishy illustrated, the book (in three parts) essentially consists of a series of separate engravings (or series of engravings) with more or less extensive and more or less scholarly comments. The 1683 book is much more sophisticated than the 1674 broadsheet or the 1679 file, but the format is essentially the same. As can be seen from the dating of some of the engravings, Meijer used many old engravings for his new book, replacing the explanations by new comments, but hardly changing the engravings themselves. His *L'arte di restituire*, therefore, is still essentially a collection of advertisements of an ambitious craftsman-engineer for whom visual representations of his plans and projects were more important than the comments and explanations.

On the other hand, elements of the book suggest that it is much more than the sample book of an engineer. First, the high quality of the engravings is quite remarkable. Almost all of them bear the inscription "Cornelius Meyer inventor & delineavit, Io.Bapt. Falda sculpsit," which indicates that Meijer hired an expert hand only to engrave the drawings, not to draw the pictures themselves.[13] Yet some of the engravings bear the inscription "Cornelius Meyer inventor et fecit," suggesting that he did execute the engravings himself, without the help of other artists. Meijer was no member of the Dutch artistic brotherhood in Rome, the Bentveughels, but he evidently had talent and moved in these circles. His engravings of technical and scientific instruments are remarkable for their fine details of surrounding persons and architectural background. It looks as if Meijer wanted to impress his readers not only with his technical skills, but also with his artistic talents, or, what is more intriguing, to use his artistic talents to create an atmosphere in which his mechanical expertise was much more easily accepted by the Roman elite.

Second, the book, especially the third part of it, contains some projects that are completely new and seem to indicate a new social and intellectual milieu in which Meijer moved. For instance, he proudly presents some of the technical projects executed for the grand duke of Tuscany, Cosimo III, in Florence and some of the Tuscan harbors. Even more interesting are the engravings of fountains, scales, couches and, quite surprising, the beautiful designs for reconstructing the main squares of Rome. On some of these squares former popes had already erected an obelisk, but now Meijer wanted to use these obelisks as sundials or stardials and to decorate them with additional sculptures or new pavements. Rather delicate was the proposal for a completely new pavement of the St. Peter's Square, one of Bernini's greatest achievements. Around the famous obelisk (relocated in the 1580s by Carlo Fontana's distant relative Domenico Fontana) Meijer wanted to decorate the pavement with the four systems of the world that were being discussed by scholars at that time, the systems according to Ptolemy, Tycho (both of them acceptable to the Church), Copernicus, and Descartes (both unacceptable) (fig. 11.2). Although strictly spreaking Copernicus's book had not been put on the Index in 1616 and even Jesuit mathematicians were allowed to discuss Copernicus as long as they considered his system as a purely mathematical hypothesis, it was still very uncommon, to say the least, to confront the pope with these world systems.

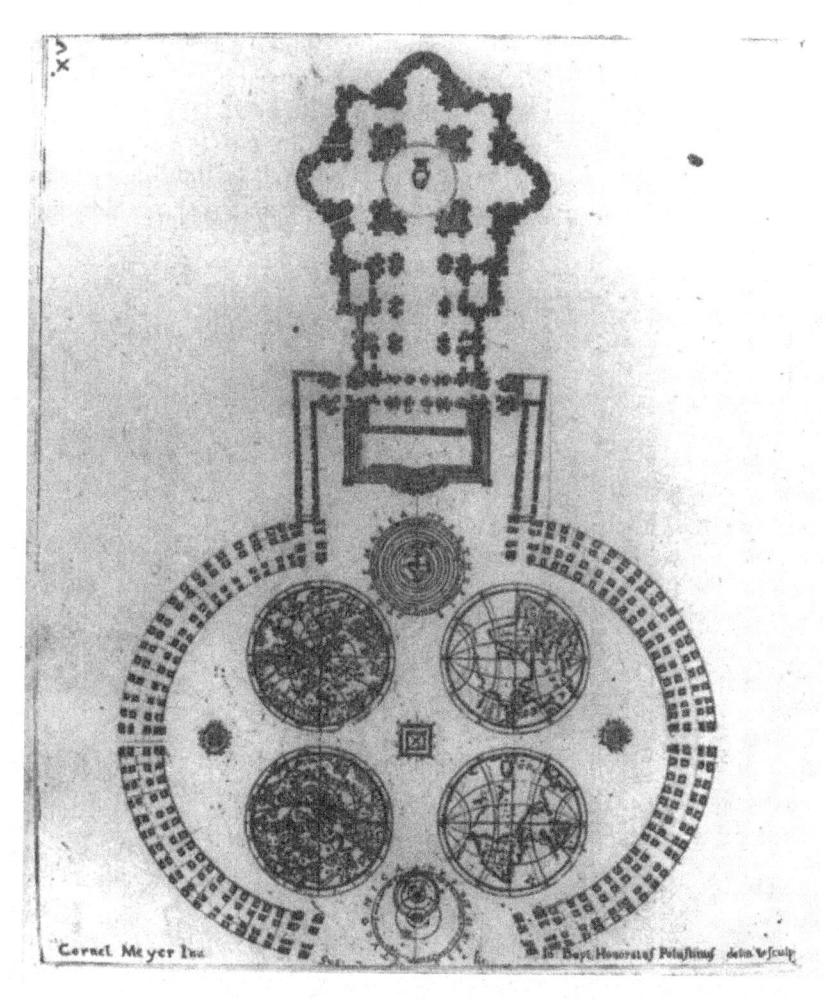

Figure 11.2 Meijer's plan for a new pavement for St. Peter's Square, displaying the Tychonic and Ptolemaic systems of the world (in the text, he also included the Copernican and Cartesian systems). From Cornelis Meijer, *L'arte di restituire* (Rome, 1685). Copyright © Amsterdam University Library.

THE ACCADEMIA FISICOMATEMATICA ROMANA

The reason for introducing these architectural designs with their scientific contents is elucidated by Meijer himself in the explanation belonging to his engraving of a balance for establishing whether a crown was made from gold or silver (Archimedes's famous device) (figs. 11.3 and 11.4). While he was writing his book on the Tiber, he says, some high officials at the papal court stimulated him to include some of these other inventions too. Evidently, he had established relations with these courtiers during his negotiations regarding the *passonata* and the project of restoring the navigability of the Tiber, and they had become interested in Meijer's other inventions too. Meijer does not say who they were, but he does mention in the book Giovanni Giustino Ciampini, a high official at the papal court and a well-known scholar. Ciampini (1633–98) is mainly known for his research on the churches of the early Middle Ages, but he was also interested in modern science.[14] His house

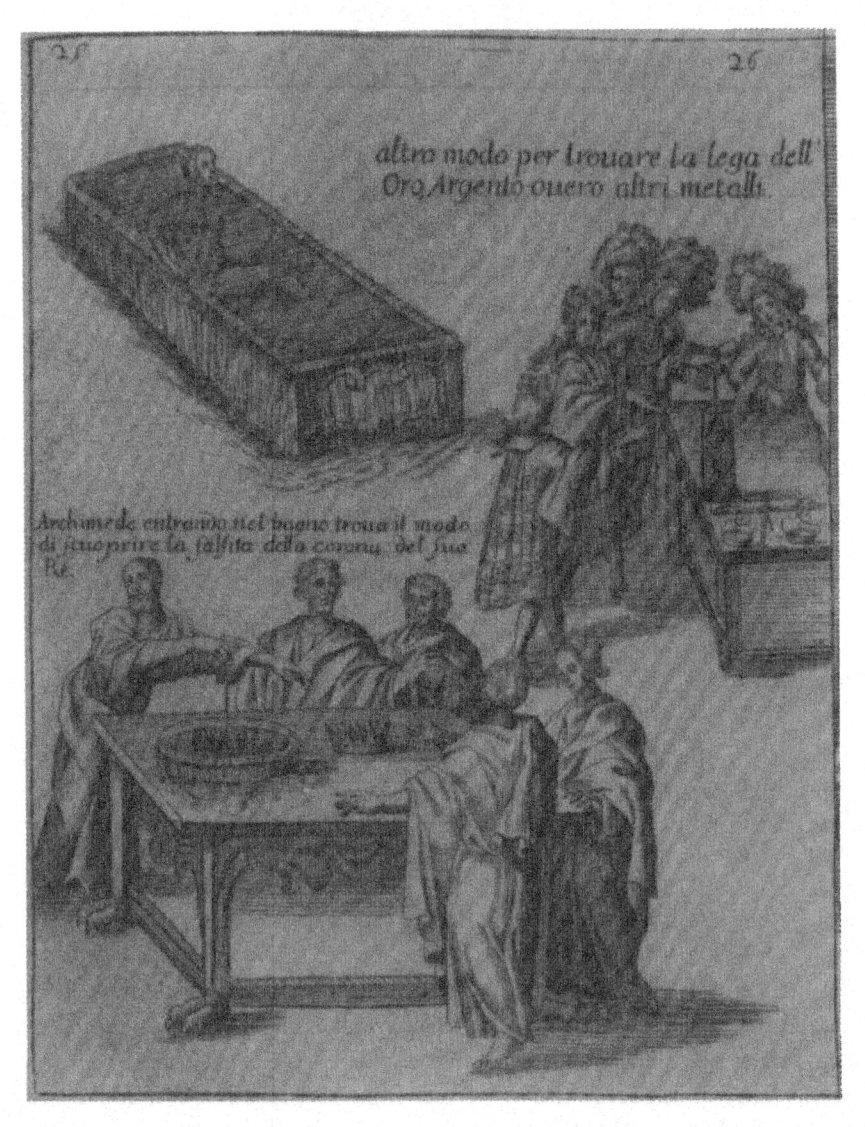

Figure 11.3 Old ways and new ways to discover the amount of gold in a certain piece of metal. From Cornelis Meijer, *Nuovi ritrovamenti* (Rome, 1689).

Klaas van Berkel

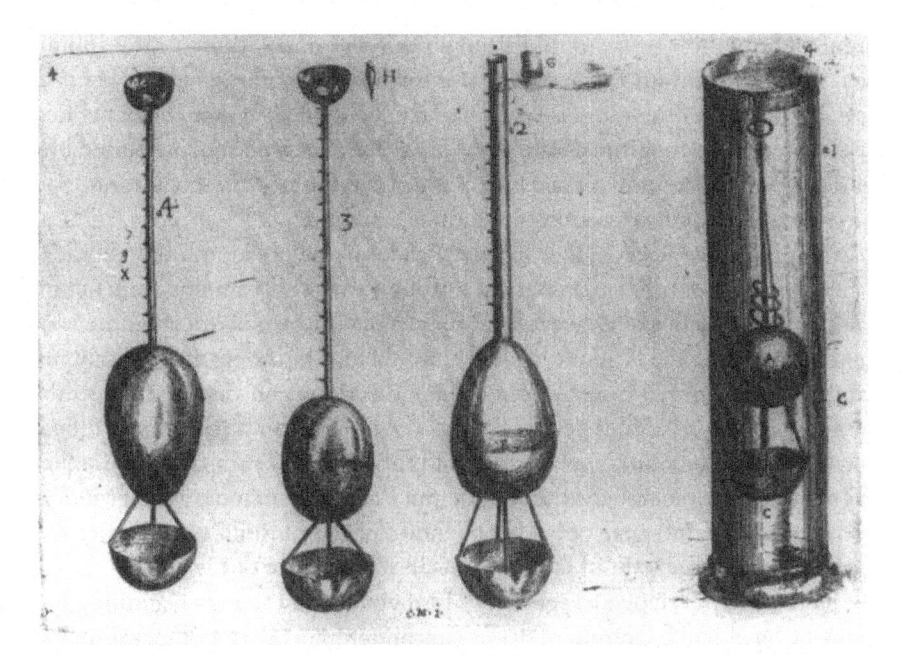

Figure 11.4 Instruments invented by Meijer to discover the amount of gold in a certain piece of metal. From Cornelis Meijer, *L'arte di restituire* (Rome, 1685). Copyright © Amsterdam University Library.

near the S. Agnese in Agone was already the meeting place of a number of learned circles when in 1677 Ciampini, in conscious imitation of the defunct Florentine Accademia del Cimento, also founded a society for the cultivation of natural science, the Accademia Fisicomatematica Romana. Ciampini owned a decent collection of scientific instruments, which he put at the disposal of the members of his academy. Although it had no official charter (even its name varied over time), the meetings of the Accademia were regulated according to strict rules. The members met every week, one of the members acted as secretary, and the discussions and suggestions for further research were carefully recorded in a large notebook, which is still extant (at least in part). Many of the members of this group of virtuosi were simply amateurs, but a small number of them might be called professionals. The Jesuit Francesco Eschinardi, professor of mathematics at the Collegio Romano and highly regarded for his astronomical research, was perhaps the most important of these professionals.[15] Although the first secretary of the Accademia had the intention to publish the minutes of the meetings, just as the Accademia del Cimento had done, the Roman Accademia as such never published anything. But some members did, for instance Eschinardi, who in the 1680s published several short pamphlets about his observations of several comets. Some of these pamphlets have the form of a letter to the Italian astronomer Giovanni Domenico Cassini, who was in charge of the obervatory of the Académie des Science at Paris. Through personal contacts like these, but also through the *Giornale de' Letterati*, a learned journal edited by Ciampini, the Accademia Fisicomatematica tried to inform scholars and scientists outside Rome of its existence and its activities.[16]

Ciampini introduced Meijer to the Accademia in 1680, not only because of his construction of the *passonata* (although that still remained his main claim to fame),[17] but also because Meijer was said to have been an active member of the Dutch scientific community before his departure to Italy in 1674. Ciampini urged him to present his inventions and discoveries to the Accademia, and as Meijer relates in his book, Ciampini also deemed them worthy of inclusion in the proceedings of the academy. From then on Meijer was a prominent member of the Accademia Fisicomatematica, as he proudly indicated on the title page of his book, and to please his fellow academicians he also included several of his inventions in the last part of his book.

Meijer soon developed a specialty of his own. From the very beginning he seems to have had a predilection for astronomy and for the observation of comets more in particular (part of the design for the new pavement of the St. Peter's Square was a list of all comets since Christ's birth up to the seventeenth century). Coincidentally, in 1680 and 1682 two (some thought three) beautiful comets appeared in the skies, and Meijer had a perfect opportunity to show the other members of the academy his expertise and his knowledge of the literature.[18] And although we should not overestimate Meijer's astronomical expertise, with the help once more of some of his Dutch friends (Abraham Genoels, a painter known for his mathematical skills) he was at least able to draw some very detailed figures of the course of some comets in his later publications (fig. 11.5). But he certainly did not restrict himself to comets. If we compare the notebooks of the first secretary of the academy and the publications of some of the members, the correspondences with the contents of Meijer's books are remarkable. The experimental work of Torricelli and that of Boyle were much discussed by the members of academy and also play a prominent part in Meijer's later works.

The works Meijer published after 1685 all follow more or less the same pattern. In 1689 he published his *Nuovi ritrovamenti* (New discoveries), essentially a collection of new inventions of very diverse character.[19] This book was expanded and republished in 1696 as his *Nuovi ritrovamenti divisi in due parti*, while in the same year he published his *L'arte di rendere i fiumi navigabili in varii modi, con altre nuove inventioni e varii altri secreti, divisa in tre parti* (The art or making the rivers navigable in various ways, with other new inventions and several other secrets, divided in three parts). Actually, these books are not really new books, because each new book consists of a

Figure 11.5 Meijer's representation of the orbits of the comets of 1682 and 1684. From Cornelis Meijer, *Nuovi ritrovamenti* (Rome, 1689). Copyright © University Library Leiden.

reprint of the former with a number of new topics and illustrations added. In general, the new material consists of two kinds of information. The first concerns new technical inventions. Meijer was hired for solving all kinds of problems all over Italy, and the results were incorporated in the new editions. The second kind of additions concerns material that had been discussed in the Accademia Fisicomatematica. There are no notebooks of the academy after the first two years, but we can reasonably assume that Meijer's books are at least in part reproducing what the members of Ciampini's academy had been discussing in the 1680s and 1690s. Of course, the books were Meijer's, and he adhered to the format he had already chosen for his *L'arte di restituire*. But we may safely assume that the other members liked his books for that very reason, because the heavy stress on the visual representation of the new experimental science was just what they needed. None of the other members is known for his artistic or representational skills; all their pamphlets are purely verbal reports on their research. Meijer is the only member with the talents to draw his own illustrations and as a craftsman-become-virtuoso the language of art was his favorite means of presenting the result of the work of the academy to the learned world. His explanations are a rambling concoction of new and old knowledge, including some fragments from ancient authors whom he evidently was not able to read, but his drawings are detailed, lifelike, and trustworthy representations of instruments and experiments. His limitations therefore were, at least in the context of the new science, at the same time his main assets.

DEFENSE AND DEFEAT

With the publication of *L'arte di restituire* Meijer undoubtedly had in mind to show the world that he was not just a plain Dutch engineer, unskilled in the arts and the sciences, but a member of the scientific elite of Rome. That is why on the title page he proudly announced himself as a member "dell' Accademia Fisicomatematica Romana." From the contents of the book it is clear that Meijer even pretended to be an architect, just as Fontana was, and it is no coincidence that he especially dwelled on the reconstruction of the pavement of St. Peter's Square, because his arch enemy Fontana had just begun to write an impressive book about St. Peter's Church.

Meijer's book certainly was a success, but his new standing as a virtuoso seemed only to rekindle the feud between Meijer and Fontana rather than end it. The rivalry between the two men appears to have inspired both of them to compose new books — books they might not have contemplated if they had not needed material to counter each other's charges. Meijer in this conflict was the underdog, but it is remarkable that Fontana, who by now had become the most important architect of Rome, an all-round artist who was in the process of seeing through the press his monumental work on St. Peter's Church, still was trying to ruin the career of someone who, as far as we can see at least, did not pose any real threat anymore to his reputation. In 1694 and in 1697 Fontana and his followers once again openly charged Meijer of having used the wrong material for his *passonata*, suggesting that within a short while it would collapse after all.[20] New investigations were ordered, with the same result as before: there was nothing wrong with the *passonata*.

Apparently, Meijer was not sure that this would be the last time that he and his *passonata* were to be criticized by Fontana and his followers. Although he had already written several memoranda to defend his *passonata*, he now mobilized all his connections in Rome to deal a final blow to all his critics and collect all the money the papal government owed him. With the linguistic, rhetorical, and juridical help of the Roman lawyer Francesco Maria Onorati, a member of the Accademia Fisicomatematica and someone who had helped Meijer before, in 1698 the engineer published an enlarged edition of an earlier Latin *Memoriale* as his *Apologia per la passonata fatta sopra il Tevere fuori di Porta del Popolo in difesa della strada Flaminiana.*[21] This publication is a very detailed and rhetorically very sophisticated reconstruction and defense of Meijer's career in Rome, with special emphasis on his building the *passonata*. The self-presentation in this volume is somewhat different compared to Meijer's other publications. He repeats the story about the *passonata* and the obstructions he had encountered during and after its construction. But he also has his readers believe that he is a descendant of a rich aristocratic family in Holland, his brother being the viceroy of the Dutch East Indies. There is no independent evidence to confirm these claims, quite the opposite, but it is clear that Meijer in his *Apologia* publicly posed as an aristocrat who was not treated accordingly by the papal bureaucrats and their Italian clients, Fontana being one of them. Fontana himself is not attacked right away; although his name is not mentioned, the architect (referred to as 'un gran Virtuoso') is even praised for his fine knowledge of architecture. But in the second half of the *Apologia* Meijer subtly points out that Fontana had overseen some details that were crucial to the construction of the *passonata* and that only the superior technical expertise of Meijer, who stood in the tradition of the celebrated Dutch engineers, had been able to build a construction strong enough to withstand the pressure of the water in the river.

In the end, Meijer was able to ward off all the charges brought against him by Fontana and others, but in an indirect way, Fontana did succeed in ruining Meijer's career in Rome. Even though the Dutch engineer proved to be able to execute several difficult constructions in several places in Italy, he never obtained the rewards promised to him by the papal administration. He constantly had to pay for his expenditures from his own pocket. In the *Apologia* he complains how he had to sell his cabinet of curiosities in Amsterdam just to stay alive in Rome. We are not able to verify this story, but it is quite sure that dealing with the pope ruined Meijer financially.

Lack of success is also what characterizes Meijer's efforts to drain the Pontine marshes — another proposal worthy of a Dutch engineer.[22] Though others had tried to drain this region to the south of Rome before and had never succeeded in doing so, Meijer was convinced that with his superior skills he would finally succeed. Already around 1680 and later in the 1690s, he drew up several contracts with wealthy Roman nobles and even dreamed of obtaining a noble title after having opened the land for cultivation. In the 1690s he indeed hired workmen to dig canals and build sluices in the marshes, but in the end the inhabitants of the surrounding villages and towns successfully obstructed these operations. They rightfully feared that they would lose the opportunity to acquire some additional income by fishing in the marshes and by herding some of their livestock in the drier sections of the plain. So by the time of his death, in 1701, Meijer had still not succeeded in draining even a small part of the marshes, and in his last will he handed over this task to his son Otto. Otto Meijer bravely continued the work, but after a few more years he too had to acknowledge defeat.

CONCLUSION

As Hoogewerff saw it, the career of Cornelis Meijer foundered on the jealousy of the Italians. Notwithstanding the success of his *passonata* near the Via Flaminia and the willingness of some amateurs of science to admit him to the Accademia Fisicomatematica, he ended up impoverished and disillusioned. His books, however, remain an important source for the history of science and technology in Rome in the second half of the seventeenth century. They contain information about the Accademia Fisicomatematica that cannot be found anywhere else. In combination with his *Apologia* these books also inform us about the social conventions regarding the practice of science and technology in the age of baroque. And finally they draw our attention to the visual aspect of science and technology. What Meijer had to say on the course of comets or the effects of air pressure or the existence of the void is not very important perhaps, but the way in which he presented his conclusions does indeed merit our attention. As I suggested, in his representation of science Meijer is still very much indebted to the customs and conventions of the class of commercially operating engineers in Holland to which he originally belonged. Yet this was exactly what the new scientific elite in Rome needed in order to present their research in a trustworthy way to the learned world. Meijer and the Accademia made a perfect fit. A closer study not only of the texts, but also of the engravings these texts pretend to explain, as well as further investigations into the contacts Meijer had both with artists and with other engineers in Holland and in Rome might eventually shed more light on the development of the visual language of the new experimental natural philosophy.

Notes

1. A recent discussion of the importance of visual language in propagating the new experimental philosophy, especially the eclectic philosophy of the Leiden professor Arnold Senguerd, can be found in Gerhard B. Wiesenfeldt, *Leerer Raum in Minervas Haus. Experimentelle Naturlehre an der Universität Leiden, 1675–1715* (Amsterdam: Edita, 2001).

2. G. J. Hoogewerff, "Cornelis Jansz. Meijer, Amsterdamsch ingenieur in Italië (1620–1701)," *Oud-Holland* 38 (1920): 83–103. This article is mainly based on Roman sources, including Meijer's writings.

3. Giuliano Briganti, *Caspar van Wittel e l'origine della veduta settecentessa* (Rome: Bozzi, 1966); An Zwollo, *Hollandse en Vlaamse vedute-schilders te Rome, 1675–1725* (Assen: Van Gor-

cum, 1973), 120ff.; Giuliano Briganti, *Caspar van Wittel*. Nuova edizione a cura di Laura Laureati e Ludovico Trezzani (Milan: Electa, 1996).

4. Ellinoor Bergvelt and Renée Kistemaker, eds., *De wereld binnen handbereik. Nederlandse kunst- en rariteitenverzamelingen, 1585–1735* (Zwolle: Waanders, 1992) 51, 249–250, 324.

5. The Dutch text reads: *Verscheyde aanwijzingen en bequame middelen, aan d'Hartogh van Venetien & om alderhande Schepen, heen en weer, over rivieren en ondiepten te halen.* A copy is to be found in the Venetian Archives. See note 6.

6. Roberto Berveglieri, "Tecnologia idraulica olandese in Italia nel secolo XVII: Cornelis Janszoon Meijer a Venezia (gennaio-aprile 1675)," *Studi Veneziani*, N.S., 10 (1985): 81–91 (with illustrations); Idem, *Inventori stranieri a Venezia (1474-1788). Importazione de tecnologia e circolazione di tecnici, artigiani, inventori* (Venice: Istituto Veneto di Scienze, Lettere ed Arti, 1995), 152–166.

7. Much has already been written on this subject. See for instance: Cesare d'Onofrio, *Il Tevere e Roma* (Rome: Bozzi, 1970), esp. 80–85; Paola C. Scavizzi, *Navigazione e regolazione fluviale nello Stato della Chiesa fra XVI e XVIII secolo (il caso Tevere)* (Roma: , 1991).

8. Roman correspondents of Leibniz, like Christian Albert Walter and Ehrenfried Walther von Tschirnhaus, repeatedly informed the German philosopher and scientist of the Dutchman and his *passonata*—strikingly without ever mentioning his name. Walter simply referred to "un habile Hollandois" (a competent Dutchman), while Tschirnhaus, whose report is quite detailed, talks about "Hollandus." G. W. Leibniz, *Sämtliche Schriften und Briefe*. Dritter Reihe, Zweiter Band (Berlin: Akademie Verlag, 1987) 33, 317, 383–384. (I kindly thank Liesbeth de Wreede for drawing my attention to these letters.)

9. Versions of the report are to be found in the Biblioteca Corsiniana and the Biblioteca Nazionale in Rome and in the Staatsbibliothek in München. They all are densely illustrated and offer a wealth of material for comparing Meijer's and Van Wittel's contributions to the final report.

10. The copy of Meijer's booklet in the Vatican Library is titled *L'arte di restituire a Roma la tralasciata navigazione del suo Tevere* (Rome: Varese, 1679), but this is only added in handwriting. The copy in the University Library at Amsterdam does not have this title, and it is probable that the title is just a mistake. In the *Giornale de' Letterati* of 1680 there is a review of a book by Meijer that bears the title *Delinationi con discorsi delle Reparationi del Tevere fatte da Cornelio Meyer Olandese con alcuni pensieri circa la disseccationi delle Paludi Pontine, e fare un nuove alveo al Fiume* (Rome: Lupari, 1679), and this is exactly what the book is about. (The review also gives the correct printer.)

11. *L'arte di restituire à Roma la tralasciata navigazione del suo Tevere, divisa in tre parti. 1. Gl'impedimenti, che sono nell'alveo del Tevere da Roma à Perugia, e suoi remedii. 2. Le difficoltà, che sono nella navigazione del Tevere da Roma fino al mare, e suoi remedii. 3. Nel quale si discorre perche Roma è stato fabricata, e mantenuta sù le sponde del Tevere, e si tratta d'alcun' altre propositioni proficue per lo stato ecclesiatico.* Dell' ingeniero Cornelio Meijer (Rome: Stamperia della Reverenda Camera Apostolica, 1683).

12. Not everybody was convinced that the *passonata* would hold. In April 1678 Von Tschirnhaus wrote to Leibniz: "Satis bene successit, sed cum non tam bene atque tam alte in nostris regionibus extructum videatur, nescio an sit futurum durabile." Leibniz, *Sämtliche Schriften und Briefe* 3.2, 389. This clearly is an echo of Fontana's (unfounded) criticism.

13. There is one engraving drawn by Caspar van Wittel and a few by other artists.

14. *Dizionario Biografico degli Italiani* 25 (1981): 136–143.

15. According to the entry in the *Dizionario Biografico degli Italiani* 43 (1993): 273, Eschinardi "fosse in qualche modo il principale animatore."

16. On the Accademia: W. E. Knowles Middleton, "Science in Rome, 1675–1700, and the Accademia Fisicomatematica of Giovanni Giustino Ciampini," *British Journal for the History of Science* 8 (1975): 138–154. Since the author was interested mainly in the history of the thermometer, his account of the activities of the Accademia is rather one-sided. More information

is offered by Salvatore Rotta, "L'accademia fisicomatematica Ciampiniana: un' iniziativa di Cristina?," in W. di Palma a.o., *Cristina di Svezia. Scienza ed alchimia nella Roma barocca* (Bari: Dedalo 1990), 99–186. As the title of the article already suggests, Christina of Sweden had nothing to do with the Accademia. Ciampini and others may have hoped to place their society under the protection of the former queen of Sweden, but she did not have the financial means to do so. On the *Giornale*: Jean-Michel Gardair, *Le 'Giornale de' letterati' di Roma (1668–1681)* (Firenze: L. Olschki, 1984), esp. ch. 7.

17. When Marcantonio Celli, fellow of the Accademia, wrote a letter to Cassini, informing him about what was going on in Rome, he also mentioned Meijer and introduced him as the man who had constructed the *passonata* and thereby had saved the Strada Flaminia.

18. There is for instance a reference to Bartholomeus Schimpffer, *Kurze Beschreibung des dunckelen Cometen so anno 1652 den 8. Decembr erschienen darauff gemeiniglich sonderliche Enderungen und Verwirrungen zuerfolgen pflegen* (Frankfurt am Main: Johann Phillips Weiss, 1653). Schimpffer, an obscure almanac maker and astrologer in Halle (Saxony), predicted that the comet would reappear in 1682 and since around that time indeed a new comet was seen (the comet of Halley), on Meijer's suggestion the members of the Accademia ordered the book from some library in Rome (nowadays it is very rare), had someone translate it, and then discussed its contents.

19. *Nuovi ritrovamenti dati in luce dall' ingegniero Cornelio Meyer per eccitare l'ingegno de' Virtuosi ad augmentarli ò aggiungervi maggior perfettione* (Rome, 1689). Among the topics discussed by Meijer in this book we find eyeglasses, couches, the furnishing of a cabinet of curiosities—including a chemical laboratory—the introduction of silkworm breeding in Italy, and even some medecine. In the context of the treatment of illnesses caused by the little animals seen through the microscope Meijer claims to have been present at some of the anatomical dissections of Jan Swammerdam (who died in 1680), which once again indicates that Meijer's interest in science dates back to his early life in Holland. Also included is a chapter in which Meijer cites a number of biblical texts on the correct payment of businessmen ('Tenor Sacrae Scripturae de Mercede')!

20. In 1694, the year in which his magnum opus on St. Peter's Church was published (*Il tempio Vaticano e la sua Origine*, in Italian and Latin), Fontana also had the time to issue a *Discorso sopra le cause delle inondazioni del Tevere antiche e moderne à danno della città di Roma, e dell' insussistente passonata fatta avanti la Villa di Papa Giulio III per riparo della via Flaminia* (reissued in 1696). See Helmut Hager, "Le opere letterarie di Carlo Fontana come autorappresentazione," in *In Urbe Architectus. Modelli, disegni, misure. La professione dell' architetto, Roma 1680–1750*, Ed. Bruno Contardi, Giovanna Curcio, (Rome: Argos, 1991), esp. 177–187.

21. The full title runs *Apologia di Francesco Maria Onorati per la passonata fatta sopra il Tevere fuori di Porta del Popolo in difesa della Strada Flaminiana con le direttione del Signor Cornelio Meyer, famoso ingegniere olandese all'eminentissimo e reverendissimo prencipe il Sig. Cardinale Gio. Francesco Albano Segretario de Brevi di nostro signore*. In Roma MDCXCVIII. In the foreword Onorati confesses to be the mouthpiece of Meijer himself, "havendo io quì quasi la sola parte di traduttore & interprete del suo linguaggio." This foreword also contains a direct reference to the Dutch as being such able hydraulic engineers: the *passonata* was built "secondo i suoi principii di far Passonate all'usanza Olandese, che in quelle parti sostengono con artificio incomparabile sopra il dorso della passonata il peso di tutte le acque di quel gran Mare che bagna l'Olanda." Onorati in his capacity of "ministro deputato per la Reverenda Camera" had been the papal supervisor during Meijer's construction of the *passonata*, which means that he had a vested interest in clearing Meijer of all charges brought against him by Fontana.

22. Meijer's efforts are relatively well documented by Hoogewerff, "Cornelis Janszoon Meijer," and J. Korthals Altes, *Polderland in Italië. De werkzaamheden der Nederlandsche bedijkers in vroeger eeuwen en het Italiaansche polderland voorheen en thans* (The Hague: Van Stockum, 1928).

Part 3

CONSUMPTION, ART, AND SCIENCE

Inventing Nature

Commerce, Art, and Science in the Early Modern Cabinet of Curiosities

PAULA FINDLEN

"But is it a basilisk?"

"It's a saltwater fish that charlatans usually arrange in the form of a basilisk, and it helps them deal with peasants in the piazza when they want to sell their balsam."

—Carlo Goldoni, *Famiglia dell'antiquario*

CURIOSITIES FOR SALE

In 1653, a curious book appeared in the city of Venice: Niccolò Serpetro's *Marketplace of Natural Marvels*. Serpetro's encyclopedia was one of many such volumes that satisfied the seemingly infinite desire for wonders in the early modern period. It followed a rich publishing history of broadsheets, natural histories, and encyclopedias of the strange and unfamiliar that characterized the sixteenth-century love affair with the marvelous, and that cataloged the many pleasurable and terrifying ways in which nature made manifest the hand of God in the world.[1] Serpetro drew liberally from this tradition to create his own theater of wonders. But he added one innovation that was entirely his own: he placed his marvels in the marketplace, a teeming piazza in which merchants and customers bargained over goods for sale, and wares were displayed for all to see (fig. 12.1). It was the most fitting location that he could imagine for the pursuit of wonder.

It is surely appropriate that a book published in the city of Venice—still a thriving center for trade and commerce despite the challenges of such northern cities as Amsterdam, Marseilles, and London, and the Spanish gateway to the Atlantic, Seville—should imagine the world of marvels to be a marketplace. Serpetro explained his metaphor as follows: "Since in a

Franco — Capelleti — Spagnolo — Turchi — Inglese

Intertenimento che dano ogni giorno li Ciarlatani in Piazza di S. Marco al Populo, d'ogni natione che mattina e sera, ordinariamente, ui concore. Giacomo Franco. Forma con Priuilegio

Figure 12.1 Charlatans selling their wares in Piazza San Marco, Venice. Source: G. Franco, *Habiti d'huomini e donne* (Venice, 1609). Courtesy of Marquand Library of Art and Archaelogy, Princeton University Library.

famous marketplace the wealthiest merchants come from many different countries to show gems and the most precious and admirable things that one finds in various provinces of the world, thus, in this work I tried to transport from the most celebrated authors the rarest and most delightful marvels that the Author of Nature has produced." He made his book a literal marketplace, dividing it into porticos, loggias, and shops so that passersby could "walk easily" among them.[2] Each chapter was an imagined purchase, or at the very least a bit of window shopping in the marketplace of marvels. Serpetro had probably taken the idea of the marketplace from works such as Tommaso Garzoni's *Universal Piazza* (1585), a popular encyclopedia that collected all the professions of the world into an imaginary piazza.[3] But he was also an astute observer of his times. Nature was for sale in many marketplaces throughout Europe. It was a commodity bought, sold, bartered, and exchanged — the centerpiece of a series of transactions that connected the world of commerce to the study of nature.

Shopping for natural curiosities was indeed possible by the time Serpetro wrote his *Marketplace of Natural Marvels*. We need only think of the Dutch tulip craze at the beginning of the seventeenth century to recall just how frenzied the market for a particular curiosity could become.[4] More generally, however, the growing popularity of cabinets of curiosities — private, princely, and, in a few cases, institutional collections that grew in size and scope throughout the early modern period — gradually transformed the act of collecting nature into a business. It produced a world of entrepreneurs who saw nature in new ways because of the culture of collecting. In February 1644, John Evelyn described the experience of walking through the merchants' stalls in the Isle du Palais in Paris. One shop, in particular, caught his attention, a place called Noah's Ark. There "are sold all curiosities naturall or artificial, Indian or European, for luxury or use, as cabinets, shells, ivory, porselan, dried fishes, insects, birds, pictures, and a thousand exotic extravagances."[5] Evelyn had found a cabinet of curiosities in which everything was for sale. Collectors missing some choice item for their cabinets could depend upon the proprietor of Noah's Ark to supply them with a sample — for the right price.

The idea of a shop filled with curiosities seemingly contradicted the humanist ideal of scientific collecting as a series of exchanges among scholars in which objects were freely given as an act of friendship; they accompanied and embellished the words that described them.[6] Many collectors accumulated the majority of their artifacts through travel and through the generosity of other scholars with whom they regularly exchanged letters, images, and specimens. But it was also possible to buy a cabinet of curiosities, or at least its most important parts, by the early seventeenth century. Such purchases were costly luxuries — not an act of scholarly inquiry into nature but a sign that the pleasures of collecting involved more than the single-minded pursuit of knowledge. If having a collection was one means by which a prince or a merchant might proclaim his ability to command the world, creating a microcosm in which to receive visitors and to demonstrate his place in a world of global commerce and conquest, then a collection was indeed worth something. Many objects did have a precise monetary value, even if scholarly collectors chose to ignore this aspect of the passion for curiosities.

The market for marvels produced more than one type of collector, and all of them in different ways responded to the exigencies of the marketplace. In addition to thinking about learned naturalists such as Ulisse Aldrovandi, who created a theater of nature in late sixteenth-century Bologna in order to know more about the natural world, we need to consider a different kind of collector who understood the idea of profiting from wonder. The early seventeenth-century Augsburg merchant Philipp Hainhofer, for example, not only acted as purchasing agent for rulers who sought out luxury goods, but explicitly made his cabinets of curiosities, filled with objects acquired from merchants at the Frankfurt fairs, to sell them. He speculated in nature. "When someone presents me with a foreign object for my *Kunstkammer*," he once said, "I experience more pleasure than if he had given me cash."[7] This comment that reflects the ways in which curiosity and commerce worked harmoniously together. Curiosities, after all, might be a good investment in terms of the favors and ultimately business they might bring from certain patrons.

Hainhofer was perhaps one of the earliest collectors, following in the wake of the Fugger merchants who had acquired many objects for princely patrons, to recognize that the value of the cabinet of curiosities was not simply intrinsic. By the late seventeenth century, tales of the fantastic sums that princes were willing to pay for a good cabinet circulated among connoisseurs of such things. The grand duke of Tuscany's efforts to acquire the Dutch naturalist Jan Swammerdam's collection of insects—and his expertise as a naturalist—for 12,000 guilders were well-known and only increased the status of this particular collection.[8] Around the same time, the duke of Modena became so fascinated with Manfredo Settala's gallery of curiosities and inventions in Milan that he attempted to purchase it. Negotiations had fallen apart by the early 1660s, but when John Ray and Philip Skippon visited the newly installed cabinet in the ducal palace in February 1664, visitors were still being told of the outrageous sums the duke had been willing to pay for a collection he never succeeded in buying.[9] The economic ability to *afford* a famous cabinet, in other words, had become a measure of one's status.

By the eighteenth century, natural history cabinets were put up for public auction, and sale catalogs began to appear with greater regularity, reflecting a full-scale commercialization of collecting culture. In the late sixteenth and seventeenth centuries, however, it was rare to have an entire cabinet made purely for profit. Individual objects might be heavily embedded in the world of the marketplace, and occasionally princes might try to buy a collection, but the majority of cabinets emerged from an individual collector's passion for things. Yet even these collectors, however removed from the world of commerce, had to contend with the ways in which their fascination with nature was fueled by a variety of individuals who had unique access to natural objects and understood the profitability of nature. No collector could entirely remove himself from the marketplace. How they interacted with it reveals a series of interesting connections between commerce, science, and art.

TRAFFICKING IN NATURE

Early modern natural history was a product of the new material abundance that flowed into European cities from all corners of the world. It extended the medieval culture of buying and selling nature into new domains because knowledge quite literally grew in proportion to the expansion of European trade.[10] While humanists who studied nature for the pure pleasure of extracting knowledge might scoff at those who used their knowledge to turn a profit, the fact remains that nature had always been a commodity to the rest of the world. Since the Middle Ages the spice trade between western Europe and the Levant– dried bits of nature that traveled thousands of miles to satisfy the taste for the exotic — had shaped the commercial image of nature. Columbus's attentiveness to the wonders of the New World in 1492 was hardly disinterested curiosity. He was not simply looking for the monsters described in Pliny's *Natural History*, but also went in search of nature for profit — cinnamon, balsam, aromatic woods, and unusual animals and plants to delight the palate as well as the eye, and to cure the diseases of the Old World with the nature of the New.[11]

The profitability of nature was closely tied to its medicinal uses. Nature provided the ingredients for a vast array of medicines in the ancient pharmacopeia, from simple herbal remedies to more highly prized items such as balsam, bezoar stones, and all of the key ingredients to create that panacea of panaceas, theriac.[12] Merchants, apothecaries, and physicians together created an economy of natural objects. They bought those parts of nature that they could not cultivate and acquire on their own and transformed them into medicines. The rarest and most exotic medicines, dependent on ingredients from the Levant and later the New World, were usually composed of costly ingredients. Serpetro's image of marvels lined up under the porticos for sale was not at all improbable: it reflected the reality of the most marvelous aspects of medicine.

If commerce and medicine established the essential contours of trafficking in nature, faith placed a high premium on a different set of unusual objects. By the thirteenth century the Crusades had created a lively trade in relics, but also in natural objects that conformed to ancient accounts of the marvels of the East.[13] The spoils of Christian conquest included a kind of mythologized conquest of nature: Egyptian crocodiles, ostrich eggs, alleged unicorn's horns, griffin's claws, and other examples of exotic nature, real and imagined, began to appear in churches and treasuries throughout western Europe.[14] While not as highly prized as sanctified relics, such objects reflected a growing interest in the fantastic parts of nature described in medieval bestiaries and other Christian allegories of nature that privileged certain animals as harbingers of God's will. The basilisks, griffins, and dragons found in the Bible and in such works as Pliny's *Natural History* became more than paper fantasies of natural omens. Increasingly, they were actual objects created to satisfy the taste for such curiosities. Such objects did not disappear at the end of the Middle Ages but enjoyed a certain revival in the age of the Reformation. In an era fascinated with reports of omens and prodigies that signified God's will in a world of divided faith, they were fully integrated into the cabinets of curiosities.

In all of these different ways, curiosity about the natural world shaped the marketplace of marvels. The fascination with wonder helped to create a kind of individual skilled in buying, selling, and creating wonder. Curiosity created its own commerce — a world of specialists in natural curiosities that we can only glimpse indirectly through accounts of nature in the early modern period. Such individuals did not aspire to interpret nature, but to sell nature to those who created knowledge out of the raw ingredients of the marketplace. Extraordinary things demanded a special expertise to acquire and invent them, which gave them economic as well as symbolic value. Understanding more precisely how learned collectors acquired the wonders that they prized brings us into closer contact with the marketplace that they were often loathe to discuss. It was a world filled with mountebanks and charlatans who cultivated ties with physicians, apothecaries, and merchants in order to sell their vision of nature to a public consumed by curiosities.

The tensions between those who sold nature and those who interpreted it are evident in letters that accompanied objects in circulation among naturalists. When a learned collector crossed the imagined boundary between science and commerce, he was subject to scathing criticism. In the 1590s, for example, naturalists complained to each other about the practices of the Basel physician Felix Platter who, according to one source, refused to make gifts of his curiosities, selling "everything he has."[15] This rather unusual comment about a learned naturalist suggests that by the end of the sixteenth century the line between science and commerce was increasingly blurred, if it had ever been clear. Buying nature in the marketplace was a commonly accepted practice among naturalists, a necessity to increase and replenish the storehouse of knowledge. Selling nature, however, was an activity unworthy of a natural philosopher. Or was it? Platter's decision to sell what he possessed suggests that it had become possible to put a price on the time and expertise required to find and cultivate something rare, even for the purposes of study.

Selling curiosities in a cabinet, or selling an entire cabinet, represents the final step in a series of transactions that began the moment a curiosity became available. Following an object from the beginning to the end helps us to understand more precisely how science and commerce intersected. Let us take the case of a curiosity that entered Ulisse Aldrovandi's collection in Bologna in 1579, a gift of one of his regular correspondents, the Genoese patrician Bernardo Castelletti. Castelletti exemplified well the meaning of friendship in late Renaissance natural history. He routinely procured new curiosities for Aldrovandi to describe in his great, unpublished natural history, and asked nothing in return but the pleasure of corresponding with a famous naturalist. The gifts he gave to Aldrovandi arrived in his hands by many different avenues, and included curiosities he purchased in the public piazzas of his city. In February 1579, Castelletti sent a letter announcing the imminent arrival in Bologna of the most marvelous fish he had ever seen: "What's more, you will have a fish that is one of the rarest and most extravagant parts of nature in the sea." He described how he acquired this rather ugly fish with bulging eyes:

> It was given to me dried, as I send it to you, by the fisherman who caught it, who, upon seeing it had such strange features, didn't throw it back into the sea, as fishermen usually do with all the other useless fish. Indeed he kept it alive as long as he could, and then had it dried to show to people as a miraculous thing.[16]

The ingredients in the story are the stuff of which cabinets of curiosities were made and replenished: a useless fish, an ambitious fisherman, an audience eager to pay to see natural oddities, and collectors who could not resist acquiring them. This was quite literally the experience of nature in the marketplace.

The dried monster made its way to Bologna and Aldrovandi added it to his museum. He may have even had his artists illustrate it and dictated a description to his scribes, in preparation for its inclusion in his *Natural History*.[17] This at least was Castelletti's fear a few years later. Apologetically and quite reluctantly, he informed Aldrovandi that the marvel had been invented by the fisherman who sold it to him. "I am sorry to have to tell you that in the description of the fish sent to you some years ago, I was deceived. . . ." Worried that he had compromised the veracity of Aldrovandi's account of nature, he confessed that his words as much as the object itself were not a reliable source of information. They, too, had been bought and sold in the marketplace: "they are those that the fisherman sold me."[18] A clever vendor of the nature's bounty had tricked a gullible humanist into believing that all the monsters found in Pliny's *Natural History* truly might be acquired for one's museum, if only one looked hard enough. Castelletti had forgotten the golden rule: *caveat emptor*.

Such episodes give us further insight into the way in which the commerce in natural curiosities responded directly to the collector's passion for the exotic and unknown. A city like Genoa was a trading zone for natural curiosities. When the grand duke of Tuscany commissioned his botanist at the University of Pisa, Francesco Malocchi, to acquire curiosities for the university garden and its museum during the summer of 1599, Malocchi planned an itinerary that made Genoa his final destination. Malocchi's buying trips were, in essence, a merchant's itinerary to the port cities of Italy. In each city, he encountered men who had curiosities to sell, and made purchases for the grand duke which were recorded in his ledger. In April 1604, for instance, Malocchi acquired an entire "whale skeleton"—a rare prize for an early modern natural history museum — in the port city of Livorno.[19] He was more successful than the French royal surgeon Ambroise Paré, who was fascinated by "a head of a large fish in the house of a rich merchant" in Lyon that he hoped to acquire for King Charles IX.[20] Unfortunately the fish was quarantined with the family during a plague epidemic, and that was the last Paré ever saw of it. These and other anecdotes suggest that naturalists routinely visited merchants who owned and sold curious things.

Knowledge of nature could not increase without the commerce in nature. Naturalists had to come to terms with the marketplace in order to pursue curiosities. Digging further into Aldrovandi's correspondence we find indications that he knew some of the famous charlatans of his day who made and sold curiosities in the piazza, and considered them an interesting source of knowledge as well as artifacts. In April 1568, for example, a correspondent from Piacenza described their mutual acquaintance "Master Leone who sells his wares in public often, and is known to all the apothecaries in Venice."[21] Leone Tartaglini of Foiano was a famous mountebank known to most collectors of natural curiosities in late sixteenth-century Italy. He inhabited the Venetian piazza famously depicted as filled with men of his profession. Naturalists traveled from cities as dispersed as Lucca, Piacenza, Bologna, and Verona to see his cabinet of curiosities in Venice, which was an early precursor to the Parisian Noah's Ark that Evelyn described. Many of the objects Tartaglini possessed were evidently for sale. Among other things, he specialized in the sort of extravagant fish that Castelletti admired and purchased in Genoa. Visitors to Venice reported that he had a book illustrating all of his dried fish — a book Aldrovandi, among others, wanted very much to see.[22] While many naturalists collected images of curiosities in order to create a complete archive of the natural world, in Tartaglini's case, such a book might have served the additional purpose of advertising the kind of nature that he sold.

The image of the seller of nature as a mountebank appears not only in descriptions of Tartaglini's activities in Venice, perhaps the most famous vendor of curiosities of whom we have a precise description, but also informed other accounts of the buying and selling of curiosities. In November 1663, the English traveler Philip Skippon encountered a mountebank named Rosachio, an astrologer who sold medicines in Piazza San Marco. Skippon was evidently fascinated by Rosachio; he followed his initial encounter with the mountebank by visiting Rosachio at home in order to see his "collection of rarities." In it was a flying serpent — or at least an alleged flying serpent since Skippon described it as having "a long furrow on either side, in which were cartilaginous parts (he said) when it was alive, that served for wings."[23] Skippon's traveling companion, the great English naturalist John Ray, evidently did not find the alleged dragon worthy of note since he neglected to include it in his own journal of the same voyage, but the fact remains that a century after Tartaglini had succeeded in getting all the great naturalists of Italy (and undoubtedly other regions) to visit his cabinet in Venice, mountebanks were still selling the same bits of artificial nature to the heirs of Aldrovandi. In the 1672 catalog to his museum in Verona, Count Lodovico Moscardo continued to discuss the "swindlers and charlatans from Dalmatia" who sold examples of the basilisk in his museum.[24]

The network of people who bought and sold nature was composed of more than just charlatans and random fishermen who showed exotic fish in the fish markets. Let us return for a moment to the fact that Master Leone of Venice was known to all the apothecaries of the city. Were they as much the source of his curiosities as he was of theirs? In his *History of Animals* (1558), the Swiss naturalist Conrad Gessner informed his readers about "apothecaries and others who usually dry rays and shape their skeletons into varied and wonderful forms for the ignorant."[25] Rather than condemning charlatans, Gessner blamed apothecaries for facilitating this trade, indeed accused them of inventing fraudulent curiosities. We can find traces of relationships among apothecaries and mountebanks in surviving correspondence. The Veronese apothecary Francesco Calzolari, for instance, was so intrigued by reports of Master Leone's activities that he sought out the artist who had illustrated the Venetian's curiosities.[26]

Scholarly collectors recognized that the pharmacy was both a world of wonder and an extension of the marketplace. They entered it expecting to find an invented nature (fig. 12.2). Visiting apothecaries was an important

𝒮𝒾𝑔𝑢𝑟𝑒 12.2   The apothecary Francesco Calzolari's museum in Verona, filled with many strange fish and reptiles hung from the ceiling. Source: Benedetto Ceruti and Andrea Chiocco, *Musaeum Franc[isci] Calceolarii Iun[ioris]. Veronensis* (Verona, 1622). Courtesy of the Biblioteca, Universitania, Bologna.

part of the collector's itinerary. John Ray took pleasure in "a so-called siren's rib" in the apothecary Jean van der Mere's collection in Delft and visited the apothecary Mario Salò in Verona, who claimed to have the "reliques of *Calceolarius* his *Museum*."[27] Possibly one of the items surviving from Calzolari's museum that did not especially impress Ray in 1663 was the unicorn's horn that Aldrovandi saw when he visited his shop at the Sign of the Golden Bell in Piazza dell'Erbe in 1571. Aldrovandi was too polite to tell Calzolari that it was a fake, but he privately noted "that there is no doubt that it is not a true example."[28] Such objects were also the ordinary stuff of any cabinet of curiosities. But apothecaries, who practiced a certain alchemy on nature to create their medicines, must have seen the fabrication of natural objects as a

Paula Findlen

demonstration of professional skill—the ability to manipulate nature. They filled their shops with those marvels, real and imaginary, that helped to sell their medicines and reminded people of the apothecary's close connections with the world of art to which they were officially joined in towns where painters and apothecaries belonged to the same guild because both transformed the raw ingredients of nature into art.[29]

Collectors understood that the more unusual nature *seemed* to be, the more likely it was a product of their own demand for a certain kind of wonder. They repeatedly offered advice on how to discern the difference between an authentic and fabricated version of nature. The Milanese physician Girolamo Cardano advised his readers to inspect the joints and sutures of marvelous creations in order to see if they had been put together by human rather than divine hands.[30] But the possibility of fraud did not make collectors any less interested in acquiring them—quite the opposite since invented bits of nature were highly prized. One of the less well-studied aspects of the cabinets of curiosities regards the significance of objects that purported to be natural while actually being artificial. These fabrications allow us to understand how commerce and science helped to create the art of nature in the early modern period.

INVENTING THE HYDRA AND THE BASILISK

The most popular fabrications of the sixteenth and seventeenth centuries were hydras and basilisks. They took their place in the cabinet of curiosities among the many different kinds of dragons that fascinated early modern collectors. Flying dragons, eagle-fish, and other hybrids of the imagination emerged from the pages of medieval bestiaries and church and princely treasuries to fill Renaissance museums. They did so according to rules of art that were best expressed in a passage from Leonardo da Vinci's notebooks. Describing how to make an imaginary animal appear natural, Leonardo wrote:

> You know that you cannot make any animal without it having its limbs such that each bears some resemblance to that of some one of the other animals. If therefore you wish to make one of your imaginary animals appear natural—let us suppose it to be a dragon—take for its head that of a mastiff or setter, for its eyes those of a cat, for its ears those of a porcupine, for its nose that of a greyhound, with the eyebrows of a lion, the temples of an old cock and the neck of a water-tortoise.[31]

The rules of good painting applied no less to the three-dimensional construction of an imaginary animal. In order to be convincing, it had to originate in nature. Leonardo's contemporary Albrecht Dürer also believed that art emerged from nature, and he strove hard to give the beasts of the Apocalypse a more anatomical appearance.[32] Leonardo's example of a dragon was hardly casual because it was indeed the imaginary animal of choice. It was the most fantastic and symbolically potent animal in the Christian imagination, worthy of multiple inventions across the centuries.

The hydra and the basilisk — two of the most elaborate kinds of dragons described in ancient and biblical sources — had a level of complexity that many other natural inventions did not. A unicorn's horn was the horn of a narwhal. A griffin's claw was often a bison's or ox's horn. Many inventions of nature, in other words, were entirely natural. They simply involved an act of reinterpretation in order to see the imaginary in the real. Objects that took shape through the manipulation and transformation of nature belonged to an entirely different category. They were truly works of art in which one could take pleasure in the possibilities that nature suggested to the human mind.

Not coincidentally, they were also objects on which one could put a price — repositories of economic as well as spiritual capital.[33] Conrad Gessner described a hydra that had been brought from Turkey to Venice in 1530 and acquired by the king of France (fig. 12.3). "It is appraised at six thousand ducats," he wrote in 1560. Like Dürer's rhinoceros, Gessner's hydra was an image derived from an image. He lifted it from broadsheets such as Dürer's popular *Whore of Babylon* (1498) that depicted the seven-headed beast of the Apocalypse with vivid clarity for a public eager to see signs of a world in turmoil. An encyclopedia such as Conrad Lycosthenes's, *Chronicle of Prodigies and Portents* (1557) was probably the more direct source for Gessner's illustration. Evading the issue of its truth or falsehood, Gessner chose instead to comment on the hydra's art. "The ears, tongue, nose, and faces are different from the nature of all species of serpents. But if the author of such an invented natural thing were not ignorant, he would be able, with great artifice, to trick observers."[34]

Aldrovandi agreed with Gessner's assessment of the hydra. After receiving a hydra from a Ferrarese noble who wanted to know if it was authentic, Aldrovandi responded that, given the confused description of the hydra among the ancients — an animal with three, four, seven, nine, or even ninety heads — it was hardly surprising that no one knew the truth about it. He reflected on how others had profited from this uncertainty: "it is no wonder that in our age some have been deceived by the miraculous artifice with which these hydras are faked from other bodies and put together, as they have also done with the flying dragon — which however does exist in nature — trying to imitate it by using a species of marine ray, as one can see in my study." His assessment of the hydra of Ferrara was mixed. The body

and tail came from the "true flying dragon that is born in Arabia and Egypt," but the heads had come from different animals and one could see that various parts of the dragon—its wings and its hind legs—had been removed to give it the appearance of a hydra.[35] It was a half-true specimen, a wonder of nature transformed into a work of art by the desire of nature's artisans to turn a profit. Better, in short, than the hydra of San Marco in Venice, which he declared to be patently false.[36] For this reason, Aldrovandi engraved it for eventual inclusion in his *History of Serpents and Dragons*.

Undoubtedly because hydras were often found in state treasuries—the Venetian doge had a fine example with nine heads, for instance[37]—visitors talked more self-consciously about their monetary worth (and went to famous naturalists such as Aldrovandi to see if they would authenticate them, which surely increased their value). Skippon, for instance, admired the seven-headed hydra in the duke of Modena's gallery, originally a gift of the Holy Roman Emperor Charles V to the Gonzaga family of Guastallo. He, too, refused to say with certainty that the hydra was a fake, though he commented on "the head being like that of fitchet, or of that kind, the body and feet were of a rabbet or hare, and the tail was made of common snake's skin, the back and neck covered with the same." But he was very precise about the origins of the hydra since it was part of a collection bought from "*Zennon* the apothecary for 300 doppii" when the d'Este family was unable to acquire Settala's collection.[38] An apothecary's hydra, of course, had its price — and it was much lower than the value of objects normally associated with a ducal treasury.

The process of inventing nature fascinated early modern naturalists. While they might condemn mountebanks for preying on the gullible and the ignorant, they could not contain their own delight in understanding how nature could be invented or suppress their admiration for the artistry involved in making monsters. As naturalists collected and inspected the variety of nature with greater regularity, they began to put into print their observations on nature's fabrications. Dragons were a focal point of this discussion and, more often than not, such discussions appeared in ichthyologies — further underscoring the idea that the point was not to talk about dragons *sui generis* but to discuss how to make them from fish. In his *Natural History of Strange Fish* (1551), Pierre Belon described the passion of many people for dragons "made for pleasure such as those that we see counterfeited with rays disguised in the manner of a flying serpent."[39] Conrad Gessner's complaint in 1558 about fraudulent apothecaries came in the midst of a lengthy discussion of dragon-making in his *History of Animals*. In a chapter on rays, he described in great detail how such monsters were made. "They bend the body, distort the head and mouth, and cut into and cut away other parts. They raise up the parts that remain and simulate wings, and invent other parts at will."[40] Understanding the possibilities of the ray as a dragon *in potentia* was the first step in appreciating the art of the dragon.

The ability of many naturalists to look critically at the anatomy of the hydra, the basilisk, and many other kinds of dragons reflected the shifting religious and intellectual climate. In the early decades of the sixteenth century, such creatures were sufficiently charged with religious meaning that it would have been heretical to suggest that they were anything less than God's will. By the 1550s, it had become possible to inspect these portents as examples of nature's variety and to suggest that human intervention made them approximate people's fantasies of a terrifying nature. Increasingly, such objects seemed to evoke pleasure more than horror.[41] The Renaissance dragon, after all, was usually no more than a couple of feet long. Cardano simply couldn't imagine how many of the specimens he saw could fly. J. C. Scaliger contented himself by observing: "The skin is like that of a ray."[42] One wanted to know *how* they were made while avoiding the question of whether they existed.

Naturalists actively collected and traded these physical talismans of the medieval and Reformation culture of portents — no longer clear demonstrations of the mysterious ways in which God's will manifested itself in the world, but increasingly desirable items for cabinets of curiosities. In 1573, the French surgeon Ambroise Paré recalled a marine monster that Cardano sent Gessner, "which had a head similar to a bear and hands almost like a monkey, and the rest of a fish."[43] Such descriptions reveal the pleasure naturalists took in understanding how harmonizing the many parts of nature into something new and unexpected might be an art unto itself. Examining the griffin's claw in the treasury of Charles V, for instance, Cardano reflected: "perhaps by carving out an ox's horn, art invents nature."[44] The ability to dissect the bestiary that made the beast gave credence to the idea that knowledge did transform how one looked at an object. If commerce responded to curiosity by inventing what people wanted to see, then science responded to art by understanding that the boundaries between nature and art were there to be crossed. We need only think of the jeweled boxes that German and Italian artisans made in the shape of crocodiles and dragons, the French artisan Bernard Palissy's ceramic re-creations of nature, or the flying dragon chandelier that Dürer designed in Nuremberg, which used the natural shape of a stag's antlers for its wings, to recognize how the idea of making art from nature was a central theme of the late Renaissance.[45]

By the time Aldrovandi's *On Fish* appeared posthumously in 1613, it reflected the new sensibility of late Renaissance natural history toward the idea of inventing nature. While indebted to all previous publications that had discussed fabulous creatures in the cabinets of curiosities, Aldrovandi's book improved upon them by showing the artifice of inventing dragons and basilisks from rays in greater visual detail. His work included no less than two images of a "ray dried and shaped in the form of a dragon" as well as a "sea-eagle" that he declared to be patently false (fig 12.4).[46] Examining these images, we can see explicit efforts to demonstrate the artifice of the object in question while retaining the canonical form of the dragon.

Aldrovandi's images of flying dragons provided the introductory material for a chapter on the basilisk in Bartolomeo Ambrosini's edited version of Aldrovandi's *History of Serpents and Dragons* (1640). A small, solitary African dragon described by Pliny and Galen, it was reputedly so poisonous that it could kill someone with its breath or its glance, dry plants, and break stones in half.[47] It quickly became the canonical example of a work of nature transformed into a work of art (fig. 12.5). Aldrovandi reported that the great physician Girolamo Mercuriale had found a "basilisk's cadaver" in the treasury of the Holy Roman Emperor Maximilian II. He (or his editor Ambrosini) tactfully chose not to comment directly on the imperial basilisk, restricting himself instead to condemning those "imposters" who frequently made basilisks "out of small dried rays."[48]

Aldrovandi's comments on the invention of the basilisk rested on the more extensive critique of this animal composed by the imperial physician Pier

Figure 12.4 The "dragon formed a ray" in Ulisse Aldrovandi's museum in Bologna. Source: Ulisse Aldrovandi, *De piscibus* (Bologna, 1613). Courtesy of Department of Special Collections, Stanford University Libraries.

Bafilifcus ex Raia effictus pronè,& fupinè pictus.

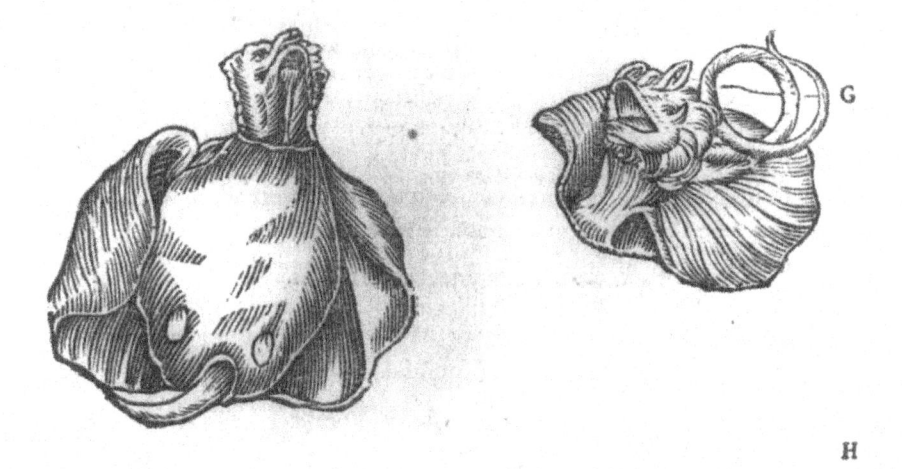

Figure 12.5 Aldrovandi's basilisk. Source: Ulisse Aldrovandi, *Serpentum et draconum historiae libro duo*, ed. Bartolomeo Ambrosini (Bologna, 1640). Courtesy of Department of Special Collections, Stanford University Libraries.

Andrea Mattioli. In the expansion of his 1544 commentary on Dioscorides's *De materia medica*, the leading handbook on medicinal simples since antiquity, Mattioli added a section on poisons. The final chapter of his popular commentary was devoted to the basilisk. "The variety of stories makes me easily believe that one can't determine anything about this animal," wrote Mattioli, "or know what its true history might be among all the stories told."[49] Nonetheless he proposed a few logical questions about the idea of the basilisk that reflected the growing numbers of specimens in cabinets of curiosities. How could something so dangerous that it could kill men instantly be so easily captured? If it were so small, how could men, observing it from a safe distance, see enough of its features to report on details such as the three points on the crested head, or the crown that it was often thought to wear? The basilisk, after all, had no Hercules to slay it like the hydra, nor a tale equivalent to the decapitation of the deadly Medusa. Only divine providence, or human delight in the endless invention of nature, could bring it into the museum.

The longevity of the basilisk, well beyond the period in which there was any doubt about its authenticity, suggests the importance of understanding the relations between science and art in the early modern period. Certainly the decision to make basilisks a prominent part of the iconography of natural history was a contributing factor. Each image created a prototype of an object that could be made by looking at its engraving, and remade by copying these images into new natural histories. Aldrovandi's fake dragons enjoyed a wide circulation in the seventeenth century. They reappeared in later editions of Aldrovandi's posthumous natural history and eventually found their way into Joannes Jonstonius's *Natural History of Serpents* (1657). In this work, Jonstonius brought together all of Aldrovandi's images to demonstrate the art of inventing nature (fig. 12.6). When it came to the basilisk, Jonstonius offered no lengthy discussion of its physical form, customs, and mythology, as earlier naturalists had done. He simply noted: "They are formed from a ray, just as one can see from this image. Preserved in the Bologna Museum."[50]

By 1622, connoisseurs of basilisks could enjoy a competing image of this dragon by turning to page 90 in the new and improved catalog of Calzolari's museum written by Benedetto Ceruti and Andrea Chiocco, two Veronese physicians in contact with the apothecary's grandson (fig. 12.7). There was a splendid portrayal of all the unique features of the basilisk, with a level of detail that no previous image had captured: the diadem decorating its crested forehead, the scales covering its wings and tail, the strange fins on which it balanced, and, most importantly, the act of flight. The engraver had succeeded in bringing the basilisk to life. Lest there be any confusion, Ceruti warned his readers: "You should know, lest any lies are discovered in our nomenclature, that this is neither a basilisk nor a dragon, but a fish from the

Figure 12.6 Joannes Jonstonius' reproduction of Aldrovandi's invented dragons. Joannes Jonstonius, *Historia naturalis de serpentibus libri II* (Amsterdam, 1657). Courtesy of the Biblioteca Nazionale Centrale, Florence.

Figure 12.7 Calzolari's basilisk in Verona. Source: Benedetto Ceruti and Andrea Chiocco, *Musaeum Franc[isci] Calceolarii Iun[ioris] Veronensis* (Verona, 1622). Courtesy of the Biblioteca Nazionale Centrale, Florence.

sea — an ill-shaped ray of course — worked into this shape by the hand of an artisan." He invited his readers to admire how Calzolari's monster, "exhibited for viewing," imitated the shape of the basilisk.[51]

Calzolari's engraved basilisk quickly supplanted Aldrovandi's illustrations as the canonical depiction of an object that *did* exist, even if the animal did not. When Lodovico Moscardo published two catalogs of his own collection in 1656 and 1672, he reproduced Calzolari's image. Of course in Moscardo's case it is not unlikely that he had Calzolari's actual basilisk, since both collectors came from the same city. It was in regard to this particular basilisk that he offered the opinion that it "had been shaped in this way by swindlers and charlatans from Dalmatia, and shown by them in public stands to the people as a true basilisk."[52] The image, in other words, now fully demonstrated the art of invention and the collector's role as a critical consumer in the marketplace of marvels.

The power of Calzolari's image and its circulation in various catalogues throughout the seventeenth-century attracted visitors to Moscardo's museum who wanted to inspect the art of the basilisk. Catalogs gave objects a double life; visitors experienced them both in word and image, before see-

---

ing them in the museum. In 1687 Maximilian Misson stood in front of Moscardo's basilisk, which he had surely encountered first in print, and discussed how it was made in greater detail than any of his predecessors: "the invention is most pleasing and a thousand people are fooled by it." He added to Gessner's original description of 1558 by noting the way in which a darted tongue was neatly fitted into the fictitious mouth, and claws and enamel eyes were added "with some other little parts dexterously put together." With great pleasure, he concluded, "And voilà! The invention of the basilisk."[53] The Verona basilisk did not disappear from view in the next century, but gained further currency as naturalists more aggressively cultivated their reputation as debunkers of ancient superstitions. When the catalogue of the Nuremberg apothecary Basil Besler and his son Michael Rupert's cabinet appeared in 1716, it also contained an image of the 1622 Calzolari basilisk, further cementing its reputation as the measure of this particular wonder (fig. 12.8).

Even museum catalogs that did not include the image of Calzolari's basilisk made reference to it as the best instance of the engraver's art captur-

Figure 12.8 Basil and Michael Rupert Besler's basilisk, with a demonstration of how it was made from a ray. Source: *Rariorum Musei Besleriani quae olim Basilius et Michael Rupert Besler collegerunt, aeneisque tabulis ads vivum incisa evvulgarunt: nunc commentariolo illustrata a Johanne Henrico Lochnero* (Nuremberg, 1716). Courtesy of the Biblioteca Nazionale Centrale, Florence.

ing the fabrication of nature. The papal physician Johan Faber, for instance, referred to the "most beautifully engraved figures" of the basilisk in flight in the Ceruti and Chiocco catalog to highlight the unusual appearance of a dragon's skeleton he included in his edition of the Spanish royal physician Francisco Hernández's famous *Treasure of Medical Things of New Spain* (1649) (fig 12.9).[54] Cardinal Francesco Barberini's dragon had been carefully inspected by Faber, who pronounced it authentic in every respect. One way to demonstrate its authenticity was to depict it in a manner different from the Calzolari basilisk because it had become the canonical image of the invention of nature.

There were many technical reasons to admire the Calzolari image. In comments such as Faber's we get a glimpse of the naturalist as a savvy consumer of the art of printing as a technique for reproducing nature. By the time Lorenzo Legati composed the 1677 catalog of Marchese Ferdinando Cospi's museum in Bologna, he was no longer satisfied with Aldrovandi's depictions of the basilisk. While referring his readers to the images of 1640—which were actually woodcuts done at the end of the sixteenth century—he told them that the image of the Calzolari basilisk more closely approximated the object he was trying to describe. "Other than being most finely engraved

Figure 12.9 Cardinal Francesco Barberini's dragon in Rome, as described by papal physician Johan Faber. Source: Francisco Hernández, *Rerum medicarum novae hispaniae thesaurus seu plantarum animalium mineralium Mexicanorum Historia ex Francisci Hernandez*, ed. Johan Faber (Rome, 1649). Courtesy of Bancroft Library, University of California, Berkeley.

in copper, it also articulates the spines and roughness of the tail that one doesn't observe in the first figures."[55] Legati did not follow Moscardo's example of including the image, on the presumption that readers of his catalog would simply turn to a copy of the 1622 catalog to confirm his opinion. In a much more decisive way, Legati reminded his audience that depicting a dubious nature was a special kind of art.

Only one seventeenth-century scholar took the image that Faber created in the 1640s to be a better likeness of a dragon. Both the image and description of Faber's dragon appeared prominently in the German Jesuit Athanasius Kircher's *Subterranean World* (1664).[56] But this was hardly surprising since Kircher was in the midst of dissecting a dragon's head with the Barberini librarian Hieronymus Lancia after a flying dragon made its appearance in Rome in 1660. Kircher was perhaps the last naturalist to believe passionately in the reality of any papal dragon he saw, even though he knew well the stories of basilisks invented from rays. His successor as curator of the Roman College museum, the Jesuit naturalist Filippo Bonanni, tactfully chose not to discuss the Barberini dragons, confining his comments instead to a splendid example of a dried ray "sold by some as a basilisk." It was surely one of the two rays "formed by art" that Giorgio de Sepi described in the 1678 catalog of Kircher's collection.[57] By the end of the seventeenth century, the vast majority of naturalists agreed with Ceruti that hydras, basilisks, and dragons existed only to the extent to which artisans and engravers could bring them to life.

MONSTROUS CODA: THE LAST HYDRA FOR SALE

No account of the early modern invention of nature, however, ends without the moral that belief is more powerful than any number of criticisms that might demolish it. The last hydra to preoccupy the community of naturalists belonged to two merchants in Hamburg. In the city of Amsterdam, the apothecary Albert Seba routinely enjoyed the company of visitors to his famous cabinet of curiosities. Around 1720, he began to hear tales of the hydra of Hamburg (fig. 12.10). At first, he dismissed it as a mere fable. A year later, a minister told him the same story and brought him an image of the hydra. But what finally convinced Seba that he needed to know more about the hydra was its price. "When I heard that it was for sale for 10,000 florins, a detail he confirmed, the immensity of the sum reawakened my desire to have a faithful copy of it." Seba's response to the hydra was not all that different than his contemporary Antonio Vallisnieri's reaction to the basilisk. Vallisnieri, one of the famed professors of natural history who practiced the kind of critical, microscopic natural history that his mentor Mar-

Figure 12.10 The hydra of Hamburg, engraved for Albert Seba. Source: Albert Seba, *Locupletissimi rerum naturalium thesauri accurata descriptio, et iconibus artificiosissimis expressio, per universam physices historiam* (Amsterdam, 1734), vol. 1, table CII. Courtesy of Bancroft Library, University of California, Berkeley.

cello Malpighi pioneered, kept a basilisk in his collection in Padua in the early eighteenth century because he could not believe the "high price" that an "Armenian trickster" had gotten for it.[58]

Commerce indeed was the final wonder of the art of inventing nature. Both truth and falsehood had their price. Seba immediately wrote to a fellow apothecary in Hamburg, asking his opinion of the hydra. "He assured me that it was in no way a work of art, but truly one of nature."[59] The apothecary Natorp provided the "faithful copy" that Seba requested for him to see what kind of hydra it was. Seba subsequently circulated it widely among connoisseurs of curiosities by making it the most dramatic illustration in the 1734 catalog of his Amsterdam collection, even though he had no direct claim on the hydra. Shortly thereafter, young Linnaeus would declare that it was probably the fabrication of monks — not unlike the "basilisk's tongue in two pieces" and the "two basilisk skeletons in pieces" that the abbot Matteo Priuli kept in his collection in Padua at the end of the seventeenth century. Debunking the hydra became part of Linnaeus's mythology as a modern naturalist.[60] Yet what we miss in such an account is Linnaeus's admiration for the hydra of Hamburg—a response to the fabrication of nature that he shared with Seba and all the naturalists who preceded them. The price on the hydra may have declined precipitously thereafter, but it was still a work of art.[61]

Notes

1. See especially Lorraine Daston and Katharine Park, *Wonders and the Order of Nature 1150–1750* (New York: Zone Books, 1998); and Jean Céard, *La nature et les prodiges. L'insolite au seizième siècle* (Geneva: Droz, 1977); Ottavia Niccoli, *Prophecy and People in Renaissance Italy*, trans. Lydia G. Cochrane (Princeton, N.J.: Princeton University Press, 1990); and William Burns, *An Age of Wonders: Prodigies, Providence, and Politics in England, 1658–1727* (Manchester: Manchester University Press, 2001).

2. Nicolò Serpetro, *Il mercato delle maraviglie della natura overo storia naturale* (Venice, 1653), n. p., "Introdutione per chi legge."

3. Tommaso Garzoni, *Piazza universale di tutte le professioni del mondo*, ed. Paolo Cherchi (Turin: Einaudi, 1996).

4. See Anne Goldgar's essay in this volume.

5. John Evelyn, *The Diary of John Evelyn*, ed. William Bray (London: Bickers and Son, 1906), Vol. 1, 51 (Paris, 3 February 1644).

6. The role of gifts in early modern natural history is discussed in Paula Findlen, "The Economy of Scientific Exchange in Early Modern Italy," in *Patronage and Institutions: Science, Technology and Medicine at the European Courts, 1500–1750* (Woodbridge, U.K.: Boydell & Brewer, 1991), 5–24; Giuseppe Olmi, "'Molti amici in varii luoghi': Studio della natura e rapporti epistolari nel secolo XVI," *Nuncius* 6 (1991): 3–31; and Brian Ogilvie, *Observation and Experience in Early Modern Natural History* (Ph.D. diss., University of Chicago, 1997), esp. 8, 129–130, 241–242.

7. Hans-Olof Boström, "Philipp Hainhofer and Gustavus Adolphus's *Kunstschrank*," in *Origins of Museums: Cabinets of Curiosities in Early Modern Europe*, ed. Oliver Impey and Arthur MacGregor (Oxford: Clarendon Press, 1983), 91. For further discussion of this approach to a cabinet of curiosities, see Pamela H. Smith, *The Business of Alchemy: Science and Culture in the Holy Roman Empire* (Princeton, N.J.: Princeton University Press, 1994).

8. See Mark Meadow's and Harold Cook's essays in this volume for more on Hans Jacob Fugger and Jan Swammerdam.

9. John Ray, *Observations Topographical, Moral, & Physiological; Made in a Journey Through part of the Low-Countries, Germany, Italy, and France* (London, 1673), 237; and Philip Skippon, *An Account of a Journey Made Thro' Part of the Low-Countries, Germany, Italy, and France*, in *A Collection of Voyages and Travels*, eds. A. and S. Churchill (London, 1752), Vol. 6, 565.

10. Many of the essays in *Cultures of Natural History*, ed. Nick Jardine, James Secord, and Emma Spary (Cambridge: Cambridge University Press, 1995), touch upon this theme.

11. The commercial aspect of Columbus's interest in nature should be considered alongside those elements described in Mary Campbell, *The Witness and the Other World: Exotic European Travel Writing 400–1600* (Ithaca, N.Y.: Cornell University Press, 1988); and Stephen Greenblatt, *Marvelous Possessions: The Wonder of the New World* (Chicago: University of Chicago Press, 1991).

12. Theriac was an ancient medicine, described in great detail by Galen and composed of numerous ingredients that allegedly cured all manner of poisons. It was increasingly taken as a preventive medicine in an era of frequent plague epidemics. See Findlen, *Possessing Nature: Museums, Collecting, and Scientific Culture in Early Modern Italy* (Berkeley: University of California Press, 1994), ch. 5.

13. Patrick Geary, *Furta Sacra: Thefts of Relics in the Central Middle Ages* (Princeton, N.J.: Princeton University Press, 1978), indicates the extent of the passion for relics whose value escalated to such a degree that people stole as well as bought them.

14. Daston and Park, *Wonders*, 69, 74.

15. This marvelous passage is discussed in Ogilvie, *Observation*, 241.

16. Biblioteca Universitaria, Bologna (hereafter BUB), *Aldrovandi*, ms. 136, Vol. 9, c.5v (Castelletti to Aldrovandi, Genova, 22 February 1579).

17. See, for example, Ulisse Aldrovandi, *De piscibus libri V* (Bologna, 1613), 401. "De centrine" describes fish he acquired from Castelletti, who called them "verae ac genuinae."

18. BUB, *Aldrovandi*, ms. 136, Vol. 9, c.129r (Castelletti to Aldrovandi, n.d.)

19. Archivio di Stato, Pisa, *Università*, 530, c.2r (*Spese occorse nel viaggio fatto da un semplicista per ritrovare piante e minerali*); 518 (16 April 1604). This material is also discussed in Lucia Tongiorgi Tomasi, "Arte e natura nel Giardino dei Semplici: dalle origini alla fine dell'età medicea," in *Giardino dei Semplici: l'Orto botanico di Pisa dal XVI al XX secolo* ed. Fabio Garbari, Lucia Tongiorgi Tomasi, and Alessandro Tosi (Ospedaletto: Pacini, 1991) 162.

20. Ambroise Paré, *On Monsters and Marvels*, trans. Janis L. Pallister (Chicago: University of Chicago Press, 1980), 128.

21. BUB, *Aldrovandi*, ms. 38, Vol. 4, f.46 (Antonio Anguissola, Piacenza, 12 April 1568). The Italian original literally describes Master Leone as someone who "monta in bancho spesso"—the origins of the word "mountebank."

22. The fascinating story of Leone Tartaglini has been reconstructed in Achille Forti, "Del drago che si trovava nella Raccolta Moscardo e di un probabile artefice di tali mistificazioni: Leone Tartaglini da Foiano," *Madonna Verona* 8 (1914): 26–51; and idem, "Il Basilisco esistente al Museo Civico di Storia Naturale a Venezia e gli affini simulacri finora conosciuti. Contributo alla storia della ciarlataneria," *Atti del Reale Istituto Veneto di scienze, lettere ed arti* 87, part 2 (1928–29): 225–238.

23. Skippon, *Account of a Journey*, 517. Compare with Ray, *Observations*.

24. Lodovico Moscardo, *Note overo memorie del Museo del Conte Lodovico Moscardo nobile veronese* (Verona, 1672), 235. Moscardo called them "ciurmatori, ò Zaratani." Achille Forti makes the interesting suggestion that the spelling of the last word indicated a kind of charlatan who came from Dalmatia into northern Italy so I have indicated this possibility in the translation. Forti, "Del drago," 30.

25. Conrad Gessner, *Historia animalium* (Tiguri, 1558), 4, 945.

26. Mario Cermenati, "Francesco Calzolari e le sue lettere all'Aldrovandi," *Annali di botanica* 7 (1908): 48 (Verona, 16 December 1571).

27. Ray, *Observations*, 27, 219.

28. BUB, *Aldrovandi*, ms. 136, Vol. 5, f. 179r. This episode is also discussed in Conor Fahy, *Printing a Book at Verona in 1622: The Account Book of Francesco Calzolari Junior* (Paris: Fondation Custodia, 1993), 20.

29. For more on this subject, see Pamela Smith's forthcoming book on artisans and science in early modern Europe.

30. Girolamo Cardano, *De rerum varietate*, in *Opera Omnia* (Leiden, 1663), Vol. 3, 342. Also discussed in Daston and Park, *Wonders*, 167.

31. Leonardo da Vinci, *The Notebooks of Leonardo da Vinci*, ed. Irma A. Richter (Oxford: Oxford University Press, 1952), 167. The original is in ms. A, f. 20r.

32. Colin Eisler, *Dürer's Animals* (Washington, D. C.: Smithsonian Institution Press, 1991), 311–312.

33. This formulation is found in Daston and Park, *Wonders*, 74, in their discussion of the medieval treasury. Since the treasury was the original location of many hydras and basilisks, it seems all the more fitting.

34. Conrad Gessner, *Nomenclator aquatilium animantium. Icones animalium* (Tiguri, 1560), 362–363. Compare with Conrad Lycosthenes, *Prodigorum ac ostentorum chronicon* (Basel, 1657 ed.), 538–539. For further discussion of the religious significance of the hydra, see *Mythical Beasts*, ed. John Cherry, (London: British Museum Press, 1995), 20, 35–36.

35. BUB, *Aldrovandi*, ms. 21, Vol. 4, c. 89v.

36. Ulisse Aldrovandi, *Serpentum et draconum historiae libro duo*, ed. Bartolomeo Ambrosini (Bologna, 1640), 387. See the second hydra, which is evidently the hydra of Ferrara: "Hydra septiceps Equitis de Corneto affectatoris olim Sereniss. Ducis Ferrariae."

37. Edward Topsell, *Historie of Four-Footed Beastes* (London, 1607), 202.

38. Skippon, *Account of a Journey*, 565. "Zennon" is probably Giacomo Zanoni, a well-known Bolognese apothecary whom many collectors visited in the mid-seventeenth century. See also John Evelyn's account of a fifteen-headed hydra in the Villa Ludovisi in Rome that he saw in 1645; (*The Diary of John Evelyn*, ed. E. S. de Beer [Oxford: Clarendon Press, 1996, 1951], Vol. 2, 391).

39. Pierre Belon, *L'histoire naturelle des estranges poissons* (Paris, 1551),18r. For a general discussion of fake animals, see E. W. Gudger, "Jenny Hanivers, Dragons and Basilisks in the Old Natural History Books and in Modern Times," *Scientific Monthly* 38 (June 1934): 511–523; Richard Carrington, *Mermaids and Mastodons: A Book of Natural and Unnatural History* (New York: Rinehart & Company, 1957); and Peter Dance, *Animal Fakes and Frauds* (Berkshire, UK: Sampson Low, 1976).

40. Gessner, *Historia animalium*, 945. Compare with Maximilian Misson, *Nouveau voyage d'Italie*, 5th ed. (La Haye, 1731), Vol. 1: 161–162.

41. See Daston and Park, *Wonders*; and Niccoli, *Prophecy*.

42. Carrington, *Mermaids and Mastodons*, 69–70. I have modified Carrington's translation of the passage in order to conform with other translations of "raia" as "ray."

43. Paré, *On Monsters and Marvels*, 109.

44. Cardano, *De rerum varietate*, 343.

45. Eisler, *Dürer's Animals*, 265, 321. An excellent example of a carved dragon can be found in the Museo degli Argenti in Florence, part of the Medicis' famous collection of worked objects.

46. Aldrovandi, *De piscibus*, 437, 443–444. I have wondered if the sea-eagle might not be Castelletti's bulging-eyed fish? The most detailed discussion of the sources of Aldrovandi's imagery can be found in Erminio Caprotti, *Mostri, draghi e serpenti nelle silografie dell'opera di Ulisse Aldrovandi e dei suoi contemporanei* (Milan: Gabriele Mazzotta, 1980).

47. For a classic description of the basilisk, see Lycosthenes, *Prodigorum*, 22; also Jacques Grevin, *De venenis libri duo* (Antwerp, 1571), ch. 18.

48. Aldrovandi, *Serpentum*, 364.

49. Pier Andrea Mattioli, *De i discorsi di M. Pietro Andrea Matthioli . . . Nelli sei libri di Pedacio Dioscoride Anazarbeo* (Venice, 1585 ed.), 1526–1527.

50. Joannes Jonstonius, *Historia naturalis de serpentibus libri II* (Amsterdam, 1657), 34.

51. Benedetto Ceruti and Andrea Chiocco, *Musaeum Franc[isci] Calceolarii Iun[ioris] Veronensis* (Verona, 1622), 90–91.

52. Moscardo, *Note*, 235.

53. Misson, *Nouveau voyage*, Vol. 1, 161.

54. Francisco Hernández, *Rerum medicarum novae hispaniae thesaurus seu plantarum animalium mineralium Mexicanorum Historia ex Francisci Hernandez*, ed. Johan Faber (Rome,

1649), 818. This text is discussed in greater detail in Silvia de Renzi, "Herodotus and the Microscope: Investigating Dragons in Seventeenth-Century Rome" (unpublished paper). I thank Dr. de Renzi for providing me with a copy.

55. Lorenzo Legati, *Museo Cospiano* (Bologna, 1677), 81.

56. Athanasius Kircher, *Mundus subterraneus* (Amsterdam, 1678), 103–108.

57. Filippo Bonanni, *Musaeum Kircherianum* (Rome, 1709), 270; Giorgio de Sepi, *Romani Collegii Societatis Jesu Musaeum Celeberrimum* (Amsterdam, 1678), 27. He concluded: "They are deformed rays and putative basilisks and, in the author's opinion, made by art and not by nature." There is no doubt that this opinion was also Kircher's, suggesting that he shared Aldrovandi's view of the distinctions between true dragons and false basilisks.

58. Antonio Vallisnieri, *Opere fisico-mediche* (Venice, 1733), Vol. 3, 370. Vallisnieri"s biographer C. Lodoli also discussed how he showed the basilisk to "reveal the monstrous deceptions perpetrated in other museums where much was made of miraculous works of nature such as basilisks, fabulous hydras, petrified bread and fungi and other similar nonsense." Ibid., Vol. 1, LVI. This latter passage is discussed in Krzysztof Pomian, *Collectors and Curiosities: Paris and Venice, 1500–1800*, trans. Elizabeth Wiles-Portier (London: Polity, 1990), 104.

59. Albert Seba, *Locupletissimi rerum naturalium thesauri accurata descriptio, et iconibus artificiosissimis expressio, per universam physices historiam* (Amsterdam, 1734), Vol. 1, table 102, 159.

60. Pomian, *Collectors*, 103. On the hydra of Hamburg, see Colin Clair, *Unnatural History: An Illustrated Bestiary* (London: Aberlard-Schuman, 1967), 211–212, 235; and Dance, *Animal Fakes*, 33–36. For an excellent introduction to Linnaeus, see Lisbet Koerner, *Linnaeus: Nature and Nation* (Cambridge, Mass.: Harvard University Press, 1999).

61. Samuel Butler's *Hudibras* recounts a less well-known story—a send-up of the whole cult of fictitious nature—about a dead rat that James Bobart found in the Oxford physick garden in the late seventeenth century and turned into a dragon to see who would believe him. Yet after he revealed the joke, the dragon remained in the cabinet of curiosities associated with the Oxford anatomy theater, "looked upon as a masterpiece of art." In Dance, *Animal Fakes*, 59.

Nature as Art

The Case of the Tulip

ANNE GOLDGAR

"When Homer sang in ancient times at Corinth, no one listened to his verses. In our own era in Paris, Poussin earned too little to live." These lines bewailing philistinism, published by Nicolas de Valnay in 1669, were written, rather surprisingly, in defense of the tulip. Valnay, contrôleur of Louis XIV's household and a member of a loose group of *curieux* devoted to flowers, expressed surprise at the preference some felt for other curiosities, such as paintings, medals, or porcelains. Look at such things as long as you like, he wrote, but you will always be looking at the same thing. Not so with the wonderful annual variety of flowers, of which the tulip was the queen. The beauties of painting, moreover, are all in design, execution, and color; but "I challenge the entire Académie de Peinture to imagine flowers better than natural ones, to execute them in complete perfection, or ever to approach the colors of Flowers." If you own a painting, you will always have only one, but bulbs have the advantage of multiplying themselves. The consequence of this (although Valnay did not put it this way) is social: you can give a rare flower to a friend and yet still keep the same thing, not a copy, for yourself. These arguments against painting, Valnay said, could also be made against medals, porcelains, and other fashionable rarities: "when reason is combined with taste, beautiful flowers will hold the first rank among the pleasures of sight."[1]

Valnay's view that the times were too "blind and insipid" for flowers like tulips—that they suffered from the poor taste of the public, as painting and poetry had also sometimes suffered—is something of an exaggeration.[2] Although the tulip would not find again such passionate advocacy as it did in the period leading up to the tulipmania of 1634–37, it enjoyed a healthy popularity, particularly among a circle of professional men, merchants, and gentry, both in France and in equivalent social groups in other European countries such as the Netherlands, England, Italy, and the German states. But what is interesting in Valnay is not chiefly the strength of his views, views expressed by other enthusiasts over the years, such as Crispijn van de Passe in the Netherlands, Jean Franeau in Flanders, Sir Thomas Hanmer in England, or the Sieur de La Chesnée Monstereul in France. The interest lies rather in Valnay's treatment of tulips as works of art. This essay will explore the complex of ideas and attitudes that allowed such a comparison, and, further, the social consequences that sprang from making it.

Grappling with the relationship between art and nature was hardly new in the seventeenth century. As Lorraine Daston and Katharine Park have delineated in a richly suggestive chapter of their *Wonders and the Order of Nature*, the opposition between the forces of nature and art was an ancient paradigm, still crucial in the seventeenth century even as natural philosophy began first to break it down and then to change its terms.[3] From the days of Zeuxis and Parrhasius, artists have made a strong case for the superiority of their craft to the creative powers of nature.[4] With the strengthening view in the Renaissance that the artist's *ingegno* was akin to that of the creating God, the view of art as surpassing nature became ever more influential.[5] Early modern comments about floral still life make this clear. Painters of flowers were considered to improve on nature if they were talented at depicting texture, and, as Paul Taylor has pointed out, the desire to idealize the flowers in paint and thus perfect imperfect nature was a powerful impulse for artists.[6] Thus the triumphs of Zeuxian grapes were brought up to date with verses praising Daniel Seghers' painted roses. According to Huygens in 1645, "Nature as judge, conceded defeat in the contest:/The painted flower rendered the real one a shadow."[7]

But art had not quite won this battle with nature, and Seghers could prove just as potent an argument for the other side. Proponents of the glories of flowers, for example, also cited Seghers, but now to stress his supposed inability to do justice to them in paint. Flower breeders John Rea and his son-in-law Samuel Gilbert favored real tulips over their portrayal by "Pater Zegers, a Jesuite in *Antwerp*, famous for painting flowers," Rea commenting of a tulip called the Agate Hanmer, "Her Native Beauties shaming Art, / Once did that famous Jesuite try / To copy out her Majesty; But falling short of his desire, / He left his Pencil to admire."[8] Despite artists' tradition of challenging God and nature with their *ingegno*, in the seventeenth century some voices, including, naturally enough, those of various botanists and gardeners, continued to maintain that art could do nothing to imitate the beauties and wonders of some natural objects.

The traditional division represented here, seen in the usual classification of collections into *naturalia* and *artificialia*, was precisely one that the later sixteenth and seventeenth centuries delighted in undermining.[9] There was a pleasure in blurring the boundaries between art and nature, to be seen in artificial objects resembling natural ones, such as Palissy's ceramics or the mechanical rainbows and songbirds to be found in the Villa Aldobrandini at Frascati.[10] More important for our purposes are the many natural objects in collections turned half into *artificialia* by gilding, etching, carving, or artistic arrangement. Coconuts, ostrich eggs, or rhinoceros horns transformed into reliquaries; nautilus shells etched and gilded into luxurious beakers; reindeer antlers fashioned into candelabra: all testified to the desire of artists and collectors to intertwine nature with art.[11]

A coconut carved with a biblical scene or a nautilus cup engraved with the image of other shells and sea creatures not only illuminates the status of objects that are half art and half nature. Such objects also demonstrate to us a desire for art to conquer nature. A nautilus shell itself was sometimes not enough; the hand of man had to alter it and beautify it as well. These attitudes have been elaborated in recent work on the *Kunstkammer* and its objects. What has not so far been examined by scholars, however, is a further step along this path. Man could impress himself upon natural objects by gilding, etching, and engraving; but there were also objects that, although remaining entirely natural, yet were evisaged as art. The tulip is one such object, fascinating and enigmatic precisely because of this special mixture of art and nature. What, then, did it mean for Valnay to place it in the same category as a painting or a piece of porcelain?

Even in 1669, when Valnay was writing, tulips remained exotic items. They had arrived in Europe in the mid-sixteenth century, either through seeds sent home by the imperial envoy Ogier Ghislain de Busbecq, as most sources recount, or, possibly, through trade between Turkey and Italy, France, and the Low Countries. The first tulip in Europe was described by Conrad Gessner in *De Hortis Germaniae* (1561) as growing in 1559 in the garden of Johann Heinrich Herwart in Augsburg. By the late sixteenth century, botanists and collectors had developed a passion for tulips. Such collectors included both professional men with an interest in plants, particularly doctors and apothecaries, as well as a variety of elite groups ranging from merchants to aristocrats. The special excitement generated by tulips stemmed first from their foreign nature; they were prized along with the other exotic bulbs that arrived in Europe, largely from the Ottoman Empire, in the same period, including flowers such as the iris, crocus, and hyacinth.

But tulips were particularly valued because of their unpredictable and exciting capacities for variation. Unlike most other flowers, tulips could change from year to year in coloration and form, and the propagation of tulips could present new forms never before seen. Already in 1597 Gerard's *Herball* reported that to recount all the different sorts of tulips "would trouble the writer and weary the Reader," and by the time of Rea's *Flora* of 1665 we hear that "so numerous are the varieties, that it is not possible that any one person in the world should be able to express, or comprehend the half of them."[12] These qualities led to high prices for many tulips and, eventually, to a futures trade in the Netherlands. But even in countries unaffected by the futures trade, the tulip remained a favorite flower until it was eclipsed by the hyacinth in the eighteenth century.

Given the reigning issues about art and nature, the question of the authorship of tulip varieties was a live one in the period. Who or what actually created the tulip? Many works on gardening alluded to tulips, and to flowers in general, as small but perfect works of God, or of both God and nature. For Petrus Hondius, whose poem *Dapes Inemptae, of de Moufe-schans* (1614) praised the garden of his patrons in Neuzen, gardening was a way of honoring the name of God and his creation.[13] Similarly, Jean Franeau, extolling the gardens of the gentry and aristocracy of the Southern Netherlands, compared a flower to a school or a beautiful book of which "the author is this great God, who, as a schoolmaster, teaches the lessons in his own words."[14] But these protestations address a countervailing trend which we have already seen in the field of painting or sculpture: the desire of man to claim credit for himself. The commercial breeder Samuel Gilbert, acknowledging in 1682 that man can play a role in gardening, hedged his bets in a verse mainly devoted to the planning, shaping, and protection he would give to a garden:

Assisting Nature by industrious Art;
To perfect every Plant in every part,
But not like some, whose crimes to rise so high
Boldly to pull down Heavens Deity.[15]

Gilbert's concern that an emphasis on man deprives God of his rightful place speaks to the questions raised by those who believed that man could, indeed, "assist nature."[16]

The actual assistance man could provide was minimal, but this relative powerlessness was not acknowledged by contemporaries. We have seen that it was the variety of tulips that made them so popular. This variety was achieved either by cross-breeding or by "breaking" tulips through an aphid-borne virus. Neither process was known in the early modern period. Gardeners had no knowledge of the sexuality of plants, so that any crosses which occurred would have to take place by accident; and although there was some speculation that beautiful tulips were diseased—"in the same way that a person in agony turns different colors when through a contagious malady he approaches death," wrote a derisive La Chesnée Monstereul in 1654—this was neither universally accepted nor understood.[17] Yet long experimentation had assured some botanists and gardeners that, if they were grown from seed rather than bulbs, certain tulips were more liable to vary in color, although such variation could take up to ten years. Jacques Garret, a Dutch apothecary living in London, was described by John Gerard as having "undertaken to finde out if it were possible, the infinite sorts by diligent sowing of their seedes, and by planting those of his owne propagation, and by others received from his friends beyond the seas, for the space of twentie yeeres, not being yet able to attaine to the end of his travaile, for that each new yeere bringeth foorth new plants of sundrie colors not before seene."[18] Later annotators of Dodonaeus's *Cruydt-Boeck* noted in 1618 that sowing seeds was an uncertain business, and that in any case tulips could get worse as well as better;[19] but the very fact that sowing seeds could produce new tulip strains produced a confidence that man could indeed use his art on the natural tulip.

Not surprisingly, much of the writing on the alteration of tulips focused on the choice of seed. If gardeners could not actually predict the outcome of sowing seed, at least they could try their art in choosing only the seed of superior tulips, and by culling bulbs of flowers that did not meet their standards. The eighteenth-century diary of the Lancashire gardening enthusiast Nicholas Blundell is full of notations such as "I Examain'd my Tulops and marked some of the best of them to be preserved & the worst to be destroyed."[20] But the idea that man could control nature went further than this. The aesthetic and commercial value of tulips, as well as the tedium of taking ten years to grow them from seed—described by the Haarlem breeder Nicolas van Kampen as "unpleasant" and "useless"[21]—led early on to more direct attempts to intervene by art into the processes of nature.

Some of these promised shortcuts to beautiful flowers, it is true, remained close to natural processes. The theory that tulips changed color through disease led to experiments in weakening flowers so that they would fall sick more easily. John Rea suggested in 1665, for example, that "more vulgar" tulips might be dug up just before flowering and laid in the sun "to abate their luxury, and cause them to come better marked the year following"; a yearly alternation of good and poor soil was thought to have the same effect.[22] Rea assured the aspirant gardener that such methods would produce tulips that "might be taken for much better flowers than they are, especially if a new name be put upon them, as some flower-merchants about *London* use to do."[23]

Other procedures to alter tulips, however, were much more self-consciously a form of art. Like an engraver carving designs on a nautilus shell, gardeners set about by intrusion to change their flowers. It was said that cutting two bulbs in half and sticking them together would produce a cross-breed; that new varieties of tulip with exotic colors could be bred by steeping the bulbs or seeds in colored water, ink, paint, or even "mixing a number of

Anne Goldgar

ingredients with pigeon dung" and burning the ground with it.[24] Many of our accounts of such interventions come, it is true, from those casting aspersions on these methods; John Evelyn, for example, warns us to "trust little by mangonisme, insuccations, or medecine, to alter the species, or indeed the forms and shapes of flowers considerably," and John Parkinson dismisses as "meere tales and fables . . . the many rules and directions extant in manie mens writings to cause flowers to grow yellow, red, greene or white, that never were so naturally. . . . [W]hen they come to the triall, they all vanish away like smoak."[25] Comments of this sort indicate, however, the prevalence of such views; and contemporary gardening books, such as Giovanni Battista Ferrari's *Flora, seu de florum cultura* of 1633, took such advice seriously.[26] Moreover, even those ridiculing these methods did not necessarily believe that there was no art to changing the appearance of tulips. La Chesnée Monstereul, who took time to ridicule the Rouennais who burned up his entire garden with a fire made with pigeon dung, affirmed flatly that, although this particular method was laughable, efficacious means of producing new tulips did exist. "It only remains for me to discuss whether by Art one can embellish those which have not yet attained their peak of perfection. . . . I have no difficulty in saying that one can, and that without doubt by Art they can be rendered capable of changing into something better."[27]

Not only did gardeners, then, give their endorsement to the idea that man's art could triumph over the processes of nature, but they consciously conceived of what they were doing in these terms. La Chesnée Monstereul's discussion of the transformation of tulips plunges straight into the topic. "There is no doubt that it is not only in this point that Art surpasses nature, of which we can see the effects, but in many other things which [Nature] begins, & which Men complete & perfect through their industry."[28] Florists and gardeners, according to other writers, "know how to aid nature by an artifice which industry and time has taught them"; flowers are "natures Choicest dishes, advantag'd by Art."[29] These gardeners were not mere spectators to the wonders of nature, but active participants in changing it, for, as Jan van der Groen wrote of gardens in 1669, "nature can, through art, be shifted, decorated, put into good order, and made ornamental and pleasurable."[30]

Thus even those pleading, as Samuel Gilbert did with such concern, that flowers were the work of God had to admit that, ultimately, "our Art, with Madam Nature joyn[s]."[31] But the power to control nature—a power of which tulips were, ironically, a poorer example than industry or agriculture—was not the end of the construction of tulips as artifacts. The language used by gardening writers and the names given to tulips by growers show a distinct mental association between the flowers and both art and craft. In floral still life, it was said that the technically gifted made roses look like silk and tulips like leather,[32] but the same kind of comparisons were applied not only to paintings but to the flowers themselves.

The trope that tulips outdid the work of any painter—"it is impossible for painters and dyers to imitate the colors of them"[33]—demonstrates a cognitive link between the flowers and the art of painting. But the mention of "dyers" in this same passage from a 1697 gardening treatise points us toward the wider associations of tulips in the period. There were constant references to the flowers as part of a wider world of man-made luxury objects. That both paintings and other *artificialia* should provide comparisons with tulips is perhaps not surprising, since painting had such strong connections with craft and with craft guilds, in the Netherlands at least. In the chief towns of Holland, painters and sculptors were members of the same guild as craftsmen such as embroiderers, glassworkers, and goldsmiths. Although painters increasingly came to emphasize the dignity of their profession, they did not seek in this period to emancipate themselves from the structure of a craft guild; indeed one artist who also was involved in the tulip trade, Frans Pietersz. de Grebber, was reported to "get by nicely on embroidery" when his skills as a portraitist were not in demand.[34] Given both the rarity and the price of tulips, however, a more important explanation for their linkage with costly crafts is surely the role of the luxury trades in the maintenance of status. Like visible material wealth, tulips were precious and costly collector's items. The close associations of tulips and luxury are evident; the names and descriptions of tulips remind us continually of a shiny, varied, patterned world of cloth, enamel work, and polished stone.

Cloth, carpets, and embroidery are among the earliest images applied to tulips and the gardens containing them. Gardens decorated with a variety of colors reminded viewers of a tapestry or carpet; Marie de Brimeu, Princesse de Chimay and a friend of Clusius', referred in 1591 to the garden he had stocked for her with plants sent from Frankfurt as "the riches of your tapestries [which] truly surpass by far those of gold & silk, as nature surpasses artifice."[35] John Parkinson was still musing in 1629 on such comparisons, and on the possibilities for garden design using tulips. "[A]bove and beyond all others, the Tulipas may be so matched, one colour answering and setting of another, that the place where they stand may resemble a peece of curious needle-worke, or peece of painting."[36] That this was not merely a metaphor is evident from the *Iardin du Roy Tres Chrestien Henry IV* of 1608, a collection of engravings of plants in the king's gardens. The author, Vallet, far from being a gardener, was a professional embroiderer, and the accompanying verses in praise of the book make much of his abilities with the needle. His designs were evidently intended at least in part as patterns for embroidery.[37]

Not only whole flower beds, but also individual tulips called to mind the luxury of elegant cloth. Clusius, in first describing his tulips in his *Rariorum plantarum historia*, resorted repeatedly to images of silk shimmering with two colors, such as a silk with a golden warp and a red weft, or a silver silk, made in the same way and known to the Germans as Silberfarb.[38] Such images quickly appeared in the vernacular. Among the earliest names to be given to tulips (the first flowers of which individual cultivars were named) were "Goude Laeckens" and "Silver Laeckens," gold cloth and silver cloth, appearing in other countries as "drap d'or" and "drap d'argent" and as "Cloth of golde" and "Cloth of sylver."[39] Other names referring to cloth included "Saey-blom" (say-flower). While says were not the most elegant of cloths, the economy of Holland depended on them; and the other materials could not have been more redolent of luxury. No cloth was more expensive or prized than silk embroidered or shot with gold or silver thread—silver tissue was the standard material of bridal gowns at the European courts[40]— and silk and satin clothing was similarly confined to the elite.[41] Like embroidery, which bespoke an ability to pay for goods whose manufacture was highly labor-intensive, clothing or furnishings made of costly materials were effective signals of leisure and high station. Fine textiles, because they demonstrated marvelous workmanship, were also commonly to be found in collections and *Kunstkammern*.[42]

It was natural for an expensive flower like the tulip to be compared with such goods, but, as Clusius's more specific descriptions indicate, it was not an idle comparison. The petals of the tulip were also thought actually to resemble silk, satin, or velvet. One Dutch gardening book recommends matter-of-factly that a good source of seed for the best tulips was a flower that was "Satijn-agtig" (satinlike),[43] and in the more florid prose of works dedicated to praising the tulip, references to elegant cloth abound. To take only one example, Jean Franeau's 1616 ode to the tulip, the *Iardin d'Hyver ou Cabinet des Fleurs*, intended to remind the growers and collectors of the aristocracy and gentry in the Southern Netherlands of their treasures during the winter months, is liberally peppered with references to embroidery, silk, taffeta, silver cloth, and silver needlework. Tulips were "dressed" in rich "mantles" which, far from being natural, were "full of artifice." The tulip called the Duc van Tholl was said to be the work of a skilled tailor: clothing worthy of a great prince or duke, so richly was it embroidered in gold. This was the work of nature, Franeau wrote, but also of "les grans," who cultivated tulips in their gardens.[44]

The luster of tulips, if it did not come from shiny satin or silk, was also said in many texts to be enamel work or vermeil, a metaphor that was mixed happily with the many references to clothing.[45] But the other favorite comparison for the tulip, with its veined and streaky markings, was polished stone such as marble and agate. Again, the names of tulips give us a hint of how they were perceived. A common designation in the Netherlands was *ghemarmerde*, marbled, and names such as Ghemarmerde de Goyer or Ghemarmerde Liefkens became usual. In French, tulips were "marbrées" or "jaspées," and whole classifications of tulips based on this comparison grew up. Besides the Morillons, or rough emeralds, a major class of French tulips (which was adopted also in English nomenclature) was the Agate. By mid-century there was an abundance of names such as Agate Morin, Agate Guerin, or Agate Picot, generally adding the name of the cultivator to the designation of Agate; La Chesnée Monstereul mentioned fifty-five Agate tulips in his list of 1654.[46] John Rea gives us a good picture of the association of the two objects; tulip petals, "warmed by the Sun, open and change into divers several glorious colours, variously mixed, edged, striped, feathered, garded, agotted, marbled, flaked, or specled, even to admiration."[47] Like tulips, stones such as agates and marbles were prized for their variation in color and their attractive veining. Polished and worked, they formed an ornament to buildings, were transformed into *pietra dura* furniture, or formed objects for the *Kunstkammer* or cabinet. We find special collections of agates in the period, such as that belonging to the goldsmith Antoine Agard of Arles, not to mention the agates and marbles in the cabinets of tulip lovers such as Christiaan Porret in Leiden or Bernardus Paludanus in Enkhuizen.[48]

The designation of tulips as *ghemarmerde*, *marbré*, or "marbled"— phrased as though they had actually undergone a process—raises, moreover, the possibility that the connection was actually with marbled paper rather than marble itself. Paper with the swirling patterns of marble had arrived in Europe around the same time as the tulip and from the same country of origin, and, like tulips, it became associated with the Dutch in the seventeenth century. Like real agates, marbled paper was valued by collectors and can be found in collections, such as that of Paludanus; Pierre de l'Estoile records instances in 1608–09 of giving a fellow Parisian collector sheets of marbled paper because "I know he is a collector like myself."[49] The resemblance between the paper and stone was remarked upon early, and one of the oldest patterns was known, like the tulip, as Agate.[50] Interestingly, Evelyn uses the word "Pennaches (as the French call it)" to describe the paper's design;[51] *panache* was the usual word for the similar patterns on tulip petals, with a broken tulip being known as *panachée*. Most suggestively, Anna Maria von Heusenstain, who frequently wrote Clusius from Vienna asking for flowers, reported in 1591 that a tulip she still lacked was called "Turkish paper" ("das tirckisch papir").[52] Although we cannot be conclusive about the connections between marbled paper and tulips, it is clear, at least, that all these objects— flower, paper, and stone—occupied a similar space of aesthetic appreciation and social and intellectual exchange.

The praise of the tulip, indeed, is reminiscent of the kind of aesthetic discussion we find about paintings in the same period. Although the Dutch

Anne Goldgar

were, as Seymour Slive has put it, "unusually inarticulate" about their art in the seventeenth century,[53] with only a handful of critical writings to help us enter the minds of artists, the same sorts of words to describe beauty (*aerdigh, fraey, schoon*) and the same values of harmony of form and clear, bright colors were applied both by a writer on painting like Karel van Mander in 1604 and commentators on the beauty of tulips.[54] Both annotations to Dodonaeus' chapter on tulips and Karel van Mander on paintings, for example, spoke of *netticheyt*, the engagement of the eye, in the case of painting in a smooth rendering of surface; the tulip was said to be "much honored in all lands for the *netticheyt* of its petals."[55] But perhaps the most important aesthetic comment common both to tulips and art was the value of *verscheydenheydt*: variety. The excitement of diversity dated back at least to Pliny,[56] and formed an important principle for a range of arts in the Renaissance, from painting to music to literature.[57] For Karel van Mander it was a crucial concept; art should found itself on nature, and "nature is beautiful through variety," both the variety of colors and of forms and attitudes.[58] He compared a painting with a field of flowers which draws the eye, like the honeybee, to dart from one point to another, eager not to miss any of the sweetness.[59] And as we have already seen, it was the variation of tulips, from year to year, from mother bulb to offset, from bloom to bloom, which made tulips so much more compelling than other flowers: "the more various, the more beautiful."[60] Again, the appreciation of tulips falls within the same aesthetic universe as the appreciation of art.

While these similarities might be put down to the paucity of critical language available to commentators, the very fact that a critical vocabulary was being applied to tulips at all demonstrates another facet of their relationship to works of art. In a period when critical discussion and connoisseurship of painting among laymen was becoming more common, alongside the rise of the virtuoso collector of *artificialia*, we also find an increasing application of specific standards to tulips.[61] Whereas in the late sixteenth and early seventeenth century writers were relatively undiscriminating about tulips, finding all a source of wonder, it did not take long for writers and enthusiasts to develop a hierarchy of varieties and a set of characteristics of a good flower. In a typical case, Peiresc complained in 1626 of seven or eight boxes of tulips he had received from his brother's estate: "I found none which were perfect of their sort. The *drap d'or* and *drap* or *toille d'argent* had so much red in them that the rest seemed nothing of any worth."[62] In guides for gardeners, some of whom might not know "either what to choose, or what to desire," as Parkinson put it, we find descriptions of the best tulips; La Chesnée Monstereul provided a chapter with the title "What the Tulip must be, both in its Colors, Panaches, and in its Form," and similarly Valnay and Van Kampen each spent some pages outlining such qualities.[63] Valnay instructed his readers that the most beautiful tulips were the "bigeares" (stripes of brown, red, violet, or other colors on a yellow background), the more nuanced the better, and the stripes or panaches had to be distinct; the colors should be as far from red as possible, although "red ones on a white ground are not to be rejected." He defined the proper form of the flower, a description of the best color for the base, and the appropriate size and color of the stamens.[64] Some of these standards might be thought to be fixed, as they resulted from observation of the best traits for breeding. Since the purpose of breeding was beauty, however, the apparent "science" of such definitions in fact demonstrates how the changing vision of floral excellence was an arbitrary matter of aesthetics. And that the standards changed over time links tulips not only to painting but also back to clothing and fashion. Rea, in 1665, remarked that the flowers described by Parkinson in 1629 had "by Time grown stale, and for Unworthiness turned out of every good Garden"; the popular flowers in his day, tellingly, were known as Modes.[65] But for a certain core of tulip lovers whom we can consider the connoisseurs, the standards hardened into what would ultimately be called "florists' flowers," with the specific requirements for shape, texture, color, and markings enforced by the development of flower shows in the eighteenth and nineteenth centuries.[66]

That the resemblance of tulips to art could extend to connoisseurship has important implications. As we have seen, the idea that art and nature were potentially oppositional is something of a cliché. So, indeed, is the suggestion that the line between these two could become blurred in the early modern period. Scholars who have written on these subjects have also approached them by commenting on artistic objects that look like nature (Palissy's ceramics) or natural objects that look like art (figured stones with apparent landscapes or animals in their markings). But with tulips, as I have argued, the tulip itself is objectified. Although the tulip resembled works of art, it did not have to, since it was in fact art itself, an item that, it was thought, could be created in its entirety by man. Moreover, once made, the tulip was the subject of criticism and discussion. Thus not only was the tulip a real art form, but it was an art that had further ramifications. The tulip as art promoted sociability.

From the beginning, the increasing interest in exotic flowers, of which tulips were the chief, fit into existing exchange relationships and engendered new ones. Dodonaeus made it clear in his *Cruydt-Boeck* that in the Low Countries the tulip was "only to be found in the gardens of the connoisseurs [*liefhebbers*],"[67] and it is evident that many of these connoisseurs knew each other and exchanged flowers. The botanist Carolus Clusius is an obvious example; his correspondence includes much evidence of the trading of bulbs and seeds, even with people he had never met.[68] Less professional plantlovers, such as Petrus Hondius, also clearly were involved both in the breeding of tulips and their exchange, and similar relationships are also obvious among collectors in other countries. Peiresc, for example, reported sending tulips to Antelmy, *conseiller* at the Parlement at Aix; Sir Thomas Hanmer's correspondence shows him sending "rootes" to friends such as John Evelyn and the parliamentary general Lord Lambert; while the anonymous accounts of an English garden from 1638–39 included both bulbs sold by the owner to "M[rs] Rous" and a large number exchanged with a "M[r] Blackley" and a "M[r] La candle": "Amanicis de Pari for Olivandesburge/Generall Gouda for Noris morilio[n]/Satanee for Gulamp van Rhine/M[r] Jullien for Semp[er] Londinu[s]."[69] Such relationships could become institutionalized in clubs such as the Society of Florists of Norwich, known to have existed since at least 1631, when Ralph Knevet's play *Rhodron and Iris: A Pastorall* was presented at their feast on the third of May.[70] Such florists were not professional growers—the word came to that meaning only later—but rather were lovers of flowers who grew them for their beauty rather than any usefulness.[71]

Whether or not tulip lovers were involved in formal societies, tulips became a route of sociability for them. Because of their bulbs, John Rea wrote in 1665, tulips could be regarded as "transferable favours from one *Florist* to another, aptly conveyable (the seasons considered) many miles distant."[72] The fellow feeling that was engendered by these exchange relationships was an important part of the interest in tulips. La Chesnée Monstereul devoted a chapter of his treatise on the flowers to pleading that tulips should not be allowed into the hands of the many. "If Tulips were made common, that would remove the most praiseworthy interaction to be found among Men, & would deprive them of the most sweet society which has ever existed among *gens d'honneur*. How much company does their rarity give to curious wits? how many agreeable visits? how many sweet conversations? & how many well-founded discussions? Certainly this is the sweetest life in the world."[73] Such interchange could be the foundation both of society and of a good collection, so that the anonymous Valnay could write of himself that "through purchases, exchanges, and accommodations, the principal stock of the only beautiful Tulips are at present in the hands of M. de Valnay" and two other persons, all officers at the Louis XIV's court.[74] In his pursuit of the tulip, someone like Valnay, breeder and *curieux*, was both artist and collector.

Valnay listed only a few *curieux* and breeders in Paris who had experimented on tulips, attempting to get more beautiful varieties as they studied each other's productions. But the best flowers remained rare, and, according to his account, one seventeenth-century collector, Lombard, who had the best stock, would not exchange or sell any of his bulbs or seed, "which increased the desire [for them] and the price."[75] La Chesnée Monstereul's argument that tulips should remain confined to a few is important to the status of these flowers as collectibles or as art. The sociability of connoisseurship is based on expertise about the rare and costly; if everyone could comment, or everyone could own these objects, there would be no point to the connoisseurship. Thus although he declared that it was possible to change tulips by art—in his case, essentially alchemy—he would not reveal the formula. "I do not want the secrets of Divinity to be known other than by Sages, so that they are not profaned by the vulgar; it being a certain thing, that according to the sentiment of the learned [Roger] Bacon, he who reveals the Mystical diminishes & reduces its majesty." He provided a mysterious and cryptic recipe, saying "those who have eyes & ears will see & hear"; no one without the requisite learning would be able to understand his formula and thus join the exalted company of the artists and the connoisseurs.[76]

But the similarity between tulip lovers and collectors of art and curiosities does not end with the behaviors of connoisseurship and exchange. In many cases, these groups did not simply resemble each other, but were actually the same. Tulip buyers were themselves collectors of art. Pierre Morin, one of the great professional florists of the first half of the century, was also "one of the most intelligent men in the world in all these rarities," including objects of art as well as shells, butterflies, and other *naturalia*.[77] But ordinary buyers of bulbs, or owners of a few tulips, prove on investigation to have been active in the purchase of artworks. A comparison of the names of tulip buyers in Amsterdam up to 1640 with those known to have bought art at auction suggests that, in Amsterdam at least,[78] among the main groups to take an interest in tulips in the period were members of overlapping networks of art collectors. The merchant Abraham de Casteleyn, for example, was involved in both breeding and purchasing tulips, but also bought art at auction and was a considerable collector of *naturalia* and *artificialia*. At his death in 1644 he left not only his cabinet of curiosities, but a carefully arranged collection of tulip bulbs whose inventory ran to thirty-nine pages.[79] Similarly, men such as Lambert Massa, Adam Bessels, Jacob Abrahamsz. van Halmael, and Jan Hendricksz. Admirael, who were mainly merchants, purchased paintings and prints at auction and even (in the case of Massa and Bessels) were connected to important families of art patrons, but were also involved in the purchase of tulip bulbs.[80] These are only some of the examples of the crossover between tulip and art collectors in Amsterdam in the first part of the seventeenth century.

The fact that many of these transactions took place during the financial craze of 1634–37 of course raises questions about the role of commerce in this relationship between tulips and art. It is hard to determine exactly why people bought tulips, even if they were collectors of art; and of course there is a commercial element even to collecting, however much the values of exchange and civility also entered into it. For tulips or for paintings, the question remains whether the reason for purchase was decoration, collecting, or profit.[81] The remark of Valnay's cited above, pointing to the increased desirability of rare tulips in Paris precisely *because* they were rare, reminds us that commerce was a factor in the love of "artistic" tulips from the beginning. Clusius, involved in exchange relationships with botanists, apothecaries, and scholars across Europe, disapproved of the commercial activities of the "rhizotomi" (root cutters), his name for the (mainly French) traveling sellers of bulbs and exotic plants, at the same time as he made purchases from them. One of his arguments was that of connoisseurship. Whereas he had always maintained a garden to supply his friends, now, in 1594, "merchants, even tailors and shoemakers and other petty people are involved, through the hope of profit. For they see that rich people will sometimes give out handfuls of money to buy some plant or other which is sought because of its rarity, so that they can preen themselves in front of their friends because they own it."[82] The implication is that exchange, not purchase, is the proper way to obtain bulbs, and that those appropriate to own such bulbs should remain select. But it is evident that, well before the speculative craze of the 1630s, beauty was in the eye of the purchaser. Commentators on Dodonaeus wrote in 1618: "In this country men love most the flamed, winged, speckled, jagged, or snipped and the most strongly variegated: and they will pay the most, not for the most beautiful or the finest, but for the rarest to be found, or those owned by only one master; these can fetch high prices."[83] And Rea's remarks in 1665, quoted above, that alternating soil can make "vulgar" tulips appear "better flowers than they are, especially if a new name be put on them," reminded the reader of a commercial advantage to the application of art.[84]

These comments point us both to the tulipmania of the 1630s and beyond. As trade in tulips heated up, some buyers, at least, wanted whatever would command the highest price. The fact that by this time some tulips were sold as futures and could change hands several times before they came to flower makes it plain that at this juncture tulips were valued by some only for their profitability. But the emphasis of the *Cruydt-Boeck* on beautiful features as well as on the price that rarity brings reminds us that beauty and profit can go hand in hand. After the crash in February 1637, tulips continued to be a favorite flower and continued to command good prices. Indeed, the consolidation of the bulb-growing industry around Haarlem dates from the period after 1637, with dynasties of commercial growers settling into what until then had been sometimes a temporary or part-time occupation. The scion of one such dynasty, George Voorhelm, was in 1752 still making arguments from connoisseurship to justify his high prices for hyacinths, by then the flower of mode.

> Is not a unique Hyacinth, which twenty or thirty people have been trying in vain to cultivate, a wonderful thing? Should not he who possesses it be

pleased with himself? Is it not very satisfying to be able to say: there are several people in my town who have magnificent Diamonds, but no one in the world who has a flower as beautiful as mine? Does not such a Flower have a real value? Is one not obliged to make more of it than of a thousand other Flowers? Could one be such an idiot as to offer it for nothing? . . . Why should one make a fuss if it is sold for a thousand Florins?[85]

Rarity, beauty, and profit thus go together; what is rare is beautiful, and what is beautiful is profitable. This is the reason for the constant changes in the fashion of flowers, for once a particular tulip is cultivated too widely, it becomes "obsolete and overdated" and must be replaced by others now claimed to be more beautiful.[86] The ultimate result, for the tulip, was the rise of the hyacinth.

The rhetoric of florists thus has considerable resonance for the commercial world. If supplies were too great, then tulips would lose their value; tulips must therefore not become common. New techniques had to be tried, and new flowers grown, if tulips were to remain profitable for those investing their time and money. As in a craft guild, the "mysteries" of the craft had to be protected, although, ironically, of course, in this case there was no proven art of creating new tulips. Such techniques as were developed were aimed to cut the cost and labor involved in production; to turn out new varieties, breeders did not want to have to wait eight or ten years to see the uncertain results of their culled seed. The interest in tulips, their praise, their production, thus all owed at least some of their impetus to commerce. But, as students of the art market have noted, such arguments can apply equally well to painting.[87]

Nicolas de Valnay, by arguing that tulips were superior to other works of art, chose to situate the flower in the milieu of aesthetics, artistic creation, collecting, and connoisseurship. In the long-standing argument over the superiority of art or nature, he chose nature; but this nature, for him and his colleagues, in fact *was* art. The apparent creation of their artwork, their knowledge of it, their criticism, all, Valnay would say, gave them rights to challenge the Académie de Peinture. And, as the comparison with the academy suggests, there were social ramifications for this identification of nature with art. Connoisseurship and collecting established social networks, to be institutionalized ultimately in florists' societies and flower shows. The commercial craze for tulips in the 1630s, with its concentration solely on profit, is *something of a diversion from these trends*, but not entirely. For tulips, as for other collectibles, commerce was always a part of the equation. La Chesnée Monstereul might protest that "well bred spirits have beauty rather than mercenary advantage as their object,"[88] but with tulips so expensive, the line between beauty and profit could blur. Perhaps Paul Contant, apothecary of

Poitiers, was more honest with himself. His cabinet and his garden were open to visitors; but he charged them admission.[89]

Notes

I would like to express my thanks to the National Endowment for the Humanities for supporting my work on collecting. I am grateful for the advice and suggestions of the editors, Paula Findlen and Pamela Smith, and of Carrie Alyea, Bertrand Goldgar, Doug Hildebrecht, Elizabeth Honig, Jennifer Kilian, Machteld Löwensteyn, Susan Merriam, Stephanie Schrader, and Betsy Wieseman. I would also like to thank Michael Montias for allowing me to compare the Montias/RKD Databank of art auctions in Amsterdam 1600–40 with my archival materials on tulip sales.

1. [Nicolas de Valnay], *Connoissance et culture parfaite des tulippes rares, des anemones extraordinaires, des oeillets fins, et des belles oreilles d'ours panachées* (Paris: Laurent d'Houry, 1688; first published 1669), "Avertissement." The book is attributed to Valnay by E. H. Krelage, *Drie Eeuwen Bloembollenexport* (The Hague: Rijksuitgeverij, 1946), 538, and Antoine Schnapper, *Le Géant, la licorne, la tulipe: Collections et collectionneurs dans la France du XVIIe siècle* (Paris: Flammarion, 1988), 44.

2. [Valnay], *Connoissance et culture parfaite*, "Avertissement."

3. Lorraine Daston and Katharine Park, *Wonders and the Order of Nature 1150–1750* (New York: Zone Books, 1998), chap. 7.

4. For Zeuxis, see Pliny, *Natural History* xxxv. xxxvi. 64–66.

5. These views are much discussed in the literature, but see, among others, Erwin Panofsky, *Idea: A Concept in Art Theory* trans. Joseph J. S. Peake (New York: Harper & Row, 1968, first published 1924), 48; Ernst Kantorowicz, "The Sovereignty of the Artist: A Note on Legal Maxims and Renaissance Theories of Art," in *De Artibus Opuscula XL: Essays in Honor of Erwin Panofsky*, ed. Milliard Meiss (New York: NYU Press, 1961) I, 268, 271; Joy Kenseth, "The Age of the Marvelous: An Introduction," in *The Age of the Marvelous*, ed. Joy Kenseth (ex. cat. Hood Museum of Art, Dartmouth College, 1991), 38; Walter Melion, *Shaping the Netherlandish Canon: Karel van Mander's Schilder-Boeck* (Chicago: University of Chicago Press, 1991), 20–21.

6. Beatrijs Brenninkmeijer-De Rooij, "For the Love of Flora: A Brief Look at Seventeenth-Century Flower Painters," in Brenninkmeijer-De Rooij et al., *Boeketten uit de Gouden Eeuw/Bouquets from the Golden Age: The Mauritshuis in Bloom* (ex. cat. The Hague, Mauritshuis, 1992), 14; Paul Taylor, *Dutch Flower Painting 1600–1720* (New Haven, Conn.: Yale University Press, 1995), 82–83.

7. Constantijn Huygens, "In praestantissimi pictoris Dan. Segheri rosas," in *A Selection of the Poems of Sir Constantijn Huygens (1596–1687)* ed. and trans. Peter Davidson and Adriaan van der Weel, (Amsterdam: Amsterdam University Press, 1996), 129.

8. John Rea, "Flora, To the Ladies." *Flora, seu, De Florum Cultura* (London: for Richard Marriott, 1665). See also Samuel Gilbert, *The Florists Vade-Mecum* (London: for Thomas Simmons, 1682), 87, who versified on tulips: "Presuming Painters find their skil out-done\At sight of these, so Pensil'd by the Sun, That *Paterzeger*, doth himself confess\He colours wants their glories to express."

9. Daston and Park, *Wonders*, 255–260, 276–277; Martin Kemp, "'Wrought by No Artist's Hand': The Natural, the Artificial, the Exotic, and the Scientific in Some Artifacts from the

Renaissance," in *Reframing the Renaissance: Visual Culture in Europe and Latin America 1450–1650*, ed. Claire Farago (New Haven, Conn.: Yale University Press, 1995), pp. 177–196.

10. On Palissy, see Daston and Park, *Wonders*, 285–286, and Kemp, "'Wrought,'" 191–193. On naturalistic automata in gardens, see John Dixon Hunt, "'Curiosities to Adorn Cabinets and Gardens,'" in *The Origins of Museums*, ed. Oliver Impey and Arthur MacGregor, (Oxford: Clarendon Press, 1985), 198–200.

11. Kemp's article, "'Wrought,'" focuses entirely on such objects. On coconuts, see especially Rolf Fritz, *Die Gefässe aus Kokosnuss in Mitteleuropa 1250–1800* (Mainz am Rhein: Verlag Philipp von Zabern, 1983). On ostrich eggs, see Isa Ragusa, "The Egg Reopened," *Art Bulletin* 53 (1971): 435–443, and Creighton Gilbert, "'The Egg Reopened' Again," *Art Bulletin* 56 (1974): 252–258. Numerous such objects are pictured in *Prag um 1600: Kunst und Kultur am Hofe Rudolfs II.* (ex. cat. Essen, 1988); see, e.g., color plates 68, 69, 71, 72.

12. John Gerard, *The Herball or Generall Historie of Plantes* (London: John Norton, 1597), 119; Rea, *Flora* (1665), 50.

13. Petrus Hondius, *Dapes indemptae, of de Moufe-schans/dat is, De soeticheyd Des Buyten-Levens, Vergheselschapt met de Boucken* (1614), (Leiden: Daniel Goels, 1621; orig. ed. 1614), 88–89, 93.

14. Jean Franeau, *Iardin d'Hyver ou Cabinet des Fleurs* (Douai: Pierre Borremans, 1616), Elegie XXVI, 2. Pagination starts over with this elegy.

15. Gilbert, *Florists Vade-Mecum* (1682), 12.

16. Gilbert's concern was not only with man's arrogance, but also with those who divided nature from God; he wished "that men may make each Clod/Speak God of Nature, make not Nature God" (ibid., 13). Such comments, besides worrying about the role of man, point to the sort of concerns with the relationship between God and nature in the later seventeenth century discussed by Daston and Park (*Wonders*, 296–301).

17. Sieur de La Chesnée Monstereul, *Le floriste françois, Traittant de l'origine des Tulipes* (Caen: Eleazar Mangeant, 1654),72; Ruth Duthie, *Florists' Flowers and Societies* (Haverfordwest: C.I. Thomas and Sons, 1988), 7–8; Krelage, *Drie Eeuwen Bloembollenexport*, 458; Elisabeth Blair MacDougall, "A Cardinal's Bulb Garden: A *Giardino Segreto* at the Palazzo Barberini in Rome," in MacDougall, *Fountains, Statues, and Flowers: Studies in Italian Gardens of the Sixteenth and Seventeenth Centuries* (Washington D.C.: Dumbarton Oaks Research Library and Collection, 1994), 241 n. 58.

18. Gerard, *Herball* (1597), 117.

19. In Rembertus Dodonaeus, *Cruydt-Boeck* (Leiden: François van Ravelingen, 1618), 367, "Biivoegsel."

20. Frank Tyrer, ed., *The Great Diurnal of Nicholas Blundell of Little Crosby, Lancashire* II, Record Society of Lancashire and Cheshire 114 (1972), 55, 28 April 1726.

21. Nicolas van Kampen, *Traité des Fleurs à Oignons* (Haarlem: C. Bohn, 1760), 71.

22. Rea, *Flora* (1665), 70–72; Gilbert, *Florists Vade-Mecum* (1682), 81–82, 85, and Van Kampen, *Traité des Fleurs à Oignon* (1760), 58–59, also recommend alternating soil or using poor soil to weaken bulbs.

23. Rea, *Flora* (1665), 71.

24. See for discussions of such methods Hanmer, *Garden Book* (1659), 17; Van Kampen, *Traité des Fleurs à Oignons* (1760), 58–59; La Chesnée Monstereul, *Le floriste françois* (1654), 175–176.

25. John Evelyn, *Kalendarium Hortense*, ed. Rosemary Verey (London: Stourton Press, 1983; first published 1664); Parkinson, *Paradisi* (1629), 23.

26. Giovanni Battista Ferrari, *Flora, seu de florum cultura libri IV* (Rome, 1633), 457–503, cited in MacDougall, "A Cardinal's Bulb Garden," 241.

27. La Chesnée Monstereul, *Le floriste françois* (1654), 163–164.

28. Ibid., 164.

29. *Nouvelle instruction pour la culture des fleurs* (Amsterdam: Henri Desbordes, 1697), 120; Gilbert, *Florists Vade-Mecum* (1682), "To the Reader."

30. Jan van der Groen, *Den Nederlantsen Hovenier* (Amsterdam: Weduwe van Gijsbert de Groot, 1721; orig. ed. 1669), "Inleydingh."

31. Gilbert, *Florists Vade-Mecum* (1682), 251.

32. Brenninkmeijer–De Rooij, "For Love of Flora," 14.

33. *Nouvelle Instruction pour la Culture des Fleurs* (Amsterdam: Henri Desbordes, 1697), 120.

34. See Hessel Miedema, "De St. Lucasgilden van Haarlem en Delft in de zestiende eeuw," *Oud Holland* 99, no. 2 (1985): 77–109; Miedema, "Kunstschilders, gilde en academie: Over het probleem van de emancipatie van de kunstschilders in de Noordelijke Nederlanden van de 16de en 17de eeuw," *Oud Holland* 101, no. 1 (1987): 1–34; Svetlana Alpers, *The Art of Describing: Dutch Art in the Seventeenth Century* (Chicago: University of Chicago Press, 1983), 100, 102; Celeste Brusati, "Stilled Lives: Self-Portraiture and Self-Reflection in Seventeenth-Century Netherlandish Still-Life Painting," *Simiolus* 20, nos. 2/3 (1990/1991): 171. On embroiderers in the St. Lucasgilde, see Saskia de Bodt, . . . *op de Raempte off mette Brodse: Nederlandse Borduurwerk uit de Zeventiende Eeuw* (Haarlem: H. Becht, 1987), 22–36. The comment on Frans Pietersz. de Grebber appears in Karel van Mander's *Schilder-boeck*; the best edition is Karel van Mander, *The Lives of the Illustrious Netherlandish and German Painters, from the first edition of the Schilder-boeck (1603–4)*, ed. and trans. Hessel Miedema (Doornspijk: Davaco, 1994), Vol. 1, f. 300 of facsimile.

35. University of Leiden (UBL), Ms. Vulc. 101, Marie de Brimeu, princesse de Chimay, to Carolus Clusius, letter 2, Leiden, 18 September 1591. *Tapisseries*, the word used here, seems to have been a usual metaphor of hers for gardens; in other letters she describes the garden she lost by moving to the north as "des belles tapisseries que jay perdu pendant ces troubles" (UBL, Ms. Vulc. 101, Marie de Brimeu to Clusius, letter 3, Leiden, 24 January 1592) and remarks that "combien q[ue] naves moien de dresser vostre tapiserÿe tellem[ent] que desireries ie ne doute que nonobstant ce elle serat tres belle" (UBL, Ms. BPL 885, Marie de Brimeu to Clusius, The Hague, 5 November 1593). That it was a more general comparison is suggested by the verb *se tapisser* used by Christiaan Porret to describe his garden: "Mon iardin commence a se tapisse[r] de petites fleurs" (UBL, Ms. BPL 2724d, Christiaan Porret to Matteo Caccini, 25 February 1611). This comparison with carpets is also discussed in Erik de Jong and Marleen Dominicus-van Soet, *Aardse Paradijzen: De tuin in de Nederlandse kunst, 15de tot 18de eeuw* (ex. cat. Haarlem, Frans Halsmuseum, 1996), 103, and MacDougall, "A Cardinal's Bulb Garden," 233.

36. Parkinson, *Paradisi* (1629), 14.

37. Pierre Vallet, *Le Iardin du Roy Tres Chrestien Henry IV Roy de France et de Navare* ([Paris]: 1608). See also Penelope Hobhouse, *Plants in Garden History* (London: Pavilion Books, 1992), 108.

38. Carolus Clusius, *Rariorum plantarum historia* (Antwerp: Plantin, 1601), II, cap. IX, sec. III, pt. 2,146; cap. VII, sec. VII, pt. 8,142.

39. The earliest use of these names I have found is 1592, when the tulip-lover Jan van Hoghelande in Leiden reported the flowering of "une [tulipe] de drap d'or fort belle" in his garden (UBL, Vulc. 101, Jan van Hoghelande to Clusius, letter 7, 20 May 1592 N.S.). The earliest I have found in Dutch is in Emmanuel Sweerts, *Florilegium* (Frankfurt am Main: Anthonius Kempner, 1612), "Catalogus den ersten Boeck," in which the *"Tulipa* geel met fleyne roode strepen/genaempt goude Laecken" stands out among a host of mere descriptions of flowers; in the French section of the tetralingual *Florilegium* it is merely called "d'orée," as a description, and the name also does not appear in the German and Latin sections. The minister Walter Stonehouse had both "Cloth of golde" and "Cloth of sylver" in his garden in

Yorkshire in 1640 ("The Garden of the Rev. Walter Stonehouse at Darfield Rectory in York-shire," *The Gardeners' Chronicle*, 29 May 1920, 268), and La Chesnée Monstereul's long cata-log of tulips in 1654 includes four types of "Drap d'argent" (*Floriste françois*, 224). Annotators of Dodonaeus's *Cruydt-Boeck* (1618 ed.) made the same comparisons: "sometimes one color shines above the other: that is the white and the yellow have something red shining through it: one like gold cloth/one like silver cloth" (*Cruydt-Boeck* [1618], 365).

40. Irene Groeneweg, "Court and City: Dress in the Age of Frederik Hendrik and Amalia," in *Princely Display: The Court of Frederik Hendrik of Orange and Amalia van Solms in The Hague*, ed. Marika Keblusek and Jori Zijlmans, (ex. cat, The Hague, Haags Historisch Museum, 1997), 203.

41. Linda A. Stone-Ferrier, *Images of Textiles: The Weave of Seventeenth-Century Dutch Art and Society* (Ann Arbor: UMI Research Press, 1985), 172, 215–216; Groeneweg, "Court and City," 201–203, 205–206; Valerie Cumming, "'Great vanity and excesse in Apparell': Some Clothing and Furs of Tudor and Stuart Royalty," in *The Late King's Goods: Collections, Pos-sessions and Patronage of Charles I in the Light of the Commonwealth Sale Inventories*, ed. Arthur MacGregor (London and Oxford: Alistair McAlpine/Oxford University Press, 1989), 322, 326; Donald King, "Textile Furnishings," in MacGregor, *The Late King's Goods*, 307–308; Alison McNeil Kettering, "Ter Borch's Ladies in Satin," in *Looking at Seventeenth-Century Dutch Art: Realism Reconsidered*, ed. Wayne Franits (Cambridge: Cambridge University Press, 1997),103–4. On the Leiden say industry, see Leo Noordegraaf, "The New Draperies in the Northern Netherlands, 1500–1800," in *The New Draperies in the Low Countries and England*, ed. Negley B. Harte (Oxford: Oxford University Press, 1997), 173–195, and Stone-Ferrier, *Images of Textiles*, 23–29; on the Amsterdam silk and silver cloth industries, see Leonie van Nierop, "De zijdenijverheid van Amsterdam, historisch geschetst," *Tijdschrift voor Geschiedenis* 45 (1930): 18–40, 151–172; and 46 (1931): 28–55, 113–143, and H. Brug-mans, *Geschiedenis van Amsterdam* (Utrecht and Antwerp: Het Spectrum, 1973) 3: 31. The bright colors associated with tulips were not as divorced from the clothing of the Dutch elite as somber but misleading paintings might suggest, as Irene Groeneweg argues in "Regenten in het zwart: vroom en deftig?" *Nederlands Kunsthistorisch Jaarboek* 46 (1995): 199–251.

42. Lorenz Seelig, "The Munich *Kunstkammer* 1565–1807," in Impey and MacGregor, *Origins of Museums*, 84–5.

43. *De Nederlandsen Bloem-Hof, of de Nauwkeurige Bloemist* (copy consulted has no title page; publication attributed by University of Amsterdam Library to Amsterdam: Harmen Machielsz and Nicolaas ten Hoorn, 1699), 7.

44. Franeau, *Iardin d'hyver* (1616), 96–104, 106, 108, 110, 114, 118, 122, 124, 125; on the Duc van Tholl, 97; on "les grans," 125. The book is filled with names of those cultivating tulips.

45. For example, Franeau, 95, 102, 104, 114, 121, 125; Rea, similarly, refers to banks of flowers as "Enamel'd" (*Flora*, "Flora. To the Ladies").

46. La Chesnée Monstereul, *Le floriste françois*, 208–213.

47. Rea, *Flora* (1665), 51.

48. Antoine Agard, *Discours et roole des medailles & autres antiquitez . . . à present rangees dans le Cabinet du Sieur Antoine Agard . . .* (Paris, 1611), 14–17, 26, 27, 31; *Catalogus oft Regis-ter vande Sonderling-Heden oft Rariteyten ende Wtgelesen Sinnelickheden . . . Die Christiaen Por-rett, wijlen Apoteker, in zijn Cunstcamer vergatert had* (auction catalogue, Leiden: Jan Claesz. van Dorp, 1628); UBL, ms. BPL 2596–9, Collectie Hunger, transcription of catalogue of cab-inet of Paludanus from ms. original in KB Copenhagen, ff. 190–203 (in original ms., ff. 130–140). On the collection of agates, see Schnapper, *Géant*, 191–192; on *pietra dura*, see C. W. Fock, "Pietre Dure work at the court of Prague and Florence: Some Relations" in *Prag um 1600*, 51–59; J. F. M. Sterck, "Dirck van Rijswijck. Een Amsterdamsch Goudsmid en Moza-ïekwerker," *Jaarverslag Koninklijk Oudheidkundig Genootschap* (1908–09), 35–54; Seelig,

Anne Goldgar

"Kunstkammer," 79. The colors of agate and marble are praised in Thomas Nicols, *A Lapidary; Or, the History of Pretious Stones* (Cambridge: Thomas Buck, 1652).

49. On the introduction of marbled paper to Europe, see Phoebe Jane Easton, *Marbling: A History and a Bibliography* (Los Angeles: Dawson's Book Shop, 1983), 33ff; Rosamond B. Loring, *Decorated Book Papers* (Cambridge, Mass.: Harvard College Library, 1942), 12–13; Richard J. Wolfe, *Marbled Paper: Its History, Techniques, and Patterns* (Philadelphia: University of Pennsylvania Press, 1990), 3–14; Graham Pollard, "Changes in the Style of Bookbinding, 1550–1830," *The Library* 5th ser. 11, no. 12 (June 1956): 79. On the role of the Netherlands, see Easton, *Marbling*, 63–66, and J. F. Heijebroek and T. C. Greven, *Sierpapier: marmer-, brocaat- en sitspapier in Nederland* (Amsterdam: De Buitenkant, 1994), 15–17; the latter authors disagree with Wolfe, who claims a more important role for Germany and France (Wolfe, *Marbled Paper*, 13). On Paludanus's early possession of marbled paper, see Heijebroek and Greven, *Sierpapier*, 14. The example of l'Estoile is from Loring, *Decorated Book Papers*, 24.

50. Easton, *Marbling*, 109, 111.

51. John Evelyn ms. in BL, "An Exact Account of the Making of Marbled Paper," quoted in Charles M. Adams, *Some Notes on the Art of Marbling Paper in the Seventeenth Century* (New York: New York Public Library, 1947), 11. Adams does not give the exact reference to the Evelyn ms.

52. UBL, Ms. Vulc. 101, Anna Maria von Heusenstain to Clusius, letter 9, Vienna, 7 May 1591. Another correspondent of Clusius's referred to a "plante . . . du papier Persien et Turquesque," but it is not clear if this was a tulip. UBL, Ms. Vulc. 101, Jacques Plateau to Clusius, letter 9, Tournay, 8 September 1592.

53. Seymour Slive, *Rembrandt and His Critics 1630–1730* (The Hague: Martinus Nijhoff, 1953), 1.

54. The chief text for the aesthetics of early seventeenth-century Dutch painting is Karel van Mander, *Den grondt der edel vry schilder-const*, the first section of his *Het Schilder-Boeck* (Haarlem: Paschier van Wesbusch, 1604). The *Grondt*, or *Groundwork*, has been edited in a separate modern version by Hessel Miedema (Utrecht: Haentjens Dekker and Gumbert, 1973), 2 vols. Miedema has also written several analyses of the chief descriptive terms in the work: Hessel Miedema, *Fraey en Aerdigh, Schoon en Moy in Karel van Manders Schilder-Boeck* (Amsterdam: Kunsthistorisch Instituut, 1984); Hessel Miedema, *Kunst, Kunstenaar en Kunstwerk bij Karel van Mander* (Alpen aan den Rijn: Canaletto, 1981), see especially 146–152, 156–159. A challenge to some of Miedema's views on Van Mander is Walter S. Melion, *Shaping the Netherlandish Canon: Karel van Mander's Schilder-Boeck*.

55. Van Mander, *Grondt*, chap. 12, stanza 21; Dodonaeus, *Cruydt-Boeck* (1618 ed.),365, "Biivoegsel." On Van Mander's use of *netticheyt*, see Melion, *Shaping the Netherlandish Canon*, 60–63. This is a concept also applied to flower painting; see Taylor, *Dutch Flower Painting*, 96, 99.

56. E.g., on shells: Pliny, *Natural History* ix.lii.

57. John Shearman, *Mannerism* (Harmondsworth: Penguin, 1967), 75, 86, 92, 100–101, 105, 139, 140–151.

58. "Door verscheydenheyt is Natuere schoone": Van Mander, *Grondt*, chap. 5, stanza 20. On this verse, see Melion, *Shaping*, 8–9, 21. A canonic example for Van Mander is the Jan van Eyck Adoration of the Lamb by the Elders in Ghent, which he valued for its clear, new–seeming colors and the variety of its composition, encompassing as many as 330 different faces. See Karel van Mander, *The Lives of the Illustrious Netherlandish and German Painters*, ed. Miedema, Vol. I, 61; f. 220 of facsimile.

59. Van Mander, *Grondt*, chap. V, stanzas 32–3. Melion comments on this passage in *Shaping*, 9.

60. Rembertus Dodonaeus, *Cruydt–Boeck* (Leiden: François van Ravelingen, 1608), 389, later annotations.

61. The subject of connoisseurship awaits full treatment, but see Zirka Zaremba Filipczak, *Picturing Art in Antwerp 1550–1700* (Princeton, N.J.: Princeton University Press, 1987); Elizabeth Honig, "The Beholder as a Work of Art: A Study in the Location of Value in Seventeenth-Century Flemish Painting," *Nederlands Kunsthistorisch Jaarboek* 46 (1995) 253–297; Elizabeth Honig, "Making Sense of Things: On the Motives of Dutch Still Life," *Res* 34 (autumn 1998): 167–183; Antoine Schnapper, *Curieux du Grand Siècle* (Paris: Flammarion, 1994). The literature on collectors is enormous, but see especially Paula Findlen, *Possessing Nature: Museums, Collecting, and Scientific Culture in Early Modern Italy* (Berkeley: University of California Press, 1994); Schnapper, *Géant*; Ellinoor Bergvelt and Renée Kistemaker, eds., *De Wereld binnen handbereik: Nederlandse kunst- en rariteitenverzamelingen 1585–1735* (ex. cat. Amsterdams Historisch Museum, 1992). Alongside connoisseurship, we can also place the setting of standards for tulips back within the context of craft guilds, whose task it generally was to maintain a level of quality in their members' product. This was true of the St. Lucasgilde, although less is said in its regulations about painting than about the other crafts included in the guild. See Hessel Miedema, "Over kwaliteitsvoorschriften in het St. Lucasgilde; over 'doodverf,'" *Oud Holland* 101, no. 3 (1987): 141–147.

62. Nicolas–Claude de Fabri de Peiresc to his brother Palamède de Valavez, Aix, 3 May 1626, in *Lettres de Peiresc*, ed. Philippe Tamizey de Larroque (Paris: Imprimerie Nationale, 1888–1898) Vol. 6: 501.

63. Parkinson, *Paradisi*, "Epistle to the Reader"; La Chesnée Monstereul, *Le floriste françois*, chap. 5, "Quelle doit estre la Tulipe, tant en ses Couleurs, Panaches, qu'en sa Forme"; Van Kampen, *Traité des Fleurs à Oignons* (1760), 60–61, "Les qualités requises pour former une belle Tulipe . . ."; [Valnay], *Connoissance et culture parfaite*, 12ff.

64. [Valnay], *Connoissance et culture parfaite*, 12–21.

65. Rea, *Flora*, "To the Reader."

66. Duthie, *Florists' Flowers and Societies*, 33, 71; Sam Segal, "Exotische bollen als statussymbolen," *Kunstschrift* 31, no. 3 (1987), 96; D. Tarver and B. Elliott, "Des Fleuristes aux Sociétés Horticoles. Histoire des Expositions Florales," in *L'Empire de Flore*, ed. Sabine van Sprang (Brussels: La Renaissance du Livre, 1996), 117–118. A possible precursor to such shows might be the use of a "theater" of tulips, arranged on racks for other collectors to examine, an invention attributed to Valnay by the *Nouvelle instruction pour la culture des fleurs* (1697), 127: "Monsieur de Valnay invented a completely lovely sort of theater, to be able to see easily and all together a whole mass of panachées mixed together according to their different colors & arranged near each other, so that, sitting in the shade & with one glance you can divert your sight with all the rarities that a large garden can produce."

67. Dodonaeus, *Cruydt-Boeck*, (1608 edition), 388.

68. Examples are numerous in the Clusius correspondence at the University of Leiden, but for several printed documents demonstrating this, see F. W. J. Hunger, *Acht Brieven van Middelburgers aan Carolus Clusius* (Middelburg: Zeeuwsch Genootschap der Wetenschappen, 1925).

69. Peiresc to Palamède de Valavez, Aix, April 10, 1626, in *Lettres de Peiresc* Vol. 6: 443; Sir Thomas Hanmer to John Evelyn, Bettisfield, 21 August 1671, quoted in introduction to Hanmer, *Garden Book*, xv; Hanmer's pocket book, quoted in introduction to *Garden Book*, xx, gives accounts of Hanmer's gifts to Lambert; BL Sloane Ms. 95, ff. 153–154, "Accounts for my Garden 1638." It should be noted that the anonymous English estate owner was clearly indulging not only in exchange but in trade of flowers. The manuscript includes entries such as "Mrs Rous hath fro[m] me 200 small Anemones to halves, and of my part m^{rs} Elizabeth Budding must have our half of the profitt. ffreeman oweth me 3£ upon bill wch is in my box, in lue whereof I have of him 2 tulips called Aggot Goblins wch I have set in my little square

north east, the wch I have agreed to have if I like them when I see their flowers, or els returne to him and have fro[m] him my three pounds." BL Sloane ms. 95, f. 148, "Accounts for my Garden 1638."

70. [Ralph Knevet], *Rhodron and Iris: A Pastorall as it was presented at the Florists Feast in Norwich, May 3, 1631* (London: for Michael Sparke, 1631). On florists' feasts, see Duthie, *Florists' Flowers and Societies*, 9–14; and Tarver and Elliott, "Des Fleuristes," 124. It is not clear in what fashion flowers were involved in the Norwich society's activities, although Knevet's play is full of floral references.

71. Duthie, *Florists' Flowers*, 5, 8. Duthie reports the earliest known use of the term as 1623, in a letter by Sir Henry Wotton, but Jean de Maes used "floriste" to describe amateur growers in 1599, reporting as well that "Je commençoie aussi à floriser . . . " (UBL, ms. Vulc. 101, Jean de Maes to Clusius, letter 5, Brussels, 8 April 1599).

72. Rea, *Flora* (1665), 50.

73. La Chesnée Monstereul, *Le floriste françois* (1654), 180–181. That these sentiments were not only French is perhaps indicated by the plagiarism of this passage (along with the rest of the book) by Hendrik van Oosten in his *Nieuwe Nederlandsche Bloemhof* (1700); see the English translation, Henry van Oosten, *The Dutch Gardener: Or, the Compleat Florist*, 2nd ed. (London: D. Modwinter, 1711), 160. The quotation here is my translation of La Chesnée Monstereul rather than from the English edition of Van Oosten.

74. [Valnay], *Connoissance et culture parfaite* (1688), 7–8.

75. *Ibid.*, 7.

76. La Chesnée Monstereul, *Le floriste françois*, 173–180; quotation on 173–174. Schnapper, *Géant*, 218–219, also discusses ambivalent attitudes of gardening treatises toward revealing their secrets.

77. Michel de Marolles, *Suitte de Memoires de Michel de Marolles Abbé de Ville–loin* (Paris: Antoine de Sommaville, 1657), 268.

78. My preliminary research on Haarlem suggests that some involved in tulip sales there may have been of a lower social station than in Amsterdam and thus less likely to be purchasers of art, although some were also from leading Haarlem families. Unfortunately auction records from Haarlem appear to have been lost, making this topic more difficult to investigate.

79. Casteleyn's inventory is in the Gemeentearchief, Amsterdam (GAA): GAA NA 939A/187ff., 28 August 1644. A tulip sale involving Casteleyn is recorded at GAA NA 341/155, 26 September 1611; he was obviously involved in tulip collecting from early on. On Casteleyn, see also Bergvelt and Kistemaker, eds., *De Wereld binnen Handbereik*, 316.

80. My list of Amsterdam purchasers of tulips is compiled from notarial transactions in the Gemeentearchief, Amsterdam (GAA), concerning sales or quarrels over sales. I am grateful to Michael Montias for allowing me to compare this list with the Montias/RKD Databank of buyers of art at auction in Amsterdam from 1600 to 1640. Notarial records about tulips and concerning those collectors listed include: on Bessels, GAA NA 951, 14 May 1637; on Admirael, GAA NA 917/272ᵛ, 16 October 1635; GAA NA 917/310, 1 December 1635; GAA, NA 918/145ᵛ, 19 May 1636; GAA NA 918/180, 12 June 1636; GAA NA 918/228, 6 July 1636; GAA NA 918/519ᵛ, 8 December 1636; GAA NA 919/64, 13 February 1637; GAA NA 919/195, 13 June 1637; GAA NA 920/334, 2 December 1638; on Halmael, GAA NA 918/554ᵛ, 31 December 1636; GAA NA 919/20ᵛ, 12 January 1637; GAA NA 919/21, 15 January 1637; GAA 919/61, 10 February 1637; GAA NA 919/61, 10 February 1637; on Massa, GAA NA 1158/144–144ᵛ, 27 December 1636. Adam Bessels was closely connected to the major collecting family, the Reynsts, as well as to well-known collectors such as Jacques Nicquet and Jean Renialme; Lambert Massa was connected to Renialme; his brother, Isaac, was painted by Hals three times, and his tulip purchase was from Susanna Spranger, sister of the important col-

lector Gommer Spranger and widow of Outger Cluyt. Cluyt was a son of Dirck Outgertz Cluyt, Clusius's assistant at the Leiden *hortus*, and had written a treatise on the tulip. There are many other similar examples.

81. On this question for Dutch paintings, see Marten Jan Bok, "Art-Lovers and their Paintings: Van Mander's Schilder–boeck as a Source for the History of the Art Market in the Northern Netherlands," in *Dawn of the Golden Age*, ed. Ger Luijten et al. (ex. cat. Amsterdam, Rijksmuseum, 1993), 136–166; Marten Jan Bok, *Vraag en aanbod op de Nederlandse kunstmarkt, 1580–1700* (Proefschrift, University of Utrecht, 1994).

82. Clusius to Lipsius, 22 October 1594, quoted in F. W. Hunger, *Charles de l'Escluse. Carolus Clusius. Nederlandsche Kruidkundige 1526–1609* (The Hague: Martinus Nijhoff, 1927, 1943), Vol. 2, 250. On the *rhizotomi*, see also Hunger, *Clusius* Vol. 1: 303–304, and Vol. 2: 251; Krelage, *Drie eeuwen*, 3.

83. In Dodonaeus, *Cruydt-Boeck* (1618 edition), 365. "Biivoegsel." This passage does not occur in the 1608 edition.

84. Rea, *Flora*, 71.

85. George Voorhelm, *Traité sur la Jacinte*, 3rd ed. (Haarlem: N. Beets, 1773; 1st publ. 1752), 21–22.

86. Gilbert, *The Florists Vade-Mecum* (1683), "To the Reader."

87. See especially J. Michael Montias, "Cost and Value in Seventeenth–Century Dutch Art," *Art History* 10, no. 4 (December 1987): 455–466.

88. La Chesnée Monstereul, *Le floriste françois* 1654), 194.

89. Paul Contant, "Le Iardin et Cabinet Poetique," in Jacques and Paul Contant, *Les Divers Exercices de Iacques et Paul Contant Pere et Fils Maistres Apoticaires de la Ville de Poictiers* (Poitiers: Julian Thoreau and la Veuve d'Antoine Mesnier, 1628), 55–56. Contant defends his decision to take money— the charge was that he was too "prompt & diligent\A prendre d'un chascun de l'or & de l'argent\Pour voir mon Cabinet"—by asking whether, if someone seeing his cabinet wanted to give him money for seeing it, he really had to refuse?

Inventing Exoticism

The Project of Dutch Geography and the Marketing of the World, circa 1700

BENJAMIN SCHMIDT

What do we talk about when we talk about the exotic? This depends, in part, on *when* we do the talking, though there may be no better time to listen in on the conversation than the late seventeenth and early eighteenth centuries, when the talk was relatively thick. Consider: Georg Rumphius—also known as *Plinius Indicus* for his monumental contribution to the natural history of the East Indies—spoke of the "imperfect chaos" of the exotic world that he assembled in his massive studies of Asian marine and plant life, *The Amboinese Curiosity Cabinet* and *The Amboinese Herbal*, both composed at the close of the seventeenth century. This and other remarks by Rumphius on the unwieldy business of ordering tropical *naturalia* reflect perhaps the finicky anxieties of a scholar. By contrast, Engelbert Kaempfer—the "Humboldt" of the Indies, as he came retrospectively to be known—praised the "pleasures of the exotic." Here the emphasis lay on the readers' reception of those tomes chock-full of Near and Far Eastern exotica compiled by Kaempfer in the late seventeenth century, and on the effect that these stunning descriptions, visual no less than verbal, presumably had upon their audience. And then there is the commentary of Arnoldus Montanus. Neither a Pliny nor a Humboldt was this modest schoolteacher turned geographer who delighted in the "novelty," "variety," and "strangeness" of those exotica collected in his vast, rambling books of "wonders" that explored the terrain of Asia, Africa, and America at the twilight of the seventeenth century.[1]

All of these observations derive from a particular context, and it is this context—time and place, purpose and perspective—that lends recognizable shape and valuable definition to that all-too-vaguely articulated concept "the exotic." All can be associated, that is, with the project of geography in the Dutch Republic, circa 1700: a singular burst of printing, painting, mapping, publishing, producing, and otherwise promoting images of the non-European world undertaken chiefly in the province of Holland around the turn of the eighteenth century. Rumphius and Kaempfer both gained their knowledge of the world while serving in the Dutch East India Company; Montanus, an accomplished armchair traveler, belonged to the stable of geographers, historians, and draftsmen who worked for the Amsterdam publisher Jacob van Meurs. Finally, all of these comments, despite their identifiably Dutch provenance, circulated throughout late Baroque Europe in various editions and multiple languages, thereby conveying to a very broad audience what indeed was meant when the exotic was talked about.

To be sure, discussions focused on the idea of the exotic, both in and of the late seventeenth century, tend to be rare and still more rarely satisfying. In the first instance, few of the contemporary commentators on matters of geography chose to elaborate on their theories of the exotic; the word itself appears only infrequently in Baroque letters.[2] In the second instance — in the, by contrast, very many critical discussions of Europe's mimetic engagement with the expanding early modern world — the exotic too often gets tucked away, neatly and nonchalantly, under the broad heading of "Europe and its Other." This permits a certain laxness concerning the Other, understood simply as the object of European imperial desire. It also allows — equally problematically — considerable leeway for that grand, elastic figure of the early modern European, who habitually goes undistinguished by gender, class, culture, and so forth. It strips the exotic and its makers of context. The comments of Rumphius, Kaempfer, Montanus, and others gain their value precisely by pointing to a more cogent idea of exoticism, which pertains more particularly to late Baroque Europe — a crucial period of geographic production and European expansion that heralded the age of empire. They indicate, too, how this idea was formulated, propagated, and marketed by the Dutch, most conspicuously around 1700.[3]

The Dutch project of geography at the turn of the eighteenth century provokes a number of observations. First, the sheer quantity of materials produced in the Republic is impressive. A veritable flood of georgraphic goods — of literary works, such as travelogues, learned geographies, natural histories, and books of "wonders"; of cartographic resources, including decorated maps, multivolumed atlases, and luxurious globes; of visual artifacts, comprising tropical painting, inexpensive prints, and coveted curiosa, (the latter often sold with the cabinets that housed them)— streamed off the presses and out of the ateliers of the Netherlands, suppliers in the province of Holland manufacturing most assiduously. Second, many of the works produced in the Netherlands share a certain bric-a-brac quality that suggests a self-conscious strategy of — for lack of a better word — exoticism. Books on the extra-European world move briskly and even programmatically among countries, customs, and creatures; the preface to one volume claims to offer only quick "morsels" of exotica, variety being the favorite spice of geographic life.[4] Paintings and prints likewise mix and match peoples and continents, embracing a lush aesthetic of eclecticism. Third, the timing of this burst of geography is significant for what it is not: coincident with any period of Dutch imperial expansion. On the contrary, the later decades of the seventeenth century witnessed a reduction of the Republic's activities abroad: the Netherlands' American colonies (in Brazil and New York) fell in the 1650s and 1660s, and the Dutch East India Company started losing relative market share at about the same time. The Republic, in other words, chose to market a world which it had a *contracting* stake in governing. Which brings up a final, crucial point: that the Dutch in fact "marketed" and sold that version of the world which their geographers so meticulously fashioned. This worked in a variety of ways. Rumphius's text very plainly promoted the valuable shells of his own cabinet of curiosities (a previous collection had been sold to Grand Duke Cosimo III of Tuscany), and Montanus—or his publisher, van Meurs—ambitiously advertised in his Asian volume the merits of another deluxe edition, *America*, by the same author-publisher team.[5] Somewhat more subtly, Kaempfer's textual descriptions of Oriental riches sold the reader on a veritable cornucopia of imports lately available in Europe, as did, in their own ways, any number of Dutch texts, which sensuously described the wondrous products of the expanding globe. Still more to the point, Dutch geography sold an *idea* of the world that appealed to readers, viewers, and consumers across Europe, and this idea marketed a world that was identifiably "exotic."

This essay investigates the development of geography in late Baroque Europe and the manner in which various modes of describing the world functioned in the decades surrounding 1700. It proposes that, in the Netherlands at this time, a category and a strategy of discourse emerged, that might best come under the rubric of "exotic." The term *exotic* has been crucial to any number of discussions of Europe's post-Columbian expansion, its establishment of commercial markets overseas, and its development of imperialist ideologies. Exoticism has served as a touchstone for analyses of colonial (and postcolonial) discourse, of European representations of the Other, and of early modern forms of geography—the evolving art and science of empire. Despite this evident centrality, however, few excavations of the term and its implications have informed the study of these topics, and certainly not the study of geography in Europe's great age of expansion. Few attempts have been made to locate the production and consumption of exotica, especially in that period bridging the Old World's initial thrusts overseas in the sixteenth and early seventeenth centuries, and the establishment of vast European empires by the later eighteenth and nineteenth centuries.

Where do we look when we look for the exotic? To track the exotic, one need look no further than the Dutch Republic, geographers nonpareil of early modern Europe, and Dutch strategies of representing the world circa 1700. Dutch geography, prominent enough in the early years of Renaissance exploration, expanded dramatically in the final decades of the seventeenth century. In an astonishing assortment of media, the Dutch described, delineated, reproduced, and otherwise propagated images of the world beyond Europe. This applies not only in terms of the great quantity of works issuing from the Republic. It characterizes also the phenomenal variety and dazzling quality of texts, images, and objects pertaining to geography (the products) and the extraordinary extent of their dispersal (their consumption). The Republic, quite simply, dominated the field. By consequence, it framed the way most Europeans viewed the globe at the turn of the eighteenth century.

Dutch geography came in various shapes and forms, genres and media. There were, to begin with, "traditional" geographies (sometimes published under the name "cosmographies"), which, in the humanist mode, sought to detail the lay of the world. These were printed texts, which became, in many instances, authoritative textbooks: Philip Cluverius's *Introductionis in universam geographiam*, which appeared in a staggering sixty-seven editions by 1725; Bernard Varenius's widely cited *Geographia generalis*; and the vast, omnibus works of Georg Hornius—"social" studies on the empires of the world, the origins of the races, the nature of world polities, and the like— that numbered forty editions in the final third of the century.[6] Next came the regional studies—fabulous, often folio works, sometimes called "atlases" and generally brimming with engraved prints, foldout maps, and panoramic views—that filled a market for "local" geographies of the non-European world: Schouten on Siam (nearly twenty editions), Nieuhof on Brazil (yet another Jacob van Meurs title), Baldaeus on Malabar (reprinted in Churchill's acclaimed *Travels*) (fig. 14.1).[7] The magnificent natural histories done in the Republic might also strive to be global, yet this genre tended to encourage studies that were site-specific: Maria Sibylla Merian's glorious *Metamorphosis insectorum Surinamensium*, Hendrik van Reede tot Drakestein's twelve-volume *Hortus Malabaricus*, and Rumphius's *Amboinsche rariteitkamer*, all of which appeared in the *decennium mirabilius* of exotic natural history, 1695–1705.[8] The Dutch also produced a notably large share of travel narratives: well over fifty editions of Willem Bontekoe's adventures in South Asia; multiple versions of Ogier Busbecq's life among the Turks; thick accounts of Cornelis de Bruyn's journeys to the Levant and Muscovy. And they were behind some of the most important travel anthologies:

Figure 14.1 Frontispiece from Philippus Baldaeus, *Wahrhaftige ausführliche beschreibung der berühmten ostindischen kusten Malabar und Coromandel, als auch der insel Zeylon* (Amsterdam, 1672). Courtesy of the Rosenfeld University. University of California, Los Angeles.

sprawling, multivolume collections, including Hartgers' "Voyages" and Commelin's "Travels" (which formed the basis of Renneville's and Churchill's similarly gargantuan collections); and the twenty-eight volume series of Pieter van der Aa, which served as a standard geographic reference work for half a century.[9] A final category that comes under the rubric of "literary" text is the Dutch books of wonders and "things-of-the-world." These described, in some cases, a single set of attributes or customs surveyed in a global setting: Balthasar Bekker on the universality of witchcraft or Bernard Picard on world religions, for example. In other cases, they jumbled together, *Kunstkammer*-like, the miscellaneous mores and disparate marvels of the world; arranged these quirky attractions with purposeful disregard for place; and finally framed them with enticing titles, such as "The Great Cabinet of Curiosities," "The Warehouse of Wonders," or, most bluntly, "The Wonder-Filled World."[10]

Also from the Netherlands came a stupendous outpouring of cartographic texts, which placed the Republic in the enviable position of mapmaker to Europe. From the workshops of Blaeu, Janssonius, and de Wit came the preeminent "grand" atlases of the later seventeenth century. Under the signs of Colom, Donker, and van Keulen one could obtain the most sought-after "water worlds," or sea atlases, on the market. Alongside these sumptuous, often folio works were simpler "minor" atlases and plain sheet maps for the cost-conscious. Available for the truly profligate, though, were the high-end wall maps, which decorated the finest homes of Europe. Elaborately decorated and often hand-colored, these could cost more even than an atlas; they also came in made-to-order "floor models": mosaics of the world mapped onto a patron's floor. Deluxe Dutch globes spun in the best studies and princely corridors of Europe; miniature "pocket" globes, meanwhile, could be conveniently carried across the continent. And, just as Dutch printers and engravers produced city views, topical news maps, and topographical panoramas (some up to 2 meters in length), so did Dutch draftsmen and painters, often working from the same original sketches, furnish more durable scenes of the identical exotic terrains done in watercolor and oil.[11]

From Dutch painters, too, came diverse visual versions of the non-European world. Tropical landscapes — a genre wholly invented by the Dutch in the second half of the seventeenth century — presented the far-flung corners of the globe in lush, opulent color (fig. 14.2). Here the very competitive market for paintings in the Republic induced innovation by encouraging artists to select, and then specialize in, a particular region or style. Frans Post, perhaps most famously, painted verdant variations of Brazilian life — though other regions had their masters. Dirk Valkenburg cornered the market for Suriname scenes; Andries Beeckman did the same for the East Indies; and Gerard van Edema applied his brush to that growing urban jungle known

Figure 14.2 Frans Post, *View of Olinda*, 1662 (canvas, 107.5 x 172.5 cm). Courtesy of the Rijksmuseum, Amsterdam.

as Manhattan, which he rendered in vaguely pastoral, *capriccio* views. Other genres also developed. Painters of the Republic reproduced on canvas the products and peoples of the world — as in Albert Eckhout's studies of the non-European inhabitants of Brazil — and the flora and fauna of the tropics. Many of these images were subsequently recycled in still lifes and other exotic compositions — Jacob van Campen's *Triumph, with Treasures of the Indies* combines elements of still-life painting with human figures bearing the rich harvest from overseas — or in delftware, tapestries, and other decorative arts (fig. 14.3).[12]

The actual objects depicted on the canvas had their market as well, which the Dutch skillfully supplied. The Republic, that is, did a brisk business provisioning the *Kunst-* and *Wunderkammern* of Europe. Rumphius's shells went to the ducal cabinet of Cosimo, who beat out Peter the Great of Russia, one of the many (and most extravagant) shoppers to visit the Netherlands in search of collectibles. Shells were certainly the best preserved exotica available and therefore the most popular items for sale. Yet a wide variety of *naturalia*, *artificialia*, and hybrid items bridging the two — finely painted animal horns, artfully crafted fossils, ingeniously worked coral — could be had for a price from Dutch collectors, who readily dispensed with their holdings in precisely these years. Tourists in the Republic also made sure to visit the splendid botanical and zoological gardens in Leiden, Amsterdam, and Rotterdam, which were well stocked with imports from the East and

Figure 14.3 Polychrome tile panel, Delft (workshop unknown), ca. 1700 (170 x 79 cm). Courtesy of the Rijksmuseum, Amsterdam.

West Indies; and they called on the renowned physicians of Holland, who possessed among the finest collections of simples and specimens in Europe. Finally, the Dutch plied a trade in the actual cabinets that contained these collectibles. Commonly constructed out of tropical woods or other imported materials, and elaborately decorated with scenes meant to evoke the distant lands from which the treasures within had derived, these cabinets offered consumers yet one more opportunity to imagine the shape of the exotic world—or at least the Dutch version thereof.[13]

The products of Dutch geography, which spanned so many genres, forms, and styles, also spanned multiple communities of readers, collectors, and consumers, reaching markets far and wide. This is easiest to see in the category of printed sources, which circulated exceptionally broadly at this time. Texts on the extra-European world—a seaman's narrative, for example—might appear originally in inexpensive octavo or duodecimo, with crude woodblock prints and the vaguest of maps. Yet these images might be redone by the same or another publisher with expertly engraved plates, detailed maps, and text printed in folio. Or the reverse: a text first offered in massive, luxury editions might be pirated by a publisher working for the lower-end market, who would offer an abridged edition at a favorable price. Plates were commonly recycled as well, with or without an accompanying text. Romeyn de Hooghe's *Les Indes Orientales et Occidentales* (1710), a tour de force of engraved exotica executed in a striking, oblong format, furnished images for any number of other texts that had little or nothing to do with de Hooghe's original commission.[14] More basically, Dutch geographic texts were recycled in translation. What is particularly impressive about this process, certainly not uncommon in early modern publishing, was the degree of control exercised by Dutch publishers over their product. Translations usually derived *from the original publisher* in the Republic, whose editions would then compete with, and generally prevail over, translations undertaken by foreign publishers. German, French, and Latin works of geography commonly came from Holland, where printers employed a core of translators. The Royal Geographer of Restoration England, John Ogilby, may have departed from this pattern somewhat by hiring his own translator, yet he commonly ordered his prints from Amsterdam and produced a final product that was (Ogilby's boastful claims of authorship notwithstanding) undeniably Dutch.[15]

In the case of other sources of Dutch geography, patterns of dissemination are perhaps less plain—yet the fact of their dispersal throughout Europe is abundantly clear. Brazilian landscapes by Frans Post shipped to Versailles, part of a spectacular trove of Dutch Americana purchased by Louis XIV. Tropical still lifes by Albert Eckhout went to Frederick III of Denmark, gaining a prime position in the royal collection in Copenhagen. And cartographic watercolors from the venerable Vingboons atelier reached Rome by order of Christina of Sweden, who abdicated her throne in Stockholm en route to becoming a leading patron of Baroque arts and letters. Dutch images, like Dutch texts, spread across the continent. They provided, in short, rich and plentiful models for those who would contemplate the exotic world.[16]

The sum of these sources and their dissemination constitutes what might be called a geographic moment, which can be traced to the final decades of the seventeenth century and early years of the eighteenth. This poses a simple pair of related questions: Why then—around 1700? And why there—the Dutch Republic?[17] That the Netherlands triumphantly concluded an epic Eighty Years' War against Spain in 1648, and that their success in foreign policy had boded well for domestic affairs, cultural no less than economic—the Dutch Golden Age—may explain in part the vibrancy of Dutch geography, which was, in essence, a cultural export with economic dimensions. Yet 1648 denotes not so much the dawn as the dusk—or perhaps, pre-dusk dimming—of that Golden Age, which was, by most measures, in a state of decline by the wonder years of Dutch geography. What *had* changed by the end of the war was the harshly polemical representations of Habsburg "tyranny," as the Dutch chose to characterize Spanish government both at home and abroad. By the second half of the century, with no need to demonize the enemy, descriptions of Spain and its empire had become more mild; Dutch geography lost its habitual Hispanophobic edge.[18] This shift accounts for questions of quality rather than quantity, however. It fails to explain the Dutch dedication to worlds overseas in the first place, and the assiduous concern of the new Republic with matters imperial.

The conclusion of the Netherlands' struggle against Spain did free up ships and soldiers, which might suggest an expansion of colonial efforts—and a parallel extension of colonial discourse in the form of geography. Yet the very opposite would seem to be the case, at least as far as Dutch overseas expansion is concerned. Dutch settlements in America collapsed, in fact, in the years immediately following the Treaty of Münster (1648)—New Holland (Brazil) succumbed to a joint Spanish-Portuguese armada in 1654, while New Netherland fell to the duke of York only a decade later—and the Dutch West India Company declared bankruptcy by 1664. In Asia, though there were no such dramatic setbacks, the Republic experienced a number of reversals and contractions and a loss of relative market share to its European competitors. By the later seventeenth century especially, the Dutch East India Company had given ground to the English and French; and if the VOC (as the Company was called) still turned a profit, it did so increasingly as middlemen in inter-Asian trade rather than masters of pan-Asian domains. Rather than land-based, imperial ambitions, the Republic cultivated more profit-minded, commercial strategies. In both the East and West Indies, the Dutch peddled the products—the stuff—of the world. And increasingly, they also plied a trade in the *image* of the world, which took the form of geography.

The image of the world marketed by the Dutch came in many forms. Yet this image, in virtually all of its permutations, shared certain qualities and followed discernible patterns that may be said to characterize the Dutch brand of geography flourishing circa 1700. These qualities and patterns, moreover, functioned to render this image — the Dutch production of the world — agreeable and therefore salable to the broad, Europe-wide audience for Dutch geography. Taken together, they constitute an identifiable and effective strategy of representation, which might be termed "exoticism."

The world according to Dutch geography was a rich, jumbled hodgepodge of peoples and places, the creatures of one land and customs of another slipping easily across borders and even continents. It was a resolutely disorderly world, not infrequently described as "strange," somewhat paradoxically as "novel," or more prosaically as "marvelous." It burst with social, cultural, and natural bric-a-brac, arranged with seemingly careless disregard for order or provenance. Dutch geography was eclectic and notably catholic: all manner of scenes and snippets of exotica, described by all manner of European observer, were made welcome. Yet there was a method to this madness, or at least a pattern to the chaotic clutter of Dutch geography.

Dutch geography emphasized, firstly, variety. The mix-and-match quality of texts and images was often by design, and difference was accentuated — not so much to distinguish the cultures and landscapes of the world as to conflate them. Distinctions, like borders, were studiously erased. Here a strategic shift becomes apparent, when works of geography from the later seventeenth century are compared with those dating from just a few decades earlier. Johan Nieuhof's masterly description of Brazil, penned originally in the middle of the century — at the height, namely, of the Dutch West India Company's (WIC) struggle against Portugal — appeared finally in 1682, combined with the author's reports on the *East* as well as West Indies. In place of the original, carefully focused narrative of the Republic's tenure, and then decline, in South America, the reader now contends with a swirl of exotic settings, ranging "from China to Peru." Orient and Occident comfortably commingle, at times with haphazard abandon. Brazilian flora segue to Chinese fauna, while Jewish merchants of Recife bump up against tobacco-addled natives of Malaysia.[19] In much the same spirit, an edition of Willem Piso's *Historiae naturalis Brasiliae*—first introduced in 1648 by a director of the WIC, who unabashedly endorsed the Netherlands' empire in Brazil—was reissued after the fall of New Holland, carrying in this later version a preface in praise of wonders and a newly appended, yet otherwise incongruous, study of Asian *naturalia*. A fresh frontispiece engraved for this second edition casually blends a heraldic Brazilian figure with a vaguely Persian one — neither, to be sure, having much to do with the natural histories within.[20] This sort of inspired eclecticism is particularly embraced on the frontispieces of (printed) Dutch geographies. The magisterial *Ceremonies et coutumes religieuses des tous les peuples du monde*, published initially in Amsterdam in 1723, opens with a fabulous melting pot of intercontinental religion; Simon de Vries's *Curieuse aenmerckingen der bysonderste Oost- en West Indische verwonderens-waerdige dingen* (Curious observations of the most exceptional East and West Indian wonders, 1682) entices the reader with a baroque blend of global goods; and Joan Blaeu's monumental *Atlas maior* (1662 and following) announces itself with an allegory of all the world's parts, offering an iconographic image and a cartographic style that would become standard for the next half century.[21]

Dutch geography collapsed distinctions, and, while efforts were certainly made to compare and contrast, this was done in a peculiar "analogistic" style that suggests, once again, a shift in discursive method. Whereas Hernán Cortés, in the early sixteenth century, found the towers of Mexico evocative of Seville and Granada — crucial loci, it should be stressed, of the Spanish *Reconquista* — Arnoldus Montanus by the 1670s associated Mexican temples with those of China and Japan. Montanus, that is, matched exotic with exotic; Cortés, meanwhile, compared newly won Spanish domains with the soon-to-be colonized province of New Spain.[22] Dutch geography, more generally, celebrated the vastness of the world and conflated global space — which offers yet another point of contrast, in this case with contempory geographic agendas. Thus, where an Athanasius Kircher or Joseph-François Lafitau infused the study of geography with a pronounced historical dimension — comparing Native Americans or Ch'ing Chinese with the Ancients — an Arnoldus Montanus or Olfert Dapper pursued the "savage" (or "civilized") American by looking to examples in Asia and Africa. Dutch cross-references tended to be spatial, not temporal; Dutch geography expanded the globe rather than excavated the past. Dapper (who, like Montanus, collaborated frequently with the indefatigable Jacob van Meurs) exemplifies this trend in his very impressive and extensive oeuvre: two tomes on Africa, an immense volume dedicated to China, three lavish works on the Near East and South Asia, two more sprawling accounts of the Mediterranean. All were done in the space of two decades, and it is no wonder that engravings of "races" tend naturally to collapse the different continents; that the term "Indian" is applied to Chinese and American indigenes alike; that the "biggest," "richest," and "most fabulous" marvels of the world seem to resurface in multiple exotic locales. How could there not be a fair amount of geographic bleeding from text to text, region to region, race to race — in some instances creating a stunning kaleidoscope of global color — for this author of thousands of wonder-filled pages, whose stream of publications would finally crest with the aptly titled, two-volume anthology *Dapperus exoticus curiosus?*[23]

The world fashioned by Dapper and his colleagues was unusually fluid and supple. It was a decontextualized space, with no obvious center and with minimal orientation. Cornelis de Bruyn, a superbly capable draftsman from The Hague, took his sketch pad on a tour of the globe and recorded, in a single whirlwind volume, his impressions of Russia, Persia, Sri Lanka, and the East Indies. In another, equally remarkable volume of travels, de Bruyn transported his readers to the Levant and North Africa, with stops en route in Habsburg Austria and Italy. In both works, de Bruyn insisted on taking the most indirect narrative routes imaginable, pausing occasionally to tidy things up with chapters devoted to "Odd Matters": miscellany that merit otherwise haphazard attention.[24] Arnoldus Montanus, who hardly ever left the bosom of Holland, almost made a virtue of discursiveness — which provoked fierce attack from competing (non-Dutch) geographers.[25] Montanus had no reason to worry: his very popular *Atlas Japannensis* spun the reader from inquests into native flora to reflections on Buddhist dogma, from volcanic topography to Tokugawa history, from snippets on local reptiles to the wisdom of Shinto priests. It went through nine editions in French, German, English, and Dutch, exasperating Montanus's critics — though not his faithful readers — for more than half a century. (His *America*, if slightly less digressive in form, turned out to be slightly less successful as well: a mere three editions in three languages.) These and other examples of Dutch geography cultivated a meandering style and flaunted a purposeful indeterminacy. They eschewed — once again, relative to other traditions of geography — the sort of "national" perspective that had characterized earlier works by Hakluyt, Purchas, Ramusio, and Herrera. Dutch geography lacked a sharp focus and avoided a straightforward narrative. Many of the texts it produced were (and still are) all but unreadable.[26]

Or rather, many of the texts resisted the sort of linear reading to which their critics may have subjected them — though this may be the point. For if Dutch geography discouraged easy, systematic study (this apropos of printed, literary materials), it did encourage a more flexible, almost casual style of perusal. Volumes of Dutch geography are, fundamentally, immense and cumbersome objects. This pertains both to the length of the text — many of the works produced in this period run nearly, and sometimes over, a thousand pages — and to its format, which often was delivered in an imposing folio. They do have outstanding indices, most include helpful tables of contents, and they often have summary chapter headings. If readers could only uncomfortably clasp one of the enormous products of Dutch geography, then, they could easily browse the volume and readily taste the diverse "morsels" of exotica (as one editor referred to them) offered within. Prefatory materials sometimes advocated just such a cursory manner of scanning the text. One author sheepishly confessed at the outset of his 938-page survey of world religions that his book was wholly wanting of an organizing principle. Another cheerfully noted his role in gathering, and then scattering, data for the soon-to-be overwhelmed reader, pointing out that no single person could possibly master the harvest of exotica that he had reaped: "*Non omnia possumus omnes.*"[27] Many of these editions sought to make matters easier on the reader by their generous inclusion of figures, engraved plates, and pull-out maps, adding a visual component to the text that further invited skimming. Indeed, the extensive illustration programs of printed Dutch geographies also lent a fluidity, and even interchangeability, to these sources. Plates produced for one volume typically reappeared in others, and a reader could hardly be faulted for eliciting only the broadest and most basic themes from the resulting, perhaps recycled product. Dutch geography in its printed form — immense, attractive, elegantly illustrated, and programmatically superficial — may represent a first generation of coffeetable books at the dawn of the age of coffee.[28]

Specimens of Dutch geography, whether *pronk* or not — the Dutch word, not easily translated, well conveys the quality of sumptuousness and ostentation inherent in so many of these objects — often drew attention to themselves. Books, images, and artifacts all had an importance in and of themselves, which came at the expense of their subject — the swirling mélange of places to which they were ostensibly dedicated — and their nominal authors. This, in turn, had the effect of effacing authorship, if not authority. Which is not to suggest that the original voyagers, draftsmen, and naturalists who produced Dutch geographies went unnamed; some did, if many did not. Yet even when original authors were cited, the text had a way of taking attention away from specific places and persons — Johan Nieuhof in the East Indies, say — and directing it on the work itself. Again, a useful contrast can be drawn with other samples of geographic literature. Dutch texts of this period rarely have recourse to what Anthony Pagden has called the "autoptic imagination": the device, so prevalent in early modern travel narratives, of privileging eyewitness evidence and first-person presence when describing new worlds.[29] Dutch texts, on the contrary, commonly obscure the author, following his (and it nearly always is a *he*) perfunctory opening remarks. This made the Indies the subject, rather than Nieuhof's personal experience there. More generally, it allowed products of Dutch geography to be more widely accessible — less rooted in a particular Dutch experience. Broad dissemination came easily to these products, if piracy, likewise, naturally followed. Thus could John Ogilby brashly claim authorship of Montanus's and Dapper's major works, which he repackaged and incorporated into his multivolume "great atlases" of the exotic world.[30]

Which brings up one more vital quality of Dutch geography: its semblance of neutrality. Dutch descriptions of the world endeavored to be disinterested. They dispensed as far as feasible with the built-in biases of geography, and they disguised where they could the Dutchness of their product — yet another strategy meant to foster Europe-wide consumption. Painters, accordingly, hid the fact of the Republic's prior presence in their renderings of exotic landscapes — as Frans Post did in his Brazilian scenes, which as often as not highlighted the *Portuguese* inhabitants of this formerly Dutch domain; and as Gerard van Edema did in his views of New York, which he undertook almost exclusively for an English clientele. Texts, too, went out of their way to be evenhanded. When Philippus Baldaeus composed a geography of Malabar (India), he opened his account with a strikingly inclusive survey of traffic to the region by "the Dutch, English, Moors, and Portuguese." Evert Ysbrand Ides frankly acknowledged the political purposes of his voyage from Moscow to Beijing (he traveled at the behest of the Amsterdam regent, Nicolaes Witsen, in an embassy of the czar), yet emphasized his chief "Obligation . . . to impart to the curious World what I saw and observ'd in my Journey"—fabulous exotica—rather than to relate the political and commercial horse-trading done for his patrons.[31] Dutch geography chose not to narrate the story of the Republic's rise overseas, and it conspicuously lacked an aggressively "national" focus. The late seventeenth-century Republic, it merits repeating, produced no Hakluyt or Herrera to sing its imperial glories. Indeed, Dutch geography in this period avoided any taint of politics or hint of polemic—at least as far as European rivalries were concerned. Studies of Japan gave reasonably sympathetic accounts of the persecution of the Catholics—when penned by Calvinist authors, no less—and of the expulsion of the Portuguese. Maps of the Americas erred on the side of neutrality when it came to charting colonial control. Even old rivals could be reconciled in the world of Dutch geography. A remarkable vignette in one widely translated travelogue describes how a Hollander and a "fine" Castilian met on a Moluccan island, where the two discussed the benefits of "amity" among Christians. They agreed that their nations, ancient and fierce rivals, might now fruitfully cooperate in the conversion of the heathen. This friendly tête-à-tête pointedly gives way to a jaunty discourse on birds of paradise and other exotica of the bountiful, and presumably mutually profitable, tropics.[32]

Such soft "internationalism," wholly foreign to earlier Dutch descriptions of Habsburg "tyranny" in the Indies, was not uncommon to the products of Dutch geography manufactured around 1700. By this time, memories of the epic struggle against Spain (concluded in 1648), of the highly charged Anglo-Dutch Wars (waged chiefly in the 1650s and 1660s), and of the French invasion of the Netherlands (1672) were quickly fading—or at least mellowing enough to permit a depiction of the world that appeared, to most European consumers, mostly inoffensive. Works of Dutch geography, despite their abundance of "color," despite their tendency toward strangeness, and despite their embracement of difference, often had a neutral, almost generic quality to them. The potpourri of countries and customs, of peoples and products, could come across finally as bland. Diffuse, digressive, often disorienting, sometimes recycled, purposely decontextualized: Dutch geography ended up being specific to none and thus palatable to all. The exotic world designed by the Dutch was a brand, ultimately, of very wide appeal.

Geography, whether local or global, has a double context: the place and time of production, and the place and time of consumption. Comprehending both of these contexts establishes a firmer foundation for understanding the nature of the imagined world (*geo*) and its description (*graphia*), a step, in turn, toward understanding that common substance of geography, the exotic. The Dutch Republic emerged as the leading geographer of Europe around the turn of the eighteenth century, a critical moment in the construction—imaginative as well as real—of the modern world. At the advent of the age of empire, as England and France especially intensified their expansion east and west, the Netherlands assumed the role of chief purveyor of words, images, and ideas concerning the globe. Europeans devoured the products of geography at the very moment that they began to gobble up the colonial world. The Republic, meanwhile, set to the task of manufacturing *representations* of that world. It is not that the Netherlands had no part in the expansion of overseas commerce at this time: the Dutch continued to trade in Asia (if less so in America and Africa) and certainly trafficked in imported non-European goods. Yet, by the late seventeenth and early eighteenth century, there was a marked shift away from expansionist, imperial, colonial projects—and an upsurge in the production of geography. The Republic, in other words, became less and less engaged in land-based empire, while becoming more and more involved in an empire of images: geography. Increasingly, the Dutch marketed, rather than colonized, the world.

The Dutch plied their trade in geography in multiple profitable ways. They sold, most basically, the actual wares of geography: books, maps, paintings, prints, and artifacts, which retailed at a considerable profit. Folio volumes—to cite but one example—fetched spectacular prices in the late seventeenth century, especially when sold in large orders. Six hundred readers signed on for François Valentijn's *Oud en Nieuw Oost-Indiën* at a cost of 38 guilders per five-volume set, netting the publisher a phenomenal gross of 20,000 guilders—this, when the average VOC sailor earned 120 guilders per annum. Servants of the Company, nevertheless, might supplement their wages by dealing in exotica on the side—such as the birds of paradise abundant in the Moluccas, or the lucrative shell collections of Rumphius, which the author sold, replenished, then sold again. Geography was good business.[33] Yet, more than the mere objects of geography, the Dutch sold the very *things* of the world in mimetic form—representations of actual, exotic merchandise—in their breathless descriptions and enticing promotions of those foreign products lately available in Europe. Dapper lavished loving attention on the Damascus bazaar, where the "choicest and dearest" things—silk garments, gold and silver jewels, sables, pearls, "and also slaves of both sexes"—could be had. One van Meurs-produced print

Figure 14.4 "Diverse Sorts of Bonnets / Verscheiden slagen van Bonnetten." Engraving from John Ogilby, *Atlas Chinensis* (London, 1671), based on Olfert Dapper, *Gedenckwaerdig bedryf der Nederlansche Oost-Indische Maetschappye, op de kuste en in het keizerrijk van Taising of Sina* (Amsterdam, 1670). Courtesy of the William Andrews Clark Memorial Library, University of California, Los Angeles.

arranged a selection of Oriental goods catalog-style, the adjacent "copy" (as it were) supplying the reader with nearly every commercial detail save the shop address where the commodities could be purchased (fig. 14.4). Other prints advertised other costly imports with monumental reproductions: the "Clove Tree" in Nieuhof's *Indien*, depicted literally on a marble pedestal; or Kaempfer's homage to the tea plant and its elaborate preparation, engraved as an impressive pull-out feature to his study of Japan. Frontispieces (and paintings) exhibit almost without fail the most stupendous riches of the globe — Japanese lacquerwood, Brazilian sugarcane, African ivory, Indian incense, Chinese porcelain, Persian carpets — which virtually spill out of the picture frame and onto the viewer's lap (see previous fig. 14.1).[34]

Most of all, though, the Dutch sold an *idea* of the globe, and that idea made the non-European world seem immensely, alluringly, and ineluctably desirable. For the world formulated by Dutch geography was not simply full of commodities, open to trade and potential profit. It was, more merely full of wonder, engagingly disheveled and charmingly chaotic. It was also cannily decentered and politically decontextualized, which transformed it, as a result, into a realm cleansed of commercial rivalries and refreshingly clear of colonial polemics. Instead of a hotly contested space of exploding imperial antagonisms, the non-European world created by the Dutch abounded with curiosities, diversions, and delight. It was, in the end, not so much the products of the world as the world as product that captivated the armchair traveler. The world of Dutch geography beckoned the consumer with what one magnificent tome of Asiana succinctly pronounced "the pleasures of the exotic": *Amoenitates exoticae*.

All of this was by design. At the turn of the eighteenth century, as European expansion and imperial jostling began significantly to intensify, the architects of Dutch geography constructed a world — pursued a marketing strategy, as it were — of extraordinarily wide appeal. The world fashioned by the Dutch was not only enticing; it was broadly inviting and readily agreeable to the avid consumers of late Baroque and early Enlightenment geography. The Dutch represented the world circa 1700 as a supremely seductive and wonderfully accessible space. To Europeans, at least, this world appeared enchantingly, amenably, and reassuringly exotic.

Notes

1. Georgius Everhardus Rumphius, *D'Amboinsche rariteitkamer* (Amsterdam: François Halma, 1705); idem, *Het Amboinsche Kruid-boek* (Amsterdam: François Changuion, 1741), from which the quotation derives (n.p.); Engelbert Kaempfer, *Amoenitatum exoticarum politico-physico-medicarum fasciculi V, quibus continentur variae relationes, observationes & descriptiones rerum Persicarum & Ulterioris Asiae* (Lemgo: H. W. Meyer, 1712); and Arnoldus

Montanus, *Gedenkwaerdige gesantschappen der Oost-Indische Maetschappy in 't Vereenigde Nederland, aen de Kaisaren van Japan* (Amsterdam: Jacob van Meurs, 1669), for which see the English edition, *Atlas Japannensis* (London: John Ogilby, 1670), 488. For Montanus's predilection for wonders, see also idem, *De wonderen van 't Oosten ofte de beschrijving en oorlogsdaden van Oud en Nieuw Oost-Indien* (Amsterdam: Cornelis Jansz, 1655); and idem, *Oud en Nieuw Oost-Indien* (Amsterdam: Cornelis Jans[z] Zwol, [1680]).

2. The term first comes into usage in the literature of natural history, a notably precocious example being Carolus Clusius's [Charles de L'Ecluse] *Exoticorum libri decem* (Leiden: Plantin Office [Raphelengius], 1605). And when "exotic" does appear in print, it tends to be in Latin: rare is an instance of the word in Dutch, German, or English vernacular letters.

3. The literature on early modern "exoticism" per se is virtually nonexistent—though the subject is skirted in the expanding field of "wonder" studies. Of the many recent titles on the latter topic, see Stephen J. Greenblatt, *Marvelous Possessions: The Wonder of the New World* (Chicago: University of Chicago Press, 1991); Lorraine Daston and Katharine Park, *Wonders and the Order of Nature, 1150–1750* (New York: Zone Books, 1998); and Mary Baine Campbell, *Wonder and Science: Imagining Worlds in Early Modern Europe* (Ithaca, N.Y.: Cornell University Press, 2000). Two very useful and provocative studies, focused on texts somewhat earlier and slightly later, respectively, than those cited in this essay, are Mary Baine Campbell, *The Witness and the Other World: Exotic European Travel Writing, 400–1600* (Ithaca, N.Y.: Cornell University Press, 1988), and Peter Mason, *Infelicities: Representations of the Exotic* (Baltimore: Johns Hopkins University Press, 1998). For more generalized overviews, see Bernard Smith, *Imagining the Pacific: In the Wake of the Cook Voyages* (New Haven, Conn.: Yale University Press, 1992), 1–39 ("Art in the Service of Science and Travel"); and G. S. Rousseau and Roy Porter, eds. *Exoticism in the Enlightenment* (Manchester: Manchester University Press, 1990), especially the editors' introduction, 1–22.

4. P[etrus] de Lange, *Wonderen des werelds* (Amsterdam: Marcus Willemsz Doornick, 1671), sig. A2v. Cf. also the translator's preface to Thévenot's *Travels*: "He [Thévenot] therein gives you a succinct account of all that is curious in every place, and a character of the several people. In short, he says enough to give one a reasonable information of those countreys, and not too much, to cloy the reader with the repetition of what hath seen before" (Jean de Thévenot, *The Travels of Monsieur de Thevenot into the Levant*, trans. Archibald Lovell [London: Henry Clark, 1687], n.p.).

5. Arnoldus Montanus, *De nieuwe en onbekende weereld: of Beschryving van America en 't Zuid-land* (Amsterdam: Jacob van Meurs, 1671). On Rumphius and his shells, see the superb introduction by E. M. Beekman to Georgius Everhardus Rumphius, *The Ambonese Curiosity Cabinet*, trans. and ed. E. M. Beekman (New Haven, Conn.: Yale University Press, 1999).

6. The classic bibliographies of Dutch geography—P. A. Tiele, *Nederlandsche bibliographie van land- en volkenkunde* (Amsterdam: Frederik Muller, 1884), and idem, *Mémoire bibliographique sur les journaux des navigateurs Néerlandais réimprimés dans les collections de De Bry et de Hulsius, et dan les collections hollandais du XVIIe siècle* (Amsterdam: Frederick Muller, 1867)—tend to adopt a less generous view of the range of "geography" than do I in this essay, and they offer, therefore, only moderate guidance. For works with any relevance to the Dutch experience in Asia, however, see John Landwehr, *VOC: A Bibliography of Publications Relating to the Dutch East India Company, 1602–1800* (Utrecht: HES, 1991); and, for books that make mention of the Americas—which applies to the geographies of Cluverius, Varenius, and Hornius—see John Alden and Dennis Landis, eds., *European Americana: A Chronological Guide to Works Printed in Europe Relating to the Americas, 1493–1750*, 6 vols. (New York: Readex Books, 1980–1997). More broadly useful is John Landwehr, *Studies in Dutch Books with Coloured Plates Published 1662–1875: Natural History, Topography and Travel Costumes and Uniforms* (The Hague: Junk, 1976).

7. Joost Schouten, *Notitie van de situatie, regeeringe, macht, religie, costuymen, traffijcquen, ende andere remercquable saecken, des Coninghrijcks Siam* (The Hague: Aert Meuris, 1638), which appeared in English, German, French, Latin, and Swedish, mostly in the second half of the century; Johan Nieuhof, *Gedenkweerdige Brasiliaense zee- en lantreize* (Amsterdam: Widow of Jacob van Meurs, 1682); Philippus Baldaeus, *Naauwkeurige beschryvinge van Malabar en Choromandel, der zelver aan grenzende ryken, en het machtige eyland Ceylon* (Amsterdam: Johannes Janssonius van Waasberge and Johannes van Someren, 1672); and cf. Awnsham and John Churchill, eds., *A collection of voyages and travels*, 4 vols. (London: Awnsham and John Churchill, 1704).

8. On all three—and on the *decennium mirabilius* more generally—see David Freedberg, "Science, Commerce, and Art: Neglected Topics at the Junction of History and Art History," in *Art in History/History in Art: Studies in Seventeenth-Century Dutch Culture*, ed. David Freedberg and Jan de Vries (Santa Monica, Calif.: Getty Center for the History of Art and the Humanities, 1991), 376–428. The *Hortus Malabaricus* first appeared in 1678, with complete editions following in 1683 and 1703.

9. Garrelt Verhoeven and Piet Verkruijsse, eds., *Iovrnael ofte gedenkwaerdige beschrijvinghe vande Oost-Indishe reyse van Willem Ysbrantsz. Bontekoe van Hoorn: Descriptieve bibliographie 1646–1996* (Zutphen: Walburg, 1996); Ogier Ghislain de Busbecq, *Itinera constantinopolitanum* (Antwerp: Christopher Plantin, 1581), which came out in a much expanded version published by Elsevier (Leiden) in 1633 that served, in turn, as the model for many later seventeenth- and eighteenth-century editions; Cornelis de Bruyn, *Reizen van Cornelis de Bruyn, door de vermaardste deelen van Klein Asia, de eylanden Scio, Rhodus, Cyprus, Metelino, Stanchio, &tc mitsgaders de voornaamste steden van Egypten, Syrien en Palestina* (Delft: H. van Krooneveld, 1698); and idem, *Cornelis de Bruins Reizen over Moskovie, door Persie en Indie* (Amsterdam: R. and G. Wetstein, J. Oosterwyk, H. van de Gaete, 1714). For the travel anthologies, see Landwehr, *VOC*, esp. 99–133.

10. Balthasar Bekker, *De betoverde weereld*, 4 vols. (Amsterdam: Daniel van den Dalen, 1691–93); and J. F. Bernard et al., eds., *Ceremonies et coutumes religieuses des tous les peuples du monde*, 8 vols. (Amsterdam: J. F. Bernard, 1723–43). For examples of the sort of "literary *Kunstkammern*" that I have in mind, see Simon de Vries, *D'edelste tijdkortingh der weet-geerige verstanden: of De groote historische rariteit-kamer der sonderlinghste natuerlijcke en boven natuerlijcke saecken, geschiedenissen en voorvallen van allerley slagh*, 3 vols. (Amsterdam: Jan Bouman, 1682–95); idem, *Wonderen soo aen als in, en wonder-gevallen soo op als ontrent de zeeën, rivieren, meiren, poelen en fonteynen* (Amsterdam, 1687); and de Lange, *Wonderen*.

11. Dutch-produced atlases are excellently cataloged in Cornelis Koeman, *Atlantes Neerlandici: Bibliography of Terrestrial, Maritime and Celestial Atlases and Pilot Books, Published in the Netherlands up to 1880*, 6 vols. (Amsterdam: Theatrum Orbis Terrarum, 1967–85); for globes, see P. C. J. van der Krogt, *Globi Neerlandici: The Production of Globes in the Low Countries* (Utrecht: HES, 1993). On Dutch cartographic materials more generally, see Kees Zandvliet, *De groote waereld in 't kleen geschildert: Nederlandse kartografie tussen de middeleeuwen en de industriële revolutie* (Alphen aan den Rijn: Canaletto, 1985); and on the exotic world more particularly, see idem, *Mapping for Money: Maps, Plans and Topographic Paintings and Their Role in Dutch Overseas Expansion during the Sixteenth and Seventeenth Centuries* (Amsterdam: Batavian Lion International, 1998), which discusses "floor" maps on 211.

12. The literature on visual exotica is uneven. For Post, see Joaquim de Sousa-Leão, *Frans Post, 1612–1680* (Amsterdam: A. L. van Gendt, 1973); and P. J. P. Whitehead and M. Boeseman, *A Portrait of Dutch Seventeenth-Century Brazil: Animals, Plants and People by the Artists of John Maurits of Nassau*, Royal Dutch Academy of Sciences, Natural History Monographs, 2nd ser., vol. 87 (Amsterdam: North Holland, 1989), which covers Brazilian iconography in toto and, in doing so, details the oeuvre of Albert Eckhout, Post's colleague who specialized in

exotic still lifes and portraits. Valkenburg, Beeckman, and van Edema are still in need of biographers and catalogers, but see the brief treatment of Valkenburg in C. P. van Eeghen, "Dirk Valkenburg: Boekhouder-schrijver-kunstschilder voor Jonas Witsen," *Oud Holland* 61 (1946): 58–69. On exotic themes in decorative arts, see the relevant chapters of Hugh Honour, *The European Vision of America* (Cleveland: Cleveland Museum of Art, 1975).

13. Patterns of Dutch collecting are surveyed in Ellinoor Bergvelt et al., *De wereld binnen handbereik: Nederlandse kunst- en rariteitenverzamelingen, 1585–1735*, 2 vols. (Zwolle: Waanders, 1992), and see especially the essays of Jaap van der Veen, "'Dit klain Vertrek bevat een Weereld vol gewoel': Negentig Amsterdammers en hun kabinetten," 232–258; K. van Berkel, "Citaten uit het boek der natuur: Zeventiende-eeuwse Nederlandse naturaliën kabinetter en de ontwikkeling van de natuurwetenschap," 169–191; and Roelof van Gelder, "De wereld binnen handbereik: Nederlandse kunst- en rariteitenverzamelingen, 1585–1735," 15–38, which notes the unique Dutch habit of selling collections to foreign buyers (this in the final decades of the seventeenth century). On "hybrid" exotica — and for a rich inquiry into collecting and exotica more generally — see Martin Kemp, "'Wrought by No Artist's Hand': The Natural, the Artificial, the Exotic, and the Scientific in Some Artifacts from the Renaissance," in *Reframing the Renaissance: Visual Culture in Europe and Latin America, 1450–1650*, ed. Claire Farago (New Haven, Conn.: Yale University Press, 1995), 177–196.

14. Romeyn de Hooghe, *Les Indes Orientales et Occidentales et autres lieux* (Leiden: Pieter van der Aa, 1710), and see also (to cite but one example) Wouter Schouten, *Oost-Indische voyagie, vervattende veel voorname voorvallen en ongemeene vreemde geschiedenissen, bloedige zee- en landt-gevechten tegen de Portugeesen en Makassaren; belegering, en verovering van veel voorname steden en kasteelen* (Amsterdam: Jacob van Meurs and Johannes van Someren, 1676), which contains selections of de Hooghe's (in this case, wholly irrelevant) images in some editions.

15. Ogilby claimed authorship of a number of Dutch works — most notoriously, perhaps, Montanus's *America* — and, even when he did relinquish claims of authority, he sometimes cited original authors inaccurately (ironically giving credit to Montanus for Dapper's *Atlas Chinensis*; see below). For a case study of the intricacies of publishing early modern geography, see Isabella H. van Eeghen, "Arnoldus Montanus's book on Japan," *Quaerendo* 2 (1972): 250–272; and compare Katherine S. Van Eerde, *John Ogilby and the Taste of His Times* (Folkestone: Dawson & Sons, 1976), 95–122, which seems to have overlooked the Dutch sources of Ogilby's "great atlases."

It may also be worth pointing out how well printers in the Republic themselves poached and appropriated works of geography not originally written in Dutch — as was the case with Charles de Rochefort's *Histoire naturelle et morale des iles Antilles de l'Amerique* (Rotterdam: Arnout Leers, 1658), the Rotterdam editions of which became signal texts for later printers. See Everett C. Wilkie Jr., "The Authorship and Purpose of the 'Histoire naturelle et morale des iles Antilles,'" *Harvard Library Bulletin*, 2nd ser., no. 3 (1991): 26–84.

16. On Post and Eckhout, see Whitehead, *Dutch Seventeenth-Century Brazil*, 162–193 and passim; for the so-called "Christina atlas," see Zandvliet, *Mapping for Money*, 179–180.

17. Freedberg poses this question implicitly, in identifying a surge of Dutch natural-history writing in the later seventeenth century ("Science, Commerce, and Art"). This is also a theme broached by V. D. Roeper and G. J. D. Wildeman, *Reizen op papier: Journalen en reisverslagen van Nederlandse ontdekkingsreizigers, kooplieden en avonturiers*, Jaarboek van het Nederlands Scheepvaart Museum (Zutphen: Walburg, 1996), which pays well deserved attention to the remarkable work of van Meurs and other Dutch printers of travel literature.

18. This pertains particularly to representations of America. See Benjamin Schmidt, "Tyranny Abroad: The Dutch Revolt and the Invention of America," *De Zeventiende Eeuw* 11 (1995): 161–174; and idem, "Exotic Allies: The Dutch-Chilean Encounter and the (Failed) Conquest of America," *Renaissance Quarterly* 52 (1999): 440–473.

19. Johan Nieuhof, *Gedenkwaerdige zee en lantreize door de voornaemste landschappen van West en Oostindien*, 2 pts. (Amsterdam: Widow of Jacob van Meurs, 1682), and see 1: 20–38 and 195–211 for Nieuhof's (or his publisher's) conflation of exotic *naturalia*, and 1: 211–226 for his survey (and confusion) of exotic "races."

20. Willem Piso et al., *Historia naturalis Brasiliae* (Leiden: F. Haack, and Amsterdam: L. Elsevier, 1648); and idem, *De Indiae utriusque re naturali et medica libri quatuordecim* (Amsterdam: L. & D. Elsevier, 1658).

21. Bernard, *Ceremonies et coutumes* (and note how the first Paris imprint of 1741 actually scotched this engraved frontispiece in favor of a more "Catholic" image of the Church); Simon de Vries, *Curieuse aenmerckingen der bysonderste Oost- en West Indische verwonderenswaerdige dingen*, 4 vols. (Utrecht: Johannes Ribbius, 1682); and Joan Blaeu, *Atlas maior, sive Cosmographia Balviana*, 11 vols. (Amsterdam: Joan Blaeu, 1662).

22. Cf. Hernán Cortés, *Letters from Mexico*, trans. and ed. Anthony Pagden, 2nd ed. (New Haven, Conn.: Yale University Press, 1986), 67, 102, 105; and Montanus, *Japan*, 91.

23. Olfert Dapper's magnificent oeuvre began, it should be added, with the first-ever Dutch translation of Herodotus (1665). See further Olfert Dapper, *Naukeurige beschrijvinge der Afrikaensche gewesten, van Egypten, Barbaryen, Libyen, Biledulgerid, Negroslant, Guinea, Ethiopien, Abyssinie* (Amsterdam: Jacob van Meurs, 1668); idem, *Naukeurige beschryvinge der Afrikaensche eylanden* (Amsterdam: Jacob van Meurs, 1668); idem, *Gedenckwaerdig bedryf der Nederlansche Oost-Indische Maetschappye, op de kuste en in het keizerrijk van Taising of Sina* (Amsterdam: Jacob van Meurs, 1670); idem, *Asia: of Naukeurige beschryving van het rijk des Grooten Mogols, en een groote gedeelte van Indiën* (Amsterdam: Jacob van Meurs, 1672); idem, *Naukeurige beschryving van gantsch Syrie, en Palestyn of Heilige Lant* (Amsterdam: Jacob van Meurs, 1677); idem, *Naukeurige beschryving van Asie* [sic] *behelsende de gewesten van Mesopatamie, Babylonie, Assyrie, Anotolie of Klein Asie* (Amsterdam: Jacob van Meurs, 1680); idem, *Naukeurige beschrijving der eilanden, in de archipel der Middellandsche zee, in en ontrent dezelv, gelegen* (Amsterdam: Wolfgang, Waesberge, Boom, van Someren, and Goethals, 1688); idem, *Naukeurige beschryvinge van Morea, eertijds Peloponnesus en de eilanden gelegen onder de kusten van Morea en binnen de Golf van Venetien* (Amsterdam: Wolfgang, Waesberge, Boom, van Someren, and Goethals, 1688); and J. C. Männling, ed., *Dapperus exoticus curiosus*, 2 vols. (Frankfurt and Leipzig: M. Rohrlachs, 1717–18).

24. Bruyn, *Moskovie*; and idem, *Klein Asia*, in which Chapter 25 is among those expressly dedicated to miscellany. On Bruyn, see Jan Willem Drijvers, Jan de Hond, and Heleen Sancisi-Weerdenburg, eds., *'Ik hadde de nieusgierigheid': De reizen van Cornelis de Bruijn (ca. 1652–1727)* (Leiden: Ex Oriente Lux, and Leuven: Peeters, 1997).

25. See, for example, the introduction by the translator to Kaempfer's history of Japan, which complains of the "large digressions" of Montanus and of the lavish plates, which are dismissed as "the greatest embellishments": Engelbert Kaempfer, *The history of Japan*, trans. J[ohann] G[aspar] Scheahzer (London: J. G. Scheuchzer, 1727), xliij–iv.

26. Smith (*Imagining the Pacific*, 23–24) makes a similar point regarding narrative ordering, though in reference to visual sources, specifically, of Dutch geography. Much the same can be said, I wish to argue, for the literary (no less than visual) texts produced at this time.

27. De Lange, *Wonderen*, sig. A2v, on bite-size exotica; J[oannes] A[ysma], *Spiegel der Sibyllen, van vierderley vertooningen* (Amsterdam: J. Aysma, 1685), sig. *3r, on disorderly organization ("in weynig regulen"); and Johan Nyenborgh, *Tooneel der Ambachten: of Den winckel der handtwercken en konsten* (Groningen: Jacob Sipkes, 1659), sig. *2, where the author quips, in Dutch as well as Latin, "Een eenig man, niet alles kan" (No one can do it all).

28. A number of authors were explicit about the importance of a visual component in geography. Kaempfer noted in his preface that "copper engravings also needed to be made [for this book], since exotica are very difficult to comprehend without the help of clarifying

illustrations": Kaempfer, *Amoenitatum exoticarum*, n.p., and see the English translation (which I have altered slightly) in Engelbert Kaempfer, *Exotic Pleasures: Fascicle III, Curious Scientific and Medical Observations*, trans. Robert W. Carrubba, Library of Renaissance Humanism (Carbondale: Southern Illinois University Press, 1996), xix. The English introduction to Bernard's *Ceremonies* likewise remarks on the essential place of pictures in geography: "no subjects stand more in need of illustration than these [geography and travel literature]; so hardly any have been ever set off with such truth and advantage." See J. F. Bernard, *The ceremonies and religious customs of the various nations of the known world*, 6 vols. (London: William Jackson for Claude du Bosc, 1733–37) vol. 4, viii.

29. Anthony Pagden, *European Encounters with the New World: From Renaissance to Romanticism* (New Haven, Conn.: Yale University Press, 1993), 51–87. Meanwhile, the "I-witness" (to adopt Clifford Geertz's pun) was making great headway in contemporary *fictional* prose—Swift's Gulliver, Defoe's Crusoe, and Montesquieu's Uzbek all claim first-person authority—just as Dutch editors were deemphasizing the traveler's position in the text. On Nieuhof's Asian narrative, which was much worked over by his Amsterdam publisher (van Meurs), see Roeper and Wildeman, *Reizen op papier*, 98.

30. Cf. Van Eerde, *John Ogilby*, 95–122, and, more generally, Adrian Johns, *The Nature of the Book: Print and Knowledge in the Making* (Chicago: University of Chicago Press, 1998), which, inter alia, seems also to misread Ogilby's title pages.

31. Baldaeus, *Malabar en Choromandel* (and cf. Churchill, *Voyages and travels*, 572); Evert Ysbrants Ides, *Drie-jarige reize naar China* (Amsterdam: François Halma, 1704) (quotation from English edition: *Three years travels from Moscow over-land to China* [London: W. Freeman et al., 1706], sig. A2v).

32. Schouten, *Oost-Indische voyagie*, 44–45. If one had to point to an "enemy" in Dutch geography of ca. 1700, it would be the Portuguese, an antagonist widely acceptable to the "new" imperialists of Enlightenment Europe. Virtually no text produced in the Republic was ever translated into Portuguese, in any event, nor were the products of Dutch geography apparently marketed for Portuguese consumption.

33. François Valentijn, *Oud en Nieuw Oost-Indiën*, 5 vols. (Amsterdam: Gerard Onder de Linden and Dordrecht: Joannes van Braam, 1724–26), which includes a subsciption list of some six hundred buyers. On prices of luxury books, see Landwehr, *Studies in Dutch Books* (81 for Valentijn's geography). Data on wages—from 9 to 11 Dutch guilders per month for a VOC sailor (or soldier) and about twice that amount for an officer—are taken from Femme S. Gaastra, *De geschiedenis van de VOC* (Zutphen: Walburg, 1991), 91; and see also Jan de Vries and Ad van der Woude, *The First Modern Economy: Success, Failure and Perseverance of the Dutch Economy, 1500–1815* (Cambridge: Cambridge University Press, 1997), 607–32.

34. Dapper, *Syrie en Palestyn*, 19; idem, *Gedenckwaerdig bedryf*, plate facing 459 ("Verscheiden slagen van bonetten"); Nieuhof, *West en Oostindien*, 2: plate facing 31 ("Nagelboom"); Kaempfer, *De beschryving van Japan: behelsende een verhaal van den ouden en tegenwoordigne staat en regeering van dat ryk* (The Hague: P. Gosse and J. Neaulme, and Amsterdam: Balthasar Lakeman, 1729), plate no. 39.

Shopping for Instruments in Paris and London

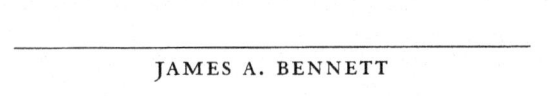

JAMES A. BENNETT

On 8 December 1768, Jean Bernoulli wrote from London:

> I've been here in London for eight days. I am still not able to tell you about astronomers or observatories, but I will share the pleasant surprise which strikes an astronomer walking through the streets of this capital. You have surely heard talk of the richness and brilliance of the shops of London, but I doubt whether you can imagine how much astronomy contributes to the beauty of the spectacle: London has a great many opticians; the shops of these artists are full of refracting and reflecting telescopes, octants, &c. All these instruments, ranged and set out with care, strike the eye at the same time as imposing reflections on the mind.[1]

He was astonished, and was confident that his correspondent would share his astonishment, that he could continue his report on the state of astronomy in Europe without yet having visited such conventional sites as observatories, academies, and the homes of astronomers. He was not surprised that instrument making flourished in London: that was well known to anyone active in practical astronomy in the eighteenth century, when London instruments were being used in observatories all over Europe. His correspondent also was familiar with this, as Bernoulli introduces the famous names as though he had met in the flesh some shared object of distant curiosity and admiration ("You know very well the name of M. DOLLOND, the celebrated artist").[2] Instead what surprised him was the commercial context for all this astronomy: the vulgar but dynamic and exhilarating world of the London shops — of Fleet Street, the Strand, Haymarket, and Piccadilly. What business did astronomy have to display its apparatus in such a context? And the display was not confined to the famous names he had known from their publications and exported instruments: there were evidently a great many more makers of unknown reputations, but whose shops seemed similarly to be filled with organized presentations of telescopes and octants. It was clear from the very first impression that the experience of an astronomer shopping in London would be very different from one in Paris.

We have become familiar with the idea that over the course of a century or so, a "public" science had been established by the later eighteenth century, and the ingredients commonly cited in its formation include societies, coffeehouses, lecture courses, museums, polite or rational entertainments, and popular books. This chapter will look at shopping for science in the seventeenth and eighteenth centuries, at the nature of the interaction between buyer and retailer, and at how and where their transaction was conducted. We will use the experiences of foreign visitors: they notice and remark on what strikes them as unexpected and distinctive, drawing attention to things that locals pass over as unremarkable and taken for granted.[3]

MONCONYS, VON UFFENBACH, AND LALANDE IN LONDON

Our first shopping visitor to London arrived in May 1663. He was Balthazar de Monconys, who was accompanying the duc de Chevreuse on a tour of Europe at the behest of his father, the duc de Luynes.[4] Monconys was a member of the Montmor Academy in Paris and was keen to meet fellows of the Royal Society: he tried to find Henry Oldenburg as soon as he arrived in London. He was an active, enthusiastic, and perceptive observer of the English scene, who deliberately set out to experience as much as he could manage, filling his days with the rich and colorful life of London — the manners of the court, the bookshops of St. Paul's, the workshops of instrument makers, the public prize fighting and bear baiting. More than anything he was taken by all kinds of "ingenuity" in London, by the activities of the Royal Society, and the inventions, experiments, and "secrets" of its fellows. His chief guides were Oldenburg, Robert Moray and William Brouncker.

On his first day in London, before he had met any of these guides, he bought a telescope from a maker close to the Royal Exchange. In the days that followed he visited more shops, bought more telescopes, and on his third day in London, before he had found Oldenburg, he made his way to Richard Reeve's workshop in Longacre, to which he had been particularly recommended. No telescopes were in stock, such was the demand, but Monconys was shown something that astonished him. He attended a demonstration of a magic lantern. It is clear from his careful description that he had never seen such a thing before — indeed his description became one of the very first published accounts of the magic lantern. He has no shortcut vocabulary to deploy, but must describe the process with deliberation; the slide, for example, is "a glass 'leaf' on which the objects are painted."[5] Not only does Monconys give us what seems to be the first recorded English instance of a magic lantern, but more important for our purposes, his account shows that more things could take place in the shops of instrument makers than buying and selling: already they could be the sites of public demonstrations in natural philosophy.

Monconys continued to visit shops and to buy instruments, while becoming caught up in the life of the London virtuosi. He began to attend meetings of the Royal Society on 13 May — an important occasion for the new society, since it was the day when the royal charter was read to the council — and returned to his lodgings by way of Reeve's shop, to see his range of microscopes. He was back at the society the following week. He met Robert Boyle then, and visited and admired Boyle's laboratory, noting his very good telescopes and two excellent microscopes. He attended the society again on 27 May, and this time the Journal Book records him contributing to the discussion. He visits other laboratories and workshops, and ventures as far as Stratford Bow to visit the inventor Johann Küffeler, where he saw a self-regulating "philosophical furnace" for experiments in natural philosophy.

Monconys records all these encounters with evident relish and enthusiasm. He was on an odyssey of discovery. Boyle tells him about dissecting the frozen eye of a bull and describes in detail an experiment of his demonstrating the weight of the air. Monconys buys sixty-six examples of what he calls "glass teardrops," known in England as "Prince Rupert's drops"— small glass vials with unusual mechanical properties that the Royal Society had investigated at the king's request and of which Robert Hooke was to publish an explanation in his *Micrographia* of 1665. The following day Monconys sees a special design of pendulum clock at Moray's house, goes with him to the laboratory of Nicaise le Fèvre, former chemist at the Jardin du Roi and now apothecary to Charles II, and from there to Oldenburg to discuss the last meeting of the Royal Society. A few days later he buys eighty-four more of the glass teardrops.

Monconys was delighted to be involved in this activity. When Samuel Sorbière, secretary of the Montmor Academy, visited London at the same time and sought out Monconys, he says, "I found him in his element, immersed in the conversation of natural philosophers and breathing nothing but machines and new experiments"[6] The shops of certain makers were an integral part of this world. When Monconys returns to Reeve's to see his microscopes, he also engages him in discussion and learns, for example, something of the technique of working gems.

Other instrument makers visited by Monconys were Ralph Greatorex, to whom he entrusted a loadstone for "arming"— that is, fitting with iron pole pieces to enhance its magnetic properties — and Anthony Thompson. He wanted Thompson to make him an example of Christopher Wren's perspectograph, even though he could not have it ready in less than fifteen days, by which time Monconys would have left England. Monconys arranged for Oldenburg to send it on to him, which he did in November 1664, but it arrived in Paris shortly after Monconys died.[7]

There are a number of things to be learned from the record of Monconys's experience in London. He was keen to acquire London instruments, and there were a number of makers to choose from. Among those Monconys visits, some — in particular Reeve, Greatorex, and Thompson — are clearly linked to members of the Royal Society and are an integral part of the virtuosi culture of London. Monconys is aware that Reeve's collaboration is central to the efforts of Goddard, Paul Neile, Moray, and Wren to develop the long refractor, efforts that had attracted the personal interest of Charles II. When Oldenburg reported observations of a transit of Mercury to Boyle in October 1664, he said that "Our Virtuosi did observe both at Gresham [College] and Mr Reeve's".[8] We know that on the occasion of an earlier transit, in 1661, Christiaan Huygens was among the observers at Reeve's shop.[9] There is evidence that Thompson's shop in Hosier Lane, Smithfield, was also a recognized meeting place, and Monconys knew that he had made the original example of Wren's perspectograph.[10] Greatorex too was one of the makers closest to the Royal Society and had worked for Wilkins, Goddard, and Boyle.

We have seen that Monconys does not only transact business with Reeve: he records things he learned from his discussions with him, and it is particularly striking that Reeve has a demonstration to offer his visitors. It is important in this context that Reeve has a shop — a business address that is more than simply a workshop. His address is known; Monconys can go there and be received before he has met his Royal Society contacts. This is a commercial space that is in the public domain, but it is a site also for the exchange of intelligence in natural philosophy and even for observation and demonstration of the kind normally associated with the Royal Society.

In these London shops there were off-the-shelf items that could be had immediately, but for more unusual instruments from the best makers, the customer would wait while his order was attended to. This was not always successful: Monconys was promised by a glassworker that he could have an example of Wren's circular thermometer — an instrument that could be made self-registering — but on returning several days later, he was disappointed. This is not surprising: it was a very unusual instrument, requiring critical shaping and balancing. Even this phenomenon of delayed orders and returning visits is linked to the different uses of the shop space. The visitor might come back not only to see or receive his completed instruments, but also or alternatively to see finished work for other customers or for stock, and a more advantageous time for a visit could be predicted on the basis of progress in the workshop. This reinforced the idea of the shop as a place of resort, where instruments and production techniques could be viewed and discussed, while the visitor's growing familiarity with the maker and his premises added to the impression of a semipublic space where he and other visitors had an interest shared with the maker himself. Monconys saw Reeve several times, and records being given specimens of materials, but so far as we know he bought nothing.

These characteristics of the London trade had developed significantly by the time the collector, connoisseur, and traveler Zacharias Conrad von Uffenbach of Frankfurt-am-Main came to London with his brother in 1710.[11] He visited the shops of John Marshall, Edmund Culpeper, John Patrick, John Rowley, and Francis Hauksbee, all of whom are remembered today as talented and original makers. In each case he seems to have gone by coach deliberately to the premises of a known maker at a known address. On one occasion they "intended to wait on" Rowley, but he was not at home.[12] On another they failed to find "the shop of the famous mechanician Moxon."[13] The Moxon who could most reasonably be described as "famous" was Joseph, who had died in 1691, but could well have had a continuing European reputation through his publications. His son James succeeded to the business, but the last record of him trading dates from 1703.[14]

Von Uffenbach's brother persuaded Marshall, on payment of 7 guineas, to teach him the art of glass cutting, not because he thought Marshall was particularly skilled in this direction — he did not — but because he was curious to learn the English practice. As a result the brothers made frequent visits to Marshall's shop, usually in the afternoons, for these practical lessons. They bought some small telescopes, and were taken by Marshall's method of demonstrating their quality: he "had had his name placed in white on the roof of a house some twenty houses from his own," which could be read easily with one of his telescopes.[15] From Culpeper, von Uffenbach bought a number of fairly routine items — an architectonic sector, a magnet, a microscope, a spyglass, a drawing pen, and an oval reading glass — but Culpeper could not help the brothers in their quest for an example of Samuel Morland's calculating machine. At Patrick's they saw many different kinds of barometer, which von Uffenbach describes in detail, while mentioning which are new inventions and what were their particular advantages, so they must have spent some time viewing and discussing them, but they seem to have bought nothing.[16]

They did buy a telescope at "an optician's called James Praun," and they asked him to repolish the lenses of instruments bought from Culpeper. It is curious that no James Praun or anyone with a name that might be so construed is known to have been trading at the time. In von Uffenbach's view

"This man is very cheap and good and, if he takes the trouble, makes a fine polish,"[17] but we must remember that he had judged Marshall's talents with glass inferior, even though he knew that "everyone makes a great to-do over him and his work."[18] Von Uffenbach's judgment reflects on his engagement with instruments, and in any case the whole account of his visit to London reminds us that he is a general connoisseur, collector, and dilettante. The telescope he buys from Praun is in keeping with this. It is a refractor with five lenses, a shagreen covered body and a number of draw-tubes. The lenses and tubes can be configured in four different ways, to yield different telescopes, which von Uffenbach describes. This delight in ingenuity, often taking the form of a multipurpose instrument that can be variously configured, was a familiar ploy to catch the dilettante shopper.

When von Uffenbach did find Rowley in, he was willing to make Morland's calculating machine for 5 guineas, but none seems to have been ordered. Rowley, who was a very resourceful and original maker, showed the brothers some long object glasses between 15 and 18 feet focal length, that he was not willing to sell. One interesting thing we learn from von Uffenbach, which does not seem to be known otherwise in the history of the telescope, is that Rowley was making a Newtonian reflector. It is generally thought that the only such attempt between Newton himself and John Hadley in 1721 was by Francis Hauksbee, who was closely associated with Newton. Although the details are slight, it seems likely that the objective mirrors were made of glass, to be silvered: von Uffenbach introduces them in the context of the long focal length objective lenses, says they are "convex-concave" and compares their polish with that of the lenses. Silvered glass mirrors for telescopes came into general use only much later but the idea was around in the early eighteenth century: John Pound mentions it as a possibility in 1723, and James Short was making such mirrors in 1734. Both Newton and Hadley used metal mirrors. Rowley valued his objective mirrors highly — at 7 or 8 guineas each.[19]

So the pattern of transactions in the shops of the makers is becoming familiar. Viewing of original pieces, discussion with the maker, instruction, and demonstration are all part of practicing the trade on the one hand and polite shopping on the other. Makers with substantial reputations were particular targets, even if such shoppers were prepared to buy elsewhere. Von Uffenbach was especially fortunate to have seen a Newtonian telescope under construction at Rowley's, and to have listened while "he praised this invention of Newton very highly, as though it were quite matchless." But he still recorded his disappointment that "there were no other instruments completed at the moment, which is greatly to be regretted, since he is considered one of the best mechanicians in England."[20] Rowley's name is found on a great variety of surviving instruments, and it is difficult to imagine that he had nothing in his shop beyond a few lenses that were not for sale. It seems more likely that von Uffenbach is ignoring the standard and routine instruments: this aspect of the shopping experience related to the original, ingenious, or ornate piece, an instrument worth a special visit, one for which the maker himself had a direct responsibility and that was not simply made or bought in as an item of stock.

Von Uffenbach witnessed the most developed example that London had to offer in this rise of polite shopping when he visited the premises of Francis Hauksbee. Hauksbee was the maker closest to the Royal Society, being employed as a demonstrator to provide experiments at the meetings. He took these experimental demonstrations from the society into the public realm with his subscription series of lecture/demonstrations, at first in collaboration with James Hodgson.[21] By 1710 Hauksbee was offering the courses on his own, and von Uffenbach's account suggests that experiments would be performed for private visitors as well as within the lecture course; we cannot be certain of that, but there is no suggestion that the audience was larger than the two brothers.

The first time they visited Hauksbee's premises in Wine-Office Court, Fleet Street, it was not by appointment, since "we did not find him in." Clearly they treated Harksbee's address like that of a shop, where they could expect to be received on demand. They were not entirely disappointed, as Hauksbee's young "cousin"—probably his nephew, also Francis Hauksbee, who was later involved in a rival lecturing enterprise—"took us up and showed us some common experiments." They then made an appointment and bought a copy of the elder Hauksbee's *Physico-Mechanical Experiments* (London, 1709), "so that after studying it at home, we might see the experiments again with great profit."[22]

When they returned, they were in the hands of a master philosophical showman: "We saw with amazement his excellent demonstrations and experiments, especially those relating to the nature of light, which were certainly very excellent and curious." Von Uffenbach followed the experiments from Hauksbee's book and was enchanted by his skill in carrying off a whole series of pneumatic demonstrations in a virtuoso display on the air-pump. Hauksbee was practiced at drawing his audience into the experiments, getting them to test the effect on the phenomena of rubbing the evacuated vessel with their fingers, or breathing on it.[23] Here is a telling early example of the commercial talent and technique of a new breed of philosophical entrepreneur: the combined use of the illustrated textbook and the demonstration to engage the potential customer for examples of the apparatus in use. Hauksbee derived income from courses and publications, but his principal aim was to sell the products he manufactured. To do so he had first to create a new market, and the policy he adopted was to transfer to his shop—with only slight modification—the traditional experimental performance demanded formerly of Robert Hooke and now of himself at the Royal Society.

An unfortunate imbalance is already evident: we are much better supplied with foreign instrument shoppers in London than in Paris. For the end of the seventeenth century, we do have Martin Lister's visit to Paris: he is interested in various trades, but he takes little notice of instrument makers. In fact the only one who figures significantly is Michael Butterfield, who was "a right hearty honest Englishman, who has resided in France 35 years."[24] Butterfield is a further example of a maker conducting experimental demonstrations on his premises—in this case with his large collection of lodestones—but it is clear that this is not typical of the Parisian scene.

The imbalance simply reflects the state of affairs in the period: informed observers did not go to Paris to shop for instruments. Long ago Maurice Daumas noted that the Parisian makers served "a small, local clientele," which he identified as the royal court, the salons of a few wealthy individuals, and the cabinets of several colleges.[25] There was practically no export trade, and the local market would not witness the consumer expansion that in England would give the hardware of natural philosophy a place in many well-to-do homes. It is only toward the end of the eighteenth century that a few visitors to Paris indicate the beginnings of a revival in the French industry.

But French visitors to London can be an indirect comment on Paris, because of the unfamiliar things they note and the contrasts they draw. Lalande came to London in 1763, the visit being in itself a comment on the relation of English to French work in precision mechanics, for his mission was in part to discover as much as he could about the chronometers of John Harrison, and in part to investigate the acquisition of astronomical instruments.[26] He was certainly struck by the vitality and confidence of the mechanical scene in London, by the distinctive and visible presence of a dynamic group of practitioners, and by the acceptance of some of them into the Royal Society. For some, such as the leading makers of astronomical instruments, involvement with the Royal Society was important, but it must be remembered that the makers had other institutions and associations and were more than able to take independent initiatives. Historians of science tend to focus on the Royal Society as the source of intellectual and cultural patronage, but it is far from clear that it had an exclusive prominence in these respects for the makers. Nonetheless, Lalande found the easy relations between *savants* and *fabricants*, between *sciences abstraites* and *sciences appliquées*, different, refreshing, and positive.

Lalande spend a good deal of time with James Short, and also with John Bird and Francis Watkins. He discussed polishing techniques several times with Short, who was his principal link to Harrison. On one occasion Short confided that giving a mirror a parabolic shape — and his reputation rested particularly on this supposed skill — was a matter of touch, not science: "it's only by feeling one's way."[27] Lalande was entertained several times by Watkins and described instruments he saw there. He also visited Jeremiah Sisson more than once and viewed his instruments. It may have been from Watkins that he learned that Sisson had gone to prison several times for not paying his workmen, and that failure to complete instruments had led him to pawn others, only to see them sold well below their market value.[28]

Bird, he discovered, would charge 1,200 French *livres* (equivalent to 50 guineas) for a quadrant of 18 inches, half to be paid in advance, and 350 pounds sterling (8,000 *livres*) for an 8-foot quadrant — that is, one like the mural instrument he had built for Greenwich. Packing would be an additional 10 pounds, and the delivery time would be two years.[29] Lalande had learned at Sisson's that it was Jonathan, rather than his infirm father, Jeremiah, who had made several well-known quadrants, including that of his mentor Pierre Charles Le Monnier; at Bird's, on the other hand, Bird told him that he had seen complaints about Sisson's work.[30] No doubt, after the order from Le Monnier and in view of Le Monnier's increasing promotion of English instruments, Lalande was seen as a serious possible source of a significant commission, so the rivalry between Bird and Sisson was understandable. A week later Bird was able to play an important card: Lalande had breakfast at Bird's with Thomas Hornsby, professor of astronomy in Oxford, and they went together by boat to Greenwich to examine the instruments there; both Bird's guests were shopping for quadrants, and both would eventually buy small and large quadrants from Bird. Lalande placed his first order two weeks later, for an 18-inch quadrant, paying the stipulated 25 guineas in advance.[31]

Lalande introduces us to some new features of the London scene. No ordinary shopper, he was favorably placed as a fellow of the Royal Society, and he carried the promise of a significant commission. His shopping technique included spending a long period in the astronomical community of London — makers and astronomers. At the same time, the situation of the makers was changing. The success of Graham's instruments at Greenwich, including the first empirical proof of the motion of the earth and the setting of a new foundation of accuracy in positional astronomy through the discoveries of aberration and nutation, had set the elite makers of precision instruments on a path that would progressively raise their status above that of the rest of the trade. Sisson and Bird had begun to reap the benefits through the beginnings of an export trade in astronomical instruments.[32] Bird would became even better known through the Board of Longitude's endorsement and publication of his construction methods.[33] But he was already able to take distinguished shoppers to the Greenwich Observatory — the perfect showroom for his quadrant and transit instrument.

Lalande's elevated position also reveals to us an aspect of the trade in instruments of natural philosophy that we have not encountered before. He went with Dr. John Pringle, physician to the queen and later to George III, to see the royal collection. According to Pringle, George had told him that he knew Lalande's works. The king was going to Richmond but had left orders that the air pump designed by Smeaton was to be made ready for Lalande, and it was George Adams, the maker of the pump and instrument maker to the king, who had the considerable task, according to Lalande's account, of getting it to work. Princely patronage for instrument makers was not typical of the London trade, but it did exist.[34]

BERNOULLI, BUGGE, AND VAN MARUM IN LONDON AND PARIS

Three of our travelers from the later eighteenth century go both to London and to Paris. The first is Bernoulli, whose surprise and delight at the vibrancy of the commercial trade in London in 1768 we have already seen. Some of the practices we have encountered with Reeve and Haukbee are now being pursued vigorously by Benjamin Martin. Bernoulli and his correspondent already know Martin's name through his publications. His shop is one of the best stocked, and he has a clientele eager for his courses on mechanics, experimental physics, and astronomy, all made doubly interesting by the beautiful instruments used for illustration. Bernoulli himself attended "with pleasure" a lecture on the forthcoming transit of Venus, where Martin used a large animated diagram on one wall of the room, which represented the progress of the transit, as it might be visible in London, up to the time of sunset. This was a "virtual" experience offered in a room of Martin's shop, available daily with no disappointment from bad weather. Bernoulli is very taken by this, and in general gives the impression of a popular, thriving, and innovative business in natural philosophy.[35] Although he judged that Martin's twenty or so books had been very well received, not everyone had been impressed. It is perhaps an indication of the circles Lalande had moved in that he had been told in 1763 that Martin "gives courses in physics ridiculously."[36]

Opposite Martin, and also well known through his publications, was Adams, who had a great number of instruments of physics, mathematics, gnomonics, and astronomy. Henry Pyefinch also had a very well-stocked shop, and Edward Nairne is mentioned as a well-known maker of telescopes and other instruments. Short has died, and Bernoulli attends the sale of his instruments.[37]

Of the mathematical instrument makers, three rivals stand above the others, and among them Bernoulli believes their reputations to stand in the order: Bird, Sisson, and Jesse Ramsden. He has clearly spent time talking to Bird and Sisson, but not Ramsden. He does describe in detail a telescope mount by Ramsden, but he may have seen this in Dollond's workshop. Among other things, he has discussed with Bird the application of achromatic lenses to divided instruments and with Sisson his method of dividing scales — a point of interest because Bird's method had now been published by the Board of Longitude, and Sisson had been trained by his own father, who had also trained Bird. For the well-informed shopper the history and workshop traditions of the London makers already fall within the orbit of connoisseurship. Bernoulli is aware of Bird's latest foreign commissions — clearly considered a mark of his distinction — and while his instruments are judged the finest, they are also the most expensive.[38]

One of the most useful aspects of Bernoulli's record is the negative report he writes on Dollond, because it illustrates part of the increasing complexity of commercial practice. Bernoulli has been to Peter Dollond's workshop: it is large and its products cover a wide range — reflecting as well as refracting telescopes, and almost all the types of optical and astronomical instruments used in England. The more valuable instruments are available only to order. It is helpful that, while the word "shop" is ambiguous in English in this period, in French Bernoulli has three words — "atelier," "boutique," and "magasin" — that he can deploy more precisely, and at this point we know he is talking about Dollond's workshop, "atelier." (Martin, Adams, and Pyefinch each have a "magasin" — a shop of a larger size than a "boutique.") For the instruments made in quantity, he cautions that people who buy English work imagining that the signature "Dollond" is enough to ensure excellence are seriously mistaken. Indeed, if they are fortunate enough to get a good instrument, this means that it was not made by Dollond's workmen at all, but that at least part of the work has been subcontracted to his brother-in-law Ramsden.[39]

Whatever the rights of Bernoulli's opinion of Dollond's workshop, we have learned that by 1769, at least in the larger enterprises, a signature does not identify the work of the master; it does not even necessarily identify the workshop where the piece was made. It has to be said that Bernoulli was not impressed by Peter Dollond, because he did not have the theoretical knowledge of his father, John. It was surprising, wrote Bernoulli, that he had managed to achieve so much in achromatic lenses on the basis of trial and error. He did not, of course, hear this from Dollond, but had been assured on good authority that a great many lenses of crown and flint grass were manufactured and successful combinations found simply on the basis of trying them out. Bernoulli did, however, have his own experience to add to this. Extraordinarily, he posed a series of questions to Dollond, questions that had been set beforehand by Béguelin. It is not clear whether Dollond realized that he was sitting an examination, but he definitely failed.[40]

Despite all this, the only purchases Bernoulli records making were of three lenses from Peter Dollond. Dollond held the patent for achromatic lenses, which is part of the explanation for widespread resentment among other opticians, as well as for the questioning and probing from foreign visitors, who believed that the theoretical advantage lay with Continental mathematicians. Sometimes shoppers were obliged to buy from a certain maker for reasons other than choice. Bernoulli could not be completely sure of the significance of Dollond's examination failure: either he could not or he would not answer, but either way he did not feel obliged to cooperate with Bernoulli's stratagem. Perhaps the strength granted to him by the patent meant that he did not need to cultivate shoppers in the fulsome manner Bernoulli had enjoyed elsewhere.

Bernoulli left England for France in May 1769, and he sees the mural quadrants by Bird and Sisson in the observatory of Le Monnier. He says he has little new to report concerning the makers of astronomical instruments. They are not as good as the English makers, who particularly excel in divided instruments, but he can at least mention Langlois and Canivet for producing distinguished work. There are amateur lens makers producing good achromatic objectives for telescopes, but no "Artists by profession." The only shop he mentions is that of Passemant, where good reflectors and refractors can still be found, though his report seems not to be firsthand. Throughout, no maker is reported as having said anything to Bernoulli: at least so far as his letters are concerned, the Parisian makers are silent.[41]

The visits to London and Paris made by the Danish astronomer Thomas Bugge were separated by some twenty years, so we will look first at his experiences in London in September and November 1777 and separately at his time in Paris. In London he visited the shops of many makers, buying books and instruments, and enjoying conversation and experiments.[42] Adison Smith "at the golden quadrant" in the Strand, who in 1764 had been one of the petitioners against the patent for achromatic lenses held by Peter Dollond, told him the makers' account of the priority of Chester Moor Hall, while taking his order for a triple prism to demonstrate Dollond's technique.[43] On his visit in 1763, Lalande also had heard of the claims on Hall's behalf from John Bevis and Short. Bugge may have caught the flavor of this dispute, for he later noted, having visited the premises of both Peter Dollond and his brother John, that "none of the Dollond brothers seems to have any theoretical knowledge."[44] It was precisely Peter's contention that any earlier lens combinations that may have existed were made empirically and not on the basis of any theoretical understanding.

Some instruments Bugge could buy directly from stock — a rule from Smith, for example, comparing English, French, Dutch, and Antwerp measure, or Dollond's form of rolling parallel rule.[45] Martin's shop was "well-supplied," and he bought a number of books there.[46] He was particularly taken with Nairne & Blunt, finding Edward Nairne a "splendid man," who could show him "many excellent objects"—a new kind of marine barometer, a dip circle, different sorts of theodolites, and a new telescope mount.[47] He returned so that Nairne could show him a number of experiments with his electrical machine, and he ordered one.[48]

Bugge was very taken with the watchmaker Alexander Cumming, buying his book on the *Elements of Clock and Watch Work*, admiring his barograph, and hearing the details of the construction of different types of compensation pendulum. Cumming showed him the observatory he had at the top of his house, with a transit instrument and an equatorial, both by Ramsden.[49] Bugge later returned and "examined his barometric clock very closely," learning along with the design details that the price for such a clock was 500 pounds.[50] On his visit to John Arnold he was told of his improvements to chronometers, was shown a demonstration of the effect of temperature on a balance spring, and made an appointment to view experiments on different types of compensation pendulum, which took place the following week.

Bugge discovered that Arnold had a transit instrument that had formerly belonged to George Graham.[51] Sisson described to him an observatory designed for Nathaniel Pigott, and showed him a transit instrument to be installed there.[52] Here as elsewhere, details of the design are carefully explained and recorded, especially where there are new ideas. These were particularly evident at Ramsden's shop in Piccadilly, where he was shown an 8-foot quadrant being constructed and noted "Ramsden's ideas about some new instruments."[53] George Adams was able to show him a transit instrument he was making for the king's observatory at Richmond.[54]

Bugge spend some 88 pounds on instruments and associated apparatus, as well as 34 pounds on books. The most expensive items were a compound microscope from Dollond at 8 guineas, lenses from Smith at 8 pounds, 9 shillings, and a range of things from Nairne and Blunt: a hydrostatic balance (7 pounds, 17 shillings, 6 pence), an electrical machine (13 guineas), a battery of nine Leiden jars (4 guineas), a mechanical model (mechanical powers) (21 pounds), and an air pump (11 pounds, 15 shillings). Nairne was able to show Bugge the instruments made for him on his last day in London, and he "found them all very pleasing."[55] He also bought a set of drawing instruments from Adams at 2 guineas.[56] It is worth emphasizing that he returned twice to see more extensive experiments — in Arnold's case certainly by appointment, and probably in Narine's as well, to judge by the extent of the experimentation and the careful notes taken by Bugge.

In July 1785 Martinus van Marum of Teyler's Museum in Haarlem was in Paris, visiting physical cabinets, attending sessions of the *Académie des sciences*, witnessing the therapeutic applications of electricity, and so on—

thoroughly occupied with the French practice of natural philosophy.[57] He is particularly interested in electricity and is curious to see the use of a machine by Nairne. It is clear that there is plenty for him to do and see and that, while there is a growing vitality that is less commercially based than in London, there are also occasional similarities to London. Courses of lecture-demonstrations continue in the tradition of Nollet, generally not conducted by makers themselves, but using a wide range of instruments. Roulant was the successor of the better-known Sigaud de la Fond and was in the middle of moving when Van Marum visited him, so not much of the collection was visible, but he did say that he had held thirteen courses in physics the previous year.

However Van Marum does visit one shop — that of Bianchi (or "Bianchy") in the fashionable shopping street the rue Saint-Honoré. As an Italian who had previously plied his trade in Amsterdam, Bianchi was something of an interloper in the Parisian scene, but he brought with him practices of the Anglo-Dutch variety that linked experimental demonstration with making and trading. Bianchi probably began as a glass worker and barometer maker in the Italian tradition, and it was the use of blown glass in electrical machines that occupied the conversations and demonstrations that engaged Van Marum and himself, continued by arrangement into a second day. We know separately that Bianchi advertised himself as a demonstrator in physics, conducted courses on experimentation in electricity, and supplied a wide range of experimental apparatus, including electrical machines, air pumps, barometers, thermometers, microscopes, and telescopes.[58] This was a real shop in the London sense — a space where the maker cultivated the customers' interests, engaged them with impressive experiments, offered them courses to deepen their commitment, and sold them philosophical instruments.

This was a single instance, the initiative of an enterprising immigrant. Otherwise, Van Marum is very largely engaged with visiting the many private cabinets; these give him his principal visual impression of natural philosophy in Paris. When he comes to London in 1790, he seems to be less motivated to make a full record of his activities, but in only a few pages of notes covering three weeks, which trail off into mere jottings, instrument makers and their shops are a prominent and recurring feature.[59] Not all are named, but the better known among those who are are Nairne, Adams, and Haas. Van Marum visits Tiberius Cavallo, who uses his extensive cabinet of instruments for a series of demonstrations. Although not generally seen as a maker, Cavallo incorporated a commercial dimension into his performance, as he takes an order for four pieces from Van Marum and will have them made. Also an Italian, his situation is not very unlike that of Bianchi in Paris.

Otherwise, the conduct of Van Marum's shopping in London is familiar to us. He returns by appointment to see more with Adams, Nairne, and Dollond. Adams was rewarded by an order for a complete table planetarium with lunarium and tellurium. Nairne "requested us to come again the next Wednesday, when he expected to have some new instruments on hand," while at Dollond's "we received from him the promise that he would show us another day what he had ready." Van Marum also went twice to Haas, but by this stage his notes are very sketchy. These visits fall within the pattern we know already of the London trade in relation to specialist shoppers. Perhaps the only new fact of commercial interest we learn from Van Marum is that Nairne is sufficiently prosperous to have a country house.[60]

CASSINI IN LONDON; COMMERCE AND NATURE

J. D. Cassini offered an analysis of the French situation in relation to the English — in effect Paris in relation to London — as he saw it when he took over the directorship of the *Observatoire de Paris* in 1784. He was deeply dissatisfied with its prospects, particularly on account of his instrumentation. The famous expeditions of the past had created an enthusiasm for instrumental improvements and had encouraged the talents of French makers, but they had now been left far behind by the English, whose technical and commercial dominance could not be ignored.

> The Observatory was then equipped with mural instruments, with large movable quadrants, the work of Langlois, of Canivet, of Lennel, who were in those days the most celebrated makers of astronomical instruments. But at the time I took over the direction of the Observatory, these old talents had been eclipsed by those of Bird and Ramsden, English artists who had carried their art to the highest perfection, leaving the French far behind them, from whom they had usurped the trade in optical and mathematical instruments almost entirely.[61]

Cassini's analysis is instructive, as is the proposal he offered to remedy the situation. French makers, he was sure, were not inferior in talent or education; the problem lay in commerce, not in mechanics. The French makers could not get a fair price for their products: French customers would not pay a fair price for French instruments. Yet at the same time he expected them to pay as patriots, rather than as shoppers. Caught up in an "antipatriotic mania," they behaved as though they were buying lengths of cloth:

> How often have I been offended by people who, begging me to procure a good instrument for them, haggle as if it were a length of cloth. What will it cost? I was asked; not as expensive, surely, as an English instrument?

Why not? I replied; do you want to be fair? if the instrument is worth nothing, don't take it: but if it is good, pay what the maker will ask, even if he were to make you pay more than for an English one.[62]

In fact it was impossible, he said, for a maker in Paris to produce the same instrument for the same price as one in London, and for three reasons: they did not have the means and the appropriate machinery, they did not have the capital to fund the first stages of construction, and they were the victims of the "Anglomania" that created a preference for English instruments.

Cassini's solution, however, was more French than English. He did not argue for, say, the abolition of the restrictive practices of the corporations, whose activities were particularly detrimental to a manufacturing trade which, if it was to progress, had to be able to bring together different skills and combine a variety of materials. He did not try to imagine how he might encourage a broader-based consumerism with respect to mathematics and natural philosophy, as his jibe about shopping for cloth makes clear. Rather he proposed the establishment of a kind of national workshop at the *Observatoire*. Here the machines that individual makers could not afford to buy would be made available to them. Two or three promising mechanics would be sent for training in the great workshops of London, to be employed in the national workshop on their return, and to maintain the momentum of improvement the workshop should be given an annual subvention from the government.

Cassini's analysis of the differences between makers in Paris and London was largely accurate, but in London capital for the machines needed for efficient production and capital for large, prestigious, and innovative instruments were generated by commerce in smaller, everyday instruments, and by the entrepreneurial development of forms of shopping that made buying instruments not so very different from buying cloth. Of course, London makers had this commercial opportunity because they were in the middle of a broader consumer revolution among the English bourgeoisie, and they could hitch themselves to this engine of capital production. But in doing so, they had taken risks that Cassini did not feel could be expected of the Parisian makers: John Cuff and Benjamin Martin were among a number declared bankrupt. Martin even committed suicide.

The workshop and an associated foundry were established at the *Observatoire* but were not successful. Yet, just as the project seemed to be faltering, Cassini had the opportunity to go to London on a plausible and legitimate mission that would take him into the heart of the instrument world. The meridians of Paris and Greenwich were to be linked by a collaborative geodetic enterprise, with Cassini in command of the French component. He would have to go to London to make the necessary arrangements, as he explained to the minister: "I will go to see these superb English instruments, to examine these masterpieces of the art, and these models which it is our first ambition to imitate in France. I will have occasion to see and to cultivate Dollond, Troughton, Ramsden."[63] He was particulaly anxious to cultivate Ramsden, for by now his reputation was unrivaled, and it was in his workshop that he hoped to place the two or three chosen Frenchmen. How could Ramsden be persuaded of such a plan? Cassini sought permission to order an instrument from him, having no doubt that he would be suitably mollified by receiving such a commission: "without doubt he will be flattered to work for the Observatoire Royal de Paris, where there is still nothing by him."[64] This would be the device for softening Ramsden's attitude to training Frenchmen. It was, admittedly, quite a step to buy an English instrument for the Paris observatory, but the long-term outcome made it worth the loss of face, and they would acquire a desperately needed modern instrument as well as a model for future imitation. Cassini left in September 1787 with permission to order a 7-foot transit instrument and to negotiate the placing of French workers in London workshops. He would be a shopper with a very particular agenda, not least because he did not really approve of shopping.

Cassini was not disappointed in Ramsden; indeed he was enormously impressed: "I recognised that despite all our efforts we would never have so consummate an artist in France; all rivalry, all comparison seemed now to me impossible faced with such a great talent."[65] Ramsden was full of ideas and conversation. The kinds of shop discussions we have noted, engaging other makers and other visitors, had become in Ramsden's case an inspirational audience for Cassini.

> Leaving one day from one of these conversations in which I loved to take part and be instructed by him, I said to a stranger, who was just as enthusiastic as I about the merit of M. Ramsden: In truth, this man is an electrical machine which you only have to touch to draw a spark. Your comparison could not be more appropriate, was the stranger's animated reply, for you could very well get nothing more than sparks here.[66]

Elsewhere the electrical machine was a star attraction in the polite entertainment offered in the shops of instrument makers; here it was a metaphor for the extraordinary maker himself. Whether at this stage Cassini appreciated the meaning of the foreigner's response is not clear, but sparks were all he could hope to draw from this machine: he would never acquire an instrument from Ramsden.

Ramsden was utterly charming and plausible. Cassini spent close to two years in London, and he visited the shop "ceaselessly." Ramsden spent a great deal of time with him, showing him instruments, promising him everything, and delivering nothing. Cassini attributed this to Ramsden's perfectionism and his fascination for new and improved designs: "Don't think that it is indifference or laziness on his part: quite the contrary. But a new idea, a difficulty to overcome or an instrument of some new type that someone proposes to him will attract all his attention and make him abandon any work he has started."[67] In this context a transit instrument, one stipulated to be modeled on the one already made for Palermo, would not excite much interest for Ramsden. Whether or not he was flattered to receive an order from the *Observatoire*, it did not represent the most exciting work he had in hand. In fact the discussions resulted in two instruments being ordered — the transit instrument and a rotatable wall with an 8-foot quadrant on one side and a complete circle on the other. The virtues of the circle over the quadrant were beginning to exercise Ramsden's interest and inform his later designs, something Cassini must have picked up from their many conversations. The instrument would permit a comparison between the circle and the quadrant, he wrote to Ramsden on his return, confirming the order: "I believe this deserves to excite your genius."[68]

Despite all Cassini's efforts to obtain his instruments, and despite Ramsden's continuing promises, only the transit instrument was completed, and it was made by Matthew Berge, Ramsden's foreman and successor in business. It was delivered in 1804, eleven years after Cassini's return and four years after Ramsden's death. Meanwhile Cassini's greater projects had been overtaken by the disruption of the Revolution. In truth Ramsden did not need Cassini's commission. He had told him in replying to his written order that he had forty or fifty men employed in his workshop. The regular business provided income for the extraordinary, but this meant that Ramsden was free to choose the extraordinary on his own terms. Cassini could have noticed this danger when he read Ramsden's reassurance that he did not need to worry about financing the work: "The regular business of my workshop provides me with the necessary income. My main objective is the perfection of instruments. This part of our profession is still in its infancy."[69]

Cassini offers more analysis than other visitors, but the general pattern of their experiences has become familiar and to some extent repetitive. It is time to stop adding examples and attempt some analysis of our own. It is evident to our shoppers that makers in London are much more engaged in entrepreneurial commerce than those in Paris; this leads both to a greater visibility, and to a more flourishing manufacturing enterprise largely invisible to visitors. In the way things are managed in London, the growth of demand for routine items enables innovation and design development for more individual and special pieces. The more successful makers are less dependent on the dictates of clients for these more ambitious designs, and in extreme cases their success and reputation were such that they could afford to ignore commissions that were not to their taste — not because they were difficult or costly to undertake, but because their design ambitions lay elsewhere. The astronomer Francis Wollaston failed to interest either Ramsden or Troughton in his proposal for an instrument and was obliged to take his custom to the less able and less prestigious maker William Cary, complaining that, "observers know best what they want; and an instrument-maker who will condescend to listen to them is a treasure."[70]

We have seen that the existence of a shop space was a valuable resource in the makers' situation. They were, after all, presented with some problems. On the one hand, they were trading in mathematics and natural philosophy — their material products were supposed ultimately to deliver more than materiality to their customers — so they needed to present a "polite" image to the world. But at the same time they ran mechanical workshops, and the skill and reliability of those who worked there was of legitimate concern to customers. A shop — an intermediate space between the street and the workshop — could be used in imaginative ways to negotiate the distance between the polite and the mechanical. The shop was a place to which visitors had unannounced access, and to that extent it was part of the public realm, but the maker controlled this space and what took place there. He could make himself and his special instruments available there in different ways, according to the importance and the purchasing potential of the customer.

As we have seen from our shoppers in London, the ways in which this access was managed included repeat visits, discussions, demonstrations, lectures, experiments, and even mechanical instruction, as well as traditional shop displays. The shop could to some extent be held ready for casual demonstration and explanation, or could be made ready for a special session arranged by appointment. Its relationship with the workshop meant that such sessions could be scheduled in sequence with workshop output. Anita McConnell's study of the London workshops cites examples of recorded premises that included a shop, a workshop, living quarters, and the possibility of other workshops nearby. These resources were augmented by links to more widespread workshops under different direction through the network of subcontracting.[71] The control the maker or retailer exercised over the shop space meant that his response could be tailored to the shopper, though in the case of the most prestigious and independent makers, this could spell frustration even for distinguished callers. Hornsby records several frustrating visits to Ramsden's premises to complain about delays, when he was kept waiting in the shop without seeing the great man, even though he was convinced that Ramsden was in a back room.[72]

This chapter has been mainly concerned with commerce; what can it say about the representation of nature? First, it is clear that there is a link between activities in the shop and those taking place at other locations in the geography of contemporary natural philosophy, including the Royal Society.

We are inclined to think of the commercial manifestation as an opportunist outgrowth from the academy —Hauksbee finding a business opportunity in the model of illustrative demonstration developed by Hooke. But while that may still be the dominant direction of influence, we need to be cautious in simply assuming that this is the whole story, not least because the chronology is not clear-cut, as we have seen through the cases of Reeve, and even earlier of Allen. Monconys could listen to the Royal Society debates about the "glass teardrops" and, had he lived, could have read about them in Hooke's *Micrographia*, but he could also buy them by the score in the shops of instrument makers. Whatever may be concluded about directionality from a more detailed study, it is clear that similar kinds of things were taking place across a range of locations, some under a stronger commercial agenda, others prioritizing natural philosophy, but for contemporary observers some morphological similarity would have been obvious. At the very least, it was the shops that disseminated a form of natural philosophical practice to a broad public; is was therefore appropriate that the popular textbooks of the eighteenth century arose largely from these commercial enterprises.

One important difference between the situations of makers in London and Paris was the guild or company regulation that applied in the two cities. In Paris, companies regulated particular trades, seeking to control the size of workshops, the provision of labor, the methods of production, and the choice of material.[73] Further, these regulations became stricter and more stringently enforced in the eighteenth century. Various companies sought to control instrument making, as a relatively new trade, but it was not clear which was most appropriate, and disputes arose that disrupted production, with makers even having tools and materials seized. As instruments were developing in the period, makers in fact needed to use a variety of skills and materials, and they did not fit into a particular category. One way of avoiding these difficulties was to achieve royal protection and work in the *Galeries du Louvre*—a further step away from the kind of brash commercialism evident in London.

The guild situation in London was very different. Here a maker needed to belong to some company or other in order to trade in the city, but it did not matter which he joined and he was not bound by any regulations governing his product. Once a successful maker belonged to a company, his apprentices would be made free of that company after completing their apprenticeship, so that dynasties of successive generations of master and apprentice would become established in the Grocers, Stationers, Merchant Taylors, or whatever.

If we consider the makers we have come across in this study, Allen was a Grocer and Clockmaker, Greatorex a Clockmaker, Thompson a Stationer, Culpeper and Adams were Grocers, Rowley a Broderer (embroiderer), Marshall a Turner, Patrick a Joiner, Moxon a Weaver and Stationer, Martin a Goldsmith, and Smith, Pyefinch, Nairne, and Watkins were Spectaclemakers. Many other seemingly unlikely trade affiliations were represented throughout the instrument makers. With the exception of the Spectaclemakers, the instrument makers did not, of course, practice any of these trades, but they did belong to the companies and assumed such obligations as holding office.[74]

Instrument historians have been unsure what to do with this information, apart from being amused at the idea of makers being classified as grocers, dyers, fishmongers, haberdashers, and so on, and using the surviving guild records as a powerful tool for dating makers and their signed instruments. However, the involvement of the makers in a variety of companies will have brought them into contact with a range of trading practices and given them a familiarity with the general commercial life of London.

One very important development in London, which is particularly evident at the beginning of the eighteenth century, is trading across the traditional distinction between mathematical and optical instruments. Mathematical instruments were made by specialist engravers, while the relative newcomers were the optical instrument makers, who had emerged from among the most skilled makers of spectacles. In addition to these two categories, there were now also instruments of natural philosophy, derived from the new enthusiasm for experiment. There is no *prima facie* reason why these three types of instrument should be retailed together and why they should eventually be accommodated by a single category, "scientific instrument"—that it seems natural to us is simply our inheritance from a conjunction formed in the eighteenth century—but the possibility was created by company regulation in London, where there were no restrictions on what company a maker might join or what he might make or sell.

Two of the makers we have encountered are particularly associated with early trading across the mathematical / optical distinction, namely Culpeper and Rowley, but it soon became widespread, and with the addition of experimental instruments of natural philosophy, it was characteristic of the operations of many makers, among whom Adams and Martin were prominent. By this account there is indeed a link between commerce and the representation of nature: the very formation of the category of scientific instrument owed something to the regulation of trading in London, while the makers' acumen in encouraging the extraordinary growth of consumer interest in natural philosophy may well be related to their association with colleagues in companies dealing with luxury consumer goods, such as the Broderers or the Merchant Taylors.

A few makers managed to trade without joining companies, especially those associated with the Royal Society, either as fellows or through their close connections with senior astronomers and observatory commissions. Among those we have mentioned, this would apply to the Sissons, Bird, Short, and Ramsden. We have seen that there were links between experimental demonstration as presented at the society and as organized in the shops of makers. Might there be another relationship with the commercial world? Might the Royal Society have acted in some respects in the role of a company, by making it possible for some makers to operate outside the usual obligations to the city? It might be said that this simply reflects the declining power of the London companies, but makers could scarcely have begun to flout their authority without some alternative form of support and patronage.

This was not a formal responsibility of the Royal Society, but by virtue of its royal charter it had the status, rights, and privileges of a chartered corporation. George Graham, a Royal Society Fellow, who established the role of the elite, specialist maker of astronomical instruments in London, was the first to employ assistants in the instrument-making side of his business without binding them as apprentices. This was how Sisson and Bird entered the trade, and they never joined a company. (Graham was a Clockmaker, having served an apprenticeship under Thomas Tompion, and took apprentices in the company for that side of his activities.) Lalande noted the status enjoyed by makers such as Sisson and Bird within the circles of the Royal Society and among the important astronomers — a *de facto* if not *de jure* measure of protection, which allowed them to avoid the attentions of the regular companies. Short was introduced to the London mathematicians through his patron in Edinburgh, Colin Maclaurin, and was a fellow before he moved permanently to London. Ramsden entered the trade through his employment by Jeremiah Sisson, and he became a fellow in his own right; his best-known employees, Matthew Berge, John Stancliffe, and Thomas Jones (a fellow), had no company affiliations.

Thus the entanglement between the Royal Society and the commercial life of the instrument makers had at least two aspects: the makers' shops had some of the functions we associate with the society in relation to natural knowledge, and the society in effect had some of the functions of a livery company.

EPILOGUE: BUGGE IN PARIS

By the time Thomas Bugge visited France at the end of the eighteenth century, the old guild structure and its regulatory apparatus had been swept away by the Revolution.[75] Already there are clear signs of a revival of the Paris workshops. Bugge's account has something of the flavor of Bernoulli's letters from London: there is plenty to say. Occasionally Bugge enters the caveat that the work is not quite as good as in London, but in general he is very positive, and some of the work he sees is excellent.

Lenoir had a large workshop, which Bugge was able to visit, and he made a wide range of mathematical and astronomical instruments. The optical instrument maker Laroche had good reflecting telescopes and achromatic refractors, and he had lots of conversation. For the first time among the records of these visitors, we hear of a French maker engaging in extended discussions and demonstrations. Dumotiez made physical instruments, which Bugge bought and recommended; he did not only offer the standard designs, but would work from the customer's drawings. Fortin was very good, though expensive, while Betalli and Perrical were excellent glassworkers. Behind these individual stories, there were general signs of a consumer market, with between twelve and fourteen shops selling instruments near the *Pont Neuf* in the *Quai de l'Horloge* and several more in the *Palais Royal*.

In 1801 Lalande announced that the work of Lenoir had demonstrated that "the French industry is no longer behind the English." This was premature, but certainly a change was under way that would bring the two traditions into much more equal competition by the midcentury. Comparison between Paris and London is not so artificial a perspective for the historian as it may appear. It was present, implicitly or explicitly, in most of the accounts we have examined, and it occasionally surfaces in remarks made by the makers themselves. As an old man, Lenoir designed a dividing engine — the machine for which the English makers, particularly Ramsden and Troughton, had been especially celebrated. It is not clear what he can have meant in technical terms, but the emotional significance of his remarks was clear when he explained, "I have not tried at all to imitate the English; on the contrary I dare to assert that my method is completely French."[76]

Notes

1. "Me voici à Londres depuis 8 jours; je ne puis vous parler encore d'Astronomes ni d'Observatoires; mais je vous serai part de la surprise agréable où est jetté un Astronome en parcourant les rues de cette Capitale. Vous avés sûrement oui parler de la richesse & de l'éclat des boutiques de Londres, mais je doute que vous vous représentiés combien l'Astronomie contribue à la beauté du spectacle: Londres a un grand nombre d'Opticiens; les Magasins de ces artistes sont remplis de Télescopes, de Lunettes, d'Octans &c. Tous ces instrumens, rangés & tenus proprement, flattent l'oeil autant qu'ils imposent par les réflexions auxquelles ils donnent lieu." J. Bernoulli, *Lettres astronomiques* (Berlin, 1771), 63.

2. "Vous connoissés très bien le nom de M. DOLLOND; l'Artiste célebre" Bernoulli, *Lettres*, 65.

3. For foreign accounts of London instrument makers, see G. L'E. Turner, "The London Trade in Scientific Instrument Making in the Eighteenth Century," *Vistas in Astronomy* 20 (1976): 173–182.

James A. Bennett

4. Balthazar de Monconys, *Journal des voyages de Monsieur de Monconys* (Lyons, 1665–66).

5. "vne feüille de verre sur laquelle ces obiects sont peints," Monconys, *Journal*, 17–18.

6. "ie le trouuay dans son élement, enfoncé dans le commerce des Physiciens, & ne respirant que machines, & que nouelles experiences." Samuel Sorbière, *Relation d'un voyage en Angleterre* (Paris, 1664), 66.

7. Henry Oldenburg, *The Correspondence of Henry Oldenburg*, ed. A. Rupert Hall and Marie Boas Hall, 9 vols. (Madison: University of Wisconsin Press, 1965–73), 2: 285–291.

8. Ibid., Vol. 2: 271.

9. A. D. C. Simpson, "Richard Reeve—the English Campani—and the Origins of the London Telescope-Making Tradition," *Vistas in Astronomy*, 28 (1985), 357–365. For more detail on Reeve, see A.D.C. Simpson, "Robert Hooke and Practical Optics: Technical Support at a Scientific Frontier," in *Robert Hooke: New Studies*, ed. Michael Hunter and Simon Schaffer (Woodbridge: Boydell Press, 1989), 33–61. The much earlier shop of Elias Allen, in the 1620s, seems to have been a place of resort for practical mathematicians, a source of news and a means of communication. See William Oughtred, *The Circles of Proportion* (London, 1633); Hester Higton, *Elias Allen and the Role of Instruments in Shaping the Mathematical Culture of Seventeenth-Century England*, Ph.D. dissertation, University of Cambridge, 1995.

10. E. G. R. Taylor, *The Mathematical Practitioners of Tudor and Stuart England* (Cambridge: Cambridge University Press, 1970), 220–221.

11. Zacharias Conrad von Uffenbach, *London in 1710 from the Travels of Zacharias Conrad von Uffenbach*, ed. W. H. Quarrell and Margaret Mare (London: Faber & Faber, 1934).

12. Ibid., 158.

13. Ibid., 146.

14. Gloria Clifton, *British Scientific Instrument Makers 1550–1851* (London: Zwemmer, 1995), 194.

15. Uffenbach, *London*, 77.

16. Ibid., 145.

17. Ibid., 173.

18. Ibid., 77.

19. Ibid., 168. For the received early history of the reflector, see Henry C. King, *The History of the Telescope* (New York: Dover, 1979), 67–92.

20. Uffenbach, *London*, 168.

21. A. Q. Morton and J. A. Wess, *Public and Private Science: The King George III Collection* (Oxford: Oxford University Press, 1993), 39–65.

22. Ibid., 77–78.

23. Ibid., 168–170.

24. M. Lister, *A Journey to Paris in the Year 1698* (London, 1699), 80.

25. Maurice Daumas, *Les instruments scientifiques aux XVIIe et XVIIIe siècles* (Paris: Presses Universitaires de France, 1953), 97–113, 339–385.

26. J. Lalande, *Journal d'un Voyage en Angleterre 1763*, trans. Helene Monod-Cassidy (Oxford: Voltaire Foundation, 1980).

27. "Ce n'est que par tatonnement." Lalande, *Journal*, 25.

28. Lalande, *Journal*, 60.

29. Ibid., 33.

30. Ibid., 32–3.

31. Ibid., 38, 42, 47.

32. J. A. Bennett, "The English Quadrant in Europe: Instruments and the Growth of Consensus in Practical Astronomy," *Journal for the History of Astronomy* 23 (1992): 1–14.

33. J. Bird, *The Method of Dividing Astronomical Instruments* (London, 1767); J. Bird, *The Method of Constructing Mural Quadrants* (London, 1768).

34. Lalande, *Journal*, 72.

35. Bernoulli, *Lettres*, 72–74.

36. "fait des cours de phis[ique] ridiculement," Lalande, *Journal*, 44.

37. Bernoulli, *Lettres*, 70, 74, 96.

38. Ibid., 126–132.

39. Ibid., 68–69.

40. Ibid., 65–66.

41. Ibid., 138–173.

42. Thomas Bugge, *Journal of a Voyage through Holland and England, 1777*, ed. K. Møller Pedersen (Aarhus: Department of History of Science, 1997).

43. Ibid., 128–131.

44. Ibid., 154–155.

45. Ibid., 128–129.

46. Ibid., 130–133.

47. Ibid., 130–133.

48. Ibid., 140–145.

49. Ibid., 162–171.

50. Ibid., 296–301.

51. Ibid., 156–161, 170–177.

52. Ibid., 178–185, 191.

53. Ibid., 184–189.

54. Ibid., 254–255.

55. Ibid., 344–345.

56. Ibid., 198–208.

57. Martinus Van Marum, *Martin Van Marum. Life and Work*, ed. R. J. Forbes, 6 vols. (Haarlem: H. D. Tjeenk & Zoon, 1969–76), Vol. 2: 220–239.

58. Maurice Daumas, *Scientific Instruments of the Seventeenth and Eighteenth Centuries and Their Makers*, trans. M. Holbrook (London: Batsford, 1972), 148, 330.

59. Van Marum, *Life and Work*, 2: 266–272.

60. Ibid., 2: 270–272.

61. "L'Observatoire avait été muni alors de muraux, de grands quarts de cercles mobiles, ouvrages des Langlois, des Canivet, des Lennel, qui étaient en ces tems-là les plus célèbres constructeurs d'instrumens d'astronomie. Mais au moment où je pris la direction de l'Observatoire, ces vieux talens étaient éclipsés par les Bird et les Ramsden, artistes anglais qui avaient porté leur art à la plus haute perfection, laissant bien loin derrière eux les Français, à qui ils avaient enlevé presqu'entièrement le commerce des instrumens d'optique et de mathématiques." J. D. Cassini, *Mémoires pour servir a l'histoire des sciences et a celle de l'observatoire royal de Paris* (Paris, 1810), 4.

62. "Combien de fois je me suis indigné contre des personnes qui, me priant de leur procurer un bon instrument, le marchandaient comme une aune de drap! Quel prix coûtera-t-il? me demandait-on; pas aussi cher, sans doubte, qu'un instrument anglais? Pourquoi non? répondais-je; voulez-vous être juste? si l'instrument ne vaut rien, ne le prenez pas: mais s'il est bon, payez-le ce que l'ouvrier demandera, vous le fit-il même acheter plus cher que s'il était anglais." Cassini, *Mémoires*, 5.

63. "j'irai voir ces superbes instrumens anglais, examiner ces chef-d'oeuvres de l'art, et ces modèles que notre première ambition est d'imiter en France. J'aurai occasion de voir et de cultiver les Dollond, les Stroughton [Troughton], les Ramsden." Cassini, *Mémoires*, 20.

64. "sans doute il sera flatté de travailler pour l'Observatoire royal de Paris, où il n'y a encore aucun de ses ouvrages." Cassini, *Mémoires*, 20.

65. "je reconnus que malgré tous nos efforts nous n'aurions jamais en France un artiste aussi consommé; toute rivalité, toute comparaison me parurent désormais impossibles vis-à-vis d'un si grand talent." Cassini, *Mémoires*, 23.

66. "Sortant un jour d'un de ces entretiens où j'aimais tant à m'engager avec lui et à m'instruire, je dis à un étranger non moins enthousiasmé que moi du mérite de M. Ramsden: En vérité, cet homme est une machine électrique qu'il suffit de toucher pour en tirer une étincelle. Rien de plus juste que votre comparaison, reprit vivement l'étranger, car vous pourriez fort bien ici ne tirer que des étincelles." Cassini, *Mémoires*, 23.

67. "Ne croyez pas que ce soit indifférence ou paresse de sa part: bien au contraire. Mais une idée nouvelle, une difficulté à vaincre ou un instrument d'un nouveau genre qu'on viendra lui proposer vont attirer toute son attention et lui faire abandonner tout ouvrage commencé." Cassini, *Mémoires*, 24.

68. "je la crois digne d'aiguillonner votre génie." Cassini, *Mémoires*, 28.

69. "Le courant de mon atelier me fournit suffisamment l'argent nécessaire. Mon principal objet en vue, c'est la perfection des instrumens. Cette partie de notre profession est encore dans son enfance." Cassini, *Mémoires*, 179.

70. See D. W. Dewhirst, "Meridian Astronomy in the Private and University Observatories of the United Kingdom: Rise and Fall," *Vistas in Astronomy* 28 (1985): 147–158.

71. Anita McConnell, "From Craft Workshop to Big Business—The London Scientific Instrument Trade's Response to Increasing Demand, 1750–1820," *London Journal*, 19 (1994): 36–53.

72. J. A. Bennett, "Equipping the Radcliffe Observatory: Thomas Hornsby and his Instrument-Makers," in *Making Instruments Count: Essays on Historical Scientific Instruments Presented to Gerard L'Estrange Turner*, ed. R. G. W. Anderson, J. A. Bennett and W.F. Ryan (Aldershot: Variorum, 1993), 232–241.

73. Anthony Turner, "Mathematical Instrument-Making in Early Modern Paris," in *Luxury Trades and Consumerism in Ancien Régime Paris*, ed. Robert Fox and Anthony Turner (Aldershot, 1998), 63–96.

74. For the makers and the London guild companies, see Joyce Brown, *Mathematical Instrument-Makers in the Grocers' Company 1688–1800* (London: Science Museum, 1979); M. A. Crawforth, "Instrument Makers in the London Guilds," *Annals of Science*, 44 (1987): 319–377; Clifton, *Directory*.

75. Thomas Bugge, *Science in France in the Revolutionary Era. Described by Thomas Bugge*, ed. M. P. Crosland (Cambridge, Mass.: Society for the History of Technology, 1969).

76. "l'industrie française ne le cède plus à celle des Anglais"; "je n'ai point cherché à imiter les Anglais; j'ose au contraire avancer que ma méthode est toute française"; Daumas, *Les instruments scientifiques*, 365.

EPILOGUES

A World of Wonders,
A World of One

LISSA ROBERTS

When nature is reborn in us, it calls itself art.
—Max Weber, American painter

W hen Copernicus placed the sun at the center of the cosmos, he was driven by an aesthetic compulsion. The efforts of other astronomers, as he told it, were "just like someone taking from various places hands, feet, a head, and other pieces, very well depicted, it may be, but not for the representation of a single person; since these fragments would not belong to one another at all, *a monster rather than a man* would be put together from them." If the world was indeed "created for our sake by the *best and most systematic Artisan of all*," as Copernicus believed, it was bound to exhibit "symmetry of its parts."[1] The task and burden of the philosophical astronomer was to uncover the cosmic order manifested in its unified arrangement. Copernicus struggled to do just this, breathing his last as *De Revolutionibus* was being printed in 1543.

This tragically heroic tale is the starting point for many renditions of the "Scientific Revolution," though authors tend not to dwell on the aesthetic dimension of its history. It is not my plan here to rehearse the generally told story of the Scientific Revolution or even to refute it. I want instead to introduce a cluster of issues that sit within the above snippet of Copernicus's text and find resonance in this collection of essays. By doing so, I hope to get at a tension that exists in our understanding of the history of early modern European art and science, one that needs to be resolved if we are to achieve the kind of historical synthesis that this book aspires to stimulate. At the risk of anticipating what I set out below, this tension can be understood briefly as existing on two related levels. Historiographically, an explanatory cleft lies between the history of the mathematical sciences, on the one hand,

and of the descriptive and experimental sciences on the other. A tandem divide separates historians who discuss the arts and sciences of early modern Europe as having been undergirded by the aesthetic principles of unity and order from those who emphasize the aesthetic principles of variety and uniqueness. Once I spell this tension out more fully, I want to indicate what I see as the potential of this book's collective vision for resolving it. And finally, I want to argue that the tension between the principles of unity and variety was already recognized and debated during the early modern period itself. What ultimately served to resolve it historically was a focus on activity, both in terms of philosophical reflection and in terms of everyday life, as increasingly dominant market activities came to shape the production of goods and ideas in a way that reflective philosophy never had the power to do on its own. This book's focus on practice, then, couldn't be more fitting.

THE ESSENTIAL TENSION?

> A man cannot tell whether Apelles, or Albrecht Dürer, were more tri-
> fler; whereof the one would make a personage by geometrical propor-
> tions; the other, by taking the best parts out of divers faces to make one
> excellent.
>
> —Francis Bacon, "On Beauty"

I begin with Copernicus's carefully chosen analogy between the astronomer's depiction of the cosmos and the anatomist's depiction of the human microcosm. Without speaking of influence, it is certainly striking that Andreas Vesalius's *De Humani Corporis Fabrica* was published in the same year as *De Revolutionibus*. A fellow Paduan (Copernicus had attended the University of Padua prior to Vesalius's arrival), Vesalius too presented an anatomized image of the body—human microcosm rather than cosmic macrocosm – that exhibited the ordered symmetry of its parts. Indeed, whether associated with Plato, Vitruvius, Horace, or any other ancient antecedent, the ideal of nature as an harmonious, unified whole that was constructed from a divinely (quasi-)mathematical blueprint was a recurrent trope during the Renaissance.[2] Not only did this feed new representations of the world, its parts, and inhabitants (and methods for investigating them), it inspired various artists and architects to adopt new principles of perspective as a foundation for their work as well.

That these were more than coincidental developments among a range of natural philosophical and artistic endeavors is attested to by repeated claims that reverberate across apparent divides. Architects drew inspiration for their designs from contemporary depictions of the human body ("nowhere

Lissa Roberts

else than that sacred temple made in the image and likeness of God, which is man—in whose make up all the other wonders of nature are comprised"),[3] while descriptions of the human body as a divinely constructed "temple" echoed Copernicus' (and others') explicit description of the cosmos.[4] From microcosm to macrocosm, from nature to products of human design, the guiding watchwords were (divinely rooted) unity and order.

Historians have argued that this perspective was crucial for the subsequent development of a unitary natural philosophy that sought to portray the universe as a system with a structure and motions that were bound by divinely ordained mathematical laws.[5] At the heart of what is traditionally presented as the Scientific Revolution stood the urge to read the divinely authored "book of nature" which, for men such as Galileo, was written in the language of mathematics. Because nature was created and maintained by unitary laws, according to this perspective, it must be possible to uncover them by examining natural phenomena in terms of the measured and measurable patterns they exhibited. Whether this was done through experimentally based induction, the application of mechanical analogy or mathematical analysis, the goal was the same—to reveal the order and unity of nature.[6]

If combined historical and historiographical scrutiny has taught us anything, it is that there are other ways to tell this story. In his classic study of European art history, for example, Arnold Hauser referred the Renaissance urge toward unity to a "spirit" very different from Neoplatonism.

> The principles of unity which now become authoritative in art . . . express the same dislike for the incalculable and the uncontrollable as the economy of the same period with its emphasis on planning, expediency, and calculability; they are creations of the same spirit which makes its way in the organization of labour, in trading methods, the credit system and double-entry bookkeeping, in methods of government, in diplomacy and warfare. The whole development of art becomes part of the total process of rationalization. . . . The things that are now felt as "beautiful" are the logical conformity of the individual parts of a whole, the arithmetically definable harmony of the relationships and the calculable rhythm of a composition . . . and the mutual relations of the various parts of the space itself.[7]

Hauser's narrative fits perfectly with the minority voice of Marxist historians of science (and their fellow travelers) mentioned by Paula Findlen and Pamela Smith in this book's introduction, who sought to root the development of modern science in the rise of capitalism. According to this version of history, it was the materially grounded march of economic development that both brought unity to a range of human endeavors and posited unity as the philosophical expression of an historic process of rationalization.

It is important to note that, while I began with a saga of intellectual struggle and then countered it with one built on the dialectic of material conditions, both these accounts privilege the linked aesthetic principles of unity and order. They portray this aesthetic as prescribing method, determining boundaries between science and craft, and giving shape to both scientific and artistic production. Strikingly, the essays in this volume imply a rather different tale of the relations between art and the study of nature. While it also comes in two (though expressly not autonomous) versions — we might call one a "history of representing" and the other a "history of intervening"—what brings both these versions together, by and large, are the inverse aesthetic principles of variety and uniqueness.[8] According to the authors in this volume, what seems to have marked and demarcated both nature and its investigation on one side, and artistic production and appreciation on the other, were the thirst for and apprehension of uniqueness and wonder.[9] Ironically, while historians' focus on the aesthetics of unity has led to an image in which a boundary separates the arts and sciences, the present focus on variety paints a picture of continuity between them.

SCIENCE: A MATRIX OF MARVELS

> . . . a marvelous museum . . . a small theater in which all the wonders of
> nature can be displayed in miniature.
> —Giralmo Porro's description of Padua's botanic garden, 1591

As was the case with so many beliefs, Aristotle's authority helped legitimate the traditional opposition between art and nature.[10] In contrast to this tradition that fostered a fascinating history of art's competition with natural beauty and wonder, the dictum that "beauty is truth" became a highly respectable one by the beginning of the eighteenth century, especially as formulated in the third Earl of Shaftesbury's aesthetics.[11] Even before his articulation of this view, however, many of the actors presented in this book accepted and modified the equation by defining beauty in terms of the individuating aesthetic principles of variety and uniqueness. Hence, the construction and increase of knowledge required, first, the collection of extensive stores of singular phenomena. On one hand, this connects with discussions of how these *naturalia, artificialia*, scientific instruments, and models (the general categories of items that stocked these collections) were identified, produced, and distributed, to which we will return. On the other hand, it leads to the question of how the increasing range of phenomena were stored, categorized, represented, and used.

The most obvious collection sites were gardens and cabinets where aristocrats, merchants and corporations (be they cities, universities or amateur societies) alike amassed and displayed their holdings. To these Claudia Swan adds mimetic illustrations and grids: representational collections in which illustrated (either pictorially or verbally) elements were laid out in a way that at least partially corresponded to their physical position in space and time. The reference to Foucault is blatant.

> The Classical age gives history a quite different meaning: that of undertaking a meticulous examination of things themselves for the first time, and then of transcribing what it has gathered in smooth, neutralized, and faithful words. . . . The documents of this new history are not other words, texts or records, but unencumbered spaces in which things are juxtaposed: herbariums, collections, gardens; the locus of this history is a non-temporal rectangle in which, stripped of all commentary, or all enveloping language, creatures present themselves one beside another, their surfaces visible, grouped according to their common features, and thus already virtually analyzed, and bearers of nothing but their own individual names.[12]

If the analogy between material sites and their representations seems only partial — painters, for example, were free to portray bouquets of blooming flowers that, in fact, blossomed at different times — the difference was actually only a matter of degree. For what all these venues had in common was that they formed an intersection of art and the objects of nature that endeavored to escape the strictures of natural time and space, and it was out of that juncture that knowledge (not to mention value) was produced.

Since the Renaissance, gardens were spoken of as embodying a "third nature"—a world borne of the marriage between the creative forces of primal nature and human artifice, dedicated simultaneously to utility and pleasure, built to grow plants out of both their native spaces and times.[13] And, as a number of essays in this collection remind us, the *Wunderkammern* of Europe were also filled with a range of items — some found in nature, others embellished or created out of whole cloth by artists, artisans, and instrument makers — drawn from around the world and across the scope of the human imagination. If gardens were experimental sites for transplanting exotics, creating new varieties and advancing "physick" through the cultivation of medicinal plants (not to mention the architectural fancies they housed), cabinets held collections that also stimulated work as well as wonder. They fed the intellectually productive fires of anatomy, natural history, and metallurgy, while stoking the skills of specimen production and preservation, of artisanal precision and presentation. Opening their doors opened the world in miniature, rearranging the matrix of space and time for the benefit of human understanding, consumption, and manipulation.

Representations of nature — be they in the form of still life paintings, anatomy sheets whose flaps could be raised to reveal bodily organs, natural histories or maps — helped to standardize portrayals of natural phenomena by adopting a naturalist style that made them, in all their uniqueness, amenable to surface comparison and categorization.[14] They also made them transportable, extending the potential for their interpretive consumption and exploitation. By domesticating the exotic and refusing to be bound by the ordering strictures of natural space and time, these representations afforded their viewers the opportunity to travel on their own terms — in the comfort of their homes and at a pace set by their leisure — through worlds laid out for their perusal and profit.

BEYOND THE GREAT DIVIDE: TOWARD A HISTORY OF DOING

> Let physicians and confectioners and the servants of the great houses be judged by what they have done.
>
> —Isak Dineson, "The Dreamers"

Before turning to the question of how the contents of these collections came to be there, I want to address another important set of contrasts between the sagas with which I began and those bound in this volume. In addition to revolving around mirror-image aesthetic principles — unity and order, on the one hand, variety and uniqueness on the other — they also appeal to different forms of natural knowledge and art. The first privileges the mathematical sciences — astronomy and physics — and unified perspective. The second focuses largely on natural history, alchemy, and medicine, along with representational description and handcrafted objects. Are we flirting here with a coupling of traditional oppositions: mathematical versus experimental sciences together with "Italianate" versus "Netherlandish" representation?

Traditionally, such a coupling worked at the expense of the "experimental sciences" and northern art. Consider Thomas Kuhn's claims, as referred to in this volume's introduction, that tied Baconians to commercial interests and thereby cut them off from the Scientific Revolution. Consider too Hauser's condescending appraisal. He writes that rationalism, the burgeoning hallmark of the Italian Renaissance, "does not remain restricted to Italian art; but in the North it assumes more trivial characteristics than in Italy, it becomes more obvious, more naive."[15]

The art historian Svetlana Alpers embraces these coupled dichotomies, but with a different strategy in mind, that of championing what she considers the descriptive nature of Dutch seventeenth-century art. Not interested in resolving these claimed distinctions, she focuses instead on presenting a more positive interpretation of experiment and description. Alpers explicitly posits a parallel between the Baconian project and Dutch painting, with its purported penchant for description and its "established alliance with those craftsmen—goldsmiths, weavers, glassblowers and geographers—whose products became the crafted objects in their representations." Bacon's world, Alpers tells us,

> is stilled, as in Dutch paintings, to be subjected to observation. Detailed descriptions, compiled almost without end and fitted into the table, displace time, since each observation is separate from the next. Indeed, despite its title Bacon's natural history displaces history. . . . It is, like the Dutch art with which we have linked it, description, not narrative.[16]

Interested to portray seventeenth-century art as essential to its contemporaries' understanding of the world, Alpers commends Bacon's dictum that "the nature of things betrays itself more readily under the vexations of art than in its natural freedom."[17]

Should we too leave these paired dichotomies unresolved, with or without debating their (hierarchical) relation? To do so, I fear, fails to answer the challenge of crafting an inclusive explanation for what has come to be called the Scientific Revolution. Given the current unpopularity of grand narratives, this is perhaps a good thing. It could well be that no overarching explanation exists—or needs constructing—for the concatenation of activities and ideas associated with the investigation and representation of nature in early modern Europe. On the other hand, this volume houses a pregnant suggestion that deserves to be fleshed out: that we replace a history of deeds by a history of doing. Once *homo faber* takes center stage, apparent oppositions begin to disappear.[18] It is unclear whether their disappearance is a simply a function of our redirected attention, but we will discover this only when such an active history is told in more detail.

Klaas van Berkel takes us a step along the way toward writing this kind of history, though he still couches the introduction to his essay in this volume in the binary terms of mathematical and experimental sciences. The major actor of his story, like so many early modern practitioners of science, did not respect the boundary that these two categories imply. Indeed, I doubt Meijer recognized the existence of such a boundary; he practiced astronomy, was a successful engineer, and published books that beautifully illustrated both his own inventions and experiments done before the Roman Accademia Fisicomatematica, of which he was a member.

While this broad range of activities is characteristic of many "scientific" practitioners in early modern Europe, whether obscure or as famous as

Galileo (consider also that Copernicus trained in both medicine and law, as well as learning to paint and translate) and deserves attention, I want to focus here on Meijer's work as an engineer. Then as now, (successful) engineering combined mathematical ability with experimental and entrepreneurial skills. Besides being honored in scientific academies across the continent, engineering was taught in courses housed (with varying degrees of official recognition) at major universities in the Netherlands during portions of the seventeenth and eighteenth century. No less a figure than Willem 's Gravesande (known generally, in caricatured fashion, for having brought Newtonian science to the Continent) taught "Dutch mathematics," as it was known, for a time at Leiden University.[19] Institutionally as well as intellectually, then, engineering existed precisely at the point denied by a historiography that categorically separates mathematical and experimental inquiries of nature, relegating it to a lesser status that bears the adjective "applied."

Chandra Mukerji's essay underlines the importance of engineering while setting it in a more blatant political context. What remains of interest throughout her essay is the depiction of knowledge as constituted by a network of specialized knowing and skills; a coordinated distribution that crossed any number of disciplinary, social, and political boundaries in order to understand nature and thereby harness it for human use. Perhaps this is the most fitting way to investigate a period during which the loci of learning, knowledge production, and application were multiplying. Focusing on activities and the networks required to accomplish them frees us from the constraints entailed in studies whose inquiries are organized in terms of either ideas or institutions.

One might respond by saying that this model is applicable only to instances involving the creation of what Cicero long ago termed a "second nature;" that is, a landscape engineered for human use.[20] Indeed, Mukerji pointedly speaks of representations of nature as tools that were expressly used to transform that which they represented. We might see the maps discussed by Alison Sandman in a similar light. Though the "network" in which they were placed housed contention over what constituted the proper representation of nature and how that representation ought to be used — for the pragmatic purpose of navigation or that of "objectively" mapping the world — and, therefore, manifested contours that could only be solidified once the controversy was ended, the final product was one that brought together the expertise of navigators, cosmographers, illustrators, and politicians in order to assert (and challenge) Spanish imperial claims that aspired to remake the entire globe.[21] We might, then, further see Benjamin Schmidt's discussion of exoticism as an inverse reflection of this process whereby the Dutch compensated for their loss of empire by informing and controlling the market for geographic representations.

But I think the true test for this approach — that is, a "history of doing" — is whether it can go beyond this level of application and resolve the claimed dichotomy of mathematics and experiment in general. This would be to argue that the application of any and all human activity to the world, whether mental or manual, includes an act of transformation that can therefore be investigated in essentially the same way. One would, in other words, have to cast mathematical physics and astronomy in the same explanatory mold as engineering and experimental manipulations of nature. And one would have to present a convincing argument that the mathematical representation of nature resulted from the same kinds of sociointellectual processes and transformed nature through its representation in a way that could further be impressed in networks of knowledge and power.

From the standpoint of intellectual history, this entails developing the claim that mathematics had evolved, by the seventeenth century, from the ancient Greek conception "as an inventory of (ideal) mathematical entities and their absolute properties" to a formal language of relations, capable of representing mathematical and nonmathematical relations alike and thereby capable of "accounting" for observable changes in nature in a powerfully general way. This need not be an idealist history, for we know that the institutional context of early modern European mathematics increasingly permitted application of a method drawn from one discipline to the subject matter of another discipline, something strictly forbidden in Aristotelian logic as leading to category mistakes.[22] It further involves that we take seriously (that is, consider as more than handy analogies) the connections between what came to be called the "mechanical philosophy" and the mechanisms — living or otherwise — that Descartes and his contemporaries experienced firsthand as well as the intimate links between Newton's alchemy and his conception of gravity as an active principle.[23] Finally, it involves writing a full-blown cultural history of the mathematical sciences; that is, a history that integratively situates them in the broader cultural context of their time and simultaneously shows their practice to have been constitutive of that culture.[24]

THE MARKET AS MEDIATOR BETWEEN UNITY AND THE UNIQUE

> If phenomena are not all linked one to another, there can be no philosophy.
> —Denis Diderot, *L'Interprétation de la nature*

If beauty and truth came to be seen as inseparable, Anne Goldgar's essay reminds us that, increasingly, so were beauty and profit. To quote her, "What is rare is beautiful, and what is beautiful is profitable." While gar-

dens, *Wunderkammern* and the like might therefore be regarded as repositories of intellectual capital, to borrow Mark Meadow's formulation, so too did
they relate to the nexus of cold, hard cash. Financing by private brokers,
trading companies, and empires made both "discovery" and control of the
globe increasingly possible and plausible. But a full range of technologies
was equally important and had, consequently, to be invented, "improved,"
and applied. These technologies varied from navigational techniques and
tools, on one side, to means of destruction and preservation on the other;
from technologies that named and represented to technologies that silenced
and produced transparence; from technologies that eliminated surprise to
those that encouraged awe.

The telos of this technological engagement with nature and its elements
was consumption, whether it involved ingesting herbals, imbibing facts, or
absorbing sights, sounds, and textures. But it was a consumption that was
conspicuous in the important sense that it gave rise to further productivity,
be it health, understanding, or enhancement of artistic and artisanal skills.
Hence production and consumption fed off each other in a spiral that had
more to do, this book argues, with the densely populated world of work and
wonder than with some grandly conceived process of rationalization.

Should we then be surprised if these developments involved an emphasis on
variety and uniqueness rather than unity and order, as implied by at least some
of the essays of this book? Or need we draw the conclusion that, in the end, this
was indeed the case? For if the market that supplied and benefited from the
growing urge to know and show appealed to its customers with the promise of
variety, so too did it see the rise of standardization. While this was perhaps
most obvious in the marketing of instruments and mechanical models, whose
operational success and popularity depended on the play between apparent
uniqueness and calibrated standards, the same can certainly be said for printed
matter, natural specimens, and handcrafted *artificialia*, all of whose value was
determined with reference to standardizing categories and notions of quality.

That we can detect the presence of a productive tension between these aesthetic ideals is clearly more than the result of historians' retrospection. Some of
the most stimulating philosophical debates of the early modern period rested
on this contest of emphasis. Spinoza, for example, who spent his days grinding
lenses in market-mad Amsterdam, spoke of God and the world in monist
terms. Leibniz, neither stranger to alchemy, automata, or imperial collections,
called this "the best of all possible worlds," by which he meant that God could
not but create a universe filled with as many distinct entities as did not involve
a contradiction. His views (and pretensions) led him to argue with Newtoni-
ans over the nature of God and God's relation to nature.[25] Is that relationship
marked by divine omniscience or omnipotence? Do we know God through
the unified order or the infinite wonders he creates?

For many, the challenge was to find a way to say both. But as the eighteenth century wore on, increasing numbers (though still relatively few) questioned the need to refer to God at all when investigating nature. Where the market led, philosophy followed. And while Adam Smith drew the "invisible hand" to bring order to a commercial world of competing individuals, Voltaire looked around him and stated with pessimistic resignation that this is indeed the best of all possible worlds.

Notes

Epigraph quoted in Martin Green, *New York: The Armory Show and the Paterson Strike Pageant* (New York: Collier Books, 1988), 249.

1. Quotations drawn from Copernicus, *On the Revolution of the Heavenly Spheres* (London: David & Charles, 1976), 25.

2. Robert Westman argues that Copernicus's appeal to unity was not so much an invocation of Neoplatonic ideals as it drew on the rhetoric of Horace, for which there was a high regard at that time. "If a painter were willing to join a horse's neck to a human head and spread on multicolored feathers, with different parts of the body brought in from anywhere and everywhere, so that what starts out above as a beautiful woman ends up horribly as a black fish, could you my friends, if you had been admitted to the spectacle, hold back your laughter? Believe me, dear Pisos, that very similar to such a painting would be a literary work in which meaningless images are fashioned, like the dreams of someone who is mentally ill, so that neither the foot nor the head can be attributed to a single form." Horace, *Ars Poetica*, lines 1–13, quoted in Robert S. Westman, "Proof, Poetics, and Patronage: Copernicus' Preface to *De Revolutionibus*," *Reappraisals of the Scientific Revolution*, ed. David C. Lindberg and Robert S. Westman, (Cambridge, Mass.: Cambridge University Press, 1990), 183. I thank Claudia Swan for also calling the link to Horace to my attention.

In a different vein, it is interesting to note that Thomas Laqueur goes so far as to argue that the unity of Renaissance portrayals of human anatomy entailed depicting the female body as a modification of the male — what he refers to as the "one-sex model." Thomas Laqueur, *Making Sex. Body and Gender from the Greeks to Freud* (Cambridge, Mass.: Harvard University Press, 1990), especially chapter 3.

3. This quotation is from Daniel Barbaro's (1567) edition of Vitruvius, cited by Jonathan Sawday, *The Body Emblazoned. Dissection and the Human Body in Renaissance Culture* (London: Routledge, 1996), 70.

4. According to Pierre Gassendi, Copernicus used the artistic skills he learned as an extension of his study of perspective to paint a self-portrait. "He [Copernicus] concerned himself with all parts of mathematics so that, at one time, he dwelt especially upon [the study of] perspective, and, at another time, he took the opportunity to learn more about the art of painting, until he became skillfully practiced; and, it may be reported, as well, that he painted himself excellently using a looking-glass. Whereupon, he began to seek advice about painting, for while contemplating travel, and above all to Italy, he resolved not only to sketch but also, insofar as he could, to represent exactly whatever he found worthy of observation." Quoted in Robert Westman, "Proof, Poetics and Patronage," 184. I chose to quote this excerpt not only as a indication of the close links between artistic composition and astronomy as discussed in my essay, but also to comment on how intriguing it is to note that Copernicus appar-

ently did not deem astronomical observation crucial to astronomy's reform (he reportedly made no more than twenty seven observations himself), but considered observation of his own surroundings to be crucial for artistic representation.

5. For the most eloquent, if complex, expression of this argument, see Amos Funkenstein, *Theology and the Scientific Imagination from the Middle Ages to the Seventeenth Century* (Princeton, N.J.: Princeton University Press, 1986).

6. While it is certainly true that Bacon did not advocate the mathematization of nature, he did nonetheless distinguish his inductive view from "empiricks" who sought nothing more than to uncover and put to use individual phenomena. See, for example, his *New Organon*, aphorism 99.

7. Arnold Hauser, *The Social History of Art* (New York: Vintage Books, 1951), Vol. 2, 15.

8. For the categories of "representing" and "intervening," see Ian Hacking, *Representing and Intervening. Introductory Topics in the Philosophy of Natural Science* (Cambridge: Cambridge University Press, 1983). Hacking uses these words as a way to activate discussions of rationalism and realism. I use them here to indicate, in an equally active way, histories of how knowledge was constructed through its representation and how that construction process was enabled through various means of intervening in nature, the workshop and the marketplace (not to mention the political realm).

9. See also Lorraine Daston and Katharine Park, *Wonders and the Order of Nature, 1150–1750* (New York: Zone Books, 1998), 15–16.

10. Aristotle, *Physics*, 2.1, 192b. 9–19.

11. J. V. Arregui, "La teologia de la belleza en Shaftesbury y Hutcheson," *Thémata* 13 (1995): 11–35; J. Stolniz, "From Shaftesbury to Kant: The Development of the Concept of Aesthetic Experience," *Journal of the History of Ideas* 48 (1987): 287–305.

12. Michel Foucault, *The Order of Things. An Archeology of the Human Sciences* (New York: Vintage Books, 1973), 131.

13. There is a growing literature on the history of gardens. See, for example, John Dixon Hunt, *Gardens and the Picturesque. Studies in the History of Landscape Architecture* (Cambridge: M.I.T. Press, 1994); Chandra Mukerji, *Territorial Ambitions and the Gardens of Versailles* (Cambridge: Cambridge University Press, 1997).

14. Here I equate naturalism with Foucault's notion of the "table." See footnote 15. For anatomy sheets, see Andrea Carlino, *Books of the Body: Anatomical Ritual and Renaissance Learning* (Chicago: University of Chicago Press, 1999). For the struggle to standardize maps, see Alison Sandman's essay in this book.

15. Arnold Hauser, *Social History*, Vol. 2, 16.

16. Svetlana Alpers, *The Art of Describing. Dutch Art in the Seventeenth Century* (Chicago: University of Chicago Press, 1983), quotations on 103 and 109.

17. Bacon, quoted in ibid., 103.

18. For a view of *homo faber*'s historical significance, see Hannah Arendt, *The Human Condition* (Chicago: University of Chicago Press, 1958).

19. P. J. van Winter, *Hoger beroepsonderwijs avant-la-lettre. Bemoeiingen met de vorming van landmeters en ingenieurs bij de Nederlandse universiteiten van de 17e en 18e eeuw* (Amsterdam: Noord-Hollandsche Uitgevers Maatschappij, 1988) (*Verhandelingen der Koninklijke Nederlandse Akademie van Wetenschappen, Afd. Letterkunde*, Nieuwe Reeks deel 137).

20. The term Cicero used was *alteram naturam*.

21. For the relation between controversy resolution and the validation of network contours in science, see Trevor Pinch, "Towards an Analysis of Scientific Observation: The Externality and Evidential Significance of Observation Reports in Physics," *Social Studies of Science* 14 (1985): 167–187.

22. Amos Funkenstein, *Theology and the Scientific Imagination*, 297–298. Funkenstein makes the general claim that a new ideal of knowledge emerged in the seventeenth century that equated knowing with doing, not only in the commonly accepted Baconian sense, but more universally as a mirror of God's active intelligence.

23. For the mechanical philosophy see, for example, Otto Mayr, *Authority, Liberty and Automatic Machinery in Early Modern Europe* (Baltimore: Johns Hopkins University Press, 1986). For Newton's conception of gravity as an active principle, see Betty Jo Tweeter Dobbs, *The Foundations of Newton's Alchemy, or the Hunting of the Greene Lyon* (Cambridge: Cambridge University Press, 1975).

24. Mario Biagioli's *Galileo Courtier* (Chicago: University of Chicago Press, 1993) is an important step in this direction but falls short of offering a cultural history of the mathematical content of Galileo's natural philosophy. Instead he couples a well done history of its cultural context with an internalist analysis of the mathematics itself.

On the needed symmetry of explanation — that is, the mutual constitution of science and society/culture — see Bruno Latour, *Nous n'avons jamais été modernes* (Paris: La Découvérte, 1991).

25. See, for example, *The Leibnitz-Clarke Correspondence* (London, 1717). For an interesting discussion of the debate, see Steven Shapin, "Of Gods and Kings: Natural Philosophy and Politics in the Leibniz - Clarke Debates," *Isis* 72 (1981): 187–215.

Questions of Representation

T his book proffers a lavish array. Like some of the subjects they treat, the essays collected here draw their materials from various parts of Europe and touch on many parts of the globe. Including discussions of a variety of disciplines, they offer an expanded view of early modern history, and at the same time enrich earlier interpretations, especially of the history of science and the history of art. Yet while they intrigue us with fascinating intellectual wares, these essays also invite us to consider further some of the larger questions that they raise. This epilogue responds to some of the selection's stimuli.[1]

Connections that may be established between individual essays and across sections of this book indicate the general direction of this collection. While not all the individual essays may be regarded as "interdisciplinary" in approach, as a whole they suggest some ways in which considerations of similar issues from multiple yet compatible points of view may mutually enhance each other. While Mark Meadow points to an agent who he believes played a key role in the establishment of early modern collections, the *Kunstkammer* (here called, resonating with the title of the book, the *Wunderkammer*), Paula Findlen discusses the trade in actual objects, the curiosities that went into what was called in English the "curiosity cabinet." While Chandra Mukerji points to the entrepreneurial interests that were involved in cartography and hence in canal construction, Benjamin Schmidt emphasizes that mapmaking itself was an important element in what he refers to as a marketing strategy.

Most obviously, all the essays presented here thus eschew approaches that may be called "internal" to the historiography of disciplines, which traced transformations, or saw developments arising from within the traditional concerns of their fields. Accordingly the trajectory of science was one that involved methods, theories, and the accumulation of knowledge.[2] Classic histories of science — for example, that of A. C. Crombie[3] — were histories of scientific ideas; at most they may have intersected with the history of ideas, as did an important older work by E. A. Burtt.[4] In the history of art a comparable "internalist" tradition was the history of style, as exemplified by Heinrich Wölfflin, Alois Riegl, or other art historians associated with Vienna, another that of iconography, the study of subject matter in art, as in the work of Émile Mâle.[5] While it may seem that such approaches have long been outmoded, and this collection parallels other recent efforts that move firmly away from internal histories, it is worth recalling that the tradition has survived, and the tendencies it expresses certainly formed a powerful force at the time many of the contributors to this collection were being educated: so suggests the simultaneous appearance of important syntheses in the historiography of art and the history of science thirty years ago.[6]

Alternative approaches were, to be sure, long available. For example, some of the intellectual origins of essays found here on the importance of practical alchemy or on systems of representation may be traced back to the works of Aby Warburg, Fritz Saxl, and other scholars associated with the Warburg Institute on astrological and occult imagery, or to that of scholars such as Erwin Panofsky on systems of representation, including studies of perspective and proportion.[7] Books by scholars such as Martin Wackernagel or Hans Floerke suggest that social and even economic histories of art were not entirely lacking earlier, either.[8] Somewhat similarly, so witness the works of Robert K. Merton and the influential study of Herbert Butterfield, cultural and social historical approaches to the history of science also existed in the earlier twentieth century.[9] Nevertheless, if a self-conscious social or economic history of art or science was practiced, it was most often to be associated with a Marxist tradition, not just in parts of Europe dominated by the Soviet Union, but in the West, both in the history of art, as exemplified by Frederick Antal and Arnold Hauser, and also in the history of science, as exemplified by J. D. Bernal.[10]

At the same time, however, and almost in the same year that older sorts of syntheses were produced — the early 1970s — newer tendencies were astir in art history.[11] A new art history brought with it a host of new or restated concerns: "gender, race, class" form a by now familiar litany. Hence, along with arguments informed by literary theory and postmodern philosophy, arrived other newer, or at least subtler, approaches to questions concerning the socioeconomic aspects of art. More recently, and more to the point of this collection, increasingly sophisticated studies of the commercial and economic aspects of art of the early modern period have also appeared. The works cited by Pamela H. Smith and Paula Findlen in their introduction are just some among the noteworthy publications which have illuminated commercial and economic aspects of art in the Low Countries, Germany, and Italy.[12]

Similar tendencies emerged more or less simultaneously in the historiography of science. While older surveys still marked out the course of scientific ideas, the same years (the early 1970s) that saw a new art history also witnessed numerous expressions of a social history of science.[13] Similar sorts of concerns were expressed: an increasing number of studies, including those by some of the contributors to this volume, deal with the institutional nexus, patronage relations, and personal networks of practitioners of science.[14] As signaled by recent books on canonical figures such as Galileo Galilei and Tycho Brahe, the social history of science has grown increasingly sophisticated, with far-reaching implications.[15] It has now been argued that even the determination of scientific "truth" may be socially constructed.

This importance of social practices for the determination of knowledge, in the thesis advanced by Stephen Shapin, recalls some of the arguments of Michel Foucault — whom Shapin indeed cites.[16] In books not however cited by Shapin, Foucault, to use his own diction, had enunciated an archaeology of knowledge,[17] and, more relevant to issues here, had suggested an "order of things" which offered a view of sequentially changing epistemic systems. For Foucault the "classic" period (roughly, of the "long" seventeenth century, to use another term initiated in francophone historiography) was marked by the episteme of representation. In the preface to Foucault's *The Order of Things* this idea was in turn "represented" by a famous painting, *Las Meninas* of Velázquez. Furthermore, Foucault also spoke of "exchanging" as well as classifying as characteristic of the classic period.[18]

Foucault thus opened the path followed by many essays in this collection. Foucault's articulation of a concern with the idea of "representation," and its manifestations in epistemology, science, and art is reflected in the general framing of the present collection; it resonates most clearly in essays like Claudia Swan's, where epistemological concerns for classification are linked to forms of artistic representation, and associated with the origins of a genre of painting, the independent still life. Likewise, Foucault's association of epistemological concepts of value with economic ones in the classic period is reflected in the coupling of commerce with representation in art and science in numerous other essays in this collection.

As the editors of this volume reiterate in their introduction, many scholars in the twentieth century were certainly concerned with the way in which art aids science, and science art, in the representation of the world. Richard Rorty's critique of the philosophical mirror of nature demonstrates that philosophers other than Foucault have also questioned the notion of representation of truth as an adequate or accurate conception for epistemology.[19] In addition to an increasing literature on the interactions of art and science, there has arisen an interest in the interrogation of the concept of "representation," its many connotations and manifestations, as well as its social construction and determination. The birth and early success of the periodical *Representations* occurred in this atmosphere, as did the work of authors who were initially associated with it.[20] Moreover, and independent of these tendencies, other discourses on the human sciences have taken newer directions into the investigation of the often fraught interactions of artistic and scientific representation.[21]

In an essay published a decade ago in a volume titled *Art in History, History in Art*, David Freedberg picked up many of these strands, and wove them together in a polemic on the relations of art, science, and commerce.[22] Speaking specifically about seventeenth-century Dutch culture, Freedberg argued that many of the interconnections that lie between these supposedly separate realms of activity had been ignored. He challenged scholars to address issues that seem to be located in such interstices between related but apparently different disciplines.

This collection replies to Freedberg's challenge, bringing together a variety of essays that link art, science, commerce, and representation. Moreover, even if it must be said that fields are not always treated in the same piece, the ways in which connections have been made also correspond to fresher socioeconomic approaches. The stress on commerce, on instruments used, and on objects studied means that practices, not theories, activities, nor attitudes, are emphasized in the historiography of science. Networks, exchanges, and extraneous objects are here the topics for history of science, as for one of art, rather than scientists, systems, or for that matter masterpieces.

In addition to merchants, mechanics—meaning those who work with their hands or have a trade, not the classic physical science called mechanics, the laws of which were adduced by Galileo and Isaac Newton—might thus seem to have taken center stage. In keeping with other recent syntheses and collections of studies, this move indicates a shift in approach away from a concern with the history of physics and astronomy, which had been a main focus for a traditional history of science, to one in which natural history and other subjects such as cartography or geography come to the fore as ways of mapping nature.[23] Similarly, even in paintings with religious subjects, not figures, but elements pertaining to what were to emerge as new, but were regarded as lower genres—landscape, animal painting, and still life—engage art history.

At the same time that these essays point to more paths for investigation, they also provoke further consideration of some of the theses which they advance. Engineers and instrument makers surface at several places in this book, as in James Bennett's essay. This corresponds to a trend in which engineers (and to a lesser degree instrument makers) have increasingly been seen not only as ancillary to the development of the natural sciences, but to epitomize the connection between art and science in the Renaissance. As instantiated by figures from Filippo Brunelleschi or Leon Battista Alberti to Leonardo da Vinci, skills in engineering and instrument making were closely associated with art and architecture in the Italian Renaissance.[24] The paradigmatic "artist-scientist-genius"[25] so personified by Panofsky half a century ago has yielded to the artist–scientist-engineer engaged in designing fortifications, making waterworks, instruments, and works of art.

Such figures were to be found over a much longer period of time and in many more places than Renaissance Florence. Although not so famous, the position of instrument maker–scientists such as Jobst Bürgi between art and science has in fact gained some attention.[26] But there are many other figures such as Simon Stevin or Salomon de Caus who could claim a place equally in histories of seventeenth-century art and architecture, as they have done in those of mechanics or mathematics. While the previous segregation of national and disciplinary historiographies seems to have led to their comparative neglect, De Caus has recently been recognized as a perspective theorist, and as designer of "mechanical contrivances," and Stevin's work has been called "deeply characteristic of Dutch activities — scientific and practical — at this time (i.e., the early seventeenth century)."[27] De Caus was also directly involved not only with hydraulic theory, but with garden (and hence garden fountain-sculpture design); Stevin also was much interested in architecture, on which he penned a treatise.[28]

With figures such as De Caus, Stevin, and their older Netherlandish contemporary Hans Vredeman de Vries, it is hard to separate the scientist or engineer from the artist or architect. Vredeman de Vries also made waterworks, served as master of fortifications (*Festungsbaumeister*) in both Wolfenbüttel and Gdańsk (Danzig), but he is equally well known, if not more famous in art and architectural history as the author of important treatises on perspective and on the architectural orders. Vredeman de Vries was also a prolific draftsman and painter.[29] Hence the story that Berkel tells here about the Netherlandish practitioner calls up a pattern established by the efforts and interests of other, more important figures; indeed, famous figures such as Andreas Schlüter remained active in the intersections of art, science, and engineering into the eighteenth century.[30]

The lengthy survival or recurrence of such supposedly distinctive Renaissance phenomena raises considerations of periodization, and thus leads to other questions about the conceptualization of this collection. The definition of commerce posited here is a broader one, that encompasses various kinds of exchange, not only of trade, for example, of trade, but also of gift-giving. Economic practices are thus described as having a longer purchase, as it were. Consequently, Weberian notions that economic rationalism could be linked with capitalism and with the Reformation (or Renaissance), and thus connected with definitions of historical periods seems to be rejected. In a world in which a prince could offer to trade a colony for a collection, or courts could bankrupt themselves with expenditures on luxuries in a desire to express their magnificence, it may well be that period distinctions based on notions of economic rationality are not the best markers of modernity.[31]

Instead, representational practices provide the basis for the period definitions assumed here. Pamela Long argues most directly for these sorts of distinctions in her essay on the relation of visual representation to the investigation of nature. She contrasts what she finds to be the use of forms of visual representation to legitimate knowledge claims in the period 1490–1540s with what she describes as the antecedent, ancient, and medieval reluctance "to use visual images to demonstrate claims" about the natural world.

But what are the implications of this thesis? Clearly many examples exist of images from antiquity and the Middle Ages that were used to illustrate scientific texts, to demonstrate an argument. As exemplified by herbals and later by *tacuina sanitatis*, numerous illuminated manuscripts pertaining to medicine and natural history survive from antiquity, and in larger numbers through the Middle Ages.[32] Moreover, other kinds of "scientific" texts, notably astrological and alchemical handbooks, were also illustrated during the Middle Ages, and there is evidence that some such sorts of works may have been in antiquity as well.[33] These are, furthermore, some of the very fields — natural history and alchemy — that form the focus for discussion in this collection.

Accordingly, the period and category distinctions employed here cannot be seen to rely simply on the presence of empirical evidence. Rather, it is the quality of the evidence concerned that is important. And this leads back, as indeed is suggested in part by Long's essay, to another look at the development of representational forms and skills. Yet such an investigation also leads further into a more extended history of artistic forms and practices, into questions of artistic endeavor of an art historical nature — one which, however, is not directly addressed in this book.[34] The thesis that there was a reluctance to rely on visual evidence for truth claims is in fact based on the evidence of theory, not practice, and the theoretical considerations seem to derive, as Long indicates, from discussions of mechanics. This raises a fundamental question: To what extent did a mathematical worldview offer a different perspective on visual representation of nature?

Mechanics and celestial mechanics, or astronomy, are also not treated in this book. But consideration of these subjects is of importance not just for their implications for questions of periodization, but also for more general issues concerning commerce and representation that are central to this collection. Astronomy had immense commercial importance in the period here discussed, certainly at least in its astrological form.[35] Almanacs, ephemerides, and horoscopes circulated widely and seem to have been avidly acquired.

New astronomical phenomena were eagerly reported and became the "hot news" of the day.[36] Astronomers were highly sought after and regarded by courts, whom they served in various capacities, not just for casting horoscopes. Significantly, Tycho Brahe received many privileges from the Danish crown; he then became the highest paid servitor of the imperial court.[37]

Moreover, attention to mechanics, especially to celestial mechanics, sheds a different light on issues of representation in art and science. Whether or not one agrees with an older thesis that regards the "Scientific Revolution" as connected with the mechanization of the world picture,[38] developments in mechanics were certainly related to advances in mathematics. These relied on other forms of representation, utilizing quantification and systems for indicating it.[39] For practitioners of mathematically based sciences such as astronomy, nature was to be read not in images, but in numbers. Ultimately the increasing sophistication and difficulties involved with mathematics, related to the development of professional specialization,[40] in fact split the union that had existed between art, science, and engineering. But such developments were not of course imaginable until the end of the early modern period.

Not all natural philosophers gave images the same meaning. Differences in opinion about the significance of visual imagery were in fact already evident in the early seventeenth century, in the "Kepler-Fludd controversy." While Fludd believed that the cosmos could be represented in images and diagrams, Kepler treated these images as at best symbolic, and denied that they, or other similar images, could represent reality (even though he himself was a master of the scientific diagram and had famously made a model of the universe based on the inscription of the Platonic [Pythagorean] solids. Mathematics, not pictures, was to be trusted in the end.[41] Considerations of cosmology had thus already led to what can be called a crisis of confidence in the image, at least in the realm of astronomy after Copernicus, at the very time in which the idea of a "true" image of nature could thrive in such fields as anatomy and natural history. While science and art could continue to coexist, this position may be regarded as the initiation of a theme, advanced by the Enlightenment, by which images would come to be regarded as deceptive.[42]

The visual revolution of our own time reminds us, however, that there are many views of the importance of image making. There are still many diverse opinions about systems of representation and their relation to nature. While new forms of biology and biotechnology have revolutionized conceptions of life itself, new kinds of visual imaging have proliferated, and those also make claims to represent reality and call for a new understanding of visuality related to newer discourses in the humanities and social sciences.[43] But the issues and apparent contradictions suggested by the early modern period are also still with us. The physical sciences still strive to produce a unified theory, and biological scientists also claim that all science, indeed all

Thomas DaCosta Kaufmann

knowledge, may be explained by a single unified theory.[44] Moreover, many of these questions, concerning computers, biotechnology, physical fusion, have vast commercial implications. A virtue of this collection of essays is that it not only stimulates reconsiderations of the historiography of worldviews, but that in so doing it encourages reconsideration of the role of representation, commerce, image-making, and science in the contemporary world.

Notes

1. The remarks made here pertain to more general issues raised by the book, and therefore refrain from commenting on more particular arguments in individual essays.

2. This distinction between an "internal" historiography of science and its alternatives is made by Thomas DaCosta Kaufmann, "Empiricism and Community in Early Modern Science and Art: Some Comments on Baths, Plants, and Courts," in *Natural Particulars. Nature and the Disciplines in Renaissance Europe*, ed. Anthony Grafton and Nancy Siraisi (Cambridge, Mass. and London: MIT Press, 1999, 401f. For the historiography of the Scientific Revolution see most comprehensively H. Floris Cohen, *The Scientific Revolution. A Historiographical Inquiry*, (Chicago and London: University of Chicago Press, 1994).

3. A. C. Crombie, *From Augustine to Galileo* (Harmondsworth: Penguin Books, 1959; 1st ed., 1952).

4. Edwin A. Burtt, *Metaphysical Foundations of Modern Physical Science*, (New York: Harcourt Brace, 1932, rev. ed.; 1st ed. 1924).

5. The works of all these scholars are now largely accessible in translation. See, for example, Heinrich Wölfflin, *Principles of Art History. The Problem of the Development of Style in Later Art*, trans. E. Hottinger (New York: Dover, 1950; 1st English ed., 1932); *Classic Art*, trans. Peter and Linda Murray (London: The Phaidon Press, 1952); *Renaissance and Baroque*, trans. Kathrin Simon, intro. Peter Murray (Ithaca, N.Y.: Cornell University Press, 1964); Alois Riegl, *Problems of Style. Foundations for a History of Ornament*, trans. Evelyn Kain, annotations and intro. David Castriota, preface Henri Zerner, (Princeton, N.J.: Princeton University Press, 1992); *The Group Portraiture of Holland*, trans. Evelyn M. Kain and David Britt, intro. Wolfgang Kemp (Los Angeles: Getty Research Institute for History of Art and the Humanities, 1999); Émile Mâle, *The Gothic Image*, trans. (New York, 1952). They have also garnered significant historiographical attention. [See, for example, For Mâle.] Germain Bazin, *Histoire de l'histoire de l'art de Vasari à nos jours* (Paris: Albin Michel, 1986), 208–210 (in a chapter titled "Les pouvoirs de l'image: l'iconographie").

6. See, for example, Richard S. Westfall, *The Construction of Modern Science. Mechanisms and Mechanics* (Cambridge: Cambridge University Press, 1971); Sydney J. Freedberg, *Painting in Italy 1500–1600 (The Pelican History of Art)* (Harmondsworth: Penguin Books, 1971).

7. Warburg's essays, including many papers touching on astrology, are now accessible in an English translation: Aby Warburg, *The Renewal of Pagan Antiquity: Contributions to the Cultural History of the European Renaissance*, trans. David Britt, intro. Kurt W. Forster (Los Angeles: Getty Research Institute for History of Art and the Humanities, 1999). See further Fritz Saxl, *Lectures* (London: Warburg Institute, 1957). Panofsky's early German essays on proportion and perspective are also available in translation: "The History of the Theory of Human Proportions as a Reflection of the History of Style," in *Meaning in the Visual Arts* (Garden City, N.Y.: Doubleday Anchor Books, 1955), 55–107; *Perspective as Symbolic Form*, trans. Christopher Wood (Cambridge, Mass.: Zone Books [MIT Press], 1991).

8. Martin Wackernagel, *The World of the Florentine Renaissance Artist. Projects and Patrons, Workshop and Art Market*, trans. Alison Luchs (Princeton, N.J.: Princeton University Press, 1981; 1st ed. Leipzig, 1938); Hans Floerke, *Studien zur niederländischen Kunst- und Kulturgeschichte. Die Formen des Kunsthandels, das Atelier und die Sammler in den Niederlanden vom 15.–18. Jahrhundert* (Munich and Leipzig: Georg Müller, 1905).

9. Robert K. Merton, *Science, Technology and Society in Seventeenth-Century England* (New York: Harper & Row, 1970; 1st ed. 1938); Herbert Butterfield, *The Origins of Modern Science* (New York: Macmillan, 1957; 1st ed. London, 1949). For the impact of the latter work, see Robert S. Westman and David C. Lindberg introduction to *Reappraisals of the Scientific Revolution*, ed. Westman and Lindberg, (Cambridge, Cambridge University Press, 1990), xvii.

10. For example, Frederick Antal, *Florentine Painting and its Social Background. The Bourgeois Republic before Cosimo de Medici's Advent to Power*, (London: Kegan Paul, 1947); Arnold Hauser, *Social History of Art*, trans. Stanley Godman (New York: Random House, 1951), 2 vols.; J. D. Bernal, *Science in History*, (Cambridge, Mass.: MIT Press, 1971), 4 vol. (1st ed. London, 1954).

11. I have dated the appearance of the "new art history," at least in its self-proclamation, to 1972 in a response to a "Visual Culture Questionnaire," *October* 77, 1996: 45–8. See further "What Is New about the 'New Art History,'" *The Philosophy of the Visual Arts*, ed. Philip Alperson (New York and Oxford: Oxford University Press, 1992), 515–520.

12. In addition to the titles cited by Smith and Findlen, see, for example, Richard A. Goldthwaite, *The Building of Renaissance Florence. An Economic and Social History* (Baltimore and London: Johns Hopkins University Press, 1980); Neil de Marchi and Hans J. Van Migroet, "Novelty and Fashion Circuits in the Mid-Seventeenth Century Antwerp-Paris Art Trade," *Journal for Medieval and Early Modern Studies* 28 (1998) 201–246; *idem*, "Exploring markets for Netherlandish Paintings in Spain and Nueva España," *Nederlands Kunsthistorisch Jaarboek* (2000): 80–111; Bernd Roeck, *Kunstpatronage in der Frühen Neuzeit* (Göttingen: Vandenhoeck & Ruprecht, 1999).

13. Alan G. R. Smith, *Science and Society in the Sixteenth and Seventeenth Centuries* (London and New York: Science History Publications, 1972). A new edition of Merton's *Science, Technology and Society* was also published in 1970.

14. Among the volume of recent literature, an exemplary collection is *Patronage and Institutions. Science, Technology, and Medicine at the European Court 1500–1700*, ed. Bruce T. Moran (Rochester, N.Y., and Woodbridge: Boydell Press, 1991), including essays by Smith and Findlen. See also their other publications, and studies by other scholars cited in essays above.

15. Mario Biagoli, *Galileo Courtier. The Practice of Science in the Culture of Absolutism* (Chicago and London: University of Chicago Press, 1993); John Robert Christianson, *On Tycho's Island. Tycho Brahe and His Assistants 1570–1601*, (Cambridge: Cambridge University Press, 2000).

16. Steven Shapin, *The Social History of Truth. Civility and Science in Seventeenth-Century England* (Chicago and London: University of Chicago Press, 1994), 36–38, citing Foucault. See further Shapin's more recent synthesis *The Scientific Revolution* (Chicago and London: University of Chicago, 1996), emphasizing the social practices of science.

17. See Michel Foucault, *L'archéologie du savoir* (Paris: Gallimard, 1969).

18. Michel Foucault, *The Order of Things. An Archaeology of the Human Sciences* (New York: Pantheon Books, 1970), English trans. of *Les Mots et les choses* (Paris: Gallimard, 1966).

19. Richard Rorty, *Philosophy and the Mirror of Nature* (Princeton, N.J.: Princeton University Press, 1979).

20. Notably Stephen Greenblatt, *Renaissance Self Fashioning From More to Shakespeare* (Chicago and London: University of Chicago Press, 1980); Svetlana Alpers, *The Art of Describing. Dutch Art in the Seventeenth Century* (Chicago and London: University of Chicago Press, 1983).

21. Exemplified by Barbara Maria Stafford, *Body Criticism. Imaging the Unseen in Enlightenment Art and Medicine* (Cambridge, Mass. and London: MIT Press, 1991); *Artful Science.*

420   *Thomas DaCosta Kaufmann*

Enlightenment Entertainment and the Eclipse of Visual Education (Cambridge, Mass. and London: MIT Press, 1994); *Good Looking. Essays on the Virtue of Images* (Cambridge, Mass. and London: MIT Press, 1996).

22. "Science, Commerce, and Art: Neglected Topics at the Junction of History and Art History," in *Art in History. History in Art. Studies in Seventeenth-Century Dutch Culture*, ed. David Freedberg and Jan de Vries (Santa Monica: Getty Center for the History of Art and Humanities, 1991), 376–428. Freedberg's essay has been excerpted, "Ciência, Comércio e Arte. Topícos negligenciados na junção da históri a[historia] com a história da arte (excertos)," in *O Brasil e os Holandeses 1530–1654*, ed. Paulo Herkenhoff (Rio de Janeiro: Sextante Artes, 1999), 192–217.

23. Grafton and Siraisi, *Natural Particulars. Nature and the Disciplines in Renaissance Europe*.

24. Bertrand Gille, *Les ingénieurs de la Renaissance* (Paris: Hermann, 1964), is an older introduction to the topic. See also for an overview Paolo Galluzzi, *Renaissance Engineers from Brunelleschi to Leonardo da Vinci* (Florence: Istituto e Museo di Storia della scienza, 1996) and Hélène Vénn, *La gloire des ingénieurs* (Paris: Albin Michel, 1993).

25. See Erwin Panofsky, "Artist, Scientist, Genius: Notes on the 'Renaissance-Dämmerung,'" in *The Renaissance. Six Essays*, ed. Wallace K. Ferguson (New York: Harper & Row, 1962), 121–182 (initially given in a lecture series at the Metropolitan Museum of Art, New York, 1951–52).

26. Because of his importance for the history of mathematics, horology, and astronomy, Bürgi, who crafted exquisite objects that became elements of princely collections, may be picked out as exemplifying this tendency. For literature on Bürgi, see Ludolf von Mackensen, ed., *Die erste Sternwarte Europas mit ihren Instrumenten und Uhren. 400 Jahren Jost Bürgi in Kassel* (Munich: Callway, 1988; 3rd improved ed.; 1st ed. 1979), and for a more recent summary *idem*, "Die Kasseler Wissenchaftskammer oder die Vermessung des Himmels, der Erde und der Zeit," in *Moritz der Gelehrte. Ein Renaissancefürst in Europa*, ex. cat. ed. Heiner Borggrefe, Eurasburg, 1997, 385–390, with catalog entries 391ff.

27. Martin Kemp, *The Science of Art. Optical Themes in Western Art from Brunelleschi to Seurat* (New Haven and London: Yale University Press, 1990), 112–118; Kemp comments: "Stevin and his fellow mathematicians were concerned with an astonishing range of applied skills and technologies—fortifications, guns, ships, canals, navigation windmills, cranes modes of transport, timepieces, surveying, accounting, banking, and certainly not least, the optical instruments such as the telescope and microscope that were been exploited to revolutionize the visual data of science"(114).

28. With characteristic insight, Frances Yates recognized De Caus's multiple talents and importance. See *The Rosicrucian Enlightenment* (London and Boston: Routledge and Kegan Paul, 1972), 11–13 passim. For De Caus, see Piet Lombaerde, "Pietro Sardi, Georg Müller, Salomon de Caus und die Wasserkünste des Coudenberg-Gartens in Brüssel," *Gartenkunst* 3, 1991: 159–171; idem, "Die Wasserkünste des Coudenbergparks in Brüssel," in *Die Wasserversorgung in der Renaissancezeit*, ed. Albrecht Hoffmann (Mainz: Von Zuben, 2000), 277–84. An edition with commentary of Stevin's architectural treatise is being prepared by Charles van den Heuvel; in the meantime see *idem*, "Stevins 'huisbouw' en het onvoltooide Nederlands architectuurtractaat. De praktijk van hat bouwen als wetenschap," *Bulletin van de Konijklijke Nederlandse Oudheidkundige Bond* 93 (1994): 1–18.

29. Vredeman de Vries is the subject of a forthcoming exhibition in Lemgo which will illuminate many of his qualities. An essay by Lombarde and Van den Heuvel promises further to relate his many-sided talents to those of De Caus and Stevin. See Petra Sophia Zimermann, "Die Palastenentwürfe des Hans Vredeman de Vries in der 'Architectura' von 1577," in *Italienische Renaissancebaukunst an Scheide, Maas und Niederrhein: Stadtanlagen–Zivilbauten–Wehranlangen: Tagungshandbuch (2. Jülicher Pasqualini-symposium vom 18. bis 21. Juni 1998 in Jülich)*, ed. Günter Bers and Conrad Doose, Jülich, 1999; 335–337 (summary on 621–622), with references to earlier studies.

30. For example, Andreas Schlüter, for whom in this regard see Thomas DaCosta Kaufmann, "Schlüter's Fate. Comments on Sculpture, Science, and Patronage in Central and Eastern Europe c. 1700," in *Künstlerische Austausch/ Artistic Exchange. Akten des XXVIII. Internationalen Kongresses für Kunstgeschichte Berlin, 15.–20. Juli 1992*, Berlin, Akademie Verlag, 1993, 199–212.

31. The first story is told by Pamela H. Smith, *The Business of Alchemy. Science and Culture in the Holy Roman Empire* (Princeton, N.J.: Princeton University Press, 1994), 171–192. The overwhelming impact of expenses on luxuries and magnificence is familiarly given as a reason for the bankruptcy of the French crown in the eighteenth century, and the same occurred elsewhere, as for example in Bavaria.

32. See, for a general introduction, Wilfrid Blunt, with the assistance of William T. Stearn, *The Art of Botanical Illustration. An Illustrated History* (London: Collins, 1950), 5ff. For an introduction to *tacuina sanitatis* and their relation to the herbal, see Luisa Cogliati Arano, *The Medieval Health Handbook* (New York and London: Barrie & Jenkins, 1976). For a recent publication related to an ancient example, see Cesare Ruffato, ed., *La medicina in Roma antica. Il Liber medicinalis di Quinto Sereno Sammonico* (Turin: UTET, 1996).

33. For an illustrated overview of alchemical manuscripts and books, see Gareth Roberts, *The Mirror of Alchemy. Alchemical Ideas and Images in Manuscripts and Books. From Antiquity to the Seventeenth Century* (London: British Library, 1994). Astrological handbooks were discussed long ago by Warburg, Saxl, and their followers; see note 7 above. For a general overview, see Kurt Weitzmann, *Ancient Book Illumination* (Cambridge, Mass.: Harvard University Press, 1959), not without questions, however.

34. For a very recent approach to the question of the origin of still life in Italy which, taking into account other literature, discusses historical and art historical questions, see Giacomo Berra, "Arcimboldi, Vincenzo Campi, Figino, Fede Galizia, Caravaggio: congiunture sulla nascita della natura morta in Lombardia," in *Vincenzo Campi: scene del quotidiano*, ex. cat., ed. Franco Paliaga, Milan and Cremona, 2000, 61–86. I deal with this in a forthcoming essay.

35. For a discussion of some aspects of the commercial relations of astrology see most recently Anthony Grafton, *Cardano's Cosmos* (Cambridge, Mass.: Harvard University Press, 1999).

36. This is the subject of ongoing research by Eileen Reeves.

37. In addition to the work by Christianson, *On Tycho's Island*, see for Brahe's later career Victor E. Thoren, *The Lord of Uraniborg. A Biography of Tycho Brahe* (with contributions by Christianson) (Cambridge: Cambridge University Press, 1990), 376ff. For the point about Tycho's salary see Alphons Lhotsky, "Die Geschichte der Sammlungen," *Festschrift des Kunsthistorischen Museums in Wien 1891–1941*, pt. 2, Vol. 1, p.295.

38. Cf. E. J. Dijksterhuis, *The Mechanization of the World Picture* (Oxford: Clarendon Press, 1961; 1st ed. Amsterdam, 1950).

39. See Alfred W. Crosby, *The Measure of Reality. Quantification and Western Society 1250–1600* (Cambridge: Cambridge University Press, 1997).

40. See J. V. Field, *The Invention of Infinity. Mathematics and Art in the Renaissance* (Oxford, New York, Tokyo: Oxford University Press, 1997), 229ff.

41. See for these points the insightful essay by Robert Westman, "Nature, Art, and Psyche: Jung, Pauli, and the Kepler-Fludd Polemic," in *Occult and Scientifc Mentalities in the Renaissance*, ed. Brian Vickers (Cambridge: Cambridge University Press, 1984), 177–230.

42. This subject has been well elucidated by Barbara Stafford, *Body Criticism*, and *Artful Science*.

43. See Barbara Stafford, *Good Looking*.

44. See Edward Osborne Wilson, *Consilience. The Unity of Knowledge* (New York: Knopf, 1997).

Contributors

Pamela H. Smith is Edwin F. and Margaret H. Hahn Professor of History at Pomona College and the Claremont Graduate University in Claremont, California. She is the author of *The Business of Alchemy: Science and Culture in the Holy Roman Empire* (1994), which won the Pfizer Prize in the History of Science in 1995, and is now completing a book on artisanal attitudes to nature in early modern Europe.

Paula Findlen is Professor of History and Director of the Science, Technology and Society Program at Stanford University. She is the author of *Possessing Nature: Museums, Collecting, and Scientific Culture in Early Modern Italy* (1994), which won the 1995 Marraro Prize in Italian History and the 1996 Pfizer Prize in History of Science, and *A Fragmentary Past: The Italian Renaissance Origins of the Museum* (forthcoming). She is currently completing a book on gender and knowledge in eighteenth-century Italy.

Antonio Barrera is assistant professor of History at Colgate University. His areas of interest are history of science and Atlantic world history. His current research concerns the interactions between the Atlantic world and the emergence of modern science, with a particular emphasis on Spain and America in the sixteenth and seventeenth centuries.

James A. Bennett is Director of the Museum of the History of Science, University of Oxford. His research interests focus on instruments, astronomy, practical mathematics, and museums.

Klaas van Berkel earned his Ph.D. at Utrecht University with a dissertation, *Isaac Beeckman (1588–1637) and the mechanization of the world picture* (1983). Since 1988, he is professor of Modern History at the University of

Groningen. With Albert van Helden and Lodewijk Palm he edited *A History of Science in the Netherlands. Survey, Themes and Reference* (1999).

Harold J. Cook is currently Director of the Wellcome Trust Centre for the History of Medicine at University College London. He has authored two books and several articles on the place of early modern medicine and natural history in the scientific revolution, and continues his investigations into those areas of inquiry during the Dutch Golden Age.

Anne Goldgar teaches early modern European history at King's College London. She is the author of *Impolite Learning: Conduct and Community in the Republic of Letters, 1680–1750* (1995) and articles on seventeenth- and eighteenth-century cultural history. She is writing a book about the social and cultural context of tulip mania.

Deborah E. Harkness is an associate professor of History at the University of California at Davis. Her previous work on John Dee has received prizes from the Renaissance Society of America and the History of Science Society, and culminated in a book, *John Dee's Conversations with Angels: Cabala, Alchemy and the End of Nature* (2000). Presently she is working on *Neighborhoods of Science: Knowledge and Practice in Elizabethan London* under the auspices of the National Science Foundation.

Thomas DaCosta Kaufmann is a professor in the Department of Art and Archaeology, Princeton University. Among his books are *The Mastery of Nature: Aspects of Art, Science, and Humanism in the Renaissance* (1993) and *Court, Cloister and City. The Art and Culture of Central Europe 1450-1800* (1995; German revised edition, 1998).

Pamela O. Long is a historian who has taught at Barnard College, St. Mary's College of Maryland, and Johns Hopkins University. She has published extensively on late medieval and Renaissance mechanical arts and is the author of *Openness, Secrecy, Authorship: Technical Arts and the Culture of Knowledge from Antiquity to the Renaissance* (2001).

Mark A. Meadow is Assistant Professor of the History of Art at University of California, Santa Barbara, and Co-Director (with Bruce Robertson) of Microcosms: Objects of Knowledge, a Special Humanities Project of the University of California Office of the President. He has published on Pieter Bruegel, Pieter Aertsen, Albrecht Dürer; on the history of collecting, the history of rhetoric, and the history of memory; on proverbs and proverb collecting, and on Renaissance epistemology. His first book is

Pieter Bruegel the Elder's Netherlandish Proverbs *and the Practice of Rhetoric* (2001).

Chandra Mukerji is Professor of Communication and Sociology at the University of California, San Diego. She has written widely on the sociology of culture and communication, and the history and sociology of science and technology. Her book publications include *Territorial Ambitions and the Gardens of* Versailles (1997), *From Graven Images: Patterns of Modern Materialism* (1983), *A Fragile Power* (1990), for which she was awarded the Robert K. Merton award, and, co-edited with Michael Schudson, *Rethinking Popular Culture* (1991).

Tara E. Nummedal has recently completed her dissertation, entitled "Adepts and Artisans: Alchemical Practice in the Holy Roman Empire, 1550–1620," at Stanford University. Her research focuses on the careers of working alchemists and their connections to broader scholarly, political, and commercial pursuits in early modern Europe.

Lissa Roberts teaches the history of science and technology at the University of Twente, the Netherlands. While more broadly interested in the cultural history of science and technology in Europe during the eighteenth century, she is currently writing a book that traces the cultural history of the introduction of the steam engine into the Netherlands.

Alison Sandman recently completed her dissertation, entitled "Cosmographers vs. Pilots: Navigation, Cosmography, and the State in Early Modern Spain," at the University of Wisconsin, Madison. Her research uses disputes about the practice of navigation to probe the construction of the idea of the utility of science and examines reasons for the growth of state patronage of science in the early phases of the Scientific Revolution.

Benjamin Schmidt is Assistant Professor of History at the University of Washington. His publications include *Innocence Abroad: The Dutch Imagination and the New World* (2001) and numerous articles on early modern cultural history. He has held recent fellowships from the NEH and Ahmanson and Getty foundations. His current research focuses on travel, expansion, and exoticism in Baroque Europe.

Larry Silver is Farquhar Professor of Art History at the University of Pennsylvania. He taught previously at Berkeley and Northwestern and is a specialist in early modern prints and paintings of Germany and the Low Countries. He has served as President of both the Historians of Netherlandish Art and the College Art Association and is also the author of *Art in History* (1993), a general survey.

Claudia Swan is Assistant Professor of Art History at Northwestern University. She is completing a book titled *Art, Science, Witchcraft; Jacques de Gheyn II and the Representation of the Natural World in the Netherlands ca. 1600*; her *Clutius Botanical Watercolors* (a compendium of sixteenth-century scientific watercolors employed in the medical curriculum at Leiden University) appeared in 1998.

Index

De Mellayne, John, 149
De Revolutionibus (Copernicus), 399–400
Dee, John, 137–138, 152
Descartes, René, 18, 224, 228, 407
Diderot, Denis, 110, 407
Digges, Leonard, 149
Dioscórides, 171
Dodonaeus, Rembertus, 121
Dollond, Peter, 380–381
Don Manuel I, 1
Dürer, Albrecht, 1–14, 19, 39–40, 65, 71–74, 308
   alchemy themes in, 41
   Madonna with the Mayfly, 29–30, 32
   Madonna with the Monkey, 31–34
   Madonna outdoors, 29–31, 34, 36, 46, 51
Dutch East India Company (VOC), 225, 348–349, 356
Dutch geography, 347–364
   exoticism/image of world, 356–360
   marketing of "World," 349, 356–360
   neutrality of, 360–362
   pronk (sumptuousness of), 359–360
Dutch Republic
   Baconians and painting, 405
   exoticism/image of world, 356–357
   geography project; *see* Dutch geography
   Golden Age of, 356
   mathematics in, 406
   natural histories of, 350
   painters of, 353
   representation of the world, 362
   traditional geographies, 350
   travel narratives, 350–352
   wonders and "things-of-the-world," 352, 364

Eamon, William, 202
Eckhout, Albert, 353, 355
Economic rationalism, 416
Eichberger, Dagmar, 73
Electricity, 383
Elias, Norbert, 4, 224
Elizabethan London
   commercial practices/advertising in, 140–142
   English alchemical tradition vs. foreigners, 151–154
   foreigners and "strange" ideas, 139, 141

husband-and-wife medical partnerships, 144
   instrument makers in, 148–149
   large-scale engineering/mechanical feats, 150
   mechanical marvels/royal patents, 147–151
   medical practitioners, 143–147
   natural science practitioners/exchange in, 137–155
   Paracelsian medicine in, 146–147
   royal patents, 142
   surgical practices, 145–146
   technical progress in, 147
Embalming methods, 230–236; *see also* Preservation arts
Entrepreneurs; *see also* Canal du Midi
   in 17th c. France, 248–249
   state-based entrepreneurialism, 249
Ercker, Lazar, 204, 212
Eschinardi, Francesco, 287–288
Evans, R. J. W., 209
Evelyn, John, 299
Exoticism, 347, 352, 364, 406
   colonialism, 349
   Dutch image of world, 356–360
   early observers of, 347

Fabrica (Vesalius), 74–78, 80
Falero, Francisco, 86–89, 100–101
Fama of the ruler, 4
Farnese, Alessandro, 190
Ferdinand I (King of Bohemia), 190
Fernández de Oviedo, Gonzalo, 7
Feudal gift economy, 4
Févre, Nicaise le, 372
Findlen, Paula, 1, 111, 297, 401, 412–413
Flight into Egypt (Dürer), 31
Flight into Egypt (Schongauer), 51
Floerke, Hans, 413
Fontana, Carlo, 280, 282, 284, 290–291
Forestry surveyor, 267
Forster, Richard, 138, 144
Foucault, Michel, 119, 403, 414
Fountain of Life, 44, 46, 52
Fountain of youth, 228
Four Elements (Hoefnagel), 36
Francis I (King of France), 1
Franeau, Jean, 327
Freedberg, David, 415

Meadow, Mark, 6, 182, 408, 412
Mechanical arts, 63, 407
   in Elizabethan London, 147–151
   in Madrid Codex I, 65, 67–71
Medical practitioners, 143–147
Medicina diastatica (Tentzel), 231
Medina, Pedro de, 89, 91–92, 94, 96
Meijer, Cornelius, 278–285, 405–406
   Accademica Fisicomatematica and, 288–289
   Apologia of, 290–292
   biography and early work of, 279–280
   conflict with Fontana, 282–283, 290–291
   defense and defeat of, 290–292
   engineering skills of, 405
   L'arte di restituire (Meijer), 289–291
   passonata in the Tiber, 280–282, 290–291
   plan for St. Peter's Square, 284–285
Merian, Maria Sibylla, 14
Merkel Centerpiece (Jamnitzer), 49
Mersenne, Marin, 19
Merton, Robert K., 15–19, 413
"Merton thesis," 15–16
Mexía, Pedro, 87, 89, 101
"Microcosms: Objects of Knowledge" (Univ. of California), 186
Micrographia (Hooke), 372
Microscopes, 372
Military cartographers, 257
Mining enterprises, 210–212
Mistrell, Eloy, 149
Modern science; *see also* Scientific Revolution
   capitalism and, 401
Monardes, Nicolás, 169, 172
Monconys, Balthazar de, 371–374
Montanus, Arnoldus, 347–349, 359–360
Montias, John Michael, 15
Morales, Garciperez, 169
Moran, Bruce, 209
Morland, Samuel, 374
Morland's calculating machine, 374–375
Mornay, Robert, 371
Moscardo, Lodovico, 315
Motion, Leonardo's studies of, 68–70
Mountebanks, 305
Moxon, Joseph, 374
Mukerji, Chandra, 18, 228, 248, 406, 412
Mummies, 230–232
Muzafar II (Sultan), 1

Mylius, Johann Daniel, 45

Nairne, Edward, 379
Narratives of place, 258–259
Natural history, 17, 302
   basilisks as iconography of, 313
   inventing nature, 310–311, 319
   science vs. commerce, 302–303
   trafficking in, 301–307
Natural History (Pliny), 301, 304
Natural History of Serpents (Jonstonius), 313
Natural History of Strange Fish (Belon), 310
Natural philosophers, 13–14, 17
Natural sciences, 9–10
   practitioners in Elizabethan London, 137–139
Naturalia, 5, 124, 402
   vs. *artificialia*, 325
   in curiosity cabinets, 182–183
   dried objects, 226–227
   medical instruction and, 113
   preparation/preservation of, 223–241
   trafficking in, 301–307
   tropical *naturalia*, 347
Naturalism, 8–9, 11, 13, 47
Naturalistic representation, 8–9, 109
   blowfish, 112–113
Nature
   art and, 65, 72, 324–328, 402
   consumption and, 18
   in *Hypnerotomachia Poliphili*, 65–67, 74
   representations as standardization of, 404
   visual representations, 417
Navigational techniques/instruments, 83, 165, 370
Neoplatonism, 44, 401
New World; *see also* Santa Domingo balsam
   commerce and knowledge in, 163–165
   empirical information/validating knowledge of, 164–165, 175
   health issues in, 163
   history of science and, 164
   medicine of, 164
   natural resources of, 164
   trading and commerce, 163
Newton, Isaac, 19, 375, 407, 415
Newton's reflector, 375
Nieuhof, Johan, 357, 360
Nonez, Hector, 144

Royal patents, 147–151
Royal Society, 371–373, 376–377, 390–391
Rudolf II (Holy Roman Emperor), 36, 182,
191, 193, 209
Rumphius, Georg, 347–349
Russwurin, Valentine, 145–147
Ruysch, Frederik, 241–242

Sadeler, Aegidius, 31
St. Johannis Kirche (Dürer), 71
Saint John the Evangelist and John the Baptist
(Altdorfer), 36–37
Saltpeter, 150
Sandman, Alison, 83, 406
Santa Cruz, Alonso de, 86–87, 89–90
Santa Domingo balsam, 164–165
Barreda's report, 170, 174
commercialization of, 169–170
crown's and knowledge production,
172–173
testing experience of, 170–175
Villasante's report on, 166–170, 174
Saxl, Fritz, 413
Schäfer, Ernst, 166
Scherdinger, Abel, 203, 205
Schlüter, Andreas, 416
Schmidt, Benjamin, 347, 406, 412
Schongauer, Martin, 51
Science
art and, 13–14, 17–19
capitalism and, 15–16
classical histories of, 413
commerce and, 15–18
construction of, 17
consumption and, 18–19
foundations of, 3
historiography of, 17, 414–415
as matrix of marvels, 402–404
Puritanism and, 15
The Science of Art (Kemp), 13
*Science, Technology, and Society in Seven-
teenth-Century England* (Merton),
15
Scientia, 47
Scientific instruments, 372, 402
as commercial enterprises, 389
in Elizabethan London, 147
foreign commissions for, 380
in France, 381
mathematical vs. optical instruments, 390

Paris shops, 377
Royal Society and, 390–391
trade affiliations for, 389–390
Scientific Revolution, 3, 11, 16, 18–19, 399,
405
early practitioners, 405–406
mechanics/mathematics and, 418
nature and, 16
social divide and scientific knowledge,
277
Sea charts
astronomical navigation and, 95–96
commerce and, 83
compass navigation, 96–97
controlling navigation, 91–97
cosmographers, 86–87
in Dutch Republic, 352
Falero's proposals, 89
information reliability in, 88–91
magnetic declination problem, 92–94
navigation and, 84
padrón real, 85–87
sea pilots and, 88, 90
Spanish-Portguese disputes, 83–84
territorial claims/disputes, 83, 97–101
Sea pilots
astronomy and, 95–96
compass navigation, 96–97
sea charts and, 88, 90
Seba, Albert, 318–319
Securie, John, 137
Seghers, Daniel, 325
Serlio, Sebastiano, 65, 74–79
Serpetro, Niccolo, 297, 299, 301
Settala, Manfredo, 300
Shapin, Steven, 414
Shoring, John, 144
Short, James, 375, 377
Silver, 210
Silver, Larry, 29
Sisson, Jeremiah, 378, 380, 382
Smith, Adam, 409
Smith, Adison, 381
Smith, Pamela H., 1, 29, 401, 413
Smythe, John, 140
Sömmering, Philipp, 203, 205, 213, 217
Sorbière, Samuel, 229, 372
Spain
in 16th century, 83–102
controlling navigation, 91–97

CPSIA information can be obtained
at www.ICGtesting.com
Printed in the USA
LVOW13s2224250118
563763LV00010BA/275/P